Lebanon

the Bradt Travel Guide

Paul Doyle

edition
2

www.bradtguides.com

Bradt Travel Guides Ltd, UK
The Globe Pequot Press Inc, USA

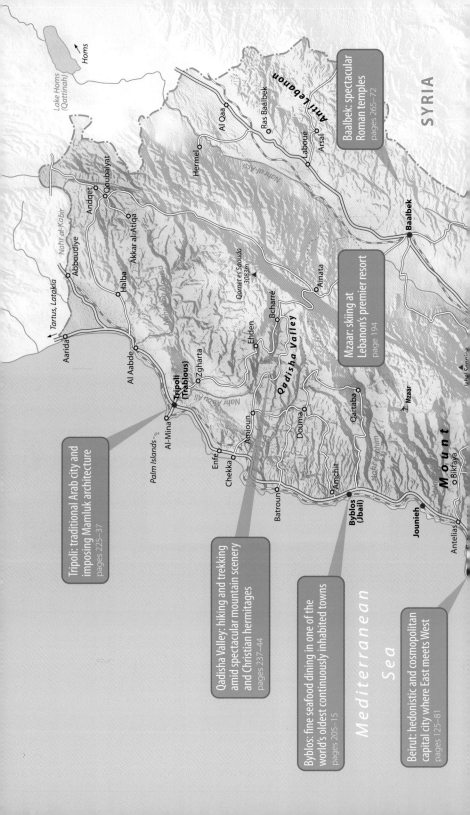

Tripoli: traditional Arab city and imposing Mamluk architecture
pages 225–37

Qadisha Valley: hiking and trekking amid spectacular mountain scenery and Christian hermitages
pages 237–44

Byblos: fine seafood dining in one of the world's oldest continuously inhabited towns
pages 205–15

Beirut: hedonistic and cosmopolitan capital city where East meets West
pages 125–81

Baalbek: spectacular Roman temples
pages 265–72

Mzaar: skiing at Lebanon's premier resort
page 194

SYRIA

Homs

Lake Homs (Qattinah)

Tartus, Latakia

Aarida

Al Aabde

Abboudiye

Andqet

Qoubaiyat

Akkar al-Atiqa

Halba

Nahr al-Kabir

Nahr abou Moussa

Zgharta

Ehden

Bcharré

Qadisha Valley

Qanrnet es Saouda 3083m

Ainata

Hermel

Al Qaa

Ras Baalbek

Laboué

Arsal

Anti Lebanon

Nahr al-Assi

Baalbek

Tripoli (Trablous)

Al-Mina

Palm Islands

Enfe

Chekka

Batroun

Byblos (Jbail)

Jounieh

Antelias

Amioun

Douma

Amchit

Qartaba

Bikfaya

Nahr Abou Ali

Nahr Ibrahim

Mzaar

Mount

Mediterranean Sea

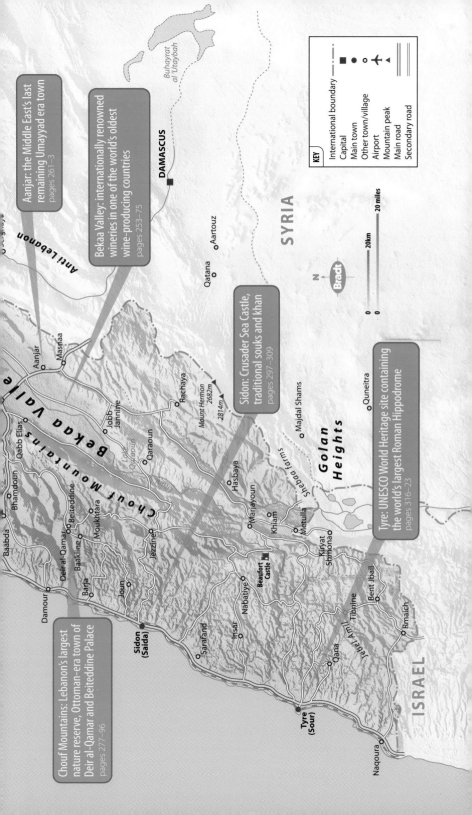

Aanjar: the Middle East's last remaining Umayyad era town
pages 261–3

Bekaa Valley: internationally renowned wineries in one of the world's oldest wine-producing countries
pages 253–75

Chouf Mountains: Lebanon's largest nature reserve, Ottoman-era town of Deir al-Qamar and Beiteddine Palace
pages 277–96

Sidon: Crusader Sea Castle, traditional souks and khan
pages 297–309

Tyre: UNESCO World Heritage site containing the world's largest Roman Hippodrome
pages 316–23

Anti Lebanon

Bekaa Valley

Chouf Mountains

Golan Heights

Jebel Amil

Shebaa Farms

DAMASCUS

Aartouz

Qatana

Rachaya

Jobb Jannine

Qaraoun

Lake Qaraoun

Mount Hermon 2682m

2814m▲

Hasbaya

Majdal Shams

Marjayoun

Khiam

Metulla

Kiryat Shmona

Quneitra

Aanjar

Mashaa

Qabb Elias

Baabda

Bhamdoun

Bhandoun

Deir al-Qamar

Beiteddine

Baakline

Moukhtara

Barja

Joun

Jezzine

Nabatiye

Insar

Sarafand

Damour

Sidon (Saida)

Qana

Tibnine

Bent Jbail

Rmaich

Tyre (Sour)

Naqoura

Beaufort Castle

Buhayrat al 'Utaybah

SYRIA

ISRAEL

N

Bradt

0   20km
0   20 miles

KEY

International boundary
Capital ■
Main town ●
Other town/village ○
Airport ✈
Mountain peak ▲
Main road
Secondary road

Lebanon
Don't
miss...

Baalbek
The Baalbek complex contains some of the largest and most impressive Roman remains in the world
(I/S) pages 265–72

Byblos
The town of Byblos has been in existence for 7,000 years, making it a contender for the world's oldest continuously inhabited town
(i/S) pages 205–15

Beiteddine Palace

The home of Lebanon's final ruling prince, Beiteddine Palace was built over a 30-year period using Italian architects and highly skilled artisans from Damascus

(PD) pages 287–90

National Museum, Beirut

Lebanon's premier museum is arguably the first sight to visit in the country, in order to gain an overview of the history and peoples that have helped to shape its development

(SS) pages 174–5

Jeita Grotto

This karstic limestone landscape, fashioned by geology, time and water, has resulted in a stunning array of stalactite and stalagmite rock formations

(PD) pages 197–8

Lebanon in colour

above left   The Martyrs' Square statue in Downtown Beirut pays homage to the Lebanese nationalists murdered here by the Ottomans in 1915–16 (PD) page 170

above right   Traditional building, Beirut; the city once boasted the nickname 'Paris of the Middle East' (d/S) page 125

right   Cafés at night, Nejmeh Place; with an ever-increasing number of bars, cafés, discos and nightclubs, Beirut's nightlife has something for everyone (SS) pages 147–50

below   A stroll along the Corniche is a ritual that should be undertaken by every visitor to Beirut (PD) pages 166–7

above left The interior of the Taynal Mosque in Tripoli is a superb example of Mamluk architecture, using alternating layers of stonework (*ablaq*) and exquisite Arabic calligraphy (PD) page 234

above right The exterior of Beirut's iconic Muhammad Al-Amine Mosque (d/S) pages 168–9

below The attractive façade of Deir Mar Antonios Qozhaya, one of the many rock-cut monasteries that have been fashioned in the Qadisha Valley since the 7th century (EK/D) page 243

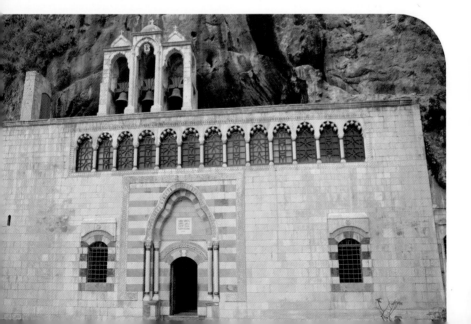

AUTHOR

Paul Doyle was born and brought up in Hampshire, England, where his youthful excursions around the county helped sow the seeds for his enduring interest in travel. Following a few years working in the aviation industry, a new departure beckoned and he decided to pursue a career as a freelance photographer. He began to work for a variety of public-sector clients, with travel to Arab lands such as Egypt, Jordan, Lebanon, Libya and Syria fitted into his schedule. His travel  photography has subsequently appeared in in-flight magazines, books and travel guides in the UK and overseas. His interest in travel writing developed out of his part-time photography degree, where his earlier social science education had been instrumental in inspiring him to undertake a final year photojournalistic project documenting the reconstruction of post-war Beirut. After more than 20 years residing in west London, Paul has now decamped back to Hampshire, where he hopes that the ongoing reconstruction at his beloved football club, Portsmouth, will lead to a similar change in the club's fortunes, and that Saturdays spent at Fratton Park may once again become tear-free.

For further information, visit www.pauldoylefoto.co.uk.

AUTHOR'S STORY

When I decided to embark on a photojournalistic study of Beirut's post-war reconstruction for my degree project in photography, Lebanon seemed to fit the bill perfectly as a destination that had been off the tourist radar for many years but was familiar to the world through the reports and images of its devastating 15-year-long civil war. I wanted to learn more about this tiny but significant country which had entered the public consciousness in an overtly negative manner. I recall one evening sitting in a bar quenching my thirst on the local brew Almaza, listening to the sound of the 1970s Bee Gees' hit 'Stayin' Alive', when it occurred to me that Beirut and Lebanon were doing much more than that. Stained by the blood of war Lebanon may have been, but the friendliness and hospitality of the Lebanese never ceased to amaze me, nor their desire to move forward and rebuild their shattered country. Lebanon without doubt represents the pinnacle of my forays to Arab countries. Despite its civil war, the country offers so much variety in cultural, historical and political terms when compared with Jordan, Syria and its other neighbours, and provides probably the best introduction to any visitor wanting to appreciate and gain a greater understanding of the Middle East. Even beyond its familiar and strategic importance in the region, another aspect of Lebanon's draw are those moments spent just walking around the capital and chatting to someone in the street or in a bar or café; you might find yourself striking up a conversation with someone on a bus or with a farmer in the Bekaa Valley leading his flock across the road. Moments like these enhance the travel experience in Lebanon and change any lingering stereotypical preconceptions. Furthermore, they come on top of other wonderful experiences the country has to offer, such as the soaring Roman temples at Baalbek or nature's remarkable handiwork at Jeita Grotto.

PUBLISHER'S FOREWORD
Adrian Phillips, Publishing Director

Lebanon offers geographical proof of the maxim 'size doesn't matter' – a tiny country that can nevertheless cater to the interests of a wide variety of tourists, from dedicated clubbers to history buffs. It has witnessed much violence, of course, and it inevitably bears the burden of events in a turbulent Middle East. But this is a forward-looking nation with arguably the greatest commitment of any in the region to the civil rights and freedoms of its people. I'm proud to see Paul Doyle's guide go into a second edition, and to see it still brimming so full of his knowledge and passion for this pint-sized country.

Second edition published January 2017 First published 2012
Bradt Travel Guides Ltd
IDC House, The Vale, Chalfont St Peter, Bucks SL9 9RZ, England
www.bradtguides.com

Print edition published in the USA by The Globe Pequot Press Inc,
PO Box 480, Guilford, Connecticut 06437-0480

ISBN: 978 1 84162 558 4 (print)
e-ISBN: 978 1 84162 798 4 (e-pub)
e-ISBN: 978 1 84162 699 4 (mobi)

British Library Cataloguing in Publication Data
A catalogue record for this book is available from the British Library

Photographs @Ministry of Tourism–Lebanon (MTL); AWL images: Michele Falzone (MF/AWL); Dreamstime: Ddkg (Ddkg/D); Edward Karaa (EK/D); Paul Doyle (PD); Shutterstock: diak (d/S), Eliane Haykal (EH/S), f8grapher (f8/S), Anton Ivanov (AI/S), irynal (i/S); JOAT (JOAT/S); lucvar (l/S); SuperStock (SS)
Front cover Bcharré and Qadisha Valley (PD)
Back cover Port of Byblos (i/S), Tetrapylon, Aanjar (d/S)
Title page Lion's head and cornice, Baalbek, Bekaa Valley (PD), Interior detail of Muhammad Al-Amine Mosque, Beirut (SS), Cedar tree (PD)

Maps David McCutcheon FBCart.S; regional maps in this guide based on ITMB Publishing Ltd map *Lebanon*; Beirut maps in this guide based on ITMB Publishing Ltd map *Beirut* and *Zawarib Beirut & Beyond*. *Colour map* Relief map base by Nick Rowland FRGS

Typeset by Dataworks, and Ian Spick, Bradt Travel Guides
Production managed by Jellyfish Print Solutions; printed in India
Digital conversion by the Firsty Group www.dataworks.co.in

Acknowledgements

A number of people and organisations have provided advice, assistance and support during this book's journey and whose input has proved invaluable. I would like to thank Serra Celikkan and Pegasus Airlines for getting me to Beirut. At Lebanon's Ministry of Tourism office a big *shukran* goes to Dana Nasr, Hala Mansour and Rasha Abou Alewi for their help and patience in answering my many questions. To Rita Salamoun and all the friendly staff at the Four Seasons Hotel and Ghazi El Aschkar, Ali and Michel at O Monot Hotel in Beirut who all made my stays unforgettable ones. At the American University of Beirut (AUB) I would like to say thank you to Clare Leader and Sana Mourad for their information and time. To the numerous Lebanese I have met along the way who provided me with hospitality, advice and support and who make this welcoming little country what it is. In particular, I would like to acknowledge Khaddouj Baz, Alya Hazeem, Mirna Alaaeddine, Najwa Harb, Norica-Daniela El Hallak, Dr Pascale Hayal Al Chibani, Dr Wessam Al Chibani and, last but not least, Tanya Saab. To visitors Gordana Mijuk and Shazia Islamshah, your menu suggestion in Kahwet Leila was spot on: the chicken livers, *tabbouleh* and Ghazal Beirut were to die for! A special thanks also to the entire editorial staff at Bradt, in particular Rachel Fielding and my Project Manager, Susannah Lord, for their editing, patience and professionalism. Finally, a warm debt of thanks to Lilian Button for her constant presence, advice and encouragement, and a big thank you, too, to those readers who took the time to write in with their comments and suggestions on the first edition of this guide.

DEDICATION

In loving memory of my father, Trevor John Doyle (1935–2012), and friend Katherine Elsa Johnson (1941–2014).

FEEDBACK REQUEST AND UPDATES WEBSITE

At Bradt Travel Guides we're aware that guidebooks start to go out of date on the day they're published – and that you, our readers, are out there in the field doing research of your own. You'll find out before us when a fine new family-run hotel opens or a favourite restaurant changes hands and goes downhill. So why not write and tell us about your experiences? Contact us on ☏ 01753 893444 or e info@bradtguides.com. We will forward emails to the author who may post updates on the Bradt website at www.bradtupdates.com/lebanon. Alternatively you can add a review of the book to www.bradtguides.com or Amazon.

Contents

HOW TO USE THIS GUIDE

AUTHOR'S FAVOURITES

Finding genuinely characterful accommodation or that unmissable off-the-beaten-track café can be difficult, so the author has chosen a few of his favourite places, and sights, throughout the country to point you in the right direction. These 'author's favourites' are marked with a ✳.

MAPS

Keys and symbols Maps include alphabetical keys covering the locations of those places to stay, eat or drink that are featured in the book. Note that regional maps may not show all hotels and restaurants in the area: other establishments may be located in towns shown on the map.

Grids and grid references Several maps use gridlines to allow easy location of sites. Map grid references are listed in square brackets after the name of the place or sight of interest in the text, with page number followed by grid number, eg: [103 C3].

LIST OF MAPS

Introduction

'If you think you understand Lebanon, you haven't been studying it long enough'
(A popular saying)

Lebanon is a pint-sized country accounting for less than 2% of the size of the landmass of its former colonial ruler, France. It may be small on a global map but, like the Tardis in the *Dr Who* TV series, appearances can be deceptive, and Lebanon manages to pack a lot in within its diminutive borders. The country's capital, Beirut, for many years the subject of a global media frenzy during the devastating 1975–90 civil war, has always attracted the vast majority of visitors drawn to its high-octane nightlife, exclusive beach clubs, fine dining and eclectic and upmarket shopping, a tradition that continues to this day. Yet with a history spanning some 7,000 years, Lebanon offers the visitor so much more than these hedonistic pursuits. Phoenicians, Greeks, Romans, the various Arab dynasties, Crusaders, Ottomans and the French have all vied for mastery of this tiny eastern Mediterranean landmass, and they have left their architectural and cultural footprints all over the country, with Lebanon's premier sites at Aanjar, Baalbek, Byblos (Jbail), the Qadisha Valley and Tyre (Sour) all given World Heritage site status by UNESCO. The must-see Jeita Grotto, by contrast, showcases history fashioned by nature, resulting in a beautiful array of stalactite and stalagmite formations. Adrenalin junkies and sporty types are also well catered for with Lebanon's numerous ski resorts suitable for the beginner and seasoned skier alike; paragliding around mountain vistas; hiking and trekking in the Qadisha Valley; or walking and cycling the Lebanon Mountain Trail (LMT) are also great ways to get off the beaten track and get up close and personal with some of Lebanon's diverse communities to experience the beauty and tranquility of rural Lebanon. There is much to entice the environmentally conscious visitor, too, with a couple of highlights being turtle conservation and eco-living, which helps support rural communities, on offer at The Orange House in Naqoura and in the Bekaa Valley town of Hermel, respectively.

It is Beirut, however, that probably offers the most visible reminders of a transformed Lebanon since the end of the civil war. The city today remains a vibrant and cosmopolitan mix of the country's religious mosaic and increasingly offers accommodation and eating options to suit all budgets. With a vibrant festival and cultural arts scene, a lovingly restored National Museum showcasing history from the Phoenician to the Mamluk period, renovated Ottoman-era architecture in the Downtown district of the capital and plenty to occupy the more active traveller such as cycling, golf, football and horse racing, the capital demands a few days' exploration by any visitor to appreciate the renaissance of this once so-called 'Paris of the Middle East'. By way of contrast, Lebanon's second city of Tripoli (Trablous) offers visitors an authentic Arab experience with traditional Mamluk-era architecture and atmospheric souks.

Of course, despite these *mezze* of attractions and pursuits for the visitor, not everything in the Lebanese garden is rosy and the country, like the region as a whole, continues to face many challenges. The sectarian divide remains a salient fact of life, as does the confessional-based system of power politics. Lebanon technically remains in a state of war with its southern neighbour, Israel, and conflict between Hezbollah and the Jewish state never seems far away. The murder of former prime minister Rafiq Hariri in 2005, undergoing the judicial process at the Special Tribunal for Lebanon (STL) in The Hague at the time of writing, has polarised the country's politicians and it remains to be seen what, if any, are the ramifications of international justice for Lebanon. Economically speaking, Lebanon has weathered the global economic downturn witnessed in recent years much better than many other countries around the world, but major infrastructure projects to improve such areas as roads, electricity, water, education and health require ongoing development. Without doubt, however, it is the ongoing turmoil in neighbouring Syria which is weighing most heavily on Lebanon's present and future development and has seriously blighted the country's tourist industry over the last few years. Lebanon is currently hosting well over 1½ million refugees from this conflict and, in addition to the strain this puts on an already challenged economy, has been exacerbated by intermittent sectarian fighting and targeted assassinations in parts of the capital and elsewhere around the country, yet overall Lebanon has remained remarkably resilient during one of the most turbulent periods in modern Middle Eastern history.

Despite these many problems that Lebanon faces – and will no doubt overcome if its history is anything to go by – the country remains essentially a safe place for tourists and other visitors. The Lebanese are invariably a cultured and welcoming people with the hassles often experienced by visitors in other parts of the region largely absent here, so do not hesitate in accepting any hospitality offered when in the country. If you have not previously been to the Middle East or perhaps have only visited places such as Dubai, Lebanon will certainly come as something of a culture shock with its intoxicating blend of tradition and modernity, the differing religious sects, a world-renowned cuisine and a country often at the heart of Middle Eastern politics. It is this infinite variety which helps to ensure that Lebanon is one of the best introductions to the Middle East you can find. If, like me, you prefer to visit less mainstream but totally rewarding destinations, I hope that you will find this guide a helpful companion on your Lebanese journey and that you leave, like I have, with an enduring fascination and love for the country and the Arab world.

Ahlan wa sahlan fi Lubnan
(Welcome to Lebanon!)

Part One

GENERAL INFORMATION

LEBANON AT A GLANCE

Full name Republic of Lebanon (Al-Jumhuriyah al-Lubnaniyah in Arabic, République Libanaise in French)

Location West Asia: 33°50′ N, 35°50′ E

Border countries Syria in the north and east, Israel in the south

Size 10,452km² (4,036 sq miles)

Geography Four main regions: long and narrow coastal plain, Mount Lebanon and Anti-Lebanon mountain ranges, separated by the Bekaa Valley

Climate Mediterranean with hot, dry summers and mild, wet winters. Heavy winter snow in the mountains

Population 6,237,738 (July 2016 estimate)

Status Republic. President and prime minister with legislative power residing with the 128 members of the unicameral National Assembly (parliament) elected through universal adult suffrage

Capital Beirut (*Bayroot* in Arabic, *Beyrouth* in French): 33°52′ N, 35°30′ E; population 2.226 million (2015 estimate)

Other main towns Baalbek, Byblos, Sidon, Tripoli, Tyre, Zahlé

Life expectancy Men 76.3 years, women 78.9 years (2016 estimate)

Economy Service sectors (banking and tourism, 69.7% of GDP), agriculture (5.6% of GDP), industry (24.7% of GDP) (2015 estimates)

Independence 22 November 1943 (from France)

Administrative divisions Eight governorates (*Muhafazat*) sub-divided into 25 districts (*Qada*)

Natural resources Iron ore, limestone, salt, arable land, water

Major rivers Litani, Assi, Moussa, Kalb, Awali, Ibrahim

GDP US$18,200 per capita (PPP) (2015 estimate)

Languages Arabic (official), French, English, Armenian

Adult literacy rate Male 96%, female 91.8% (2015 estimate)

Religion 18 officially recognised sects including Shi'ite and Sunni Muslim, Christian Maronite, Druze, Alawite

Currency Lebanese lira (LL), also known as the Lebanese pound (LBP)

Exchange rate £1 = LBP1,937.56, US$1 = LBP1,506.50, €1 = LBP1,6925.34 (October 2016); for current rates see www.xe.com

National airline Middle East Airlines – Air Liban (MEA; *www.mea.com.lb*)

Airport Rafiq Hariri International Airport, Beirut (IATA/ICAO airport codes: BEY/OLBA; *www.beirutairport.gov.lb*)

International telephone code + 961

Highest point Qornet es Saouda 3,083m (10,115ft)

Time GMT/UTC +2 winter (October–March); GMT/UTC +3 summer (April–September); US Eastern Standard Time (EST) +7

Electrical voltage 220v AC, 50Hz – European round two-pin plugs

Weights and measures Metric

Flag Two horizontal red bands (top and bottom), white band in the middle containing a cedar tree, Lebanon's national emblem

UNESCO World Heritage sites Aanjar, Baalbek, Byblos, Qadisha Valley and the Forest of the Cedars, Tyre

Ministry of Tourism website www.mot.gov.lb

National anthem 'Kulluna lil-watan' (All of Us, For Our Country!). Adopted 12 July 1927 by Presidential decree; words by Rachid Nakhlé (1873–1939)

Public holidays See pages 99–100

1

Background Information

GEOGRAPHY

Lebanon is a tiny country (ranked 170 in the world out of 257 nations according to Central Intelligence Agency (CIA) country comparison figures), making it easy to visit in a short space of time. Traffic permitting, it is perfectly feasible to travel from the extreme north to the far south of the country in 3–4 hours. Yet, despite its extremely compact size – around a third the size of the landmass of the US state of Maryland and a quarter the size of Switzerland – Lebanon possesses remarkable topographical diversity, ranging from rocky coastal landscapes, snow-capped mountains, fertile plains, lush valleys, rivers and waterfalls, all packed into a mere 10,452km^2. Roughly rectangular in shape, Lebanon's geography extends approximately 225km from Nahr al-Kabir (the Great River) on the northern border with Syria to Naqoura near the Israeli border in the south and averages just over 50km in width. Its northeastern border with Syria extends for some 403km, whilst the southern border with Israel stretches for 81km. Together with Israel and the Occupied Palestinian Territories, Jordan, Syria and Turkey, Lebanon forms part of the Levant – the 'land of the rising sun' – at the eastern end of the Mediterranean Sea and lies within the Fertile Crescent, a band of rich agricultural land that extends from Egypt to Iraq.

Lebanon can be divided into four main geographical regions with an approximate north–south configuration. The mainly narrow and broken maritime plain on the country's Mediterranean coast reaches its widest point of only 6.5km at the northern city of Tripoli. This region is home to the capital, Beirut, together with the country's other main towns and centres of population such as Byblos, Sidon, Tripoli and Tyre, which have their origins in ancient port settlements. Innumerable non-navigable rivers such as the Litani, Moussa, Ibrahim, Kalb and Awali make their exit here into the Mediterranean Sea from the mountains. Inland from the coast, the western Mount Lebanon range of mountains runs almost the entire length of the country and accounts for more than a third of Lebanon's landmass. The often wild and rugged terrain in this region has served throughout history as a point of refuge and safe haven for religious groups such as the Druze and Maronite Christians fleeing persecution and has been at the epicentre of Lebanon's historical, economic and social development. Like most of the country, this area is composed of limestone rock from the Jurassic and Cretaceous periods and reaches its and Lebanon's zenith at Qornet es Saouda (the Black Horn, 3,083m) in the northern section of the range northeast of Bcharré which remains blanketed with snow for much of the year. Known as *Jebel Lubnan* in Arabic, these mountains give Lebanon its name: *lubnan* meaning 'white' and referred to in the Bible (Jeremiah 18:14) as the 'snow of Lebanon'. Consequently, the Mount Lebanon area has a well-developed ski industry with a number of popular resorts dotted around the highest mountain peaks, with the ski season normally running

3

from around mid-December to mid-April. The section southeast of Beirut contains the picturesque and lush green relief of the Chouf Mountains, where unique and favourable geological conditions have enabled cultivation and human settlement to flourish at higher altitudes of up to 1,500m. The Chouf is also one of the main locations for Lebanon's national emblem, the ancient cedar tree (*Cedrus libani*); evergreen, coniferous trees that can attain heights of over 40m. Progressive deforestation by man since the Phoenician period has severely depleted the number of trees, but an active regeneration programme is ongoing. To the south of the Chouf and the Litani River is the last of the three principal sections of the Mount Lebanon range, Mount Amil (Jebel Amil), whose peaks merge into the Upper Galilee in modern-day northern Israel.

Forming a natural geological boundary with neighbouring Syria, eastern Lebanon is composed of the Anti-Lebanon mountain range (Lubnan ash-Sharqi in Arabic). Lower in height than the Mount Lebanon range, geologists believe that at one time the two formed a single structure. This eastern range of mountains is considerably more arid with meagre vegetation compared with that of Mount Lebanon, and many peaks retain a carpet of snow for much of the year. The highest point of the Anti-Lebanon range is reached at Mount Hermon (Jebel al-Sheikh, 2,814m) in the southeastern part of the country which straddles the Lebanese–Syrian border. On the western slopes of Mount Hermon lies the fertile valley known as Wadi al-Taym adjoining the southeastern Bekaa Valley, which has historically been an important place of refuge and settlement for the Shi'ite and Druze religious communities. Southwest of Mount Hermon is possibly one of the geographically smallest territorial disputed areas in the Middle East: that of the c22km^2 Shebaa farms. This slender portion of land, occupied by Israel along with the Syrian Golan Heights (Al-Jawlān in Arabic) captured during the 1967 Six Day War between the two countries, is claimed by Lebanon as sovereign territory but disputed by Israel, who claim the area falls within Syria's borders.

Sandwiched between the Mount Lebanon and Anti-Lebanon mountain ranges is Lebanon's agricultural and wine-producing heartland, the Bekaa Valley, ancient Rome's breadbasket and situated only 30km or so east of Beirut. The valley extends some 125km from north to south and varies in width from around 8km to 16km. A plateau, the Bekaa can nevertheless still reach a height of over 1,000m above sea level in parts. It comprises the northern extremity of the Great Rift Valley, which runs from the Jordan Valley in Syria to Mozambique in east Africa. The Bekaa accounts for around 40% of Lebanon's arable farmland; and its well-watered plains, facilitating the production of potatoes, tomatoes, olives, wheat and grapes, are thanks to the country's two main rivers having their source in the region: the Orontes (Assi) or Rebel River, named for the unusual direction of flow northwards into Syria and Turkey, and the Litani, which flows south from near Baalbek before finally meandering west and emptying into the Mediterranean Sea some 10km north of the southern city of Tyre. Where the flow of the Litani nears the Chouf Mountains is the artificial 11km^2 Lake Qaraoun, created in 1959 for the purposes of irrigation and hydro-electric power generation. Extending for some 140km in length, the Litani is Lebanon's largest river and the only major river in the Near East not crossing an international boundary.

CLIMATE

Unlike the overwhelming aridity of neighbouring Arab states in the region, Lebanon's climate is as diverse as its terrain. Temperatures and precipitation differ markedly from region to region, with the country's Mediterranean climate and weather systems broadly coinciding with its topographical zones, though modified locally owing to the great variations in the country's geography.

Nevertheless, Lebanon as a whole enjoys around 300 days of sunshine annually, making the country virtually a year-round travel destination.

THE COAST The coastal areas of the country experience a typical Mediterranean climate system, similar to that enjoyed by other areas sharing similar latitudes such as Los Angeles in California. Summer (June–September) on the coast is characterised by hot, dry and humid conditions, especially during July and August, though they are often modified slightly by sea breezes. Beirut, for example, has average summer temperatures ranging from 28°C to 35°C, and from June to September rain is virtually unheard of. The winter months (December–March) see temperatures drop to more palatable levels of between 11°C and 18°C (though Beirut has in the past recorded a January temperature of 25°C); but the flip side to this is that these months can see the heaviest and most concentrated periods of precipitation, and even a sprinkling of snow is periodically possible as far south as Beirut. Beirut, for instance, receives more rainfall than the city of Manchester in the UK, with more than seven inches in both December and January, but has only half the number of rainy days. This plentiful precipitation together with an absence of frost has helped to ensure the agricultural importance of the coastal districts, with many citrus fruits, banana plantations and vegetables cultivated there. Springtime (April–May) in the coastal districts is pleasantly warm with temperatures of between 15°C and 25°C, and as the winter rains recede the whole country begins to blossom with an assortment of vegetation and wildflowers. However, in spring and early summer the coastal areas can witness the onset of a hot, dust-laden and oppressive wind from the Sahara desert, the *khamseen*, which – though not good news for those suffering from conditions such as asthma – apparently has the strength to remove flowers and facilitate fruit growth. This wind has reputedly endured for up to 50 days (*khamseen* means 50 in Arabic) but for the most part is far more short-lived, lasting a week or so at most. Autumn (October–November) on the coast is also characterised by pleasant weather with lower temperatures than in summer, between 13°C and 28°C, less humidity and minimal rainfall.

INLAND Inland from the coast, the higher altitudes of the Lebanon and Anti-Lebanon mountain ranges considerably modify the country's basic Mediterranean climatic pattern. During summer, the mountains have a pleasantly cool and alpine feel with temperatures between 6°C and 22°C, providing a welcome respite from the more sultry conditions on the coast. Whilst daytime temperatures can often approximate those on the coast, the mountain air is much drier with a consequent decrease in humidity, and by nightfall temperatures have dropped much lower. In winter the dominant polar air masses prevail and, combined with the effects of altitude, it is much cooler than on the coast with most precipitation falling as snow from about mid-December onwards. This heralds the start of Lebanon's ski season, which can run until mid-April or even later, with some peaks, such as Mount Hermon, remaining snow-covered for the majority of the year. If you want to live the cliché and ski in the morning and take a dip in the Mediterranean Sea in the afternoon, then this is the time to do it. Autumn and spring both bring very pleasant weather, with temperatures varying from 0°C to 20°C and are the ideal seasons to indulge in outdoor activities such as hiking, trekking and exploring Lebanon's natural beauty and its array of archaeological sites.

Lying between the two mountain ranges, the Bekaa Valley is characterised by a more continental climate with extremely hot and dry summers. The town of Ksara near Zahlé, for example, has an average July temperature of around 31°C, comparable to Beirut on the coast, but minus the humidity due to the rain shadow effect produced by the Mount Lebanon range, which blocks the moisture-laden winds arriving from the sea. Night-time temperatures fall dramatically, however, and can be quite cool like the mountains, often necessitating a jumper or fleece for the evenings. The winter months in the Bekaa can also be very severe and are characterised by cold, windy and sometimes wet conditions with frequent snowfall. Ksara, for instance, has a recorded minimum temperature of 3°C in December, some 10°C lower than in the capital.

NATURAL HISTORY AND CONSERVATION

Whilst Lebanon may lack the predominantly dry conditions of neighbouring states in the region, the country more than makes up for this by being the most heavily wooded country in the Middle East: the Mount Lebanon and North Lebanon regions have the highest concentration of forested areas. The marked variations in topography, varying between upland, lowland and plateau, together with equally diverse meteorological conditions and a large water resource in an otherwise severely depleted region have helped to ensure Lebanon's rich biodiversity. Species range from sub-tropical to alpine. Combine this with a government and a variety of NGOs actively conserving the country's natural beauty and promoting the importance of the environment and sustainability issues, and Lebanon has all the ingredients for those interested in an ecotourism adventure.

FLORA The coastal areas of Lebanon are particularly lush and are an important agricultural region. Among the vegetation that grows and is cultivated here are orange, lemon, banana, palm and olive trees. In the mountains, pine, juniper, oak, fir, beech and cypress trees are abundant and comprise just a portion of Lebanon's estimated 2,600 species of flora, of which 12% are endemic. Lebanon's most famous flora, and the country's national symbol, is the cedar tree (*Cedrus libani*; box, pages 292–3), which are found in a number of areas, the most well known being in the environs of Bcharré in northern Lebanon and the Chouf Mountains southeast of Beirut. Progressive deforestation since biblical times, which saw the ancient Egyptians use the resin from the tree to embalm their pharaohs and the Phoenicians use the wood to build their ships, has severely depleted the cedars' numbers but many still remain and some are estimated to be around 2,000 years old. The much drier Bekaa Valley lacks any significant tree population and the flora here is mainly characterised by fields of vegetation and vineyards. Springtime throughout the country sees smaller vegetative types such as poppies, anemones (a type of buttercup), narcissus, clematis, cyclamen, wild herbs, shrubs and the vibrant Lebanon violet carpeting the landscape.

FAUNA The mountain and rural landscapes of Lebanon provide a haven for a range of animal life such as deer, wild cats, porcupines, badgers, foxes, squirrels, hedgehogs, hares, wolves, wild boar, goats and gazelles. The country's plentiful rivers are well stocked with eels, bass and mullet, and a variety of turtles such as the endangered green sea turtle (*Chelonia mydas*) and the loggerhead turtle (*Caretta caretta*) lay their eggs on the Palm Islands Nature Reserve off the coast of the northern city of Tripoli and in southern coastal regions such as Tyre and Naqoura; the Mediterranean monk seal (*Monachus monachus*) also frequents the coastal areas.

A number of snake species have been identified which range from the non-venomous large whip snake (*Coluber jugularis*), Lebanon's biggest serpent, which can grow to more than 2m in length, to the much smaller, though venomous, Palestinian viper (*Vipera palaestina*), as well as many types of lizard including the vibrant Levant green lizard (*Lacerta media*) and the Mediterranean chameleon (*Chamaeleo chameleon*). Snakes are particularly prevalent during the warmer summer months, and to help avoid being bitten the usual advice about wearing shoes or boots in areas where they are known to reside, and not to poke around in crevices with your hand, obviously applies (see page 77 for more details on snakebites).

A more unusual mammal you may be fortunate to encounter in Lebanon is the rock hyrax (*Procavia capensis*), which has been spotted in a number of areas such as the Chouf, Jabal Moussa and Horsh Ehden nature reserves. This small, rodent-like creature, similar in size to a domestic cat, has brown fur and its hoof-like toes can be likened to those of a horse. Despite the hyrax's small size, modern DNA techniques have revealed that the elephant is its nearest relative.

For ornithology enthusiasts, Lebanon's varied geography and its location on the important north–south African–Eurasian migration route offer a wealth of bird habitats and sighting possibilities. At the time of writing, Lebanon has some 15 sites which BirdLife International (*www.birdlife.org*) has designated as Important Bird Areas (IBAs). In total, BirdLife International have identified 294 different bird species, including the Syrian serin (*Serinus syriacus*), Bonelli's eagle (*Aquila fasciata*) and the chukar (*Alectoris chukar*), around the coastline and inland regions of Lebanon, with numerous other types observed at the Palm Islands Nature Reserve off the coast of Tripoli, such as finches, ospreys, broad-billed sandpipers, mistle thrush and tern, choosing to build their nests on the islands; whilst further south at the Tyre Coast Nature Reserve there are nesting sites for many birds on their annual migration routes. Cuckoos, eagles, kites, falcons, quails, vultures and woodpeckers are present in the mountains and nature reserves such as those in the Chouf and Horsh Ehden. In the marshlands of the Bekaa Valley, ducks, flamingos, herons, storks, buzzards, hoopoes, kestrels and golden eagles all use the area as a stop-off point on their annual migratory routes, flying north in spring (early March–mid-April) and south in autumn (mid-September–mid-October), prime birdwatching seasons.

ENVIRONMENTAL ISSUES AND CONCERNS Awareness of the impact of man's activities on the environment is much greater in Lebanon than in some Arab nations. The country's Ministry of Environment (*www.moe.gov.lb*), the government agency responsible for raising awareness of and protecting the country's natural world, often in conjunction with NGOs and voluntary organisations, has embarked on a large number of projects from general environmental awareness programmes to tackling climate change, wetlands and woodlands conservation schemes, forest-fire management plans and waste-management programmes for the olive oil industry to name a few. In 2001, the government allocated substantial funds to the ongoing National Reforestation Plan (NRP), aiming to increase Lebanon's forested areas

MAIN NATIONAL PARKS AND PROTECTED AREAS

- Aammiq Wetlands (pages 263–5)
- Bentael Nature Reserve (page 214)
- Chouf Cedar Reserve (pages 293–5)
- Horsh Ehden Nature Reserve (page 247)
- Jabal Moussa Biosphere Reserve (page 216)
- The Orange House Project (page 319)
- Palm Islands Nature Reserve (pages 235–7)
- Arz Tannourine Nature Reserve (page 244)
- Tyre Coast Nature Reserve (pages 322–3)

from its then 13.3% to 20% by 2030, replacing those trees and other flora lost or damaged through persistent deforestation, fires, wars, climate change, etc. Lebanon is also party to a number of international agreements concerning environmental issues such as biodiversity, climate change (Kyoto Protocol), hazardous waste, law of the sea, ozone layer protection, ship pollution, environmental modification and marine conservation. Moreover, Lebanon's plethora of well-established and protected nature reserves together with initiatives like the Lebanon Mountain Trail (LMT; box, page 235) benefit both the environment and rural communities and contribute to the country's ecotourism potential. In February 2013, Lebanon advanced in its quest to protect the sustainability of its natural environment by becoming the 178th state to join CITES (Convention on International Trade in Endangered Species of Wild Fauna and Flora; *www.cites.org*), who estimate that Lebanon has more than 100 species, eg: jungle cat, red fox, jackal, greater flamingo, and numerous birds of prey, reptiles and plants, under threat from continued trade.

However, despite these achievements, Lebanon still has some way to go. Recycling facilities and services, for example, are nowhere near what they are in western Europe or North America, and domestic and industrial waste continues to be disposed of into rivers, valleys and by roadsides, etc, with no consideration of the environmental impact. Along the coastline you will see discarded bottles, plastic bags and other refuse, all easily recyclable given the necessary infrastructure. In Beirut, air pollution from high-density car use and industry is a particular concern: in the hot summer months the air can be quite thick. Continued hunting and pesticide use are also issues that need to be confronted. The prognosis for Lebanon's environmental future was addressed at an October 2010 conference, the first in the country to highlight both the prevailing issues and possible solutions, and which drew attention to the worldwide problem of global warming, which in Lebanon's case could lead to the extinction of five plant species and significant reductions in annual snowfall, with the economic impact of a much shorter winter ski season (pages 192–5). On a local level, the conference drew attention to the high levels of pollution in the cities, the need for improved water purification systems, the ongoing need to protect the country's green spaces and the task of reducing Lebanon's 700+ rubbish tips, which pose a serious threat to both the environment and human health.

The most recent major damage to Lebanon's environment, however, came not from climate change or environmental mismanagement, but from the 34-day conflict in July 2006 between Israel and Hezbollah (box, page 32). Over a period of two days, the Israeli air force bombed the 40,000m² thermal power plant at Jiyeh, 30km south of Beirut, resulting in around 15,000–20,000 tonnes of oil being spilled into the Mediterranean Sea, creating a slick 10km wide and extending 150km along the Lebanese and Syrian coasts, and which threatened at one point to engulf Turkey and Cyprus. Scores of fish were killed and disruption caused to other marine life such as the already endangered green sea turtle. The one 'plus' point was that the type of oil released was of the heavy variety, which meant it sank quite quickly to the seabed before it could spread more widely to the beaches. Nonetheless, with a clean-up operation running into hundreds of millions of dollars, work is still ongoing to completely decontaminate the affected coastline and recover from the most devastating environmental disaster the eastern Mediterranean has ever seen.

HISTORY

Lebanon as an independent state is a recent creation, but its shores have been populated since the dawn of time, with the country's history telling of wave after wave of mostly foreign conquest and occupation. Lebanon's location within the Fertile Crescent also assures it of a place among the Cradles of Civilisation, for it was in this region that one of the oldest civilisations on earth has been recorded: the Sumerian people from Mesopotamia in modern-day Iraq c5000BCE. This early non-Semitic tribe is credited with the invention of the wheel, the measurement of time and its division into hours and minutes, as well as the oldest known form of writing, a wedge-like cuneiform script inscribed on clay tablets to aid business transactions. The Sumerians also used slaves to cut down and export Lebanese cedarwood.

Furthermore, the origins of the world's three monotheistic religions and civilisations – Judaism, Christianity and Islam – are inextricably linked to the history of the Middle East.

Lebanon's history can be seen in the architectural and cultural achievements left by a succession of foreign invaders and rulers. More than 400 years of Turkish rule have left an indelible footprint of Ottoman-style architecture in Beirut and the Chouf Mountains. The ancient Phoenician ramparts are less conspicuous, but the Temple of Echmoun (pages 307–9) in Sidon and the Temple of Baalat Gebal (page 212) in Byblos remain the most visible reminders of this once innovative civilisation. The relatively short-lived Roman occupation has bequeathed some of the most awe-inspiring architecture to be seen in the Middle East, at Baalbek. The onset of Muslim rule in the 7th century has left a unique and delicate archaeological legacy at Aanjar in the Bekaa Valley in the form of an Umayyad trading town, courtesy of the first of the Arab dynasties. Two centuries of Crusader presence in Lebanon has left imposing monuments in Byblos, Sidon, Beaufort and Tripoli, whilst the French colonial era has left a range of Parisian-style architecture in the capital. With such a rich and varied history, Lebanon is an ideal destination for aficionados of archaeology and culture in one of the region's smallest, yet most fascinatingly diverse, countries.

PHOENICIAN SETTLEMENT Although archaeological evidence unearthed in the coastal town of Byblos testifies to the existence of Neolithic dwellings dating back more than 7,000 years, it wasn't until c3000BCE that anything like permanent city-states were established on Lebanon's shores. Descendants of the Semitic Canaanites, who inhabited the land of Canaan – broadly comprising modern-day Israel and the Levant – the seafaring Phoenicians are widely considered to be the first settlers in Lebanon and established maritime trading colonies at Tyre, Sidon, Beirut and Byblos. For centuries they traded with Egypt, exporting Lebanese cedarwood, which was used to build King Solomon's Temple, in exchange for gold and other precious metals from the Nile Valley.

A quasi-autonomous people, the ancient Phoenicians lacked an overall sense of political unity, with their cities being overseen by hereditary kings and dominated by an economic elite. The least despotic of Lebanon's succession of invaders and occupiers over the years, their autonomy was, however, frequently interrupted by more omnipotent civilisations wanting access to the flourishing Levantine sea trade. In c1600BCE, tribal warriors from central Asia, the Hyksos, conquered and ruled both Egypt and Phoenicia for a century before Egypt regained control. The Hittites, from Anatolia in modern-day Turkey, who are credited with instigating the Iron Age, conquered the region in c1200BCE before Egyptian rule was once again restored. Out of the turmoil that engulfed the eastern Mediterranean around this time came the destruction of the Hittite Empire by the elusive Sea Peoples, probably from north Africa, and the decline of Mycenaean or late Bronze-Age Greek civilisation, which heralded the start of a golden era of stability and prosperity for the Phoenicians. This innovative and enterprising race expanded its maritime trading activities by sailing all over the Mediterranean, founding colonies on the islands of Cyprus and Malta, and in Tarshish in Spain, and by c814BCE had founded ancient Rome's nemesis, Carthage in present-day Tunisia. Phoenician ships, with their uniquely designed hulls, were able to cope with the rigours of long and often arduous sea journeys. The Phoenicians were also the first people to use the Pole Star for celestial or night-time navigation.

Revered as superb artisans and craftsmen using a variety of indigenous and imported materials to manufacture a range of luxury and utilitarian goods, the Phoenicians forged trading partnerships with peoples as diverse as the Israelites, and the Euboens and Nuragic peoples from Sardinia. Ivory was imported from Africa, India and Syria and fashioned into ornate items of furniture. Glass-making, metalwork and wine production were also important aspects of the Phoenician economy. But perhaps their most important aesthetic and economic product was the purple dye that was applied to clothing to create eye-catching garments coveted by royalty and the rich. (It was from the Greek word for purple, *phoinikes*, that gave the Phoenicians their name.) The dye was extracted from the hypobranchial glands of the murex mollusc, which was caught in nets off the Lebanese coast. Once the shells of the trapped mollusc had been smashed, they were allowed to dry out before salt water was added to produce the purple colour. Owing to the small amount of dye procured from each shell, production was necessarily on a huge scale; and at the southern city of Sidon, a mound of waste murex shells more than 40m high has been discovered. The whole process was also a very pungent one and the famous Greek geographer Strabo (circa 64BCE–circa CE23) offered the following observation on his visit to Tyre: 'The great number of dyeworks renders the city unpleasant as a place of residence, but the superior skill of the people in the practice of this art is the source of its wealth.'

Perhaps the greatest legacy of the Phoenicians today, however, is their invention of a 22-letter phonetic alphabet, devised to aid record-keeping and communication in business transactions. Though not the first people to assign spoken words to written form, the system they devised was the forerunner to all later alphabets, including our modern Roman one.

An important part of Phoenician life was their worship of a range of gods such as Melqart (God of the City), Astarte (God of Fertility), Echmoun (God of Healing) and Baal (Storm God). Despite these, however, this interlude of innovation and considerable economic and cultural achievement, the Phoenicians' mastery of the sea and their independence once again came under threat from the Assyrians from modern-day northern Iraq, who had succeeded the Sumerians c3000BCE. At its zenith, the Assyrian Empire embraced Iraq, Iran, Arabia, Turkey, Syria, Lebanon, Egypt and Cyprus. The Assyrians, like earlier powers, eager to gain access to the sea trade and expand their influence from a basically landlocked empire, under the Great King of Assyria, Ashurnasirpal II, burdened the Phoenician states with heavy tributes of silver, gold, tin, bronze and ivory to their powerful invaders. From c612–538BCE the Babylonians from southern Iraq broke the stranglehold of the Assyrians on Phoenicia and imposed another round of tributes on the Phoenicians. The arrival of the Persians in 539BCE, under Cyrus the Great, was initially a cathartic experience for the Phoenicians from Babylonian domination and they supported the Persians during the Greco-Persian Wars (490–49BCE), supplying their navy with ships and manpower. However, revolts and rebellions against the empire ensued as heavier and heavier tributes were imposed, continuing until the arrival of the Greeks on Lebanon's coast.

GREEK AND ROMAN CONQUEST Despite his forces being outnumbered two to one, the Macedonian general, Alexander the Great (July 356BCE–June 323BCE), dealt a crushing blow to the Persian Empire under Darius III, King of Persia, at the Battle of Issus in November 333BCE. Shortly afterwards, Alexander took the Phoenician city-states of Byblos and Sidon with ease, but the southernmost port of Tyre chose to staunchly resist the iconic leader. Tyre's reaction to the forces of Alexander was initially one of acquiescence, but when he declared his intention to offer a sacrifice to their god Melqart, this fell on deaf ears with the city's citizens. In Alexander's eyes, Tyre was too important a city to leave untouched; as a stronghold of the Persian navy, if left undefeated it would leave his forces vulnerable to a rearguard attack whilst *en route* to his conquest of Egypt. Negotiations with the Tyrians having failed, a seven-month-long siege of the city ensued – the longest and most protracted of Alexander's short but illustrious military career. Although many of Tyre's women and children were evacuated to Carthage, the remaining 40,000 or so Tyrian citizens stayed in the city; but with Alexander's overwhelming military might of more than 200 ships, the general proceeded to massacre around 8,000 people and consigned the remainder to a life of slavery.

Phoenician identity and independence was now on the wane and soon replaced by Greek cultural influences. Alexander's untimely death in 323BCE at the age of nearly 33 meant that his Hellenistic empire was split between his three generals – Antigonous, Ptolemy and Seleucus. Seleucus gained control of Phoenicia, and the Hellenistic Seleucid Empire held sway over the region, interrupted by frequent power struggles with the Ptolemies until 64BCE, when the emerging power of Rome under the general Pompey incorporated Lebanon together with Palestine in the south into the Roman province of Syria. The onset of Roman rule ushered in the period known as the Pax Romana, characterised by an increase in population and an era of peace and prosperity as the Phoenician people were given Roman citizenship and their economic and artisanal activities were permitted to flourish once again. This more sanguine period of colonisation also saw the Roman Empire establish a School of Law in Beirut which was revered throughout the empire. This period was also characterised by the building of huge and lavish temples; those at Baalbek testify to the optimism and ambition of Rome. The year CE395, however, marks an important stage in Lebanon's history at which the Roman Empire finally split into a western region (with its capital remaining in Rome), and an eastern portion known as the Byzantine Empire with its capital in Constantinople (modern-day Istanbul). One of the most salient points in this period of Roman rule was the widespread diffusion of Christianity – a faith and its followers who were until then much-persecuted – both within Lebanon and throughout the wider empire under the emperor Constantine 1 'The Great' (c27 February CE280–22 May CE337). Constantine credited his conversion to Christianity, in CE312, to divine intervention by Christ, an instructive vision which, he alleged, helped to facilitate his victory the next day at the Battle of Milvian Bridge and he formally endorsed the 'new' religion in the Edict of Milan in CE313 which permitted Christians, as well as followers of other faiths, to confess and practise their beliefs openly. By CE380, Christianity had become the Roman Empire's official religion. However, during the 5th century, fierce ecumenical discussions and schisms ensued including those relating to Christ's true nature and will.

From these theological conflicts arose a splinter group from the orthodox Christian Church, the Maronites, who take their name from a hermit called Saint Maroun. Because of the strict orthodox Christianity imposed by the Byzantine rulers, the Maronites came into conflict with the emperor Justinian II and were forced to take refuge in Lebanon's mountainous regions, which remain to this

c3000BCE	Settlement of the Semitic Canaanite peoples in modern-day Lebanon
c2500BCE	Phoenicians establish colonies at Tyre, Sidon, Byblos and Beirut and develop enduring trade relations with Egypt
c1550BCE	Egypt expands its empire and assumes control of Phoenicia
c1200–842BCE	Phoenician independence returns and they invent a 22-letter alphabet
842BCE	Assyrians, under King Ashurnasirpal II, conquer Phoenicia
814BCE	Phoenicians found Carthage in modern-day Tunisia
539–332BCE	Persian Empire conquers and rules Phoenicia
332BCE	January–July. Alexander the Great conquers Tyre after seven-month siege and Lebanon comes under Greek rule
64BCE–CE395	Pompey the Great conquers Phoenicia, and Lebanon becomes part of the Roman province of Syria, ushering in a Pax Romana
CE395–636	Roman Empire divides into two parts and Lebanon comes under the control of the eastern (Byzantine) Empire with its capital in Constantinople (modern-day Istanbul)
CE551	Earthquake and tsunami destroy Beirut resulting in 30,000 deaths in the city
CE636	Battle of Yarmouk marks the first wave of Arab conquests following the death of the Prophet Muhammad. Caliphate of Rashidun defeats the Byzantine armies in a six-day war and ends Byzantine rule in Anatolia (present-day Turkey)
CE652 (up to 1516)	A succession of Arab armies and dynasties sweep across the Middle East and beyond in a combination of conquest and peaceful conversion to the new faith of Islam
1095–1291	Crusaders (Franks) from western Europe embark on a series of conquests to liberate the Holy Land from Islamic rule. In Lebanon, they capture Tripoli, Beirut, Sidon and Tyre
1250–1516	Mamluk dynasty of former slaves
1348–49	'Black Death' slashes Lebanon's population by a third
1516–1918	Ottomans defeat Mamluks and rule over Lebanon
1633	Ottomans depose Druze emir Fakhreddine Maan II
1635	13 April. Ottomans execute emir Fakhreddine Maan II
1843	1 January. Ottomans carve up Mount Lebanon into separate Druze and Maronite administrative districts (qaim-maqamats), the first time Lebanon had been geo-politically divided along sectarian lines
1860	Druze/Maronite sectarian Mountain War
1918	Ottoman defeat in World War I and loss of Arab territories
1920	League of Nations places Lebanon under French Mandate rule
1926	23 May. Lebanon adopts its first constitution and becomes a republic
1932	31 January. Lebanon's last census shows Christians slightly outnumbering Muslims
1943	22 November. Lebanon gains independence from France; National Pact amends 1926 constitution
1945	Lebanon becomes a founding member of the United Nations (UN) and Arab League

1948	State of Israel is formed and 120,000 Palestinian refugees flee to Lebanon
1958	15 July. Operation Blue Bat. c14,000 US Marines land in Beirut to support pro-Western government and quell Arab nationalism
1967	Further intake of Palestinian refugees to Lebanon following Israel's victory in Six Day War, which fuels increasing Palestinian militancy
1970	Black September. Palestine Liberation Organisation (PLO) expelled from Jordan and sets up new headquarters in Beirut
1975	13 April. Start of Lebanon's 15-year civil war
1976	June. Syrian forces enter Lebanon, heralding start of Syria's long history of involvement in Lebanese affairs
1978	March. Israel launches Operation Litani to destroy PLO infrastructure south of the Litani River; UNIFIL created
1982	6 June. Israel invades Lebanon in Operation Peace for Galilee; Yasser Arafat and PLO leave Lebanon 16–18 September. Massacre of Palestinians at Sabra and Shatila refugee camps in Beirut by Christian Phalange
1983	23 October. 247 US servicemen and 58 French paratroopers killed in co-ordinated suicide bomb attacks in Beirut
1989	4 November. Lebanon's parliament ratifies Taif Agreement recalibrating the constitution to end the civil war
1990	13 October. End of 15-year civil war
1991	May. Lebanon and Syria sign the Brotherhood, Cooperation and Coordination Agreement September. Lebanon and Syria sign a Common Defence and Security Agreement
1992–96	Prime Minister Rafiq Hariri is the driving force behind post-war economic recovery; Israel–Hezbollah conflict continues for supremacy of south Lebanon
2000	25 May. Israel withdraws the last of its forces from south Lebanon
2005	Former prime minister Rafiq Hariri and 21 others killed by a car bomb in Beirut on Valentine's Day; Cedar Revolution calls for end to Syrian military/intelligence presence and justice for Hariri; Lebanon's politics splits into pro-Western 'March 14' and Hezbollah-dominated 'March 8' factions
2006	July–August. 34-day war between Israel and Hezbollah
2007	30 May. UN Security Council Resolution 1757 establishes Special Tribunal for Lebanon (STL) to investigate Hariri murder May–September. Lebanese army hostilities with Fatah al-Islam at Nahr al-Bared Palestinian camp near Tripoli
2008	21 May. Doha Agreement ends 18-month political crisis and averts possible civil war
2011	January. Collapse of 2009 pro-Western 'March 14' unity government following resignation of 'March 8' alliance members over STL 15 March. Start of uprising in Syria June. STL announce indictments against members of Hezbollah; Premier Najib Mikati forms Hezbollah-dominated cabinet

continued overleaf

2012–13	Syrian conflict embroils Lebanon – assassinations and car bombings, sectarian fighting between Alawites and Sunnis; influx of Syrian refugees; collapse of Mikati government; Hezbollah fighters enter Syria to support regime of Bashar al-Assad
2014	16 January. STL starts *in absentia* trial for five accused members of Hezbollah
	15 February. After 11 months of political stalemate a government of national interest is formed

day a place of sanctuary and pilgrimage. A weakened Byzantine Empire, a result of both internal religious disharmony and repeated incursions from eastern invaders, heralded the start of a new chapter in Lebanese, and Middle Eastern, history; one that would usher in both a new language and a new religion.

ISLAMIC CONQUEST AND RULE The transition to Islamic rule and the consequent Islamisation of Lebanon was a remarkably peaceful event compared with many earlier periods of Lebanese history. Islam was founded in CE610 by the Prophet Muhammad following a series of visitations from Jibril (Archangel Gabriel to Christians and Jews), who had revealed the final and true word of God to him, and these words were eventually written down in a series of verses known as the Koran, the sacred book of Islam (page 49). Muhammad then began the process of unifying the people and pantheistic faiths of Arabia who had hitherto worshipped some 360 different deities. After a period of struggle and conversion, Islam eventually became the third monotheistic faith after Judaism and Christianity, and the new religion spread like wildfire from the desert regions of the Arabian Peninsula. The seeds of Islam were planted in Lebanon some four years after the death of the Prophet Muhammad (in CE632) at the Battle of Yarmuk in CE636, the present-day border between Jordan and Syria. This early six-day war between the expanding Muslim forces and those of the Byzantine Empire saw the Arab armies emerge victorious and led to the decline of a Byzantine Empire already weakened by its long wars with the Persians, paving the way for the march west of the Muslim conquerors. In CE638 the hallowed city of Jerusalem, for centuries under Christian control, was also seized by the Muslim forces in the name of Islam.

The first Arab dynasty, the Umayyad Caliphate (CE661–750), led initially by the governor of Syria Muawiyya (died CE680), was established in Lebanon by CE661 and ruled from their capital in Damascus. Theirs was a huge empire, extending from India to central Asia and incorporating north Africa, Spain and Portugal. In CE732, the Umayyads were engaged in the Battle of Tours in France, where their advance was only halted by the Christian ruler Charles Martel (circa CE688–22 October 741). Some scholars have suggested that, if Martel had lost this battle, western Europe itself may well have come under the banner of Islam. Nonetheless, despite less than a century of Umayyad rule, under the caliph Abd al-Malik (reigned CE685–705) they made Arabic the formal language, introduced an Islamic currency, overhauled the tax system and generally ruled with a degree of tolerance towards other faiths such as Christians. In terms of architecture the Umayyads have left an impressive legacy, which more than hints at the monumental ambitions for their empire. The iconic Dome of the Rock (Qubbat al-Sakhrah) in Jerusalem's old city – located on

2015	Israeli airstrikes on Qunaitra in the Golan Heights kill six Hezbollah fighters; Hezbollah retaliates, killing two Israeli soldiers in Israeli-occupied Shebaa farms; Lebanon hosting c1.6 million Syrian refugees
	August. Demonstrations over rubbish disposal and ongoing presidential vacuum leads to violent street protests and calls for corrupt and incompetent government to resign
2016	Ongoing war in Syria and presidential vacuum continue to impact on Lebanon's present and future

the Temple Mount (Al-Haram Ash-Sharif), a site sacred to both Muslims and Jews – was completed in CE691 and the extensive Umayyad Mosque in Damascus's old city was commissioned during the reign of the sixth caliph, Khalid ibn al-Walid (reigned CE705–715). In Lebanon, too, the UNESCO-listed graceful palace in the Bekaa Valley town of Aanjar is also a must-visit site and the only remaining example of an inland trading town from the Umayyad period. Internal strife and economic decline, however, set in during the CE740s and seriously weakened the Umayyads' power base, and the final caliph, Marwan II, was overthrown following a coup in CE750 which saw Abdu'l Abbas as-Saffah found the Abbasid caliphate (CE750–1258). Ruling initially from Kufa and later from Baghdad in Iraq, the Abbasids governed the whole of the previous Umayyad dynasty, with the exception of Morocco and Spain. Although Lebanon's historical record is relatively quiet during the Abbasid reign, the caliphate's more fundamentalist rule was less tolerant than under their Umayyad predecessors, prompting intermittent rebellions from Lebanon's Christians. More broadly, this period of Arab rule is often referred to as the Golden Age of Islam for it saw great advances in literature, philosophy and the natural sciences, especially chemistry, mathematics and medicine, along with the blossoming of economic activity, in particular in the port cities of Tyre and Tripoli. After about CE860, however, the empire was weakening and, as wholesale decline accelerated, a number of smaller dynasties began to hold sway including the Tulunid and Ikhshidids in Egypt who would come to control swathes of southern Syria between CE868 and 969. The Fatimid dynasty (CE909–1171), with its capital initially in Tunisia, defeated the Ikhshidids in CE969. This Shi'ite Ismaeli caliphate, claiming descent from the Prophet Muhammad's daughter, Fatima, moved their capital to Cairo in CE973 and by the early CE980s had established control over Lebanon. In contrast to the preceding few centuries, the Fatimids placed more emphasis on commerce than military endeavours and Lebanon's coastal port cities were increasingly used for a flourishing trade with Europe and beyond. It was also during this period that the enigmatic Druze faith emerged, an offshoot of Ismaili Shi'ism (page 52). As Fatimid power eventually fragmented and weakened, they were usurped by the rising power of the Sunni Seljuk Turks (1058–1157), a group of Turkish chieftains who had conquered Persia and established their capital at Isfahan (modern-day Iran). In 1055, and again in 1058, they assisted the Abbasids in quelling internal schisms in their capital, Baghdad, and in return the Abbasids deferred to the Seljuk ruler as 'Sultan' or ruler of the State of Islam. The Seljuks went on to expand their territory into Fatimid domains during the 1070s, defeating them in Syria, occupying Aleppo and Damascus, and in 1071 the Seljuks, led by their second Sultan Alp Arslan (c1030–1072), achieved a significant victory over the Byzantines at the Battle of Manzikert in Armenia (Malazgirt in modern-day Turkey) – they now called their new state in Anatolia the sultanate of Rum, or 'Rome', a name that the Byzantines had continued to use. Though Fatimid power and influence was significantly weakened, the ongoing conflict between these rival Sunni states and the Shi'ite caliphate would soon prove to have extremely important repercussions, with the arrival of the crusaders from western Europe on Lebanon's shores *en route* to their conquest of Jerusalem.

CRUSADES For 200 years Lebanon would become embroiled in the battle between Christian and Muslim forces for supremacy of the Holy Land and, in particular, the hallowed city of Jerusalem (al-Quds in Arabic) – a site sacred to Christians, Jews and Muslims which had been in Islamic hands for more than 400 years, following its capture by the Caliph Omar from the Byzantines in CE638. There seems to be no single event that prompted thousands of armed and unarmed Christians to embark on an arduous three-year, c2,000-mile journey to reclaim lost land and restore Christianity's former dominance. In 1009, the Fatimid caliph known to history as 'mad' Al-Hakim had ordered the destruction of Jerusalem's Church of the Holy Sepulchre (the site of Christ's alleged crucifixion and resurrection) and went on to further harshly oppress the local Christian population. More salient perhaps was the ongoing expansion of territory by the Seljuk Turks, epitomised in 1071 when the Byzantines, under Emperor Romanus IV, were decisively defeated at the Battle of Manzikert (modern-day Turkey) led by Seljuk sultan Alp-Arslan. This loss drove the Greek Christian Emperor Alexius I Commenus (c1056–1118) to seek military assistance from Pope Urban II (c1035–1099) and the Roman Catholic Church, in order to stem the tide of Byzantium's losses and restore authority to the eastern realm of Christianity. A meeting was convened in March 1095 at the Council of Piacenza in northern Italy, attended by senior clergy as well as thousands of lay people. Despite existing doctrinal and ecclesiastical differences between the Western and Eastern branches of Christianity, Pope Urban reacted positively, and a few months later, in November, he convened the Council of Clermont in central France, where he delivered an impassioned speech imbued with anti-Islamic rhetoric, calling for an armed expedition to recover 'Jerusalem the Golden' from Muslims, who he said were 'alien to God'. Emphasising that those who 'take the Cross' would atone for past sins and be granted redemption, Urban's maligning and stern words were given extra cogency. His sermon was deemed utterly compelling by his audience and, overwhelmed with religious hysteria, the assembled crowds chanted the words 'Deus Vult!' (God wills it!), which quickly resonated around Europe, galvanising knights, infantrymen, and ordinary men, women and children, giving birth to the First Crusade (1096–99), which set off in the autumn of 1096.

An initial and disorganised 'People's Crusade', led by the charismatic and oddball preacher Peter the Hermit and impoverished knight Walter the Penniless, set off in May 1096 but was decisively cut down by the Seljuk Turks almost as soon as they had entered the Muslim world. The more organised armed pilgrims that followed, numbering up to 100,000 knights, infantrymen, peasants and noblemen were drawn mainly from Germany, France (hence the name Franks, which their Muslim foes called them) and Italy and included such figures as Count Raymond of Toulouse, Godfrey of Bouillon, Stephen of Bois and Bohemond of Taranto. The crusaders reached the epicentre of the eastern Greek church – Constantinople – in November 1096, then proceeding to conquer Nicaea (Iznik in present-day Turkey) in June 1097 and, after a hard-won battle at Dorylaeum (Eskisehir in modern-day Turkey) in July 1097, finally reached the heavily fortified and revered city of Antioch (Antakya in modern-day Turkey), which after an eight-month siege came under crusader control in June 1098. Continuing south along the coast, the crusaders finally reached their goal, Jerusalem, and, following a six-week siege, captured the holy city on 15 July 1099, unleashing a barbaric wave of attacks and slaughter not only on the city's Muslim population but also on local Christians and Jews. Despite immense losses in battle and from those due to exhaustion and starvation *en route* to the Holy Land, the first crusade was a resounding success, helped in no small way by the chaos and internal conflicts that existed in the Islamic world between the Shi'ite Fatimids and the Sunni Seljuk Turks, who failed to present a united front to repel the invaders. By the time Jerusalem fell, the Christians had established three overseas settlements, or *outremer*, which they built to defend and govern their newly acquired territories: County of Edessa (1097), Principality of Antioch (1098), and the Kingdom of Jerusalem (1099), which incorporated Beirut and southern Lebanon. Following the fall of Tripoli in 1109, the County of Tripoli completed the quartet of crusader states, which included the towns of Byblos and Batroun. Following the seizure of Jerusalem by the crusaders, military orders such as The Knights Templar and the still active Knights of St John (aka Hospitallers) arose to defend the city and provide medical assistance to pilgrims, whilst a series of strategic fortifications to defend their territories were built by the Franks to make up for their lack of numbers, such as those still standing and visitable in Lebanon at Beaufort, Byblos, Sidon, Tripoli et al.

But within 50 years the crusaders' fortunes would begin to turn: the powerful and ruthless warlord Zangi (c1084–1146) – *atabeg* (governor) of Aleppo (Syria) and Mosul (Iraq), nominally in league with the Seljuks – with a thirst for conquest and territorial gains, and boasting a 20,000-strong force, dealt the first hammer blow to the crusaders, capturing the County of Edessa in December 1144. This prompted Pope Eugenius III to launch a Second Crusade (1145–49), led by French King Louis VII, his wife Eleanor of Aquitaine, Germany's King Conrad III and some 60,000 soldiers. Suffering complete military humiliation after their failure to capture Damascus, the crusaders were now on the defensive as Zangi's youngest son, Nur ad-Din, assumed control of Damascus in 1154, and in 1169 despatched his Kurdish general Yusuf al-Din ibn Ayyub (better known to the world as Saladin; c1137/38–93), to Egypt, where he defeated the Fatimids in 1171, returning Sunni Islam to Egypt and becoming its new sultan. With Nur ad-Din's death in 1174, Saladin returned to Syria and, using a combination of diplomacy and military force, succeeded in uniting the various Muslim factions from Egypt to Iraq. Further military successes followed, with victory over the crusaders at the Battle of Hattin on 4 July 1187, and the fall of both Beirut and Sidon soon after. On 2 October, less than a century after its conquest by the crusaders, Saladin and the Ayyubid dynasty, which he had founded, won back Jerusalem.

Upon hearing of the loss of Jerusalem, Pope Urban III promptly died of a heart attack, through shock. His successor, Pope Gregory VIII, exhorted the Third Crusade (1187–92), sometimes referred to as the King's Crusade, which would see Richard I ('the Lionheart'; 1157–99), King of England, do battle with Saladin's forces. Despite having already seized Cyprus, Acre and Jaffa *en route* to Jerusalem by 1191, the pragmatic 'Coeur de Lion' was aware that, even if captured successfully, it would be almost impossible to retain control of the city. Thus, he signed the Treaty of Jaffa with Saladin on 2 September 1192, whereby Muslim control of the holy city would be preserved in return for pilgrims' unencumbered access and Christian control maintained in the coastal areas north from Jaffa to Tyre. Although there would be a further six crusades to the region resulting in relatively minor gains for the European invaders, they would never again fully recapture Jerusalem (except for a limited period of quasi control following the Sixth Crusade (1228–29) led by German Emperor Frederick II); and, following Saladin's death in 1193, his Ayyubid dynasty stuttered on for over half a century until overpowered by the rising power of the Mamluks.

MAMLUKS Ruling Egypt and Syria from their capital in Cairo for more than 250 years, the elite class of soldiers and warriors who comprised the Mamluk sultanate were not Arabs but former Turkish and Circassian slaves (Mamluk variously means 'owned', 'possessed' or 'slave' in Arabic) from the Christian lands of central Asia and the Caucasus. As was the convention of the times since the Abbasid era, young boys were often captured and brought to Cairo. Here, they were schooled in Islam and trained to the very highest standards in combat and warfare and owing total devotion to their masters. Eventually overpowering their Ayyubid owners, they succeeded the dynasty founded by Saladin and became a repressive and revered fighting force. Perhaps their greatest warrior was al-Zahir Rukn al-Din or Baybars (1223–77; ruled 1260–77), who possessed an impressive CV of military achievements: beating the French Crusader army of King Louis IX at the Battle of Mansourah on 8 February 1250 during the Seventh Crusade (1248–54); defeating the Mongol army at the Battle of Ayn Jalut on 3 September 1260; and, by the time of his death, many notable victories over the crusaders, including winning back Arsuf, Beaufort, Crac des Chevaliers, Haifa, Jaffa and Antoich in 1268. Qalawun (died 10 November 1290) succeeded Baybars as sultan in 1279 until his death and, together with his son al-Ashraf Khalil (d1293), proceeded to clean up what remained of the crusaders' *outremer*, taking back Latakia in 1287, Tripoli in 1289 and sacking their last remaining stronghold at Acre in 1291, the final nail in the coffin for the crusader presence in the Levant which soon saw the Franks evacuate their posts at Beirut, Sidon and Tyre. Military prowess and successes aside, the Mamluks also left a wonderful legacy of mosques and other architecture extant still today, with Lebanon's second city of Tripoli adorned with numerous beautiful examples of their building works. By the early 16th century, however, the Mamluks' hold on power was broken by the expansionist ideology of an empire, which was to change the face of Lebanon and the Middle East for the next four centuries and beyond: the Ottoman Empire.

OTTOMAN EMPIRE The Ottoman Empire traces its origins back to 1299 at Sogut in northwest Anatolia, about 150 miles from Istanbul, a then rural backwater of nomadic horsemen and tribal warriors. Named after its founder Osman (1258–c1324/26), his followers were known as Osmanlis (rendered in English as 'Ottoman'), and from these humble beginnings this Sunni Muslim dynasty morphed into an empire spanning three continents encompassing some one million square miles to become the world's last Islamic empire and superpower. Within a couple of years of its founding, the Ottomans had achieved a notable victory over the already ailing Byzantine Empire, and by 1326 Osman's son, Orhan, had established Bursa as the nascent empire's new capital. In 1453, under the 7th Ottoman sultan, Mehmed II 'the conqueror' (1432–81), he had achieved what previous Muslim armies of the Umayyad and Abbasid dynasties, as well as the Mongol Empire, had failed to do and captured Constantinople from the Byzantines, following a 54-day siege, which sounded the death knell for the late or eastern Roman Empire. The Ottomans now made their capital Istanbul, ruling from the Topkapi Palace overlooking the city and the Straits of the Bospherous. In this new epicentre of Ottoman power and rule, a *harim* of Christian slave women from Europe were used to ensure heirs for the empire, whilst the equally unsavoury and still common custom of *devershirme* or 'boy levy' saw young Christian children conscripted from their homelands in the Balkans and the Caucasus and brought to Istanbul, where they were schooled in Islam to serve the empire, with the most capable recruited into the elite Janissary military regiment. Although the Ottomans had quashed the last remnants of the Roman Empire, they still faced threats to the east from the opposing Shi'ite Persian Safavid Empire (1501–1722), which ruled from what is now modern-day Iran. Despite an important military victory over the Safavids in 1514 which served to subdue the challenge to their rule, the Ottomans decided to turn their attention south towards Mamluk-occupied lands to further cement their power and territorial supremacy over the Muslim world and which heralded a marked change in direction for future Ottoman rule over the soon-to-be-acquired Arab Lands. On 24 August 1516, at Marj Dabiq, some 40km north of the city of Aleppo in northwest Syria, a 60,000-strong army commanded by the 9th Ottoman sultan, Selim I 'the Grim' (ruled 1512–20) confronted a 20,000-strong Mamluk army led by its 49th sultan, al-Ashraf Qansuh al-Ghwari. The Mamluks, though courageous and highly skilled warriors, were not only outnumbered but also outgunned as the Ottoman forces had, in addition to their own skilled and disciplined army, modern firepower in the form of rifles. It wasn't long before numerical supremacy and the tools of modern warfare comprehensively cut down the Mamluk ranks, whose crushing defeat paved the way for Ottoman dominance over Syrian and Arab lands for the next 400 years, including Islam's holiest sites of Mecca, Medina and Jerusalem. This period ushered in the Golden Age of Ottoman rule: with Selim's son, Süleiman the Magnificent (c1494–1566; ruled 1520–66) in the west and al-Kanuni or 'the lawgiver' to the Turks, for his legal and administrative reforms, the empire reached its apogee and limits of expansion, with Iraq, Hungary, Greece and much of the North African Maghrib (excluding Morocco) added to the sultanate. Ottoman rule over Lebanon, as in many of its extensive territories, which stretched from Asia Minor to southeastern Europe, has been described as one of 'benign neglect', with existing power structures in lands under its authority permitted to retain a degree of autonomy as long as local rulers deferred to the power of the Sublime Porte (government) and sultan, and paid their taxes in full and on time.

In Lebanon the Ottomans allowed the existing feudal rule of the Druze Maan family to continue to oversee the Mount Lebanon region on their behalf. The Maans' most famous member was the emir Fakhreddine II (box, pages 284–5), who proved a good choice as proxy leader for a time until his expansionist and territorial ambitions posed a threat to Ottoman power, leading to his execution in Istanbul in 1635 after 45 years of rule. Following a period of struggle, rule passed to Fakhreddine's nephew for the next two decades, after which his grandson, Ahmad Maan (1658–97) took the helm and sought to perpetuate his grandfather's quest for independence for Lebanon from the Ottoman yoke. After his death without a male heir, the Maan dynasty declined and power was delegated to the related Sunni Shihab family. The pinnacle of their power was reached in 1788 with the ascent of Bashir Shihab II. Dubbed the 'Red Emir' for his omnipotent and often brutal suppression of his opponents including cutting their throats, the Shihabs had adopted Christianity by the end of the 18th century and forged an alliance with Egypt's rebel pasha Muhammad Ali to expel the Ottomans from Lebanese soil in 1831. The shift of power to the Shihabs and the harshness of their rule led to sectarian conflict between the Christians and the increasingly alienated Druze. To counter the threat to their economic interests, the Ottomans, aided by Britain and Austria, banished Bashir Shihab from Lebanon and he was exiled in Malta, signalling the demise of emirate rule in Lebanon. In order to fill the power vacuum, the Ottomans decided to divide up Mount Lebanon into Christian north and Druze south administrative and political districts (*qaim-maqamats*) in 1843, but this served merely to accentuate sectarian divisions and regular conflict as both areas possessed majority Christian populations. This paved the way for the 'events of 1860', which saw unprecedented ethnic cleansing between Christians and Druze costing 5,000 lives, the destruction of 200 villages and the displacement of 100,000 people in the Mount Lebanon region alone.

In 1861, the Ottomans, assisted by France who sent their forces to Beirut to support the Christians, once again reorganised Mount Lebanon into a singular unit or *mutasarrifiyah* under a Christian governor, and assisted by a council consisting of 12 members numerically representative of the country's sectarian communities implemented with European guarantees. Until the instability created by the outbreak of World War I, this new arrangement worked and this period saw a return to peace and economic prosperity, particularly in the capital which witnessed the growth of its silk and publishing industries, as well as the establishment of the Syrian Protestant College, a revered seat of learning, which opened its doors in 1866, later to be renamed the American University of Beirut (AUB). The Ottomans sided with the Central Powers during World War I, but following the defeat of Germany in 1918, Ottoman rule ended, to be replaced by another foreign power, France, which would also impose its hegemony on Lebanon.

FRENCH MANDATE The instruments for more than two decades of French rule in Lebanon were drawn up even before World War I had ended. In anticipation of an Allied victory, Britain and France held a series of meetings between 1915 and 1916, to discuss how they might divide up the former Ottoman lands between them following Germany's defeat. The end agreement of negotiations between British diplomat Sir Mark Sykes (1879–1919) and his French counterpart François Georges-Picot (1870–1951) resulted in the Sykes–Picot Agreement of 1916, where it was agreed that Lebanon along with Syria would be mandated to France and the UK would get Palestine and Iraq. For France, who had long cherished an expansion of its existing colonial presence in Arab lands, notably Algeria, Morocco and Tunisia, it also offered the opportunity to further strengthen its ties with the Christian Maronites. At the San Remo Conference in Italy between 9 and 26 April 1920, which was expressed by the Treaty of Sèvres, France was finally granted Lebanon and Syria and it could now realise its ambitions to impose its hegemony over the new State of Greater Lebanon (Etat du Grand Liban) with the initial avowed aim of supporting the Maronites', and Lebanon's, goal of achieving complete independence.

The passage of time, however, saw France begin to impose its own agenda on Lebanon. In line with Maronite wishes at the 1919 Paris Peace Conference, France extended Lebanon's borders beyond the Mount Lebanon area to encompass its 'natural boundaries' including Beirut, the eastern Bekaa Valley to the Anti-Lebanon Mountains, Sidon, Tyre and Tripoli, thereby sowing the seeds of discontent from the numerically superior Pan-Arab Muslims, who had no inclination to be part of a Christian-dominated order. Opposition from Muslims reached fever pitch in the summer of 1925, which saw violent conflicts between the Druze, who felt betrayed after French promises of autonomous rule failed to materialise, and the French, who harshly suppressed the Druze resistance. From hereon, France began to export its own culture and politics, with the flag becoming the French tricolour; new infrastructure emerged such as roads, healthcare, agricultural methods, a rise in the standard of living, and adoption of the French penal code, and the French language became compulsory in schools. But perhaps the most important aspect of French rule took place in 1926 when it initiated the still-current 'confessional' based political system, whereby power was apportioned along religious or sectarian lines heavily biased in favour of the Maronite population and the country became the Lebanese Republic.

Although the 1936 Franco-Lebanese Treaty guaranteeing Lebanon's future independence was signed in both Beirut and Damascus, its ratification was blocked by Paris. With the advent of World War II in 1939 and the invasion of France in May 1940 by German forces, France, along with Lebanon, experienced a period of Vichy rule until the Free French forces under General Charles de Gaulle (1890–1970) and Britain reclaimed Lebanon in June 1941 and promised the country complete independence. This was music to the ears of Lebanese nationalists, who now took matters into their own hands and began to prepare the road to an independent Lebanon, free of French influence and control.

INDEPENDENT LEBANON   In the aftermath of the Allied powers' victory over Vichy forces, Lebanon remained, in practice, under French rule, but in 1943 nationalist politicians held elections which voted in Bechara al-Khoury (1890–1964) as the country's first president, who in turn selected Riad al-Solh (1894–1951) to become the first prime minister. In their quest to gain absolute autonomy from France the constitution was redrafted to exclude the French mandate. Arabic was now made the official language and the Lebanese flag was redrawn into its current red and white stripes with a cedar tree in its centre. French anger at the changes prompted the speedy arrest of the president and prime minister by French forces; they were later released from detention in the Bekaa Valley town of Rashaya but only after much internal dissent and British pressure on the French. Independence was formally declared on 22 November 1943, but it would be another three years before the French military and security services departed Lebanon. Yet the changes and reforms to the constitution brought about by the new country enshrined the basic principles that had already been drawn up in 1926. The new unwritten National Pact of 1943 established in the new country the same confessional principles that had been drawn up under the French. It was agreed that the president would be a Maronite Christian, a Sunni Muslim would have the post of prime minister and the parliamentary speaker would be a Shi'ite Muslim, with the Druze also allocated cabinet posts. Such a system, something of a white elephant in Middle Eastern politics dominated by more authoritarian regimes, proved a remarkably stable system for a time and, with the end of World War II in 1945, Lebanon became a founding member of both the newly formed United Nations (UN) and the 22-member Arab League in the same year. Economic prosperity and political stability was a hallmark of this early period of independence and not even the creation of the State of Israel in 1948 after the first Arab–Israeli war, which saw the initial influx of around 120,000 Palestinians from their former homeland, was sufficient to yet upset the economic and political applecart, though even at this early stage the Lebanese government refused the refugees citizenship of Lebanon.

BACKGROUND TO CIVIL WAR   The long, protracted Lebanese civil war continues to cast an equally long and dark shadow over the country. Images and stories of wanton death and destruction, hostage-taking, and the murder and displacement of innocent people are horrors difficult to convey in words. With the country in the throes of recovery, traversing the heavily restored and pristine Downtown area of Beirut, once the epicentre of the conflict, it is hard to imagine the horrors once perpetrated there. Moreover, to this day there is still ongoing debate in political and scholarly circles as to what caused the war in the first place, with the different factions all having their own versions to tell. The following therefore is a timeline of the 'events' that started off with violence born of internal schisms in the country but which eventually embroiled a number of countries from Europe, the region and beyond.

Since independence in 1943, Lebanon's demographic balance had begun to shift dramatically. Through a combination of high Christian emigration and higher birth rates amongst Muslims, the latter were widely believed to be numerically superior to their Christian counterparts, thus reversing the findings of the 1932 census. Christian concern that this posed a potential threat to their dominance was exacerbated by the presence of some 127,600 Palestinian refugees by 1950. During this period the Pan-Arab stance of Egypt's president Gamal Abdel Nasser (1918–70), which sought to unify Arab nations whose ideology was successful in ousting the pro-Western government in Iraq in 1958, also found favour amongst Lebanese Muslims which brought them into conflict with their own pro-Western economy and government dominated by president Camille Chamoun (1900–87). Sectarian conflict resulted in street battles and in 1958, Chamoun became the first leader to evoke the Eisenhower Doctrine, inviting US forces into the country to quell the Muslim rebellion. US President Dwight D Eisenhower (1890–1969) quickly sanctioned Operation Blue Bat, which saw some 14,000 US Marines land in Beirut which quickly suppressed the uprising and US forces withdrew on 25 October. Yet this did little to ameliorate the growing schisms within Lebanese society which would be flagged up to more devastating effect within two decades.

The 1960s and 1970s witnessed, by and large, an age characterised by relative stability and prosperity and Lebanon emerged as the Middle East's financial centre. Economic prosperity and tourism ushered in a golden era, and Beirut was often referred to as the 'Paris' of the Middle East for its affluence and style. Though Lebanon took no part in the 1967 Six Day War (5–10 June) with Israel which saw the Jewish state capture the Sinai Peninsula, Gaza Strip, the West Bank, East Jerusalem and the Golan Heights, the country saw a further influx of Palestinian refugees, whose increasing radicalisation manifested itself in cross-border attacks on northern Israel from its bases in southern Lebanon, and the Palestinians found an ally in the Muslim faction the National Movement (NM) led by Kamal Jumblatt (1917–77). No such alliance took place with the Christians, who feared for the Muslim and Palestinian threats to their dominance in the country, and fighting erupted between the groups once again in 1969. This was only halted following Nasser's intervention which brokered the Cairo Agreement in November, permitting the Palestine Liberation Organisation (PLO) to launch attacks against Israel from Lebanese territory, much to the chagrin of the Maronite Christians. This volatile mix was added to again in 1970, following the PLO's exodus from Jordan during Black September in which some 3,000 Palestinians had died in clashes with Jordanian forces who had no intention of allowing a militant Palestinian group to operate from its soil. By 1975, the total Palestinian presence in Lebanon numbered some 350,000 and, with their new headquarters established in Beirut, continued to launch attacks and raids into northern Israel which continued with the onset of the 1973 October (Yom Kippur) War, though once again Lebanese forces took no part in that conflict. By March 1975, unofficial estimates made the Muslim population a majority over the Christians.

CIVIL WAR By March 1975, the demographic realities of the country had been translated into yet another conflict in which the Christian-controlled army violently suppressed a strike by fishermen in the southern port city of Sidon, which served to exacerbate an already tense situation. Less than four weeks later, on Sunday 13 April 1975, Muslim militiamen launched an attack on the Maronite leader Pierre Gemayel (1905–84) who founded the Kataeb Party (aka Phalangist Party) in the

1930s, which he survived, but which killed his personal bodyguard, among others, and is widely held to be the straw that broke the camel's back and ignited the flames of conflict in Lebanon. In reprisal, Christian Phalangist gunmen laid siege to a bus carrying Palestinians through the Christian neighbourhood of Ain Al-Remmaneh in Beirut, killing all its 28 occupants. From this point on this first stage of the war was characterised by a plethora of tit-for-tat killings, which would claim the lives of some 30,000 people with over 70,000 wounded until the first ceasefire, of which there were many, in October 1976. People were killed purely on the basis of their religious affiliation. On Black Friday, Beirut saw ten Christians massacred which was followed by the even more horrific Black Saturday in December, following which Christian militiamen, in retaliation for the death of four of their fighters, proceeded to kill more than 300 Muslims with the latter responding by killing a similar number of Christians. The carnage continued almost unabated and in January 1976, Christians entered the Muslim enclave of Quarantina in Beirut, killing hundreds of Palestinians and razing the town to the ground. This was followed by Palestinians entering the town of Damour south of Beirut, killing 500 of this town's Christian inhabitants. In June, Christian forces entered the Tal Al-Zaatar Palestinian refugee camp in east Beirut, killing some 3,000 of its 30,000 population during a two-month siege of the area. Eventually whole swathes of the capital were engulfed in the conflict with few areas spared. The city became partitioned into a Muslim west and Christian eastern sector with the no-man's-land in between dubbed the 'Green Line'.

FOREIGN INTERVENTION Towards the end of 1976, Lebanon had degenerated into a totally anarchic and chaotic state, with the Christian-dominated economic and political elite increasingly concerned at their inability to oust the Palestinians from Lebanon. The war entered a new phase in June with the entry of Syrian forces, initially in support of the Christians to prevent Israeli involvement in the event of a Muslim victory, and to secure its own hegemony over the country which would come to endure for nearly 30 more years. Some 26,500 Syrian troops entered the country along with an additional 3,500 committed by other Arab League states as part of the League's peacekeeping force, but to no avail. With no end in sight to continued Palestinian attacks from Lebanon on northern Israel, its southern neighbour entered the fray for the first time in March 1978. In an operation code-named Operation Litani, Israeli forces crossed the border into southern Lebanon in response to a Palestinian guerrilla attack on an Israeli bus travelling on the Haifa–Tel Aviv road which killed 37 Israelis. The avowed aim of the military action was to destroy PLO infrastructure south of the Litani River and set up a security zone to protect its northern border. Given the escalating situation Israel, under pressure from the United Nations to withdraw its forces, it did so, leaving its self-imposed 'security zone' in the hands of its Christian proxy militia, the South Lebanon Army (SLA), to assist in protecting its northern border areas. A UN peacekeeping force, the United Nations Interim Force in Lebanon (UNIFIL) was also established following UN Resolution 425, to maintain some semblance of order and peace with the 'interim' period remaining to this day. North of the Litani the fighting raged on with innumerable ceasefires coming and going. Syria became more and more drawn into the conflict as its relationship with the Phalange became strained, resulting in conflict between the two as well as Israel.

With the strengthening of the relationship between Israel and the Christians between 1977 and 1980, their alliance saw an opportunity to despatch the Palestinians, and Syria, from Lebanon once and for all. The momentum for this was the reshuffling of the Israeli cabinet in 1981 which saw the hard-line Yitzhak Shamir (1915–2012) become foreign minister and Ariel Sharon (1928–2014) granted the post of defence minister, both of whom saw the elimination of the PLO and Syria as a necessary step to eventual peace with Lebanon and the installation of a favourable Christian order, which resulted in the most intense period of fighting yet in the conflict. Although Israel's second 1982 invasion of the country had been in the planning stage for some months between Sharon and Gemayel, its stimulus was the assassination attempt on Israel's ambassador to Britain, Shlomo Argov (1929–2003), near London's Dorchester Hotel on 3 June by the Palestinian splinter group of Abu Nidal (1937–2002). Three days later Operation Peace for Galilee was put into effect, a much more wide-ranging and intense invasion than its 1978 effort. According to United Nations figures, 17,000 Lebanese and Palestinians were killed and a further 30,000 wounded during the ten-week Israeli operation, which dealt a heavy and decisive blow to the major cities in the south. As the PLO fighters retreated, they were pursued north to Beirut by the Israeli army and its 1,200 tanks where they laid siege to the capital, shelling PLO areas and cutting off food, fuel, water and other utility supplies. Following an international outcry over the operation, US intervention brought about a ceasefire and Yasser Arafat (1929–2004) and his PLO were allowed to leave Beirut under the protection and supervision of a multi-national force comprising US, French and Italian troops to other Arab states including Algeria, Iraq, Sudan, Yemen and Tunisia (the latter where the PLO set up its new headquarters). Born in Cairo, Arafat, the first representative of an NGO to address the United Nations General Assembly in 1974 and controversial Palestinian leader, founded his Fatah ('conquest') organisation in 1959. 'Fatah' was an inverted acronym of *Harakat Tahrir Filastin*, the Palestine Liberation Movement, which supported armed struggle to liberate Palestinian lands from occupation, and, following internal conflicts, Arafat would eventually become chairman of the PLO (founded in 1964) in 1969 until his death. Although Arafat would later come to share the Nobel Peace Prize in 1994 with Israel's Prime Minister Yitzhak Rabin (1922–95) and Foreign Minister Shimon Peres (1923–2016) following the 1993 Oslo Accords, in which the PLO recognised the right of Israel to exist with the Jewish state formally acknowledging the PLO and the Palestinians' right to self-determination, the departure of around 11,000 of his compatriots from Lebanon signalled the death knell for Arafat's longtime and passionate quest for a state and a homeland for the Palestinian people. The multi-national force left soon after the PLO's evacuation and Bashir Gemayel (1947–82) was elected president on 23 August 1982, only to be assassinated at his Kataeb Party headquarters three weeks later before he could become inaugurated, sparking outrage and calls for revenge and leading to Israel's return to the capital. Retribution duly arrived in horrific fashion only two days later when some 150 Christian militiamen entered the Palestinian refugee camps at Sabra and Shatila, where, over the course of just three days, they perpetrated an orgy of torture and killing against innocents which shocked the world and claimed up to 2,000 lives, many of those women and children. In its aftermath, eyewitness accounts and international investigations seemed to confirm that this macabre act, and a war crime, had at the very least tacit Israeli approval; in Tel Aviv alone, half a million Israelis demonstrated at the role of the Israel Defence Force (IDF) in the massacre, which resulted in Sharon stepping down from his post, but with no-one brought to justice for the crimes. The killing spree also led to the return of a 6,000-strong multi-national peacekeeping force in an attempt to broker a peace deal between the warring militias a week after Amin Gemayel (b1942) had succeeded his brother, Bashir, as the new president. Obliged to enter into the 17 May Agreement of 1983 by the US to guarantee the security of Israel's border in the north, the agreement was opposed by Muslims and Syria who soon attacked Christian neighbourhoods in Beirut. Meanwhile, fighting took place between Christian and Druze militias in the Chouf Mountains and despite its hitherto claims to be an honest broker in the war, the USS battleship *New Jersey* used its colossal 16-inch guns to batter Druze positions in the Chouf from the Mediterranean, which served to further Muslim hostility towards the US and its perceived support of Israel.

Although not the first suicide bombing on Lebanese soil during the civil war, it was a tactic and weapon which was to increase in frequency and severity by groups hostile to US interests. In April 1983, a suicide bomber killed 63 people, a death toll that included all the leading CIA agents in the region and destroyed the US embassy in Beirut. This was followed on 23 October by simultaneous suicide attacks on the US marine barracks near Beirut airport which killed 247 US servicemen. A truck laden with explosives was also driven into the headquarters of the French military, killing 58 French paratroopers. These attacks were deemed to be the work of the hitherto shadowy groups of Islamic Jihad and Hezbollah (box, pages 34–5), Lebanese Shi'ite organisations influenced by the Iranian Revolution and progressively radicalised by the Israeli presence in south Lebanon. During 1984, the Multi-National Force (MNF) departed Lebanon and the Israelis vacated the security zone in the south. Fighting continued between militias throughout the rest of the 1980s, with vestiges of the PLO in conflict with the Shi'ites and the Syrians increasing their stranglehold on the country. The Christians, despite their own internal conflicts, fought both. Some of the most intense fighting during this period was in the so-called 1985–87 'War of the Camps', which pitted the Shi'ite Amal militia against the Palestinians in west Beirut and the south of the country. Amal (Movement of the Dispossessed or Harakat al-Mahrumin in Arabic) had been founded back in 1975 by a theologian of Iranian origin called Musa al-Sadr (b1928–disappeared in Libya in 1978) as offering 'hope' to the impoverished Shi'ites by staving off Palestinian influence and thus the return of Israeli reprisals. Over the course of two years, in which the more moderate and secular Amal was also engaged in heavy fighting with the Druze and Hezbollah, it is estimated that the camp battles cost the lives of some 3,000 people. To get a sense of the sheer carnage and mayhem, which was Beirut around this time, the 2001 film *Spy Game* with Robert Redford and Brad Pitt is well worth watching.

With Amin Gemayel's tenure as president coming to an end on 22 September 1988, additional chaos and crisis ensued with Gemayel's appointment of the vehemently anti-Syrian general Michel Aoun (b1935) as the new prime minister. Aoun embarked on a 'War of Liberation' with military assistance from Iraq, who sought retribution for Syrian support for Iran during the 1980–88 conflict against the Syrian presence, in an attempt to unite the nation, but to no avail. In the absence of agreement across the sectarian divide the Muslims set up their own counter government in west Beirut, led by Prime Minister Salim al-Hoss (b1929), and intense fighting not seen since Israel's 1982 invasion once again arose between the militias across the Green Line. Following a ceasefire in September 1989, the Arab League initiated talks with the Lebanese politicians in the Saudi Arabian town of Taif to help resolve the conflict and pave the way for national reconciliation. Following 22 days of negotiations, this culminated in the Taif Agreement (officially, the Document of National Accord) which preserved Lebanon's confessional-based political system but led to an equitable 50:50 distribution of parliamentary seats from the previous 6:5 ratio in favour of the Christians. The Agreement also stipulated that all militias must lay down their weapons – except Hezbollah, who were permitted to continue their *jihad* of liberation against the Israeli occupation of south Lebanon. On 4 November, the accord was ratified by the Lebanese parliament. René Moawad (1925–89) was elected as the new president but assassinated a mere 17 days after taking office. Though Aoun was one of many other suspects, no-one has ever been charged with the killing of Moawad. Within 48 hours, Elias Hrawi (1925–2006) replaced him, whose pro-Syrian stance brought him on a collision course with the anti-Syrian Aoun, who was finally forced to go into exile to Paris following heavy Syrian bombardments and internal schisms with the Lebanese Forces (LF) commander Samir Geagea (b1952). With the civil war formally ending on 13 October 1990, the death toll was deemed to have cost somewhere between 100,000 and 200,000 lives, with many more wounded and displaced from their homes.

POST-WAR DEVELOPMENTS With an end to general hostilities a semblance of normality began to return to the country not witnessed for a decade and a half. It was a tenuous peace, however, and sporadic outbursts of fighting continued. The various militias began the process of disarmament, in accordance with the Taif Agreement, except for Hezbollah who were permitted to retain their arms to continue their struggle against Israel, and the south of Lebanon remained a volatile area. By the summer of 1992, the remaining Western hostages were released from their captivity and plans began in earnest to rebuild the devastated country and economy.

Following the first elections since the war, in 1992, the new billionaire prime minister Rafiq Hariri (1944–2005) initiated Solidere, a joint stock company charged with rebuilding Beirut's Downtown district with the aim of rejuvenating the capital which, it was hoped, would percolate through to drive economic growth and prosperity. It has proved controversial, amid rumblings about corruption and kickbacks, but it has undoubtedly transformed the aesthetics and the fortunes of Downtown Beirut. Meanwhile, Syria cemented its continuing presence in the country and in May 1991 signed the Brotherhood, Cooperation and Coordination Agreement, which was supplemented in September 1991 with a military treaty called the Common Defence and Security Agreement. In the south, fighting between Israel, its proxy the South Lebanon Army (SLA) and Hezbollah continued with major incursions by Israel in 1993 (Operation Accountability) and 1996 (Operation Grapes of Wrath); the latter provoking worldwide condemnation for its killing of more than 100 innocent civilians on 18 April sheltering at a United Nations (UN) base in Qana.

In May 2000, following public concern in Israel at its high military losses in Lebanon, its forces withdrew from the majority of the south of the country, which also saw the collapse and surrender of the SLA to Hezbollah. Israel remains in control of the small enclave known as the Shebaa farms, which remains a source of conflict and justification for Hezbollah's continued military action against Israel. Meanwhile, although dissent at another continuing occupying force, namely Syria, had been simmering away since the end of the civil war, when Damascus sanctioned extending the pro-Syrian Emile Lahoud's (b1936) term as president, the UN Security Council's Resolution 1559 calling for all foreign presence to cease in Lebanon, Rafiq Hariri resigned from office in opposition to Syria's ongoing presence. Just five months later, on Valentine's Day 2005, a one-tonne car bomb killed the former leader along with 21 other people and injured 226 others close to Beirut's Saint George's Hotel Yacht Motor Club in Ain Mreisse, widely attributed to Syrian involvement, and setting in motion a chain of events that would transform the country's political landscape. The outpouring of grief which followed Hariri's killing resulted in the resignation of Prime Minister Omar Karami (1934–2015) on 28 February amid criticism of his government's handling of the murder and soon erupted into larger-scale protests and demonstrations beginning with the pro-Syrian and Hezbollah organised protest in Beirut on 8 March, a date coinciding with the seizure of power in Syria of the Ba'ath Party in 1963, which was attended by up to 500,000 people who lauded Syria's near 30-year presence in the country and its contribution to stabilising the country. One month to the day after Hariri's murder, on 14 March, a more extensive counter demonstration and protest was attended by around a million Lebanese citizens from across the sectarian divide – about a quarter of the then country's population – who took to the streets in Martyrs' Square in Downtown Beirut to protest at alleged Syrian involvement in the assassination and demanded that the totality of Syrian presence in the country end. This mass wave of demonstrations and protests, Independence Intifada (*intifadat al-istiqlal*), came to be more popularly dubbed the Cedar Revolution and engendered the country's still current opposing political groupings known as the March 8 and March 14 Alliances; the former pro-Syrian led by Hezbollah and Amal whilst the latter a pro-Western grouping, led by Saad Hariri, the son of the murdered ex-premier, and his Future Movement, the Druze leader Walid Jumblatt (b1949), and Samir Geagea, committed to terminating Syria's occupation and meddling in Lebanese affairs. Following continued internal and foreign outcry, especially from the USA and France, Syria finally succumbed to the pressure and withdrew its 14,000 military and known security personnel from Lebanon on 26 April 2005, ending a 29-year military and hegemonic occupation which also saw the return of the banished Aoun to Lebanon.

In the wake of the Hariri assassination, the resulting Cedar Revolution and the departure of all known Syrian military and intelligence personnel from Lebanon, the country continued to be dogged by political turmoil and violence, which over the next decade and to the present day, heightened by the Arab Spring and war in Syria (pages 29–33), would dramatically expose the deep fault lines now running through Lebanese politics and society. Whilst the May/June 2005 parliamentary elections – the first in the post-civil-war era without Syrian interference – went ahead and resulted in a convincing victory for the March 14 alliance (winning 72 of the 128 parliamentary seats), which installed former Finance Minister Fouad Siniora (b1943) as prime minister, targeted assassination attempts and murders, with the finger of blame once again pointing at Syria, continued throughout the year alongside the preliminary UN investigations into Hariri's murder. On 12 July anti-Syrian Defence Minister Elias al-Murr (b1962) survived a car bomb attack; on 2 June, journalist and Syrian critic Samir Kassir (1960–2005) was killed in a car bomb attack in east Beirut; and, on 21 June and 28 December respectively, anti-Syrian and Communist Party leader George Hawi (1938–2005) and Christian leader and journalist Gebran Tueni (1957–2005) suffered similar fates.

The following few years proved to be no less challenging and eventful for Lebanon. In February 2006, Aoun and his Free Patriotic Movement (FPM) changed direction and allied with Hezbollah and the March 8 faction in opposition, and in July Hezbollah and Israel engaged in devastating month-long hostilities (box, page 32), which, for a short-time at least, diverted attention away from the UN investigation into Hariri's murder. Following the July war's ceasefire in August, however, conflict between the two March camps deepened, with March 8 ministers from Amal and Hezbollah resigning their cabinet posts in the government in protest at the government's endorsement of a UN tribunal to investigate the Hariri killing, and with March 14 castigating Hezbollah for instigating such a high economic and human cost of their summer war with the Jewish state and their omnipotence in defiance of seeking any legal government approval for such a costly conflict. These events led to the beginning of a near 18-month political deadlock within the country, which witnessed street protests and sit-ins led by Hezbollah and its March 8 supporters. Crises of one sort or another continued to afflict Lebanon throughout 2007, with death and destruction rearing their heads again in May, this time at

1

the Palestinian refugee camp of Nahr al-Bared, near the northern city of Tripoli, between Sunni militants and the Lebanese army (pages 227–8) in which Syria was again allegedly involved. The cessation of the camp hostilities in September was soon followed by a six-month presidential hiatus following the expiration of Emile Lahoud's term of office towards the end of November, with the opposing March political factions unable to agree on Lahoud's successor and March 8 lobbying for a greater share of power in parliament as a pre-condition to accepting March 14's proposed presidential candidate, Michel Suleiman (b1948). The year 2007 drew to a close with the assassination on 12 December of army officer General François al-Hajj (1953–2007), whilst 2008 began as the previous one had ended, with the murder on 25 January of police Captain Wissam Eid (1976–2008), an investigator in the Hariri murder investigation who had been responsible for proposing the examination of mobile phone data, which, he later claimed, could be linked to Hezbollah and which now forms a substantial part of the ongoing investigation. Just a few months later, on 5 May, the government of Fouad Siniora attempted to reign in Hezbollah by dismissing Shi'ite airport security chief General Wafik Shkair for his perceived links to the Party of God and to close down the groups' telecommunications network. This was too much for the Shi'ite party to bear who deemed the decisions a 'declaration of war' against the 'resistance' and on 8 May launched Operation Smashing the Balance (*amaliyat kasr al-tawazun*), in which Hezbollah and its armed allies, including Amal, overran parts of Sunni west Beirut, including the area around the prime minister's building and the future offices of March 14. Armed clashes in the capital and elsewhere resulted in around 70 deaths before an interim ceasefire ensued and the government revoked its decisions. Not for the first time in its tumultuous history, however, Lebanon's descent into the abyss was thwarted by outside intervention, this time by Qatar, who invited the opposing factions to Doha to broker an end to the conflict and the 18-month political crises. The resulting Doha Agreement, signed on 21 May 2008 by all parties, defused the dispute and finally resulted in the inauguration on 25 May of Michel Suleiman as Lebanon's 11th President and the formation of an interim 30-member cabinet of national unity with a greater share of parliamentary power granted to March 8; it also paved the way for the 7 June 2009 elections, which saw March 14 again emerge victorious (winning 71 of the 128 parliamentary seats) with Saad Hariri becoming the country's 51st prime minister and finally forming a government of national unity in November.

The Hariri government, however, was plagued with conflicts and disagreements from the start, not least over the continuing UN investigation into his father's murder which had commenced its work as the Special Tribunal for Lebanon (STL) in March 2009 (box, pages 30–1). Amid suspicions that the STL was shortly going to point the finger of blame at members of Hezbollah for Hariri's killing (later confirmed on 29 June), the Party of God's leader, Hassan Nasrallah, asked the government to reject the tribunal as an Israeli–American conspiracy. Falling on deaf ears, on 13 January 2011, 11 cabinet members from the March 8 political alliance promptly quit the government, leaving Saad Hariri no choice but to resign as prime minister. With the earlier defection of Walid Jumblatt's Progressive Socialist Party (PSP) bloc to March 8 from March 14, the former coalition now became the majority; Hezbollah, along with Aoun and Jumblatt, nominated Najib Mikati (b1955) to serve his second term as prime minister, and he finally managed to form a cabinet on 13 June following a five-month political impasse. Mikati's tenure lasted until 22 March 2013, when he resigned after failing to implement electoral reform for the upcoming June elections and citing irreconcilable differences between the opposing March political camps, particularly in relation to matters of security. Following cross-party support, on 6 April 2013 current prime minister, Tammam Salam, was nominated to succeed Mikati, but internal disputes delayed Salam's formation of a government of national interest until 15 February 2014. Salam's government entered a political fold in which deep divisions between the March 8 and 14 factions, together with the ongoing STL, and disputes over electoral reform were exacerbated by the conflict now raging across the border in Syria, of particular concern the divergent views of the March political camps over the military support provided by Hezbollah to help ensure the survival of the Assad regime, the huge influx of Syrian refugees, security issues and the economic and social impact of the war. Added to this volatile mix of issues would be the forthcoming political vacuum, created by the inability of parliament to elect a new president following the end of Michel Suleiman's term of office on 25 May 2014, and a mass demonstration of Lebanese in Downtown Beirut in August 2015 over garbage collection and politicians' ineptness and corruption. At the time of writing, Salam and his cabinet have assumed the duties of the president in the interim, as permitted by the constitution, and amid security concerns and heightened tensions in the light of the situation in Syria, in November 2014 parliament extended its current mandate until June 2017.

ARAB SPRING AND WAR IN SYRIA When 26-year-old street trader Muhammad Bouazizi (29 March 1984–4 January 2011) publicly set himself on fire in the central Tunisian town of Sidi Bouzid on 17 December 2010 to protest at police brutality, corruption and injustice, he probably couldn't have foreseen the impact that his extreme form of protest would have on other parts of north Africa and the wider Arab world. His actions quickly resonated across the country, culminating in mass resistance and uprisings – dubbed the Jasmine Revolution – which saw the rebellion rapidly spread across the Middle East galvanising support in the form of popular protest against long-time simmering opposition and resentment at years of despotic rule and human rights violations, as well as a host of other economic and social disadvantages experienced by the Arab peoples. This 'Arab Spring', referring to the mass flowering of protests of discontent, soon resulted in the popular overthrow of autocratic regimes not only of President Zine al-Abidine Ben Ali's 23 years of authoritarian rule in Tunisia, but also in Egypt, Libya and Yemen, and served to incite smaller but still significant opposition protests in other Arab and Gulf countries such as Bahrain. As far as Lebanon was concerned, the impact was initially negligible, given the country's more pluralistic make-up, with current political debate hitherto dominated by internal political meanderings and the forthcoming STL (box, pages 30–1). All this would soon change, however.

Across the border in Syria, the seeds of discontent against oppressive rule were sown, when, in March 2011, in the southern city of Deraa close to the Jordanian border, 15 pupils daubed revolutionary slogans on the wall of their school ('the people want to bring down the regime'), resulting in their arrest and the subsequent torture and killing of dozens of demonstrators by security forces. Nationwide protests and opposition to the dictatorial rule of President Bashar al-Assad (b1965) rapidly ensued, and Syria has since descended into a seemingly never-ending and increasingly brutal and complex civil war. Into its sixth year at the time of writing, this conflict is currently the world's worst humanitarian disaster and the latest statistics make for sombre reading: more than 400,000 people killed (a figure already far eclipsing the worst estimates of Lebanon's death toll from its own 15-year civil strife); around seven million people internally displaced within Syria; and well over 4.59 million Syrian refugees eking out a harsh and tenuous existence outside the country, mainly

The Special Tribunal for Lebanon (STL) is the first international tribunal to preside over an act of terrorism in peacetime. It is independent of, but backed by, the United Nations (UN), established on 30 May 2007 by UN Security Council Resolution 1757, following a request by the Lebanese government on 13 December 2005, with a mandate 'to prosecute persons responsible for the attack of 14 February 2005 resulting in the death of former Prime Minister Rafiq Hariri and in the death or injury of other persons.' The STL officially commenced its work on 1 March 2009 with a remit that has scope to be broadened to include investigations into attacks in Lebanon which occurred between 1 October 2004 and 12 December 2005 and beyond if evidence becomes available that they are 'connected' and are of a 'similar nature and gravity' to the Hariri murder. As a hybrid court, comprising both Lebanese and international judges and other staff, the STL uniquely uses Lebanese national criminal law – but excluding forced labour and the death penalty – with a maximum sentence of life imprisonment, with any eventual convicted person(s) serving their sentence in a country designated by the STL president from a list of countries who have said they would be willing to accept the guilty person(s). As the STL is not a UN institution, its annual funding (€62.8 million in 2016) is similarly hybrid with 51% of its annual budget paid for by voluntary contributions from states such as the UK, other EU nations and the US, with the Lebanese government meeting the remaining 49% of the cost. Nearly nine years after Hariri's killing and a number of setbacks and indictments, the trial finally got underway on 16 January 2014, held 'to ensure justice, fairness and security', at Leidschendam, near The Hague, in the Netherlands, with five members of Hezbollah being tried as individuals, as opposed to Party of God members, *in absentia* at the time of writing; the first international criminal court since the post-World War Two Nuremberg Trials of Nazi war criminals to hold such *in absentia* proceedings.

Yet what seems *prima facie* to be merely a quest for justice has from the STL's inception polarised Lebanon's delicate sectarian balance, with tensions pervading Lebanese politics ever since the 2005 attack. In the wake of Hariri's killing, a series of demonstrations and rallies in March 2005 culminated in the so-called Cedar Revolution, calling for the withdrawal of all Syrian military and intelligence personnel and an end to Syrian meddling in Lebanese politics, with many blaming Syria, and later Hezbollah, for the bomb attack on Hariri. Lebanon's political scene

in Jordan (c650,000), Turkey (c2.5 million) and Lebanon (c1.6 million), with Iraq, Egypt and Libya hosting smaller numbers of Syrian migrants. The exodus fleeing the conflict, however, has extended beyond the region to mainland Europe and the UK, where around 10% of Syrians have sought safe haven, dividing EU nations over responsibility for the resettlement of these displaced people. What began as a call for the removal of President Assad has developed in to full-blown sectarian conflict – a schism between Sunnis and Shi'ites, which dates back to the dawn of Islam some 1,400 years ago (page 48) –pulling in regional and world powers, with additional complications created by the rise of a multitude of armed factions, most notoriously the extremist and Sunni jihadist group Islamic State (IS; aka Daesh), in 2013, who declared a 'caliphate' the following year after its seizure of large areas of Iraq and Syria.

In order to try to distance itself from the fallout from the Arab uprisings, especially the Syrian war, Lebanon's cross-party National Dialogue Committee issued the Baabda Declaration on 11 June 2012 to express the country's neutrality divided into a pro-Western and anti-Syrian March 14 alliance supported by the US, Saudi Arabia and former prime minister Saad Hariri (b1970), son of the slain premier, who have an 'unswerving commitment to international legitimacy' and the STL. The opposing pro-Syrian March 8 faction, dominated by Hezbollah, totally reject the very existence of the STL, which its leader Sayyed Hassan Nasrallah has designated an 'Israeli project' serving Western interests, designed to 'guillotine the resistance'. They point also to the 'false witnesses', which they say wrongly implicated Syria in the 2005 attack, and steadfastly refuse to hand over any of the current accused to the STL. Following talk in 2010 of the STL about to indict members of Hezbollah, 11 cabinet members of the March 8 camp resigned in protest at the government's refusal to condemn the STL and the government collapsed on 13 January 2011 with March 8 nominee Najib Mikati (b1955) finally forming a cabinet on 13 June 2011, but resigning over forthcoming elections in March 2013. Following an 11-month political impasse, current prime minister Tammam Salam (b1945) finally formed a government of 'national interest' in February 2014, amid the current ongoing STL proceedings and the war in neighbouring Syria. Whilst somewhat overshadowed by the latter events and elsewhere in the region, the STL nonetheless remains a political hot potato in Lebanon. The announcement in January 2014 that the STL have charged a journalist and the Al-Jadeed TV station with contempt of court for 'knowingly and wilfully interfering with the administration of justice' relating to witness broadcasts in August 2012 has possible ramifications for press freedom in Lebanon and beyond. Both stood trial in The Hague on 16 April 2015, the STL setting yet another example of its 'special' character by becoming the first international court to indict a company, with the Contempt Judge on 18 September 2015 acquitting the TV station but fining the journalist €10,000 with an appeal by both the prosecution and defence ongoing at the time of writing. Amid continuing debate over the STL's costs (US$400+ million to date), the odds against the accused ever appearing in court let alone serving a prison sentence, and its political neutrality, the STL itself remains optimistic, with Tribunal spokesperson Marten Youssef commenting that: 'Justice is not a waste of time, even if it's *in absentia*. Part of the process is the discovery of the truth – this is what the victims are waiting for. And if there are convictions, that will live with the culprits for the rest of their lives.' For further details and to keep abreast of developments visit the official STL website (*www.stl-tsl.org*).

and a 'disassociation' policy towards these conflicts in order 'to avoid the negative repercussions of regional tensions and crises to preserve its own paramount interest, national unity and civil peace…' Yet as the war in Syria has evolved, with the huge influx of Syrian refugees and a deteriorating security situation which has seen intermittent violence and assassinations around the country, its impact on Lebanon has become more and more palpable. On 19 October 2012, a car bomb in the east Beirut neighbourhood of Achrafieh killed Wissam al-Hassan (1965–2012), Head of Lebanon's Internal Security Forces (ISF), a known opponent of the Assad regime who was instrumental in implicating Syria for the 2005 assassination of former premier Rafiq Hariri. This was followed in June 2013 by battles in the southern city of Sidon between the Lebanese Army and the radical Sunni sheikh Ahmad Al-Assir, aligned with rebels in Syria and a staunch opponent of Lebanon's Shi'ite Hezbollah, with the ensuing fighting killing dozens, including several Lebanese soldiers. Since 2013 the active military engagement of Lebanon's Hezbollah – for

Popularly known as the July War by the Lebanese and the Second Lebanon War in Israel, this 34-day conflict between Israel and Hezbollah was the most recent large-scale battle between these implacable foes. The start of the war on 12 July was in response to the Shi'ite party's military wing crossing the border into Israel killing three IDF (Israel Defence Force) members, wounding two and abducting a further two soldiers, ostensibly to pressurise the Jewish state into releasing Lebanese and Palestinian prisoners held in Israel. Israeli reprisals were rapid and severe with the avowed aim of the wholesale destruction of Hezbollah which went far beyond what even the Party of God had expected. The Israeli military launched large-scale air and sea strikes on the south of the country, Beirut airport and beyond, with the two sides fighting fierce ground battles in the hills of south Lebanon which saw Hezbollah launch more than 4,000 of its Iranian-supplied Katyusha rockets into northern Israel. There were many low points in this war, the nadirs being Hezbollah's rocket attacks, which killed eight Israeli civilians on 16 July in the northern Israeli city of Haifa, followed by Israel's 30 July airstrike on the southern village of Qana which killed 28 civilians, including 16 children; this latter attack provoked an international outcry which served to hasten the end of hostilities. By the end of the war some 1,191, mainly Lebanese, civilians had been killed and some 160 Israelis, mainly IDF members, with 4,405 Lebanese and 4,262 Israelis wounded. Lebanon's infrastructure was decimated with many of the country's roads and around 100 bridges destroyed. Almost one million Lebanese had been displaced and 30,000 homes were destroyed. The intense Israeli air bombardment of Lebanon's main power plant at Jiyeh resulted in an environmental catastrophe unprecedented in the eastern Mediterranean (page 8). According to the UN, the economic cost of the war to Lebanon was estimated at cUS$5 billion, severely disrupting the hitherto promising post civil war tourist recovery. In south Lebanon a large number of unexploded cluster bombs and other ordnance still pose a threat to locals and visitors alike. Although an Israeli naval blockade remained in place until 8 September, United Nations Security Council Resolution 1701 on 11 August led to a final ceasefire three days later. Despite both sides claiming victory, Israel's aim of destroying Hezbollah had not been achieved and the party's standing remained strong in the wake of its self-confessed 'divine victory' with its Shi'ite supporters as it did with many other Lebanese. The UN call for the disarmament of all militias had also not been accomplished. The end result of this conflict was merely a more intense UN peacekeeping force in the south and, for the first time in many years, the deployment of Lebanese forces around the country. Meanwhile, both Israel and Hezbollah have been busily replenishing their arsenals with Hezbollah now possessing more sophisticated and longer-range weapons, whilst Israel's receipt of military aid from the US continues apace…

whom the Baabda Declaration was, in the words of Hezbollah MP Muhammad Raad merely 'ink on paper (and) born dead' – in Syria in support of the Alawite regime of President Assad, the group's main patron along with Iran and Russia, has also had repercussions, including the 12 November 2015 twin suicide bombing in the Shi'ite-dominated south Beirut suburb of Bourj Brajneh which killed 43 people and injured 239 others. Responsibility for the attack was claimed by IS in revenge for

Hezbollah's military presence in Syria. The northern city of Tripoli has not escaped the conflict and has been intermittently mired in sectarian fighting between its opposition Sunni and pro-Assad Alawite communities; most devastatingly to date, on 23 August 2013, Tripoli was the scene of twin bomb attacks near two mosques during Friday prayers which resulted in 47 deaths with hundreds more injured. The high human cost of the spillover from the Syrian conflict has been equally devastating for Lebanon economically, with the World Bank estimating that since 2012 the economic cost to Lebanon amounts to more than US$13.1 billion, equating to around 11% of the country's GDP. As the fighting in Syria shows little sign of any denouement at the time of writing, regional and world powers remain militarily and politically embroiled and divided, with countries such as Qatar, Jordan, Saudi Arabia, Turkey, the US, the UK and France supporting the Sunni rebel militias against Assad, whilst Iran, Lebanon's Hezbollah and Russia are allied with the Assad regime. By the early part of 2016, various attempts at a peaceful solution to the war and the refugee crisis – from talks in Geneva, a security conference in Munich to a one-day London conference aimed at 'Supporting Syria and the Region' – had failed to deliver any definitive and long-term tangible results, though a call for the imminent 'cessation of hostilities' did see the guns fall a little more silent for a brief period; but achieving a comprehensive and lasting peace presents a much more challenging prospect. For readers who would like more information on the impact of the Arab Spring and the Syrian conflict on Lebanon, an excellent and detailed analysis is given in Maximilian Felsch and Martin Wählisch's *Lebanon and the Arab Uprisings: In the Eye of the Hurricane* (Oxon: Routledge, 2016).

GOVERNMENT AND POLITICS

Lebanon has its constitutional antecedents in the 19th century during the Ottoman era with the partitioning of Mount Lebanon into separate Christian and Druze regions to help stave off sectarian conflict. But the country didn't adopt its first political constitution until 23 May 1926 during the French Mandate era (pages 20–1) which transformed Lebanon into a republic and laid the groundwork for the present-day system of **confessionalism** (aka consociationalism), an organisation of government that proportions political power amongst the various religious groups. Following independence from France in 1943, the National Pact (al Mithaq al Watani) – the outcome of an unwritten or gentlemen's agreement between the Maronite, Shi'ite and Sunni religious leaderships – further cemented religion and politics with a number of additional amendments (notably the 1989 Taif Agreement, the accord reached in the Saudi Arabian town which ended the 1975–90 civil war, and which modified the 1943 Pact but left the confessional basis of sectarian power-sharing intact; and the 2008 Doha Agreement, which made further revisions to the 1943 Pact).

According to the constitution, present-day Lebanon is a republic and parliamentary democracy. Under the terms of the country's confessional-based system, the main religious communities are allotted the highest government posts: the president must be a Maronite Christian, the prime minister a Sunni Muslim and the parliamentary Speaker (aka President of Parliament) a Shi'ite Muslim, with these three key posts comprising the 'troika' of Lebanese politics. The power to make laws, set policies, approve the annual budget, vote for a new president, nominate a new prime minister, etc resides within the **legislative branch** of government and the unicameral (single chamber) National Assembly or Chamber of Deputies (Majlis al-Nuwab in Arabic, Assemblée Nationale in French) and commonly referred to as the parliament, whose 128 seats are divided equally

Designated a foreign terrorist organisation by the US and many other Western countries, Hezbollah – literally, the Party of God – continues to be one of the most enduring and high-profile aspects of late 20th-century Lebanese history and politics with which most Westerners are familiar. This Lebanese Shi'ite military and political organisation, formed in 1982, traces its origins back to the 1979 Islamic Revolution in Iran which overthrew the country's shah and ushered in the fundamentalist Islamic Republic of Iran, led by Ayatollah Khomeini (1902–89), who espoused the concept of Wilayat al-Faqih, or supreme spiritual leader, to govern the religious class. Lebanon's Shi'ites, long the most impoverished, powerless and poorly educated among Lebanon's religious mosaic, saw this Iranian ideology and success story as hope for a greater voice and participation in their country's affairs, which they had hitherto lacked. These ideas was given the catalyst to be translated into practice following Israel's June 1982 invasion of Lebanon designed to eliminate finally the Palestine Liberation Organisation (PLO) from the country. The overwhelming Israeli firepower and the long and destructive siege of Beirut only served to galvanise an already dispossessed and radical Shi'ite population, who had also long suffered from Israeli reprisals brought about by the cross-border conflict between Israel and the Palestinians since the late 1960s. The fertile Bekaa Valley provided, in the strategic town of Baalbek, an equally fertile educational, theological and military training ground for Iranian Revolutionary Guards to help support their Lebanese Shi'ite compatriots in expelling Israel from Lebanon and fighting Western, especially US, hegemony and interference in the country and the region.

From Hezbollah's inception, the group implemented a back-to-basics Islamic ideology with their role model the 'martyr' Imam Hussein, the Prophet Muhammad's grandson, slain fighting the Umayyad dynasty at the Battle of Karbala in southern Iraq in CE680 and upheld as the ultimate sacrifice against injustice and oppression. Whilst Hezbollah's resistance to Israeli occupation and US support for the Jewish state involved hijackings, the kidnap of Western hostages and, until then, unheard of 'martyrdom operations' (suicide bombings) during the 1975–90 civil war, the organisation has consistently denied involvement in the October 1983 suicide bomb attacks that devastated the French paratrooper and US marine barracks in Beirut. Yet, ever since the fledgling organisation first went public with the publication on 16 February 1985 of its Open Letter, declaring itself the Islamic Resistance (al-Moqawama al-Islamiyah; www.moqawama.org), in which it explicitly espoused its ideology and political goals including fighting Israel's occupation of south Lebanon and its enduring ties with Iran, Hezbollah has always been about much more than its military wing (Jihad Assembly, or Special Security Apparatus), including its ambitions to be a leading player in the wider Islamic world and for the establishment of an Islamic state in Lebanon, but insists this will only be achieved by consensus: 'Hezbollah

between the Christian and Muslim faiths with further divisions within each sect. Parliament meets for two three-month sessions annually, in March and October, with additional sittings convened by the Speaker as required. The Speaker, elected by parliament, serves for a renewable term of four years and has a powerful role in overseeing the entire workings of parliament with the power to veto the entire political process. Parliamentary elections are held every four years and all Lebanese citizens over the age of 21 years (women were given the vote in 1952) are eligible to does not wish to implement Islam forcibly but in a peaceful and political manner, that gives the chance to the majority to either accept or refuse. If Islam becomes the choice of the majority only then will it be implemented.' Since 18 February 1992 the organisation has been led by its charismatic secretary-general Hassan Nasrallah (b31 August 1960), following the assassination of his predecessor Abbass Al Moussawi (1952–92), who was killed by Israeli helicopter gunships along with his wife and one-year-old child. Born into humble origins in the Quarantina district of east Beirut, Nasrallah, the son of a fruit and vegetable salesman and eldest of nine children, had an interest in politics and religion from an early age, initially joining the Shi'ite group Amal at the age of 15, and travelling to the Iraqi city of Najaf at 16 to commence his theological training before returning to study at Baalbek in Lebanon's Bekaa Valley, and later the Iranian city of Qom. Overwhelmingly elected leader by the group's seven-member Majlis al-Shura (Consultative Council), Nasrallah's impassioned rhetoric and speeches have helped endear him within and outside Hezbollah's Shi'ite heartlands. Together with his oratorical skills, the organisation operates a sophisticated and highly adaptable communication and media apparatus. Since 1984 it has published its own weekly newspaper al-Intiqad (originally al-Ahd or The Pledge), to which was added a radio station, Al-Nour ('The Light') in 1988 and the TV station Al-Manar (The Beacon) in 1991. It is also rarely shy of lauding its military and political prowess as can be seen at the Mleeta visitor complex in south Lebanon (pages 315–16), a striking visual celebration of Hezbollah's role in expelling Israeli forces from the south of the country in May 2000 (with the exception of the still-contested Israeli-occupied Shebaa farms).

In addition to operating a number of schools, clinics, hospitals and social welfare programmes including low-cost housing, and with support from its Iranian patron compensating those left impoverished and homeless by the summer 2006 hostilities with Israel (box, page 32), Hezbollah has since 1992 gradually entered the political fold, and the group's political faction (Loyalty to the Resistance Bloc), which forms part of the March 8 political alliance (pages 26–7), currently has two cabinet members and 14 seats in parliament, up from eight seats in the 2005 elections. A formidable voice in the country's affairs, the group has often been dogged by controversy, notably following the assassination of former premier Rafiq Hariri in 2005 and the resulting STL, which has indicted Hezbollah members for the killing (box, pages 30–1), the summer 2006 war with Israel, and the 2008 anti-government conflict in Beirut. Equally contentious is Hezbollah's armed wing currently fighting alongside its other main backer, Syria, in that country's ongoing civil war in support of President Bashar al-Assad (pages 29–33); and the recent declaration by Arab Gulf states and the Sunni-dominated Arab League also labelling the group a terrorist organisation.

vote. The **executive branch** of government comprises the president, prime minister and the cabinet. Based in the presidential palace at Baabda in Mount Lebanon, the president is elected by parliament following a two-thirds majority vote for a six-year *ahd*, or term, but is not permitted to stand for consecutive terms of office. As 'the head of the state and the symbol of the nation's unity' the president is also commander-in-chief of the armed forces and custodian of the constitution, but has considerably reduced powers since the 1989 Taif Agreement. Prior to Taif, he (and in theory, she) was solely responsible for the appointment of the prime minister and deputy prime minister, but now simply announces the successful candidate for prime minister following the parliamentary majority nomination. The prime minister, as head of the government with primary executive power, then chooses a 30-member Council of Ministers (cabinet), who like parliament are also subject to sectarian quotas, after consulting with both the president and parliament. The prime minister and his cabinet are based in the Grand Serail in Downtown Beirut.

The **judicial branch** of government, with personnel also proportioned along sectarian lines, uses a mixture of Canon (religious) law, civil law, Ottoman law (and the Napoleonic Code). As laid down in the constitution, the judiciary is independent of the other two branches of government, though in practice political pressure often prevails in areas such as the appointment of key staff members. The Lebanese court system comprises four Courts of Cassation (Supreme Court) presided over by three judges (sometimes fewer in the case of more minor civil or criminal matters), and there are courts for civil, commercial and penal (criminal) matters. There are also a number of religious courts representing the various sects which hear personal status cases such as child custody, divorce and inheritance matters; whilst military courts deal with military affairs and have the power to indict civilians in security matters such as spying or treason. Matters relating to business and corporate legal affairs are dealt with by the Arbitration Courts. There are no trials by jury and a ten-member Supreme Judicial Council oversees the appointment and promotion of judges, whose performance is monitored by a Judicial Inspection Unit. A ten-member Constitutional Council, whose members are appointed by parliament and the cabinet to serve five-year terms, rule on the legality of laws and deal with disputes arising from parliamentary and presidential elections, whilst a 15-member Supreme Council, comprising seven elected members of parliament and eight high-ranking judges, presides over matters against the president and prime minister as required. At the time of writing Lebanon had around 10,000 practising lawyers, who must be registered with one of the country's two Bar Associations, located in Beirut and Tripoli, who are also responsible for providing *pro bono* or free legal advice and representation to citizens in both civil and criminal cases, as stipulated by the country's constitution.

At a local level, Lebanon is divided into eight *muhafazat* or governorates with each administered by a governor (*muhafiz*) appointed by the Council of Ministers and these, with their capitals in brackets, are: Akkar (Halba), Baalbek–Hermel (Baalbek), Beirut (Beirut), Bekaa (Zahlé), Mount Lebanon (Baabda), North Lebanon (Tripoli), South Lebanon (Sidon) and Nabatiye (Nabatiye). These main administrative regions are further sub-divided into 25 smaller *Qada* or districts headed by a Qa'em Maqam (District Chief) with further divisions into numerous smaller Municipal Councils responsible for the provision of local planning issues and services and containing locally elected officials led by a mayor. Unlike central government, seats on the local council are not constitutionally subject to sectarian quotas, with municipal elections held every six years.

CURRENT AFFAIRS AND DOMESTIC POLITICS In its Preamble the 1989 Taif Agreement states that 'the abolition of political confessionalism is a basic national goal and shall be achieved according to a gradual plan'. Yet following the 2005 Cedar Revolution (page 27), sectarian politics has become even more entrenched and polarised with the pro-Syrian Hezbollah and Amal Movement-led March 8 alliance facing off against the pro-Western March 14 coalition led by former prime minister Saad Hariri's Future Movement, evoking the principle sectarian rivalry that dominates Lebanese politics today. This continued schism has proven to be a double-edged sword for Lebanon.

Loyalty remains with the sect rather than any overarching notion of nationhood or a clear idea of what it means to be 'Lebanese', with conflicts and disagreements more often than not resolved by the notion of 'no victor no vanquished' (*la ghalib la maghlub*); but when this attainment of consensus and compromise proves elusive, invariably violence has ensued as witnessed by the armed conflicts of 1958, 1975–90, 2006 and 2008. Ironically, this is also a blessing for the country since, along with a limited presidential term, it has helped Lebanon stave off dictatorship and autocracy so widespread in other countries of the region, as brought to the fore in late 2010 with the onset of the Arab Spring which engulfed many Arab nations. The Arab world's sole Christian presidency has been vacant since May 2014 following the expiration of Michel Suleiman's (b1948) six-year term and has left parliament unable on numerous occasions (43 at the time of writing and the longest in Lebanon's history) to muster the required quorum (86 out of 128 MPs) to vote for a new head of state due to the March 8 and 14 political groups' opposing agendas and choices to succeed Suleiman. Similarly, the ongoing trial at the STL (box, pages 30–1) also continues to divide these two rival blocs over its legitimacy, with Christian blocs backing whichever March alliance most closely reflects their interests.

In the meantime, current prime minister Tammam Salam (b1945) and his cabinet are temporarily assuming the duties of the president, as permitted by the constitution, and have extended their terms of office until 2017. Yet this has also served to reinforce Lebanon's weak form of governance as, in the absence of a president, not a great deal can be achieved from the Grand Serail, demonstrated most recently by the crisis over refuse collection and disposal following the closure of a Beirut landfill site and the inability of politicians to agree on a solution. As the rubbish piled up in the streets of the capital and elsewhere and the public health concerns stemming from this, thousands of people descended on parliament in Downtown Beirut to demonstrate politicians' weakness, and corruption, as well as their inefficiency in an array of public services. The burgeoning You Stink protest movement, whose name owes as much, if not more, to government failings as to the rotting garbage on the streets, had banners proclaiming 'Ali Barber and 128 thieves' and demanded wholesale political change, an end to corrupt politicians and a more secular political system. Nepotism, however, continues to endure in Lebanese politics: names such as Arslan, Hariri, Gemayel and Jumblatt et al have featured for years on the Lebanese political stage and their owners are probably in no hurry to see the back of a system that has got them to where they are today. As British journalist and long-time resident of Beirut Robert Fisk (b1946), once put it, 'Lebanon is like a Rolls-Royce with square wheels … it's praiseworthy but doesn't run well.'

ECONOMY

As the majority of the world's economies floundered in the wake of a global economic downturn not witnessed for a generation, Lebanon was one of only seven countries to record economic growth in 2008. And for the period 2007–2010 the economy experienced an average growth rate of 8%. Unlike many of its Arab neighbours who derive their revenues and wealth from huge oil and natural gas deposits, Lebanon's economy has traditionally derived primarily from its unique geography and location at the crossroads of Asia, Africa and Europe, together with a long history of mercantile activities and a resourceful population.

The mainstay of Lebanon's long-standing *laissez-faire* economy is the service sector, with banking, finance and tourism accounting for around three-quarters of the country's GDP. Lebanon's resilient and successful banking system offers many advantages to investors, including no restrictions on foreign investment or movement of capital, a strict banking code guaranteeing secrecy, and a country free from any international trade sanctions. An additional and vitally important revenue stream for the economy are the remittances the country receives from the estimated 10–15 million Lebanese diaspora, many of whom left Lebanon during the civil war for a better life in Europe, the Americas and Australia, and who now occupy high-salaried positions overseas or have established their own successful businesses. The money these expatriates send home to family members in Lebanon is immense, around US$7–8 billion annually (World Bank estimate) representing nearly 20% of the country's GDP, one positive aspect of Lebanon's 'brain drain', which has seen such foreign capital inflows benefiting both the real estate and banking sectors. Tourism, employing around half a million people or 38% of the workforce, has long been a salient part of the Lebanese economy and, although the industry receded following the 2006 summer conflict between Israel and Hezbollah (box, page 32), this sector recovered quite quickly and in 2009 the United Nations World Tourism Organisation (UNWTO) ranked Lebanon in first place for world tourism growth. According to figures from the Lebanese Ministry of Tourism, revenues from tourism reached US$8 billion in 2010, the year that also witnessed the country's highest ever number of visitors, well in excess of two million. However, since that period internal political conflicts and schisms combined with the adverse knock-on effect from the Arab Spring, particularly the ongoing war in neighbouring Syria, have led to a marked decrease in the number of tourists and visitors to the country, over security concerns, with many hotels and restaurants around the country feeling the economic effects of low room occupancy and empty tables. At the time of writing, Lebanon is hosting well over 1½ million refugees fleeing the Syrian conflict and, in addition to the increased strain this is placing on the country's already stretched infrastructure and public services, the World Bank and the UN estimated to the end of 2014 the cost to Lebanon was some US$7.5 billion together with an increase in unemployment to around 20%, twice the current rate. Consequently, GDP growth for 2015 was estimated at 2% by the International Monetary Fund (IMF) and 4% in the medium term, with reduction of the public debt, modernising reforms and political stability the key factors weighing heavily on Lebanon's future economic prospects.

Lebanon's industrial sector accounts for around 24.7% of GDP, with exported goods centred on tobacco, jewellery manufacture, cement, chemicals, textiles, paper and electrical machinery together with wood and furniture. The country's main trading partners for exports in descending order of size in 2015 were: Saudi Arabia, United Arab Emirates, Iraq, Syria, South Africa. For imports they include China, Italy, the US, France, Germany and Greece. At around 5.6% of GDP, agriculture may be the smallest sector of the economy but it still contributes significantly to Lebanon's well-being with over a third of the country's land area given over to this sector. Owing to Lebanon's location within the Fertile Crescent, with its well-watered soils and favourable climate, it has the highest proportion of land given over to agriculture in the Arab world. Consequently, a wide variety of crops are grown, including citrus fruits, grapes, apples, vegetables, potatoes, olives, tobacco and wheat, alongside livestock farming of sheep and goats. It is viticulture, however, that is probably Lebanon's best-known agricultural product, with the wineries in the Bekaa Valley such as Ksara, Kefraya and Musar having well-established local and international reputations.

Whilst Lebanon may have been relatively insulated from the global economic crisis that afflicted many countries from 2008, it continues to suffer from an economic hangover from the civil war years of 1975–90. Not surprisingly, this

15-year conflict had a high economic as well as human cost, cutting national output by half, destroying the majority of the nation's infrastructure and severely devaluing the Lebanese currency from a pre-war LBP2.50 to US$1 to the current rate of LBP1,505.39 (August 2016 estimate) to US$1. To meet these ongoing challenges, the government has had to borrow heavily and tap into its foreign exchange reserves to fund major reconstruction projects such as those in Downtown Beirut, the area most heavily damaged during the civil war (pages 22–6, and 167–70). The result is that public debt remains high and in 2015 was 138.8% of GDP, the fourth highest in the world and more than any other Arab country. The main challenges for the Lebanese economy are to alleviate this debt, implement ongoing reforms such as privatisation, the overhaul of major infrastructure (electricity, roads and water), internal political stability, and to weather the storm wrought by the ongoing war in neighbouring Syria.

Despite the testing times ahead, one recent development could transform Lebanon's economic and social landscape. For a country whose major natural resource has traditionally been water, the potential presence of vast hydrocarbon (oil and natural gas) deposits off the Lebanese coast and inland – initial estimates based on ongoing geo surveys put the figure in excess of 30 trillion cubic feet of natural gas and 660 million barrels of oil from just 10% of currently surveyed Lebanese waters – has been met with much enthusiasm by businessmen and politicians alike. Other areas are being studied including the Bekaa Valley, with numerous international oil and gas companies from 20+ countries including Chevron, Exxon Mobil, Shell, Total and the National Iranian Drilling Corporation having already bid for the rights to drill. Some analysts estimate that the value of natural gas alone could be worth up to US$600 billion. However, it is very early days with many hurdles to overcome (including ongoing maritime disputes with neighbouring Israel over a c850km^2 area predicted to be rich in natural gas alone) before Lebanon sees any petrodollars; whilst continued political in-fighting, the war in Syria and sectarian conflicts have all served to damage confidence and hamper progress towards the final awarding of drilling licences to interested companies.

LEBANON ONLINE

For additional online content, articles, photos and more on Lebanon, why not visit www.bradtguides.com/lebanon.

2

Lebanese People and Culture

PEOPLE

In Lebanon, the issue of the sectarian balance of the population is also a highly political one in this confessional-based society. No formal headcount has been undertaken since the last census in 1932 during the French Mandate era, with little prospect of another any time soon. Christians remain sensitive about their diminishing numbers relative to other sects, whilst the Shi'ite and Sunni sects are in no hurry to see their relative numerical sizes known. According to the latest available data from 2016, however, the overall population stood at 6,237,738 with nearly 88% of people residing in urban areas and well over two million resident in the capital, Beirut. There is a roughly 50/50 split between males and females and the population, in common with many Arab countries, is predominantly a youthful one with more than 25% of people aged under 14 years and around 68% of the population aged between 15 and 64 years. In 2014 Lebanon's population growth rate was estimated at 9.37%, the highest in the world, owing to the continuing influx of Syrian refugees fleeing their country's hostilities, a rate that has since slowed considerably to 0.85% since stringent border controls were introduced. According to the latest 2015 figures Lebanon had 605 people/km^2 making the country the tenth most densely populated in the world. An astonishing figure is the additional c10–15 million Lebanese, or those of Lebanese descent, living outside the country, the largest number living abroad of any Arab nation. Many of these have fled the country over the years – a mass migration which began in the 19th century, to escape wars, unemployment, and political and sectarian repression – and have settled in North and South America (an estimated seven million Lebanese or those of Lebanese descent reside in Brazil alone), Australia, New Zealand and Europe. A large number of these diaspora continue to retain close ties with their country by frequent visits and remitting significant sums of money 'home' to family members.

ARABS Ethnically, Arabs – an eclectic name for equally diverse religious and ethnic groups – comprise some 95% of Lebanon's total population. Out of this total some 54% are Muslim, spread across the different denominations such as Sunni, Shi'ite, Druze and Alawite, with the remainder, around 40.5%, composed of myriad Christian sects such as Maronite (21%), Greek Orthodox (8%) and Greek Catholic (5%) plus around 6.5% of smaller Christians sects such as Armenians and Copts. Many Christians, however, often eschew the word 'Arab' in favour of being identified with their ancient Phoenician roots, while the Druze, an offshoot from Shi'ite Islam comprising some 5.6% of the population and concentrated mainly in the Chouf and Metn mountains and Wadi al-Taym further south, are considered by many to be so far removed from Islam's basic tenets so as to constitute an entirely separate religion (page 52). There are also differences between the Sunni and Shi'ite sects and this variety adds to the cosmopolitan mix, rendering Lebanon a fascinating place for visitors, evident in its contrasting architectural styles (churches, mosques, temples) and costumes, together with a variety of celebrations and festivals.

ARMENIANS The Armenian diaspora are Lebanon's largest ethnic minority comprising an estimated 120,000+, around 3% of the country's population. They are mostly concentrated around the Bourj Hammoud district in east Beirut and the coastal Metn region northeast of the capital with smaller numbers resident around the cities of Aanjar in the Bekaa Valley, Byblos and Tripoli. The Armenians fled to Lebanon in great numbers in 1915 because of the genocide in Ottoman Turkey, in which it is estimated that between 1 million and 2 million Armenians were killed. They are mostly Christian, adhering to either the Armenian Catholic or Armenian Orthodox faith and they now have a thriving community, which is fully integrated into Lebanese society. They have managed to remain largely aloof from the country's sectarian rivalries. The Armenian Haigazian University (*www.haigazian.edu.lb*) in Beirut continues to teach their language and culture; banks, shops and street signs still bear the Armenian script; and they are well represented in the media with their own daily and weekly publications, radio stations and television coverage. In accordance with Lebanon's confessional constitution, the Armenians are allocated six seats in the 128-member parliament: five for the Armenian Orthodox and one for the Armenian Catholic faith.

PALESTINIANS Not so fortunate as the Armenians are the c485,000 (August 2016 estimate) United Nations Relief and Works Agency (UNRWA) registered Palestinian refugees, the vast majority Sunni Muslims, many of whom eke out a miserable existence in Lebanon's 12 refugee camps (box, page 43) scattered across the country. Many of these are those who fled what is now Israel in 1948 following the *nakba* or 'disaster' of the first Arab–Israeli war, with later influxes from the 1967 Six-Day War (5–10 June) and the expulsion of Palestinians from Jordan during Black September in 1970. More recently, the civil war in Syria which began in March 2011 (pages 29–33) has seen a further 53,000+ Palestinians enter Lebanon from that country in order to escape the ongoing hostilities, and with little end in sight to the Syrian war, at the time of research, this number will potentially increase. Unlike the Armenians, the Palestinians are unwanted in Lebanon and possess little or no civil or political rights, no access to social services, and they are forbidden by law from engaging in dozens of occupations including professions such as dentistry and medicine, engineering, law, etc. They rely almost entirely on aid from UNRWA, with Lebanon having the highest percentage of refugees in the region living in abject poverty and registered with UNRWA's Special Hardship programme. In June 2010, thousands of refugees took to the streets of Beirut to protest their plight and demand a degree of integration and civil rights they have hitherto lacked. Although a new labour law was subsequently passed the same year to facilitate access to the jobs market for Palestinians, this has so far had negligible impact on the plight of the available and large Palestinian workforce.

JEWS Despite the recent history of conflict between Lebanon and Israel, Jews have a history of settlement in the country dating back millennia and, although a much diminished presence today, they were once highly assimilated into the Lebanese sectarian mosaic. During the early years of Islamic rule,

UNRWA provide economic, educational, social and medical assistance to some of the five million registered Palestinian refugees in Jordan (10 camps), Syria (9 camps), the West Bank (19 camps) and Gaza Strip (8 camps), as well as to the c485,000 Palestinians currently residing in Lebanon in its 12 refugee camps listed below. For further information on UNRWA, the work that it carries out and the camps detailed below, contact the UNRWA Lebanon Field Office in Beirut (*Bir Hassan, Ghobeiry, Beirut (nr the Sports stadium);* 01 840 490; www.unrwa.org).

- **Beddawi** 5km north from Tripoli (16,500+ refugees)
- **Bourj Brajneh** southern suburbs, Beirut (17,945+)
- **Bourj Shemali** 3km east of Tyre, southern Lebanon (22,789+)
- **Dbayeh** 12km east of Beirut (4,351+)
- **Ein el Helwe** near Sidon, southern Lebanon (54,116+)
- **El Buss** 1.5km south of Tyre (11,254+)
- **Mar Elias** south of Beirut (662+)
- **Mieh Mieh** c4km east of Sidon (5,250+)
- **Nahr al-Bared** c16km north of Tripoli (5000+ and rising following post-conflict camp reconstruction)
- **Rashidieh** c5km from Tyre (31,478+)
- **Shatila** southern suburbs, Beirut (9,842+)
- **Wavel** near Baalbek, Bekaa Valley (8,806+)

settlement in the southern cities of Sidon and Tyre was positively encouraged by both the Umayyad and Abbasid dynasties to help in the development of their cities. During the Ottoman era Jews were, like the Christians, part of the *millet* system as 'People of the Book' and granted considerable autonomy in their affairs in exchange for payment of taxes (*jizya*) and deference to the Porte in Istanbul, and a Jew even administered customs during the early period of Turkish rule. The cosmopolitan and tolerant emir Fakhreddine Maan II (box, pages 284–5) could count Jews among his inner circle, though the Christian–Druze Mountain War of 1860 forced many to flee the Chouf town of Deir al-Qamar to Beirut, Sidon and Tripoli. By 1914 Jews comprised around 3% of the population of Beirut. Following the end of Ottoman rule after World War I, the French Mandate (1920–43) period witnessed a further escalation of the Jewish population, together with the building of synagogues and schools, which peaked at around 14,000 in the mid 1950s and this despite the creation of the State of Israel in 1948 with Lebanon being the only Arab country to see a growth in the Jewish population. The seeds of decline for the Jewish community, however, were sown following the political impact of the 1967 Arab-Israeli Six-Day War and later during Lebanon's own 1975–90 civil war, particularly Israel's 1982 invasion, which saw most Jews depart the country. Trappings of Beirut's once flourishing Jewish community remain, however, centred on the recently restored Maghen Abraham Synagogue in Wadi Abou Jmil Street in the Downtown district of the capital (page 170). For an excellent study of the history and politics of the Jewish presence in Lebanon, see Kirsten E. Schulze *The Jews of Lebanon: Between Coexistence and Conflict* Sussex: Sussex Academic Press, 2001 (2nd edition, 2009).

MIGRANT WORKERS In addition to the increasing number of Syrian workers in the country escaping their nation's civil war, especially on construction sites in the cities and undertaking agricultural labour in the Bekaa Valley, it is estimated that there are around 200,000 additional foreign workers in Lebanon. These are mostly from countries such as Ethiopia, Nepal, the Philippines and Sri Lanka, a small proportion of the millions of mainly women workers who have journeyed from Africa and Asia in search of employment and a better life. They generally work as domestic maids and servants in private households and businesses, work that is often viewed as demeaning and degrading by Lebanese. Some live in with their employer, whilst others rent accommodation elsewhere. You can often see them around the streets of Hamra in west Beirut dog walking or pushing a pram in their trademark pink or black-and-white uniforms, and on their day off strolling round the city. At present, foreign domestic workers are mainly sponsored by their employer under what is called the *kafala* system, yet are excluded from Lebanon's labour laws designed to protect other workers' rights. Consequently, they work at the behest of their omnipotent employer and their plight is not always a happier one. According to Human Rights Watch (*7th Fl, Saga Bldg, Damascus Rd, Beirut;* ✆ *01 217 670; www.hrw.org*), many have their passport and mobile phones confiscated by their employer, are forced to work up to 18 hours a day and denied any time off; they often have to endure late or even non-payment of wages whilst others experience psychological, physical and even sexual abuse at the hands of their employer which has led to an alarming suicide rate amongst this vulnerable group of imported labour. Some progress has been made in recent years with the Lebanese government regarding this exploitation of domestic workers, and a number of local NGOs are actively engaged in trying to bring the country's labour laws in line with accepted international legislation such as that proposed by the International Labour Organisation (ILO; *www.ilo.org*) guaranteeing basic human rights such as a minimum wage, working hours and adequate time off.

WOMEN On the surface, Lebanese women seem to experience freedoms and opportunities unrivalled in the Middle East, adding yet another dimension to the country's contradictions. In Beirut especially, girls and young women walk the streets of Downtown and dance the night away at bars and nightclubs in skimpy tops and short skirts, whilst bronzed, bikini-clad beauties adorn the beach clubs and swimming pools in the capital and beyond. The plethora of beauty and fashion services available in the capital and elsewhere where females can be manicured from head to toe seem to belie the lifestyles of their Arab sisters in other parts of the region. Despite these outward appearances, however, and for a country where women are estimated to make up over half of the total population, females continue to experience disadvantage and discrimination in many aspects of daily life. Although Article 7 of the Lebanese Constitution asserts equality for all citizens regardless of gender, with women given the right to vote back in 1952, women's participation in the political sphere remains woeful. In 2005 women made up only six of the 128 parliamentary members and a mere four in 2009, whilst the government of current prime minister, Tammam Salam, contains just one female cabinet member. In 2014 the World Economic Forum ranked Lebanon as the world's second worst nation in terms of women's political participation and to date the country has yet to see a female prime minister or president. Perhaps unsurprising given this gender gap in politics, it was only in 1994 that a law was passed permitting women to own their own business without the prior approval of their husband. Away from their under-representation in politics, many of

Lebanon's women are less restricted than they were by religion and tradition and now comprise around half of all university graduates, and many have risen to the highest echelons of their professions in such fields as law, the media, medicine and science. Culturally, too, women from across the sectarian divide have excelled in literature with authors such as the Christian Emily Nasrallah (b1931) and the Shi'ite Hanan al-Shaykh (b1945) both contributing to the understanding of women and society during the 1975–90 civil war. In the visual arts, filmmakers such as Nadine Labaki (b1974) and Jocelyne Saab (b1948) have won international critical acclaim for their cinematic works. As elsewhere in the world, however, Lebanon's women continue to be plagued by such familiar issues as domestic violence, unfair marriage laws and workplace discrimination, but many women now run a number of pressure groups and organisations dedicated to fighting the female corner for improved equality and participation in Lebanese society; and, although much remains to be done to readdress the balance in this male- and sectarian-dominated nation, Lebanon's women continue to make some positive strides forward.

SYRIAN REFUGEES Lebanon's population has swelled significantly over the past few years owing to the spillover effect from the ongoing hostilities in neighbouring Syria which began in March 2011 (pages 29–33), which has resulted in a refugee and humanitarian crisis unprecedented in the modern era. The country is at the time of writing hosting c1.6 million Syrians who have fled their country's war zone and who are now housed in makeshift camps and other often substandard accommodation at c1,600 locations around Lebanon, mostly in the Bekaa Valley and northern Lebanon with smaller concentrations in Beirut and south Lebanon. These refugees now make up around one in five of the country's overall population. With little denouement to this conflict in sight at the time of writing, it remains difficult to assess the long-term impact of the refugee situation and future resettlement issues, but it is certainly accentuating Lebanon's pre-existing economic and social problems, and augmenting political and sectarian schisms within Lebanese society.

LANGUAGE

As stated in Article 11 of the constitution, 'Arabic is the official national language' of Lebanon. The largest of the Semitic family of languages, which also includes Hebrew, Aramaic and Syriac, Arabic is also the native language spoken by well over 300 million people, mainly in north Africa and the Middle East, but there is a great variety of spoken dialects around the region from Morocco to Oman. The specific type of Arabic spoken in Lebanon is known as Levantine Arabic which is also the *lingua franca* of Jordan, Syria and of the Palestinians in the Occupied Territories and beyond. In Lebanon's schools, study of Arabic is a compulsory part of the curriculum for all school children.

During the French Mandate (1920–43) era (pages 20–1) French was an official language and compulsory in schools, and the linguistic impact of colonial rule retains its importance to this day, particularly amongst the Christian Maronite community in areas like east Beirut and the Mount Lebanon region, where street and shop signs and people with French names such as Antoine, Michel and Pierre are often encountered. The French-language daily newspaper *L'Orient Le Jour*, the francophone Saint Joseph University (USJ) and the leading business school Ecole Supérieure des Affaires (ESA) all testify to the continued importance of the French language in Lebanon. As the international language of business, English has had a high profile for many years and continues to gain ground on French in popularity, particularly amongst the entrepreneurial and younger generation,

MIXED BLESSINGS

Despite its veneer of Western cosmopolitanism, openness and tolerance, Lebanese couples from different faiths are still not permitted to marry, unless one partner converts – impossible in the Druze faith, which has forbidden conversion from outside sects since 1043 – or the ceremony takes place overseas, which the law will accept. This is because in 1936 a law was issued during the French Mandate period, decree RL60, which meant that marriage became controlled and regulated by the various religious authorities, each sect having its own laws, which also govern related areas such as adoption, child custody, divorce, inheritance and domestic violence. Only religious, not civil, weddings are thus allowed under Lebanese law, and even for couples that share the same faith, marriage comes at a potentially high economic and human cost. On the death of a Sunni husband, for instance, his widow may receive a maximum of only 50% of her late husband's estate; whilst the Christian Maronite sect prohibits divorce. In the Druze religion, renowned for its steadfast sense of tradition and unity, marital union outside one's own sect is strongly discouraged. The 2014 wedding of US actor George Clooney (b1961) to the human rights lawyer Amal Alamuddin (b1978), descendant of an affluent Druze family from the Chouf town of Baakline, was met with the usual fanfare and glitz associated with celebrity and Hollywood weddings in the west but received with far less enthusiasm amongst the Druze community themselves with one elderly Druze lady in Baakline purportedly commenting: 'Aren't there any young Druze men left? God give you better luck, my girl.'

Civil rights opponents of the present system have campaigned since the 1950s to abolish what they view as an archaic, morally unjust and unequal system, which serves, among other things, to perpetuate already deep sectarian divisions in Lebanese society, and which disadvantages women at the cost of securing a better national, rather than sectarian identity. Times seem to be changing, albeit slowly, and in 2009 the then interior minister, Ziad Baroud, announced that people would have the choice whether to declare their religious affiliation on their national ID cards. In 2013, this helped to facilitate the country's first-ever civil marriage, between a Sunni and Shi'ite Muslim couple who, having removed their religious affiliation from state records were then able to marry at a local notary, exploiting a loophole in the law stating that those who are not part of a religious community would be subject only to civil law in such personal status issues, and their union was later duly ratified by the government. But for the time being at least, in the absence of civil marriages becoming enshrined in law or for those unwilling to strike their sect from the record, star-crossed lovers will have to continue to pop over to places like nearby Cyprus, where, for around US$2,000, they can tie the knot and be back in Lebanon in time for the wedding breakfast.

and it is the main language of instruction at two of the country's top universities – the American University of Beirut (AUB) and the Lebanese American University (LAU). A common linguistic trait of many young Lebanese is to skilfully mix and match Arabic, French and English during the course of a conversation or even within a single sentence. Thus, the greeting '*Hi, Habibi, ça va?*' combines the English 'Hi' with the Arabic 'baby/darling' and the French 'How are you?' Such versatility in the use of language has caused concern in some circles that the younger generation are losing contact with their linguistic roots, preferring English and French, to the detriment of their Arab and national identity.

Although comprising only a small part of the total population, the Armenian diaspora in the Bourj Hammoud district of east Beirut, the Metn region and Aanjar in the Bekaa Valley continue to honour their linguistic roots by speaking Western Armenian, an Indo-European language identical to that spoken in the Republic of Armenia and the disputed south Caucasus region of Nagorno-Karabakh. Educational institutions such as the Haigazian University in Beirut continue to teach the Armenian language, and the script is also visible on many banks, shops and road signs in their community heartlands. The Armenian language is officially recognised as a minority language by the Lebanese government.

LEARNING AND USING ARABIC Many Lebanese are bilingual or even trilingual, meaning that you can often get away with no knowledge of Arabic at all in places like Beirut, where English and French are widely spoken. Nevertheless, it can be useful to have at least a smattering of Arabic in case the need arises outside of the main cosmopolitan urban areas. The Arabic language comes in a number of guises and a distinction is drawn between Classical Arabic (CA) – essentially a written form, used in early Arabic poetry, and the language in which the Koran was reputed to have been revealed to the Prophet Muhammad. CA's descendant, Modern Standard Arabic (MSA), is, as its name implies, the contemporary form of Arabic, and is one of the six official languages of the United Nations. It is also principally a written version of the language, used in books, magazines and newspapers, but can also be heard over formal public address systems and in radio and TV broadcasting. Like CA, it is standardised throughout the Arab world: thus a daily Lebanese Arabic newspaper is perfectly intelligible to an Arab reader in Iraq or Libya, or vice versa. However, it is the colloquial, spoken, form of the language that can vary greatly from country to country, and even within a country. The enigmatic Druze sect, for instance, has its own distinctive dialect. Though rarely used in written form, colloquial Arabic when transliterated into English can show great variety, which for the visitor can be confusing when it comes to identifying street and place names, for example. Happily, despite some small differences, spoken Levantine Arabic is not too dissimilar to MSA, and learning a few stock words and phrases can only serve to enhance your cultural and travel experience. For practical information on the everyday use of Arabic, see pages 325–35; and pages 111–12 for details of Arabic language courses and tuition available in Beirut.

RELIGION

Lebanon has the most religiously diverse population in the Middle East with 18 different officially recognised sects in the country: Muslim (Twelver Shi'ite, Sunni, Druze, Ismaili and Alawite), Christian (Catholic Maronite, Greek Orthodox, Melkite Catholic, Armenian Orthodox, Armenian Catholic, Syrian Catholic, Syrian Orthodox (Jacobites), Roman Catholic, Chaldean (Assyrian Catholics), Assyrian, Copts, Protestant), and Judaism. As the last official census was held by the French way back in 1932, it is a tricky business to ascertain the exact numbers of each sect. Although the census showed a slight majority in favour of the Christian Maronites, it is now generally recognised that, owing to differences in birth rates and the high rates of emigration amongst Christians, Muslims comprise the majority of Lebanon's religious groups. According to the latest (2012) estimates, the various Christian sects account for 40.5% of the population, whilst Muslims make up 54%, evenly split between the Sunni and Shi'ite faiths. Supplementing these main Christian and Muslim sects are a negligible number of Jews (pages 42–3), Baha'is, Buddhists, Hindus and Mormons.

One of the defining characteristics of Lebanon has been the history of co-existence between such diverse faiths over the years, characterised by periods of harmony, often for pragmatic reasons, and discord, as witnessed during Lebanon's 15-year civil war, and, now, the ongoing civil war in Syria which has pitted Alawites against Sunnis. Whilst the post-civil war era has seen remarkable stability relative to the smouldering resentment of that period, the importance of religion in both daily and political life remains as entrenched as ever for most Lebanese. The country remains governed along 'confessional' lines, as it has since the country's first constitution of 1926, meaning that politics and religion remain virtually inseparable. The social fabric of life is also touched by faith, and couples from different sects are not permitted to marry outside their own religion (box, page 46). In order to understand Lebanon and its people better, a general awareness and understanding of Islam and the basic tenets of the main sects are useful.

ISLAM With more than 1½ billion Muslims, nearly a quarter of the world's population, Islam, the third and youngest of the monotheistic faiths after Judaism and Christianity, is the world's second-largest religion after Christianity and the world's fastest-growing faith. Contrary to widespread belief, the majority of Muslims reside not in the Middle East or north Africa but in the Asia–Pacific region, where Muslims make up nearly two-thirds of the world's Islamic population, with Indonesia being the most populous Muslim country. The founder of Islam (literally, 'submission' or 'surrender' to God) was merchant Arab Abū al-Qasim Muhammad ibn Abdullah ibn Abd al-Muttalib ibn Hashim – better known as the Prophet Muhammad – who was born in the city of Mecca in Saudi Arabia around CE570. According to Islamic history, Muhammad was orphaned by about the age of six and was reared briefly by his grandfather, Abd al-Muttalib, and then by his uncle Abu Talib. Born into the Bani Hashim branch of the influential and wealthy Quraysh trading empire, Muhammad carved out a successful career in commerce, earning respect amongst his peers for his honesty and fairness. At the age of 25, Muhammad married a wealthy widow, Khadija, who bore him four daughters and the youngest, Fatima, would prove to be very important to Islamic events and history. According to Muslim tradition, Muhammad had been prone to seeking solace and spiritual contemplation in nearby Mount Hira and, in CE610, at the age of about 40, he received the first of a series of visitations from Jibril (Archangel Gabriel to Christians and Jews), who revealed to him, in the Arabic language, the word of God; these visitations would continue for the remaining 22 years of Muhammad's life. Although God's word had been received by earlier prophets such as Adam, Abraham, Jacob and Moses, his words had been corrupted and distorted over time and Muhammad thus represents the last and true final prophet. Jesus, for example, is recognised as just another one of these prophets but is not accepted to be the son of God in Islam, as he is in Christianity. Accordingly, both Christians and Jews were given due recognition as recipients of earlier revelations such as the Gospels and Torah, respectively, and given the status of Ahl al-Kitab or 'People of the Book.' In CE622, following a period of persecution and struggle in which the Prophet and his initially small band of followers fought against sceptics and unbelievers, Muhammad and his entourage embarked on the Hegira (migration) some 300km north from Mecca to the fertile oasis town of Yathrib (later named Medina or City of the Prophet). This epochal event marks the beginning of the burgeoning Islamic community, or *umma*, and the birth of the Islamic calendar. Eventually, these words

THE FIVE PILLARS OF ISLAM

Underpinning the practice of Islam are five obligations, known as the Five Pillars of Islam, which every devout Muslim must follow in order to lead a moral and virtuous life. These are:

Shahada The first and most fundamental principle of Islam is the admission of faith, the *shahada*, or 'Two Testimonies', in which the true Muslim asserts that 'there is no God but God and Muhammad is His messenger'. This basic tenet forms a vital part of the *muezzin* calling the faithful to prayer from the mosque.

Salat Both men and women must pray five times a day: at dawn (*fajr*), midday (*zuhr*), mid afternoon (*asr*), sunset (*maghrib*) and nightfall (*isha*), alone anywhere or in a mosque reciting passages from the Koran, whilst bowing and prostrating in the direction (*qibla*) of the *kaaba* in Mecca.

Zakat Almsgiving to the poor or to those less fortunate has equated historically to the giving of a proportion of one's annual income, but in practice is often left up to the ethical and moral choice of the individual. The large international Muslim charities such as Islamic Relief often dispense *zakat* to help alleviate the suffering of the poor and refugees in countries such as Syria and in Africa.

Sawm The holy lunar month of Ramadan, the ninth month of the Islamic calendar, commemorating the revelation of the Koran to the Prophet Muhammad. Between sunrise and sunset each day during the month of Ramadan adult Muslims must fast, abstaining from eating and drinking, smoking and sex. Each day the fast is broken by an evening *iftar* meal. The very young and old, those who are in poor physical or mental health, menstruating, pregnant or breast-feeding women are excused from the obligation to fast.

Hajj This pilgrimage (*hajj*) to Mecca should be undertaken at least once during a Muslim's lifetime, for those physically and materially able, and who then receive the status of *hajji*.

of God were written down to form the Koran, or 'recitation', Islam's sacred book, which is considered by Muslims to be the actual and unchangeable word of God; in contrast to the Bible, whose 66 books were penned by numerous writers and was centuries in the making, the Koran took around three decades to complete. The book's content is divided into 114 *suras* (chapters), containing the recitations that Muhammad had received in both Mecca and Medina, with those in Medina having a more pragmatic rather than spiritual content. Underpinning the whole text is the belief, like Christians and Jews, in one God, together with the obligations that every Muslim must observe to follow an Islamic way of life, enshrined in the *'rkaan al-'islaam*, or Five Pillars of Islam (box, above).

In addition to the revelations, Jibril took Muhammad on the so-called Night Journey from Mecca to Jerusalem astride the winged horse-like beast with a human face, *al-Buraq*. There he met all the prophets since Abraham, ascended to heaven from the Dome of the Rock on the city's Al-Haram ash-Sharif, or Noble Sanctuary (Temple Mount to Jews), and had a lone audience with God, thus making Jerusalem the third most sacred city in Islam after Mecca and Medina. Muhammad died, without a male heir, on 8 June CE632. Within a short time, the new religion experienced a major rupture centred on the future leadership of the nascent Islamic community, and which endures to this day in the division of Islam into the two main Sunni and Shi'ite sects, as well a plethora of splinter groups.

SUNNI MUSLIMS Muhammad left no clear directions as to who should succeed him and lead the fledgling Islamic community, and after his death a period of confusion and uncertainty ensued. But following the tribal customs of the age, the Prophet's friend and early convert to the new faith Abu Bakr was elected to become the first caliph, or leader. Although his reign was short, lasting only from CE632 to 634, he succeeded in continuing to unite the faith of Islam. Upon his death he was succeeded by Omar ibn al-Khattab, whose ten-year tenure (CE634–644) witnessed a remarkable expansion for the growing Islamic faith and inflicted crushing defeats on both the Byzantine and Sassanian Empires, and conquered Jerusalem in CE638. His murder resulted in the election of Uthman ibn Affad, a member of the influential and powerful Umayyad family and part of the Quraysh tribe, who initially continued Omar's expansionism until his progressively weak leadership, and nepotism in granting the most sought-after positions to family members, resulted in his assassination in CE656. Uthman's successor, and fourth caliph, was Muhammad's cousin Ali ibn Abi Talib, who ruled from CE656 to 661. He was married to Muhammad's daughter Fatima, and his election would prove to be the catalyst for major ongoing internal conflicts within Islam (see Shi'ite Muslims, below). For Sunnis, these first four caliphs to succeed Muhammad represent the *Rashidun*, or 'Rightly Guided' leaders (caliphs) to succeed the Prophet. For this majority, orthodox, sect, who comprise some 85% of the world's Muslims, great emphasis is placed on leaders who uphold the customs or *sunna* of the Prophet expressed through the *hadith* or words and deeds of Muhammad. In Lebanon, Sunni heartlands are most evident in the coastal cities of Beirut, Sidon, Tripoli and the far north, rural inland areas around the western Bekaa Valley, the Chouf and in districts that are 'home' to Palestinians who are themselves overwhelmingly Sunni. Traditionally the most affluent and educated of the two main sects, Sunnis represent an estimated 27% of Lebanon's Muslim population and are an important religious group and as per the country's constitution, the prime minister is always a Sunni Muslim.

SHI'ITE MUSLIMS In contrast to the Sunnis, Shi'ites reject the legitimacy of the first three caliphs under Abu Bakr, Omar and Uthman. In their eyes, only direct familial descendents of the Prophet Muhammad can rightfully claim to succeed him. For Shi'ites it was Ali, the Prophet's cousin and son-in-law, who was the first legitimate caliph. Ali's election, however, would soon prove to be both problematic and perennially divisive for Islam, not least from members of the Umayyad family who questioned Ali's validity as leader and sought justice for the murder of their kinsman Uthman. The Umayyad governor of Syria, Mu'awiya ibn Abi Sufyan, eventually met with Ali at Siffin on the banks of the upper Euphrates river in Iraq, and following a period of fighting they managed to broker a truce – though some of Ali's faction disapproved of his willingness to relegate the Will of God to human arbitration and Ali was later stabbed to death by one of his own followers in CE661, with Mu'awiya declaring himself the new caliph. This faction has since become known as the 'Partisans of Ali' or 'Shi'ite Ali', from where the name Shi'ite derives. Hassan ibn Ali (died CE669), Ali's oldest son, succeeded him for a brief period but rescinded his claim to the leadership in a treaty with Mu'awiya and he lived out his remaining years in Medina. Hassan's acquiescence to the Umayyads, however, did little to quell the dispute over how and who should rightfully succeed Muhammad. Upon the death of Mu'awiya in CE680, Hussein ibn Ali, Muhammad's grandson and the second son of Ali, mounted a rebellion against the Umayyad clan. The latter were now led by Mu'awiya's successor, Yazid, and in October CE680 the two opposing factions met at Karbala on the banks of the Euphrates River in Iraq. Hussein's forces numbered just 72 and were no match for the Umayyads' 4,000-strong army, and following the ensuing slaughter Hussein's decapitated head was taken to Damascus. The Battle of Karbala and the slaying of Hussein, along with the death of Ali, rank amongst the most important events in the Shi'ite calendar, with both seen as examples of martyrdom. In Lebanon, as elsewhere in the Middle East and beyond, the annual 'festival' of Ashura at Nabatiye in south Lebanon (page 323) is celebrated in memory of the slaying of Hussein and is a moving and remarkable visual and vocal display of faith, with young boys and men flagellating themselves whilst mourning his passing. The majority of Shi'ites are known as Twelver Shi'ites, since, following Ali, Hassan and Hussein, they recognise a further nine imams, with the twelfth, Muhammad al-Muntazar, deemed to have gone into hiding during the 9th century and who will one day return as the *mahdi*, or one who is 'rightly guided' to rule over an egalitarian and just society until the day of judgement. Although worldwide Shi'ites represent only around 15% of all Muslims (concentrated mainly in Azerbaijan, Bahrain, Iran and southern Iraq), they are possibly Lebanon's largest religious sect comprising perhaps up to 40% of the total population, with their heartlands in the southern suburbs of Beirut, Baalbek and the northeastern Bekaa Valley and in numerous towns and villages in south Lebanon. Unlike the orthodox Sunnis, they have always been the more marginalised faction, experiencing both economic and social disadvantage; but since the 1970s and 1980s the rise of groups such as Amal (Hope), led by current parliamentary speaker Nabih Berri (b1938), and Hezbollah (Party of God; box, page 34), has raised the profile of the country's Shi'ites with the latter especially now a powerful, albeit controversial, voice in the Lebanese parliament. As enshrined in the constitution the Parliamentary Speaker is always a Shi'ite Muslim.

ALAWITES The Alawites (aka Alawis or Nusayris) are a minority sect derived from Twelver Shi'ite Islam. Their beliefs and origins are shrouded in mystery, but it is thought they originate in the 9th-century teachings of Muhammad ibn Nusayr al-Namiri. Alawites revere the Imam Ali, the Prophet Muhammad's cousin and son-in-law, investing him with god-like attributes as the highest of the succession of divine beings (hence the term Alawite or Alawis, meaning 'followers of Ali'). This particular veneration of Ali, the 'bearer of divine essence', has resulted in some esoteric beliefs and doctrines – the non-practice of the Five Pillars of Islam as these are deemed merely symbolic, and the celebration of Christmas, Easter and the Zoroastrian new year – which are rejected by some mainstream Shi'ites and seen as heretical by most Sunnis, who deem Alawite beliefs incompatible with Islam. Like the Druze (page 52), they also believe in reincarnation. Consequently, Alawites have been subjected to oppression and persecution throughout history by the Crusaders, Saladin's Ayyubid dynasty, the Mamluks and during Ottoman rule, though they did achieve a degree of autonomy and increased status during the French Mandate era to help the French imperialists stave off the Arab nationalist tendencies of the Sunnis. Numbering around four million worldwide, the Alawite sect, whose presence in Lebanon dates from sometime after 1070, are thought to comprise somewhere between 70,000 and 120,000 people, around 1.5–2% of the Lebanon's population, concentrated mainly in Tripoli and the Akkar district in the far north of the country; there is also a sizeable community of around 500,000 in Turkey. One of the country's 18 officially recognised sects, the Lebanese constitution allocates Alawites two of the 128 seats in the Lebanese parliament. The largest concentration of this sect, however, is in Syria, where Alawites comprise between 12% and 15% (circa three million people) of the population living mainly in the northwest coastal districts of Latakia and Tartus with further concentrations in Damascus, Hama and Homs. With the rise to power in 1970 of the Alawite Hafez al-Assad (1930–2000) in a military coup and his succession in June 2000 by his son Bashar al-Assad, this numerically much smaller sect has dominated Syrian political and economic life in this Sunni-majority country for well over 40 years and the current conflict in Syria, although it has a number of strands running through it, and whose tensions have now spilled over into Lebanon, at times with devastating consequences (pages 29–33), has the Sunni–Alawite conflict as a salient ingredient.

DRUZE This enigmatic but highly influential sect, numbering around 200,000, 5.6% of Lebanon's total population, was founded in Cairo in the 11th century as a splinter group from the Shi'ite Ismaili faith after the Fatimid caliph, al-Hakim (CE996–1021), proclaimed himself to be God's incarnation on earth and thus the final imam. Prior to his death, Hakim despatched two envoys, Hamza ibn Ali and Muhammad ibn Darazzi (from whom the name Druze derives), to spread his ideology in Syria, which included modern-day Lebanon, and converted many Ismailis, setting in motion a theology and practice considered by many Sunni Muslims to be so far removed from the *umma* or customs of Islam so as to constitute an entirely separate religion. Widely seen as a highly secretive sect, even amongst themselves, Druze are divided into an elite 10–20% (*al-uqqal* or the knowledgeable) and the chosen remainder (*al-juhhal* or the ignorant), to whom the elite are entrusted to haemorrhage knowledge of the faith which is contained in the six holy works of the *Kitab al-Hikma*, or Books of Wisdom. It is known that the Druze retain an Islamic identity but reject its Five Pillars and believe in reincarnation (*tanasukh*). Conversion from other faiths is not permitted and you can only be Druze by birth, with intermarriage between sects also prohibited (see box, page 46). For Druze the main holy day is not Friday as in mainstream Islam, but Thursday evening, when they pray secretly, not in mosques, but in inconspicuous places like halls, known as *khalwats*. Concentrated mainly in the Chouf and Metn regions and further south at Wadi al-Taym, a valley adjoining the Bekaa Valley on the western flank of Mount Hermon, the Druze are probably the most easily identifiable sect with men dressed in trademark baggy trousers called Sarawak, sporting eccentric moustaches and beards and white caps, and women wearing white veils and long, flowing black dresses. Despite a long history of persecution, the Druze have nonetheless been a significant part of Lebanon's religious mosaic and since the Taif Agreement of 1989 have seen their allocation of six seats in the 128-member Lebanese parliament rise to eight. During Ottoman rule they found a voice and a national hero in the form of the emir Fakhreddine Maan II (box, pages 284–5) and they continue to play an active role in modern-day politics under their current leader Walid Jumblatt (b1949; box, page 291). Jumblatt has been quoted as saying that Druze 'is not a secretive religion, that is apart from the Secret Books… You could say our faith is inspired by Neo-Platonism, and that in some respects it reflects the teachings of Socrates and Plato…' The worldwide Druze population comprises around one million people, with concentrations of more than 100,000 in the Galilee and the Israeli-occupied Golan Heights, around half a million in Syria, together with smaller communities in Jordan, North and South America, Australia, Africa and Europe.

CHRISTIANS Of the numerous Christian denominations in the country, the Maronites are the largest group comprising around 21% of Lebanon's population, with sizeable communities in east Beirut, Batroun, Byblos, Jounieh and throughout the Mount Lebanon region, Zahlé in the Bekaa Valley, and Bcharré in northern Lebanon. As an eastern branch of the Roman Catholic Church, the Maronites trace their roots back to the 4th-century hermit Saint Maroun (died CE410), who lived along the Orontes River in Syria. As their ecclesiastical views on the nature of Christ's divine and human will brought them into conflict with mainstream Christian orthodoxy, they retreated to the rocky and wild terrain of the Qadisha Valley in northern Mount Lebanon around the period of the Arab invasions in the 7th century to continue to practise their doctrines free from persecution. Although they reunited with the mainstream Roman Catholic Church in the 11th century, welcomed the European Crusaders during the Middle Ages and recognise the authority of the Pope, important differences and autonomy remain, including their retention of the liturgy in the Syriac language and no requirement to take a vow of celibacy for non-ordained priests. Each year on 9 February a national holiday is held in Lebanon to remember the Maronites' founder, Saint Maroun, which is celebrated with a feast. The Maronites are an important religious group in Lebanon, and as enshrined in the 1943 National Pact, the president is always a Maronite Christian.

EDUCATION

Lebanon has a long and established history as a centre of educational excellence throughout the Arab world. During Roman rule, Beirut's School of Law was one of the most prestigious in the entire Roman Empire. In 1866, a Protestant missionary founded the American University of Beirut (AUB), which to this day is widely recognised as the finest educational institution in the country and was ranked in second place (behind King Abdulaziz University in Saudi Arabia) in the UK's *Times Higher Education* World University Rankings 2015–16 of the top 15 institutions in the Arab world. Also highly respected is the francophone St Joseph University (USJ) in the capital, founded by Jesuit Fathers in 1875, with a wide range of faculties teaching classes in Arabic and English, in addition to French as the main language of instruction. The Lebanese American University (LAU), whose origins also date back to Ottoman times, is modelled on the US education system, with classes taught in English, and is a highly valued institution both within and outside the country. The Armenian Haigazian University has a wide-ranging faculty and its courses and facilities attract both Armenian and non-Armenian students from around the world. Outside Beirut the predominantly English-language University of Balamand (UoB), established since 1988 near the northern city of Tripoli, has also gained an excellent reputation for its wide-ranging faculties and high-quality facilities. With a mercantile tradition stretching back millennia, Lebanon also fittingly boasts the country's and the region's number one institution for business education, the Ecole Supérieure des Affaires (ESA), founded in 1996 in an intergovernmental agreement between Lebanon and France. The ESA's leafy 35,000m² campus in Beirut is located on the site of a former hospital and offers an extensive portfolio of courses, in English and French, including the MBA and DBA with an equally extensive network of international academic and corporate links.

This tradition continues today, where education is a highly prized asset accompanied by high academic standards. Considerable investment and restructuring of the education system is ongoing, and this is reflected in a combined literacy rate of nearly 94% for adults over the age of 15 years, one of the highest in the Middle East. Generally, women outperform men in all sectors of education yet only account for around a quarter of the labour force, with very few women going into self-employment or attaining the highest positions in politics. Lebanon's education system is overseen by the Ministry of Education and Higher Education (MoEHE), and under Article 10 of Lebanon's constitution, schooling is free for all Lebanese children regardless of gender, ethnicity and religious affiliation. For Palestinian refugees registered with UNRWA, children are entitled to free education at one of their 70+ schools and vocational training centres at their 12 refugee camps dotted around the country. Palestinian children not registered with UNRWA are entitled to attend one of the many state schools and learn alongside other Lebanese pupils. Each year the European Union (EU) awards a number of university scholarships to those Palestinian students who have successfully completed their education at either an UNRWA or Lebanese state school.

SCHOOLING At the time of writing Lebanon has nearly 3,000 schools nationwide with state schools outnumbering those run by the private sector. The vast majority of all schools offer co-educational schooling for both boys and girls and the various religious sects. However, given the private sector's higher-quality facilities and its philosophy of encouraging more independent and analytical thinking than its public-sector counterparts, around 70% of all pupils are educated privately with annual fees ranging from around US$1,500 to US$15,000. Some of the current problems being addressed is that the school curriculum hasn't kept pace with developments in the arts, sciences and technology despite a law stating that courses are to be updated every four years – this hasn't happened since 2000. Additional issues that the system needs to address are the high pupil dropout rate, a lack of facilities and qualified personnel to meet the challenges of pupils with special needs and helping to foster more critical thinking amongst pupils. Nonetheless, in 2014 the World Economic Forum (WEF) ranked Lebanon 13th out of 148 countries in its 'Quality of educational system' survey. All pupils must attend six years of primary school education (ages 6–12, grades 1–6), followed by three years at intermediate school (ages 12–15, grades 7–9), at the end of which students sit and must pass the Lebanese Brevet or intermediate test prior to entering secondary school (ages 15–18, grades 10–12). At the end of a student's three years at secondary school, they take either the Lebanese Baccalaureate exam, which is modelled on the French educational system, or, for those following a more technical and/or vocational educational path, are awarded a technical baccalaureate. Unsurprisingly, there are marked variations in educational attainment across the country, with much lower literacy rates, lower attainment levels and higher dropout rates in poorer regions such as the Bekaa Valley, and north and south Lebanon when compared with Beirut and the Mount Lebanon areas, a problem which the government is attempting to address by lowering the age at which children start school and easing the child's passage between the different grades.

UNIVERSITY AND HIGHER EDUCATION Successful completion of the Baccalaureate is a prerequisite for university entry; students wishing to embark on higher education may also have to sit an additional university entrance exam and, in the case of foreign students, undergo proficiency in the Arabic language at some establishments. At present, Lebanon has around 40 higher education institutions, including universities and a host of more vocational seats of learning, but only one of these is state run – the Lebanese University, founded in 1951, with campuses in Beirut and around the country. The Lebanese University, owing to its lower course fees and opportunities for combining work and study, accounts for nearly 40% of Lebanon's university student intake. As in many other countries, university study usually lasts for three years but will be much longer for those studying to enter professions such as architecture, engineering, law or medicine, which can involve up to seven years of study. One area of concern is that many of these fee-paying establishments are mainly pegged to a political or religious group, which serves to fuel sectarianism and hinders opportunities for national solidarity and integration. An additional and perennial issue for Lebanon is the way the country haemorrhages many of its most highly qualified and skilled personnel. Owing to low wages and a lack of career progression, it is perhaps no surprise that only just over half of graduates gain employment with the consequence that many well-educated Lebanese leave the country to take up more rewarding and better-paid positions overseas, especially in Europe and the Gulf.

CULTURE

Cultural life in Lebanon is infused with confusions and contradictions, making this small country a fascinating mosaic of cultural mores for visitors. For a country that has been to hell and back many times throughout its history, a perhaps surprising, yet salient, aspect of cultural life is the overwhelming sense of friendliness, hospitality and openness of its people – evidenced by the warm and smiling 'Welcome to Lebanon', or an offer of a drink or meal – traits you can find from Tripoli to Tyre and across the religious spectrum. Greetings, too, can maybe be more gregarious than you might expect in an Arab country, with three kisses on the cheek and a hug a common welcome to friends and family, though a normal handshake is customary for an initial welcome.

Lebanon's culture has been described as akin to *fattoush*, the world-renowned *mezze* dish containing a variety of contrasting ingredients borne of the country's many influences over the millennia. You have the overwhelming Arab influence, of course, most apparent in the use of language, and the numerous mosques and churches of differing styles reflecting the various Muslim and Christian sects. Alongside this is the French influence from the colonial era, seen in the cuisine, and in the language and street names still apparent in Beirut neighbourhoods today; whilst the country's Armenian presence has left a similar legacy in the regions of Lebanon in which they live.

Whilst Beirut basks in its renewed status as the party capital of the Middle East, where alcohol is freely available, the southern city of Sidon has a more conservative and reserved café culture and where alcohol is currently available at only one establishment. The family remains the bedrock of Lebanese society across all regions and religious groups, creating a sense of community within and outside the home; even in the capital people will often have an extended family living close by. Traditionally, sons and daughters generally live at home until they marry, with the expectation that they will do so within their own sect, though times are slowly changing on this point (box, page 46). The importance of family life is extended to visitors, too, as Lebanese adore children, and yours will be made a fuss of. Lebanese women espouse a beauty and a glamour that can seem to belie their Arab traditions and they are generally less constrained by religion than many of their Arab sisters. A visit to the Gemmayze or Achrafieh districts in east Beirut, for instance, where there are immaculately manicured and stylishly dressed young women in short skirts, evokes Lebanon's cosmopolitanism. It is not unusual to see a woman sitting alone in a bar or café, and there is no stigma or taboo attached to this as perhaps you might find in Western culture. Though women, as in many cultures, are still constrained by their gender into defined roles such as homemaker, many Lebanese women hold down careers in the media, government departments and the scientific professions, but again, as in other countries, the top echelons of business and politics remain a primarily male preserve.

Lebanon remains a male-dominated society, as are most Arab countries, and one area where this is most noticeable, or, more accurately, absent, is the issue of homosexuality. As it is deemed to be an act against nature according to Lebanese law and punishable by prison, you will be very unlikely to see any gay cruising on the streets of the capital or elsewhere in the country, but obviously it still occurs and Beirut has a handful of venues that are gay-friendly and increasingly there are organisations and information websites available offering advice and support. As a gay visitor, however, discretion is advised and public displays of affection should be avoided (pages 81–2).

VISUAL AND PERFORMING ARTS For aficionados of **archaeology and architecture** Lebanon is an open-air museum. The country's long history of invasion and occupation has left a rich historical legacy of fine castles, churches, mosques, palaces and temples all over the country. The Crusader castles at Beaufort, Byblos and Tripoli, the Phoenician Temple of Echmoun near Sidon, the soaring Roman temples at Baalbek and the world's largest Roman Hippodrome in the southern city of Tyre are just a few highlights testifying to Lebanon's cultural past; whilst a visit to see the Umayyad-era trading town of Aanjar in the Bekaa Valley affords a beautiful and rare insight into the very early years of Islamic rule. Supplementing these in situ remains are those contained in Lebanon's variety of museums, particularly the National Museum in Beirut, which houses an eclectic array of finds from the Phoenician to the Mamluk periods.

In Downtown Beirut, restored Ottoman-era architecture is apparent along with Roman-era baths overlooked by modernity. Lebanon's most contemporary famous architect is Bernard al-Khoury (*www.bernardkhoury.com*) who divides his time between Beirut and New York. He has been involved with innumerable architectural projects since the end of the civil war, with perhaps his most famous creation, the BO18 dance club in the capital, constructed on a wartime site and using coffin-like seating, and with a fully retractable roof.

One of the reasons for Beirut once being dubbed the 'Paris of the Middle East' was its flourishing **art scene**, which has certainly seen a revival. There are numerous and popular art galleries which showcase both Lebanese and international talent, the largest of these being the Beirut Arts Centre, which has multi-media shows across a range of genres and has attracted worldwide media attention. One of Lebanon's most famous female artists is Beirut-born Saloua Raouda Choucair (b1916), who fuses abstract and Islamic styles working with a range of media – clay, painting, wood and textiles – with her work showing her passion for geometry and mathematics through the use of lines and curves. Educated at the École des Beaux-Arts and the Atelier d'Art Abstrait in Paris, Choucair's work was relatively unknown outside her native Lebanon until relatively recently, when her extensive corpus of work was the subject of a major six-month exhibition at London's Tate Modern Gallery during 2013.

There is an equally flourishing **theatre** scene catering for both mainstream and independent audiences. In Beirut theatre lovers should check out what's currently showing at the Al Madina, Babel, Monot and Sunflower Theatres, which are just a few of the many excellent venues for a variety of plays and acts including puppetry and experimental productions.

Though the Lebanese **film industry** is nowhere near as prolific as Bollywood or Hollywood – Lebanon released 22 feature films in 2012 – there are a number

FAYROUZ

To Beirut – peace to Beirut with all my heart
And kisses – to the sea and clouds,
To the rock of a city that looks like an old sailor's face.
From the soul of her people she makes wine,
From their sweat, she makes bread and jasmine.
So how did it come to taste of smoke and fire?

Born on 21 November 1935 in Beirut, the Lebanese singer Fayrouz – the name is Arabic for 'turquoise' and was given to her by an early musical mentor for the precious quality of her haunting and silky voice – was christened Nouhad Haddad, the elder of two children who would become Lebanon's and the Arab world's best-known and best-loved diva. Winner of a string of musical accolades, Fayrouz was born into a poor working-class family in the capital's deprived quarter of Zoukak Al Blat: her father was a typesetter for a local print shop and her mother a full-time housewife. By all accounts, Fayrouz was a shy child with a love for singing from an early age. By the age of ten she was regularly performing at school concerts, and by 14 was discovered by a scout from the Lebanese Conservatory and soon became a vocalist in the chorus at a radio station. It was her long-time collaboration with the well-known musical Rahbani Brothers, Assi and Mansour, whom she met there, that helped to propel her onto the national and international stage. She married Assi in 1954, with whom she had four children. They composed many of her songs together over the years which Fayrouz performed at many of the world's most prestigious venues including New York's Carnegie Hall, the London Palladium and the Royal Albert Hall in the UK. Her soprano repertoire, consisting of some 800 songs, ranged from folk and jazz to religious songs characterised by a non-partisan message but always linked to hope, peace and unification. Her first live concert performance was at the Baalbeck Festival in 1957 which was followed by regular appearances at the Beiteddine Festival. Exiled in Paris during the civil war, she famously performed in front of some 40,000 adoring fans upon her return in 1994, in Martyrs' Square in Beirut, a performance she said would happen only once the fighting had stopped, and she delighted the audience with her oft-played song 'Bhibbak ya Lubnan' ('I love you, Lebanon'). Since the death of her husband in 1986, her musical compositions have been produced by her eldest son, Ziad, an accomplished composer and musician in his own right who fuses jazz and oriental music styles. Today, into her 80s, Fayrouz remains a much-revered cultural and political icon and her velvety lyrics championing the causes of justice, liberty and love continue to resonate with the Lebanese.

of independent production companies making experimental and independent movies. The work of director Ziad Doueiri (*West Beirut*, 1998) and actress-turned-director Nadine Labaki (*Caramel*, 2007) is well worth seeing for their contrasting narratives, themes, and issues of civil war and social issues respectively. Beirut also hosts two annual film festivals, attracting Lebanese as well as international filmmakers (box, pages 176–7).

In 2010, Lebanese cinematographer Muriel Aboulrouss picked up the Bayard d'Or for Best Cinematography for her work on the film *Stray Bullet* (2010) at the

Festival International du Film Francophone de Namour in Belgium which was also screened at the British Film Institutes (BFI) London Film Festival in the same year. The songs of Fayrouz (box, page 57), Lebanon's and the Arab world's best-loved singer, continue to delight audiences, but numerically speaking there can't be many who can touch the achievements of the late Lebanese actress and diva Jeanette Gergis al-Feghali (1927–2014). Better known to her fans as Sabah (Arabic for 'morning') her 60-year career took off in the 1950s, when she appeared in numerous Egyptian movies; she went on to act in over 80 films, released more than 50 albums and had a repertoire of around 3,000 songs to her name, the first released when she was aged just 13, in 1940. Oh, and she married ten times!

The colourful, vibrant and internationally renowned **Caracalla Dance Theatre Company** (*www.caracalladance.com*) fuses eastern and western styles and its performances, prolific all over the world, are well worth seeing, whilst the *dabke*, a group dance often performed at weddings or other family gatherings and occasions, is Lebanon's national folk dance and well worth trying at one of the many venues around the country.

LITERATURE Lebanon has a literary tradition as old as the Lebanese themselves, with Lebanon's forays into the written word dating back to the ancient Phoenicians, whose 22-letter alphabet formed the basis for our modern alphabet. As a seat of scholarly learning since Roman times, and Beirut a hub of printing and publishing in the 19th century, it is a tradition that lives on. Of course, mention must be made of the Koran, the seminal work of Islamic literature, which remains an important source of motivation in life for many Lebanese Muslims just as it does in the wider Muslim world. The Lebanese are quite avid readers of newspapers, magazines and books as the number of bookshops in Beirut will testify, with stores selling works in the three main languages of Arabic, English and French. Lebanon's most famous and iconic writer, Khalil Gibran (box, pages 250–1), spent much of his life out of the country but captured the hearts and minds of the Lebanese with his almost mystical and heartfelt prose, which dealt with universal human themes such as love, pain and relationships. A tortured soul, his works have been translated into numerous languages and inspired other cultural mores. There are also a number of more contemporary Lebanese writers worth seeking out. The novels, short stories and playwriting of former *An-Nahar* newspaper journalist Hanan al-Shaykh (b1945) deal with an eclectic array of women's lives and issues encompassed in works such as *The Story of Zahra* (1980), *Women of Sand and Myrrh* (1989), *Beirut Blues* (1992) and, more recently her widely acclaimed *The Locust and the Bird: My Mother's Story* (2009). Elias Khoury (b1948), a novelist, playwright, political activist and intellectual, has written a number of works that focus on the civil war and Lebanese society. Perhaps Lebanon's most celebrated modern writer is Beirut-born Amin Maalouf (b1949), who moved to Paris shortly after the outbreak of the country's civil war. A former director of newspaper *An-Nahar*, Maalouf has written a number of works including the celebrated *The Crusades through Arab Eyes* (1984) and *The Rock of Tanios* (1993), which won the 1993 Prix Goncourt for his fictional tale of rebellion and sectarianism in a Lebanese village during the 19th century. For readers interested in more academic and scholarly literature, Lebanese authors such as Albert Hourani (1915–93), Kamal Salibi (1929–2011) and Fawwaz Traboulsi (b1941) have written some excellent books on the Arabs and Lebanese history, and their works are for this reason listed on pages 350–1.

SOME LESSER-KNOWN FACTS ABOUT LEBANON

- Hollywood actor Keanu Reeves was born in Beirut on 2 September 1964
- The country we now call Lebanon is mentioned more than 70 times in the Bible
- 'The Lebanon', a song by UK band *The Human League*, reached number 11 in the UK charts in 1984
- Lebanon holds the Guinness World Record for producing the largest pile of *hummus* at 10,452kg, equal to the country's total land area
- Lebanon receives an annual rainfall quota of c860mm per annum
- There are c10–15 million more Lebanese people living outside the country than in Lebanon itself
- All of Lebanon's 15 rivers originate entirely from within the country's own borders
- The world's tallest matchstick model was made by Lebanon's Toufic Daher, who used around six million matches to construct a scaled replica of the Eiffel Tower, measuring 6.53m tall
- Lebanon is the smallest country in continental Asia
- Mnesarchus, father of Greek philosopher and mathematician Pythagoras (c570–475BCE) was born in Tyre
- Lebanese composer Gabriel Yared (b1949) won the Academy Award, a Golden Globe and a Grammy Award for his film score for *The English Patient* (1996)
- Lebanon's gold reserves are the second largest in the Middle East and North Africa (MENA) region

SPORT AND ADVENTURE Lebanon's varied geography and climate afford the country a wonderful array of possibilities for outdoor pursuits, for participants and spectators alike, and in which the Lebanese indulge with a passion. During the hot summer months, Lebanon's extensive coastline offers both locals and visitors innumerable opportunities: for beach worshippers, sunbathing and swimming; and, for the more adventurous, activities such as boating, paragliding over the Bay of Jounieh and the Cedars, jet-skiing, waterskiing and rafting. Scuba diving is an increasingly popular summer activity and pastime, with the long-established National Institute for Scuba Diving (NISD) in Beirut providing courses and dives for both novice and experienced divers. A couple of highlights include Shark Point, off the Beirut coast, to observe Moray eels, sting rays and the Small-Tooth Sand Tiger and Grey Nurse sharks; and, a little further off-shore, the wreck of the World War II Vichy French submarine *Le Souffleur*, sunk by its British counterpart. For those who prefer their activities a little drier, there are numerous caves and potholes/sinkholes affording several opportunities for exploration, with a number of speleo clubs and organisations (*www.alesliban.org; www.cavediverslebanon.blogspot.com; www.cavinglebanon.com; www.speleoliban.org*) able to assist with visits to areas such as Afqa Grotto, the Balaa Sinkhole near Tannourine and the Qadisha Valley.

During the winter months the country's six mountain ski resorts (a seventh is under construction) cater to the beginner as well as the more seasoned skier, with well-developed après-ski facilities – skiing is a popular leisure activity among the Lebanese. Golf, weekly horse-race meetings in Beirut, the annual Beirut International Marathon, attracting international as well as local runners, are also popular events, as is football (soccer) and basketball, the latter a sport at which

Lebanon has particularly excelled in recent years, winning the FIBA Asia Stankovic Cup in 2010, beating Japan 97–59 in the final and defeating Palestine 88–79 in 2015 to win the WABA (West Asia Basketball Association) title for the fourth time.

The increasing awareness of and concern for the environment has led to a marked increase in a culture of conservation and sustainability in Lebanon, with many NGOs and smaller groups springing up to champion the cause of the great and healthy outdoors and they regularly run on- and off-road cycling trips, walks, hikes and treks the length and breadth of the country, in addition to numerous events for caving enthusiasts in the Mount Lebanon region. The country's many nature reserves such as those in the Chouf and Horsh Ehden epitomise Lebanon's growing appeal as an adventure and ecotourism destination.

3

Practical Information

WHEN TO VISIT

As the only Arab nation to experience all four seasons, Lebanon really is a 'go anytime' destination, and deciding on which season to go depends almost entirely upon your own interests and priorities. The dry **summer** months (June–September) tend to be a popular with visitors, but it can be extremely hot and humid on the coast with temperatures in Beirut often well in excess of 30°C, which is fine if you just want to while away the days by the pool or on the beach and catch some Mediterranean rays; but it can be oppressive and uncomfortable, and a retreat to the mountains for the cooler alpine air (6–22°C) affords a range of alternative outdoor activities such as hiking, rafting, trekking and mountain biking. Summer, however, is also the main season for Lebanon's slew of annual artistic and cultural festivals such as those at Baalbek, Beiteddine, Broummana, Byblos and Tyre.

Winter (December–March) on the Mediterranean coast sees temperatures plummet to milder, more palatable levels (11–18°C) than in summer, but this season is often accompanied by the heaviest rainfall – though this tends to be in short bursts rather than the prolonged periods that often characterise many countries in northwest Europe. The winter months also herald the start of the ski season in the mountains, where temperatures range from around –5°C to 5°C. Lebanon has a range of well-equipped resorts, the best of these at present being Mzaar, with snow often remaining on the highest peaks until late April or even May. The latter part of the winter ski season also affords visitors the opportunity to indulge in the cliché of skiing in the morning and swimming in the Mediterranean in the afternoon. For classical music lovers, February sees the start of the five-week prestigious Al Bustan International Festival of Music and the Performing Arts, which attracts musicians and performers of international repute.

Autumn (October–November) sees cool temperatures in the mountains (5–20°C) and warm weather (13–28°C) on the coast, though with the increased risk of some rainy days. The pleasant temperatures make this is a good time for exploring Lebanon on foot, whether visiting the country's wealth of archaeological sites or hiking in one of the country's many nature reserves. Autumn is also wine-tasting time in the Bekaa Valley, along with the annual olive harvest. And being outside the main summer and winter tourist seasons, the price of hotel accommodation is often reduced during this period.

Without doubt **spring** (April–May) is an ideal time to visit Lebanon as the country is carpeted with beautiful and varied flora, the stifling summer heat has yet to arrive, and the winter rains have disappeared. Temperatures in coastal areas range from 12°C to 25°C, whilst the more mountainous regions experience temperatures ranging from 0°C to 15°C. Snow remains on some of the mountain peaks, which make an extremely picturesque backdrop when visiting some of the country's ancient sites. Spring also presents a wealth of possibilities for outdoor enthusiasts such as mountain biking, caving, paragliding and rafting. This is also a great time for visiting nature reserves such as Horsh Ehden (page 247) and the Chouf Cedar Reserve (pages 293–5), and ideal for hiking in the UNESCO World Heritage site Qadisha Valley (page 237) or perhaps walking a section(s) of the excellent Lebanon Mountain Trail (LMT; box, page 235).

The onset of the holy month of Ramadan in Lebanon, while not a time to be avoided as in some other Arab countries, nevertheless requires visitors to be sensitive to fasting Muslims. It would be polite to avoid drinking, eating or smoking during daylight hours in more devout Muslim neighbourhoods. Also be aware that some stores shut for a few hours during the daytime, but reopen later in the day.

HIGHLIGHTS

You didn't decide to visit Lebanon to marvel at picturesque and undulating rocky desert landscapes or ride a camel, which is just as well, because Lebanon is the only country in the Middle East which is entirely without a desert. However, with an annual sunshine quota of around 300 days, a liveable cliché of skiing in the morning and swimming in the Mediterranean in the afternoon, world-class archaeological sites, breathtaking natural scenery and a diverse and cultured people, the absence of an oasis of sand and palm trees isn't going to spoil your visit too much. As the initial point of entry to Lebanon for the vast majority of visitors, Beirut warrants a few days of exploration at least by any visitor in order to appreciate the country's turbulent past and its optimism for the future. Nowhere is this hope more apparent than in the restored Downtown district of the city. Given Lebanon's compact size, the capital also makes an excellent base for organising daytrip excursions to other areas of the country if time is precious.

The following are my pick of the highlights to visit in Lebanon:

AANJAR (pages 261–3) This unique 8th-century Islamic trading town in the Bekaa Valley is the last remaining Umayyad-era site in the entire Middle East.

BAALBEK (pages 265–72) Step back in time and admire soaring Roman columns and well-preserved temples, which are amongst the finest in the world.

BEKAA VALLEY VINEYARDS (pages 258–61) As one of the oldest places in the world for wine production, a visit to at least the Ksara or Kefraya vineyards affords an important insight into this still flourishing aspect of Lebanese culture.

BYBLOS (pages 205–15) This ancient and charming Phoenician port with Crusader castle, fine fish restaurants and souks is enchanting at any time, but particularly at sunset.

CHOUF MOUNTAINS (pages 277–96) A beautiful, scenic region and the location for ancient cedar trees, the lovely old Ottoman-era town of Deir al-Qamar and the opulent Beiteddine Palace, home to some of the world's finest Byzantine mosaics.

JEBEL SANNINE (pages 192–5) The location for some of Lebanon's best winter ski resorts.

JEITA GROTTO (pages 197–8) Majestic and stunning stalactites and stalagmites, and former finalist for the title of one of the world's 'New 7 Wonders of Nature'.

QADISHA VALLEY (pages 237–44) Picturesque mountain scenery in this UNESCO World Heritage site containing churches, grottos, hermitages, villages and waterfalls.

SIDON (pages 297–309) This traditional port city has busy, traditional souks, a museum and a photogenic Crusader-era sea castle.

TRIPOLI (pages 225–37) Lebanon's second city has history aplenty with labyrinthine, anachronistic souks, an imposing Crusader castle, Mamluk-period architecture, working *hammams* (baths), travellers' inns or *khans*, *madrasas* and mosques.

TYRE (pages 316–23) A UNESCO World Heritage site containing the world's largest Roman hippodrome.

SUGGESTED ITINERARIES

The suggestions below are just that: suggestions. Lebanon is so small, around half the size of the landmass of Wales, that it is easy to mix and match these attractions as you are never more than about 3 hours away from even the most remote areas, traffic permitting.

LONG WEEKEND/SHORT CITY BREAK With its compact size, a little over 5 hours' flying time from London and a negligible time zone impact on European visitors, Lebanon is an ideal short city break destination. Explore the Downtown area of Beirut, the restored Ottoman-era architecture and the Al-Omari mosque; stroll the tree-lined Corniche, go (window) shopping in upmarket Verdun and explore the excellent Beirut National Museum. For a change of pace, take a short drive up the coast to Byblos – stopping off *en route* to visit the natural marvel of Jeita Grotto – to experience this quiet, picturesque port, with fine fish restaurants, before heading back to Beirut after dinner to experience the pulsating nightlife in Achrafieh, Downtown, Hamra or Gemmayze. Another day could be spent on a day trip to Baalbek, visiting the wineries and Roman temples and, if time permits, a visit to the Chouf town of Deir al-Qamar and the nearby Beiteddine Palace.

ONE WEEK A week-long itinerary would allow you to see most of Lebanon's main sites (and sights), whether you employ the services of a local tour operator, take public transport or go for the self-drive method, and could include the following: two nights in Beirut; one night in Byblos including a stop on the way to see the Jeita Grotto; two nights in Tripoli with a sidetrip to Bcharré and the Qadisha Valley; one night in Baalbek, and return to Beirut via a day trip to the Chouf Mountains to see the quaint little Ottoman-era town of Deir al-Qamar and the nearby Beiteddine Palace. A further day could be spent exploring the archaeological sites and souks in the southern towns of Sidon and Tyre.

TWO WEEKS This is the ideal timescale to see and fully appreciate everything that Lebanon has to offer at a more leisurely pace, by organised tour, public transport, self-drive or perhaps a combination of all three. A comprehensive circular tour in spring or summer could commence in Beirut before travelling north up the coast to the port of Byblos, stopping off at Jeita Grotto, before continuing north to Tripoli to see the Crusader castle, souks and Old City. From Tripoli, head southeast towards Bcharré to visit Horsh Ehden Nature Reserve, Qadisha Valley and the legendary cedar trees. Continue the journey southeast to visit the Roman temples at Baalbek before heading towards Zahlé to take in the wineries and the unique Umayyad town of Aanjar. Head back to Beirut at the start of the second week, and from there travel south to the coastal towns of Sidon and Tyre for their ancient ruins and ports. On the way back up to Beirut, stop off to admire the Chouf Mountains, Chouf Cedar Reserve and the beautiful Ottoman-era Beiteddine Palace and picturesque town of Deir al-Qamar.

ONE MONTH If you are fortunate enough to have four weeks to spare in Lebanon, then this will give you enough time to explore in depth the country's cocktail of natural and manmade attractions, and also experience many of the places off the beaten tourist track. Such a time frame will also afford you maximum flexibility to swap and change your schedule at will and perhaps stay longer than anticipated in areas that particularly interest you. The following itinerary can be used as a starting point for your own Lebanese forays.

Beirut (*7 nights*) Not only is a week plenty of time for exploring the capital, it also gives a great opportunity to experience this revitalised city in depth, with its varied shopping districts, pulsating nightlife venues, fine and eclectic dining, art galleries and an active and flourishing film and theatre scene. The engaging National Museum demands a couple of hours of any visitor's schedule and could be combined with a trip to the Lebanese Museum of Prehistory. If arriving in summer (June–September), there are plenty of festivals within easy reach of the capital to keep you entertained.

Byblos (*2–3 nights*) To experience the culinary delights of this delightful and romantic little town which is easily combined with a visit to the nearby natural limestone wonder of Jeita Grotto and the Téléférique cable car ride from Jounieh to Harissa.

Sidon and Tyre (*4 nights*) A few days in the less-visited south of the country offer a great contrast to cosmopolitan Beirut and here you will gain a much more authentic Middle Eastern flavour of the country.

Bekaa Valley (*5 nights*) Perhaps using Zahlé as your base, you can take day and half-day trips to Aanjar, Baalbek and the many wineries. Self-drive car hire or car with driver is an ideal way to explore this region, though minivans and taxis are available.

Chouf Mountains (*3 nights*) Savour a still-feudal region with breathtaking scenery and a slew of beautiful sites. This is a great place to relax if you have hitherto overindulged in the hedonistic capital.

Tripoli (*4 nights*) From here explore the atmospheric souks, citadel and perhaps, if arriving in Lebanon during summer, take a trip to the offshore Palm Islands Nature Reserve.

Qadisha Valley (*3–4 days*) The Qadisha Valley is perfect for hiking, especially during springtime. An alternative itinerary during the winter ski season would be to take to the slopes at the Mzaar and/or the Cedar resorts.

LEBANON MOUNTAIN TRAIL (LMT) The 470km LMT is divided into 27 sections of hiking and walking routes which pass through more than 75 towns and rural villages from the extreme north of the country down the backbone of Lebanon to the far south. Each designated route can be undertaken in around a day and offers an alternative and fascinating glimpse into less-visited rural communities, with opportunities to stay in less mainstream lodgings such as guesthouses, family homes and monasteries at prices to suit most budgets. For outdoor types, travellers wishing to gain an alternative insight into the country and those wishing to give something back by helping rural economies, this itinerary could prove a very rewarding journey, taking in some of Lebanon's most beautiful and least-visited areas. For more details on the LMT, see box, page 235.

TOUR OPERATORS

With a long and established history of tourism to the country, Lebanon has for many years been well served by tour operators from around the globe offering a range of itineraries, with/without return flights, catering to a wide range of budgets and interests from adventure travel, archaeology, cultural tours, gastronomy and winery tours to those companies providing bespoke itineraries and long weekend city breaks to the capital. For those travellers who demand more flexibility in their travel plans rather than roaming with the tourist hordes, it could be worth considering using the services of a local guide with/without a vehicle. This is also of course an excellent way to give something directly back to the local economy and these, where applicable, are detailed in the relevant regional chapters.

The following companies have all previously offered a wide range of Lebanon tours but, at the time of writing, the conflict in neighbouring Syria, together with the general instability in the region, continues to impact negatively on parts of Lebanon, and many of these operators have put their tours on hold for the time being pending an improvement in the overall security situation, so it is worth keeping an eye on their websites in case the situation changes.

UK

Abercrombie & Kent St Georges Hse, Ambrose St, Cheltenham, Gloucestershire GL50 3LG; `01242 547700, 0845 485 1630; e info@abercrombiekent. co.uk; www.abercrombiekent.co.uk

Adventure Worldwide Long Barn South, Sutton Manor Farm, Bishops Sutton, Alresford, Hampshire SO24 0AA; `01962 737565, 0845 301 4737; e sales@adventureworldwide.co.uk; www. adventureworldwide.co.uk

Andante Travels The Clock Tower, Unit 4, Oakridge Office Park, Southampton Rd, Whaddon, Salisbury, Wiltshire SP5 3HT; `01722 713800; e tours@ andantetravels.com; www.andantetravels.co.uk

Audley Travel New Mill, New Mill Lane, Witney, Oxfordshire OX29 9SX; `01993 838400; e arabia@ audleytravel.com; www.audleytravel.com

Black Tomato 40–42 Scrutton St, London EC2A 4PP; `020 7426 9888; e info@blacktomato.com, enquiries@blacktomato.com; www.blacktomato.com

Corinthian Travel Ground Fl, 118 Tachbrook St, London SW1V 2ND; `020 3583 6089; e info@ corinthiantravel.co.uk; www.corinthiantravel.co.uk

Cox & Kings 6th Fl, 30 Millbank, London SW1P 4EE; `020 7873 5000; e sales@coxandkings.co.uk; www.coxandkings.co.uk

Exodus Grange Mills, Weir Rd, London SW12 0NE; `0845 287 3629; e sales@exodus.co.uk; www.exodus.co.uk

Explore! Nelson Hse, 55–59 Victoria Rd, Farnborough, Hampshire GU14 7PA; `0844 499 0603; e res@explore.co.uk, sales@explore.co.uk; www.explore.co.uk

Far Frontiers Travel Ltd Ninestone, South Zeal, Devon EX20 2PZ; `01837 840640; e fiona@ farfrontiers.com; www.farfrontiers.com

Greentours Leigh Cottage, Gauledge Lane, Longnor, Buxton, Derbyshire SK17 0PA; `01298 83563; e enquiries@greentours.co.uk; www.greentours.co.uk

iExplore TUI Travel Hse, Crawley Business Qtr, Fleming Way, Crawley, West Sussex RH10 9QL; e help@iexplore.co.uk; www.iexplore.co.uk

Intrepid Travel 76 Upper St, Islington, London N1 0NU; `0845 287 1190; e enquiries@ intrepidtravel.com; www.intrepidtravel.com

Kirker Holidays 4 Waterloo Court, 10 Theed St, London SE1 8ST; ✆020 7593 1899; e travel@kirkerholidays.co.uk; www.kirkerholidays.com

Martin Randall Travel Voysey Hse, Barley Mow Passage, London W4 4GF; ✆020 8742 3355; e info@martinrandall.co.uk; www.martinrandall.com

Original Travel 21 Ransome's Dock, 35–37 Parkgate Rd, London SW11 4NP; ✆020 3642 3251; e ask@originaltravel.co.uk; www.originaltravel.co.uk

Pax Travel 57–59 Rochester Pl, London NW1 9JU; ✆020 7485 3003; e info@paxtravel.co.uk; www.paxtravel.co.uk

Pettitts Bayham Hse, 12–16 Grosvenor Rd, Royal Tunbridge Wells, Kent TN1 2AB; ✆01892 515966; e pettitts@btconnect.com; www.pettitts.co.uk

Quintessentially Travel 29 Portland Pl, London W1B 1QB; ✆0845 269 1152; e info@quintessentiallytravel.com; www.quintessentiallytravel.com

RB Collection 2 Boley Park Shopping Centre, Ryknild St, Lichfield, Staffordshire WS14 9XU; ✆01543 258631; e vip@rbcollection.com; www.rbcollection.com

Red Spokes Cycling Adventure Tours 29 Northfield Rd, Stamford Hill, London N16 5RL; ✆020 7502 7252; e office@redspokes.co.uk; www.redspokes.co.uk

Responsible Travel 1st Fl, Edge Hse, 42 Bond St, Brighton, Sussex BN1 1RD; ✆01273 823700; e rosy@responsibletravel.com; www.responsibletravel.com

Simoon Travel Limited 21 Ransome's Dock, 35–37 Parkgate Rd, London SW11 4NP; ✆020 7978 0508; e amelia@simoontravel.com; www.simoontravel.com

Steppes Travel Travel Hse, 51 Castle St, Cirencester, Gloucestershire GL7 1QD; ✆01285 880980; e enquiry@steppestravel.co.uk; www.steppestravel.co.uk

Taste Lebanon Tumbling Fields Hse, Tumbling Lane, Tiverton, Devon EX16 4LN; m 07545 980 508 (UK), 71 131 114/115 (Beirut); e info@tastelebanon.co.uk; www.tastelebanon.co.uk

Travel the Unknown Hyde Park Hse, 5 Manfred Rd, Putney, London SW15 2RS; ✆020 7183 6371; e info@traveltheunknown.com; www.traveltheunknown.com

Trip Feast Hyde Park Hse, 5 Manfred Rd, Putney, London SW15 2RS; ✆020 7183 5153; e info@tripfeast.com; www.tripfeast.com

The Ultimate Travel Company 25–27 Vanston Pl, London SW6 1AZ; ✆020 7386 4646, 020 3432 9037; e enquiry@theultimatetravelcompany.co.uk; www.theultimatetravelcompany.co.uk

Voyages Jules Verne 21 Dorset Sq, London NW1 6QE; ✆0845 166 7003; e sales@vjv.co.uk; www.vjv.com

Wild Frontiers 78 Glentham Rd, London SW13 9JJ; ✆020 7736 3968; e info@wildfrontiers.co.uk; www.wildfrontierstravel.com

World Discovery 32 Rothes Rd, Dorking, Surrey RH4 1LD; ✆01306 888799; e enquiries@worlddiscovery.co.uk; www.worlddiscovery.co.uk

World Expeditions 81 Craven Gardens, Wimbledon, London SW19 8LU; ✆020 8545 9030; e enquiries@worldexpeditions.co.uk; www.worldexpeditions.co.uk

REPUBLIC OF IRELAND

Citiescapes Suite 30, The Hyde Bldg, The Park, Carrickmines, Dublin 18, Ireland; ✆+353 1 294 1000; e book@citiescapes.ie; www.citiescapes.ie. Previously offered a 9-night tour of Lebanon (commencing from Syria) visiting Beirut, Byblos, Chouf Mountains, & Baalbek from €2,199 inc return flights from Dublin, Cork or Shannon via London (Heathrow) & accommodation. They have also run a Greece, Cyprus & Lebanon cruise (€999pp including return flights from Dublin to Milan), which included a day in Beirut.

The Irish Lebanese Cultural Foundation 3 The Sycamores, Freshford Rd, Kilkenny, Ireland; ✆+353 87 809 0088; e irishlebanese@hotmail.com; www.irishlebanese.com. This active cultural organisation has regularly run a couple of 9-day/8-night tours each year, usually in Mar & Oct, costing around €1,200 inc accommodation & return flights to Beirut from Dublin via London (Heathrow).

USA AND CANADA

Bestway Tours & Safaris Suite 206, 8678 Greenall Av, Burnaby, British Columbia, Canada V5J 3M6; ✆+1 604 264 7378, +1 800 663 0844 (toll free within USA & Canada); e bestway@bestway.com; www.bestway.com. A specialist, small-group cultural tour operator who previously ran a number of trips, some in conjunction with Jordan & Syria, ranging from 8 to 17 days with prices from US$1,895 exc return flights.

Caravan-Serai Tours 3806 Whitman Av, N, Seattle, WA 98103, USA; ✆800 451 8097; e info@

caravan-serai.com; www.caravan-serai.com. At the time of research this cultural tour operator provided a number of Lebanon itineraries (some combined with Jordan & Syria) but had yet to finalise detailed itineraries & prices for these tours, which range from 5 to 12 days.

Geographic Expeditions PO Box 29902, 1008 General Kennedy Av, San Francisco, CA 94129–0902, USA; 415 922 0448, 888 570 7108 (toll free); e info@geoex.com; www.geoex.com. From April to November this adventure-orientated company offers an 8-day Lebanon, Past & Present itinerary covering the major sights of the country with an emphasis on culture, gastronomy & walking. Prices start from US$4,325 inc hotel but exc return flights.

Travcoa 100 North Sepulveda Bd, Suite 1700, El Segundo, CA 90245, USA; 888 978 6904 (within Canada & USA), +1 310 730 1416 (worldwide); e info@travcoa.com; www.travcoa.com. Specialising in luxury & upmarket travel, this company previously offered a 5-day Cedars of Lebanon tour taking in the main sites at Baalbek, Jeita Grotto, Byblos, Sidon, Tyre & a winery. Prices started from US$1,995 exc return international flights but inc accommodation.

TOURIST INFORMATION

Lebanon's official **Ministry of Tourism Office** [163 F4] (*550 Central Bank St, Hamra, Beirut;* 01 343 073, 01 340 940/1/2/3/4, *Tourist Hotline, dial 1735 within Lebanon;* e *info@ destinationlebanon.gov.lb, mot@destinationlebanon.gov.lb; www.destinationlebanon.gov. lb, www.mot.gov.lb;* ⊕ *08.00–15.00 Mon–Thu, 08.00–13.00 Fri–Sat*) is an excellent and friendly resource when in the country, and from the English-speaking staff you can obtain a range of free brochures and maps, including those showing Beirut bus maps and routes (ask for *khaariTa*), hotel, entertainment and restaurant information for all areas of Lebanon in a variety of languages (Arabic, English, French, German, Italian and Spanish). If you are planning on an extensive tour of Lebanon, the Hamra office is the place to go to collect most of your material as stocks of brochures and maps etc are not normally as plentiful, and in some cases non-existent, in the regional offices and at the archaeological sites themselves. The Ministry of Tourism also maintains an office at Beirut airport [127 E7] which is situated to your left as you emerge into the arrivals hall (page 130). Additionally, there is a regional network of tourist information offices at Baalbek, Batroun, Byblos (Jbail), Jeita Grotto, Niha in the Chouf Mountains, Sidon (Saida), Tripoli (Trablous) and Zahlé in the Bekaa Valley, and these are detailed in the relevant regional chapters.

The Lebanese Ministry of Tourism also maintains two overseas offices, in Egypt (*Lebanon Tourist Office, 1 Talaat Harb St (Midan Al Tahrir), Cairo;* f +20 2 393 7529) and in France (*Office du Tourisme du Liban, 124 Rue du Faubourg St Honoré, 75008 Paris;* +33 1 4359 1036, +33 1 4359 1213/1214; e *libanot@aol.com; www.destinationliban.com*).

RED TAPE

ARRIVING BY AIR Citizens of all countries require a visa to enter Lebanon. Nationals of Bahrain, Kuwait, Oman, Qatar, Saudi Arabia and the United Arab Emirates (Gulf Co-operation Council States) and Jordan are issued with a three-month visa, free of charge, upon arrival at Beirut international airport. Nationals of the following countries are currently issued with a free, single-entry, one-month visa, upon arrival at Beirut international airport which is renewable for up to three months, upon production of a valid passport valid for at least six months: Andorra, Antigua and Barbuda, Argentina, Armenia, Australia, Austria, Azerbaijan, Bahamas, Barbados, Belarus, Belgium, Belize, Bhutan, Brazil, Bulgaria, Canada, Chile, China, Czech Republic, Costa Rica, Croatia, Cyprus, Denmark, Dominican Republic, Estonia, Finland, France, Great Britain, Georgia, Germany, Greece, Hong Kong,

Hungary, Iceland, Ireland, Italy, Japan, Kazakhstan, Kyrgyzstan, Latvia, Lithuania, Liechtenstein, Luxembourg, Macedonia, Macau, Malaysia, Malta, Mexico, Moldova, Monaco, Montenegro, Netherlands, New Zealand, Norway, Palau, Panama, Peru, Poland, Portugal, Russia, Romania, Saint Kitts and Nevis, Samoa, San Marino, Serbia, Singapore, Slovakia, Slovenia, South Korea, Spain, Sweden, Switzerland, Tajikistan, Turkmenistan, Ukraine, USA, Uzbekistan, Venezuela.

It is also possible to obtain a Lebanese visa in advance of travel from the Lebanese embassy or consulate in your own country (see opposite). It is essential to note, however, that if your passport contains evidence of a visit to Israel (including entry/exit stamps from the land border crossings between Egypt and Israel or Jordan and Israel), permission to enter Lebanon *will* be refused. The information in this section can change at any time and it is a good idea to check with the Lebanese embassy or consulate in your own country for the most up-to-date regulations prior to finalising your travel arrangements. The website of the General Directorate of General Security in Lebanon (*www.general-security.gov.lb*) has comprehensive visa information and regulations pertaining to citizens of most countries in Arabic, English and French. In the UK, the Foreign and Commonwealth Office (FCO) website (*www.gov.uk/foreign-travel-advice/lebanon*) is an especially good source of ever-changing country-specific officialdom and timely security information. In the USA, the Department of State operates a couple of informative websites (*www.state.gov* and *www.travel.state.gov*), which also contains country-specific information and travel advice for US citizens. For Australian citizens visiting Lebanon, the government website of the Department of Foreign Affairs and Trade (*www.smartraveller.gov.au*) should be consulted for a range of entry, visa and security information for Lebanon.

ARRIVING BY ROAD As it is not possible to enter Lebanon from the country's southern border with Israel, your only option to enter Lebanon by land is from its northeastern neighbour, Syria. At the time of writing, the ongoing hostilities in that country makes travel between the two countries a potentially very dangerous undertaking and cannot be recommended.

VISA EXTENSIONS In practice, at the time of research, your free, one-month tourist visa is actually valid for three-months! So, unless you are planning to stay in the country longer than this, the following details will not apply to you. To extend your original one-month visa beyond its three-month validity you will need to visit the **General Directorate of General Security** [127 H6] (*Bldg 1, 2nd Fl, Bd Sami El-Solh (nr Palace of Justice), Beirut;* ✆ *01 425 610 ext 1276/1273; www.general-security.gov.lb;* ⏱ *08.00–14.00 Mon–Thu, 08.00–11.00 Fri, 08.00–13.00 Sat*). You will need to produce your passport, passport-sized photo, photocopies of your passport ID page and the original visa entry stamp page a few days prior to the expiry of your original one-month visa. Official policy is subject to change and a quick check on the above website or telephone call to the Directorate could prove invaluable.

BUSINESS VISAS For those foreign nationals travelling to Lebanon intending to work, there is, not surprisingly, a little more bureaucracy involved than with obtaining a tourist visa. In the first place, you will need to apply to the Lebanese embassy in your home country for a business/work visa and obtain a letter of invitation from the company sponsoring you which needs to be approved by Lebanon's Ministry of Labour. Being granted a work visa generally confers resident status. A good starting point is to take a look at the website of the **General Directorate of General Security** (*www.general-security.gov.lb*) which has an extensive section on the types of work visa for Lebanon. In the UK, the **Arab British Chamber of Commerce** (*Visa Section, 43 Upper Grosvenor St, London W1K 2NJ;* \ *020 7235 4363; www.abcc.org. uk*) provides a visa service for companies based in the UK, or their overseas offices, and comprehensive details on the application process are available on its website.

CUSTOMS AND DUTY-FREE Personal items such as photographic still and video cameras, laptop computers and the like, are excluded from any form of customs duty. The current duty-free allowances for the most common types of goods being taken **into Lebanon**, whether arriving in the country via air, land or sea, are as follows: two bottles of spirits or four litres of any other alcoholic beverage, 800 cigarettes or 50 cigars or 1,000g of tobacco. These allowances can change from time to time and current allowances are displayed on the Lebanese customs website (*www.customs.gov.lb*). It should go without saying that items such as arms and ammunitions, narcotics and any form of pornographic material printed or otherwise must not be brought into the country. From **Lebanon to the UK** the duty-free allowances are currently 200 cigarettes or 50 cigars or 250g of tobacco, 16 litres of beer, one litre of spirits or two litres of fortified wine and four litres of non-sparkling wine. To keep up to date with periodic changes to UK customs and duty-free regulations visit www.gov.uk/duty-free-goods.

LEBANESE EMBASSIES AND CONSULATES ABROAD Lebanon has an extensive network of embassies and consular representation in overseas countries, and most foreign nationals will have no problem obtaining a visa in advance for travel to Lebanon. At the present time, however, as tourist entry visas for many countries and their citizens can be issued upon arrival at Beirut airport or at the land border crossing posts, there seems little need to obtain one in advance, which, in the case of UK passport holders will currently cost £25 for a three-month, single-entry tourist visa (£50 multiple entry). As the visa application process and policy can change at any time, it is a good idea to check before you travel. For a comprehensive and worldwide listing of Lebanese embassies and consulates abroad, visit the following websites: http://embassy.goabroad.com/embassies-of/Lebanon; www. embassy-finder.com; and www.embassypages.com/lebanon. For a list of foreign embassies and consulates in Beirut and environs see also pages 156–7.

GETTING THERE AND AWAY

BY AIR Lebanon's sole commercial international airport is Beirut's **Rafiq Hariri International Airport** [127 E7] (IATA/ICAO airport codes: BEY/OLBA; \ *01 628 000, dial 150 within Lebanon; www.beirutairport.gov.lb*), which is served by many of the world's major international airlines; and this is the way the vast majority of visitors will arrive. From the UK there are daily non-stop flights departing from London (Heathrow) airport (LHR) and the flying time is a little under 5 hours. Lebanon's national carrier Middle East Airlines (ME) flies from Terminal 3, whilst the UK's British Airways (BA) uses Terminal 5. From London Gatwick airport (LGW) and London Stansted airport (STN) the Turkish budget carrier Pegasus Airlines (PC) flies daily to Beirut via Istanbul. From continental Europe Beirut is a little over 4 hours from Paris and Spain, a little under 4 hours from Frankfurt and around 3 hours from Rome. There are currently no direct flights to Lebanon from North America which means that for US and Canadian citizens a stopover in one of the main European capitals such as London, Paris or Rome

3

will be required in order to complete your onward journey via a connecting flight. For travellers visiting Lebanon from Australia, Emirates (*www.emirates. com*) and Etihad Airways (*www.etihad.com*) both fly regularly from Brisbane, Sydney and Melbourne to Beirut via their national hubs at Dubai and Abu Dhabi respectively. As there are also no direct flights at present to Beirut from New Zealand, visitors will need to pick up a connecting flight from Australia, fly via a European destination such as Paris or London, or arrive in a nearby city such as Amman (Jordan), Cairo (Egypt) or Istanbul (Turkey) to pick up a connecting flight to Beirut.

Beirut airport adopted its present name in honour of the country's assassinated former prime minister. Its bright, airy and modern interior is the culmination of a ten-year reconstruction plan, which has totally transformed the former drab and outdated building into a major regional hub. Although the airport still feels a little spartan, it nonetheless has a good range of facilities to offer the traveller including airport lounges, banking and foreign exchange facilities, a post office, disabled access (elevators, ramps, airline wheelchairs and on-request ground assistance) and a full range of duty-free shopping (m *03 145 465; www. beirutdutyfree.com*), which is on a par with most European and North American airports. There are also prayer rooms for both Christians and Muslims above the duty-free area on the departures level. The airport also boasts a range of car-hire companies together with cafés and restaurants in both the arrivals and departure halls. In general, customs, health and visa procedures are courteous, efficient and hassle-free. The airport's website (*www.beirutairport.gov.lb*) also provides live departure and arrival flight information, which is updated regularly.

When departing Lebanon, you will need to complete a short pink country exit form available all over the departures hall, and official advice is to be at the airport about 3 hours before your flight is scheduled to depart. The journey time to the airport by taxi from Beirut's Downtown area is approximately 20–30 minutes, depending on traffic, and the fare should cost no more than US$20–25.

The major international carriers listed below all operated regular flights to Beirut at the time of writing. In addition, the following airlines all fly regularly into Beirut: Aeroflot, Air Algerie, Air Arabia, Air Baltic, Air Germania, Air Maroc, Armavia, Bahrain Air, Belavia, Bulgaria Air, Czech Airlines, EgyptAir, Emirates, Ethiopian Airlines, Etihad Airways, FlyDubai, Gulf Air, Iran Air, Iraqi Airways, Kuwait Airways, Malev Hungarian Airlines, Olympic Airways, Oman Air, Qatar Airways, Royal Jordanian Airlines, Saudi Arabian Airlines, Syrian Arab Airlines, Tarom, Tunis Air, and Yemen Airways.

✈ **Air France** (IATA airline code: AF) www.airfrance.com. The French national carrier flies direct to Beirut daily from Paris, Charles de Gaulle Airport (IATA airport code: CDG).

✈ **Alitalia** (AZ) www.alitalia.com. Italy's national airline has direct daily flights to Beirut from Rome's Leonardo da Vinci International Airport (Fiumicino; FCO).

✈ **British Airways** (BA) Waterside, PO Box 365, Harmondsworth UB7 0GB; ☎0844 493 0787; www.ba.com. BA, a member of the Oneworld Alliance, is Heathrow's largest airline & operates a modern fleet of Airbus A321 aircraft with daily direct flights to Beirut from Terminal 5.

✈ **Lufthansa German Airlines** (LH) www.lufthansa.com. Germany's national carrier has daily direct flights to Beirut departing from Frankfurt Main International Airport (FRA).

✈ **Middle East Airlines** (ME) ☎020 7467 8000, 020 7467 8010 (within the UK), 01 628 888, 01 623 929 (within Beirut); e lontome@mea.aero; www.mea.com.lb. The national carrier operates a modern fleet of Airbus A330s, A321s & A320 aircraft & flies direct every day, departing & arriving at respectable times from Terminal 3 at Heathrow. The airline also has an excellent network of routes across more than 20 countries in the Middle East, Africa, North & South America, connecting more than 30 of the world's major cities via code-share agreements with its *SkyTeam* alliance partner airlines.

✈ **Pegasus Airlines** (PC) ☎ 0845 0848 980 (within the UK), 00 961 1 369 869 (within Lebanon); e customer@flypgs.com; www.flypgs.com; see ad, 3rd colour section. This privately owned Turkish-based budget airline, flying to more than 100 cities in more than 40 countries, operates daily flights from both London (Stansted) (STN) and London (Gatwick) (LGW) airports to Beirut via Istanbul's Sabiha Gökçen International Airport (SAW). At the time of writing a return flight to Beirut could be obtained for under £400, but this can involve a stopover of around 3–4hrs in Istanbul before the onward connecting flight to Beirut/London.

✈ **Turkish Airlines** (TK) ☎ 0844 800 6666 (sales & reservations, Birmingham, Manchester, Gatwick & Heathrow Airports); e info-uk@thy.com; www.turkishairlines.com. Turkey's national carrier flies from Birmingham, Manchester, London Gatwick (North Terminal) and London Heathrow (Terminal 3) to Beirut via Istanbul, but this can involve a lengthy stopover of over 4 hours at Istanbul's Ataturk airport (IST) before the connecting flight to Beirut.

✈ **Vueling Airlines** (VY) Parque de Negocios Mas Blau II, Pla de l'Estany 5, 08820 El Prat de Llobregat, Barcelona, Spain; ☎ +34 93 378 7878, 807 200 100 (reservations number within Spain); www.vueling.com. This Spanish airline operates twice-weekly (Mon & Fri) direct flights between Barcelona (BCN) & Beirut with return flights to Barcelona departing on Tue & Sat at the time of writing.

BY ROAD After flying, overland travel is the most popular and accessible way for visitors to arrive in Lebanon. Although Lebanon shares an 81km land border with its southern neighbour, Israel, the two countries remain in a state of war and, despite the Israelis withdrawing the majority of their military presence from Lebanese soil in May 2000, it is still not possible to enter Lebanon from Israel, a state of affairs highly unlikely to change any time soon. The result is that entry to Lebanon by road is only possible via its northeastern neighbour, Syria, from one of Lebanon's four main border crossing points. At the time of research, bus and taxi travel between Lebanon and many towns and cities in Syria was possible but it cannot be recommended until the cessation of the ongoing hostilities in that country.

From Jordan Bus and taxi services operating between Jordan and Lebanon's Charles Helou bus station in Beirut were suspended at the time of research owing to border restrictions, once again linked to the Syrian conflict.

From Turkey There are regular bus services to Lebanon (Beirut and Tripoli) from the Turkish cities of Antakya and Istanbul which ply the route to and from the capital's Charles Helou bus station [173 B2] and Tripoli.

BY SEA Lebanon's principal ports of entry for commercial sea-going traffic are Beirut and Tripoli, but the country is not overly well served by boat. Nevertheless, there are a few possible options if you would like to visit part of the country this way, perhaps combining Lebanon with other countries in the region; but choices are fairly limited at present. As companies offering cruise itineraries that include Lebanon may well increase in the future, you may wish to check on the following two websites for developments: www.cruiseexperts.org and www.choosingcruising.co.uk. The companies listed on page 72 have all previously offered cruise itineraries that include a short stopover in Lebanon.

From Cyprus For those resident or holidaying on the island of Cyprus and perhaps pondering the idea of a short visit to Lebanon, the following companies have previously offered seasonal cruises from the island's largest port of Limassol, with short stopovers at the port of Beirut, where a range of optional shore excursions are available. In addition to those operators below, it may be worth keeping an eye on the following two Cyprus-based organisations as they periodically post information regarding cruises to Lebanon and other areas of the eastern Mediterranean: **Cruise Cyprus** (*PO Box 40218, Larnaca, Cyprus;* \+357 24 665 408; e *info@cruisecyprus.com; www.cruisecyprus.com*) and **Varianos Travel** (*PO Box 22107, 8 C Pantelides Av, 1517 Nicosia, Cyprus;* \+357 2268 0500, +357 2266 7772; e *info@varianostravel.com; www.varianostravel.com*).

Celestyal Cruises Ampatielou 8, Piraeus, Greece; \+30 210 458 3400; www.celestyalcruises. com. This company, formerly called Louis Cruises, previously operated short cruises departing from Limassol to Beirut. These were suspended at the time of writing, but check their website for updates. **Salamis Cruise Lines** PO Box 50531, Salamis Hse, 1 G. Katsounotos St, Limassol 3607, Cyprus; \+357 258 60000; e cruisereservations@ salamis-tours.com; www.salamiscruiselines. com. In June 2015 this company was offering short 3-day/2-night cruise itineraries departing from Limassol to Beirut with optional shore excursions available to Harissa, Jeita Grotto & Byblos. Check the website for upcoming tours, prices & itineraries.

From Turkey
At the time of writing, the Turkish company **Akgünler Denizcilik** (*www.akgunlerdenizcilik.com*) operated a twice-weekly ferry service (*Sun & Tue*) from Turkey's southern port of Tasucu to Lebanon's second city of Tripoli, with a sailing time of around 12 hours.

From the UK
The shipping operators below have all previously offered the cruise itineraries described with the prices indicated and which dock at Beirut for one to two days with shore excursions around the capital, as well as to many other areas such as Baalbek, Byblos, Jeita Grotto and Tripoli. Although some of these have temporarily suspended their port of call to Lebanon, it may be worth checking periodically with these companies to see if the situation has changed.

MSC Cruises Queen's Hse, 55–56 Lincoln's Inn Fields, London WC2A 3LJ; \0203 426 3010; e info@msccruises.co.uk, mscdirect@msccruises. co.uk; www.msccruises.co.uk. During the months of Apr, Jul, Sep & Oct this company has formerly run an 11-night Mediterranean cruise departing from the Italian port of Genoa which included a full day in Beirut before the ship continues on to Egypt, Greece & back to Genoa. Optional half- & full-day shore excursions to Jeita Grotto, Byblos & Baalbek were also available. Cruises including Lebanon were suspended at the time of writing, but keep an eye on their website in case this changes. *£899–1,099 exc return flights from the UK.*
Noble Caledonia 2 Chester Close, Belgravia, London SW1X 7BE; \020 7752 0000; e info@ noble-caledonia.co.uk; www.noble-caledonia. co.uk. At the time of writing the company offered a couple of 25–27-night cruises around the eastern Mediterranean which included a 2-day stopover in Lebanon with shore excursions around Beirut, Baalbek & Byblos. *From £3,995 inc return flights to Athens from the UK.*
Swan Hellenic Compass Hse, Rockingham Rd, Market Harborough, Leicestershire LE16 7QD; \0844 209 9000, 01858 898299; e info@ swanhellenic.com, reservations@swanhellenic. com; www.swanhellenic.com. A stylish cruise company who offered a 15-day Pyramids & Petra itinerary in October 2014 which includes a full day in Beirut with shore excursions around the capital & Byblos. *From £3,190 inc return flights to the seaport of departure in Piraeus, Greece.*
Thomson Cruises Thomson Cruise Service Centre, Mariner St, Swansea SA1 5BA; \0871 231 5938; www.thomson.co.uk. As part of their 7-night Myths & Legends itinerary in April 2016, the Thomson Spirit ship docks at Beirut on day 2 where optional full-day shore excursions were available of the capital, Byblos & Jeita Grotto. *From £464 pp inc return flights from the UK to Limassol (Cyprus).*

Generally speaking, Lebanon is a healthy country with life expectancy and infant mortality rates much better than other countries in the region, and you are no more likely to fall ill or contract an infectious disease than anywhere else in the Mediterranean region. The standards of healthcare are high with many medical personnel having been educated overseas, many in Europe, and several also speak English and French in addition to their native Arabic. Lebanon currently has some 174 healthcare and medical facilities around the country with around 33 doctors and 34 hospital beds per 10,000 of the population and spends some 7% of its GDP on healthcare; above average figures for the MENA (Middle East and North Africa) region. Emergency and routine medical treatment is available to overseas visitors, but as Lebanon does not have any reciprocal healthcare agreements with either North America or Europe, payment for any medical care received will be required at the time you are treated. It is therefore essential to have comprehensive medical insurance in place prior to visiting Lebanon.

TRAVEL PREPARATION Before your departure, it would be advisable to be up to date with your vaccinations against tetanus, polio and diphtheria, which are now available as an all-in-one vaccine, Revaxis, and which is valid for ten years. It is also a good idea to be up to date with hepatitis A vaccine, and longer-stay travellers, those visiting friends and relations, and more remote travellers may be recommended typhoid vaccine. If travelling for more than two months, a hepatitis B vaccine is recommended which is given as a course of three injections over a minimum of three weeks and can be administered as a combined dose with hepatitis A. These schedules are restricted for those aged 16 years and above. Longer hepatitis B schedules over a minimum of eight weeks are needed for younger people. Vaccination against rabies (pages 73–5) is ideally recommended for everyone, as there is a worldwide shortage of part of the post-exposure rabies treatment. It is especially recommended if you are planning to visit remote rural areas of Lebanon and will be more than 24 hours away from medical assistance, and definitely if you are working with animals. The pre-exposure course consists of three doses of vaccine over a minimum of 21 days but even two doses of vaccine at least seven days apart can be helpful. There is no risk of yellow fever in Lebanon and no vaccine certificate requirement.

MALARIA Lebanon is not in a malaria zone, so there is no risk of contracting the condition in the country. Nevertheless, there may be other mosquito-borne diseases present, such as dengue fever, so it is worth having an insect repellent to hand.

RABIES Rabies is carried by all mammals (beware the village dogs that are used to being fed in the parks), including bats, cats, monkeys, etc, and is passed on to humans through a bite, scratch or simply saliva on skin. You must always assume any animal is rabid and seek medical help as soon as possible. Meanwhile, scrub the wound with soap under a running tap or while pouring water from a jug. Find a reasonably clear-looking source of water (but at this stage the quality of the water is not important), then pour on a strong iodine or alcohol solution of gin, whisky or rum. This helps stop the rabies virus entering the body and will guard against wound infections, including tetanus. What treatment you need depends on whether you have had any pre-exposure vaccine. If you have not had any, then you are going to need four to five doses of rabies vaccine given over a month and will probably need Rabies Immunoglobulin (RIG) especially with bites and scratches. The RIG is hard to come by and very expensive and may well not be available in Lebanon. Having at least two doses of vaccine removes the need for

Any prolonged immobility, including travel by land or air, can result in deep-vein thrombosis (DVT) with the risk of embolus to the lungs. Certain factors can increase the risk and these include:

- History of DVT or pulmonary embolism
- Recent surgery to pelvic region or legs
- Cancer
- Stroke
- Heart disease
- Inherited tendency to clot (thrombophilia)
- Obesity
- Pregnancy
- Hormone therapy
- Older age
- Being over 6ft (1.8m) or under 5ft (1.5m) tall

A DVT causes painful swelling and redness of the calf, or sometimes the thigh. It is only dangerous if a clot travels to the lungs (pulmonary embolus; PE). Symptoms of a PE – which commonly start three to ten days after a long flight – include chest pain, shortness of breath, and sometimes coughing up small amounts of blood. Anyone who thinks that they might have a DVT needs to see a doctor immediately.

PREVENTION OF DVT
- Wear loose comfortable clothing
- Do anti-DVT exercises and move around when possible
- Drink plenty of fluids during the flight
- Avoid taking sleeping pills unless you are able to lie flat
- Avoid excessive tea, coffee and alcohol
- Consider wearing flight socks or support stockings (*see www.leghealthwarehouse.com*).

If you think you are at increased risk of a clot, ask your doctor if it is safe to travel.

RIG in most cases but four to five doses of vaccine are still required. Having all three pre-exposure doses reduces treatment down to two doses of vaccine about three days apart. Remember the fatality rate of rabies is nearly 100% so always have a low threshold for thinking you could have had a rabies exposure.

Pre-exposure vaccinations for rabies are ideally advised for everyone, but are particularly important if you intend to have contact with animals and/or are likely to be more than 24 hours away from medical help. Ideally three doses should be taken over a minimum of 21 days, though even taking one or two doses of vaccine may be better than none at all in some circumstances. Contrary to popular belief, these vaccinations are relatively painless.

If you are bitten, scratched or licked over an open wound by a sick animal, then post-exposure prophylaxis should be given as soon as possible, though it is never too late to seek help, as the incubation period for rabies can be very long. Those who have not been immunised will need a full course of injections as well as rabies immunoglobulin (RIG), but this product is expensive (around US$800) and may be hard to come by – another reason why pre-exposure vaccination should be encouraged. If you have had the full three doses of pre-exposure vaccine, then you will not need the RIG, but just two further doses of vaccine three days apart. It is important to tell the doctor if you have had pre-exposure vaccine. And remember that, if you do contract rabies, mortality is 100% and death from rabies is probably one of the worst ways to go.

LEISHMANIASIS Leishmaniasis is spread through the bite of an infected sandfly. It can cause a slowly growing skin lump or ulcer (the cutaneous form) and sometimes a serious life-threatening fever with anaemia and weight loss (Kala-azar). Infected dogs are carriers of the infection. Sandfly bites should be avoided whenever possible. The female sandflies or 'no-see-ums' (as they are called) are usually more of a problem at night and when the wind dies down on the beach. The first line of defence is to apply insect repellents containing 50–55% DEET to exposed skin. Wear long-sleeved shirts, long trousers, and socks in the evenings.

PROTECTION FROM THE SUN During the height of summer temperatures can soar to 30–35°C or even higher, especially on the coast, and for those unused to these temperatures or from more temperate climates, the intensity of the heat could be a real problem. It would be sensible to pack some suncream and to keep out of the sun during the middle of the day if possible, but if you must expose yourself to the sun, build up gradually from 20 minutes per day and wear a T-shirt and apply suncream (at least SPF25, but preferably 30 and a UVA of four or more stars) and use waterproof suncream if swimming. Exposure to the sun can age the skin, making people permanently wrinkly; and increases the risk of skin cancer. Cover up where possible and wear long, loose-fitting clothes and a hat. Prickly heat or heat rash is a related problem identified by a fine pimply rash on the trunk; cool showers, dabbing dry, and talc will all help. Treat the problem by slowing down to a more relaxed schedule, wearing only loose, baggy, 100% cotton clothes and sleeping naked under a fan; if it's bad you may need to check into an air-conditioned hotel room for a while.

PERSONAL FIRST-AID KIT

A basic kit could contain the following:

- A good drying antiseptic, eg: iodine or potassium permanganate (don't take antiseptic cream)
- A few small dressings (Band-Aids)
- Suncream
- Insect repellent; impregnated bednet or permethrin spray
- Aspirin or paracetamol
- Antifungal cream (eg: Canesten)
- Ciprofloxacin or norfloxacin, for severe diarrhoea
- Antibiotic eye drops, for sore, 'gritty', stuck-together eyes (conjunctivitis)
- A pair of fine-pointed tweezers (to remove hairy caterpillar hairs, thorns, splinters and such like)
- Alcohol-based hand rub or bar of soap in a plastic box
- Condoms or femidoms

DRINKING WATER Tap water is not generally drinkable so stick with bottled mineral water, which is plentiful, cheap and available in hotels, restaurants, supermarkets and corner shops all over the country and often from Lebanon's own mountain springs such as Mount Sannine and Tannourine.

SMOKING Smoking is widespread in Lebanon, as in most Arab countries, with around 40% of men and almost a third of women being regular smokers, and is currently the number-one cause of death in the country. A 2010 World Health Organisation (WHO) study ranked Lebanon as one of the world's most prolific nations for smoking, which claims more than 3,500 lives each year. Consequently, you will find many people lighting up in bars, cafés, restaurants, hotels and internet cafés, so passive smoking can be an issue in all these establishments. Many Lebanese smoke well-known American brands such as Kent, Marlboro and Winston. In September 2011, however, Lebanon followed the example of Syria and the United Arab Emirates by becoming the Arab world's third country to pass a law banning smoking (including the *nargileh* or *sheesha* pipe) in public places, legislation that includes an advertising and sponsorship ban on tobacco companies. The new legislation, known as Law 174, came into force in September 2012, imposing substantial fines on both establishment owners (*LBP1 million–4 million*) and individuals (*LBP135,000*) who flout the ban, but many people seem to think that the rules won't be enforced and many people and establishments will ignore them anyway, which proved to be precisely the case in some instances during the author's most recent visit.

STOMACH UPSETS Although hygiene standards in Lebanon's cafés, hotels and restaurants are generally excellent, a change in climate, diet and routine can all upset the normal digestive pattern and, apart from being caught short, you are unlikely in Lebanon to experience anything more serious beyond having a brief bout of diarrhoea. If you do experience diarrhoea, the best advice is to drink plenty of fluids such as coke, orange squash or water to help stave off the worst effects of dehydration and to stick to plain foods such as biscuits until the condition passes.

HIV/AIDS The incidence of this life-threatening condition in Lebanon is extremely low. According to the latest available 2014 estimates, there were some 1,800 people living with HIV/AIDS in Lebanon, around 0.06% of the total population, mainly the outcome of homosexual sexual transmission. Lebanon's Ministry of Public Health instigated the National AIDS Control Programme (NAP) back in 1989 and this is an ongoing initiative to help educate and limit the spread and prevalence of the disease. As having unprotected sex with an infected person exposes you to risk of catching the disease, the only sure way to be safe is to abstain from any sexual contact. If you must indulge, use condoms or femidoms, which help to reduce the risk of transmission. If you notice any genital ulcers or discharge, get treatment promptly since these increase the risk of acquiring HIV. If you do have unprotected sex, visit a clinic as soon as possible; this should be within 24 hours, or no later than 72 hours, for post-exposure prophylaxis. The chances of contracting HIV through infected needles or by blood transfusion is practically zero in Lebanon with no fresh cases of HIV infections transmitted this way since 1993.

JELLYFISH In the height of summer, during July and August, jellyfish can be a nuisance for swimmers as the creatures embark on their annual migration northwards along the Mediterranean coastline. Although not generally life-threatening, their stings can be extremely painful and medical assistance should be sought at the earliest opportunity. An antiseptic cream is usually sufficient to treat more minor stings.

SNAKEBITE Lebanon has a number of poisonous species of snake which often inhabit archaeological sites, rocky and rural terrain, though no variety is of the highly venomous type. The main toxic ones to give a wide berth should you encounter them on your travels are the Montpellier snake (*Malpolon monspessulanus*), the blunt-nosed viper (*Vipera lebetina*) and the Palestinian viper (*Vipera palaestina*). Snakes rarely attack unless provoked, and bites in travellers are unusual. To prevent bites, wear stout shoes and long trousers when you are in areas where snakes are known to be present. Most snakes in Lebanon are harmless and even venomous species will dispense venom in only about half of their bites. If bitten, then, you are unlikely to have received venom; keeping this fact in mind may help you to stay calm. Many so-called first-aid techniques do more harm than good: tourniquets are dangerous; suction and electrical inactivation devices do not work. The only treatment is antivenom. In case of a bite that you fear may have been from a venomous snake:

- Try to keep calm – it is likely that no venom has been dispensed
- Prevent movement of the bitten limb by applying a splint
- Keep the bitten limb BELOW heart height to slow the spread of any venom
- If you have a crêpe bandage, wrap it around the whole limb (eg: all the way from the toes to the thigh), as tight as you would for a sprained ankle or a muscle pull
- Evacuate to a hospital

And remember:

- NEVER give aspirin; you may take paracetamol, which is safe
- NEVER cut or suck the wound
- DO NOT apply ice packs
- DO NOT apply potassium permanganate

If the offending snake can be captured without risk of someone else being bitten, take this to show the doctor – but beware since even a decapitated head is able to bite.

MEDICAL FACILITIES IN LEBANON In the capital, the 350+ bed **American University of Beirut Medical Centre (AUBMC)** [162 E3] (*Cairo St, Hamra, Beirut;* ✆ *01 350 000;* e *aubmc@aub.edu.lb; www.aubmc.org*) is a highly respected teaching hospital with a full range of medical departments, including 24-hour emergency admissions. The smaller and nearby 106-bed **Clemenceau Medical Centre** [163 G3] (CMC; *Clemenceau St, Hamra, Beirut;* ✆ *01 372 888, hotline dial 1240 within Lebanon;* e *info@cmc.com.lb; www.cmc.com.lb*), affiliated with John Hopkins International in the USA, is another facility providing cutting-edge medical technology with well-qualified staff and has consistently been recognised as one of the top-ten World's Best Hospitals for Medical Tourism by the Medical Travel Quality Alliance (MTQUA; *www.mtqua.org*). In the Achrafieh district of east Beirut **Hôtel-Dieu de France** [172 C6] (*Alfred Naccache St, Achrafieh, Beirut;* ✆ *01 615 300;* e *info@hdf.usj.edu.lb; www. hdf.usj.edu.lb*) offers similar facilities. In addition to these hospitals, private doctors and dentists abound, working in both general and more specialised fields, and you will see their plaques advertising their services on buildings around the country. The **Syndicate of Hospitals** (*www.syndicateofhospitals.org.lb*) in Lebanon is also a good source of information and they have contact numbers for medical facilities for all regions of the country. The **British embassy** in Beirut [138 C6] (*Embassy Complex, Serail Hill, Downtown, Beirut;* \ *01 960 800;* f *01 960 855; www.gov.uk/government/ world/organisations/british-embassy-beirut*) should also be able to provide you with a comprehensive list of nationwide hospitals, with their full contact details. The website of the **US Embassy** in Beirut [127 H3] (*Rue Amin Gemayel, opp Awkar Municipality Bldg, Awkar;* \ *04 542 600/543 600;* f *04 544 136; www.lebanon.usembassy.gov*) has an excellent and more comprehensive listing of nationwide hospitals together with a list of doctors and dentists, plus personnel working in more specialised fields of medicine. In the regional chapters that follow, details of the main local hospitals and health care facilities have also been included where applicable.

PHARMACIES Well-stocked pharmacies are abundant, with many remaining open until late in the evening and a few even open 24/7. There are an increasing number of pharmacies that can also undertake minor medical procedures for less serious complaints. Contraceptives, tampons and sanitary towels are widely available in most pharmacies and supermarkets around the country.

TRAVEL CLINICS AND HEALTH INFORMATION A full list of current travel clinic websites worldwide is available on www.istm.org. For other journey preparation information, consult http://travelhealthpro.org.uk (UK) or http://wwwnc.cdc. gov/travel/ (US). Information about various medications may be found on www. netdoctor.co.uk/travel. All advice found online should be used in conjunction with expert advice received prior to or during travel.

SAFETY

The words 'Beirut' and 'Lebanon' continue to resonate with images and reports of danger, terrorism and war nearly three decades after the end of the 1975–90 civil hostilities. Memories still linger in the minds of hostages such as John McCarthy, Terry Waite and a host of other individuals who had their freedom forcibly taken away during a period of utter chaos and hatred in Lebanon's history. Thankfully, these events are in the past and, although it cannot be said that the country's internal problems and wider Middle East peace issues have been completely solved, as witnessed by the intensity of the 2006 summer conflict between Israel and Hezbollah and the current spillover from the Syrian conflict, the fact remains that foreign tourists and visitors are not targets for abductions or violence. The occupation of parts of the country by Syria ended in 2005 and the Israelis withdrew the vast majority of their forces from south Lebanon in May 2000. With the exception of a tiny parcel of land called the Shebaa farms (pages 4 and 301), over which Israel maintains a military presence, the only 'occupying' force in Lebanon now is the United Nations Interim Force in Lebanon (UNIFIL), who are located in a Security Zone in south Lebanon, monitoring the security situation between Israel and Hezbollah. The main problem in the south is the amount of unexploded ordnance left over from the 2006 July War between Israel and Hezbollah rather than any tangible threat to visitors (page 301). In Beirut especially, but also in many other parts of the country, you will no doubt come across soldiers, armoured vehicles and checkpoints, which, while it can be a little unnerving initially, is nothing to be worried about. You will find the Lebanese army courteous towards visitors, though you should always carry your passport (or a photocopy) in case you are asked for ID. At the time of writing, the main concern for visitors to Lebanon is the seemingly never-ending hostilities in neighbouring Syria which, in addition to a rising death toll in Syria itself estimated to exceed 400,000, according to UN estimates, and the influx of more than 1.06 million refugees to Lebanon, have resulted in violent incidents centred around the northern city of Tripoli, where the Alawite sect, from the regime of President Bashar al-Assad, have frequently clashed with the opposition Sunnis, resulting in numerous fatalities (pages 33 and 228). Beirut, too, is not immune from the war's spillover, as witnessed most spectacularly in October 2012 when a massive car bomb claimed the lives of many people including the chief of the Lebanese security services; and the twin suicide bombing in November 2015 which claimed the lives of 40+ people in the southern suburb of Bourj Brajneh. Widespread sectarian unrest in the southern city of Sidon in June 2013, again linked to Syria's civil war, also resulted in numerous deaths but was quickly quashed by the Lebanese army. Not surprisingly, then, the current UK Foreign and Commonwealth Office (FCO) (e *traveladvicepublicenquiries@fco.gov.uk; www.gov.uk/foreign-travel-advice/lebanon*) travel advice, in common with other countries' travel warnings, is to avoid all travel to the southern suburbs of Beirut, Tripoli, Palestinian refugee camps, the Bekaa Valley, south of the Litani River and anywhere within 5km of the Syrian border. Until the situation in Syria stabilises, when in Lebanon stay abreast of current developments by checking the daily press such as the English-language *Daily Star*, or tuning into local radio stations and/or the BBC news website (*www.bbc.co.uk*). But perhaps just as valuable is to get advice and information from local people.

As regards crime against the person, Lebanon is probably one of the safest countries in the world, with a very low crime rate compared with countries such as the UK and USA. There have been reports in the past of occasional bag-snatching and a spate of robberies in shared (*servees*) taxis in Beirut, but these are rare exceptions and Lebanon remains an inherently safe country for visitors. Like anywhere in the world, however, it pays to be vigilant.

DRIVING With some 1.4 million cars on Lebanon's congested roads, the accident rate is high and in 2008 car accidents were the number one cause of death in the country. Whilst road signs, traffic lights and speed cameras are becoming more widespread, these are often ignored by drivers. The Lebanese are not known for following rules, and when you factor in a lack of anticipation of other road users, speaking on a mobile phone whilst driving, not wearing a seat belt (assuming one is fitted) and a tendency towards road rage, the mix becomes potentially even more dangerous. Although the police will often stop and enforce the road laws, the following general advice should be observed by anyone travelling by taxi or hire car with a driver in Lebanon:

- If possible sit in the back of the car, but if you must sit in the front, wear a seat belt if there is one.
- Travel by day, not by night. Street and road lighting is often inadequate, especially in more remote mountain and rural areas.
- Avoid drivers who have been drinking.
- There are positive signs of things changing, however, and there are now a couple of well-established charities and pressure groups that have emerged to campaign for improved standards of driving on Lebanon's sometimes hazardous roads:

Kunhadi (Youth Awareness on Road Safety) 1st Fl, Feghali Bldg, Damascus Rd, Hazmieh, Beirut; ☏ 05 450 516; m 71 264 415; e kunhadi@kunhadi.org; www.kunhadi.org.

Founded in 2006, this campaigning charity is highly regarded for its many publicity initiatives in raising awareness amongst young drivers of a variety of road safety issues, such as drink-driving,

improved roads, new & improved traffic laws, new speed limits, the use of radar to track speeding drivers, & visits to schools & universities to educate potential & younger drivers in safe road use.
YASA (Youth Association for Safety Awareness) 2nd Fl, Akl Bldg, St Rock St, Hazmieh, Beirut; ⚲05 452 587; m 03 601 972; e yasa@ yasa.org; www.yasa.org. Part of the international NGO network, YASA Lebanon was set up in 1996 to combat 'reckless driving' & focuses on campaigns designed to foster improved child & pedestrian safety, the education of drivers in following the rules of the road, the perils of drink-driving & safe vehicle operation & maintenance. For visitors considering a self-drive tour of Lebanon, the YASA website, like Kunhadi above, provides some very useful background information on what to expect from 'going it alone' on Lebanon's roads

POLICE AND MILITARY You will find that the police mostly keep a low profile and are not as visible a presence on the streets as in many Western countries. You will most likely see them on some street intersections directing and controlling the flow of traffic, and they are generally hospitable and helpful to foreigners. More conspicuous is the presence of the army, armoured vehicles and numerous checkpoints around the country. Although this might initially be a little intimidating to the first-time visitor, it is perfectly normal in this part of the world, and, apart from the occasional checks at checkpoints, their presence will have minimal impact on your visit. Like the police, the Lebanese Army are generally courteous and helpful to foreigners.

TRAVELLERS WITH DISABILITIES

Lebanon is not the most disability-friendly nation in the world. Facilities are still a little thin on the ground for those with accessibility needs, though things are changing, albeit slowly. At present, Beirut airport, the National Museum, the AUB Museum, the History of Money Museum, the children's science museum Planet Discovery and the Sursock Museum, as well as some other parts of the rebuilt Downtown district of Beirut all have a range of facilities such as wheelchair and lift access; and even the Chouf Cedar Reserve now has a specially designated short trail for wheelchair users and others with a range of physical disabilities. Most of the luxury hotels have lifts and even a few of those at the budget end of the market, but comprehensive and specially adapted facilities for those with physical disabilities are still not the norm. Negotiating the streets of Beirut as well as other areas of the country, not to mention the often undulating terrain of Lebanon's archaeological and historical sites, would make for a challenging experience at best for the disabled traveller – pot-holes, the lack of street lighting, uneven road surfaces, chaotic traffic and no buses or taxis with adapted facilities would in all probability detract from what would otherwise be an enjoyable visit. Sadly, for the time being at least, solo disabled travel to Lebanon cannot be recommended.

For additional resources and general information for travellers with disabilities, see box, opposite.

WOMEN TRAVELLERS

Whether travelling solo or as part of a group tour, female travellers will find Lebanon a breath of fresh air compared with some other Arab countries where women are often given less-than-fair treatment. In a country justly famed for its cosmopolitanism and hospitality and an extremely low crime rate against the person compared with many Western countries, female travellers constantly state that they have encountered an easy-going and safe place to visit without the constant pestering and hassles that they have experienced in countries like Morocco. In terms of dress, pretty much anything goes in Beirut, and at times, with the revealing and fashionable clothing worn by many young women, you would hardly know you are in an Arabic country. That said, a short, skimpy top or skirt would be totally inappropriate attire in a mosque or in more conservative towns such as Baalbek, Sidon or Tripoli, though even here you can still see fashion-conscious and sexily dressed local women. If using taxis, it is probably a good idea where possible to sit in the back of the car in order to avoid potentially giving the wrong impression. Though Lebanon has a certain machismo, bars are by no means a male domain and as a lone woman you should not expect any more unsolicited attention than you would get back in your own country. With a vibrant café culture in the capital, you often see many lone Lebanese females passing time over a beer or cappuccino in a relaxed manner, usually accompanied only by an iPhone, laptop or both.

GAY AND LESBIAN TRAVELLERS

Lebanon's culture of openness and tolerance doesn't generally extend to the gay community, with attitudes to homosexuality still lagging some way behind those in many Western countries. As is the case in Islam generally, homosexuality is illegal under Lebanese law with Article 534 of the Lebanese Penal Code stating that homosexuality is a sexual act 'contradicting the laws of nature'; and the country does not have an overtly 'gay scene' where 'outed' homosexuals can freely mingle. Public displays of affection are taboo, and could cost you your liberty, with up to one year in prison, though in practice as a visitor you are more likely to be subject to deportation and/or a fine. There are, however, some recent positive signs of change including a more enlightened and supportive media, together with the groundbreaking statement from the Lebanese Psychiatric Society in July 2013 who declared that same-sex relationships are not a form of mental illness and require no therapeutic input, making Lebanon the first Arab country to announce that homosexuality is not a disease. However, whilst there are a number of what might be termed 'gay-friendly' establishments in Beirut (page 147), discretion remains, for the foreseeable future, the order of the day for both Lebanese and foreigners alike, as discrimination and raids by police and security forces on known and suspected gay haunts continue to occur, including the widely publicised arrest and detention in 2012 of more than 30 men at the CinePlaza cinema in Beirut who were subject to intimate physical examinations. The following organisations and websites are well worth a look, with a cornucopia of gay and general human rights information on Lebanon and the wider Arab world.

Bint el Nas (Arabic for 'Daughter of the People') www.bintelnas.org. For LBTQ (Lesbian, Bisexual, Transgender & Queer) women in Lebanon.

GlobalGayz e micamm@globalgayz.com; www.globalgayz.com. A very useful website, which keeps itself updated with news & issues relevant to the LGBT community around the region & the world with helpful information on culture & lifestyle issues for gay & lesbian travellers.

Helem (Arabic acronym for Lebanese Protection for Lesbians, Gays, Bisexuals & Transgenders) 1st Fl, Zico Hse, Yamout Bldg, 174 Spears St, Beirut; ☏01 745 092 (noon–20.00); m 70 123 687 (24hr helpline); e board@helem.net; www.helem.net

Human Rights Watch 7th Fl, Saga Bldg, Damascus Rd, Beirut; ☏01 217 670; www.hrw.org

International Lesbian, Gay, Bisexual, Trans and Intersex Association (ILGA) 5th Fl, 20 Rue Rothschild, 1202 Geneva, Switzerland; ☏+41 2273 13254; www.ilga.org. A global campaigning organisation whose website contains useful, country-specific information on a range of issues affecting gay people from attitudes & human rights to local laws worldwide.

Meem e coordinator@meemgroup.org; www.meemgroup.org. Community support group for lesbian, bisexual, queer & questioning women & transgender persons in Lebanon, this group is currently limited to Lebanese women or those of Lebanese descent only, residing within or outside Lebanon.

Proud Lebanon m 76 608 205; e info@proudlebanon.org; www.proudlebanon.org. An NGO that campaigns for & supports the LGBT community & other marginalised groups in Lebanon.

Purple Roofs PO Box 19341, Sacramento, CA 95819, USA; e wheretostay@purpleroofs.com; www.purpleroofs.com. A good source of worldwide travel information for gays & lesbians including gay-friendly lodgings, entertainment venues & tour operators, etc in Lebanon.

LEBANON FOR FAMILIES

In common with many other Middle Eastern countries Lebanon is a very family-friendly destination. The Lebanese adore children and the hospitality extended to adult visitors applies equally if not more so to parents with children. For visitors from many European countries the flight time is a relatively short 3–5 hours with a negligible time-zone impact. Visa, arrival and transfer formalities are hassle-free, and English and French are widely spoken and understood. All this, together with a year-round cordial climate compared with many other countries in the region and a variety of activities with lots for kids to see, at often discounted rates, means that Lebanon has plenty to offer parents travelling with children and looking for a long weekend break or an extended holiday.

ACCOMMODATION With accommodation options catering to all budgets, families are spoilt for choice and kids can often stay for free in their parents' room or receive child discounts at some of the high-end hotels; many will also provide cots, childcare and babysitting services upon request. At the budget end, too, family rooms are frequently available and these can be a good option for meeting up with other families. In Beirut, **Saifi Urban Gardens Hotel** ✻ (pages 143–4), **Port View Hotel** (page 143) and the **Four Seasons Hotel** ✻ (page 140) are particularly recommended options, whilst elsewhere around the country smaller, family-run hostels, hotels and guesthouses (page 95) off the beaten track also afford a home-from-home experience in more authentic surroundings.

HEALTH Lebanon presents no major health hazards specific to children, though the risk of rabies must be borne in mind as children are significantly more vulnerable than adults. Please refer to pages 73–8 for more detailed information on rabies and vaccine-preventable diseases, plus other health issues and medical facilities in Lebanon.

The intense summer heat and humidity in Beirut needs to be borne in mind and it would be wise to carry an adequate supply of suncream and bottled water. There is an excellent nationwide network of modern pharmacies, many with long opening hours, which stock disposable nappies, a range of baby foods and all the usual medicines for a range of common and other minor ailments. The larger supermarkets and Lebanon's many large, modern shopping malls are also a good source of baby supplies, and many have baby-changing facilities and extensive play areas for youngsters. There is, however, a real dearth of public toilets in the country, and those that do exist are hardly toilet heaven, so, if you or your younger ones get caught short, use the nearest café, restaurant, shopping mall or hotel and in rural or remote areas avail yourself of a nearby bush or such like and carry a supply of paper tissues and/or toilet paper.

EATING AND DRINKING Children will be positively welcomed at most cafés and restaurants and many of these have family sections where you will often see parents with their offspring dining out much later than you would normally expect to see in many Western countries. Lebanon's wide-ranging and healthy cuisine comprising fish, meat, vegetable dishes and fruit should satisfy the fussiest of eaters, and these are supplemented by equally eclectic international choices and, of course, the fast-food chains (McDonald's, KFC, Burger King, et al) are ubiquitous. For some healthy, filling and tasty family eats in good surroundings, the author particularly recommends trying the following varied options in the capital: fine seafood dining in the family-friendly **La Paillote** ✳ (pages 144–5), the down-to-earth bistro **Le Chef** ✳ (pages 146–7) for delicious home-cooked food, the weekly **Souk el Tayeb** (page 153) farmers' market to sample local organic produce, the delightful, laid-back **Al Falamanki** (page 145) garden café to sample an excellent and wide-ranging menu in atmospheric, traditional Lebanese surroundings and **Barbar** (page 146) for varied tasty and filling snacks and meals. Outside of the capital, soak up the atmosphere at the picturesque port of Byblos whilst enjoying delicious fish dishes and *mezze* at the **Fishing Club (Pepe's)** ✳ (page 209); try **Chez Sami** ✳ (page 201) in Jounieh for delicious seafood in scenic surroundings and enjoy the sweets and desserts from **Abdul Rahman Hallab & Sons** (page 231) in Tripoli.

SHOPPING There is no shortage of retail outlets for those travelling with children, including the large **Virgin Megastore** ✳ (page 153) in Downtown Beirut, which will be multi-media heaven for kids, and branches of the UK chain Mothercare at the capital's **ABC Achrafieh** (page 152) and **City Mall** (page 154); whilst the **Beirut Souks** (page 153) have a wide range of clothing outlets for all age groups. The sprawling **Sunday Market** or Souk al-Ahad (page 152) is also sure to entertain the kids, who will enjoy exploring this treasure trove of goods and slice of Lebanese life. Outside the capital, Sidon and Tripoli will hold a different appeal for many youngsters, with locally produced soap products on sale at Sidon's **Soap Museum** (page 306) and the delicious sweets from Tripoli specialists **Abdul Rahman Hallab & Sons** ✳ (page 231).

FAMILY-FRIENDLY ACTIVITIES AND SITES The following are by no means exhaustive but pointers to a small selection of things to see and do which should cater to a wide range of age groups and interests.

Animal Encounter ✳ (page 191) A terrific venue for animal-loving kids with a wide range of species at this centre dedicated to animal welfare and to educating people about the animal and natural world.

Beirut (pages 125–81) Take a tour of history at the country's premier **National Museum** ✳ (pages 174–5); join local families and stroll (or bike) the **Corniche** (pages 166–7); admire the **Pigeon Rocks** (page 166) and take a ride on the Ferris wheel at the **Luna Park** ✳ (page 166); take a walking tour of the rebuilt Downtown district and visit the children's interactive science museum, **Planet Discovery** ✳ (page 167) and/or the similarly hands-on indoor city theme park **KidzMondo** ✳ (page 168) followed by a visit to the similarly hands-on **History of Money Museum** ✳ (page 164) to see if your kids really are worth their weight in gold; explore the newly developed **Zaitunay Bay** (page 168) for a range of culinary options together with a number of artistic and entertainment offerings for both adults and children; and/or visit the nearby child-friendly **Saint-George Yacht Club & Marina** (page 152). For a respite away from the hustle and bustle of the city, visit the capital's **public gardens** (pages 179–80) and stroll the verdant campus of the **American University of Beirut** ✳ (AUB; page 165).

Beirut Marathon (box, page 176) This well-established annual running event through the streets of the capital also has a number of shorter-distance races for active children in the 7–17-year age range.

Camping An increasingly popular activity for kids and adults alike. Organisations such as **Camping Les Colombes** ✳ (pages 215–16), **Lebanese Adventure** (page 137) and **Sharewood Camp** (page 190) offer a range of summer and other camps throughout the year, together with plenty of educational, ecotourism and leisure activities to keep the kids happy.

Jeita Grotto ✳ (pages 197–8) An extraordinary display of stalactites and stalagmites which will enthral both kids and parents. The nearby **Hall of Fame** (page 198) is home to some of the world's most renowned celebrities and people immortalised in talking and moving silicone and would make an enjoyable side trip for all the family.

Jounieh International Festival (page 203) Held annually throughout the town in July, this is a very family-friendly festival with plenty of activities to keep kids amused, including a spectacular firework display, street entertainers, etc.

Lebanon Mountain Trail (LMT) (box, page 235) Some sections of the LMT are suitable for older and active children with the numerous hiking trails affording an educational and less mainstream view of Lebanon and its rural communities, allowing kids to really 'get back to nature' and learn about the great outdoors and the natural world.

Moussa Castle ✳ (pages 285–6) Learn how one man's childhood dream was translated into reality in a fairytale setting.

The Orange House ✳ (box, page 319) An excellent rural retreat and edifying experience not far from the southern city of Tyre where kids can experience eco-living and assist with the care of new turtle hatchlings.

Palm Islands ✳ (pages 235–7) Kids will enjoy the summer boat trips out to these islands off the northern coast of Tripoli which are rich in flora and fauna.

Pleasure flights Although not the cheapest of site-seeing attractions, if your budget permits these could make for an unforgettable experience for all the family. A number of companies offer scenic flights (usually for up to three or four people), departing from and arriving back at Beirut airport, which fly over coastal and inland areas and afford excellent birds-eye views of areas such as Jounieh, the Chouf, the Cedars, Tripoli, etc. Take a look at the following websites for more details: www.skileb.com, www.beirutwings.com.

Téléférique ✳ (page 203) Vertigo sufferers aside, a thrilling experience for youngsters as the cable car passes between high-rise buildings *en route* from Jounieh to Harissa.

Theatre Athénée ✳ (page 202) A colourful and specialist children's theatre in Jounieh which also holds drama workshops for kids aged 4 years and above in Arabic, French and English or a mixture of the three.

Waterparks Those at **Rio Lento** ✳ (page 197) and **Watergate Aqua Park** (page 141) have a range of watery fun activities and are great places to cool off if visiting during the hot summer months.

FURTHER INFORMATION There are a few books suitable for young children to read either before, during or after their visit to enhance their experience. A good educational read for the 6+ years age group is *Play and Learn about Lebanon* (Beirut: Turning Point Books, 2009), an interactive and colourful tome covering Lebanon's main towns, cities and places of interest. An excellent book to help children learn about the realities of war is *Sami and the Time of the Troubles* by Florence Parry Heide & Judith Heide Gilliland (New York: Clarion Books, 1992) which tells the nicely illustrated tale of ten-year-old Sami and his family living in Beirut during the chaotic events of the 1975–90 civil war and their attempts to carve out a degree of normalcy in their lives amidst the carnage all around. In *Oranges in No Man's Land* by Elizabeth Laird (London: Macmillan, 2016) a story of bravery and the human spirit is told through the eyes of ten-year-old Ayesha, who braves the Green Line during the 1975–90 civil war as she embarks on a journey to get medical assistance for her sick grandmother. Though published a few years ago, Joanne Sayad's *Gotta Love Lebanon: The Family Guidebook* (Beirut: Turning Point Books, 2012) remains a useful reference for its focus on the specifics of family travel relevant to all budgets and highlighting those lesser-known activities and places to see. If visiting the Ministry of Tourism office in Beirut's Hamra district (page 135) during your stay, try to get hold of an up-to-date copy of the free *Kids & Teens Guide* (online version at *www.aboutleb.com*), which is packed full of activities, things to see and do, shopping, and eating and drinking options for those travelling with children.

Lebanon has a plentiful supply of shopping malls, supermarkets, stores and pharmacies, especially in Beirut, and you can find almost anything you will need for your visit, including items such as condoms or tampons. If you are currently taking any form of prescribed medication, it may be better to bring with you an extra supply (and a copy of your prescription) as not all pharmacies will dispense additional supplies should you run out. As you cannot buy Lebanese currency overseas it would be a good idea to bring US dollars in cash as these are easily exchanged, unlike travellers' cheques, and readily accepted in 99.9% of places. A credit/debit card is also useful. Essential is a good, worldwide travel insurance policy, which will cover you both for medical emergencies and for any pursuits such as skiing or extreme sports you are planning to undertake; remember to take with you a copy of the full details, including the insurer's telephone number and the policy number.

It would be a good idea to be sensitive to the time of year you are visiting and to bring sufficient clothing appropriate to the season, with summer (June–September) and winter (December–March) being the main considerations, though you will have no problem obtaining any items you forget to bring. In summer, do not underestimate both the heat and humidity, especially in Beirut and along other parts of the Mediterranean coast. A hat and suncream are essential luggage items, together with loose-fitting and light-coloured cotton garments to help offset the worst effects of the sun's intensity. A strong pair of sandals would also be beneficial. Inland and mountainous areas can be decidedly cooler in the evenings, and even in the height of summer a thin jumper may be required. The winter months with their consequent drop in temperature and advent of often heavy rainfall mean a waterproof jacket and/or umbrella will also be essential. For light sleepers, a pair of earplugs could prove useful if staying near a mosque and you want to sleep through the dawn call to prayer, or at hotels where your room is overlooking the street with noisy traffic or late-night revellers. If you are planning on skiing in season, then bring appropriate clothing, though equipment can often be rented from the resorts themselves.

Whatever time of year you decide to visit, a good pair of walking boots or at least a sturdy pair of training shoes or such like will make your progress around Beirut's often pot-holed streets and the country's mountainous and historical sites a much more comfortable experience. If you are planning to enjoy some formal dining out in restaurants, or perhaps a visit to one of the capital's numerous nightclubs, more formal attire such as trousers, jacket and even tie may be required at some of the more upmarket establishments. These places often insist on smart or at least casual dress, much like in cities such as London, New York or Paris, and jeans and trainers are a definite no-no at Lebanon's Casino du Liban. Similarly, more customised clothing, especially for women, is the order of the day when visiting sensitive or religious sites such as mosques. For women, a headscarf will often be required and it would be sensible to 'dress down' at these places into more conservative attire. As power cuts and electricity rationing occur regularly throughout the country, a useful accessory to bring would be a small torch, perhaps of the Maglite variety, for help in negotiating the sometimes dark streets of the capital as well as in more remote areas of the country.

If taking your mobile phone, laptop, video or still camera (or any other electronic device) to Lebanon, a power adaptor plug will be essential to include in your luggage. Lebanon's power supply works on the European-style round two-pin plug system and, once again, adaptor plugs are readily available almost everywhere in the country should you forget to bring your own. Lebanon is an extremely beautiful country, with a stunning range of natural scenery, as well as an array of manmade architecture, which can make for a very photogenic experience – therefore bringing a camera is almost as essential as packing your passport (see also pages 104–6). If you can, bring an SLR (Single Lens Reflex) camera, either digital or film, together with a plentiful supply of memory cards or slide/negative film. In Beirut especially, memory cards, slide, colour and black-and-white film can be obtained in shops, and photo labs often offer a full range of processing services for film, as well as the option of 'burning' your memory cards to CD/DVD.

MAPS As part of their Arab World Map Library series, **GEOprojects** (*www.geo-cartographers.com*) based in Beirut publish a number of very useful maps including a 2014 Lebanon country map (9th edition, available in Arabic, English or French, scale: 1:200,000) which has a decent city map of Beirut on the reverse side (scale: 1:10,000), with lots of useful background and listings information of use to visitors. Their double-sided 2015 Beirut city map (9th edition, scale: 1:10,000) is even more detailed, providing the visitor with both business and tourist information on the map's reverse side. The company also produced in 2012 a selection of smaller, double-sided mini maps for specific districts of the capital including Achrafieh in east Beirut (2nd edition, scale: 1:9,000/1:6,000), Downtown Beirut (2nd edition, scale: 1:6,000/1:3,000) and Hamra, Ras Beirut and Verdun (2nd edition, scale: 1:8,700/1:5,000). These should all be available in Beirut bookshops or you can order online from the company's website.

International Travel Maps and Books Ltd (ITMB) (*12300 Bridgeport Rd, Richmond, BC, Canada V6V 1J5;* ℡*604 273 1400;* e *map@itmb.com, itmb@itmb.com; www.itmb.ca*) produce an excellent 2015 Lebanon country map (scale 1:190,000) containing an equally excellent city map of Beirut (scale 1:8,300) on the reverse side and which has been used to produce some of the maps used in this guide. The map is available from the publishers themselves (*US$12.95; £8.95; €9.50*) via mail or online order. In the UK, **Stanfords** travel bookshop (*12–14 Long Acre, London WC2E 9LP;* ℡*020 7836 1321;* e *sales@stanfords.co.uk; www.stanfords.co.uk*) is also a stockist and offers online ordering. If you are planning on doing a lot of exploring and walking around the capital and its environs, a useful companion to the ITMB country map above is the excellent street atlas *Zawarib Beirut & Beyond* (*US$12/LBP18,000;* see page 132 for more details), which will ensure your travails around the city are made considerably easier; this very useful navigational tool is also available from Stanfords bookshop in London and via online mail order. **Explorer Publishing** (*St 1, Al Quoz Industrial Area 3, Dubai, UAE;* ℡*+971 (0) 4 340 8805;* e *info@askexplorer.com, sales@askexplorer.com; www.askexplorer.com*) have produced a 2012 Lebanon Road Map (scale: 1:250,000), which is useful for those touring the country by self-drive. The map should be available from Waterstones or Stanfords bookshops in the UK & from the publishers themselves by international mail order (*c€13.95/cUS$14.95*).

In addition to the above, the Lebanese **Ministry of Tourism** has a range of free maps in various languages which you can pick up at their desk in the arrivals hall at Beirut airport, or at their main office in the Hamra district of west Beirut (page 135). Bookshops such as the excellent **Librairie Antoine** (page 155) on Beirut's Hamra Street should also stock all or most of the above-mentioned maps.

MONEY

The Lebanese currency is known as the Lebanese Lira (LL), but commonly referred to as the Lebanese pound (LBP). For many years the exchange rate has been pegged to the US dollar, simmering at a relatively stable LBP1,500 to US$1. In October 2016, the exchange rate for the euro, sterling and the US dollar were as follows: €1 = LBP1,6925.34; £1 = LBP1,937.56; US$1 = LBP1,506.50. Lebanese currency is issued as banknotes in denominations of LBP1,000, LBP5,000, LBP10,000, LBP20,000, LBP50,000 and LBP100,000, and there are also coins to the value of LBP25, LBP50, LBP100, LBP250 and LBP500. Though the LBP25, LBP50 and LBP100 coins were still in circulation at the time of writing, they will rarely, if ever, be encountered except perhaps when given as change in supermarkets or the like. If paying for goods or services in US dollars, you will usually receive any change in LBP. It is currently not possible to pre-order Lebanese currency outside the country. However, US dollars are universally accepted throughout Lebanon at restaurants, hotels and stores, and the two currencies are virtually interchangeable for all practical purposes. It is a good idea to keep a supply of small-denomination notes and/or coins – US or Lebanese – for tipping, bus and taxi fares.

CHANGING MONEY Banks are plentiful throughout all the major towns and cities. Opening hours can vary slightly between banks but are generally 08.00–14.00 Monday to Friday and 08.00–noon or 13.00 on Saturday, and closed on Sundays. The banks will exchange major foreign currencies such as the US dollar, sterling and euros. ATMs are also ubiquitous, including at some of the luxury hotels, and you can withdraw cash in both Lebanese currency and US dollars 24/7 in most areas. The current official bank at Beirut airport is BankMed (\ *01 629 360/1/2;* \ *03 760 026; www.bankmed.com.lb;* ⊕ *08.30–14.00 Mon–Fri, 08.30–noon Sat*), which has a kiosk (⊕ *24hrs daily*) just before passport control and provides a currency-exchange service in US dollars, euros and sterling, and there is a 24-hour ATM adjacent to the kiosk itself dispensing cash in both US dollars and Lebanese pounds. An alternative to ATMs and the banks are the many private money-changers, operating especially in the Hamra district of west Beirut, who will exchange currency for variable commission rates.

CREDIT CARDS All the major credit card companies such as American Express, Diners Club, MasterCard and Visa are accepted almost everywhere, except at perhaps the smallest hotels or stores.

INTERNATIONAL MONEY TRANSFER Sending and receiving money internationally can be done through Western Union Money Transfer (*www.westernunion.com*), whose main agent in Lebanon is **Online Money Transfer** (OMT; \ *01 391 000; www.omt.com.lb*), easily recognised by their large yellow signs. They have hundreds of offices all over the country and work in partnership with major banks such as BLC Bank, Credit Libanais, First National Bank & Lebanon & Gulf Bank and at other locations such as shops, post offices and other retail outlets. Opening hours can vary between locations, but some OMT offices remain open for business until 22.00 and some are open on Sundays. The OMT website contains a useful list of locations, telephone numbers and opening hours. If using **MoneyGram** (*www. moneygram.co.uk*), they have numerous outlets in Lebanon including at many branches of Lebanon's postal service, **LibanPost** (*www.libanpost.com*).

TRAVELLERS' CHEQUES It is not advisable to bring travellers' cheques with you to Lebanon as the vast majority of banks will not change them (unless, in a minority of cases, you have an account with the bank). At the time of the author's last visit he could not find any money-changers in Beirut or elsewhere in the country who were willing to swap travellers' cheques for hard currency; so stick to bringing your money in US dollars or use your credit/debit card at the many ATMs and banks scattered all over the country.

BUDGETING

For the first-time visitor to Lebanon the price of hotels and restaurants, the largest costs usually incurred by tourists, can come as a bit of a surprise compared with some other countries in the region, with accommodation costs generally on a par with those in western Europe or North America. That said, though the market is dominated by mid range and luxury establishments, there is also an increasing supply of budget accommodation, especially in the capital, where a double room can be obtained for less than US$60 per night and a dorm room for under US$20 per person per night, though don't expect any frills. At the luxury end of the hotel scale, a double room in high season can easily cost you anywhere between US$200 and US$500+. Mid range establishments probably offer the best-value accommodation options as they tend to offer a decent standard of comfort for around US$130–150 for a double room in high season. Outside the main summer tourist season prices can fall substantially, as they can for those planning an extended stay, and it is always worth asking about discounted room rates, whatever your budget. In all cases check whether the obligatory 10% government tax is included in the room rates you have been quoted.

If you are on a self-catering visit, there is a plentiful supply of supermarkets and stores throughout the country. The plethora of nationwide shopping malls and Lebanese chains such as Spinneys, TSC and Goodies all stock a wide range of food, cosmetics, clothing and general household items, pretty much like the chain stores in western Europe and North America, with prices generally comparable. Eating out can cost as little or as much as you like. A tasty and filling street snack in Beirut can cost around US$4–5, but restaurants will obviously cost more. A main course for two people in a decent eatery will cost around US$30–35, whilst in more expensive eating establishments you could easily pay double that. The western fast-food chains such as Burger King, Domino's Pizza, KFC and McDonald's are well represented in Lebanon, and once again prices are on a par with what you would pay back home.

Alcohol is widely available, though not particularly cheap in Lebanon and a small bottle of local Almaza beer can cost up to US$5 in many bars but will be cheaper if bought in a supermarket. The national drink, *arak*, an aniseed-flavour beverage often served with *mezze*, can also vary widely in price from around US$3–9+ for a glass, depending upon the variety, with a bottle costing somewhere between US$50 and US$90. Wine is a popular drink, especially those from the vineyards of Ksara, Kefraya and Musar in the Bekaa Valley, and is served in many establishments. A bottle from one of these labels can cost around US$50 or more in a restaurant, whilst from the supermarket a 750ml bottle from the Kefraya label will typically set you back less than US$20.

Transportation around the country is both plentiful and cheap, with the public buses and taxis the principal options available to the visitor. The buses cover most areas of the country and are great value. Within Beirut the bus fare to any area should not exceed LBP1,000 and you can travel by bus to almost any part of the country and not pay more than LBP7,000 (as at the time of research), though the journey will obviously take longer than by taxi. A bus to Bcharré in north Lebanon from Beirut is currently LBP7,000 whilst an air-conditioned bus to the southern city of Sidon from the capital costs LBP2,500. Taxi fares are subject to some negotiation, but generally speaking a shared (*servees*) taxi within the central Beirut area is LBP2,000 but will cost more if used as a taxi. Car-hire costs also vary according to season. In general, expect to pay somewhere around US$30+ in low season and US$40+ in high season for a small three-door Hyundai, Renault or Kia Picanto. If you are after renting a vehicle with more bells and whistles such as a BMW, Mercedes, Porsche or Range Rover, expect to pay around US$150+ in low season, US$200+ in high season. There are plenty of companies and thus plenty of competition, so it pays to shop around for the best deal. A car with driver will add a minimum of US$30 to the cost of car hire.

Admission fees to Lebanon's many archaeological and touristic sites, museums and natural wonders represent excellent value for money. A number of these are free and the current maximum charge for entry is LBP18,150 to see the impressive stalactites and stalagmites at Jeita Grotto.

TIPPING Tipping, or *baksheesh*, is as prevalent in Lebanon as it is in many other countries of the world. Although the amount you should leave for services rendered is by no means an exact science, invariably depending on the quality of service you have received, gratuities to airport and hotel porters are normally around US$1–2 per item of luggage. In restaurants, where an additional service charge (usually 10–15%) has *not* already been added, a tip of around 5–10% of the total bill is usual practice. There is no expectation or requirement to tip bus or taxi drivers.

GETTING AROUND

Lebanon is a very small nation and its c7,000km of paved roads, though often pot-holed and narrow with hairpin mountain bends, are going to be your principal means of travelling around the country by whatever mode of transport you choose. Officially, driving is on the right-hand side of the road, though this can change at any time depending on the whim of the driver. Traffic lights, signs and speed-restricted areas have increased in recent years, but often have the status of ornamental features rather than any real practical value given the often appalling standards of driving amongst many Lebanese who more often than not flout the 'rules' of the road. Traffic conditions, especially in Beirut, are also overwhelmingly characterised by congestion and chaos, not to mention the environmental impact of not so environmentally friendly cars, which account for around 40% of CO_2 emissions in the capital. That said, public transport is

SOME SAMPLE DAY-TO-DAY COSTS			
Bottle of water	LBP1,000	Beirut to Tripoli	LBP2,000–5,000
Tampons	LBP5,000	within Beirut	LBP1,000
Bottle of beer	LBP7,500	*Servees* taxi in Beirut	LBP2,000
Can of coke	LBP1,000	Basic hotel	
Cup of coffee	LBP5,500	(double room)	LBP65,000
Cup of tea	LBP5,000	Mid range hotel	
Loaf of bread	LBP3,000	(double room)	LBP175,000+
Mars bar	LBP1,000	Luxury hotel	
Snack	LBP4,000	(double room)	LBP300,000+
Nargileh	from LBP8,000	National Museum	
Glass of *arak*	from LBP5,500	(Beirut)	LBP5,000
.20L of petrol	cLBP22,000	4GB memory card	LBP15,000
20L of diesel	cLBP13,300	Aspirin (pack of 20)	LBP2,300
Newspaper	LBP2,000	Burning memory	
Internet café	LBP3,000/hr access	card to CD/DVD	LBP6,000
Bus fares		Pack of 4 AA batteries	LBP5,500
Beirut to Sidon	LBP1,500–2,500	Postcard	LBP1,000

plentiful and cheap in most areas of the country and you will not have to wait long to depart to your chosen destination.

BY AIR There are no internal commercial air services within Lebanon (though scenic and pleasure flights departing from and arriving back to Beirut airport are available; see page 85 for more details).

BY BUS Whilst travelling by bus may be a slower means of getting around Beirut and the rest of the country, the flip side is that it is also one of the cheapest, with fares currently ranging from LBP1,000 for journeys within Beirut rising to a maximum of LBP7,000 to almost any destination in the country, making bus travel an ideal choice for those on a tight budget with more time to spare. The standard of bus ranges from modern air-conditioned coaches to antiquated, non-air-conditioned rust buckets belching out their less-than-ecofriendly choking fumes.

There are a range of privately owned buses and minivans which ply their trade around Beirut and nationwide. Apart from the general lack of published route timetables for these buses, another downside for the visitor is that many of these vehicles don't have clearly defined numbers or route information displayed in languages other than Arabic, meaning that, away from a bus station, invariably you may need to flag down the bus and ask the driver where they are going. Travel on these buses is sometimes a cramped affair and you just hail a ride and get off anywhere along the buses route – but they are a great way to meet and chat to the locals.

Beirut has three main bus stations within an easy walk or a short taxi ride of most areas in the city and these tend to be set up to serve specific destinations within Lebanon and countries beyond (pages 132–3). None of these venues is particularly salubrious, so don't expect ultra-comfy waiting rooms and restaurants, but they are adequate enough for the purpose. The main and best-organised of the three stations is Charles Helou station [172 B2], a short walk east from Downtown, which has clearly defined zones and is generally for buses serving destinations north of the capital and to neighbouring countries. Dora [173 H2], east of Downtown near Bourj Hammoud, is also a hub for buses and taxis serving destinations north of Beirut. Whilst the Cola bus and taxi station [127 E7], southwest of Charles Helou, is a transport hub for destinations generally south and east of the capital. In many cases buses and taxis depart only when they are full, though this does not necessarily mean an extended wait.

BY BIKE In a country where the car is considered king, cycling as a mode of transport is still very much in its infancy but nonetheless growing in popularity among the outdoor-loving Lebanese. However, with erratic standards of driving, congestion problems, the current state of Lebanon's roads and the absence of widespread dedicated cycle lanes, bike travel is not yet the best or easiest option for a comprehensive sightseeing visit in the capital or a nationwide tour of the country. Having said this, there are still some excellent localised possibilities for the adventurous, environmentally concerned and healthy visitor to explore Lebanon on two wheels. Cycling along the Corniche in Beirut is a popular, if often congested, route, with cyclists vying for space with joggers and pedestrians, and bikes can now be hired by the hour, and half or whole day near the Corniche (page 134). But for the real cycle enthusiast the main draw of cycling in Lebanon will be the many opportunities available outside the capital. Given Lebanon's undulating terrain, for those with their own or rented mountain bike or other sturdy cycle, areas such as the Chouf Cedar Reserve, Horsh Ehden Nature Reserve and the Cedars provide

3

often challenging but scenically spectacular off-road biking adventures. It is also possible to cycle to the top of the country's highest mountain peak at Qornet es Saouda (3,083m) for the spectacular panoramic vistas, whilst more low-lying areas such as the equally scenic Bekaa Valley, with its much lower traffic densities compared with Beirut, are ideal for those cyclists seeking a two-wheeled experience on less demanding terrain. The Lebanon Mountain Trail (LMT; box, page 235) also has cycle-friendly routes for those keen to get off the beaten track. With ample opportunities for bike hire and/or repairs to your own bicycle in Beirut, there are now also organisations and tour operators both within and outside Lebanon who offer specialist biking activities and tours (pages 66 and 134–5).

BY CAR Hiring a car in Lebanon is both straightforward and a distinct advantage if you are planning on doing a lot of touring and want the freedom to just up and go at your leisure rather than being tied to public transport. It is also an excellent choice if you want to visit more out-of-the-way places that are less accessible by public transport or taxi, and to areas such as the Chouf Mountains, where transport is virtually non-existent after dark. There are a huge variety of vehicles available for hire ranging from small three-door Renault Clios to luxury BMWs, Mercedes, 4x4s and family vans. All the major car-hire companies such as **Avis** (*www.avis.com.lb*), **Budget** (*www.budget.com.lb*), **Europcar** (*www.europcarlebanon.com*) and **Hertz** (*www.hertz.com*) are well represented, with offices at the airport, in Beirut itself and many have other branches around the country. Supplementing these are the innumerable **local companies** all vying for your custom – so shop around for the best deal. As a guide, however, at the time of research rates for self-drive hire ranged from around US$30–40/day upwards for a small car such as a Kia Picanto or Renault Twingo to around US$400+ for a 4x4, BMW or Range Rover. Discounts are often available in low season, and year-round for three or more consecutive days of car hire. During the busy summer and holiday periods try to book car hire well in advance as at these peak times the availability of small cars can be at a premium. Hiring a car with a driver will obviously cost more and as a rough guide you should expect to factor in an extra US$30+ per day depending on which company you use, with perhaps an optional meal and small tip for the driver if you are happy with their service. Although precise terms and conditions vary slightly between the different companies, drivers normally need to be aged between 21 and 25 years and to have held a valid international driving licence for a minimum period of between one and three years. Whichever company and type of car you use, one of the key points to note, apart from the potential hazards of actually getting behind the wheel in Lebanon (page 79) is to familiarise yourself thoroughly with the company's insurance policy and be sure what is included, such as the policy excess amount (and, just as importantly, what is not!), before you sign any documents. By European and US standards fuel costs represent good value and, although prices often fluctuate, as a general guide 20 litres of diesel or petrol will cost around LBP13,300 and LBP22,000 respectively.

ON FOOT Walking has the obvious benefits of being free, healthy and the most environmentally friendly method of getting from place to place. An additional plus point, given Lebanon's compact size and variable terrain, is that walking can also be one of the most pleasurable ways to explore many parts of the country. To get a flavour of the people and this cosmopolitan country, a leisurely stroll around some of the different neighbourhoods of Beirut (eg: Hamra and west Beirut, Achrafieh, Downtown, Gemmayze or Bourj Hammoud) is highly recommended for the first-time visitor. This can be a challenging and confusing endeavour, given the often distinct lack of road and street signs, traffic congestion, the driving skills of the Lebanese which leave much to be desired, the generally poor state of the city's roads and the intense heat and humidity of the summer months. However, by timing your walks to avoid the hottest times of the day and perhaps catching a bus or taxi to your district(s) of interest and commencing your tour from there will help get around these issues. Though their walks were on hold at the time of writing, **WalkBeirut** (page 135), previously allowed you to explore the capital and its history by taking part in an organised tour of the city and was highly recommended for the first-time visitor to Beirut. Away from the capital, Lebanon's other major towns such as Baalbek, Byblos, Sidon, Tripoli, Tyre and Zahlé are all eminently walkable, and in fact this is the best way to see and experience their principal areas of interest with perhaps only a short taxi ride required to more outlying areas. The country's upland and lowland regions provide excellent possibilities for dedicated and adventurous walkers keen to explore some of Lebanon's natural landscapes and off-the-beaten-track rural areas on foot. Nature reserves such as those in the Chouf, Horsh Ehden and the UNESCO-listed Qadisha Valley in north Lebanon all present great hiking and trekking challenges for the committed walker. There are also now many organisations, such as the excellent Lebanon Mountain Trail (LMT; box, page 235), who offer Lebanese and visitors alike the opportunity to engage in extended hikes and treks the length of the country, taking in more rural and less-visited areas with the option of staying in equally varied and less mainstream accommodation *en route*.

HITCHING As with walking, hitching has the (potential) benefit of being free; but the practice in Lebanon is nowhere near as prevalent as in many western countries, so the time you will have to wait for a lift once you have stuck your hand out by the side of the road (which will also of course attract the attention of passing buses and taxis) is anyone's guess. As in any country in the world, however, the general advice has to be that lone female travellers should never accept a lift from a male driver(s). For those visitors on a tight budget and whose means do not stretch to hiring a vehicle, however, hitching could be a viable way of travelling around many parts of the country especially in those areas (eg: Chouf region) that have a dearth of public transport options or even at night if you have missed the last bus, as this author did on more than one occasion. It is important to clarify before accepting a lift, however, whether the driver will require payment as some private cars may expect to be paid for a potentially unexpected source of extra revenue. If a couple or family with children stop to offer you a lift, it is almost certain no payment will be expected and you will just be made to feel welcome, with the added benefit of getting to know local people. As regards the safety aspects of hitching in general, Lebanon is probably as safe as it gets anywhere else in the world. The author has hitched solo on a number of occasions around the country, by day and night and was greeted with nothing but hospitality and kindness, and the most 'traumatic' experience he can relay was feeling obliged to take an extended tour of my enthusiastic driver's plumbing supplies shop when we arrived back in Beirut from our night-time journey from the Chouf Mountains.

BY RAIL You will not be able to travel by train within Lebanon; nor are there any rail links with neighbouring Syria or Israel. Although Lebanon was the first Middle Eastern country to establish rail travel in 1895 during the Ottoman era, when services commenced from Beirut to Rayak some 20km south of Baalbek in the Bekaa Valley, the civil war together with the 2006 Israeli–Hezbollah conflict derailed the entire system, which is now rendered totally unusable: the last service was in 1997. Although there has been intermittent talk and feasibility studies undertaken for reinstating the network, the logistics and cost of doing so means that rail travel in Lebanon remains a distant prospect at best.

For rail enthusiasts, the **Rayak Railway Museum Project** (m *03 212 885;* e *contact@rayakrailway.org; www.rayakrailway.org*) is a committed group of volunteers attempting to transform the rusting rolling stock, ticket office, buildings and hotel at the Bekaa Valley's famous old station into a museum. Their ambitions extend to at least a partial renaissance of Lebanon's once-extensive domestic and international rail network. Take a look at the website for lots of fascinating background information and old photos on the past history of rail travel in Lebanon.

BY TAXI Taxis are the most ubiquitous form of transport for getting around in Lebanon. Often ageing Mercedes with red number plates distinguishing them from other cars, they cruise the streets of Beirut and all the other main cities and towns nationwide; they congregate at bus stations and can also be pre-booked by phone or in person from any of the numerous taxi firms that exist throughout the country. Taxis are quicker than using the bus but will cost much more than the bus fare. In order to avoid overpaying for your taxi journey, it is essential to learn the 'language' of taxi travel, as this directly impacts on the price you will pay the driver. The more expensive option is to hail (or phone) a taxi to take you to your destination in which case you will have the vehicle to yourself at a fixed and agreed price. The more common (and cheaper) scenario is to flag down a taxi and ask for *service* (pronounced '*servees*') and tell the driver where you want to go. For most short journeys the fare is fixed at LBP2,000 though you may be charged a *serviceain* or twice the normal service fare (LBP4,000) to more outlying areas and perhaps as much as LBP10,000–15,000 if your destination is even more remote or not on the driver's route. With both *servees* and *serviceain* the driver is at liberty to pick up and put down other passengers *en route*, so you can often find yourself sharing the car with other people and taking a little longer to reach your destination.

ORGANISED TOURS There are an ever-burgeoning number of tour operators all over the country offering itineraries to suit most budgets and interests ranging from half- and full-day visits around the capital and surrounding areas to those offering fully inclusive budget as well as luxury tours lasting a week or more. There has also been an increase in recent years of organisations offering tours that take in areas off the beaten track with a more adventurous, rural and eco-friendly slant. The various tour companies can be a good way of structuring your visit and getting around Lebanon if time is precious, and leaves someone else to take care of the transport problems. For a list of local tour operators, see pages 136–40.

ACCOMMODATION

Aside from your airline ticket, the cost of accommodation, pretty much like anywhere else in the world, is likely to be your largest single financial outlay during your visit. Fortunately, with Lebanon's constantly evolving tourist industry and popularity there continues to be an ever-increasing range of hotels and other lodging options catering for most budgets and interests ranging from large, five-star luxury establishments and chains to smaller hostels, eco-lodges and camping, serving travellers with shallower pockets and an interest in more authentic surroundings. Not surprisingly, the widest choice of accommodation is in the capital, Beirut. Here, the ongoing trend is for visitor accommodation aimed firmly at the middle- and high-income-bracket traveller as the city attempts once again to provide the chic and luxurious offerings that helped engender Beirut's pre-war label of 'the Paris of the Middle East'. The big international chains such as Four Seasons, Hilton, Intercontinental, Mövenpick, Radisson, Ramada and Rotana are all represented in the capital and a double room in any of these, with all the usual refinements and facilities you would expect to find in their western equivalents, can easily cost upwards of US$200 a night. Some prices include the obligatory 10% tax or service charge levied on rooms, but it is still a good idea to check at the time of booking. All the major credit and debit cards are universally accepted at these establishments but payment can also be made in US dollars or Lebanese pounds (LBP). In the high season of summer and over some public and religious holidays, hotel prices can rocket, sometimes by as much as 50% and often doubling in price, but outside these times it is worth enquiring about room discounts, especially if you are planning on staying longer than a few nights. During these peak times accommodation in all price categories can also get very busy and it pays to book in advance during these periods if you can.

Less common, though steadily becoming more widespread, are hotels catering for the more price-conscious visitor. Accommodation in the mid range and budget categories tend to proliferate around the Hamra and Gemmayze districts in west and east Beirut respectively and generally are clean and functional, albeit without the five-star bells and whistles of jacuzzi, swimming pools, health spas, etc. Mid range establishments normally all come with en-suite facilities and vary in price from around US$100–150 a night for a double room, though with a little shopping around and staying for a few consecutive nights you could net a cheaper price. In the budget category, a double room in the capital, almost always with shared bath and toilet facilities, can be obtained for around US$50 whilst a dorm room can be found for less than US$20. As with the five-star options, it is still a good strategy to enquire about discounted rates for extended and/or low-season stays.

Away from the capital your choices of accommodation become more limited, with the luxury hotel offerings a little thin on the ground; but on the plus side prices drop considerably even in main towns like Tripoli, Tyre, Sidon and Byblos, which generally are home to smaller B&B and boutique type options which often have a more atmospheric and local feel. The chains are mostly conspicuous by their absence though the Intercontinental Group has a well-located five-star offering in the ski-resort town of Faraya, whilst the Eddé Sands Hotel and Wellness Resort attempts to recreate the hedonistic pursuits of 1960s Byblos in modern and luxurious surroundings. The budget traveller is becoming increasingly well catered for as a growing number of hostels provide an affordable alternative to the hotels. The **Lebanese Youth Hostel's Federation** (LYHF), part of the worldwide network of Hostelling International (*5th Fl, Ameen Centre, Moustafa Kamal St, Hamra, Beirut;* \ *01 750 676;* m *03 313 377;* e *lyhf@hostelslebanon.org; www. hostelslebanon.org*), runs a growing number of hostels throughout the country at budget prices and you can book rooms via their website, which has a detailed listing of nationwide hostels. Similarly, camping, formerly quite alien to most Lebanese, is also growing in popularity as people become more environmentally aware with both a concern for protection of the environment and a desire to experience the wonders of the great outdoors. A short taxi ride north of Byblos, in the village of Amchit, there is the popular and long-established **Camping Les Colombes** ✳ \ *09 622 401/2;* e *contact@campinglescolombes.com; www.campinglescolombes. com*), which has a range of budget-priced options from camping to deluxe chalets with jacuzzi. For even less mainstream accommodation with the knowledge that your stay will also be supporting less prosperous rural communities around Lebanon, the excellent **DIYAFA Association** (\ *01 382 590/1;* e *info@diyafa.org;*

www.diyafa.org) has an extensive countrywide network of guesthouses, outside the capital, at prices catering for both the budget and mid range traveller as well as those seeking a more authentic living experience. You can book online via their website, which has a complete listing of participating lodgings. Complementing these options is the popular and expanding **L'Hote Libanais** (m *03 513 766; www. hotelibanais.com; online booking only*), which offers B&B lodgings where guests stay as part of the family, with the main aim being that visitors experience Lebanon as the locals do.

For those contemplating an extended stay in Lebanon, perhaps a month or more, there is the additional accommodation option of renting an apartment for the duration of your visit. Apartments to rent are quite plentiful, especially in Beirut and also along the coast and in the mountain areas. Prices per week or month can be comparable to what you would pay in many western cities and countries, so don't necessarily expect bargain-basement prices. A good place to start your search is the classified advertising section in Lebanon's English-language newspaper *The Daily Star*, which will give you some idea of rental prices. A company that comes highly recommended by many visitors is **Beirut Flats** (*Ain Mreisse, Beirut;* ✆ *01 363 200/1, 01 369 210;* e *info@beirutflats.com; www.beirutflats.com*), who have nicely furnished and utility-equipped apartments, including laundry and dry-cleaning facilities, with sea views, within walking distance for the Hamra and Downtown areas of the capital. Also take a look at **Ahlein** (e *feedback@ahlein.net; www.ahlein.net*), which has an extensive range of properties for both rent and sale throughout Lebanon. The Hamra office of the Ministry of Tourism in west Beirut (page 135) should also be able to provide you with a recommended listing of available furnished apartments.

EATING AND DRINKING

FOOD   Few people depart Lebanon with anything other than positive experiences of Lebanese cuisine. As with many other aspects of Lebanese culture its eating and drinking options are incredibly diverse, mirroring the Arab, Turkish and, more recently, French presence on its shores. When you factor in the country's own favourable geographic and climatic conditions, which help to nurture a range of tasty and healthy ingredients such as cheese, chicken, fish, lamb, olives, wheat and a host of fresh fruit and vegetables, Lebanon's gastronomy is quite justifiably renowned throughout the Middle East, and beyond. Like the French, the Lebanese take their food very seriously and lunch or dinner can be a lengthy and sociable occasion. The favourite and main meal of the day is the eclectic *mezze*, a wide array of up to 40 small savoury dishes, served hot and/or cold. These typically consist of salad-based plates such as *fattoush* and *tabbouleh*, the well-known *hummus* dip, grilled aubergine known as *moutabel*, olives and the creamy, cheese-based *labneh*.

ACCOMMODATION PRICE CODES		
Based on a double room per night in high season:		
Luxury	$$$$$	LBP300,000+
Upmarket	$$$$	LBP225,000–300,000
Mid range	$$$	LBP150,000–225,000
Budget	$$	LBP75,000–150,000
Shoestring	$	LBP45,000–75,000

The most popular meat dishes are chicken and lamb, which often accompany a *mezze*. The national dish is known as *kibbeh*, minced lamb and onions fried into conical-shape mortars which are served hot or cold and even raw. A main course may also consist of a fish dish, fried or grilled, with the coastal regions of Byblos and Tyre serving locally caught fresh fish in extremely picturesque settings. At Aanjar in the Bekaa Valley trout is farmed and is a speciality of the area. Desserts often pander to the Arabic sweet tooth and a popular option is *baklava*, a very sweet and syrupy pastry with pistachio nuts. The *knefeh* is another favoured dessert consisting of pastry with cheese and/or cream and a drizzling of syrup and is also sometimes eaten for breakfast. Assorted fresh fruit is also a popular dessert. Patisseries abound around the country serving a variety of cakes and sweets, with many towns having their own local delicacy such as the sweets of Tripoli and the crumbly, sugary biscuit *sanioura* from Sidon. A common and filling breakfast will often be *manoushe*, a type of pizza topped with cheese or herbs such as thyme. Other popular snacks, perhaps already familiar to many people, are *shish tawouk* and *shawarma*.

Lebanon is an ideal country for alfresco dining and great for lingering over a meal amid fantastic surroundings, whether it is in Downtown Beirut among the restored Ottoman-era façades, admiring the sunset from the capital's Corniche, whilst the Mediterranean waves lap at the coastline next to you, or eating fine fish overlooking the ancient Phoenician ports of Byblos and Tyre. Supplementing these authentic culinary experiences are a range of more international eating options, with the fast-food chains of Dunkin' Donuts, Hardee's, KFC, McDonald's, Burger King, Pizza Hut, Subway and TGI Fridays never too far away. More formal dining is also plentiful, ranging from French, Italian, Chinese and Japanese restaurants, offering a more home-from-home experience. Enjoying a street snack is another popular option and one indulged by many Lebanese. When strolling Beirut's Corniche you will invariably come across street vendors selling *kaak*, a tasty sesame seed bread and an ideal 'snack on the go'. When in Beirut do also check out Barbar (page 146) in Hamra for its wide range of great-value tasty sandwiches and snacks and the Bourj Hammoud district in east Beirut for some delicious traditional Armenian cuisine such as the spicy sausage *sujuk*.

Vegetarians Following a meat-free diet and lifestyle will in no way preclude you from enjoying the wide range of excellent Lebanese cuisine. The country's geography and climate, coupled with its agricultural output of an abundance of fruit and vegetables, ensures that vegetarians are well catered for in Lebanon. Many *mezze* dishes are in any case vegetable based such as *hummus, fattoush, moutabel* and *tabbouleh*, the latter being an extremely popular dish, and you will have little problem avoiding meat dishes in most Lebanese restaurants, though restaurants catering solely for vegetarians are not widespread. In Beirut, the weekly Souk el-Tayeb (*www.soukeltayeb.com*) and

RESTAURANT PRICE CODES

Based on the average price of a main course for two people (no drinks):

Expensive	$$$$$	LBP75,000+
Above average	$$$$	LBP60,000–75,000
Mid range	$$$	LBP45,000–60,000
Cheap and cheerful	$$	LBP30,000–45,000
Rock bottom	$	LBP15,000–30,000

Earth Markets (*www.earthmarkets.net*; pages 154 and 231) are both good sources of fresh fruit and vegetables and other meat-free products from farmers around the country, and great places to shop for a picnic or if you are on a self-catering visit, with Earth Markets also occurring weekly in the northern city of Tripoli. To the south of the capital in Sidon and beyond there are also a number of other specialist vegetable markets, or *souk al-khodra*. In common with many Mediterranean countries, olive oil is widely used and is drizzled over dishes such as *labneh*, which is delicious when scooped up with bread. An absolutely fantastic website and blog to have a look at is Mama's Lebanese Kitchen (*www.mamaslebanesekitchen.com*), which features Lebanese recipes from Lebanese mum Esperance, who hails from the north of the country near Bcharré, and who shares her foody passion with a whole host of vegetarian (and meat) recipes and cooking methods, including a vegetarian potato *kibbeh* and the delicious *mujaddara* comprising lentils, rice and onion garnish amongst many others.

DRINK Unlike many of its Muslim neighbours, Lebanon is far from being a 'dry' country, with bars, cafés and restaurants serving a wide choice of alcoholic beverages, though in more conservative towns, such as Sidon in the south, the availability of beer, spirits or wine is limited to just one venue at the present time. The national drink is *arak* (box, page 274), a high-alcohol and potent aniseed-flavoured beverage resembling Greek *ouzo* or French *anise*, which is often drunk as an accompaniment to a *mezze* meal owing in part to its palate-cleansing properties between dishes. Beer is predominantly Almaza, a refreshing local bottled and draught lager, which is available in bars and supermarkets almost everywhere; though brands such as Heineken and Mexican beer and even draught Guinness are also available. As one of the oldest countries in the world for wine production, Lebanon produces some excellent-quality brands with labels such as Kefraya, Ksara and Musar perhaps already familiar to some international visitors due to their availability overseas; these too are widely available in bars and restaurants all over Lebanon. On the non-alcoholic front, soft fizzy drinks such as Coca-Cola and Pepsi are equally ubiquitous as are a range of freshly squeezed lemon and orange juices. Among the hot drinks, traditional Arabic or Turkish coffee (*ahweh*), drunk very strong with copious amounts of sugar in small cups or glasses, is very popular with the Arab sweet tooth. Western-style coffee such as Nescafé is also widely available, though often whitened with powdered rather than 'real' milk (ask for coffee with *haleeb* if you don't want powdered milk). The coffee chains such as Costa and Starbucks, together with Dunkin' Donuts are the places to go if you need your latte, americano or cappuccino fix. Tea (*shai*) is also widely drunk without milk and, like coffee, is served in small glasses, often with the addition of mint and sugar. A vibrant and diverse café culture is alive and flourishing in Lebanon, a hangover from French colonial days. This ranges from the youth patronising the western-style chains as a meeting place to socialise and while away a few hours checking emails etc, on their laptops, to the independent cafés in Beirut offering a range of both alcoholic and non-alcoholic drinks with meals and cakes, served in more intellectual surroundings often accompanied by independent film showings and live music. In more traditional cities such as Sidon and Tripoli, for instance, cafés fill up with the older generation playing cards and backgammon whilst drinking tea. An integral part of this cultural scene is also indulging the great Arabic tradition of smoking the *nargileh* pipe (aka *argileh*, hubbly bubbly, water pipe, *sheesha*), with its aromatic range of flavours hanging heavy in the air. In Beirut, Kahwet Leila (page 146) in Gemmayze just east of Downtown has a terrific local ambience serving *arak* and numerous flavours of *nargileh* in addition to its excellent food. Whilst the 24/7 Al Falamanki café (page 145) in the capital's Achrafieh district has a nice retro feel serving a good range of beverages in a cosy indoor and outdoor setting and is a great venue to visit, where you can puff on a *nargileh* to the accompaniment of the music of Fayrouz.

PUBLIC HOLIDAYS AND ANNUAL FESTIVALS

Lebanon's cosmopolitan makeup means that the country has an extremely varied diary when it comes to public holidays, with the full range of Armenian, Christian and Muslim holidays celebrated (see box, below, for the principal ones). Generally speaking, all banks, government departments and schools will be closed, but invariably many shops and restaurants remain open and with a little advance planning the impact of these public holidays on your visit should be negligible. It is also worth noting that, as with the variable Islamic holiday dates mentioned below, the Catholic and Orthodox Christian Easter holiday period (Good Friday, Easter Sunday and Easter Monday) are also celebrated at different times by these sects during the months of March and April.

ISLAMIC HOLIDAYS WITH MOVABLE DATES There are also a number of annual Islamic public holidays, which follow the Muslim lunar or Hegira calendar, as opposed to the Gregorian or western calendar, and these change annually moving back around 10–11 days each year depending upon the first sighting of the new moon. Notable Islamic holidays with their upcoming and estimated future dates in brackets are as follows:

Eid al-Fitr	The end of Ramadan, marked by three days of feasting and the giving of gifts (25 June 2017, 15 June 2018, 4 June 2019, 24 May 2020)
Eid al-Adha	The Feast of Sacrifice which marks the end of *hajj*, the pilgrimage to Mecca, and usually lasts for around three days (1 September 2017, 21 August 2018, 11 August 2019, 31 July 2020)
Ramadan	The ninth month of the Islamic calendar during which Muslims believe the Koran was first revealed to the Prophet Muhammad (27 May 2017, 16 May 2018, 6 May 2019, 24 April 2020)
Ras as-Sana	Islamic New Year (21 September 2017, 10 September 2018, 30 August 2019, 20 August 2020)

FIXED-DATE HOLIDAYS

1 January	New Year's Day
6 January	Armenian Orthodox Christmas
9 February	Feast of Saint Maroun (patron saint of Christian Maronites)
March/April	Easter (Good Friday, Easter Sunday and Easter Monday celebrated on different days each year by the Catholic (Western) and Orthodox (Eastern) branches of the Christian church)
1 May	Labour Day
6 May	Martyrs' Day
25 May	Resistance and Liberation Day
15 August	Assumption of the Virgin Mary
1 November	All Saints' Day
22 November	Independence Day
25 December	Christmas Day

Ashura	The tenth day of the Islamic New Year mourning the death of the Prophet Muhammad's grandson, Imam Hussein (30 September 2017, 20 September 2018, 10 September 2019, 30 August 2020) (page 323)
Mawlid an-Nabi	Prophet Muhammad's birthday (30 November 2017, 19 November 2018, 9 November 2019, 29 October 2020)

FESTIVALS AND EVENTS In addition to the main public and Muslim holidays, which for the visitor mostly have the practical impact of shortening shop opening hours and inflating hotel prices, the Lebanese love a festival and their zest for enjoying life can be seen in the extensive cocktail of annual arts, cultural and sports festivals all over the country, many of which have attracted celebrities and stars of international repute. Some of these use Lebanon's array of archaeological sites, such as those at Baalbek, Beiteddine, Byblos and Tyre, for a dramatic and atmospheric backdrop to the festivities. Not surprisingly, many of these festivals take place during the warm summer months, and the listings below are some of the main ones, all of which are covered in detail in the relevant chapters together with those additional festivals that have a more local character and flavour.

January–March

Al Bustan International Festival of Music and the Performing Arts (page 190)
www.albustanfestival.com
Beirut Fashion Week (page 176)
www.beirutfashionweek.com
Mzaar Winter Festival (page 194)
www.skimzaar.com

April–June

Beirut International Platform of Dance (page 176) www.maqamat.org
Beirut International Tango Festival (page 176) www.tangolebanon.com
The Garden Show & Spring Festival (page 177) www.the-gardenshow.com

July–September

Baalbeck International Festival (page 272)
www.baalbeck.org.lb
Batroun International Festival (page 225)
www.batrounfestival.org
Beiteddine Art Festival (page 290)
www.beiteddine.org
Broummana Summer Festival (page 190)
www.brummana.org.lb

Byblos International Festival (page 215)
www.byblosfestival.org
Cedars International Festival (pages 249–50)
www.cedarsinternationalfestival.org
Deir al-Qamar Festival (page 286)
www.deirelqamarfestival.org
Ehdeniyat International Festival (page 246)
www.ehdeniyat.com
Jounieh International Festival (page 203)
www.jouniehinternationalfestival.com
Lebanon Water Festival (page 204)
www.lebanonwaterfestival.com
Tyre & South Festival (page 323)
www.tyrefestival.com
Zouk Mikael International Festival (page 205) www.zoukmikaelfestival.org

October–December

Beirut International Documentary Festival (Docudays) (page 177) www.docudays.com
Beirut International Film Festival (page 176)
www.beirutfilmfestival.org
Beirut International Marathon (page 176)
www.beirutmarathon.org
Vinifest (page 177) www.vinifestlebanon.com

SHOPPING

Lebanon offers a diverse and comprehensive shopping experience catering to both the mainstream shopper in search of designer brands as well as the less commercially minded consumer interested in more authentic, locally produced products, but don't always expect bargain-basement prices as costs are often on a par with those in Europe and North America. One plus point for shopaholics, however, provided your stay in the country doesn't exceed three continuous months, is that at the time of writing you are entitled to claim back the obligatory 10% VAT which is levied on any purchases you make (excluding services such as the cost of car hire, hotel accommodation, food and petrol); look out for the Tax-Free Shopping sign at well over a thousand participating outlets around the country and you can obtain a refund of the VAT at Beirut airport on your departure from the country or at any of Lebanon's land border crossings. Shop and store opening hours are also similar to Europe but can vary enormously; but generally speaking the large shopping malls open from 09.00/10.00 to 22.00/ midnight daily, though some will close at 19.00/20.00 outside Beirut. Many general stores and bookshops open 09.00–20.00 Monday to Saturday. Corner shops and supermarkets often have more variable trading times and you will generally be able to find a small store or supermarket open until midnight; some even stay open 24/7. The large supermarket chain Spinneys (*www.spinneys.com*) currently has eight branches in Lebanon and all have long opening hours, with most branches open 08.00–23.00/midnight. Pharmacies, especially in Beirut, are usually open 08.00–midnight and a few are open 24 hours. The capital obviously has the widest and most concentrated selection of shopping. The ABC Group (*www.abc.com.lb*), the large Middle Eastern retail chain, has a big presence in Beirut with a selection of malls selling all manner of international designer brands and labels akin to that of many western malls. In July 2013, the UK's Marks and Spencer (M&S) opened their first branch in the capital's City Centre Mall. In the Downtown district, Virgin's flagship Megastore (*www.virginmegastore.com.lb*; page 153) offers its usual range of entertainment products – books, magazines, music CDs and films – and is also the venue to buy tickets for many of Lebanon's festivals and sometimes performances at some of Beirut's theatre venues.

The Achrafieh and Verdun districts are two of the places to visit for upmarket clothes and jewellery items, along with the many outlets in the Downtown area such as the Beirut Souks, which opened to great fanfare in late 2010 and unashamedly caters for the larger wallet. The pristinely restored Saifi Village (aka Le Quartier des Arts) on the outskirts of Downtown houses art galleries, antique shops, boutiques and craft stores within its eminently walkable and perfectly manicured environs. For those in search of more traditional items in the form of glassware, old postcards, *nargileh* (aka *argileh*, hubbly bubbly, water pipe, *sheesha*) pipes, mosaics, traditional clothing such as *kaftans* and tablecloths, etc, head for the Lebanese and Oriental Artizans and Maison De L'Artisan in Ain Mreisse or L'Artisan du Liban in Achrafieh, the latter able to deliver purchases worldwide. A little further afield, east Beirut's Bourj Hammoud district has a range of traditional Armenian goods at competitive prices. The capital also hosts a number of weekly markets selling everything from CDs to organic farm produce. The main ones to look out for include the Sunday market or Souk Al Ahad in east Beirut, the twice-weekly Souk el Tayeb on Saturdays in Downtown and in west Beirut every Wednesday, and the Tuesday Earth Market in the capital's Hamra district (see pages 152–4 for more details). Beirut is also home to some excellent bookshops selling some very nice coffee-table tomes, DVDs and maps of the country which can make great gifts. The Librairie Antoine bookshop (page 155) in Hamra is a good starting point though there are many other good book stores in the capital where it is possible to purchase some excellent rare and out-of-print works.

Outside the city, a less mainstream shopping aesthetic and authentic souvenirs await in the souks of Byblos, which is the place to buy rare books, fish fossils, stones and glassware items. Further north, Tripoli's anachronistic markets (souks) are famed for their sweets, soap, herbs and spices, and a range of metal products, still locally produced in almost medieval surroundings; this is a good place to purchase a range of different styles and colours of the *nargileh* pipe to take home as a souvenir. If you are seeking precious metals such as gold, Tripoli also has a whole souk given over to its sale with prices often cheaper than you would find in some other countries in the region and often lower than in Europe and North America. The town of Jezzine in the south is famed for its beautifully decorative and hand-crafted cutlery and other utilitarian items. To the west of Jezzine, the coastal city of Sidon is well known for its soap products – it even has a museum dedicated to the craft – and is a great place to pick up all manner of 'smellies' to take home. For wine lovers, the Bekaa Valley has been home to a flourishing viticulture since Phoenician times and is the site of more than 30 vineyards, including the renowned Kefraya, Ksara and Château Musar labels; a bottle or two of these wines and/or *arak* can make excellent presents and souvenirs. Lebanon's wines are also on sale in the duty-free at Beirut airport if you don't manage a visit to one of the wineries.

A local NGO, **Consumers Lebanon** (*9th Fl, Estral Centre, Hamra, Beirut;* ⟍ *01 750 650;* e *info@consumerslebanon.org; www.consumerslebanon.org*) works to represent the interests of consumers, campaigning around a range of issues and rights, and is a useful point of contact for any queries or problems regarding any purchases you may make whilst in Lebanon.

ARTS AND ENTERTAINMENT

Lebanon's diverse and eventful history has left the country with an equally eclectic and rich artistic and cultural legacy. Superb architecture adorns many parts of the country, left by a succession of conquering civilisations. Four of these sites – the Umayyad-era town of Aanjar, the Roman temples at Baalbek and the Phoenician ports of Byblos and Tyre – have been given prestigious World Heritage site status by UNESCO. A variety of religious and other sites such as mosques, Druze hermitages, Christian Maronite churches and Crusader castles add extra interest. Supplementing these in situ cultural icons are some excellent museums such as the National and AUB museums in Beirut. Outside the capital, Sidon's soap museum (page 306) and the Khalil Gibran Museum in Bcharré (pages 240–1) are important reminders of Lebanon's artisanal and literary past. Museum and site opening hours differ slightly across the country, with many closed on Monday, including Beirut's National Museum, Beiteddine Palace, the Gibran Museum in Bcharré and Jeita Grotto. There is no shortage of other cultural pursuits, and for those with an interest in the visual arts like cinema and theatre most tastes are catered for, from the mainstream Hollywood blockbusters screened at the numerous multiplex cinemas around the country to more independent and avant-garde film showings. The theatres stage a wide range of productions in Arabic, English and French and range from dance, musicals, children's theatre to more experimental plays, as well as stand-up comedy, with venues such as the Metro Al Madina, Babel and Monot theatres in Beirut (page 150) popular with the Lebanese, the latter theatre staging some excellent productions of late by The Actors Workshop Beirut (*www. theactorsworkshopbeirut.com*). The long-established and world-renowned Caracalla Dance Theatre Company (*www.caracalladance.com*) is well worth seeing for their colourful and brilliantly choreographed dance routines, and if they are performing in the country during your visit, they shouldn't be missed. The Lebanese National Higher Conservatory of Music (*www.conservatory.gov.lb*) put on more than 100 concerts of oriental and world music annually and have a flourishing educational programme designed to nurture young musical talent. Art galleries are also widespread, especially in Beirut, with many specialising in showing the work of young and upcoming Lebanese artists across a range of themes and media; the state-of-the-art Beirut Art Centre (*www.beirutartcenter.org*) in particular is well worth a visit. Lebanon's cocktail of annual festivals stage performances of classical and contemporary music, poetry readings, puppetry, film and theatre. Some of these take place within the environs of the country's architectural sites and palaces such as the Roman temples at Baalbek in the Bekaa Valley and the Ottoman-era Beiteddine Palace in the Chouf Mountains, which complement the regular arts scene very nicely. Full details of current and forthcoming entertainment, cultural events and festivals can be found in Lebanon's English-language newspaper the *Daily Star* and the fortnightly French language magazine *Agenda Culturel*. It is also worth keeping an eye on the various cultural and information centres and institutes in Lebanon as they often organise a wide range of artistic and cultural events. The French Cultural Institute (Institut Français du Liban; *www.institutfrancais-liban.com*) is particularly active in this respect, with branches in Baalbek, Beirut, Deir al-Qamar, Jounieh, Nabatiye, Sidon, Tripoli, Tyre and Zahlé organising a wide range of art and entertainment programmes throughout the year.

Around the capital, Beirutis have a long-established and well-deserved reputation for being partygoers and night owls and their appetite for enjoying life, so evident in the pre-war years of the 1960s and 1970s when the capital was dubbed the 'Paris of the Middle East', is now once again much in evidence. With an ever-increasing number of bars, cafés, discos and nightclubs catering to a wide range of tastes, the *joi de vivre* rarely gets going until late and continues often until dawn. Gouraud Street in Gemmayze, Mar Mikhael, Achrafieh and the Downtown district are often a pulsating mass of hedonism at nights and at weekends. Music at the nightclubs ranges from house and techno to 70s and 80s pop, and jazz and blues enthusiasts are well-catered for, too, at the long-established Blue Note Café in Hamra (page 148) – which hosts both local and international bands and musicians. Nightly entertainment also comes in the guise of the 'Super Nightclubs', which can be found in areas of Beirut but are especially prevalent in the town of Jounieh, where the entertainment on offer is of a different kind. More or less exclusively patronised by males, they invariably feature provocatively dressed eastern European females, who will befriend you in return for a (overpriced) drink and, of course, additional 'services' are sometimes also available. In the district of Maameltein, near Jounieh, the iconic Casino du Liban (box, page 204) provides potentially the most lavish night out in Lebanon with restaurants, slot machines, gaming tables and cabaret for the well-heeled visitor. At the other end of the entertainment spectrum the internet is as popular in Lebanon as it is elsewhere in the world and numerous internet cafés, some open 24/7, are usually filled with younger Lebanese surfing the web or playing the latest computer games, especially in the evenings.

Football (soccer), though not as passionately followed as in the UK, Italy or Spain, is a popular spectator sport and Beirut's two main soccer teams, Beirut Ansar and Beirut Nejmeh, both have a strong following and approximate the UK's Portsmouth and Southampton in their rivalry. Other sports around the capital attracting enthusiastic audiences and participants are golf and horse racing, with the latter taking place on Sunday near the National Museum and which makes for a great afternoon's entertainment. The sport at which Lebanon most excels, however, is basketball. It has a loyal following, and in 2010 the Lebanese national team had one of their most successful seasons, winning the FIBA Asia Stankovic Cup, beating Japan 97–59 in the final, and they followed this up in 2015 by winning the West Asia

Basketball Association (WABA) cup by beating Palestine 88–79 in the final. Lebanon's extensive Mediterranean coastline ensures that a range of watersports from jet skiing to snorkelling and scuba diving are exceedingly popular during the warm summer months, whilst inland the country's many rivers provide ample opportunities for kayaking and rafting. Given Lebanon's undulating and rugged terrain, locals and visitors alike are increasingly enjoying the many caving, hiking, paragliding and trekking possibilities that the country's geography makes possible, and there are now many tour operators who specialise in just these activities with the wild landscape of the UNESCO World Heritage site listed Qadisha Valley in northern Lebanon combining both outdoor entertainment and cultural insight into early Christian settlement in the country. Lebanon is also one of the only places in the Middle East where you can ski (not counting the artificial 'snow' venues in places like Dubai), and the country's six resorts (a seventh is under construction) are popular for both the snow as well as the *après ski* offerings. Once again, there are tour companies who specialise in offering holidays catering to just these interests and activities.

PHOTOGRAPHY

During the country's long and bloody civil war years, pictures – both still and moving – had a great impact on shaping Lebanon's image to the world; bombed-out buildings and cars, pictures of corpses, the pain felt by both Lebanese and Palestinian refugees, etc defined Lebanon as a place to be avoided at all costs, and such stereotypes persist to some extent to this day. Of course, icons of war, such as the still-standing bullet and shell-shocked Holiday Inn hotel in Beirut, remain a constant visual reminder of the country's battle-scarred past and it continues to be an oft-photographed subject. But like the transformed and pristinely manicured Downtown district of the capital – once a rubble of death and destruction – changed circumstances provide the visitor the chance to capture images that show another side of Lebanon, whether it's through the beauty of its natural and urban landscape or its architectural legacies in places such as Baalbek, Tripoli and Tyre.

Whilst the markets and shopping areas of Beirut won't yield authentic pictures of anachronistic Arab souks, those in cities such as Sidon and Tripoli will, and they offer the photographer an opportunity to capture traditional day-to-day life in these areas which can say so much more than a pretty sunset postcard picture over the Mediterranean. Lebanon's architectural legacy is plentiful and extremely photogenic, and any keen photographer would not want to miss the country's premier sites at Baalbek, Byblos, Tripoli or Tyre for example. Lebanon's plentiful year-round festivals provide further opportunities to capture the Lebanese *joie de vivre* and cultured side of their country.

EQUIPMENT AND TECHNICAL ISSUES Assuming that your photographic ambitions extend beyond capturing a few moments in time on your camera-ready mobile phone, the following general points should prove useful for those wishing to take home some treasured memories from their visit. Ideally, an SLR (Single Lens Reflex) camera with interchangeable lenses is the best equipment to take with you as it offers the most flexibility with regard to picture taking. To maximise your picture-taking opportunities, a couple of lenses that span the 20–200mm range should be sufficient to capture those mountain and valley vistas and some close-up and intimate portraits and other details. Although Lebanon has a good variety of wildlife, this is not a Kenyan safari and you will not generally require an extreme (and potentially extremely expensive!) 400–600mm telephoto lens. As digital image capture is now the norm in photography, bring sufficient memory cards and batteries with you for the duration of your visit, though these are available in Lebanon and easily obtained, especially at the photo stores in Beirut. If you still use a film camera, black-and-white, colour negative and slide film were still available in Beirut at the time of writing, and even E6 (slide processing) can be undertaken.

Dust and humidity can be a problem in the summer months and it pays to look after your equipment by keeping it protected in a bag. Digital cameras are susceptible to dust, which can easily implant itself onto the camera's sensor and show up later as spots and blotches on the image, necessitating quite a bit of computer clean-up time in software such as Adobe Photoshop. To help prevent this, try to keep your lens attached to the camera at all times as it will help seal the camera from foreign intruders. Obviously this is easier if you have two camera bodies, and it will save you from changing lenses periodically. A tripod, sometimes a useful accessory, can also be an essential item if you are particularly keen on photographing, for example, inside Lebanon's many museums or the caves at the Ksara winery in the Bekaa Valley or have an interest in landscape and night-time photography and don't want to use a flash gun, which can potentially destroy the atmosphere of your shot. Regrettably, some excellent photographic opportunities where a tripod would be needed at one of Lebanon's premier natural sites, the stalactites and stalagmites at Jeita Grotto, are strictly forbidden.

As is the 'rule', the time of day at which you undertake the bulk of your outdoor picture taking has a marked effect on their quality. Generally speaking, for outdoor photography, early morning and late afternoon will provide more pleasing pictures as these times avoid the heat of the day and ensure the light is at its most attractive, and you will avoid the extremes of contrast and the sometimes 'washed-out' look to your images which can result from shooting during the day. During the day when the light is at its most intense, it would perhaps be a good time to consider photographing more indoor type subjects such as covered markets (souks) or other shaded areas of interest, though these may at times again necessitate the use of a tripod or subtle use of a flash gun. In general, unless there are particular aesthetic or other reasons, try to take all your pictures at the lowest ISO speed rating possible, as this will allow for bigger and higher-quality enlargements later for any of your favourite images. An ISO speed rating of 100–400 with modern digital cameras usually yield excellent quality images for printing out later.

Although you should try to bring everything that you will need with you such as memory cards and/or film stocks, spare batteries, charger, etc, Beirut has a good supply of photographic shops where you can purchase additional items and spares; many will burn your images to disc and provide prints, with some offering the usual 1-hour service you can find back home. A couple of excellent tried-and-tested shops in the capital worth noting are: **Photo Nubar** [162 C4] (*Makdissi St, Hamra;* \ *01 353 742;* m *03 490 303;* ⊕ *09.00–18.00 Mon–Fri, 09.00–15.00 Sat, closed Sun*), who are also an authorised Nikon reseller and offer a range of services including processing and sales of black-and-white and colour film; and, next door to Costa in Hamra, **Lord's Photo** [162 E4] (*Hamra St, Hamra;* \ *01 348 734;* e *vatche.vg@gmail.com;* ⊕ *09.00–19.00 Mon–Fri, 09.00–14.00 Sat–Sun*), who sell 4, 8, 16, 32 and 64GB Compact Flash (CF) and Secure Digital (SD) memory cards and offer C41 colour negative and E6 slide processing. Passing your photographic equipment through airport X-ray machines is a mandatory aspect of the travel process. If you are still shooting film, ask for a hand check (which may or may not be granted), especially if you are travelling for an extended length of time by plane as part of a regional Middle Eastern tour. One pass of film through

3

modern X-ray machines is usually OK but a number of bursts could fog your film, especially if shot at a high ISO (speed) rating. If, as most people now are, you are using digital equipment, X-ray machines should not present any problems.

PHOTOGRAPHIC ETIQUETTE Generally speaking, your picture-taking experience in Lebanon will be a varied and pleasurable experience with boundless photographic opportunities, and there are few areas of the country off limits to photographers. However, there are a few points to bear in mind when choosing where to aim your camera and lens and which could save you some hassle later. In a country where issues of security are paramount, you would be advised to refrain from trying to take photographs at the airport, at any military installations you may come across and of soldiers at the many checkpoints that you will doubtless see around the country. It is perfectly OK to ask to take a photograph of military personnel but the likely response will be a flat 'no', and if so you should heed the answer and not try to sneak a shot. Similarly, if you are seen taking photographs of the Grand Serail (prime minister's office) building and the area around Nejmeh Place in Downtown Beirut, which contains the parliament building, it is possible that you will be told to stop by soldiers as this author was. The likely worst case scenario is that you will be questioned, asked for your ID and perhaps told to delete the image(s) from your memory card. If this happens it pays to be polite with the authorities and co-operate. With Lebanon's wide-ranging groups and religious sects, people photo opportunities abound. However, some common sense and sensitivity is required when photographing conservatively dressed women and religious groups in case of causing offence. Asking their permission first in some cases can save you from causing offence which obviously runs the risk of spoiling the moment, but this is a decision only the photographer can determine and much depends on the specific situation. If having photographed a person or group they ask you to send them a copy, it would be courteous to do so.

MEDIA AND COMMUNICATIONS

Lebanon has a long and established media history, which reached its zenith during the latter stages of the Ottoman era, and by 1914 Beirut had a prolific output of some 168 daily and weekly newspapers, journals and magazines. The country has always been well known for the freedom granted to print and other media outlets and was the first Arab nation to grant private-sector radio and television station broadcast rights. In 2016, Reporters Sans Frontières (*Reporters without Borders; Middle East & North Africa, CS 90247, 75083 Paris Cedex 02, Paris, France;* +33 1 4483 8478; e *index@rsf.org; www.rsf.org*) ranked Lebanon 98th out of 180 countries surveyed in its annual world Press Freedom Index survey, which saw Finland top the list of countries enjoying the highest level of journalistic independence, and the east African state of Eritrea the least. After Tunisia (96th), this gave Lebanon the highest press freedom in the Arab world. Despite these relatively positive figures, however, dark clouds remain over issues of censorship and press freedom. The assassinations in 2005 in Beirut of prominent newspaper journalist and academic Samir Kassir (1960–2005) and newspaper chief executive Gebran Tueni (1957–2005) still remain unsolved crimes. More recent events, too, have highlighted the continued challenges and dangers facing Lebanese journalists covering important stories. The September 2015 conviction of Al-Jadeed (*www.aljadeed.tv*) TV journalist Karma Khayat at the Special Tribunal for Lebanon (STL; box, pages 30–1) for contempt of court and the obstruction of justice has proved widely controversial for the enduring impact this could have for freedom of information. During the demonstrations in Downtown

Beirut in 2015 led by the You Stink group which blamed the government for inefficiency and corruption surrounding the waste crisis, several journalists covering these protests were subjected to violence and deliberate damage to their equipment by the police and internal security forces. Intermittent detention and interrogation, often without legal representation, has been accentuated by the Arab Spring and, in particular, the ongoing civil war in neighbouring Syria which has impacted on Lebanon's media as it has its politics, and harsh treatment remains a sporadic but salient fact of life for many Lebanese journalists.

NEWSPAPERS There are a wide range of daily newspapers published in Lebanon in the country's three main languages of Arabic, English and French, together with a handful of Arabic and French weekly news digests. None is state-owned, but nevertheless they tend to reflect their owners' sectarian bias. Lebanon's sole English-language daily since 1952 is the *Daily Star* (*LBP2,000; 3rd Fl, Markaziah Bldg, Gelias St, Downtown, Beirut;* \ *01 985 313;* e *editorial@dailystar.com.lb; www.dailystar.com.lb*) offering national and international news coverage together with a good round-up of sport and cultural events in the country. This is the most useful newspaper for the English-speaking visitor and highly recommended for those seeking to keep up to date with current affairs and events whilst in Lebanon. Founded in 1924, the daily broadsheet most useful for the French-speaking visitor is *L'Orient Le Jour* (*LBP2,000; Damascus Rd, Baabda;* \ *05 956 444; www. lorientlejour.com*), which offers similar coverage, in French, to the *Daily Star*. Some of the principal Arabic newspapers include *Al Akhbar* (*www.al-akhbar. com*), *Al Anwar* (*www.alanwar.com*), *Al Diyar* (*www.addiyaronline.com*), *Al Liwaa* (*www.aliwaa.com*), *Al Mustaqbal* (*www.almustaqbal.com*), *Albalad* (*www. albaladonline.com*), *An-Nahar* (*www.annahar.com*; website in Arabic, English & French), *As-Safir* (*www.assafir.com*) and *El Shark* (*www.elsharkonline.com*).

The international press is also well represented in Lebanon with newspapers such as the UK's *Daily Telegraph, Daily Mail, Financial Times, Guardian* and *The Times*, as well as the USA's *International Herald Tribune* and *International New York Times*, alongside French dailies *Le Monde* and *Le Figaro*, all easily available, though sometimes a day or so after publication, in bookshops in Beirut such as Librairie Antoine or from one of the many book and magazine street vendors in the capital.

MAGAZINES Apart from the whole gamut of Lebanese magazines, you will notice a huge range on street bookstalls, as well as bookshops, of glossy publications from all over the region but especially from the Gulf. These tend to be centred on celebrity, lifestyle and women's issues and feature the usual attractive girl on the front cover. For French speakers, the pocket-sized bi-weekly French-language *Agenda Culturel* (*LBP5,000;* \ *01 369 242/3; Maktabi Bldg, Rue Clemenceau, Beirut;* e *news@agendaculturel.com; www.agendaculturel.com*) is a good source of 'what's on' information covering the artistic and cultural spheres. For the business visitor, there are a handful of monthly English-language magazines which could prove useful reading, including *Lebanon Opportunities* (*LBP9,000; 2nd Fl, Piccadilly Centre, Hamra, Beirut;* \ *01 739 777;* e *infopro@infopro.com. lb; www.opportunities.com.lb*), which has a range of articles and features on the economic, business and real-estate sectors in Lebanon. The *Executive* magazine (*LBP10,000; 7th Fl, Sehnaoui Centre, Achrafieh, Beirut;* \ *01 611 696;* e *editorial@ executive.com.lb; www.executive-magazine.com*) also has wide-ranging coverage of banking, corporations, finance, consumerism, real estate, etc, from both Lebanon and around the region.

As with newspapers, many of the major quality international magazines such as *Der Spiegel, The Economist, Newsweek, Paris Match* and *Time* should all be available from the many booksellers and stalls, especially in Beirut.

RADIO The proliferation of radio stations which resulted from the civil conflict of 1975–90, producing anarchy across the airwaves as well as on the streets, is well and truly over, and nowadays, following government regulation in 1996 which required all radio stations to be licensed, the number of broadcasters has been cut drastically from over a hundred to just over a dozen or so. The only state-owned broadcaster, run by the Ministry of Information, is **Radio Liban** (◼ *Radio-Liban-962-FM-107317089328047; 96.2FM, 837MW*), which broadcasts a wide range of music and programmes, including an hourly news service, in Arabic, Armenian, English and French. Of the privately owned stations, **Sawt El Ghad** (*www.sawtelghad.com; 96.7FM, 97.1FM*) broadcasts 24/7 broad-based entertainment and educational programmes in Arabic and English, with live phone-ins, chat and hit Arabic, English and French music. Among the other stations of most interest to the visitor and broadcasting a mix of news, music and entertainment, are: **Voice of Lebanon** (*www.vdl.com.lb; 93.3FM (Beirut), 93.6FM (Northern Lebanon), 93.1FM (Bekaa Valley & Southern Lebanon, Arabic, English & French*); **Pax Radio** (*www.paxradio. net; 103.0FM, 103.3FM, 24/7 pop music*); **Melody FM Lebanon** (*www.melody.fm; 99.5FM, 99.7FM, 99.9FM, 24/7 Arabic and international chart and pop music*); **Radio One** (*www.radioone.fm; 105.5FM; in English*), Lebanon's version of the UK's mainstream station; **Mix FM** (*www.mixfm.com.lb; 104.4FM, 104.7FM (Beirut), 104.5FM (Zahlé), 104.7 (Northern Lebanon); in English*), a 24/7 mainstream music broadcaster 'providing a soundtrack to the lives of the Lebanese'; **Voice of Van** (*www. voiceofvan.net; 94.7FM, 95.0FM; in Arabic, Armenian & English*), a 24/7 Armenian broadcaster covering news, chat, music and social issues; **Nostalgie Liban** (*www. nostalgie.fm; 88.1FM; in English & French*), an easy-listening station serving up a diet of retro and modern music; and **Virgin Radio Lebanon** (☏ *04 716 944;* ▫ *70 895 895;* e *info@virginradiolb.com; www.virginradiolb.com; 89.5FM*), a mainstream station playing an extensive range of new and commercial hits including '10 Hits in a Row'. The **BBC World Service** (*www.bbc.co.uk/worldserviceradio*) is also available in Lebanon on MW1323kHz and the **BBC Arabic** station is available on 93.1FM. **Radio Sawa** (*www.radiosawa.com*), which replaced Voice of America's Arabic programming in 2002, broadcasts regional and world news in Arabic, along with a mix of western and Arabic pop music 24/7 to its mainly youthful Arabic audience. In Lebanon you can tune in on the following frequencies: 87.7FM (Beirut, Tripoli and western Bekaa Valley) and 98.3FM (Zahlé).

TELEVISION Like the radio stations, television was completely unregulated until the mid 1990s, when the government stepped in and made it obligatory for television companies to possess a licence to broadcast. The result of these stricter controls is that there are now far fewer than the 50 or so TV stations which existed in the country during and just after the civil war. Those which air now serve up a diet of the usual entertainment, films, news, sport and documentaries. The state-run broadcaster is **Tele Liban** (*www.teleliban.com.lb*), which screens its programmes in Arabic, English and French. The remaining stations are privately owned but are usually pegged to a sectarian or political bias. Thus the Arabic language channel **Al Manar TV** (*www.almanar.com.lb*) or 'the beacon' has a strong ideological attachment to Hezbollah and has been frequently targeted by the Israelis during periods of conflict between the two foes. A favourite of

Sunni Muslims is **Future TV** (*www.futuretvnetwork.com*), launched and formerly owned by Rafiq Hariri in 1993 during his political tenure, and which broadcasts in Arabic, Armenian, English and French. A popular choice among the Christian community and probably the country's most watched channel is the Pan-Arab **Lebanese Broadcasting Corporation International** (LBC; *www.lbcgroup.tv*), broadcasting mainly family programmes in Arabic. The remaining stations include the Arabic language channel **Murr TV** (*www.mtv.com.lb*), also has a Christian bias and owned by politician Gabriel Murr; the news channel **National Broadcasting Network** (NBN; *www.nbn.com.lb*) founded by Nabih Berri the current Parliamentary Speaker is biased toward Shi'ites and the Amal movement; and **Orange TV** (*www.otv.com.lb*), with programmes in Arabic, English and French. In addition to these local channels, satellite television is widespread in many homes and in the numerous hotels in Beirut and around the country, so it is usually possible to tune in to the many international TV stations such as CNN, the BBC, Al Jazeera and EuroNews, together with a whole host of sports channels.

INTERNET The advent of the internet has been embraced in Lebanon with as much enthusiasm as in many other countries in the world. According to the latest available figures from Internet World Stats (*www.internetworldstats.com*), Lebanon's 'connected' population numbered around 4,545,007 in June 2016 with some 2,600,000 Facebook users as of November 2015. There are innumerable internet cafés around the country with even the smallest town usually having at least one 'wired' establishment; and some, particularly in the capital, stay open until the wee hours or even 24/7. Reliable Internet Service Providers are plentiful should you be thinking of opening an account whilst in Lebanon (see page 160). Connection speeds are generally reasonably fast, though be prepared on occasions to experience depressingly slow response times; but, as Lebanon is well embarked on ongoing investment in the latest technology, this should progressively make slow response times a thing of the past. For those with their own laptops and enabled mobile phones, Wi-Fi is increasingly ubiquitous around the country in bars, cafés, restaurants and hotels. A number of these establishments will allow free access for customers, though some of the top-end hotels will charge heavily for the service. At the time of writing, internet access rates ranged from around LBP1,500/hour to LBP3,000/hour in the majority of internet cafés around the country, but some of the more expensive hotels will charge you considerably more. For those who prefer to gain their information and news from the internet, an excellent source and website, www.yalibnan.com, offers less partisan news coverage than many of the newspapers, with good coverage of Lebanese and regional daily current affairs and comment.

MOBILE PHONES Mobile-phone use in Lebanon is widespread and even many companies and organisations prefer cellular contact to that of landline communication. At the time of writing, there were an estimated 4.4 million mobile phone users in Lebanon compared with 970,000 fixed telephone lines. Generally speaking, national and international coverage and reception is excellent and you should have no problem using your own mobile phone in the country (assuming you have unlocked and enabled roaming on your phone) for making/receiving calls and sending/receiving text messages – assuming you don't mind the size of the bill that will land on your door mat when you arrive home. For those who do, it is easy to buy a Lebanese SIM card (and consequently a new number), and this will save you money if you plan to use your phone a lot. At the present time, Lebanon's two mobile operators are **Alfa** (m *03 391 111, free 24hr helpline within Lebanon using an Alfa line: 111;* e *alfa.customercareteam@ alfamobile.com.lb; www.alfa.com.lb*), who launched their 4G+ service in 2015, and **touch** (m *03 800 111; dial 111 within Lebanon for customer care service;* e *info@touch.com.lb, electroniccustomersupport@touch.com.lb; www.touch.com.lb*). Both operators provide a range of pay-as-you-go and other services for business and personal customers and have numerous outlets, with many other service centres in Lebanon's main towns and cities. The whole process is generally very straightforward, involving a minimum of bureaucracy to get yourself set up on the Lebanese mobile network. Prices can vary, so it is a good idea to shop around for the best deal, which usually involves paying somewhere between US$30 and US$50 for a new SIM card, and thus a new number, which will include around US$22 of phone credit included in the price of the card. You then have one month to use up your credit with the option to recharge your phone with additional credit when you have depleted the original card. Some places may ask for a copy of your passport details for identification purposes.

TELEPHONES Lebanon's state-owned telecommunications provider is **OGERO** (Organisme de Gestion et d'Exploitation de l'ex Radio Orient; *PO Box 11–1226, Bir Hassan, Beirut;* \ *01 840 000, 1515 (24/7 call centre within Lebanon); International Operator dial 100; www.ogero.gov.lb*), which was founded in 1972. Since the end of the civil war it has transformed the country's battered and antiquated telephone system into a modern and reliable service with a full range of digital and internet services available to both business and personal customers at numerous sales offices nationwide. All landline and mobile telephone numbers in Lebanon consist of six digits preceded by the two-digit mobile code or for the area you are dialling (see opposite). At the time of writing, the tariff for national landline-to-landline calls is LBP49/minute (07.00–21.00) and LBP28/minute (21.00–07.00), and the cost of a landline call to a local mobile network is LBP166/minute. Calls from a landline to international landlines are, with a few exceptions such as those to Antarctica and Western Samoa, standardised at LBP600/minute at peak times (07.00–22.00), and LBP400/minute off-peak (22.00–07.00). For those needing to make internal or international calls from Lebanon without incurring the often extortionate costs of using their own mobile phone provider, or who prefer not to buy a Lebanese SIM, OGERO offers two types of pre-paid calling-card, still available from OGERO offices and some stores displaying the OGERO sign, but increasingly tricky to find given the proliferation of mobiles. The Kalam card, available as a pre-paid LBP15,000 or LBP45,000 card, can be used from any fixed-line phone, private or street payphone, and is activated by inputting a PIN number and then dialling the number you want to call; the Telecarte card, available in LBP10,000 and LBP30,000 denominations, can be used *only* for street payphones. Unless absolutely vital, making calls from your hotel is not recommended, especially the mid range and luxury establishments, as they can work out very expensive.

Telephone codes and numbers to call Lebanon from abroad To call Lebanon **from the UK**, dial 00 (international access code), then 961 (Lebanon country access code), followed by the regional code or mobile prefix, omitting the initial 0 in both cases, and finally the six-digit telephone number. For example, to call the Hotel Albergo (page 141) in Beirut from the UK, you would dial: 00 961 1 339 797. To call Lebanon **from the USA**, dial 011 (international access code), then 961 (Lebanon country access code) followed by the regional code or mobile prefix, omitting the initial 0 in both cases, followed by the six-digit telephone number. For example, to call the tourist office in Beirut (page 135) from the USA, you would dial: 011 961 1 343 073. To call Lebanon **from other countries**, see www. countrycallingcodes.com for a worldwide listing of international access codes and dialling procedures.

Local area/regional codes in Lebanon Regional codes in Lebanon cover a wide geographic area. Thus the code for the Bekaa Valley (08) covers the areas of Baalbek, Chtaura, Hermel and Zahlé. Similarly, the area code for Beirut (01) applies to east, west, north and south Beirut. If making phone calls within Lebanon, you need to dial the initial zero for both area codes and mobile phone prefixes.

Beirut	01
Mount Lebanon (Beit Mery, Broummana)	04
Mount Lebanon (Jounieh, Byblos, Amchit)	09
North Lebanon (Batroun, Tripoli, Bcharré)	06
Bekaa Valley (Aanjar, Baalbek, Zahlé)	08
Southern Mount Lebanon (Deir al-Qamar, Beiteddine, Baakline, Moukhtara)	05
South Lebanon (Jezzine, Sidon, Tyre)	07
Mobile phone codes	03, 70, 71, 76, 78, 79, 81
International operator	100
Directory enquiries	120

Emergency and other useful telephone numbers

Emergency services
Civil defence ☎125
Fire brigade ☎175
Police ☎112
Lebanese Red Cross ☎01 372 802/3/4/5 (general), 140 (emergency)

Information services
Ministry of Tourism ☎01 343 073
Ministry of Tourism Hotline ☎1735
Ministry of Tourism Police ☎01 752 428/9
Weather forecast ☎1718

Utilities
Electricity hotline (Electricité du Liban; EDL) ☎1707
International operator ☎100
OGERO (telephone company) ☎1515

Travel
Rafiq Hariri International Airport–Beirut
☎01 628 000; dial 150 within Lebanon
General Security (visas) ☎01 425 610 ext 1276/1273; dial 1717 within Lebanon

Embassies
🅔 **Australia** ☎01 960 600
🅔 **Canada** ☎04 726 700
🅔 **France** ☎01 420 000
🅔 **Germany** ☎04 935 000; m 03 600 053 (24hr emergency line)
🅔 **Italy** ☎05 954 955
🅔 **Netherlands** ☎01 211 150; m 70 189 389 (24hr emergency line)
🅔 **Spain** ☎05 464 120
🅔 **Switzerland** ☎01 324 123, 01 324 129
🅔 **UK** ☎01 960 800
🅔 **USA** ☎04 542 600, 04 543 600

ARABIC-LANGUAGE TUITION AND TRANSLATION IN BEIRUT

AMBergh Education Solna Torg 19, SE-171 45 Stockholm, Solna, Sweden; ☎+46 8 612 2330; e arabic@ambergh.com, info@ambergh.com; www.ambergh.com. This Swedish company, in partnership with language learning centres around the country & region, offers individual & group tuition from beginner to advanced level in Lebanese colloquial Arabic & Modern Standard Arabic in the capital. They can also help arrange accommodation & volunteering opportunities with a range of vulnerable groups. Check their website for further information & details of upcoming courses & prices.

American Language Centre (ALC) [163 F3] 102 Maamari St, Hamra, Beirut, nr the American University of Beirut (AUB); 01 741 262; e alc@ alc.edu.lb; www.alcbeirut.com. Offers regular beginners, intermediate & advanced courses in spoken (colloquial) Lebanese Arabic.

American Lebanese Language Centre (ALLC) [173 H7] 7th Fl, Confidence Centre, Dimitri Al Hayek St, Sin El Fil, Beirut; 01 500 978; e info@allcs.edu.lb; www.allcs.edu.lb. Part of the worldwide network of International House World Organisation (IHWO) of adult education schools, this centre offers a range of short courses in Arabic tailored to beginner- & intermediate-level students. Courses usually run for 2 hrs, 2 evenings per week for 2/3 months with fees around US$260.

Berlitz Language Centre [162 C3] 1st Fl, Marbella Bldg, Sidani St, Hamra, Beirut; 01 751 689/90; e info@berlitz-lebanon.com; www.berlitz-lebanon. com. This long-established & internationally renowned school, founded in 1878, offers a range of Arabic language courses from beginner to advanced level for both groups & individuals wanting private tuition. Also caters for business travellers needing to master the basics quickly. See their website for course details & current fees.

Centre for Arab & Middle Eastern Studies (CAMES) [162 D2] American University of Beirut (AUB), Bliss St, Ras Beirut; 01 350 000; e cames@ aub.edu.lb; www.aub.edu.lb. In addition to its range of other courses, CAMES offers an extremely intensive but popular annual Summer Arabic Programme in Colloquial Lebanese Arabic & Modern Standard Arabic with 8 different levels of tuition according to the students' prior knowledge of Arabic. The course takes place Mon–Fri over a 7-week period during Jun & Aug with the 6hrs of daily classroom-based study needing to be supplemented by up to 5hrs of home study each evening. These are not the cheapest Arabic courses in town, & the basic tuition fees for summer 2016 were US$3,284 for the colloquial Lebanese Arabic course & US$4,925 for the Modern Standard Arabic course (both courses exc accommodation, flights, textbooks, meals & field visits outside Beirut). The AUB website has comprehensive information about the courses including an online application form & details about student accommodation options on/off the AUB campus.

Saifi Institute for Arabic Language [172 C2] 1st Fl, Saifi Urban Gardens Bldg, Pasteur St, Gemmayze, Beirut; 01 560 738; e info@saifiarabic. com; www.saifiarabic.com; ⏰ 09.00–18.00 Mon– Fri, private lessons held on Sat. Located adjacent to the Saifi Urban Gardens Hotel (pages 143–4), the institute offers a range of excellent & competitively priced group & private Arabic language courses from beginner to advanced level with glowing reports from students who have attended their classes praising the quality of their tuition. Take a look at their website for the latest course information, schedules & pricing together with some useful information on living & studying in the capital.

SINARC (Summer Institute for Intensive Arabic Language and Culture) [162 C5] Lebanese American University (LAU), Chouran, Beirut; 01 786 456; e mimi.jeha@lau.edu.lb, sinarc@lau.edu. lb; www.lau.edu.lb. The university's highly regarded & intensive 6-week SINARC course usually takes place annually between Jun & Jul catering for the beginner to advanced proficiency levels & includes coverage of the cultural & social aspects of Lebanon & the region. The course runs Mon–Fri & the fees in 2016 were US$4,183, exc meals, flights & course materials. Autumn, winter & spring courses are also offered. Check the university's website for the current schedule, pricing & online application form.

POST Lebanon's national postal service is run by the privately owned company **LibanPost** (*main headquarters: LibanPost, Beirut Sorting Centre, Tahwitat Al Ghadir, Beirut International Airport;* 01 629 628/9, *dial 1577 within Lebanon for customer care call centre,* ⏰ *08.00–17.00 Mon–Fri, 08.00–13.00 Sat;* e *customercare@libanpost.com; www.libanpost.com*) who operate an ever-growing network of post office branches nationwide. Lebanon's postal system has undergone considerable modernisation and expansion since the company was set up in 1998 following the devastation wrought by the country's 1975–90 civil war, and can now boast a high quality service and system on a par with those in western Europe and North America, handling some 2,000 tonnes of mail annually, and has received numerous accolades and awards for the quality of its services. Their distinctive blue-and-yellow logo is dotted around the city streets, postboxes and on buildings where you can post mail to towns and cities both within Lebanon as well as destinations overseas. The system offers a full range of services including parcel posting, mail tracking, poste restante and a mail redirection service, as well as being a point of sale for mobile phone recharge services. LibanPost is also an agent for Western Union for international money transfer. Sending a 50g postcard to the UK and Europe costs LBP1,750 and to the USA and Canada LBP2,500. The price of sending a 20g letter to Europe, Canada and the USA is LBP2,750 (50g is LBP5,000). Delivery times for letters and postcards to most overseas destinations are generally between four and seven days. To send mail within Lebanon, a 20g letter costs LBP1,000 (50g is LBP1,750) and to other countries within the Middle East LBP1,750 (50g is LBP3,000). If posting mail from the blue-and-yellow post boxes there are daily collections except on Saturday, Sunday and public holidays. Generally, post offices are open from 08.00 to 17.00 Monday–Friday and from 08.00 to 13.30 on Saturday, and are closed on Sunday. Some post office branches and kiosks, such as those at Beirut airport and in some shopping malls, have longer opening hours, and these times, where applicable, are detailed in the relevant regional chapters.

ELECTRICITY

Lebanon's power supply has been run since 1964 by the much maligned and state-owned **Electricité du Liban** (EDL; *Al Nahr St, Beirut, opp Port View Hotel;* `01 442 720, customer service hotline ` *1707, customer complaints hotline 1708;* e *info@edl. gov.lb; www.edl.gov.lb*) and uses the same voltage as that within continental Europe (220v, 50Hz). The electrical system is the usual European-style round two-pin plugs. Power cuts and electricity rationing, however, are still a part of everyday life in Lebanon. In Beirut they occur daily for 3 hours, usually alternating between the hours of 06.00 and 09.00, 09.00 and 12.00, or 12.00 and 15.00. Outside the capital, power cuts and electricity rationing can last considerably longer, and outages of up to 10 or even 20+ hours a day are not unheard of. The larger hotels, restaurants, cafés and stores often have their own generators, which usually kickstart supplies within a few minutes. EDL's website has a comprehensive listing of telephone numbers for its regional offices around the country; useful for those visitors considering renting (or buying) a property for the duration of their stay in Lebanon.

BUSINESS

Lebanon offers many advantages for the aspiring foreign businessman including its greatest asset, the country's highly literate, skilled and often trilingual (Arabic, French and English) workforce. Although many Lebanese have emigrated over the years, they have maintained close links with their country through the income they send 'home', and the business acumen and experiences that they have gained overseas have often percolated through to their homeland. They can be shrewd and perceptive business people and much business activity can be expected to be conducted within a very hospitable and social atmosphere, including lunches and dinners, before any deal is done. Dress codes are often formal, though in the heat of summer it is common to dress down into more informal attire, and common greetings such as handshaking are accepted etiquette. The Lebanese, like many in the Arab world, also have a love of business cards, so bring plenty with you.

Business in Lebanon is far from being a male-only domain and the visiting female executive will generally experience no issues or problems when mixing with the cosmopolitan Lebanese. The liberal economic system is an extension of the cosmopolitan nature of the country itself: a long-established *laissez-faire* economy, strict banking secrecy laws, little or no restrictions on the movement of capital and a highly competitive corporation tax of just 15%.

It is true, however, that periodic internal political and regional instability remain perhaps the principal factors undermining investor confidence, as witnessed recently with the Arab Spring and, in particular, the ongoing conflict in Syria, whose economic, social and security knock-on effects have severely damaged the real-estate and tourism sectors especially, but with equally negative impacts on the construction and retail sectors, too. As with many other Arab countries, however, Lebanon has weathered the global economic downturn much better than many of the world's major economies, and the country remains ripe for future foreign business activity and investment. Currently, and no doubt for the foreseeable future, some of the main areas of opportunity are in the fields of major reconstruction projects such as aviation, construction (hotels, commercial and residential buildings), education, electricity, health care, roads, ports and telecommunications. The recent explorations and potential presence of substantial hydrocarbon deposits (oil and natural gas) off the Lebanese coast is obviously an emerging market for the fossil-fuel industry and one that has the future potential to transform the economic and social landscape of Lebanon, though hampered at present by the ongoing presidential vacuum and the political instability affecting the country due to the ongoing hostilities in Syria (pages 29–33).

The list of Lebanese government departments and other organisations on page 115 should also prove useful for those visitors arriving in Lebanon for business. Some additional web resources for the visiting business executive are given on pages 114–15 together with some supplementary governmental websites (pages 354–5), as well as visa information for the visiting executive (pages 68–9). Generally speaking, working hours of government departments are 08.00–14.00 Monday–Thursday, 08.00–11.00 Friday and 08.00–13.00 Saturday.

When in Lebanon, the monthly *Executive* magazine (*LBP10,000; 7th Fl, Sehnaoui Centre, Achrafieh, Beirut;* ☏ *01 611 696; www.executive-magazine.com*) is well worth seeking out. It is widely available in Beirut bookshops and at many of the top-end hotels, and is a good source of information across the gamut of business and economic issues throughout Lebanon and the wider region. Another excellent monthly publication with an equally good and informative website is *Lebanon Opportunities* (*LBP9,000; 2nd Fl, Piccadilly Centre, Hamra St, Beirut;* ☏ *01 739 777;* e *opportunities@infopro.com.lb; www.opportunities.com.lb*), which has good coverage of economics, finance, tenders, conferences, exhibitions and the real-estate sector, etc and is available in most good bookshops.

USEFUL CONTACTS
UK
Arab British Chamber of Commerce (ABCC) 43 Upper Grosvenor St, London W1K 2NJ; ☏ 020 7235 4363; e info@abcc.org.uk; www. abcc.org.uk. An excellent resource that publishes a range of business magazines, hosts events & offers a variety of export, translation & visa services to prospective investors & businesses.
Economist Intelligence Unit 20 Cabot Sq, London E14 4QW; ☏ 020 7576 8181; e london@ eiu.com; www.eiu.com. Authoritative and up-to-date economic analysis, data & risk forecasting.
Middle East Association (MEA) 6th Fl, 27 St James's St, London SW1A 1HA; ☏ 020 7839 2137; www.the-mea.co.uk. Another long-established organisation, which works across the MENA region enhancing & promoting trade & economic activities with a number of states, including Lebanon. They publish a range of material inc an annual yearbook, *Gateway: The MEA Guide to Doing Business in the Middle*

East and North Africa & run many events & conferences across a number of business areas.

Oxford Business Group 131 Great Titchfield St, London W1W 5BB; ☎ 020 7403 7213; e consultancy@oxfordbusinessgroup.com, sales@oxfordbusinessgroup.com; www. oxfordbusinessgroup.com. Authoritative and up-to-date economic analysis, data & risk forecasting.

UK Trade & Investment (UKTI) 1 Victoria St, London SW1H 0ET; ☎ 020 7215 5000; www.ukti. gov.uk. A useful government website resource for UK businesses looking to invest in Lebanon, inc a downloadable *Doing Business in Lebanon* guide (*www.gov.uk/government/publications/exporting-to-lebanon*), which contains useful country background, etiquette, contact information, markets & opportunities useful for first-time investors.

USA

National US–Arab Chamber of Commerce (NUSACC) Suite 1220, 1101 17th St NW, Washington DC 20036; ☎ 202 289 5920; e info@nusacc.org; www.nusacc.org. Serving a similar role to the ABCC in the UK.

Lebanon

Association of Lebanese Industrialists (ALI) 5th Fl, CCIABML Bldg, 1 Justinian St, Sanayeh, Beirut; ☎ 01 350 280/1/2; e ali@ali.org.lb; www.ali.org.lb

Beirut Stock Exchange (BSE) Block 1, 4th Fl, Azarieh Bldg, Azarieh St, Al Bachura, Beirut; ☎ 01 993 555; e bse@bse.com.lb; www.bse.com.lb

Business News 2nd Fl, Piccadilly Centre, Hamra St, Beirut; ☎ 01 739 777; e infopro@infopro.com.lb; www.businessnews.com.lb

Central Bank (Banque Du Liban) [163 F4] Masraf Lubnan St, Hamra, opp Ministry of Tourism, Beirut; ☎ 01 750 000; www.bdl.gov.lb

Chamber of Commerce, Industry & Agriculture of Beirut & Mount Lebanon [163 G4] CCIABML Bldg, 1 Rue Justinien, Sanayeh, Beirut; ☎ 01 353 190; e information@ccib.org.lb; www.ccib.org.lb

Chamber of Commerce, Industry & Agriculture of Tripoli & North Lebanon Bechara El-Khoury Bd, Tripoli; ☎ 06 425 600; e info@cciat.org.lb; www.cciat.org.lb

Council for Development & Reconstruction (CDR) [138 D5] Tallet al-Serail, Riad al-Solh, Downtown, Beirut; ☎ 01 980 096; e infocenter@cdr.gov.lb; www.cdr.gov.lb

Ecole Supérieure des Affaires (ESA) [163 F3] 289 Clemenceau St, Beirut; ☎ 01 373 373; e esa@esa.edu.lb; www.esa.edu.lb. Lebanon's & the region's leading business school also hosts a number of conferences & workshops together with its annual Career Fair, which attracts both Lebanese & international businesses to its campus.

Investment Development Authority of Lebanon (IDAL) [139 E7] 4th Fl, Lazarieh Tower, Al Amir Bachir St, Riad al-Solh, Downtown, Beirut; ☎ 01 983 306/7/8; e invest@idal.com.lb, export@idal.com.lb; www.idal.com.lb. Lots of useful information on applying for work and residency permits as well as general information on doing business in Lebanon.

Lebanese Customs [139 H4] ☎ 01 700 115; e info@customs.gov.lb; www.customs.gov.lb

Lebanese Petroleum Administration (LPA) e info@lebanon-exploration.com, info@lpa.gov.lb; www.lebanon-exploration.com, www.lpa.gov.lb

Lebanon Gas & Oil m 03 824 079; e info@lebanongasandoil.com; www.lebanongasandoil.com

Ministry of Economy & Trade [139 E7] 5th Fl, Lazarieh Tower, Riad al-Solh, Downtown, Beirut; ☎ 01 982 360/1/2/3/4/5; e info@economy.gov.lb; www.economy.gov.lb

Ministry of Finance [139 E5] MOF Bldg, Riad al-Solh Sq, Downtown, Beirut; ☎ 01 981 001; e infocenter@finance.gov.lb; www.finance.gov.lb

Ministry of Industry Sami Solh Av, Badaro, Beirut; ☎ 01 423 338, 01 427 006, 01 427 046; www.industry.gov.lb

Ministry of Telecommunications [139 E5] 1st Fl, Ministry of Telecom Bldg, Riad al-Solh Sq, Downtown, Beirut; ☎ 01 979 979; www.mpt.gov.lb

Solidere (The Lebanese Company for the Development and Reconstruction of Beirut Central District) [139 F4] Bldg 149, Saad Zaghloul St, Downtown, Beirut; ☎ 01 980 650/660; www.solidere.com

Other resources

www.transparency.org An NGO committed to eradicating corruption around the globe. Publishes the annual *Corruption Perceptions Index* for more than 100 countries, inc Lebanon.

www.worldbank.org World Bank entry on Lebanon, giving statistics & reports across economic, social & other indices.

TRADE CONFERENCES, SHOWS AND EXHIBITIONS In Beirut especially, there are now a number of regular and annual trade conferences, shows and exhibitions across a wide range of industries and business concerns as Lebanon is well embarked on making the country once again a regional hub for business and investment in the Middle East. A few useful organisations and venues are given below.

Beirut International Exhibition & Leisure Centre (BIEL) [139 G1] Majidieh, Downtown, Beirut; ℡ 01 995 555; e leb@biel-group.com; www.biel-group.com. Lebanon's premier conference, trade & exhibition venue.
Iktissad Events Minkara Centre, Madame Curie St, Hamra, Beirut; ℡ 01 353 577, 01 740 173/4; www.iktissadevents.com. Organises a number of conferences & exhibitions annually at various venues in Lebanon & the region across a range of business sectors.
International Fairs & Promotions (IFP) IFP Group Bldg, 56th St, Hazmieh, Beirut; ℡ 05 959 111;

e projectlebanon@ifpexpo.com, info@ifpexpo.com; www.projectlebanon.com, www.ifpexpo.com. One of the largest trade fair organisations in the region, the IFP Group organises a number of events & shows including the established event for the construction industry, Project Lebanon.
Promofair 5th Fl, Media Centre Bldg, Accaoui, Achrafieh, Beirut; ℡ 01 561 600/1/2/3/4; e info@promofair.com.lb; www.promofair.com.lb. This large Lebanese company uses the BIEL venue above for its exhibitions & fairs across areas such as weddings, and the motor-vehicle & real-estate sectors, etc.

BUYING PROPERTY

Lebanon's real-estate sector, along with tourism, has been one of the many economic success stories in recent years and a walk around the capital reveals endless construction sites and cranes building a range of apartment blocks and new residential developments. In the first quarter of 2010, Lebanon achieved a record number of over 22,000 transactions worth more than US$2 billion, and there were some 350 building projects under construction in Greater Beirut alone. Though recent instability in the region, mainly due to the ongoing conflict in Syria, led to a near 20% decline in the number of transactions in 2013, this still important market is complemented by favourable interest rates and competition amongst the banks, who offer loans of between 50% and 85% of a property's value. The good news for the prospective foreign purchaser is that there are no restrictions on foreign property ownership in line with Lebanon's liberalised economy and the desire to encourage foreign investment. Overseas purchasers are permitted to own land up to a maximum of 3,000m² with larger plots requiring prior permission from the Council of Ministers. If you don't have your own personal contacts or knowledge, you will probably need to avail yourself of the services of a reputable real-estate broker. The property-buying process in Lebanon is not dissimilar to that in western countries, with all the usual formalities being broadly similar. A good starting point for your forays into the Lebanese property market is the classified advertising section of the *Daily Star* newspaper which has a range of apartments and houses for sale and will give a good idea of asking prices. For more in-depth details about the real-estate sector, the following monthly publication is worth seeking out in Beirut: *Lebanon Opportunities* (*LBP9,000; 2nd Fl, Piccadilly Centre, Hamra, Beirut;* ℡ *01 739 777;* e *infopro@infopro. com.lb; www.opportunities.com.lb*). The property portal www.lebanon.com/realestate is a cornucopia of nationwide properties for sale and rent, whilst the *Global Property Guide* (*www.globalpropertyguide.com/Middle-East/Lebanon*) has a range of data on the current state of the market together with a guide to the buying process. Another useful website is www.realestate.com.lb, which advertises properties for sale and rent and has a list of real-estate agents and developers.

For anyone considering setting up home, either temporarily or permanently in Lebanon, a useful publication to get hold of is *At Home in Beirut: A Practical Guide to Living in Beirut* (*LBP25,000; Beirut: Turning Point Books, 2010*). In its fourth edition at the time of writing, this is an excellent handbook for locals and foreigners alike who need to get to grips with the various bureaucracy, formalities and more mundane matters such as where to get your washing machine repaired. The book should be available in Beirut bookshops, from online retailers such as Amazon (*www.amazon.com*) or from the publishers themselves (*www.tpbooksonline.com*).

CULTURAL ETIQUETTE

The Lebanese are a very tactile people and greetings between friends and family usually commence with a series of the French-style three kisses on the cheek, whilst a smile and a handshake and simple *marhaba* (hello) are accepted etiquette between both men and women who are less familiar with each other for an initial meeting - which is all something of a contrast to the more reserved cultures of the UK, Europe and North America. The main exception to this occurs in more traditional areas and amongst married or traditional Muslim women, who will refrain from kissing or shaking hands with a man; a lowering of the head and the placing of their arm and hand across their chest normally indicates this. Displays of more overtly romantic affection, however, are more variable. In Beirut couples can often be seen holding hands and kissing, especially in the Downtown and east Beirut districts of the city. Yet in areas such as Tripoli, Sidon and the Bekaa Valley such behaviour would be frowned upon and could offend Muslim sensibilities. In these areas, discretion or abstinence is therefore advised. The same is also true for homosexual partners where any outward display of your sexual orientation would be seen as even less acceptable than for heterosexual couples, and once again discretion or abstinence is the order of the day. You may also come across people of the same sex holding hands or walking together with their arms around each other. This is perfectly normal behaviour, as witnessed in other countries in the region, and does not necessarily have any romantic or sexual connotations. Although Lebanon is often seen as one of the most liberal and open-minded of Arab societies, traditional values and the importance of the family are entrenched aspects of the country's lifestyle. The Lebanese adore their children, who often live with them until getting married. If visiting as a family, you can expect a lot of interest and fuss to be made of your offspring; this is simply an extension of the Lebanese love of children and a display of genuine hospitality. If you get invited to someone's home for a drink or meal, do not hesitate to accept, though it is courteous to bring a small gift such as flowers or chocolates to show your appreciation. During the period of Ramadan (pages 49 and 99), be sensitive to fasting Muslims in certain more staunch neighbourhoods by refraining from eating and drinking in public during daylight hours.

Many Lebanese are trilingual, speaking English and French in addition to their native Arabic. '*Hi habibi, ça va?*' ('Hi baby, how are you?') may be a cliché of many a Lebanese marketing brochure but can often be heard especially around the youthful areas of Hamra and Bliss streets in the capital. Learning a few words and phrases of Arabic will not only enhance your visit and win you a few friends, but will also often assist you in negotiating daily situations with hotels, buses, taxis, etc. You'll also encounter, especially when using taxis, a slight tipping of the head backwards and raised eyebrows accompanied by a 't'-type sound, signifying 'no', when they

3

are not travelling in the direction you request. Whatever language you converse in, certain subjects such as politics and religion are obviously hot potatoes in this part of the world and need to be approached with caution and common sense. Whilst certainly not taboo, it is best to steer clear of controversial issues unless you know the person well.

Among both males and females there is a high number of smokers in the country and, although a 2011 law prohibited lighting up in public places, the fact remains that you will no doubt still come across cafés, bars, restaurants, taxis and internet cafés that will still be quite smoke-filled places which is not welcome news for those trying to quit.

Driving standards leave much to be desired in a country where the car and bus are such ubiquitous modes of transport. Traffic lights, road markings and signs are becoming more widespread but are in many cases ignored by motorists and even bus drivers. Driver temperament is often one of tunnel vision, with speeding commonplace and a general lack of anticipation or courtesy towards other road users, including pedestrians. In the frequent traffic jams of Beirut the atonal symphony of vehicle horns testifies to an absence of patience being a virtue.

Despite being a very open and tolerant country relative to some of its neighbours, Lebanon remains a Muslim destination, and observing certain dress codes and behaviour are essential for a rewarding visit. For visiting religious shrines such as mosques, this means 'dressing down'. Women should wear a headscarf, and both males and females must remove their shoes before entering. Revealing and skimpy attire appropriate to a night out in Downtown or east Beirut is completely unsuitable (and offensive) when visiting a holy site.

One aspect of Lebanese daily life you should avoid replicating is the habit of some Lebanese to engage in the environmentally unfriendly practice of just dumping their rubbish wherever they see fit. In many places around the country you will see piles of plastic bags, empty mineral water bottles and other garbage strewn around; the author has even witnessed taxi drivers just throwing their empty water bottles out of their car window. Keep hold of your rubbish and dispose of it in the proper manner in a bin when you can.

Lebanon is an extremely photogenic country and, generally speaking, you will have no problems photographing any of the main tourist sites. However, for those who deem the airport, government buildings, army checkpoints or soldiers themselves as equally photogenic 'sites', this view will not often be shared by the Lebanese authorities, so exercise caution if turning your lens to these subjects or be prepared to be questioned, and possibly to delete your pictures from your memory card (see page 106 for more details on photographic etiquette).

TRAVELLING POSITIVELY

Walking around the immaculately restored buildings of Downtown Beirut or gazing up at the plethora of glittering high-rise five-star hotels that dot the city, you could be forgiven for thinking that Lebanon is far from being a needy nation. Similarly, with its high adult literacy rate, advanced health care facilities and the billions of dollars that pour into the country each year from the Lebanese diaspora, Lebanon can evoke an aura of prosperity, and street beggars are a rarity compared with many other countries in the region. However, appearances can be deceptive, and beneath the wealthy veneer Lebanon remains an emerging country, following the cessation of civil war hostilities, with issues of human poverty, the environment and the sectarian divide remaining prominent facts of life.

All these concerns ensure that there are plenty of opportunities for the visitor to put back into the country at least as much as they take out. It may be a cliché, but buying Lebanese produce, such as at Beirut's weekly farmers' market, Souk el Tayeb (page 153), or purchasing your souvenir craft items from Lebanese artisans at the city's L'Artisan du Liban (page 152), is a fantastic way of ensuring that your money goes to some of those who need it most. There are also opportunities to purchase Palestinian products such as a variety of embroidered items, with funds fed back into refugee camps to help this much impoverished diaspora. Furthermore, buying organic produce is one way of offsetting Lebanon's excessive use of pesticides.

Your choice of accommodation, too, can have a real and positive impact on the local economy of more impoverished rural areas, and staying in lodgings that are part of the DIYAFA Association (page 95), for example, is a great way of enhancing your travel experience whilst at the same time giving something back. An increased awareness in recent years of man's impact on the natural world has led to a consequent increase in organisations campaigning on behalf of the environment, and you may want to help them with a donation or by volunteering.

Apart from the thousands of Syrian refugees currently residing in Lebanon who have fled their country's ongoing conflict, probably the most visible area of concern is that of Lebanon's 450,000+ Palestinian refugees. Scattered across a dozen camps around the country (box, page 43), their living conditions are not what any human being should have to endure. Accordingly, there are several organisations, including of course the **United Nations** (*Lebanon Field Office: Ghobeiri, Bir Hassan, opp City Sportive, Beirut;* ☎ *01 840 490;* f *01 840 466; www.unrwa.org*), operating around the country that work to improve the lot of the Palestinians.

There are many organisations working for various good causes in Lebanon, and the following list should provide useful pointers to your own particular area or areas of interest if you wish to partner up with a charitable group.

American Near East Refugee Aid (ANERA)
US Headquarters: 1111 14th St, NW, Suite 400, Washington DC 20005, USA; ☎ (202) 266 9700; e anera@anera.org; www.anera.org; Lebanon Field Office: 3rd Fl, Forest Bldg, Badaro-Alam St, Beirut; ☎ 01 382 590/1; e communication@ aneralebanon.org; www.anera.org. An American NGO that works with Palestinian refugees across a wide range of areas such as educational provision, health, housing, employment & vocational training in Lebanon, Gaza & the West Bank & provides humanitarian aid & support to refugees in Jordan.
Animals Lebanon PO Box 113-5859, Hamra, Beirut; ☎ 01 751 678; e contact@animalslebanon. org; www.animalslebanon.org. Well-respected organisation dedicated to the care & protection of all wild & domestic animals. There are opportunities to donate, sponsor & volunteer for the charity, inc running the Beirut Marathon, campaigning & administrative work.
Association for Forests, Development & Conservation 1st Fl, Madi Bd, Sagesse St, Jdiedeh, Beirut; ☎ f 01 898 475/6; m 03 848

412; e afdc@afdc.org.lb; www.afdc.org.lb. Formed in 1992 after devastating forest fires, this association runs a wide range of environmental, rural development & educational programmes. Volunteering opportunities are available.
Beirut for the Ethical Treatment of Animals (BETA) PO Box 26, Hazmieh, Beirut; m 70 248 765; e donate@betalebanon.org, volunteer@ betalebanon.org, contact@betalebanon.org; www. betalebanon.org. For animal lovers, this very active charity needs donations & volunteers to help promote its animal welfare & educational campaigns & action against abuse of animals, & to help with its re-homing programmes for dogs & cats.
Canadian–Palestinian Educational Exchange 612 Markham St, Toronto, ON M6G 2L8, Canada; e info@cepal.ca; www.cepal.ca. A range of volunteer teaching opportunities, for Canadian nationals 18+ years only, to live & work in the Palestinian camps at Bourj Brajneh & Shatila in Beirut, & the Wavel refugee camp in Baalbek in the Bekaa Valley. Volunteering opportunities are usually available during summer & autumn

& run for around 2–5 months. Full details on the application procedure available on the website.

Caritas Lebanon Dr Youssef Hajjar St, Sin el Fil, Beirut; ☎ 01 499 767, 01 483 305; e donate@caritas.org.lb, executive@caritas.org.lb, info@caritas.org.lb; www.caritas.org, www.caritas.org.lb. Caritas is Latin for 'charity', & this long-established & worldwide network of organisations with a Catholic ethos works to combat social injustice & poverty across the age spectrum. Caritas is located nationwide providing health, social & humanitarian programmes for the less fortunate, inc assistance to Lebanon's migrant workers. Opportunities exist to help run its summer camps & to assist with other practical projects such as renovating houses & environmental clean-up projects.

Children & Youth Centre Shatila (CYC) Shatila Camp, Beirut; m 03 974 672; e cyc@cyberia.net.lb; www.cycshatila.org. Established in 1997, CYC is an NGO striving to better the lot of Palestinian children & youths at Beirut's Shatila camp and at the Nahr el-Bared camp in north Lebanon. Ample opportunities for volunteering (fundraising, IT, performing arts, sports, teaching English, etc) as well as donations to the organisation. CYC also run a 5-bedroom guesthouse at Shatila where, for US$15 pp per night (discounts available for group & long stays) in clean, but basic accommodation, travellers & volunteers can experience life at the camp first hand.

Children's Cancer Centre of Lebanon Bldg 56, American University of Beirut Medical Centre (AUBMC), Clemenceau St, Beirut; ☎ 01 351 515; m 70 351 515; e cccl@cccl.org.lb; www.cccl.org.lb. The centre is always in need of funds & there are also opportunities to interact with patients & tutor arts & crafts lessons, fundraising & events.

Friends of the Disabled Association (FDA) 1st Fl, Hallak-Daouk Bldg, Dannawi St, Mseitbeh, Beirut; ☎ 01 815 526; e info@friendsfordisabled.org; www.friendsfordisabled.org. Works with children & young people with a variety of special needs at their I'dad Centre at Mechref Village in the Chouf district. Plenty of volunteering opportunities available for visitors from gardening, arts & crafts, music tuition to a range of sporting activities to help promote the children's personal & social development.

Greenline 3rd Fl, Yamout Bldg, 174 Spears St, Sanayeh, Beirut; ☎f 01 746 215, 01 752 142; e greenline@greenline.org.lb; www.greenline.org.lb. A local, independent NGO concerned with all things environmental with a wide-ranging campaign & outreach programme to local schools etc.

Indyact 4th Fl, Jaara Bldg, Nahr St, Rmeil, Beirut; ☎ 01 447 192; e info@indyact.org; www.indyact.org. Founded in 2006 after the Jiyeh oil plant destruction by the Israeli air force, this umbrella group addresses environmental, social, cultural & women's issues & is in need of both financial & volunteer assistance.

Insan Association 7th Fl, Maalouf Bldg, Adib Ishak St, Achrafieh, Beirut; ☎f 01 333 091; e insan@insanlb.org; www.insanassociation.org. A range of volunteering & donation possibilities with this human rights organisation concerned with the plight of Lebanon's Palestinian refugees & other marginalised & vulnerable groups such as migrant workers.

Kafa (Enough Violence & Exploitation) 1st Fl, Beydoun Bldg, 43 Badaro St, Beirut; ☎f 01 392 220/1; m 03 018 019 (helpline); e kafa@kafa.org.lb; www.kafa.org.lb. Run by a group of professionals & human rights campaigners, this organisation campaigns for a more egalitarian society & to stop violence against women, children & other vulnerable groups in Lebanese society.

The Learning to CARE Institute PO Box 175 159, Nahr St, Mar Mikhael, nr Electricité du Liban, Beirut; ☎f 01 560 993; m 03 757 098; e admin@learningtocare.com; www.learningtocare.com. A relatively new organisation specialising in consulting & training across a whole gamut of volunteering opportunities in Lebanon & the wider Arab world. Plenty of useful generic information on their website for the prospective volunteer.

Lebanese Autism Society [172 A2] Sacré-Coeur College, Gemmayze, Beirut; ☎f 01 449 988; m 03 232 427; e info@autismlebanon.org, volunteering@autismlebanon.org; www.autismlebanon.org. Volunteers required in the areas of fundraising, campaigns & to help out on their annual summer camp for children affected by autism.

Lebanese Red Cross [163 H5] Spears St, Qantari, Beirut; ☎ 01 372 802/3/4/5, 140 (24/7 emergency response); e info@redcross.org.lb; www.redcross.org.lb. You'll doubtless see during your visit the red-&-white vehicles of the Red Cross, who operate their free emergency service throughout the country. Although volunteering opportunities for non-Lebanese citizens are limited, they are always in need of funds & medical supplies, & donations can be made via their website.

Lebanon Trust Christy Kinsella (Chairman), 17 Whitestown Crescent, Blakestown, Blanchardstown, Dublin 15, Ireland; e info@lebanontrust.org, laura@lebanontrust.org; www.lebanontrust.org. Founded by former UN peacekeepers in Lebanon, the Trust relies on an international network of volunteers to raise funds through various events in their home countries. The money raised is then channelled into helping Lebanon's needy children, in particular funding kindergartens at the Shatila refugee camp in Beirut & the Bourj Shemali refugee camp near the southern city of Tyre. The charity also provides financial support for its work with children at the Father Andeweg Institute for the Deaf (FAID; ℡ *05 920 735;* f *05 920 625;* e *faid.amt@intracom. net.lb; www.faid-lb.org*). Every year, usually in the autumn, the charity organises visits to Lebanon for these volunteers to see how the money raised is spent & to gain practical experience of working on these projects. Volunteer speech therapists & teachers are in particular demand.

Migrant Workers Task Force (MWTF) e mwtaskforce.lb@gmail.com; www.mwtaskforce. wordpress.com. An organisation striving to better the conditions of Lebanon's 200,000+ migrant workers & enhance their future personal & professional development. This charity runs language classes in Arabic, English & French, computer literacy & cookery tuition with volunteering opportunities available for people who can offer these skills.

Operation Big Blue Association (OBBA) 4th Fl, Toufic Tabbarah Centre, Al Zarif, Beirut; ℡ 01 742 700, 01 751 760; m 03 747 789; e info@operationbigblue.org; www.operationbigblue. org. A Lebanese NGO working alongside numerous government & non-governmental organisations including the navy, Red Cross & UNIFIL promoting & protecting the environment; in particular through its annual clean-up days all along the coast, rivers & other areas collecting discarded waste. Opportunities exist to help with collecting the rubbish & for making monetary donations to the organisation.

Palestinian Human Rights Organisation Mar Elias Camp, Beirut; ℡ 01 306 740; e info@palhumanrights.org, phro@palhumanrights. org; www.palhumanrights.org. Volunteering & internships available for graduates & students especially those specialising in the social sciences, law, politics, international relations & related fields.

René Moawad Foundation 844 Alfred Naccache St, Achrafieh, Beirut; ℡ 01 613 367/8/9; e rmf@rmf.org.lb; www.rmf.org.lb. Set up in 1991 as an NGO by MP Nayla Moawad & named after her husband & former Lebanese president, René, who was assassinated in 1989 only 17 days after being sworn in, the foundation carries out its work in the fields of economic, health, social & rural development remaining true to her husband's principles of unity & equality.

Right to Play International HQ: 14th Fl, 18 King St East, Toronto, Ontario M5C 1C4, Canada; ℡ +1 416 203 0190; e canada@righttoplay.com; www. righttoplay.ca; Lebanon Field Office: 9th Fl, Block B, Al-Sabbah Centre, Corniche al-Mazraa, Beirut; ℡ 01 313 346; www.righttoplay.com. Aims to foster play & sport amongst disadvantaged & marginalised children & communities in Lebanon & around the world, including Jordan & the Palestinian Territories (West Bank & Gaza), to foster social change & promote life skills. Overseas volunteers often required; details on their website. Also has offices in Africa, Germany, Netherlands, Norway, Switzerland, Latin America, the UK & USA.

Society for the Protection of Nature in Lebanon (SPNL) 6th Fl, Awad Bldg, Abdel Aziz St, Beirut; ℡ 01 343 740, 01 344 814; e news@spnl.org; www.spnl.org. An environmental NGO whose work aims to protect & sustain Lebanon's diverse natural & animal kingdom. Volunteers from a range of backgrounds are required for a number of ongoing projects such as protection of the sea turtle, wild cat, otter, & the Syrian serin, as well as assisting with the preservation of forests & outreach programmes.

Teach a Child El Khalil Bldg, Makdissi St, Hamra, Beirut; ℡ 01 747 266; e info@teach-a-child. org; www.teach-a-child.org. An NGO providing financial & other support to disadvantaged children to enable them to attend school. Donations are accepted via their website; various volunteering opportunities available.

Universities Trust for Educational Exchange with Palestinians (UNIPAL) BCM Unipal, London WC1N 3XX, UK; e info@unipal.org.uk, volunteers@unipal.org.uk; www.unipal.org.uk. This UK-based organisation arranges volunteer placements for native English speakers 20+ years to teach English & a range of other subjects & topics to Palestinian children in refugee camps.

See the website for details & online application form & guidance notes for prospective volunteers. **World Vision UK** Opal Drive, Fox Milne, Milton Keynes MK15 0ZR, UK; ☎01908 841000, 01908 841010; e info@worldvision.org.uk; www. worldvision.org.uk. The world's biggest children's charity with a Christian ethos has been working in Lebanon since 1975. Currently providing child protection, education, health, food & a host of other welfare programmes to the large number of Syrian refugee children & their parents living in Lebanon, the charity welcomes monetary donations as well as clothing & other useful items plus fundraising initiatives carried out in your own country. Lots of helpful & useful information on the website.

Part Two

THE GUIDE

4

Beirut

Telephone code 01

Framed by the blue waters of the Mediterranean Sea and the often snowy peaks of Mount Sannine, Lebanon's capital and most populous city, Beirut – 'Bride of the East' to the ancient Phoenicians – commands a proud and enduring presence at the midway point on the Lebanese coastline. This much-vilified city of over two million people boasts more than 5,000 years of recorded history. However, it is only the last few decades with which most foreigners are acquainted as sectarian divisions and foreign interference thrust Beirut and Lebanon onto the international stage with the start of the country's 15-year civil war. Lebanon's descent into anarchy soon made the country a byword for man's inhumanity and the very notion of Beirut and tourism became one of the modern era's best-known oxymorons.

The *al hawadith* or 'events', as the Lebanese call the 1975–90 debacle, which left around 85,000 people dead in Beirut alone and forced up to one million people to flee the country, effectively cut Lebanon off from the outside world. The city's notorious Green Line, which demarcated Christian east and Muslim west, became an icon of smouldering resentment. Similarly, the Downtown district sunk into a maelstrom of death and destruction not seen in any Arab city in the modern history of the Middle East conflict. With the onset of peace, however, came the inexorable drive towards rebuilding the city – both physically and psychologically – and Beirut today is probably the most transformed city in the entire region.

Whilst present-day Beirut may lack the old-world charm of Cairo, Marrakesh or Tangier, a visit to the high-octane Achrafieh, Gemmayze and Mar Mikhael districts suggests the city is once again flaunting the cosmopolitan and hedonistic lifestyle that gave the capital its pre-war reputation as 'the Paris of the Middle East'. The epicentre of reconstruction is Downtown, which now boasts beautifully restored Ottoman- and French-era architecture, souks and an abundance of five-star hotels complemented by a chic café culture and modern restaurants. On bustling Rue Hamra, once known as Beirut's Champs Elysées, coffee, conversation and shopping take precedence, while further east the neighbourhood of Bourj Hammoud is an example of an integrated diaspora, a displaced Armenian people who have made Beirut their home whilst preserving their own cultural identity. In upmarket Verdun, Beirut bling competes with international designer fashion labels. The southern suburbs of the city, however, provide a poignant reminder of a city still wearing its past on its sleeve. Here, thousands of Palestinian and Shi'ite Muslim refugees live in abject poverty; posters of martyrs killed fighting Israel in the south of the country line the streets together with effigies of Iran's Ayatollah Khomeini, providing the most visible reminders that, for all its renaissance, Beirut remains embroiled in the wider Middle East peace process.

For decades Beirut was touristically a no-man's-land. With the capital now restored, it merits at least a few days of any visitor's time. Put aside any preconceptions of drug-crazed gunmen and terrorists roaming the streets and

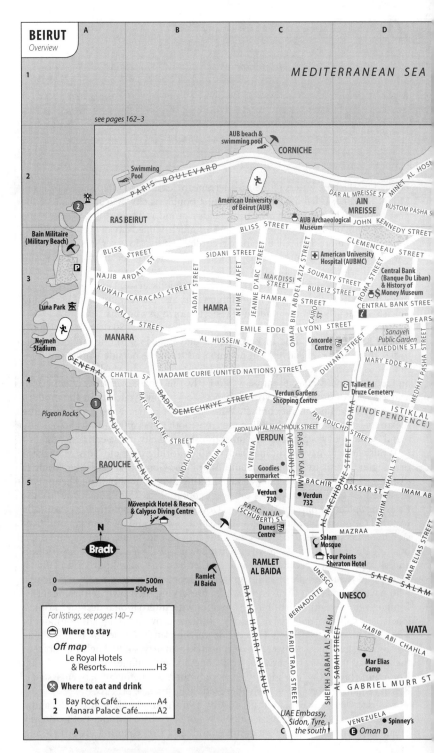

A B C D

1

MEDITERRANEAN SEA

see pages 162–3

AUB beach &
swimming pool

CORNICHE

2

Swimming
Pool

PARIS BOULEVARD

DAR AL MREISSE ST

MINET AL HOSN

American University
of Beirut (AUB)

AIN
MREISSE

RAS BEIRUT

AUB Archaeological
Museum

RUSTOM PASHA S

JOHN KENNEDY STREET

Bain Militaire
(Military Beach)

BLISS STREET

CLEMENCEAU STREET

American University
Hospital (AUBMC)

BLISS STREET

SIDANI STREET

Central Bank
(Banque Du Liban)
& History of
Money Museum

NAJIB ARDATI ST

SADAT STREET

YAFET

JEANNE D'ARC STREET

MAKDISSI
STREET

SOURATY STREET

RUBEIZ STREET

ROMA STREET

3

KUWAIT (CARACAS) STREET

NEHME

HAMRA

OMAR BIN ABDEL AZIZ STREET

CENTRAL BANK STREET

Luna Park

HAMRA

STREET

CAIRO
ST

AL QALAA STREET

EMILE EDDE (LYON) STREET

SPEARS

Nejmeh
Stadium

MANARA

AL HUSSEIN STREET

Concorde
Centre

DUNANT STREET

Sanayeh
Public Garden

ALAMEDDINE ST

MEDHAT PASHA STREET

GENERAL

CHATILA ST

MADAME CURIE (UNITED NATIONS) STREET

MARY EDDE ST

4

DE GAULLE AVENUE

RAFIC ARSLANE

BADR DEMECHKIYE STREET

Verdun Gardens
Shopping Centre

Tallet Fd
Druze Cemetery

ISTIKLAL
(INDEPENDENCE)

Pigeon Rocks

ABDALLAH AL MACHNOUK STREET

IBN ROUCHD STREET

ROMA

STREET

ANDALOUS

BERLIN ST

VIENNA

VERDUN

RASHID KARAMI

(VERDUN) ST

HASHIM AL KHALIL ST

5

RAOUCHE

STREET

Goodies
supermarket

BACHIR

AL RACHIDINE STREET

QASSAR ST

IMAM AB

Mövenpick Hotel & Resort
& Calypso Diving Centre

Verdun
730

RAFIC NAJA
(SCHUBERT) ST

Verdun
732

MAZRAA

MAR ELIAS STREET

N

Dunes
Centre

Salam
Mosque

Four Points
Sheraton Hotel

SAEB SALAM

Bradt

Ramlet
Al Baida

RAMLET
AL BAIDA

UNESCO

6

0   500m
0   500yds

BERNADOTTE

UNESCO

RAFIQ HARIRI AVENUE

WATA

HABIB ABI CHAHLA

For listings, see pages 140–7

Where to stay

Off map
Le Royal Hotels
& Resorts..................H3

FARID TRAD STREET

SHEIKH SABAH AL SALEM

AL-SABAH STREET

Mar Elias
Camp

GABRIEL MURR ST

7

Where to eat and drink
1 Bay Rock Café.................A4
2 Manara Palace Café........A2

UAE Embassy,
Sidon, Tyre,
the south

VENEZUELA

Spinney's

Oman

A B C D

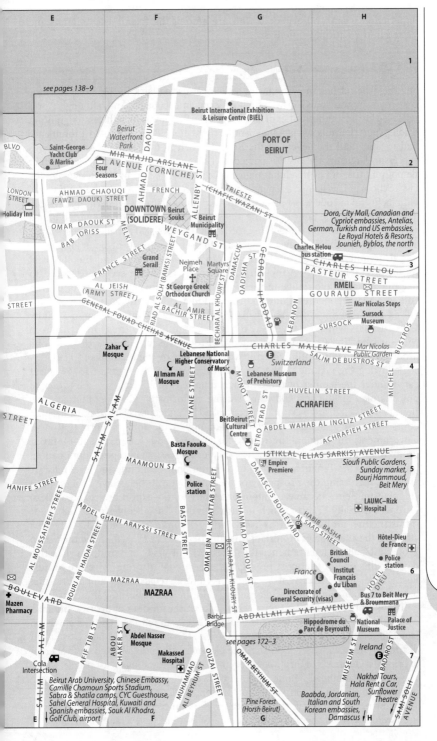

see pages 138–9

Beirut International Exhibition & Leisure Centre (BIEL)

Beirut Waterfront Park

PORT OF BEIRUT

Saint-George Yacht Club & Marina

BLVD

LONDON STREET

Holiday Inn

Four Seasons

MIR MAJID ARSLANE AVENUE (CORNICHE)

AHMAD CHAOUQI (FAWZI DAOUK) Street

AHMAD DAOUK

FRENCH

ALLENBY ST

TRIESTE (CHAFIC WAZANI) ST

DOWNTOWN (SOLIDERE)

Beirut Souks

OMAR DAOUK ST

BAB IDRISS

MELKI

FRANCE STREET

Beirut Municipality

WEYGAND ST

Grand Serail

Nejmeh Place

Martyrs' Square

RIAD AL SOLH (BANKS) STREET

St George Greek Orthodox Church

AL AMIR BACHIR STREET

AL JEISH (ARMY STREET)

AL AMIR STREET

BECHARA AL KHOURY ST

DAMASCUS

QADISHA

GEORGE HADDAD

LEBANON

Dora, City Mall, Canadian and Cypriot embassies, Antelias, German, Turkish and US embassies, Le Royal Hotels & Resorts, Jounieh, Byblos, the north

Charles Helou bus station

CHARLES HELOU PASTEUR STREET

RMEIL

GOURAUD STREET

Mar Nicolas Steps

Sursock Museum

SURSOCK

STREET

GENERAL FOUAD CHEHAB AVENUE

Zahar Mosque

Lebanese National Higher Conservatory of Music

Al Imam Ali Mosque

CHARLES MALEK AVE

Mar Nicolas Public Garden

SALIM DE BUSTROS ST

Switzerland

Lebanese Museum of Prehistory

HUVELIN STREET

ACHRAFIEH

BUSTROS

MICHEL

ALGERIA STREET

STREET

SALIM SALAM

TYANE STREET

MONOT STREET

PETRO TRAD ST

BeitBeirut Cultural Centre

ABDEL WAHAB AL INGLIZI STREET

ACHRAFIEH STREET

Basta Faouka Mosque

MAAMOUN ST

ISTIKLAL (ELIAS SARKIS) AVENUE

Empire Premiere

Siouﬁ Public Gardens, Sunday market, Bourj Hammoud, Beit Mery

HANIFE STREET

Police station

BASTA STREET

OMAR IBN AL KHATTAB STREET

DAMASCUS BOULEVARD

MUHAMMAD AL HOUT ST

HABIB BASHA AL SAAD STREET

LAUMC–Rizk Hospital

Hôtel-Dieu de France

ABDEL GHANI ARAYSSI STREET

BOURJ ABI HAIDAR STREET

AL MOUSSAITBEH STREET

MAZRAA

MAZRAA

BECHARA AL KHOURY ST

British Council

Institut Français du Liban

France

Directorate of General Security (visas)

Police station

Bus 7 to Beit Mery & Broummana

HOTEL DIEU

BOULEVARD

Mazen Pharmacy

SALIM SALAM

AFIF TIBLST

ABOU CHAKER ST

Abdel Nasser Mosque

Makassed Hospital

Barbir Bridge

ABDALLAH AL YAFI AVENUE

Hippodrome du Parc de Beyrouth

National Museum

Palace of Justice

MUSEUM STREET

Ireland

BADARO ST

Cola Intersection

Beirut Arab University, Chinese Embassy, Camille Chamoun Sports Stadium, Sabra & Shatila camps, CYC Guesthouse, Sahel General Hospital, Kuwaiti and Spanish embassies, Souk Al Khodra, Golf Club, airport

MUHAMMAD ALI BEYHUM ST

OUZOU STREET

see pages 172–3

OMAR BEYHUM ST

Pine Forest (Horsh Beirut)

Baabda, Jordanian, Italian and South Korean embassies, Damascus

Nakhal Tours, Hala Rent a Car, Sunflower Theatre

SAMI-SOLH AVENUE

Beirut

4

experience a city and a people who are among the friendliest, tolerant and varied in the entire Middle East.

HISTORICAL OVERVIEW

Although Beirut has shown signs of settlement dating back to the Stone Age, the first city-state was founded by the Phoenicians in c3000BCE. And, although it was upstaged by the southern cities of Sidon and Tyre, Beirut was nonetheless a significant trading port for this ancient mercantile civilisation. Beirut's rise to prominence had to wait until the advent of the Roman epoch in 64BCE. Thanks to Pompey's successor, Augustus, the city was named after his daughter, Julia, and given the rather flamboyant title of Colonia Julia Augustus Felix Berytus. During the Roman era the city's School of Law gained a reputation for being one of the finest in the empire, and with its Justinian code was a precursor to much of our current Western legal system. The city continued to flourish during the eastern or Byzantine Roman period until a massive earthquake and tsunami in CE551 killed some 30,000 Beirut citizens, shortly after which the School of Law was relocated to the southern city of Sidon for safety.

Beirut sunk into relative obscurity until the rise of Islam and the conquest by the Arabs in CE635. Although the Maronite Christian sect were forced to flee the city and take refuge in the Lebanese mountains, the transition to Arab rule was a largely peaceful one and ushered in a range of dynasties, which have left an indelible mark on the city. Arab rule was briefly interrupted in 1110 by the Crusaders whilst on their way to Jerusalem to liberate the Holy Land from Muslim rule. The Crusaders assumed control of Beirut, along with Lebanon's other coastal towns, until Arab rule was reinstated by the Mamluks in 1291.

Following the sacking of the Mamluk caliphate by the Turks in 1516, Beirut came under the banner of the Ottoman Empire, which remained the principal power broker for the next 400 years. During the formative years of Ottoman rule, Beirut and its environs were mainly controlled by indigenous Druze and Christian emirs who were granted considerable autonomy by the Sublime Porte (Ottoman Government) in Istanbul in return for prompt and full payment of taxes. From 1839, however, the Ottomans, wary of increasing European domination, implemented the Tanzimat, a series of constitutional, economic and legal reforms aimed at increasing the prosperity of the capital and to help stave off European colonialism. Beirut became an important centre for the export of Lebanese silk to Europe, especially France, which in turn attracted foreign investment for major infrastructure projects such as roads and telecommunications. The city also attracted the attention of Protestant Missionaries who, in 1866, founded the Syrian Protestant College, later renamed the American University of Beirut, which to this day remains one of the most prestigious educational institutions in the Middle East. Beirut also underwent a *nahda* or cultural renaissance, and the capital became a major centre for a wide-ranging printing and publishing industry.

The advent of World War I once again changed the fortunes of the city. Ottoman control had by this time reached its nadir against Arab rebellion and the governor, Jamal 'the butcher' Pasha, publicly hanged several Lebanese in 1915 in the Downtown district for siding with the Allies. An Allied blockade of the port followed, in an attempt to bring the Ottomans to their knees, together with a devastating locust plague, which engendered widespread famine. This, combined with outbreaks of bubonic plague, meant that by the end of the war tens of thousands of Beirutis had perished.

Following World War I, the European victors proceeded to divide up much of the Levant between them, and the League of Nations gave France a mandate to rule over Lebanon; its linguistic and architectural influence can still be discerned in the city today. French rule continued until 1943, when Lebanon finally gained full independence from France. The city once again became a financial, cultural and intellectual centre of the Arab world, until simmering discontent finally boiled over and culminated in the tragic events of 1975, plunging the city into a lawless state for the next 15 years. Tit-for-tat killings, a *mêlée* of foreign involvement, bombings and hostage-taking created feelings of general insecurity that percolated through the city to become a way of life for the majority of the people. After the 1989 Taif Agreement, which ended the fighting, the capital embarked on the Herculean task of reconstruction, much of it inaugurated by the country's then prime minister, Rafiq Hariri, whose initiatives have largely transformed the city into some semblance of its former prosperous self. Hariri's assassination on Valentine's Day 2005 ushered in the Cedar Revolution, a mass protest of Lebanese in the Downtown district which blamed Syria for the murder of their former prime minister and demanded the withdrawal of all Syrian military and security personnel from Lebanese territory. The following year, a month-long confrontation between Israel and Hezbollah once again threatened to destabilise the entire country. Less than two years later, widespread internal conflict and possible outright civil war between the government and Hezbollah was only narrowly averted by the signing of the Doha Agreement, on 21 May 2008. Yet, since these events, Beirut and Lebanon have enjoyed considerable stability and hopes for continued peace are high. In 2010, Lebanon received its highest ever number of visitors, with more than two million arriving in the country. With the the *New York Times* listing Beirut as the first of 44 destinations to visit in 2009 and UNESCO designating the city World Book Capital in the same year for 'emphasising cultural diversity and dialogue', it seemed that Beirut and Lebanon were at last regaining their reputation for events other than death and destruction.

TRAVEL ADVICE

At the time of writing, a heightened sense of security prevails across Lebanon, mainly due to the spillover effect from the conflict in neighbouring Syria which has seen a number of assassinations, car bombings, rocket and suicide attacks in parts of Beirut and elsewhere in the country. Consequently, the UK's Foreign and Commonwealth Office (FCO), in common with many other countries' travel guidance, 'advises against all travel to the southern suburbs of Beirut'. The areas to be avoided include south of the Camille Chamoun Sports Stadium and east of the main airport road which includes the localities of Ghobeiry, Chiah, Haret Hreik, Bourj Brajneh, Mreijeh, Roueiss and Laylakeh. Other areas to steer clear of in the southern suburbs include west of the airport road to the coast and south from Adnan Al Hakim Road to Abbass Al Moussawi Road. Whilst the Downtown district of the city is certainly not off limits to visitors, protests related to the garbage crisis (page 29) in late 2015 quickly morphed into demands for wholesale political change and, whilst not targeted at foreign visitors or tourists, these have the potential to be ongoing and have turned violent, with numerous casualties resulting from clashes between demonstrators, police and security forces. Keep up to date with all these issues via local media reports and advice from local people; and check the regularly updated travel advice from the FCO website (*www.gov.uk/foreign-travel-advice/lebanon*), or read the guidance from your own country's travel advisory service.

Beirut HISTORICAL OVERVIEW

4

Despite the Arab uprisings, which began in 2010 and which quickly resonated with many countries in the region, and with war still raging next door in Syria, Lebanon remains more shaken than stirred and, although the Syrian conflict has certainly reverberated around parts of the country, including in Beirut, the cosmopolitan and welcoming nature of the Lebanese themselves remain constant.

GETTING THERE

BY AIR Lebanon is served by numerous international airlines from major cities in Europe, the Middle East, Africa and the Far East. There was just one budget airline serving the capital at the time of writing, but the Ministry of Tourism are keen to attract low-cost carriers such as easyJet and Ryanair to Beirut, and with the former already flying to the Jordanian capital, Amman, bucket-shop deals could become a reality in the future. At present, however, there is sufficient competition among the major carriers to ensure that cut-price deals are often available, and with a little shopping around, a return airfare from London to Beirut can be obtained for around £400. In the UK, the weekly free *TNT Magazine* (*www. tntmagazine.com*) has listings for cheap flight deals. Online, it is worth browsing www.alternativeairlines.com, www.tripadvisor.co.uk, www.expedia.co.uk, www. kayak.co.uk, www.lastminute.com, www.opodo.co.uk, www.travelrepublic.co.uk, www.skyscanner.net and www.travelocity.com for the best deals.

As has been the case for many years now, there continue to be no direct flights to Beirut from/to the USA and Canada. However, the national carrier, Middle East Airlines (MEA), has code-share agreements with partners such as Air France (*www.airfrance.com*), Alitalia (*www.alitalia.com*), Delta (*www.delta. com*) and KLM (*www.klm.com*) to ensure efficient connections with many of the major cities in Canada, the USA and Beirut.

Rafiq Hariri International Airport, Beirut [127 E7] (*IATA/ICAO airport codes: BEY/OLBA;* \ *01 628 000, dial 150 from within Lebanon; www.beirutairport.gov.lb*) Lebanon's only commercial international airport is located in the southern suburbs of the city in the district of Khaldeh, some 7km from Beirut's Downtown area. It's bright and airy, and the modern interior is the result of an extensive reconstruction plan, which has totally transformed the former drab and outdated interior, and it is now used by many of the world's major international airlines. Upon arrival, formalities are usually quick and efficient. A white entry form for foreigners, available just before passport control, must be filled out with your personal and passport details, and the address of where you are staying in Lebanon. Once at passport control, your passport will be stamped with a **one-month Lebanese visa**, permitting you to stay in the country for up to two months before you need to apply for an extra one-month extension, which will allow you to stay in the country for a total of up to three months.

Once through customs and passport control, the arrivals area is very well organised. To your right are numerous car-hire companies and opposite is a duty-paid shop selling stationery, newspapers, magazines, postcards and local Alfa and touch mobile-phone services. Opposite the shop is Café Akle (\ *01 628 240;* ⊕ *24hrs daily*), serving a range of hot and cold drinks, and snacks. To your left, and facing Café Matik (⊕ *24hrs daily*), is the office of the **Ministry of Tourism** (\ *01 629 769;* e *airportoffice.mot@gmail.com;* ⊕ *08.30–19.00 Mon–Sat, closed Sun & public holidays*), which has helpful staff and a range of printed material in a variety of languages which you can take away. Across the hall from the tourist office is another duty-free shop selling confectionery, cold drinks, biscuits, tobacco and a range of fluffy toys. There are also numerous public payphones located in the arrivals hall, with a bank of seven located adjacent to the Sûreté Générale opposite Café Matik. **BankMed** (✆ *01 629 360/1/2;* m *03 760 026; www. bankmed.com.lb;* ⊕ *08.30–14.00 Mon–Fri, 08.30–noon Sat*) is the current official airport bank and they have a couple of 24hr ATMs by the arrivals hall exit.

Although there are **bus links** from the airport to the city centre, a better option, especially if you arrive in the early hours and/or have a lot of luggage, is to take a **taxi** to the city centre, west or east Beirut which should cost between US$20 and US$25, depending on your haggling abilities (pages 133–4), but be prepared to be quoted much more by the army of taxi drivers who will invariably descend upon you in arrivals! Another option is to arrange for a pre-booked hotel to organise your transfer from the airport. Most of the hotels, including the budget ones, now offer this service, which can work out cheaper than using the airport taxis. The journey time to the Downtown area of Beirut is about 15–20 minutes, depending on traffic and the time of day you arrive.

Upon departure from Beirut, a pink exit form must be completed with the same details as the white entry form. This is submitted to passport control, who will then place an exit stamp in your passport. The departures terminal is similarly very well organised and has a branch of **Libanpost** (✆ *01 629 369; www.libanpost.com;* ⊕ *08.00–20.00 Mon–Sat, 08.00–17.00 Sun*), and also a large and extremely well-stocked duty-free shop, where you can pre-order any items you wish to purchase (✆ *01 629 520 ext 276, 24hr customer service* m *03 145 465;* e *shop&collect@pac.com.lb; www.beirutdutyfree.com*).

Major airlines in Beirut

✈ **Air France (IATA airline code: AF)** [139 F4] Foch St, Downtown; ✆ 01 977 900/977; www. airfrance.com

✈ **Alitalia (AZ)** [139 F4] 170 Saad Zaghloul St, Downtown; ✆ 01 966 175/6; e customer. relationslb@alitalia.it; www.alitalia.com

✈ **British Airways (BA)** [163 F3] Block B, 10th Fl, Gefinor Centre, Clemenceau St, Hamra; ✆ 01 747 777; www.ba.com

✈ **EgyptAir (MS)** [139 E5] Riad al-Solh Sq, Downtown; ✆ 01 980 165, 01 980 465; www. egyptair.com

✈ **Emirates (EK)** [163 F3] Block D, Ground Fl, Gefinor Centre, Clemenceau St, Hamra; ✆ 01 734 500; www.emirates.com

✈ **Etihad Airways (EY)** [138 C4] Ground Fl, Zein Bldg, Omar Daouk St, Bab Idriss, Downtown; ✆ 01 989 393, 01 975 000; e beytkt@etihad.ae; www.etihad.com

✈ **Lufthansa German Airlines (LH)** [163 F3] Block B, 10th Fl, Gefinor Centre, Clemenceau St, Hamra; ✆ 01 347 007; e beyteam@dlh.de; www. lufthansa.com

✈ **Middle East Airlines-Air Liban (ME)** [163 F3; 138 D4] Gefinor Centre, Clemenceau St, Hamra; ✆ 01 629 999, dial 1330 within Lebanon (24hr customer care call centre); e salesleb@mea.aero; Abdeel Hamid-Karami St, Downtown; ✆ 01 976 976; e babidriss@mea.aero; www.mea.com.lb

✈ **Oman Air (WY)** [163 F3] Block D, Ground Fl, Gefinor Centre, Clemenceau St, Hamra; ✆ 01 753 581/2/3/4; e resbey@omanair.com; www. omanair.com

✈ **Pegasus Airlines (PC)** ✆ 01 369 869; www. flypgs.com; see ad, 3rd colour section.

✈ **Royal Jordanian Airlines (RJ)** [162 B3] Bliss St, Hamra; ✆ 01 379 990/1; e beytsrj@ rj.com; www.rj.com

BY ROAD Lebanon shares land borders with both Israel and Syria. However, in the absence of a comprehensive Middle East peace settlement, it is not possible to enter or exit Lebanon from Israel, despite Israel's military withdrawal from the majority of the south of the country in May 2000. At present, then, Syria remains the only option for direct entry to Beirut by land. Although there are both regular bus and taxi services to Beirut from the Syrian cities of Aleppo, the capital Damascus,

Hama, Homs, Latakia and Tartus, the ongoing war there means that travel to Syria, let alone from Syria to Lebanon, cannot be recommended until such time as there is a cessation of hostilities or an improvement in the overall security situation. There are also buses and taxis from Jordan arriving in Beirut, but these were suspended at the time of research, once again linked to the situation in Syria.

BY SEA For details of cruise companies visiting Beirut, see page 71.

GETTING AROUND

There is no shortage of transport options to help you get around and explore the capital, with the principal modes of transport being buses and taxis, which represent good value for money and are frequent, making most areas of the city easily accessible to the visitor. However, for those intending to do a lot of exploring, perhaps on foot or by bike, navigating the city can sometimes be a real headache. Whilst some roads and streets are named, many others are not or just give their number or a sector name denoting the city location, which is not particularly helpful for the first-time visitor. Whilst the maps in this book should meet the needs of many visitors, an additional and a very useful companion to have in hand is *Zawarib Beirut & Beyond* (*4th Fl, Mikhael Bldg, Monot St & USJ St, Yassouieh, Achrafieh;* \ *01 336 180;* m *03 079 906;* e *info@zawarib.net; www. zawarib.net;* f *zawarib*), which is akin to a *London A–Z* street map. Although the latest 2010 edition (scale: 1:4,500/1:9,000), which covers some 150km^2 of Beirut plus the outlying areas of Aley, Beit Mery, Broummana and Jounieh, is a few years old now, it remains a useful and detailed navigational tool. The same company produces a series of seasonally updated and free pocket-sized fold-out pamphlets covering most areas of the city of interest to visitors, from Ras Beirut in the west to Downtown, Gemmayze, Achrafieh, Mar Mikhael and Bourj Hammoud districts in the east. The pamphlets should be available at the Ministry of Tourism office in Hamra (page 135) and at many hotels, especially those in the budget category; on the author's last visit, Pension al-Nazih (page 144) and Saifi Urban Gardens (page 143) both had a plentiful supply. The book also contains a directory of emergency and useful telephone numbers, a bus map and a list of banks, foreign embassies, government departments and hospitals along with their telephone details. Available in bookshops throughout the capital and by international mail order, it costs LBP18,000 (*US$12*). Stanford's travel bookshop in London (page 344) is also a stockist, with mail order available (*£13.99*).

BY BUS A comprehensive network of buses operates in the capital, serving most areas of interest to the visiting tourist. Although they are often crowded affairs and not always the quickest way of getting around the city, they are the cheapest, with the current maximum fare at the time of writing to almost any destination within Beirut costing no more than LBP1,000, making the buses ideal for the budget traveller. The buses run daily, generally from around 05.30 until mid–late evening, departing at regular intervals every 10–15 minutes. The downside to the buses is the general lack of published timetable and specific route information, with many buses displaying these details and their number in Arabic only. For a comprehensive list of buses and their routes within Beirut and environs, see box, pages 136–7.

Bus stations Beirut's network of buses is complemented by three main bus stations, or hubs, which double as taxi waiting areas, with each tending to be set up to serve specific destinations within Lebanon and to some countries beyond. For some buses you may have to wait until the bus (or taxi) fills up before departing, though this does not necessarily mean a long wait.

Charles Helou [172 B2] (*Charles Helou Av, Rmeil, a short walk east of Downtown*) Named after a former Lebanese president, this bus station is just a few minutes' walk east from Downtown, but this busy, drab and grey-looking terminus is anything but stately and is long overdue a facelift. Clearly signposted in French 'Gare Routière Charles Helou', with its Arabic equivalent alongside, the station is, however, quite well organised compared with the others, and serves for transport to areas north of the capital, along with buses and taxis to a number of international destinations including Jordan and Syria. There are a number of companies who operate services, and they have ticket booths where you can purchase your ticket in advance of travel. Timetables were, with a few exceptions, scarce at the time of writing – it is best just to ask at one of the ticket booths – but services to all destinations are plentiful and frequent. The station also has a money exchange bureau and a couple of cafés serving the usual range of refreshments.

Charles Helou bus station is divided into three clearly signposted zones based on the destinations served: **Zone A** is for buses and taxis to Jordan (suspended at the time of research), and Syria (Damascus, Hama, Homs, Latakia and Tartus); **Zone B** for buses to Syria, and Lebanon's second city of Tripoli; and **Zone C** for bus and taxi services to Byblos, Jounieh, Tripoli and Syria (only by taxi at the time of writing to Damascus (*LBP30,000*), Homs (*LBP40,000*), Latakia (*LBP40,000*) and Tartus (*LBP30,000*)).

Cola intersection [127 E7] (*Pl de la Resistance et de la Liberation, Salim Salam St, Wata*) More open-plan and chaotic than Charles Helou, Cola is generally for buses, minivans, service taxis and taxis to destinations in southern Lebanon including the Chouf (Kfarhim, Beiteddine, Baakline), Sidon and Tyre. Minivans and taxis, however, also travel to destinations in the Bekaa Valley (Chtaura, Baalbek, Zahlé), and you can also find buses and vans travelling to Jounieh, Byblos and Tripoli.

Dora [173 H2] (*Dora Hwy, Bourj Hammoud*) A little more remote than the other stations, Dora is a large, busy roundabout beneath a flyover, a short distance past the imposing Forum de Beyrouth building on your left if approaching from the west, and is festooned with banks and cheap eateries, as well as of course dozens of taxis, buses and minivans. Dora, like Charles Helou, serves destinations north of Beirut including Jounieh, Byblos, Amchit, Bcharré and Tripoli.

BY TAXI Taxis – with **red number plates** – are everywhere and a good way to travel around the city as they cover all areas of the capital and operate on the usual hail-and-ride principle. You basically have three choices: a taxi, a *servees* (collective/shared) taxi or a *serviceain*. With the first option you flag down a taxi and ask for 'taxi', agreeing a price to your destination before getting inside the car. The fare for journeys to most places within the city should be around LBP5,000–10,000. To outlying suburbs the cost can be anywhere between LBP10,000 and LBP20,000. The cheaper option is to flag down a passing taxi and ask for *servees* to your destination and, once again, agree the price before setting off. Unlike with a taxi, the driver is at liberty to pick up and put down passengers *en route*, but the upside is that you often get the opportunity to chat to the locals. The current cost of a *servees* taxi within the central Beirut area is LBP2,000, but can be more if travelling to more outlying areas of the city, in which case a *serviceain* fare will apply, which equates to twice the price of a servees (*LBP4,000*).

If you wish to pre-book a taxi, the following selection of companies all have good reputations, but it is still a good idea to agree the price to your destination over the phone before confirming your booking. Some of these companies can also arrange car hire and tours around the country.

🚕 **Allo Taxi** 📞 01 517 030, dial the hotline 1213 within Lebanon; e callcenter@allotaxi. com; www.allotaxi.com.lb. Operating 24hrs daily, this large & well-established company is a good & efficient option.

🚕 **Charlie Taxi** 📞 01 285 710; m 03 285 710; e operations@charlietaxi.com; www. charlietaxi.com

🚕 **Lebanon Taxi** Hamra; 📞 01 353 153; e lebanontaxi1955@gmail.com; www. lebanontaxi.com

🚕 **Trust Taxi** Sassine St, nr Hotel Dieu, Achrafieh; 📞 01 613 573, 01 613 398; m 03 601 806; e info@trust-taxi.com; www.trust-taxi.com

🚕 **White Taxi** Sin El Fil; 📞 01 513 593; m 71 722 199; e reservation@whitetaxi.me; www.whitetaxi.me

CAR HIRE

Renting a car in Beirut couldn't be easier as there are plenty of companies offering the service, both with and without a driver. Whichever firm you choose, you will need to be over 21 years old (in some cases over 23) and have a valid – preferably international – driving licence. Car hire is a great alternative to a taxi if you are planning an extended tour of the country, but not really worth your while (or your sanity) for travelling around the capital's congested streets: in Beirut, stick to taxis and buses. The following list of agencies is far from exhaustive, but represents those companies that have good reputations and deliver reliable and friendly service. Rates can start for a small car from around US$30 per day rising to US$300+ for a luxury vehicle with all the bells and whistles. In all cases it is best to check whether insurance is included in the price of car hire.

🚗 **Advanced Car Rental** [139 F6] Azarieh Bldg, Downtown; 📞 01 999 884/5; m 70 151 510; e rent@advancedcarrent.com; www. advancedcarrent.com

🚗 **Avis** [163 H2] Ain Mreisse, inside the Phoenicia Hotel; 📞 01 363 848; e beyhotels@ avislebanon.com, reservations@avislebanon.com; www.avis.com.lb. See the Avis website for details of additional branches in the capital.

🚗 **Budget** [127 E7] Airport, arrivals hall; 📞 01 629 890; e airport.budget@budget.com.lb; www.budget.com.lb

🚗 **City Car** [127 E7] Airport, arrivals hall; 📞 01 629 900; m 03 629 900; e citycar@citycar.com.lb; www.citycar.com.lb

🚗 **Europcar-Lena Car** [127 E7] Airport, arrivals hall; 📞 01 629 888; m 03 670 323; e airport@ europcar.com.lb; www.europcarlebanon.com

🚗 **Hala Rent a Car** [127 H7] Sami El Solh Av, Badaro; 📞 01 381 345; m 03 272 817; e rent@ halacar.com; www.halarentacar.com

🚗 **Hertz** [127 H7] Sami El Solh St, Badaro; 📞 01 427 283; e hertz@cyberia.net.lb; www.hertz. com. They also have an office in the arrivals hall at the airport (📞 01 628 999).

BY BIKE

With an awareness of the growing problem of congestion and pollution in the city, and people wishing to get and keep fit, cycling is becoming increasingly popular. You will see many cyclists around the Corniche: the 'classic' bike route is from Ain Mreisse and along the Corniche all the way to Raouche, and beyond. The following companies rent out bikes and/or organise city tours.

🚲 **Beirut by Bike** [163 F2] Abdel Nasser St (behind the mosque), Ain Mreisse; 📞 01 365 524; m 03 435 524, 71 435 524, 76 435 524; e info@ beirutbybike.com; www.beirutbybike.com;

f BeirutByBike; ⏰ 08.00–midnight daily. This family-friendly company has bikes & accessories available for hire (LBP7,000/hr, LBP14,000/2hrs & LBP50,000/day), catering for all age groups, &

also organises biking events around the city, often in aid of good causes. A night bike ride takes place every Fri night between 20.00 and 22.00. They also have 2 other branches in the Downtown area at the entrance to the Beirut International Exhibition & Leisure Centre (BIEL) & at Beirut Souks. Keep an eye on their website for details of upcoming cycle events.

Bike Generation [172 D7] Elias Hrawi St, nr Beit al-Tabib, Tahwita, Furn Al-Chebbak; ☎01 398 442; m 70 885 969; e bikinfo@bikegeneration-me.com; www.bikegeneration-me.com; ⊕ 10.00–20.00 Mon–Fri, 08.00–20.00 Sat. Bike shop stocking an extensive range of leading brands of pedal power. They also arrange cycling tours &

have an excellent servicing department for spares & repairs. *Bike hire: LBP5,000/hr & LBP22,500/day for mountain bikes; LBP10,000/hr & LBP45,000/day for road bikes; helmet rental LBP5,000/day.*

Cyclosport [172 B2; 139 H6] Gouraud St, Gemmayze; ☎01 446 792; m 03 613 215; e info@cyclosportlb.com; www.cyclosportlb.com; ⊕ 10.00–22.00 daily. This long-established & respected shop offers a wide range of pedal power from road to mountain bikes which can be rented by the hour for LBP7,000 & by the day for LBP30,000 including helmet. They also run a cycling club catering to both the beginner & seasoned bike rider with regular cycling events organised. *Bike hire: LBP7,000/hr, LBP30,000/day inc helmet.*

BY FOOT Beirut's compact size makes it an ideal city to explore by foot, though the summer heat and humidity can be uncomfortable. Walking either early in the morning or late afternoon can make travel by foot more bearable. Seeing the city this way also has the advantage of bypassing the capital's often congested traffic, especially around the narrow roads of the Hamra area in west Beirut. Any concerns you may have about street crime are unwarranted as Beirut is an incredibly safe city to walk around, day or night, and you will feel safer here than in many western cities such as London or New York. Pages 161–76 provide pointers to the main areas of interest in the city which you can reach by foot. Although their organised walks were suspended at the time of writing pending an improvement in the overall security situation, **BeBeirut** (m *70 156 673;* e *walk@bebeirut.org; www.bebeirut.org*) – who commenced walking tours of the city in April 2009, taking in areas not on the 'normal' tourist trail, from Yasser Arafat's once café of choice to the little-explored Jewish quarter – gave an edifying view of the city by local people who actually live there. Founded by Ronnie Chatah, a graduate of the American University of Beirut (AUB) and son of former finance minister Muhammad Chatah (1951–2013), who was killed by a car bomb on 27 December 2013, the company's previous 4-hour 'WalkBeirut' tours of the city, in English, are highly recommended for first-time visitors. The tours formerly ran weekly, on Sunday from 14.00 to 18.00, leaving from the Gefinor Centre in Hamra, near the offices of Middle East Airlines. The cost of the walk was LBP30,000 (*US$20*), including a map of the walking tour area. Note that children must be over 12 years of age and the euro is not accepted for payment. It could be worth keeping an eye on their website to check the latest information regarding the possible resumption of these walks.

Fortunately, **Alternative Tour Beirut** (m *71 273 712;* e *alternativebeirut@gmail. com;* f *alternativetourbeirut*) have filled the organised walking void and offer off-the-beaten-track walking tours of the city every Saturday (*LBP25,000 pp; approx. 4hr duration*) from noon til 16.00, meeting by the Mar Nicolas Steps [172 C3] in Gemmayze, near the Le Chef restaurant.

TOURIST INFORMATION

Lebanon's official Ministry of Tourism Office is based in Hamra [163 F4] (*550 Central Bank St;* ☎*01 343 073, 01 340 940/1/2/3/4, Tourist Hotline, dial 1735 within Lebanon;* e *info@destinationlebanon.gov.lb, mot@destinationlebanon.gov.lb; www. destinationlebanon.gov.lb, www.mot.gov.lb;* ⊕ *08.00–15.00 Mon–Thu, 08.00–13.00*

BUS 1: HAMRA–KHALDEH Caracas, Radio Liban, Bristol Hotel, Verdun, UNESCO, Cola roundabout, Sports City, Bir Hassan, Airport Bridge, Ghobeiry, Moucharafieh, Kafa'at, Lebanese University, Kfarshima, Choueifat, Khaldeh

BUS 2: HAMRA–ANTELIAS Hamra (Emile Edde St), Radio Liban, Tallet Al Druze, Mar Elias, Sassine Square, Rmeil, Mar Mikhael, Jdeideh, Nahr Al Maut, Zalka, Jal Al Dib, Antelias

BUS 4: AUH (AMERICAN UNIVERSITY HOSPITAL)–CHOUEIFAT AUH, Wardieh, Radio Liban, Sanayeh, Riad Al Solh, Tayouneh, Chiah, Mar Mikhael Church, Kafa'at, Lebanese University

BUS 5: AIN MREISSE–CHOUEIFAT Ain Mreisse, Manara, Bain Militaire, Raouche, Verdun, UNESCO, Cola roundabout, Shatila roundabout, Rassoul Al Aazam, Cocodi, Mreijeh, Airport roundabout, Hay Al Seloum, Choueifat

BUS 5: RADIO LIBAN–FANAR Radio Liban, Tallet Al Druze, Mar Elias, Sassine, Corniche Al Nahr, Jdeideh, Fanar

BUS 6: COLA–JBAIL (BYBLOS) Cola roundabout, Barbir, National Museum (Mathaf), Fiat Bridge, Corniche Al Nahr, Dora roundabout, Nahr Al Maut, Zalka, Jal Al Dib, Antelias, Dbayeh, Jounieh, Maameltein, Boire, Nahr Ibrahim, Jbail (Byblos)

BUS 7: NATIONAL MUSEUM (MATHAF)–BHARSAF National Museum (Mathaf), Fiat, Jisr Al Wati, Hayek, Mkalles, Mansourieh, Montazah, Monteverde, Ain Saade, Beit Mery roundabout, Broummana, Baabdat, Bhannes, Dahr Al Sowan, Bharsaf

Fri–Sat). The Ministry also has an office in the arrivals hall at Beirut airport (\ *01 629 769;* e *airportoffice.mot@gmail.com;* ⊕ *08.30–19.00 Mon–Sat, closed Sun & public holidays*), where visitors can obtain information on all regions of the country and advice from the helpful staff. In addition to their range of brochures and pamphlets, the Ministry also produce some weightier tomes with extended listings of hotels, cafés and restaurants, and other useful contact information. Ask them for a copy of their annual *Lebanon Tourism Guide*, which provides information in a slimmer, pocket-sized format. Their generally excellent website also provides a wealth of information for all regions of the country which can help you to plan and tailor your visit to your own interests, though the website could be updated a little more frequently. There are also local tourist information offices in Baalbek, Batroun, Byblos (Jbail), Jeita Grotto, Niha, Sidon (Saida), Tripoli (Trablous) and Zahlé (for further details, see the respective regional chapters).

LOCAL TOUR OPERATORS

Barakat Travel & Holidays [139 E6] Block A2, Ground Fl, Azarieh Bldg, Downtown; \01 972 111; m 70 972 111; e tours@barakat.travel; www. barakat.travel. A well-respected company offering competitively priced (*US$40–50*) full-day tours to all of Lebanon's major sites including Baalbek, Byblos, Jeita Grotto, the Chouf & Bekaa Valley wineries, plus their Panoramic City Tour of Beirut (*US$40*).

BUS 8: AUH (AMERICAN UNIVERSITY HOSPITAL)–AIN SAADE Al Riyadi Sporting Club, Hamra, Radio Liban, Tallet Al Druze, Mar Elias, Bechara Al Khoury, Sassine Square, Corniche Al Nahr, Jdeideh, Fanar, Ain Saade

BUS 9: BARBIR–NAHR AL MAUT Barbir, National Museum (Mathaf), Chevrolet, Sin El Fil roundabout, Mkalles roundabout, Hayek roundabout, Salome roundabout, Dekwaneh, Sabtieh, Jdeideh, Nahr Al Maut

BUS 12: HAMRA–BOURJ BRAJNEH Wardieh (Hamra), Radio Liban, Tallet Al Druze, Mar Elias, Cola roundabout, Shatila, Moucharafieh, Haret Hreik, Bourj Brajneh

BUS 14: COLA–QMATIYE Cola roundabout, Shatila, Tayouneh, Chevrolet, Galerie Semaan, Al Sayad, Hazmieh, Yarze, Jamhour, Aaraya, Kahaleh, Aley, Qmatiye

BUS 15: COLA–QMATIYE Cola roundabout, Sports City, Bir Hassan, Moucharafieh, Mar Mikhael Church, Galerie Semaan, Al Sayad, Hazmieh, Yarze, Jamhour, Aaraya, Kahaleh, Aley, Qmatiye

BUS 15: AIN MREISSE–DORA Ain Mreisse, Manara, Al Riyadi Sporting Club, Raouche, Verdun, UNESCO, Cola, Barbir, National Museum (Mathaf), Fiat, Jisr Al Wati, Salome, Dekwaneh, Sabtieh, Jdeideh, Dora

BUS 24: RADIO LIBAN (HAMRA)–NATIONAL MUSEUM (MATHAF) Radio Liban, Bristol Hotel, Verdun, UNESCO, Cola, Barbir, National Museum (Mathaf)

BUS A: DORA–AIRPORT Dora, Quarantina (Hwy), Martyrs' Square, Bechara Al Khoury, Barbir, Shatila, Rassoul Al Aazam, Cocodi, Mreijeh, Airport

Cleopatra Tours Tayouneh; ✆ 01 393 969, 01 393 919; m 03 727 286; e info@cleopatratours. com; www.cleopatratours.com. Runs excellent & wide-ranging tours.

Concord Travel [163 E4] 8th Fl, Saroulla Bldg, Hamra St, Hamra; ✆ 01 730 074; m 03 334 337; e tours@concordtravel.com.lb; www.concordtravel. com.lb. Tour operator offering individual & group daily & extended tours (inc special Honeymoon packages) throughout Lebanon, plus tours combined with Jordan & Syria. They can also assist with airport transfer, hotel, apartment bookings & civil marriage ceremonies for Lebanese couples in Cyprus.

Esprit Nomade Adventures m 03 223 552; e coord@esprit-nomade.com, nomade@ esprit-nomade.com; www.esprit-nomade.com. Specialist ecotourism operator.

Kurban Tours Downtown; ✆ 01 368 958; m 03 510 333; e info@kurbantours.com; www. kurbantours.com. Excellent-value nationwide

tours taking in all the highlights of Lebanon. As a destination management company, they also specialise in events & group tours for business.

Lebanese Adventure m 03 214 989/234 178; e infos@lebanese-adventure.com; www.lebanese-adventure.com. As its name suggests, specialises in w/end activity-based tours inc trekking, camping, hiking & rafting all over the country.

Lena Tours & Travel Ground Fl, St George's Centre, Sin El Fil; ✆ 01 496 696; m 03 670 321; e info@lenatours.com, res.supervisor@lenatours. com; www.lenatours.com. A one-stop shop for countrywide tours, car hire & hotel bookings for business & leisure travellers.

Liban Trek ✆ 01 329 975; m 03 291 616; e info@libantrek.com; www.libantrek.com. Founded in 1997, this is Lebanon's first ecotourism operator, providing a regular & varied countrywide programme of birdwatching, camping, biking, hiking, caving, skiing, snowshoeing, etc.

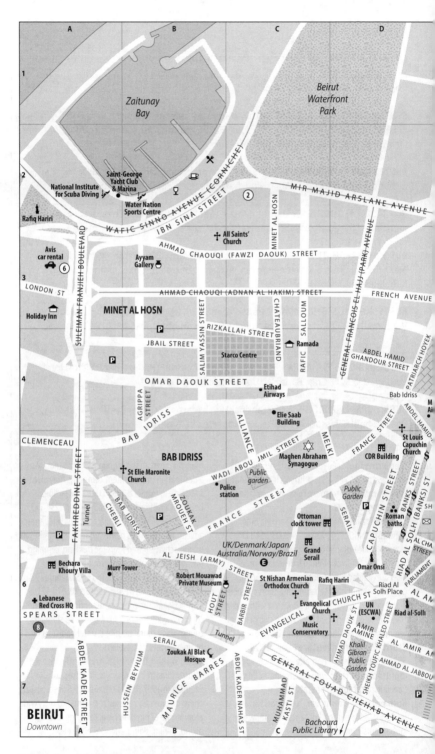

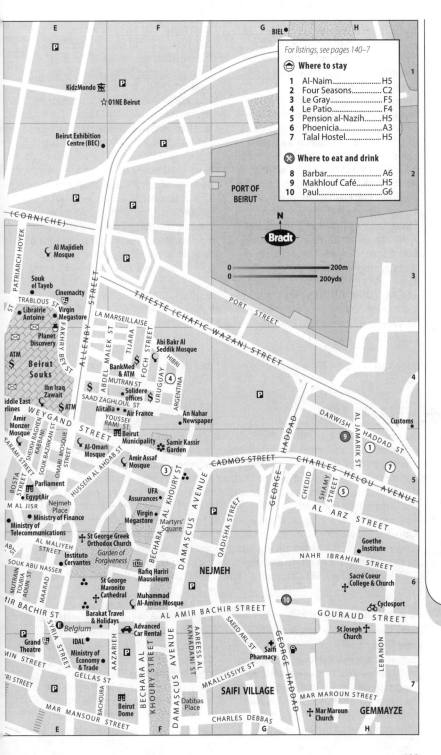

For listings, see pages 140–7

Where to stay

1	Al-Naim	H5
2	Four Seasons	C2
3	Le Gray	F5
4	Le Patio	F4
5	Pension al-Nazih	H5
6	Phoenicia	A3
7	Talal Hostel	H5

Where to eat and drink

8	Barbar	A6
9	Makhlouf Café	H5
10	Paul	G6

N

Bradt

| 0 | | 200m |
| 0 | | 200yds |

BIEL

PORT OF BEIRUT

KidzMondo
☆ 01NE Beirut

Beirut Exhibition
Centre (BEC)

(CORNICHE)

Al Majidieh
Mosque

Souk
el Tayeb
Cinemacity

TRABLOUS ST
Librairie
Antoine
Virgin
Megastore

Planet
Discovery

ATM

Beirut
Souks

Ibn Iraq
Zawait

iddle East
rlines

Amir
Monzer
Mosque

WEYGAND STREET

Parliament

EgyptAir
Nejmeh
Place
Ministry of Finance

Ministry of
Telecommunications

AL MALIYEH
STREET
Instituto
Cervantes

Barakat Travel
& Holidays

Belgium

IDAL
Grand
Theatre

Ministry of
Economy
& Trade

GELLAS ST

Beirut
Dome

MAR MANSOUR STREET

LA MARSEILLAISE

TRIESTE (CHAFIC WAZAN) STREET

PORT STREET

Abi Bakr Al
Seddik Mosque

BankMed
& ATM

MUTRAN ST
Solidere
offices

Alitalia
Air France

An Nahar
Newspaper

Beirut
Municipality

Al-Omari
Mosque

Amir Assaf
Mosque

Samir Kassir
Garden

CADMOS STREET

UFA
Assurances

Virgin
Megastore
Martyrs'
Square

St George Greek
Orthodox Church

Garden of
Forgiveness

Rafiq Hariri
Mausoleum

St George
Maronite
Cathedral

Muhammad
Al-Amine Mosque

NEJMEH

AL AMIR BACHIR STREET

Advanced
Car Rental

SAIFI VILLAGE

Dabbas
Place

CHARLES DEBBAS

DARWISH

Customs

CHARLES HELOU AVENUE

AL ARZ STREET

NAHR IBRAHIM STREET

Goethe
Institute

Sacré Coeur
College & Church

GOURAUD STREET

Cyclosport

St Joseph
Church

Saifi
Pharmacy

MAR MAROUN STREET

Mar Maroun
Church

GEMMAYZE

139

Nadia Travel & Tourism New Jdeideh, Monte Lebanon Centre;☎ 01 887 878; m 03 220 398; e nadiatravel@nadiatravel.com; www. nadiatravel.com. A good range of full- & half-day tours of the main sites.

Nakhal Tours [127 H7] Du Parc Bldg, Sami Solh Av, Badaro, nr the National Museum;☎ 01 382 444, 01 389 389, dial 1270 within Lebanon; m 03 234 747; e dailytours@nakhal.com.lb; www.nakhal. com. One of Lebanon's long-established operators (since 1959) conducting year-round daily tours to Lebanon's main attractions the length & breadth of the country. Both half- & full-day tours are offered accompanied by multi-lingual guides (Arabic, English, French & Turkish). Highly recommended & excellent value including lunch with all full-day tours. For Lebanese couples they can also take care of all the arrangements for civil marriages in Cyprus.

Tania Travel [162 D3] Sidani St, Hamra;☎ 01 739 682; m 03 686 121, 03 976 757; e taniahamra@ taniatravel.com; www.taniatravel.com. Daily tours visiting Aanjar, Baalbek, Bcharré, Cedars, Jeita Grotto, Byblos, Beiteddine, Sidon & Tyre. From US$75 including transport, lunch, guide & admission fees to sites. Excellent value.

Wild Discovery [172 C2] Pasteur Bldg, Pasteur St, Gemmayze;☎ 01 565 646, 01 444 744 (Corporate dept); m 03 852 815; e info@wilddiscovery.com. lb; www.wilddiscovery.com.lb. Offers an excellent & competitively priced selection of half- & full-day tours for individuals & groups, taking in all of Lebanon's main & less-visited sites, with private & bespoke tours also available. As part of its ever-expanding portfolio, this dynamic company can also devise the full-range of travel services for corporate & other organisational bodies. Highly recommended.

LOCAL TOUR GUIDES The following friendly and knowledgeable freelance multi-lingual guides based in Beirut both have a Masters degree in Archaeology, 15 years' experience and are fully licensed by the Ministry of Tourism to conduct guided tours nationwide.

Dana Nasr m 03 740 268; e dananasr.mot@ gmail.com

Hala Mansour m 03 921 774; e halamansour. mot@gmail.com

WHERE TO STAY

As the capital city, Beirut obviously has the greatest number and variety of accommodation offerings and its ever-evolving hospitality industry now caters to the whole gamut of visitors ranging from the business executive, the well-heeled tourist, families with children of all ages to the backpacker travelling on a shoestring budget. The Corniche, Downtown and Achrafieh districts of the city tend to proliferate with the luxury chain and boutique hotels, whilst the Hamra district in west Beirut has the majority of the mid-range and budget offerings and is nicely located for the American University of Beirut (AUB), shopping, cafés, restaurants, art galleries and theatres. At the lower end of the market, the Gemmayze and port areas have a decent selection of hostels offering cheap rooms and dorms for the backpacker and is convenient for the Charles Helou bus and taxi station and just a short stroll from the Downtown area.

LUXURY

✻ ⌂ **Four Seasons Hotel** [138 C2] (230 rooms & suites) 1418 Professor Wafic Sinno Av, Minet Al-Hosn;☎ 01 761 000; e reservations.bei@ fourseasons.com; www.fourseasons.com/beirut; see ad, 3rd colour section. This towering hotel, affording wonderful ocean & city views opposite Zaitunay Bay & an easy stroll from Downtown, offers all you would expect from this chain – classy, homely & ultra-luxurious rooms & excellent rooftop pool (May–

Oct), spa & attentive service. With state-of-the-art business & conference facilities & a range of services for children, this hotel is an excellent choice for solo travellers, couples, corporate visitors & families alike. $$$$$

⌂ **Gefinor Rotana** [163 F3] (159 rooms & suites) Clemenceau St, Hamra;☎ 01 371 888; e gefinor.hotel@rotana.com; www.rotana.com. An excellent & luxurious hotel well suited to business travellers, with extensive business &

conference facilities, easy access to Downtown & the Hamra district. Good leisure facilities & a scenic rooftop pool. **$$$$$**

🏠 **Hotel Albergo** [172 A4] (33 suites) 137 Abdel Wahab Al Inglizi St, Achrafieh; 📞 01 339 797; e albergobeirut@albergobeirut. com, albergo@relaischateaux.com; www. albergobeirut.com. For those seeking luxury with individuality, this boutique hotel offers it in spades. The rooms, each with its own character, have been meticulously & individually furnished. More sedately & nicely located than most, the hotel also has a small but great rooftop pool with an adjacent bar & lounge area surrounded by greenery. A delightful place you won't easily forget with its equally memorable Al Dente restaurant (page 144). **$$$$$**

🏠 **Le Bristol** [163 E6] (151 rooms & suites) Rue Madame Curie, Verdun; 📞 01 351 400; e sales@lebristol-hotel.com; www.lebristol-hotel. com. This longstanding & popular hotel, ideal for business & leisure visitors alike, has previously hosted the likes of Prince Albert of Monaco, Emperor Haile Selassie & Dizzy Gillespie. It re-opened in June 2015 following a 2-year cUS$30 million refurbishment, which retains its classical opulence alongside a newfound modernity. State-of-the-art conference facilities for 1000+ delegates, rooftop swimming pool & a good selection of restaurants. **$$$$$**

🏠 **Le Commodore** [162 D4] (204 rooms & suites) Commodore St, Hamra; 📞 01 734 700/734; e info@lecommodorehotel.com; www. lecommodorehotel.com. A landmark hotel that was home from home for foreign journalists during the 1975–90 civil war, this is a much-renovated but still excellent 5-star option in the centre of Hamra for both business & leisure travellers, with a range of facilities you would expect for the price such as outdoor swimming pool, spa, business meeting rooms & a range of Lebanese & international culinary options. **$$$$$**

🏠 **Le Gray** [139 F5] (87 rooms & suites) Martyrs' Sq, Downtown; 📞 01 971 111, 01 962 828; e info@ legray.com, reservations@legray.com; www.legray. com, www.campbellgrayhotels.com. In an excellent central Downtown location, this boutique offering from hotelier Gordon Campbell Gray evokes colourful minimalist chic with all the luxurious accoutrements you would expect, such as rooftop pool & Bar 360 affording panoramic views of the city. Ideal for business travellers & tourists. **$$$$$**

🏠 **Le Patio Hotel** [139 F4] (41 rooms & suites) Uruguay St, Marfa, Downtown; 📞 01 999 209; e info@le-patiohotel.com; www.le-patiohotel. com. A luxurious boutique hotel situated adjacent to the souks & other attractions of the Downtown area. Tastefully decorated rooms with all the bells & whistles you would expect for the price. Amenities for guests include a compact rooftop pool & bar during the summer months offering panoramic views of the city, plus sauna, health club & an all-day restaurant serving local & international cuisine. B/fast is an extra US$22, free Wi-Fi. **$$$$$**

🏠 **Le Royal Hotels & Resorts** [127 H3] (231 rooms & suites) Leisure Hills Complex, Dbayeh; 📞 04 555 555, 04 555 030/032/034; e info@ leroyalbeirut.com, reservation@leroyalbeirut. com; www.leroyalbeirut.com, www.leroyal.com. An imposing & classically furnished luxurious hotel on the outskirts of the city, ideal for business travellers, with excellent facilities as well as a ballroom adjoining the 20,000m² **Watergate Aqua Park** for families. Conveniently located for Byblos, Casino du Liban & Jeita Grotto. **$$$$$**

🏠 **Le Vendôme Beirut** [163 G2] (73 rooms & suites) Minet Al-Hosn, Ain Mreisse; 📞 01 369 280; e levendome@levendomebeirut. com; www.levendomebeirut.com. Scenically located overlooking the Corniche, this recently renovated, luxurious boutique hotel has a classic French flavour & feel. **$$$$$**

🏠 **O Monot Hotel** [172 A3] (41 rooms & suites) Monot St, Saifi; 📞 01 338 777; e omonot@omonot. com, reservations@omonot.com; www.omonot. com; see ad, 3rd colour section. This luxury boutique offering, a stone's throw from Downtown & round the corner from Monot Theatre & the Lebanese Museum of Pre-history, has commanding views over the city from its lovely rooftop bar & pool, ultra-modern & spacious rooms all the facilities you would expect backed up by excellent customer service from the friendly staff. An excellent choice for business & leisure visitors. **$$$$$**

🏠 **Palm Beach Hotel** [163 H1] (87 rooms & suites) Ain Mreisse; 📞 01 372 000; e info@ palmbeachbeirut.com; www.palmbeachbeirut. com. There is no denying this hotel is in a great location, overlooking the Corniche with fantastic Mediterranean vistas. It has recently undergone a much-needed refurbishment with a much improved business centre for up to 80 people & a superb rooftop pool with bar & lounge area. **$$$$$**

Phoenicia Hotel [138 A3; 163 H2] (506 rooms & suites) Minet Al-Hosn, Downtown; 01 369 110; e phoenicia@phoeniciabeirut. com; www.phoeniciabeirut.com, www.ihg.com. A favourite of well-heeled Gulf Arabs & the venue for many a high-profile political meeting, this marble adorned hotel is in a great location & oozes luxury, with terrifically spacious & recently refurbished rooms & great sea views. Presidential Suite US$4,500 per night inc b/fast. **$$$$$**

Raouché Arjaan by Rotana [162 A5] (175 rooms & suites) Raouche Bd, Raouche; 01 781 111; e raouche.arjaan@rotana.com; www. rotana.com. Another excellent hotel from the Rotana chain with all their usual high-quality business & leisure facilities including rooftop pool & in a great location overlooking the Mediterranean & Pigeon Rocks. **$$$$$**

Riviera Hotel [162 A2] (120 rooms & suites) Av de Paris, Corniche El Manara; 01 373 210; e info@rivierahotel.com.lb, sales@ rivierahotel.com.lb; www.rivierahotel.com. lb. First opened in 1956, the name & ambience continue to evoke the era when Beirut was a hedonist's playground, nowhere more apparent than its famed Beach Lounge, reached by underground walkway beneath the Corniche, which has swimming pools, jacuzzi & sun beds, with jet skiing & scuba diving available. Recently renovated to a more contemporary style with state-of-the-art business facilities. **$$$$$**

Villa Clara [173 F2] (7 rooms) Khenchara St, Mar Mikhael; 70 995 739; e olivier@villaclara.fr; www.villaclara.fr. Very chic, very French & very nicely located for the entertainment & nightlife in nearby Mar Mikhael. The hotel's restaurant serves excellent French cuisine, completing the package & making this a good choice for an extended stay. B/fast inc, free Wi-Fi. **$$$$$**

UPMARKET AND MID RANGE

Lancaster Tamar Hotel [172 D7] (151 rooms & suites) Bd General Emile Lahoud, Hazmieh; 05 458 000; e info@lancastertamar. com, sales@lancaster.com.lb; www.lancaster.com. lb/tamar. A bright & warm hotel offering excellent business & leisure facilities & attentive service. Good location for the airport, Downtown & local shopping malls. Good value, inc comprehensive buffet b/fast. Free Wi-Fi. **$$$$**

35 Rooms [163 E4] (35 rooms, suites & penthouse) Baalbek St, Hamra; 01 345 676; m 70 444 688; e stay@35rooms.com; www.35rooms.com. This hotel won't be to everyone's taste with its over-the-top, garishly decorated, though spotlessly clean, rooms with AC & Wi-Fi, but it's in a terrific central Hamra location. **$$$**

Casa D'Or Hotel [162 D4] (82 rooms & suites) Jeanne D'Arc St, Hamra; 01 347 850, 01 746 400; m 03 348 300; e casador@cyberia.net.lb; www.casadorhotel.com. Long-established hotel in the heart of Hamra, the rooms are functional & clean with AC & TV, though unremarkable, given the price. Location is this hotel's greatest asset. Buffet b/fast inc, free Wi-Fi. **$$$**

Embassy Hotel [162 D4] (50 rooms) Makdissi St, opposite Libanpost, Hamra; 01 340 814; m 03 242 281; e info@embassyhotellebanon.com, reservations@embassyhotellebanon.com; www. embassyhotellebanon.com. A clean & adequate mid range offering in a great central Hamra location but the rooms, all with AC & TV, are quite ordinary & in need of a makeover considering the price. B/fast US$9, Wi-Fi US$4/hr or US$15/day. **$$$**

Hayete Guesthouse [172 C4] (4 rooms) Furn Al-Hayek St, Achrafieh; 01 331 530; m 70 271 530; e info@hayete-guesthouse.com; www. hayete-guesthouse.com. A good alternative to mainstream hotels, this guesthouse provides charming, individually decorated & clean rooms in a good location for the bars & nightlife of Achrafieh & Gemmayze. All rooms have AC, & laundry facilities & b/fast are available. Free Wi-Fi. **$$$**

Lancaster Hotel [162 B7] (100 rooms & suites) Australia St, Raouche; 01 790 810; m 70 337 000; e sales@lancaster.com.lb; www.lancaster. com.lb. Recently renovated with extra rooms added, this hotel has warm, tasteful décor & is ideal for both business & leisure travelers, offering more comfort & style than some of the other mid range options. Complimentary airport pickup for guests. **$$$**

Mayflower Hotel [162 D3] (82 rooms) Nehme Yafet St, Hamra; 01 340 680; e res@ mayflowerbeirut.com; www.mayflowerbeirut. com. A long-established & iconic hotel in the heart of Hamra which has had some well-known guests over the years including the former British/Russian spy Kim Philby, former Formula 1 world champion Graham Hill & writer Graham Greene. The rooms, all with AC & free Wi-Fi, are however quite ordinary & unexciting, but there is the atmospheric Duke of Wellington British-style pub & a decent restaurant. **$$$**

BUDGET

🏠 Cedarland Hotel [163 E3] (70 rooms) Abdel Aziz St, Hamra; \01 340 233/4; e info@ cedarlandhotel.net; www.cedarlandhotel.net. Although the rooms are clean & spacious they have rather bland décor, but this remains a good budget choice with all rooms having AC, TV & bathroom & represent excellent value for money in a great central Hamra location. Discounts are often available for extended stays. B/fast US$7, Wi-Fi LBP20,000/day. **$$**

🏠 The Grand Meshmosh Hotel [172 C3] (17 rooms) Mar Nicolas Steps (about a third of the way up the steps on your left), off Gouraud St, Gemmayze; \01 563 465; m 03 493 222; e michebli@yahoo.com; 🇫 GrandMeshmosh. An excellent & family-friendly addition to Beirut's budget accommodation scene. Opened in January 2016, the location is nice & quiet yet near to Gemmayze's & Mar Mikhael's buzzing bar & restaurant scene, whilst the Sursock Museum is even closer. The rooms, all with AC, are clean & tastefully decorated & there is an indoor communal room with TV & a pleasant courtyard meeting & dining area for guests. Highly recommended. Laundry LBP10,000 for up to 10kg. Dorm room US$28pp. Discounts available for stays of 7 nights or more. B/fast inc, free Wi-Fi. **$$**

🏠 Hamra Urban Gardens [163 F4] (58 rooms & suites) Muhammad Abdel Baki St, Hamra; \01 742 390; m 03 039 978; e hello@hamragardens. com; www.hamragardens.com. Opened in September 2016, this well-located hotel in the heart of Hamra offers cosy, spacious & clean rooms (all en suite) & is an ideal choice for individuals & families on a budget looking for an authentic, friendly & homely Lebanese experience. The hotel also boasts an 85m² rooftop pool, gym. Their Beit Em Nazih café serves great-value *mezze* & there is live music every Fri & Sat night. Dorm room US$18pp. B/fast inc, free Wi-Fi. **$$**

🏠 Hostel Beirut [173 E3] (7 rooms) Akram Al-Eid Bldg, Geitawi, very close to Geitawi pharmacy & Geitawi hospital; \01 568 966; e hostelbeirut@gmail.com; www.hostelbeirut. com. A decent & welcoming hostel, nicely located for the bars & cafés in the Mar Mikhael neighbourhood. An especially good choice for

those travellers who want to give something back as the profits generated by the hostel go towards helping refugees gain an education. Dorm rooms from US$20; b/fast inc, free Wi-Fi. **$$**

🏠 L'Hotel Libanais m 03 513 766; e hotelibanais@hotmail.com; www.hotelibanais. com. A great alternative to conventional hotels, this organisation offers rooms in private houses with local families, enabling a more intimate insight into the city & the country, & you are welcomed as part of the family. The company also runs a nationwide network of private lodgings, accommodation in monasteries, ecolodges, guesthouses & characterful small hotels. For B&B accommodation, a minimum 2-night stay is required & booking is via the website only. **$$**

🏠 Marble Tower Hotel [162 D4] (53 rooms) Makdissi St, Hamra; \01 346 260, 01 354 586; e info@marbletowerhotel.com; www. marbletowerhotel.com. In a great central Hamra location close to the AUB, this cosy hotel has comfortable & clean rooms with AC & TV & is a good choice for both business & tourist visitors. At the time of research, a new restaurant was under construction which, when completed, will offer a meal for 2 people for US$20. B/fast inc, free Wi-Fi. **$$**

🏠 Port View Hotel [172 D2] (27 rooms) Gouraud St, Gemmayze (opposite Electricité du Liban); \01 562 722, 01 567 500; e portviewhotel@hotmail.com; www. portviewhotel.com. Well located for Gemmayze's nightlife, the rooms are clean & comfortable with AC, TV & free Wi-Fi. The new bar area is a pleasant place for relaxing. A good budget option for families, with adjoining double & triple rooms. B/fast inc. **$$**

🏠 Regis Hotel [163 H2] (18 rooms) Rue Razi, Ain Mreisse, nr Palm Beach Hotel; \01 361 845; e regishotel@regishotel-lb.com; www.regishotel-lb.com. Good central location with excellent proximity to the Corniche & Hamra district. Clean, basic & friendly with TV & AC in all rooms & a pleasant communal area for guests. Free Wi-Fi in the lobby, but US$5/day in room. The hotel also arranges airport pickup for US$25 & transfer to the airport for US$15. A laundry service is also available (*US$5 for up to 5kg wash load*). **$$**

✳ 🏠 Saifi Urban Gardens [172 C2] (15 rooms & dorms) Pasteur St, Gemmayze; \01 562 509; e hello@saifigardens.com; www.saifigardens. com. A gem of a place ideally located for Charles Helou bus station, Downtown & Gemmayze's nightlife. Excellent, clean rooms (all en suite), rooftop bar, the excellent Café Em Nazih (page 146) & on-site Arabic-language school for all levels (pages 111–12), this friendly establishment is highly recommended for its concept of encouraging interaction & learning amongst travellers. One of Beirut's best budget options. B/fast inc. Dorm room US$18pp. Discounts available for weekly & monthly stays. Free Wi-Fi. They have recently opened another equally excellent hotel, Hamra Urban Gardens (page 143). **$$**

🏠 **University Hotel** [162 D3] (25 rooms & suites) Bliss St (opposite AUB main gate), Hamra; 📞01 365 390/1/2; e info@university-hotel.net; www.university-hotel.net. A good budget option on this busy street. Clean & presentable rooms, all with AC & TV. Internet access available for cUS$3/day. Used by many AUB students but manages to retain a reasonably quiet ambience! No b/fast is served but there are numerous eateries all along Bliss St. **$$**

SHOESTRING
🏠 **Al-Naim Hotel** [139 H5; 172 B2] (12 rooms) Al Jamarik St, nr port & Talal Hostel; 📞01 587 375; m 71 896 754; e alnaimhotel@hotmail.com. Very basic lodgings in a building with a certain rustic charm & convenient for Charles Helou bus station. Rooms are clean, & adequate for those on a budget.

The Makhlouf Café (page 147) directly opposite is a good option for breakfast. Dorm room US$10pp; b/fast US$5 extra, Wi-Fi LBP10,000/day. **$**

🏠 **Pension al-Nazih** [139 H5; 172 B2] (10 rooms) Charles Helou Av, Gemmayze; 📞01 564 868; m 03 475 136; e halaassali@hotmail.com; www.pension-alnazih.8m.com. A spotlessly clean backpacker favourite, with AC & TV in all rooms, making this an excellent choice & conveniently located for Charles Helou bus station, Downtown & Gemmayze's bars & restaurants. Wi-Fi (*US$9/day*) & laundry facilities (*US$5 for small loads, US$10 for large loads*), and airport pickup (*US$30*) are available. A taxi to the airport costs US$15. Dorm room US$17pp; b/fast US$6 extra. **$**

🏠 **Talal Hostel** [139 H5; 172 B2] (20 rooms) Charles Helou Av, Gemmayze; 📞01 562 567; m 70 562 567; e info@talalhotel.com; www. talalhotel.com. An excellent & friendly option for backpackers, with basic but clean rooms, all with AC & TV, near Charles Helou bus station, Gemmayze's nightlife & Downtown & very close to Pension al-Nazih (above). No meals are provided, there's complimentary use of kitchen facilities for guests wishing to cook their own food. Airport pickup (*US$20*) & drop-off service (*US$15*) available. Dorm room US$17pp; Wi-Fi US$1/hr. **$**

✕ WHERE TO EAT AND DRINK

Beirut has a burgeoning eating-and-drinking scene and new establishments are sprouting up (and closing down) all the time. There is a huge choice both in price and also type of cuisine, including the famous Lebanese *mezze*. Most of the international fast-food and drink chains such as KFC, McDonald's, Nando's, TGI Fridays, Costa, Starbucks et al are all represented in the city, as are more independent eateries serving French, Italian, Chinese and Japanese food, including sushi. As with shopping, different areas of the capital tend to have their own distinct flavour. The following selections of restaurants and watering holes are by no means exhaustive – in Beirut you are never far from somewhere to eat or drink and, unlike in many Arab or Middle Eastern countries, alcohol consumption is not taboo. Bear in mind, though, that some of the places listed get very busy at certain times, especially at weekends, and it is probably always best to book a table in advance.

EXPENSIVE
✕ **Al Dente** [172 A4] 137 Abdel Wahab Al-Inglizi St, Achrafieh; 📞01 202 440; e restaurant@ albergobeirut.com; www.albergobeirut.com; ⏰ 13.00–15.00 & 20.00–23.00 Sun–Fri, 20.00–23.00 Sat. Legendary restaurant, part of the Hotel Albergo (page 141), serving excellent Italian

cuisine in retro surroundings every bit as luxurious as the hotel itself. **$$$$$**

✳✕ **La Paillote** [163 H1] Ain Mreisse, opposite Palm Beach Hotel; 📞01 369 113; m 03 326 246; e info@lapaillote.net, restaurantlapaillote@gmail.com; 📘 lapaillotebeirut; ⏰ noon–midnight daily.

An excellent seafood restaurant still going strong since it first opened in the early 1960s. Serves delicious fish dishes ranging from crab, sea bass, oysters & shrimps to octopus, plus their catch of the day. A cosy & characterful interior with good service makes this venue an excellent choice for family dining too. They offer a good selection of wines and *arak* from the Bekaa Valley & there is usually a female singer from 21.00 on Fri & Sat nights. $$$$$

✖ **Manara Palace Café** [126 A2] Manara, opposite Riviera Hotel, Corniche; 01 364 949; m 03 753 887; e issaahmad00@gmail.com; 24hrs daily. A large & excellent eatery by the lighthouse on the Corniche for inside & al fresco dining whilst watching fishermen cast their nets into the Mediterranean. Great food including a wide selection of fresh fish, & there is live Arabic music & dancing from 22.00. This is also a good place to puff on one of their numerous flavours of *nargileh* (*LBP12,000–15,000*). $$$$$

ABOVE AVERAGE

✖ **Abdel Wahab** [172 A4] 51 Abdel Wahab Al-Inglizi St, Achrafieh; 01 200 550/1; noon–midnight daily. Often touted as the best place to experience a wide variety of Lebanese cuisine amid authentic Ottoman-era decor, with the grills & *mezze* amongst the best in the city. Advance booking advisable. $$$$

✖ **Al Falamanki** [172 A5] 9th Fl, Block D, Sodeco Sq, Damascus Rd; 01 323 456, 01 397 167; m 03 080 908, 70 605 090; e info@ alfalamanki.com; www.alfalamanki.com; 24hrs daily. An excellent, traditional Lebanese café with a laid-back but very friendly & sociable atmosphere. They have an eclectic & delicious menu of Lebanese meat & vegetarian dishes using locally sourced ingredients. The garden area is a terrific place to relax whilst puffing on one of the many flavours of *nargileh* (*sheesha*) (from cLBP12,000) amidst the card & backgammon players. Highly recommended for a slice of Lebanese life. $$$$

✖ **Bay Rock Café** [126 A4] General De Gaulle Av, Raouche; 01 796 700; 10.00–03.00 daily. This café, overlooking the Pigeon Rocks & the Mediterranean, affords one of the best views in the city & this alone is reason enough to visit. Another reason is the excellent & varied Lebanese & international cuisine on offer including *mezze,* steaks & a range of beverages ranging from the local Almaza brew to *arak* &

a selection of wines from the Bekaa Valley. This laid-back, relaxing venue ups the entertainment ante at weekends, with belly dancers on Sat & karaoke on Sun. $$$$

✖ **Paul** [139 G6; 172 A2] Gouraud St, Gemmayze; 01 570 170, 01 582 222; 08.00– midnight daily. Established in the capital since 2001, this very popular French bakery franchise is an excellent choice for b/fast, with delicious cakes, pastries & coffee & a nice sociable ambience with outdoor seating & wheelchair-friendly toilets. The continental brunch of juice, bread, eggs, croissants & coffee is good value at US$15pp. Other branches available, eg: at Zaitunay Bay. $$$$

✖ **Seza** [173 F2] Patriarch Aarida St, Mar Mikhael; 01 570 711; m 03 251 257; e seza@ bistroarmenien.com; www.bistroarmenien.com; noon–15.00 & 20.00–midnight Tue–Sun. Excellent Armenian cuisine is complemented by the equally delightful surroundings in this cosy & intimate little bistro. $$$$

✖ **Urbanista** [162 D3] Bliss St, Hamra; 01 367 871; www.weare-urbanista.com; 07.00–midnight Mon–Sat, 08.00–midnight Sun. A very popular Western-style café serving varied international dishes including their excellent salad & b/fast menu in a very social & laid-back atmosphere. Upstairs & outside seating makes this a good choice for people-watching over the ever-busy Bliss St. $$$$

MID RANGE

✖ **Barometre** [162 E3] Blue Bldg, Makhoul St, Hamra; m 03 678 998; e springpink22@hotmail. com; 09.00–02.00 daily. Catering to a mainly 25+ age group, this cosy little bar plays jazz & oriental music, & Fri & Sat are disco nights. The daily platter is good value & a *nargileh* costs LBP10,000. $$$

✖ **Bread Republic** [162 D4] Hamra St, opposite Bank Audi, Hamra; 01 739 040; e info@ breadrepublic.com; www.breadrepublic.com; 07.00–01.00 daily. Excellent artisan bakery/café with outdoor seating which uses organic ingredients for their delicious range of pastries & snacks. The coffee & range of freshly squeezed juices are good here too & located in the same alleyway as the weekly Tue Earth Market (page 154). They have another branch in Achrafieh [172 B4] (*07.30–late daily*). $$$

✖ **De Prague** [163 E4] 166 Makdissi St, opposite Vinci clothing store & HSBC Bank, Hamra;

4

01 744 864; m 03 575 282; ◷ 09.00–late daily. With its colourful & cushioned seating, this is a cosy & homely venue serving good coffee, club & steak sandwiches, & cakes & croissants; they do a good Lebanese b/fast too. Patronised by a predominantly young, intellectual clientele, this is also a good place for Wi–Fi users in a quiet café without the distraction of daytime music. $$$

✖ **Kababji** [162 D3; 163 E4] Saroulla Bldg, Hamra St; 01 741 555; m 03 265 100, 71 008 090; e info@kababji.com; www.kababji.com; ◷ 08.00–midnight daily. Tasty & filling Lebanese food & grills from this chain eatery in unpretentious surroundings. See their website for numerous other branches around the city including in Bliss St near the AUB & in Downtown at Beirut Souks. $$$

✳✖ **Kahwet Leila** [172 B2] Gouraud St, Gemmayze; 01 561 888; m 70 184 033; www.kahwetleila.com; ◷ 10.00–midnight Mon–Thu & Sun, 10.00–01.00 Fri–Sat. A wonderfully retro & authentic traditional Lebanese restaurant with great service, backed up by an equally wonderful & wide-ranging menu including *mezze*. With its numerous flavours of *nargileh* (*LBP16,500–20,000*) this is also a great venue to just sit back, puff on a *sheesha* & soak up the laid-back atmosphere amidst the Arabic music playing in the background. In the authors' view, one of Beirut's best eating & drinking options. $$$

✖ **Napoletana** [162 D4] Hamra St, Hamra; 01 741 138; www.boubess.com; ◷ noon–23.00 daily. An excellent & family-orientated pizzeria serving generous portions accompanied by excellent service in the heart of Hamra. $$$

✖ **Tawlet** [173 F2] Ground Fl, Chalhoub Bldg, Nahr St, Mar Mikhael; 01 448 129; m 76 472 465; e info@tawlet.com; www.tawlet.com, www.soukeltayeb.com; ◷ 13.00–16.00 Mon–Fri, noon–16.00 Sat. Also known as the Farmer's Kitchen, this is a terrific place to sample authentic & traditional home-cooked regional Lebanese cuisine prepared by chefs from all over the country. The menu changes regularly & they also offer cookery & wine-appreciation classes. An excellent initiative from the organisers of the Souk el Tayeb farmers' market (page 153). Recommended. $$$

✖ **Varouj** [173 H3] Maracha Royal St, nr Royale Cinema, Bourj Hammoud; m 03 882 933; ◷ 12.30–16.30 & 19.30–23.30 Mon–Sat. This compact little restaurant with rustic charm serves an excellent selection of traditional Armenian cuisine in informal & homely surroundings. Advance booking advised given its small size. $$$

CHEAP AND CHEERFUL

✖ **Barbar** [163 E5 & H5; 138 A6] Nr Hamra Mosque & at Spears St, Hamra; 01 753 330, 01 744 341, 01 379 778; ◷ 24hrs daily. Beirut's quintessential street snacking experience with a delicious array of meat, fish, & rice dishes & sandwiches. $$

✖ **Café Em Nazih** [172 C2] Ground Fl, Saifi Urban Gardens Hotel, Pasteur St, Gemmayze; m 76 711 466; www.saifigardens.com; ◷ 08.00–04.00 daily. Located inside the Saifi Urban Gardens Hotel, this friendly café with a nice local vibe is highly recommended for the quality of its home-cooked *mezze* & platters at great-value prices. A great venue to meet & interact with your fellow travellers too. Every Wed is quiz night while on Fri & Sat the place comes alive to the sound of live music. $$

✖ **Café Younes** [162 D4 ; 163 E3] Nehme Yafet St, Hamra; 01 347 531, 01 750 975; Omar Bin Abdel Aziz St, Hamra; 01 742 654; e info@cafeyounes.com; www.cafeyounes.com; ◷ 08.00–23.00 Mon–Sat, 10.00–23.00 Sun. A long-established, unpretentious & friendly café offering a range of fresh coffee ground on the premises, with equally tasty sandwiches & cakes. They host monthly poetry readings & exhibit a variety of local artists & photographers' work. Highly recommended. $$

♀ **Captain's Cabin** [162 C3] Adonis St, nr TSC Supermarket on Sadat St, Hamra; 01 740 516; m 03 431 749; ◷ 17.00–late daily. Opened in 1964, this atmospheric & terrific nautical-themed bar resembles a British pub complete with pool table, dartboard & summer garden area. Owned & run by the friendly André, this is a great place for an easy-going few drinks or even a night out. $$

♀ **Godot** [172 C3] Gouraud St, Gemmayze; 01 575 770; e cocoelio@hotmail.com; ◷ 17.00–02.00 Fri–Sat, 17.00–01.00 Sun–Thu. A welcoming little hostelry, which gets very busy with live music on Thu & Fri nights, serving Almaza beer (*LBP7,500*), *arak* (*LBP13,500 a glass, US$90 a bottle*) & a wide range of spirits & fresh fruit cocktails; bar snacks are also available (*sandwiches LBP13,500*). $$

✳✖ **Le Chef** [172 B3] Gouraud St, Gemmayze; 01 445 373, 01 446 769; ◷ 07.00–midnight Mon–Sat. A delightful & unpretentious, intimate, friendly little restaurant which has been satisfying Beirut's diners with its generous portions since 1967. Fantastic home-cooked Lebanese cuisine with an ever-changing menu. Highly recommended. $$

♀**Torino Express** [172 C3] Gouraud St, Gemmayze; m 03 248 606; ⏰ 10.00–01.00 Mon–Fri, 10.00–02.00 Sat–Sun. One of Gemmayze's long-established drinking dens, this small, laid-back bar by day, gets very busy in the evenings serving beers, champagne, spirits & cocktails accompanied by a good range of music by the ever-rotating DJs. Sells a small selection of bar snacks, with sandwiches from US$5. $$

ROCK BOTTOM

✗**Makhlouf Café** [139 H5; 172 A1] Al Jamarik St, nr port & Talal Hostel, opposite Al

Naim Hotel; ☎ 01 444 952; m 03 423 179; ⏰ 07.00–04.00 daily. A friendly, convenient & great-value choice for a hearty Lebanese b/fast, serving freshly squeezed orange & grapefruit juice, with sandwiches costing LBP3,000–6,000. $

♀**Rabbit Hole** [162 C4] Makdissi St, Hamra; m 03 286 977, 70 151 328; ⏰ 15.00–late Mon–Sat, 17.00–late Sun, happy hour 16.00–20.00 Mon–Sat, 17.00–20.00 Sun. With free Wi-Fi, this small, intimate but lively bar caters to a predominantly young Beiruti crowd with the low-key lighting adding a nice atmosphere. An Almaza beer costs LBP7,000 & bar snacks including chicken & steak sandwiches LBP10,000–15,000. $

ENTERTAINMENT AND NIGHTLIFE

In contrast to many other countries and cities in the Arab world and the Middle East, which have a dearth of nigh-time entertainment options, Beirut embraces hedonistic pursuits in all their infinite variety, and if your penchant was just for these aspects alone, you could easily spend a week in the capital, not set foot inside a museum, and still depart feeling you have had a great time. New places and nightspots are opening up at a frenetic rate and the following listings are by no means exhaustive but represent a selection of venues for a contrasting evening's entertainment. The Hamra district in west Beirut has a good selection of cosy, neighbourhood bars, a longstanding and excellent live jazz café and a couple of decent theatres staging a varied selection of performances; whilst the Gemmayze and Mar Mikhael areas are festooned with bars and live music venues open to the wee hours. For dedicated clubbers, the Downtown area won't disappoint. In addition to looking at the informative website, www.BeirutNightlife.com, which keeps itself updated with most things nocturnal in the city, it is also worth keeping an eye on the various cultural centres' websites (pages 158–9), which often put on a range of cinematic and live events. Publications such as the English-language *Daily Star,* the French-language daily *L'Orient Le Jour* and the bi-weekly *Agenda Culturel* are also good sources of information for up-and-coming cultural and entertainment events.

MUSIC AND NIGHTCLUBS

☆ **Acid** [173 H7] Sin el Fil, adjacent Futurscope Exhibition Hall; m 03 115 777; e acidnightclub@ hotmail.com; www.acidnightclub.blogspot.com; ⏰ 22.00–06.00 Fri/Sat; admission US$20 before midnight. A popular, tactile & gay-friendly club with a spectacular sound & laser show. Very loud & crowded with the DJ spinning a range of techno, house, funk & oriental discs.

☆ **B018** [173 G2] Charles Malek Av, Quarantina, nr Forum de Beirut; ☎ 01 580 018; m 03 810 618; f B018Beirut; ⏰ 22.00–08.00 Thu–Sat. The brainchild of Lebanese architect Bernard Khoury,

this club pounds out the tunes until the wee hours when the retractable roof opens to reveal the city skyline at dawn. A Gothic-like interior with seating resembling coffins, this place is something of a unique institution & like Acid is a gay-friendly establishment.

☆ **Behind the Green Door** [172 D2] Nahr St, Mar Mikhael (opposite Electricité du Liban); m 70 856 866; f BTGDoor; ⏰ 21.00–04.00 Fri & Sat. The name apparently derives from a cult 1980s 'artistic' porn movie & its green, purple & red velvety, boudoir-like interior does have a certain

4

seductive appeal. Attracting a predominantly student, 25+ & well-heeled clientele, this venue has character & is certainly less mainstream than most & worth a visit especially if your musical tastes embrace loud dance, indie & rock music to the wee hours. Fri nights in Aug get very busy & it's advisable to book ahead.

☆ **The Blue Note Café** [162 D3] Makhoul St, nr the American University of Beirut, Hamra; ☎ 01 743 857; www.bluenotecafe.com; ⊕ noon–midnight Mon–Thu, noon–02.00 Fri–Sat; 'live music charge' US$25. Long-established, intimate & homely venue for live jazz, oriental & Latin music on Thu–Sat nights. They also serve a good selection of Lebanese *mezze* & steak dishes which make this a popular haunt for dining amidst the live music where a meal for 2 costs around US$45. Reservations recommended at weekends.

♥ **Dany's** [162 D4] Alleyway off Makdissi St, Hamra; ☎ 01 740 231; m 76 997 992; e info@danyslb.com; www.danyslb.com; 🄵 Danys. Hamra; ⊕ 10.00–02.00 Mon–Sat, 17.00–02.00 Sun. Extremely popular & friendly café/pub, which has been keeping the Hamra set happy since 2008. Highly recommended for its jovial & relaxing atmosphere, with outdoor seating available. Tue is quiz night & happy 'hour' (50% off drinks) is a very extended 10.00–20.00 daily. Snacks & sandwiches available (*LBP6,500–LBP12,000*).

☆ **Music Hall** [138 B/C4] Starco Centre, Omar Daouk St, Downtown; ☎ 01 361 236; m 03 807 555; e musichall@elefteriades. com, bookbeirut@themusichall.com; www. themusichall.com; ⊕ 22.00–late Thu–Sat.

A live-music venue with state-of-the-art sound system & large stage showcasing Lebanese & international musical talent & genres (Latin, jazz, reggae, pop, gipsy, etc). The deep red décor lends this place a warm & slightly retro feel & is an extremely popular nightspot for music lovers in the heart of Downtown. Lebanon's Libanjazz (*www.libanjazz.com*) & the French Cultural Institute organise events here. Dinner for 2 costs around US$120. Advance booking recommended.

☆ **01NEBEIRUT** [139 E1] Waterfront, Downtown; m 03 939 191; e info@sky-management.net; www.o1nebeirut.com; ⊕ Nov–May 21.30–05.00 Fri–Sat; admission free, but a charge is made for group table bookings (*table for 4 approx US$400*). It's hard to miss this huge circular clubbing venue on the waterfront, & for graffiti lovers it's a tourist attraction in its own right with many international artists flown in from around the globe to decorate its very garish & striking façade. With a state-of-the-art visual & sound system, dedicated clubbers will no doubt party to the wee hours as the DJs spin the house, pop & rock discs. Drinks are pretty pricey, though, with an Almaza costing US$12, vodka US$16 & a glass of wine US$10.

☆ **Palais by Crystal** [172 A4] Monot St, Achrafieh; ☎ 01 338 964; m 03 854 455; www. thecrystalgroup.net; ⊕ 23.00–late Thu–Sat. Set in a very modern, chic venue, this place caters to an equally chic & sophisticated glamorous, clubbing clientele belting out a wide range of sounds.

CINEMAS The capital offers a huge range of film entertainment catering to all tastes ranging from the latest Hollywood releases to less mainstream movies, including the opportunity to sample home-grown talent from the likes of director Jocelyne Saab and actress/director Nadine Labaki. The vast majority of films are shown in English with Arabic and/or French subtitles and most cinemas are equipped to screen the latest 3D and digital films. The English-language *Daily Star* newspaper publishes details of current and future showings together with periodic articles related to film.

Cinemacity [127 H3] (10 screens) 3rd Fl, City Mall, Dora Hwy; ☎ 01 899 993; e info@cinemacity. com.lb; www.cinemacity.com.lb; ⊕ generally 13.00 with last screening around 22.30 daily; admission LBP8,000–18,000.
Cinemacity [139 E3] (12 screens) Beirut Souks, Downtown; ☎ 01 995 195; e info@

cinemacitybeirut.com; www.cinemacitybeirut. com. All the latest mainstream blockbusters are shown here.
Empire Dunes [126 C5] (5 screens) Dunes Centre, Verdun St, Verdun; ☎ 01 792 123, dial 1269 within Lebanon; e info@empire.com.lb; www.empire.com.lb

Empire Premiere [172 A5] (6 screens) Sodeco Sq, Damascus Rd, Achrafieh; ☎ 01 616 707; www. empirepremiere.com

Grand ABC Cinema [172 C/D4] (7 screens) ABC Mall, Achrafieh St, Achrafieh; ☎ 01 209 109; http://lb.grandcinemasme.com

Grand Concorde [163 F5] (8 screens) Concorde Centre, Dunant St, Verdun; ☎ 01 343 143; http://lb.grandcinemasme.com

Metropolis Art Cinema [172 C3] (2 screens) Ground Fl, Sofil Centre, Av Charles Malek, Achrafieh; ☎ 01 204 080 (cinema), 01 332 661 (main office); e info@metropoliscinema.net; www. metropoliscinema.net. An exception to the 'rule', this 2-screen cinema (267 & 274 seats) screens films across a wide range of genres including independent & art-house movies & is a venue for film showings during Beirut's annual film festivals. For film buffs they also have a library (⊕ *18.00–22.00 daily*), where you can browse a wide range of books, magazines & posters & buy DVDs & soundtracks.

CINEMA CLUBS The venues below all offer a more independent and avant-garde film experience for those interested in alternative visual arts a little different from the mainstream offerings.

Academie Libanaise des Beaux-Arts (ALBA Ciné-Club de L'Alba) ALBA Campus, Av Emile Edde, Sin El Fil; ☎ 01 480 056, 01 489 207/8/9; m 03 899 195; e alba@alba.edu.lb; www. alba.edu.lb (in French); admission free. Screens alternative & modern classic films every Fri at 19.00.

Art Lounge [173 G2] Quarantina; m 03 997 676; e info@artlounge.net; www.artlounge.net. This extensive 900m² converted warehouse is a holistic venue for arts & culture, & in addition to its regular art exhibitions hosts regular film nights screening independent & less mainstream movies. Their website posts details of both past & current cinematic offerings.

De Prague Cineclub [163 E4] 166 Makdissi St, Hamra; m 03 575 282; admission free. Nightly screenings at 21.00, but note that the films are shown without sound but subtitled in Arabic, English or French.

THEATRES Along with many other aspects of Lebanese culture, theatre has both a long tradition and a very diverse artistic and cultural output, reflecting the cosmopolitan makeup of the country as a whole. Prior to the civil war years of 1975–90, theatre in its many forms – from avant-garde, experimental to musical productions – was a flourishing industry in Beirut with the likes of the Rahbani brothers, Roger Assaf and the 1970 founding of the Caracalla Dance Theatre evoking the capital's and the country's freedom of artistic and intellectual expression. In the present era, too, theatre remains a burgeoning performing art form across a range of genres, experimental and cultural themes with performances staged in the country's three main languages of Arabic, English and French, with performances of interest to both adults and children alike. The listings below consist of some of the main theatrical venues to be found in the city, but it's also worth keeping an eye on the French Cultural Institute's website (*www.institutfrancais-liban.com*) who periodically put on concerts and other productions. In most cases tickets for performances can be obtained from the venues themselves and sometimes, depending on the type of performance, from the Virgin Megastore (page 153) in Downtown, www. ticketingboxoffice.com or from one of the branches of Librairie Antoine bookshop (page 155). The back page of the English-language *Daily Star* newspaper also contains details of current and forthcoming performances and cultural events.

🗹 **AUB (American University of Beirut) Theatre** [162 D2] Bliss St, Ras Beirut; ☎ 01 374 374 ext 4350/1 (Dept of Fine Arts & Art History); e faah@aub.edu.lb; www.aub.edu.lb. Students & faculty members put on a handful of shows annually, usually during May, in the 250-seat West Hall auditorium on the AUB campus. The works performed range from concerts to dance, & plays are mostly in English, though plays in Arabic & French are also performed.

🎭 **Babel Theatre** [163 E4] Marignan Centre, Cairo St, Hamra; 📞 01 744 033; 📱 71 144 767; 📧 babeltheatre@yahoo.com; ⬛ babeltheatre. An excellent 300-seat theatre, founded in 2007 & converted from an old cinema, stages performances across a range of genres including plays, stand-up comedy, poetry readings, dance, film screenings & experimental works. Holds drama workshops & acts (no pun intended) as a vehicle for self-expression for writers & artists from Arab countries where this is often problematic.

🎭 **Lebanese American University (LAU)** [162 C5] Al Hussein St, Qoreitem; 📞 01 786 464 ext 1172; 📱 03 791 314; 📧 theatre.festival@lau. edu.lb; www.eventscal.lau.edu.lb. Students from the Department of Communication Arts stage a variety of productions at the university's 344-seat Gulbenkian & 393-seat Irwin theatres. Admission is usually free & tickets are obtained from the university itself. The university also hosts visiting theatrical productions & holds its annual festival of theatre on campus. Previous productions have included J M Barrie's *Peter Pan*.

🎭 **Metro Al Madina** [163 E4] Saroulla Bldg, Hamra St, Hamra; 📱 76 309 363; 📧 info@ metromadina.com; www.metromadina.com. Having undergone an extensive refit in recent years, including new seating, this excellent performance venue hosts a number of live cabaret acts, concerts, dance, plays, educational workshops, cinema screenings, conferences, lectures, etc in Arabic, English & French within a multi-faceted approach to the arts which creates 'a culture of diversity and openness' for both Lebanese & Arab world artists.

🎭 **Monot Theatre** [172 A4] St Joseph University St, Achrafieh; 📞 01 202 422; 📧 monot@usj.edu. lb; www.usj.edu.lb/monnot; 🕐 11.00–17.00 Mon, 11.00–23.00 Tue–Sun, Aug closed. This very active venue has 2 theatres (c285 & c80 seats) & annually stages numerous concerts, dance shows, exhibitions, plays & films mainly in Arabic, Armenian & French but occasionally in English & has staged productions with performers from the excellent Actors Workshop Beirut (*www. theactorsworkshopbeirut.com*).

🎭 **The Sunflower Theatre** [127 H7] Sami Solh Av, Tayouneh; 📞📠 01 381 290, 01 391 290; 📱 71 997 959; 📧 info@khayal.org; www.khayal. org. Another theatre with a prolific output of performing arts, staging around 3 performances a month in its 300-seat auditorium. This is also the venue for the excellent & much-loved **Lebanese Puppet Theatre** founded in 1992 which puts on a wide range of child-friendly productions dealing with a range of issues from the environment, children's & general human rights to fables.

CONCERTS

Lebanese National Higher Conservatory of Music (LNHCM) [127 G4; 172 A4] Monot St, Achrafieh; 📞 01 217 289; 📧 info@conservatory.gov. lb; www.conservatory.gov.lb. In addition to being a centre of excellence for the education & training of future musicians, the orchestra has a very prolific output & between Oct & Jun performs in excess of 100 concerts across both Arabic & World Music genres. Times, venues & performance details are usually available on the LNHCM website.

SPORT AND ACTIVITIES The beautiful game – **football (soccer)** – though not as religiously followed as in countries like Italy, Spain or the UK, nevertheless enjoys a popular following in Beirut though there are no players who are household names outside the country, whilst Lebanon's August 2016 FIFA (Fédération Internationale de Football Association; *www.fifa.com*) World Ranking of 149 (out of 205 countries) does not exactly make the country one of the giants of the sport. The city's two most famous football teams are Beirut Al-Ansar and Beirut Al-Nejmeh; the former holding the Guinness World Record for winning the most consecutive domestic league titles (11 between 1988 and 1999). The best place to find out when and where they are playing is to have a look at the *Daily Star* newspaper for venues and kick-off times.

Although primarily a male preserve, **horse racing** is a passionately followed sport with up to ten races per meeting at Lebanon's only racecourse, the **Hippodrome du**

Parc de Beyrouth [127 G7] (*Abdallah Al-Yafi Av, just behind the National Museum;* ✆ *01 632 515;* e *sparca@cyberia.net.lb, sparca.leb@gmail.com; www.beiruthorseracing. com; races commence Jul–Aug 13.30 Sat, Sep–Jun 12.30 Sun; admission LBP15,000*). This is a great way to spend an afternoon amongst the raucous Beirutis betting with a frenzy, but don't expect facilities characteristic of Newmarket or Ascot in the UK.

For aficionados of **golf** the **Golf Club of Lebanon** [127 E7] (*Bourj Brajneh, sandwiched between Ouzai Bd & Hafez Al Assad Av (New Airport Hwy) a short distance north of the airport;* ✆ *01 822 474, 01 826 335;* m *03 609 412;* e *info@ golfcluboflebanon.com; www.golfcluboflebanon.com;* ⊕ *07.00–19.00 daily*) was founded back in 1923 and is located in a very scenic and tranquil setting, and has the country's sole 18-hole championship course. Non-members are permitted to use the course, which at the time of writing cost US$40 during weekdays and US$60 at weekends and public holidays for adults (see the website for further information on their guest policy and current fees for adults and children). Equipment hire is available as an optional extra. The club also has a number of other facilities which can be used by guests, including tennis courts, a squash court, snooker tables, a swimming pool, a well-equipped gymnasium, a small football pitch & playground for children together with a restaurant serving Lebanese and international dishes.

For those with a penchant for **sub-aqua**, there are plenty of opportunities for both novice and experienced divers to don wetsuit and aqualung. The **National Institute for Scuba Diving (NISD)** [138 A2] (*Zaitunay Bay;* ✆ *01 739 203;* m *03 204 422;* e *info@nisd-online.com; www.nisd-online.com*) has been running courses and dive expeditions since the 1980s and has three boats which conduct open dive visits around the waters of the capital, as well as in the north and south of the country, including dives to see the sunken Vichy French submarine *Souffleur* from World War II. The **Calypso Diving Centre** [126 B5] (*Mövenpick Hotel & Resort, General de Gaulle Av, Raouche;* m *03 805 054;* e *info@calypsolb.com; www.calypsolb.com*) also has a good reputation for quality tuition and offers beginner courses and dives from shore and boat, as well as underwater videography and exploration of wrecks. An excellent one-stop shop for most water-based activities is the **Water Nation Sports Centre** [138 B2] (*Zaitunay Bay;* ✆ *01 379 770;* m *03 204 455;* e *info@waternation. com; www.waternation.com.lb;* ⊕ *office hours 11.00–19.00 daily*), which offers jet and water skiing, parasailing, sailing, scuba diving courses catering for most levels, boat and yacht rental plus fun water activities for kids and a summer camp.

BEACH CLUBS With Beirut being a coastal city, the capital is a hedonist's and sun-worshipper's paradise, and in true Lebanese fashion beaches are places to be seen at as much as they are for rest and recreation. All of the following have ample facilities (except an abundance of sand) and, although there is a free public beach at Ramlet Al Baida, it is distinctly lacking, and most people gravitate towards the private clubs simply for the caché of being private and stylish!

Madame Bleu [163 G1] Ain Mreisse; ✆ 01 366 222; m 03 374 437; e info@madamebleubeirut. com; www.madamebleubeirut.com; ⊕ May–Sep 09.30–18.30 daily; admission LBP40,000 Mon–Thu, LBP55,000 Fri–Sun & public holidays. Has a nice open-air restaurant, jacuzzi, swimming pool, dancing & DJ.

Mövenpick Hotel & Resort [126 B5] General de Gaulle Av, Raouche; ✆ 01 869 666; e hotel.beirut@

moevenpick.com; www.moevenpick-hotels.com; ⊕ 07.00–20.00 daily. Although it is only open to hotel guests, this has Beirut's sole beach club located directly onto the sea. Part of the Swiss hotel chain, it offers a varied experience with a marina, private beach, 4 swimming pools & a host of activities ranging from banana-boat rides to water skiing.

Riviera Hotel [162 A2] Av de Paris, Ras Beirut, Corniche; ✆ 01 373 210; m 03 322 600; e info@

riviera-yachtclub.com, prive@rivierahotel.com.
lb; www.rivierahotel.com.lb; ⊕ May–Oct
08.00–late daily; admission: adults LBP30,000
Mon–Fri, LBP40,000 Sat/Sun, children LBP25,000
Mon–Fri, LBP25,000 Sat/Sun, hotel guests free.
Once epitomising Beirut's 'Paris of the Middle East'
image, their recently renovated Beach Lounge has
3 swimming pools, jacuzzi, pool bar, a VIP lounge,
jet skiing & scuba-diving activities.
Saint-George Yacht Club & Marina [138 A2]
Ain Mreisse; m 03 958 379; e hotel@stgeorges-

hotel.com; www.stgeorges-yachtclub.com;
⊕ 09.00–18.00 daily; admission: adults
LBP35,000 Mon–Fri, LBP40,000 Sat/Sun, children
LBP30,000 Mon–Fri, LBP35,000 Sat/Sun. Discounts
available for families & groups of 4 or more people.
This former playground of the rich & famous &
overlooked by the equally famous ruined shell
of the St George Hotel remains one of the best
options with adult & children's swimming pools,
bar, restaurant & an overall cordial atmosphere.

SHOPPING

If the concept of retail therapy had a capital city, then Beirut would certainly be among the shortlist of contenders. The late Syrian poet and writer Nizar Qabbani (1923–98) once commented that it was *de rigueur* for any businessman to take his wife's shopping list with him when visiting Beirut. In fact, most Beirutis are inveterate shoppers and there is no shortage of opportunities to check out the latest Beirut bling, international fashion labels, textiles and crafts. The main thing to bear in mind when shopping in the capital is that, for the most part, it is not the traditional or exotic experience characteristic of many other Arab and Middle Eastern cities. If you think of Dubai, London's Oxford Street or New York's Fifth Avenue, you will get some idea of the retail experience that awaits you in the city. The following areas are among the most popular shopping neighbourhoods in the city but new chains and stores are constantly opening so the shops mentioned represent just a selection of what's on offer. For a good overview of the city's shopping scene have a look at *Shop Beirut* (2010) by Marwan Naaman, available via Amazon and at many Beirut bookstores.

ACHRAFIEH Situated just east of Downtown, this Christian area is an attractive district home to designer clothing, jewellery, and antique and home-furnishing stores, especially around the Sassine Square area. The one-stop **ABC Mall** [172 D4] (*Alfred Naccache St, Mar Mitr;* \ *01 212 888;* e *info@abc.com.lb; www.abc.com.lb;* ⊕ *10.00–22.00 daily*) sells a comprehensive range of international fashion labels for men, women and children. The complex also boasts cinemas, restaurants, a post office and free parking. Described as the 'social working class in Lebanon' is the weekly **Souk Al-Ahad** [173 F6] or Sunday market (*Jisr Al Wati, Beirut River, nr Achrafieh*) which, unlike the majority of Lebanese shopping, sacrifices aesthetics for utility; the market is more akin to a giant car boot sale in the UK, selling almost everything imaginable from plugs to clothing at much cheaper prices than elsewhere. Take a service taxi from the museum or Dora station. If you want to buy local arts and crafts whilst at the same time supporting the endeavours of local craftsmen, then visit **L'Artisan du Liban** [172 C2] (*Rue Montée Accaoui, St Antoine Centre, Achrafieh;* \ *01 564 907;* e *lartisan@lartisanlb.com;* f *l'artisanduliban;* ⊕ *09.30–19.00 Mon–Fri, 09.30–17.00 Sat*), which has a terrific selection.

BOURJ HAMMOUD This area provides a contrasting shopping aesthetic to most other shopping districts in the city and is a world away from the malls and trendy streets of Verdun and Downtown. With its distinctive Armenian cultural identity, the area offers more competitively priced jewellery, clothing and craft stores centred on the busy Arax and Armenia streets where you can pick up more bargain-priced items (page 175).

right   Aanjar is, uniquely in Lebanon, the product of only one historical period: the 8th-century Umayyad caliphate (AI/S) pages 261–3

below   The Crusader Sea Castle at Sidon was built by the Crusaders in 1228, using the foundations of a much earlier Phoenician temple (d/S) page 305

bottom   Tyre's Roman Road and 20m-tall Triumphal Arch date back to the time of the emperor Hadrian in the 2nd century (Ddkg/D) pages 321–2

left As an in situ open-air and subterranean museum of war, the 60,000m² complex at Mleeta must rank as one of the most unique and extraordinary shrines to military endeavour in the world (PD) pages 315–16

below Once dubbed the 'Queen of the Seas' for its mercantile and seafaring activities, Tyre was previously a flourishing commercial centre for international trade and appears in the classical writings of Herodotus and Homer (PD) pages 316–23

bottom The pretty town of Deir al-Qamar preserves its rich legacy of Ottoman-era architecture in one of Lebanon's most serene settings (PD) pages 280–6

right   The reward for visitors who have survived the 600m ascent on the Téléférique from Jounieh to Harissa is the 19th-century 15-tonne statue of the Virgin Mary (SS) page 203

below   The Bekaa Valley town of Zahlé is one of the best places in the country to sample *mezze*, wine and *arak* (PD) pages 253–8

bottom   After Cairo, Tripoli contains the largest and most significant set of Mamluk-period architecture in the world (MF/AWL) pages 225–37

above   **Carpet makers, Tripoli; Tripoli's souks are well worth a look, even if it's just to watch the craftsmen at work** (SS) page 234

left   **Druze man; the Druze sect was founded in Cairo in the 11th century as a splinter group from the Shi'ite Ismaili faith** (SS) page 52

below   **Sidon's atmospheric souks offer a range of foodstuffs and traditionally crafted products** (PD) page 306

above left A popular Lebanese dessert is *baklava*, a very sweet and syrupy pastry with pistachio nuts (SS) page 97

above right The Lebanese favourite, and main meal of the day, is the eclectic *mezze*, a wide array of small savoury dishes, served hot or cold (PD) page 96

right Traditional Arabic or Turkish coffee is drunk very strong with copious amounts of sugar in small cups or glasses (JOAT/S) page 98

below *Ka'ik* bread is sprinkled with sesame seeds and sold by the many street vendors who perambulate the Corniche in Beirut (PD) page 166

above Lake Qaraoun, Lebanon's largest artificial lake, used to generate electricity and irrigate agricultural land in the Bekaa and the south, is also a delightful spot for lakeside dining (MTL) page 265

left Mzaar is Lebanon's premier, most modern, glitzy and best-equipped ski resort (EK/D) pages 194–5

below Château Ksara celebrated its 150th anniversary in 2007, and is Lebanon and the Middle East's oldest winery and largest producer (PD) page 259

above Separated by the Mount Lebanon and Anti-Lebanon mountain ranges, the Bekaa Valley is an elongated plateau that reaches up to 1,000m above sea level in places (SS) pages 253–75

right Lebanon's most famous flora, and the country's national symbol, is the cedar tree (*Cedrus libani*) (PD) pages 292–3

below The 12km² Arz Tannourine Nature Reserve is rich in biodiversity and well worth a visit (EK/D) page 244

The Balaa Sinkhole, a relatively recent
discovery, plunges more than 250m below
ground level amidst cascading waterfalls
(d/S) pages 193–4

DOWNTOWN Beirut Central District (BCD) or Solidere, as it is also known, provides the core of the city's upmarket retail experience. Interspersed with a couple of luxury hotels and pavement cafés are a range of local and internationally known fashion labels and brands. Shopping highlights include:

Beirut Souks [139 E4] 149 Saad Zaghloul St; 01 989 040/1; e info@beirutsouks.com.lb; www. beirutsouks.com.lb; ⊕ 10.00–22.00 daily. Spread over more than 100,000m², this glitzy market area, in addition to its numerous high-end shopping options, houses many cafés, restaurants, cinemas, ATMs & a post office (see page 167 for more details).
Elie Saab [138 C4] Elie Saab Bldg; 01 981 982; e boutique.bcd.lb@eliesaab.com; www.eliesaab. com; ⊕ 10.00–19.00 Mon–Sat. (See box, page 155, for details of Lebanese designer Elie Saab.)
Saifi Village [139 G7] A short walk southeast of Martyrs' Sq; 01 980 650; e info@solidere.com.lb; www.saifivillage.com; ⊕ 10.00–19.00 Mon–Sat. See page 170 for more details.
Souk el Tayeb [139 E3] Trablous St, Beirut Souks; 01 442 664; e info@soukeltayeb.com; www. soukeltayeb.com; ⊕ 09.00–14.00 Sat. Launched in 2004, this is Lebanon's first weekly farmers' market, selling a wide range of quality organic & non-

organic local produce, handicrafts & children's items from farmers all over the country. This is a great place to support those working in less prosperous rural economies. They also hold an additional farmers' market every Wed (*between 13.00 & 19.00*) at the Gefinor Centre in west Beirut [163 F3].
✴ **Virgin Megastore** [139 F5] Opera Bldg, Martyrs' Sq; 01 999 666; e virgin@retail-me.com; www.virginmegastore.com.lb; ⊕ 10.00–22.00 Mon–Thu & Sun, 10.00–23.00 Fri–Sat. Part of the international chain of shops, this one is reputedly the largest outside the UK, stocking the usual range of music & movie DVDs, books, magazines, newspapers & electrical goods. This is also the place to book tickets to a wide range of festivals & theatrical events throughout the country. Virgin also have additional branches at ABC Achrafieh, City Mall in Dora, ABC Dbayeh, Beirut Souks in Downtown & the Duty-Free area at the airport.

HAMRA Although usurped in recent years by the rapidly developing areas of Downtown, Achrafieh and Verdun, this is still a hive of retail activity with some 200 stores, and its hustle and bustle is more akin to a Western high-street shopping experience. The main streets for all kinds of goods, including clothes, are Rue Hamra and Bliss Street. There is also the **ABC Mall** [172 D4] (*Hamra St;* 01 340 254; e info@ abc.com.lb; www.abc.com.lb; ⊕ 10.00–20.00 Mon–Sat), which specialises in women's wear. For those seeking less mainstream items, the **Oriental Art Centre** [162 D4] (*Rue Makhoul, Hamra;* 01 349 942; ⊕ 09.00–13.00 & 15.30–18.00 Mon–Sat) sells retrospective items such as old postcards and photographs of a bygone age in the Middle East. Just north of Hamra, opposite the Palm Beach Hotel, the **Lebanese & Oriental Artisans (Artisans du Liban et d'Orient** [163 H1] (*Ain Mreisse, Minet Al Hosn;* 01 362 644; m 03 250 268; e khalil_a_sattar@hotmail.com; ⊕ 10.00–18.00 *Mon–Fri, 10.00–14.00 Sat*) has been specialising in authentic souvenir items made by artisans from Lebanon and the region since the 1950s and is an Aladdin's Cave of postcards, silver jewellery, kaftans, *nargileh* pipes, decorative backgammon sets, etc and can deliver items overseas. A short walk further west and opposite the Le Vendôme hotel, is the more modern shop of **Maison De L'Artisan** [163 G1] (*Ain Mreisse, Minet Al Hosn;* 01 368 461/2; e info@mda.gov.lb; www.mda.gov.lb; ⊕ 09.30–18.30 Mon–Sat), which sells a range of items made by Lebanese artisans including glassware, cutlery from Jezzine, and soap from Sidon and Tripoli. For traditional Palestinian embroidered items, head to **INAASH** [162 B3] (*Sidani St;* 01 740 609, 01 744 609; e contact@inaash.org; www.inaash.org; ⊕ 08.00–15.00 Mon–Fri, 08.00–13.00 Sat), which features the craft endeavours of Palestinian women making cushion covers, scarves, jackets and handbags with the proceeds helping to support the Palestinians in Lebanon's refugee camps, as well as preserving an important aspect

Beirut SHOPPING

4

of Palestinian heritage. The **Earth Market** [162 D4] (*Alleyway joining Hamra St & Makdissi St, facing Bread Republic;* m *03 688 258;* e *barbaram@cyberia.net.lb; www. earthmarkets.net, www.fondazioneslowfood.com*) takes place every Tuesday between 09.00 and 14.00. Farmers and other local vendors sell their produce including Arabic bread, homemade honey and jam, and fresh fruit and vegetables.

VERDUN A very modern development since the 1990s boasting predominantly luxury boutiques and related outlets from many of the world's top-end designer brands, Rue Verdun is the place to start your forays into high-class chic. The large shopping mall, **Dunes Centre** [126 C5] (*Verdun St;* ✆ *01 785 310/1;* e *info@ dunes.com.lb; www.dunes.com.lb;* ⊕ *10.00–22.00 daily*) offers designer brands plus a range of cafés and restaurants, a multi-screen cinema, ATMs and an on-site Holiday Inn Hotel. **Verdun 730** [126 C5] and **Verdun 732** [126 C5], either side of Rachid Karame (Verdun) Street, are other ultra-modern shopping areas.

SUPERMARKETS Although there are many corner shops and mini-markets dotted around the city, for more extensive food and grocery shopping Beirut is also well supplied with supermarkets offering both local and international products. Those listed here are just a snapshot of what's available and the Hamra neighbourhood has a particularly plentiful supply.

7 Days [162 D3] Ghandour Bldg, Jeanne D'Arc St, Hamra; ✆ 01 751/2 053; m 76 944 330; ⊕ 07.00–02.00 daily. A small grocery store but stocks most items such as toiletries, beverages & sandwiches for most day-to-day needs. Will deliver to home & hotel.

City Mall [127 H3] Dora Hwy; ✆ 01 905 555; e citymall@citymall.com.lb; www.citymall. com.lb; ⊕ 10.00–22.00 Sun–Thu, 10.00–23.00 Fri–Sat. This beast of a shopping mall boasts more than 150 shops selling the latest designer brands, electrical items & jewellery. There are numerous fast-food chains & restaurants, & the multiplex Cinemacity (page 148) screens the latest mainstream film releases.

Co-op [162 D4] Makdissi St, Hamra, opposite Marble Tower Hotel; ✆ 01 348 465; ⊕ 07.00–23.00 Mon–Sat, 08.00–21.00 Sun, summer 07.00–23.00 Sun. Excellent range of fruit & vegetables, & general groceries, household, toiletry & clothing items. There is also an in-store branch of Western Union Money Transfer.

Goodies [162 D7] Verdun St, Verdun; ✆ 01 796 797; e info@goodies.com.lb; www.goodies.com.lb; ⊕ 07.00–20.00 Mon–Sat. Part of the international chain of supermarkets selling a comprehensive range

of groceries & general household & cosmetic items. They also have a branch in the Duty-Free area at Beirut airport (✆ 01 629 250).

Idriss Supermarket [163 E4] Souraty St, Hamra (opposite Bank of Beirut); ✆ 01 743 770, 01 745 255; m 70 918 441; e info@idriss.net; www.idriss. net; ⊕ 07.30–22.00 Mon–Sat, 08.00–17.00 Sun. A long-established & well-stocked supermarket with a range of fruit, vegetables & meats. They also offer free delivery to home or hotel.

Spinney's [172 D4] Mar Mitr St, Achrafieh; ✆ 01 210 110, Hotline within Lebanon 1521; e info@spinneys-lebanon.com, customer.service@ spinneys-lebanon.com; www.spinneys-lebanon. com; ⊕ 08.00–23.00 daily. A branch of the nationwide Lebanese chain, this supermarket stocks the full range of everyday groceries.

TSC Plus [162 C3] Sadat St, Hamra; ✆ 01 746 989, 01 746 874; e customerservice@tsclebanon. com; www.sultan-center.com; ⊕ 07.00–midnight daily. This is a good, mid-sized supermarket selling a wide range of items including fruit, vegetables, toiletries, beers & spirits, newspapers & magazines at competitive prices. Other branches available; see their website for contact details.

BOOKSHOPS AND LIBRARIES Beirut has a great selection of bookshops stocking a wide range of English-language reading matter, and they are also a great place to catch up with newspapers and magazines. There are also a smattering of public libraries

Born in Beirut on 4 July 1964, Elie Saab is Lebanon's best-known couturier famous for his modern, elegant and feminine designs. With boutiques in Beirut, Paris and Harrods in London, his career direction appeared to be sewn up at the tender age of nine. Using his mother's curtains and tablecloths, he would sketch designs and make items of clothing for his sisters. Following a brief sojourn to Paris in 1981 to study fashion, he returned to Lebanon after a year to open his first atelier in Beirut. Later that year he enjoyed instant success with his first collection shown at the Casino du Liban. In 1997, he became the first foreign designer to become a member of the Camera Nationale della Moda (National Chamber for Italian Fashion), and showcased his first collection outside Lebanon in Rome. Renowned for his evening gowns, and more recently for his range of *Le Parfums*, Saab also became the first Lebanese designer to have one of his creations worn by an Oscar winner, Halle Berry in 2002, when she won the Best Actress award. Other 'A' list celebrities who have adorned themselves with Saab's finery include Angelina Jolie, Catherine Zeta-Jones, Elizabeth Hurley, Gwyneth Paltrow, Nicole Kidman, Julia Roberts, Helen Mirren, Nelly Furtado and Queen Rania of Jordan. Saab has also made the journey from the runway to the shipping lanes, designing luxurious yachts evoking the same chic and elegant designs for the high-end boat market and extending 'the experience of luxury beyond the conventional limits of fashion' (*www.eliesaab.com*).

worth visiting which will appeal to adults and children alike. If outdoor book shopping appeals, then head to the capital's Achrafieh district for the popular monthly **Monot Street Book Market** [172 A3] (*Monot St, Achrafieh, facing RectoVerso Library;* ✆01 330 994; m 03 271 500; ⊕ 10.00–18.00). First launched in 2011, it takes place on the first Saturday of each month with street vendors selling a range of tomes at good prices.

The following bookshops and libraries are among the best in the city and all stock books in English, Arabic and/or French.

Bachoura Public Library [138 D7] 3rd Fl, Civil Defence Bldg, nr fire station, Bachoura; ✆01 667 701; e bachoura@assabil@gmail.com; www.assabil. com; ⊕ 09.00–18.00 Tue–Fri, 09.00–17.00 Sat. Launched in 2001, this is Beirut's first public library holding a varied selection of books, newspapers & magazines in many different languages in addition to Arabic, English & French. The library holds weekly storytelling sessions for children aged 4–9 on Fri at 16.00. Internet access available.

Books & Pens [162 D3] Jeanne D'Arc St, opposite main entrance to the AUB, Hamra; ✆01 741 975; ⊕ 08.00–22.00 Mon–Fri, 08.00–20.00 Sat. Although predominantly specialising in art supplies & stationery, they also sell a selection of general books & magazines.

Geitawi Public Library [173 E3] Jesuit Public Garden, Geitawi; ✆01 562 677;

e biblioashrafieh@yahoo.com; www.assabil. com; ⊕ 09.00–18.00 Tue–Fri, 09.00–17.00 Sat. Nicely located within this leafy public garden, the library hosts regular storytelling & writing workshops & has a good selection of works in Arabic, English & French, & there is a special children's area. Internet access available.

Librairie Antoine [162 D4] Hamra St, Hamra; ✆01 341 470/1; e contact@antoineonline. com; www.antoineonline.com; ⊕ 08.30–20.00 Mon–Sat, 15.00–20.00 Sun. This brilliant store is a book-lover's delight & has been established for over 80 years selling an eclectic range of tomes in Arabic, French & English, & is particularly strong on the history, politics & culture of Lebanon & the region. This is also the best bookshop in town to pick up copies of local & international newspapers & magazines. Antoine has numerous other outlets around the city including Achrafieh (*ABC Mall* [172 D4] & *Sassine Sq* [172 C5]), Verdun (*Dunes Centre* [126 C5]) & at Beirut Souks [139 E4] in Downtown.

Librairie Internationale [163 F3] Block D, Gefinor Centre, Clemenceau St, Hamra; 01 743 285/6; e info@librairieinternationale.com; www.librairieinternationale.com; 08.00– 17.00 Mon–Sat. Though not one of the capital's largest bookshops, this long-established store still manages to pack in an excellent selection of works on Lebanon & the Middle East in English & French. They also stock a decent selection of magazines & English-language newspapers.

Librairie Orientale [172 C4] Achrafieh St, Achrafieh; 01 200 875, 01 333 379; 08.30–19.00 Mon–Fri, 08.30–14.00 Sat; www. librairieorientale.com.lb. Maps, travel books, newspapers & magazines in Arabic, English & French. They also have another good branch on Hamra St, Hamra (*opposite Bread Republic;* 01 736 524; 08.30–19.00 Mon–Fri, 08.30–14.00 Sat).

Librairie Stephan [172 C4] Achrafieh St, Achrafieh; 01 335 503; e sales@librairiestephan. com; www.librairiestephan.com; 08.00–20.00 Mon–Sat. Long-established store stocking books & magazines for adults & children including academic & current affairs titles in Arabic, English & French. They also stock the *New York Times*.

Maliks [162 D3] Bliss St, opposite main gate of the AUB, Hamra; 01 741 975; e aub@maliks. com, maliks@maliks.com; www.maliks.com; 07.30–22.00 Mon–Fri, 08.00–17.00 Sat. This branch stocks a small selection of academic books but will order any title. Also sells office supplies & stamps, & provides a while-you-wait passport photo service (*US$10 for 8 photographs*), as well as copying, a courier service, internet facilities & will burn images to CD/DVD. Numerous other branches including in Achrafieh & Verdun.

RectoVerso Library/Bookshop [172 A3] 58 Monot St, Achrafieh; 01 330 994; m 71 347 716; e info@rectoversolibrary.com; www.rectoversolibrary.com; 13.00–18.00 Mon–Fri, otherwise by prior appointment. Founded in 2009, RectoVerso is the brainchild of art historian & critic Cesar Nammour & former German Foreign Office official Gabriela Schaub (the co-founders of the MACAM Museum near Byblos; page 214). Doubling as both a library & bookshop, this tiny venue with around 900 books, specialises in the whole gamut of Lebanese art & artists from calligraphy to sculpture. There is also a café & free Wi-Fi. Highly recommended for art lovers.

Virgin Megastore [139 F5] See listing on page 153 for details.

Way In Bookshop [162 D4] Hamra St, facing Hamra Sq, Hamra; 01 345 856, 01 753 665; e wayin@live.com; 09.00–20.00 Mon–Sat, 11.00–20.00 Sun. Stocks an excellent range of political, fiction & non-fiction books in Arabic, English & French, together with postcards, stationery items & an extensive selection of Lebanese & international newspapers & magazines.

OTHER PRACTICALITIES

FOREIGN CONSULATES AND EMBASSIES IN BEIRUT AND ENVIRONS

Argentina [172 B3] Sursock St, Achrafieh; 01 210 803; e elbno@mrecis.gov.ar; www. elbno.mrecic.gov.ar; 08.30–12.30 Mon–Fri

Australia [138 C6] Embassy Complex, Serail Bldg, Downtown; 01 960 600, 01 960 670 (visa); f 01 960 671; e austemle@dfat.gov. au; www.lebanon.embassy.gov.au; 08.30– 16.00 Mon–Thu, 08.30–13.30 Fri

Austria [172 B3] 8th Fl, Tabaris Bldg, Charles Malek Av, east of Saifi Village, Achrafieh; 01 213 017, 01 213 052; f 01 217 772; e beirut-ob@ bmeia.gv.at; www.bmeia.gv.at/en/embassy/ beirut; 08.30–13.00 Mon–Fri

Belgium [139 E6] Al Amir Bachir St, Downtown; 01 976 001; f 01 976 007; m 03 727 789 (24hr emergency number); e beirut@diplobel.fed.be; www.diplomatie. belgium.be/lebanon; 07.30–15.00 Mon–Fri

Canada [map, pages 184–5] 2nd Fl, Coolrite Bldg, Seaside Rd, Jal Al Dib Hwy; 04 726 700; f 04 710 595; e beirut-cs@international.gc.ca; www.lebanon.gc.ca; 08.30–11.30 Mon–Fri

China [127 E7] 72 Nicolas Sursock St, Mar Elias; V f 01 850 316; e chinaemb_lb@mfa. gov.cn; http://lb.china-embassy.org/eng/qwls/; 09.00–noon Mon–Fri

Denmark [138 C6] Embassy Complex, Serail Bldg, Downtown; 01 991 001/2/3/4/5, 01 991 008 (visa section); f 01 991 006; e beyamb@um.dk; www.libanon.um.dk;

⏱ 08.00–15.45 Mon–Thu, 08.00–14.00 Fri, consular department 09.00–noon Tue–Thu

🇪 **France** [172 B7] Rue de Damas, nr University of St Joseph & French Cultural Centre; Achrafieh; ☎ 01 420 000/060; f 01 420 013; e admin-francais.beyrouth@diplomatie.gouv.fr, admin-francais.beyrouth@diplomatie.gouv.fr; www.ambafrance-lb.org; ⏱ 08.15–13.00 & 14.00–17.00 Mon–Fri

🇪 **Germany** [127 H3] Maghzal Bldg, nr Jesus & Mary School, Mtayleb, Rabieh; ☎ 04 935 000, 01 935 004 (visas); m 03 600 053 (24hr emergency number); f 04 935 001; e info@beirut.diplo.de; www.beirut.diplo.de; ⏱ 07.30–11.30 Mon–Fri, 12.30–14.30 Mon–Thu.

🇪 **Ireland** [127 H7] (consulate) Badaro St, opposite IMPEX (car dealer), Badaro; ☎ 01 395 005; f 01 392 005; e irishcon.leb@hotmail.com; ⏱ 09.00–13.00 Mon–Fri

🇪 **Italy** [127 H7] Rue du Palais Presidentiel, Baabda; ☎ 05 954 955; f 05 959 615/6; e amba.beirut@esteri.it, cons.beirut@esteri.it; www.ambbeirut.esteri.it; ⏱ embassy 09.00–13.00 Mon–Fri, consular section 09.00–noon Mon–Fri

🇪 **Japan** [138 C6] Embassy Complex, Serail Bldg, Downtown; ☎ 01 989 751/2/3; f 01 989 754; www.lb.emb-japan.go.jp; ⏱ 08.00–16.00 Mon–Fri, visa section 08.00–noon Mon–Fri

🇪 **Jordan** [127 H7] Southeast of the Presidential Palace, Baabda; ☎ 05 922 500; f 05 922 502; ⏱ 08.30–14.30 Mon–Fri

🇪 **Kuwait** [127 E7] Bir Hassan; ☎ 01 822 515/6; f 01 840 613; e info@kuwaitinfo.net; ⏱ 08.30–14.00 Mon–Fri

🇪 **Netherlands** [172 C3] Netherlands Tower, Charles Malek Av, Achrafieh; ☎ 01 211 150; f 01 211 173; e bei@minbuza.nl; www.lebanon.nlembassy.org; ⏱ 08.30–16.30 Mon–Fri; consular & visa section 09.00–12.30 Mon–Fri by prior appointment only

🇪 **Norway** [138 C6] Embassy Complex, Serail Bldg, Downtown; ☎ 01 960 000; f 01 960 099; e emb.bey@mfa.no, visabeirut@mfa.no; www.norway-lebanon.org; ⏱ 08.30–16.00 Mon–Fri; consular section 09.00–11.00 Tue–Fri, 14.00–15.00 Mon–Thu

🇪 **Republic of Cyprus** [127 H3] 5th Fl, El Hajal Tower, Jal Al Dib Hwy, Jal Al Dib; ☎ 04 718 363; f 04 718 365; e info@cyprusembbeirut.org; www.cyprusembbeirut.org; ⏱ 08.00–15.00 Mon–Fri

🇪 **Republic of South Korea** [127 H7] Rue du Palais Presidentiel, Baabda; ☎ 05 953 167; f 05 953 170; e lbkor@mofat.go.kr; www.lbn.mofat.go.kr; ⏱ 08.00–16.00 Mon–Fri

🇪 **Spain** [127 E7] Chehab Palace, Hadath; ☎ 05 464 120, 05 462 811; m 03 110 074 (24hr consular assistance emergency number); f 05 467 454; e emb.beirut@maec.es; www.exteriores.gob.es/Embajadas/Beirut; ⏱ 08.30–15.00 Mon–Fri, visa section 09.00–noon Mon–Fri

🇪 **Switzerland** [172 A3] Bourj al-Ghazal Bldg, General Fouad Chehab Av, Achrafieh; ☎ 01 324 123 (visas), 01 324 129; f 01 324 167; e bey.vertretung@eda.admin.ch; www.eda.admin.ch/beirut; ⏱ 08.30–11.00 Mon–Fri

🇪 **Turkey** [127 H3] 1st St, Rabieh; ☎ 04 528 061/2/3; m 76 084 388 (24hr emergency number); f 04 407 557; e ambassade.beyrouth@mfa.gov.tr; www.beirut.emb.mfa.gov.tr; ⏱ 09.00–15.00 Mon–Fri

🇪 **UK** [138 C6] Embassy Complex, Serail Bldg, Downtown; ☎ 01 960 800 (24hr); f 01 960 855; e consular.beirut@fco.gov.uk (visa queries); www.gov.uk/government/world/lebanon; ⏱ 08.00–16.00 Mon–Thu, 08.00–14.00 Fri, consular section 09.00–noon Mon–Thu

🇪 **United Arab Emirates (UAE)** [126 C7] Ramlet Al Baida, Jnah; ☎ 01 857 000; f 01 857 009; e eembassy@uae.org.lb; ⏱ 08.30–noon Mon–Fri

🇪 **USA** [map, pages 184–5] Rue Amin Gemayel, opposite Awkar Municipality Bldg, Awkar; ☎ 04 542 600, 04 543 600; f 04 544 136, 04 544 861; e beirutacs@state.gov, beirutpd@state.gov; www.lebanon.usembassy.gov; ⏱ 08.00–11.00 Mon, Tue, Thu

BANKS Given the importance of financial institutions as one of the mainstays of the Lebanese economy it will come as little surprise to learn that banks proliferate throughout the city and country and transactions are usually carried out very efficiently with services easily up to the standards of most European and US banks. There are also innumerable 24hr ATM machines for cash withdrawals throughout Beirut dispensing money in both Lebanese pounds or US dollars. Opening hours can vary between different banks and even between different branches of the same bank, but generally speaking they are open between 08.00/08.30 and 14.00/15.00 Monday to Friday and 08.00–noon/13.00 on Saturday, with some banks located in shopping malls having longer opening hours. The following are a small selection of some of Lebanon's main banks and their conveniently located branches in the capital.

$ **Bank Audi** [162 D3] Bliss St, Hamra; ☏ 01 361 714/5; e contactus@banqueaudi.com; www.banqueaudi.com. Lebanon's largest bank with around 80 branches nationwide & more than 20 in the capital.

$ **Bank of Beirut** [139 F4] Foch St, Downtown; ☏ 01 958 704, dial 1262 within Lebanon (24hr customer service); www.bankofbeirut.com. Has nearly 60 branches & ATMs all over the country.

$ **Bank of Beirut & Arab Countries (BBAC)** [163 F3] 250 Clemenceau St, Hamra; ☏ 01 360 460, 01 366 630/1; e clemenceau@bbac.com.lb; www.bbacbank.com

$ **BankMed** [139 F4] Weygand St, Beirut Souks, Downtown; ☏ f 01 992 061/2/3/4; www.bankmed.com.lb. At the time of writing BankMed had over 50 branches countrywide,

around half in Beirut, & whose market share is around 10% of Lebanon's banking system.

$ **Banque Bemo** [172 D5] Bemo Bldg, Elias Sarkis Av, Achrafieh; ☏ 01 200 505; www.bemobank.com. One of Lebanon's smallest banks with just 9 branches located nationwide, but most have an ATM machine.

$ **Blom Bank** [163 E7] Rachid Karami St, Verdun; ☏ 01 738 938; e mainbranch@blom.com.lb; www.blombank.com. One of Lebanon's oldest banks, it was voted Best Bank in Lebanon & the Middle East in 2013 by *The Banker* & *Euromoney* & has many ATMs & branches nationwide.

$ **Byblos Bank** [163 E7] 1st Fl, Byblos Bank Bldg, Rachid Karami St, Verdun; ☏ 01 205 050; www.byblosbank.com.lb

$ **HSBC** [163 E3] Rbeiz Bldg, Abdul Aziz St, Hamra; ☏ 01 760 000; www.hsbc.com.lb

COURIER SERVICES When time is of the essence, or bulky or valuable items need to be sent, there are a number of courier companies that can arrange this. The 'big three' all have offices in Beirut.

DHL ☏ 01 629 700; e beyalert@dhl.com; www.dhl.com.lb. DHL has a plentiful supply of offices throughout the city & these are listed on their website.

Federal Express (FedEx) ☏ 01 487 087; www.fedex.com/lb

UPS Azouri Bldg, 711 Alfred Naccache St, Achrafieh; ☏ 01 218 575; e info@unitedcouriers.net; www.ups.com/lb

CULTURAL AND INFORMATION CENTRES

British Council [172 B7] 8th Fl, Berytech Bldg, Damascus Rd; ☏ 01 428 900; e general.enquiries@lb.britishcouncil.org; www.britishcouncil.org.lb; ⏲ 08.00–17.00 Mon–Fri, 08.00–14.30 Sat

Goethe-Institut Beirut [138 H6; 172 B2] Nahr Ibrahim St, behind Sacré Coeur College & Church, Gemmayze; ☏ 01 446 092; m 71 457 490, 71 457 498; e info@beirut.goethe.org; www.goethe.de/beirut; ⏲ 09.00–17.00 Mon–Thu, 09.00–13.00 Fri. Offers a number of German language courses, as well as a varied range of events across the cultural spectrum. Also has a well-stocked library.

Institut Français du Liban [172 B7] Espace des Lettres, Rue de Damas, nr National Museum; ☏ 01 420 200, 01 420 230; e info.beyrouth@if-liban.com; www.institutfrancais-liban.com; ⏲ 10.00–18.00 Mon–Fri, 10.00–13.00 Sat. A very active cultural centre, which hosts a regular range of conferences, events & lectures together with dance, film & theatre showings & a range of language courses.

Instituto Cervantes [139 E6] 2nd Fl, Bldg 287, Rue Maraad, Downtown; ☏ 01 970 253; e cenbei@cervantes.es; www.beirut.cervantes.es. Runs a range of Spanish language courses & hosts many cultural events from concerts to films.

Italian Institute of Culture Beirut
[163 F5] Najjar Bldg, Roma St, Hamra; ☎ 01 749 801/2; e iicbeirut@esteri.it; www.iicbeirut. esteri.it; ⏰ office 10.00–21.00 Mon–Fri. In addition to running Italian language courses, the institute works in partnership with many of Lebanon's most prestigious universities &

organisations including UNESCO, Sursock Palace & the Lebanese National Higher Conservatory of Music & has its own stand at the annual Beirut International Book Fair.
Ministry of Culture [163 E5] Hatab Bldg, Rue Madame Curie, Verdun; ☎ 01 744 250/1/2/3; www.culture.gov.lb

DOCTORS AND HOSPITALS

✚ **American University of Beirut Medical Centre (AUBMC)** [163 E3] Cairo St, Hamra; ☎ 01 350 000, dial 1242 within Lebanon; e aubmc@aub.edu.lb; www.aubmc.org. This private 350+ bed teaching hospital provides a full range of medical departments & services, including accident & emergency, & has a prestigious reputation throughout Lebanon & the Middle East.

✚ **Clemenceau Medical Centre** [163 G3] Clemenceau St, Hamra; ☎ 01 372 888, 24hr hotline number within Lebanon 1240; e info@ cmc.com.lb; www.cmc.com.lb. With its glass façade, mature leafy trees & salubrious interior, you could be forgiven for thinking that this is the latest 5-star offering from an international hotel chain. In fact this 106-bed facility is a well-respected hospital, affiliated with John Hopkins International in the US, with state-of-the-art medical facilities & well-qualified staff.

✚ **Home Visiting Doctor** Achrafieh; hotline m 70 112 116; e drghabre@hotmail.com; www. homevisitingdoctor.com. Offers a 24hr call-out service to homes & hotels with full nursing support.

✚ **Hôtel-Dieu de France** [172 C6] Rue Alfred Naccache, Achrafieh; ☎ 01 615 300; e hdf@usj.edu. lb; www.hdf.usj.edu.lb

✚ **Lebanese American University Medical Center (LAUMC)-Rizk Hospital** [172 B5] Zahar St, Achrafieh; ☎ 01 200 800; e info@umcrh.com; www.umcrh.com

✚ **Najjar Hospital** [163 F4] Abdul Baki St, nr Gefinor Centre, Hamra; ☎ 01 340 626; e najjarhp@ inco.com.lb. A 61-bed private modern hospital offering a comprehensive & state-of-the-art range of medical facilities including emergency admissions.

✚ **Pasteur Medical Centre (Doctors at Home)** [172 C2] Pasteur St, opposite Saifi Urban Gardens Hotel, Gemmayze); ☎ 01 444 400; m 03 609 998. A 24hr emergency call-out service with doctors charging US$100 for a day/ evening visit. Nursing care charged at US$50/day or US$100 for an overnight stay.

✚ **Sahel General Hospital University Medical Centre** [127 E7] Airport Av, Ghobeiry; ☎ 01 858 333; e info@sahelhospital.com.lb; www.sahelhospital.com

✚ **St George Hospital University Medical Centre** [172 D3] Rue Rmeil, Achrafieh; ☎ 01 441 000, 01 575 700; ☎ 1287 within Lebanon; www. stgeorgehospital.org

INTERNET Ubiquitous throughout Beirut and other cities in the country, you should have no problem gaining access to the internet, including Wi-Fi, at most hotels, cafés and restaurants. The area around the vicinity of the American University of Beirut (AUB) is an especially good source of internet cafés and there are an increasing number of Internet Service Providers (ISPs) for those with wireless-enabled laptops. A selection of ISPs and internet access locations is listed below. The cafés are a small selection of the many available in the capital, with all offering decent internet facilities with charges generally around LBP2,000–3,000/hr. In the evening especially, some cafés are often patronised by the younger generation playing computer and video games, with a consequent increase in noise (and smoke) levels, so choose your time carefully if you require more sedate email checking and surfing time. As well as the following dedicated internet venues (overleaf), are an increasing number of cafés and some hotels now offer free Wi-Fi for those with their own laptops/phones.

Internet Service Providers

Cyberia 7th Fl, Block A, Hamra Sq Bldg, Hamra St; 01 517 027, 01 744 101, 01 727 575 (24hr technical support); e info@cyberia.net.lb, support@cyberia.net.lb; www.thisiscyberia.com. One of Lebanon's largest ISPs.

Destination 01 577 222; m 03 234 716; e help@destination.com.lb; www.destination.com.lb

Iconet Data Management (IDM) 01 512 513, dial 1282 within Lebanon for 24hr technical support; e support@idm.net.lb, ccu@idm.net.lb (customer care unit); www.idm.net.lb

Mobi 01 296 060 (sales), 01 296 029 (24hr support); e info@mobi.net.lb, sales@mobi.net.lb, customercare@mobi.net.lb; www.mobi.net.lb

Terranet 01 577 511, dial 1293 within Lebanon for 24hr customer care hotline; e info@terra.net.lb; www.terra.net.lb

Internet cafés

Bits 'n' Bytes [162 D3] Sidani St, Hamra; 01 742 211; m 03 432 697; ⊕ 10.30–05.00 daily. Good, high-speed access with plenty of computers & refreshments available.

Firewall [162 D3] Sidani St, Hamra; 01 739 497; e firewall.lb@gmail.com; ⊕ 10.30–02.00 Mon–Sat, 17.00–02.00 Sun

Sky Net Internet Café [162 D3] Sidani St, Hamra; 01 341 412; ⊕ 10.30–04.30 daily

LAUNDRETTES   Although there is no shortage of dry cleaners in the capital and most hotels, including those in the budget category, provide a laundry service, outside of these the city is not exactly awash with laundrettes, and if you want to avoid the often steep costs charged by the mid range and luxury hotels for washing and drying your clothes, the following friendly & efficient option offering a same-day service is highly recommended:

Laundromat.SM [162 D3] Jabre Doumit St, nr Mayflower Hotel & just around cnr from La Cigale Patisserie, Hamra; 03 376 187, 03 467 547; ⊕ 08.00–18.00 Mon–Sat, inc public holidays. This excellent laundry offers free

collection & delivery within the Hamra area & also an ironing & dry-cleaning service. *Self-service wash loads less than 4.5kg LBP5,500, loads of 4.5–8kg LBP7,000, exc detergent, dryer LBP3,000/10mins.*

PHARMACIES

Berty Pharmacy [172 C4] Achrafieh St, opposite ABC Mall; 01 200 767; e info@phberty.com; ⊕ 08.00–23.00 daily. An excellent pharmacy with a comprehensive supply of medicines.

Mazen Pharmacy [127 E6] Bd Saeb Salam, Mazraa; 01 313 362, 01 700 077; e info@mazenpharmacy.com; www.mazenpharmacy.com; ⊕ 24hrs daily

Pharmacie Idéale [172 C2] Gouraud St, Gemmayze; 01 443 357, 01 583 082; ⊕ 05.00–23.30 daily

Pharmacie Vitale [172 B3] Gouraud St, Gemmayze; 01 446 043, 01 564 037; ⊕ 08.00–22.00 Mon–Sat

Phoenicia Pharmacy [163 H2] Nr Regis & Phoenicia hotels, Ain Mreisse; 01 363 644, 01 369 936; e phoenicia-pharmacy@hotmail.com; ⊕ 08.00–midnight daily. Excellent selection of baby supplies, cosmetics & general medicines.

Ras Beirut Pharmacy [162 B5] Sadat St, facing Lebanese American University, Hamra; 01 788 383, 01 869 830; ⊕ 08.00–midnight daily. Good range of prescription & non-prescription drugs.

Saifi Pharmacy [139 G7; 172 A2] George Haddad St, Saifi Village, Downtown; 01 988 588; e info@saifipharmacy.com; ⊕ 08.00–02.00 Mon–Sat, 10.00–18.00 Sun. Modern pharmacy stocking a good range of medicines, baby provisions & cosmetics.

Sami Pharmacy [162 A4] Manara, opposite Luna Park; 01 342 888, 343 888; m 71 343 888; e sami@samipharmacy.com; www.samipharmacy.com; ⊕ 24hrs daily. A well-stocked & ultra-modern pharmacy with staff who can also check blood pressure & glucose levels; there is also a small consulting room for treatment of minor ailments.

Wardieh Pharmacy [163 F4] Souraty St, Hamra; 📞01 343 679, 01 751 343/345; ⊕ 24hrs daily. Good pharmacy. Close to the American University Hospital (AUH) & Clemenceau Medical Centre (CMC).

POST Lebanon's postal service is operated by **Libanpost** (📞 *01 629 629, dial 1577 within Lebanon for customer care centre;* e *customercare@libanpost.com; www. libanpost.com;* ⊕ *08.00–17.00 Mon–Fri, 08.00–13.30 Sat*) and their branches, post boxes and vans are easily recognised by their distinctive blue-and-yellow logo. The company has a growing number of branches, kiosks and post boxes throughout the city and nationwide, providing an efficient and comprehensive range of postal services including *post restante*, redirection of mail, mobile phone services and MoneyGram online money transfer services to name but a few. The official post office branch opening hours throughout the country are 08.00–17.00 Monday to Friday and 08.00–13.30 on Saturdays, with all branches closed on Sunday except at Beirut international airport, which is open 08.00–20.00 Monday to Saturday and 08.00–17.00 on Sunday. However, Libanpost also operates an increasing number of smaller kiosks located at some of the large shopping malls both inside and outside Beirut, and these are open 10.00–22.00 daily and are included in the regional chapter listings where applicable. The following post office outlets are in convenient and central locations in the capital's main areas and districts.

ABC Mall [172 D4]; 📞01 219 210; ⊕ 10.00–22.00 daily
Achrafieh [172 D5] Ogero Bldg, Sassine Sq; 📞01 321 657, 01 202 019
Beirut Souks [139 E4] 📞01 983 733; ⊕ 10.00–22.00 daily
Bourj Hammoud [173 H3] Ghanaja Bldg, Armenia St; 📞01 260 543
Dora [127 H3] City Mall; 📞01 873 547; ⊕ 10.00–22.00 daily

Downtown [138 D5] Ogero Bldg, Riad al-Solh St; 📞01 992 777
Gemmayze [172 C2] Zoghbi Bldg, Gouraud St; 📞01 442 902, 01 564 343
Hamra [162 D4] Nejmeh Library Bldg, Makdissi St; 📞01 354 706
Rafiq Hariri International Airport [127 F7] Upstairs in departure terminal; 📞01 629 369; ⊕ 08.00–20.00 Mon–Sat, 08.00–17.00 Sun

WHAT TO SEE AND DO

The Lebanese capital is not exactly endowed with a *mezze* of historical sights and attractions in the traditional sense. Whilst icons of the rejuvenation of the city are a key feature of Downtown and icons of war like the still-standing but bullethole-ridden Holiday Inn Hotel in Ain Mreisse possess a certain war kitsch, the city's pull lies in its people and its quartet of neighbourhoods. These highlights offer the visitor a fascinating and insightful glimpse into a people and a city that continue to fall victim to stereotypes based on events that occurred well over 25 years ago. A visit to the National Museum should help to emphasise the diversity and richness of the country's history, whilst a night out in the districts of Achrafieh, Gemmayze and Mar Mikhael will dispel notions that the main preoccupation of the Lebanese are guns and conflict. Here, life is lived with a capital 'L', from clubbing to shopping. Strolling the tree-lined Corniche in west Beirut is to experience a cosmopolitan and laid-back feel to the city as both Christians and Muslims freely mingle.

WEST BEIRUT Called *Gharbiye* in Arabic, this predominantly Muslim area broadly covers that part of the city west of Downtown between Ain Mreisse and

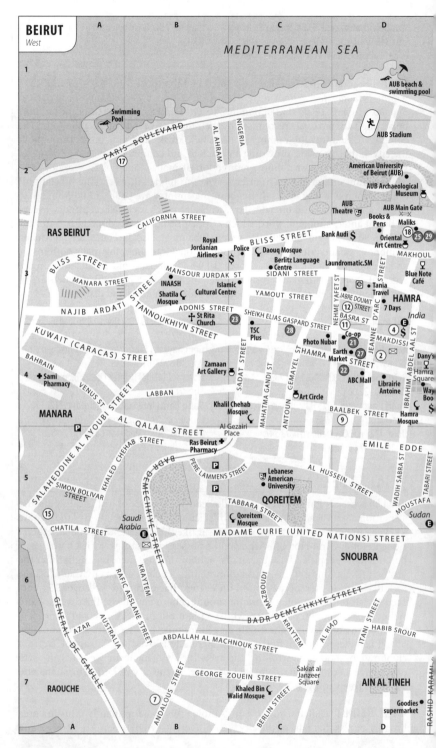

BEIRUT
West

MEDITERRANEAN SEA

A B C D

1

2

3

4

5

6

7

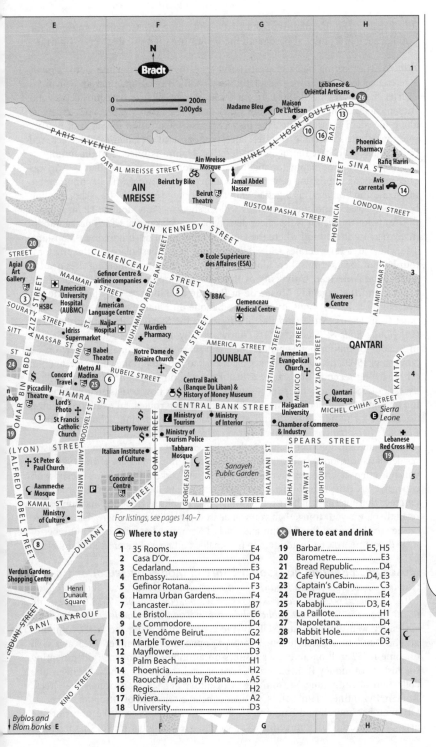

For listings, see pages 140–7

Where to stay

1	35 Rooms	E4
2	Casa D'Or	D4
3	Cedarland	E3
4	Embassy	D4
5	Gefinor Rotana	F3
6	Hamra Urban Gardens	F4
7	Lancaster	B7
8	Le Bristol	E6
9	Le Commodore	D4
10	Le Vendôme Beirut	G2
11	Marble Tower	D4
12	Mayflower	D3
13	Palm Beach	H1
14	Phoenicia	H2
15	Raouché Arjaan by Rotana	A5
16	Regis	H2
17	Riviera	A2
18	University	D3

Where to eat and drink

19	Barbar	E5, H5
20	Barometre	E3
21	Bread Republic	D4
22	Café Younes	D4, E3
23	Captain's Cabin	C3
24	De Prague	E4
25	Kababji	D3, E4
26	La Paillote	H1
27	Napoletana	D4
28	Rabbit Hole	C4
29	Urbanista	D3

4

Ras Beirut – the 'headland' of the city – and along the Corniche south to the public beach at Ramlet al Baida and incorporating the busy district of Hamra.

Hamra The beating heart of west Beirut takes its name from the word '*ahmar*', a reference to the reddish hue of the area's soil. This commercial and financial district has always been the hangout for a cosmopolitan, artsy, intellectual and student population. Thronged with shops, cafés, restaurants and money-changers along the main Hamra Street, the district is also the location for most of Beirut's mid range hotels, cinemas, theatres, late-night bars and art galleries. Once eclipsed by Gemmayze in east Beirut for its nightlife, Hamra is once again beginning to reassert itself as the haunt for night owls. If proof were needed that Beirut was once a thriving publishing centre, a stroll along Hamra Street with its innumerable magazine and book stands together with a whole range of quality bookshops selling both mainstream and specialist titles will surely dispel any doubts. Hamra's main downside for the visitor is the sheer density of vehicular traffic which packs into its many narrow streets and where the atonal symphony of horn honking is constant. The whole area reverberates with life and is one of the best places in the city for a tour by foot for its atmosphere alone, though there are a few engaging sites nearby, such as the **American University of Beirut** ✳ (see opposite), which shouldn't be missed, and the engaging **Musée de la Banque du Liban** ✳ (**History of Money Museum**; see below) housed within the Banque du Liban. For a bit of peace and quiet from Hamra Street and the city, head for the **Sanayeh Public Garden** [163 G5] (*Emile Edde St, Sanayeh*). Also known locally as the René Mouawad Garden in honour of the former Lebanese president who was assassinated nearby on 22 November 1989, this 20,000m² space dates back to 1907 and is the city's oldest public park. Having recently undergone a major renovation programme costing well in excess of US$2 million, the park re-opened in 2014. It now boasts an amphitheatre for staging cultural performances, cycle and running routes, an exhibition centre, fountains, a children's playground and a wall of fame paying tribute to famous Lebanese personalities – a great and green retreat for families and children.

Less than 2km south of Hamra is the relatively new area of **Verdun**; an exclusive residential and shopping district which dates from the latter part of the 1990s and which is often described as Beirut's version of New York's Fifth Avenue. Packed with expensive apartment buildings, cafés and restaurants, Lebanese and international designer clothing stores, it has a rather soulless feel despite its affluence, but if upmarket retail therapy is your thing, then you will be in shopaholic heaven here. The epicentre of the area is around Rue Verdun and Rachid Karami, where there are a number of large department stores in addition to the smaller and no less expensive boutiques.

Musée de la Banque du Liban (History of Money Museum) ✳ [163 F4]
(*Central Bank (Banque du Liban), Hamra, opposite the Ministry of Tourism Office;* ☏*01 750 000 ext 6020;* e *sharb@bdl.gov.lb; www.bdl.gov.lb;* ⊕ *08.30–13.00 Tue–Thu, 08.30–noon Fri–Sat, closed public holidays; admission free; wheelchair access*). This extremely well-designed and state-of-the-art museum using the latest computer graphics and smart-screen touch displays, opened in November 2013 at a cost of some US$2 million and takes visitors on an interactive journey documenting the history of money in Lebanon, the region and the world. Whilst having a fine collection of coins ranging from the 5th-century Persian era through the Greek, Roman, Byzantine, Islamic and Crusader epochs, a selection of Ottoman and post-Ottoman banknotes, and banknotes – some of which approach the status of fine art – from more than 200 countries, past and present, what makes this museum

even more absorbing is its hands-on approach, making a visit engaging for both adults and children alike. Highlights include: being able to handle an actual 3kg gold bar; taking part in a budgeting game to see how wisely you can make as well as spend money; a weighing machine that will convert your body weight into gold and Lebanese pounds; and having your photograph taken and printed out on a banknote of your choice, or having your portrait enlarged on screen and embellished with Lebanese banknotes. A short but highly informative 10-minute film documents the history of Lebanon's system of currency in the post-Ottoman period together with the history and role of the Banque du Liban since its founding in 1964.

American University of Beirut (AUB) ✳ [162 D2] (*Bliss St, Ras Beirut;* ✆*01 340 460, 01 350 000 ext 2677 (Visitors' Bureau for guided visits);* e *communications@ aub.edu.lb, visitors@aub.edu.lb; www.aub.edu.lb;* ⊕ *approx. 08.00–22.00 daily, 10.00–16.00 Mon–Fri for guided visits; admission free; upon entering proceed to the signposted Office of Protection, leave your passport & you will be given a visitors' card which you present on leaving to reclaim your passport. The Visitors' Bureau, on your right at the bottom of the steps after coming through the main gate, offers free 2-hr tours of the campus conducted by students; there is a small post office,* ⊕ *08.00–17.00 Mon–Fri, next to the student canteen where staff will forward mail to the Downtown branch of LibanPost for onward delivery*) The AUB, Lebanon's oldest university, is renowned as the most prestigious institution of higher education in the country and the Middle East, and celebrated its 150th anniversary in December 2016. Founded in 1866 by the US Protestant missionary Daniel Bliss (1823–1916) along with six other American Protestant missionaries, it was originally called the Syrian Protestant College but changed its name to the American University of Beirut in November 1920. Initially employing Arabic as the main language of instruction until 1879, its c130 subjects are now taught in English and, since its founding, more than 65,000 students, including many Arabic and Lebanese politicians, writers and philosophers, from around 100 countries have graduated from the AUB. As a private (and costly) non-sectarian seat of higher learning for all, the AUB has had a colourful and eventful past, and, since the early 1880s, its history has often been embroiled with events in Lebanon's wider political and religious sphere. During the 1975–90 civil war, the university remained open but was intermittently targeted by those hostile to American interests including the kidnapping and assassination, respectively, of AUB presidents David Dodge (1922–2009) on 19 July 1982 who was released a year later, and Michael Kerr (1931–84) who was murdered in his office on 18 January 1984. A car bomb on 8 October 1991 destroyed the AUB's original College Hall building (subsequently rebuilt in 1999) allegedly by still-unknown belligerents who opposed the 1989 Taif Agreement, which ended the country's civil war.

A highly recommended site to visit, the AUB is a lovely and walkable retreat from the busy city with the university's campus comprising beautifully manicured and verdant gardens spread over more than 60 acres overlooking the Mediterranean Sea, with its own student and public beach. In what must be a delightful place to study, the campus grounds are well worth a couple of hours of wandering to get a glimpse of student life and take in the attractive neo-Ottoman architecture. The excellent on-site archaeological museum (page 166) is a further reason to visit. It is also worth checking out the AUB's website as they frequently hold lectures on a range of interesting topics which visitors are often welcome to attend. The AUB student canteen (⊕ *07.00–17.00 Mon–Fri*) is a great place for a tasty and filling meal of chicken burgers and such like at student prices!

AUB Archaeological Museum [162 D2] (*Bliss St, Ras Beirut;* ↘ *01 350 000 ext 2660/1, 01 759665;* ✉ *museum@aub.edu.lb; www.aub.edu.lb/museum_archeo;* ☉ *summer 10.00–16.00 Mon–Fri, during Ramadan 10.00–15.00 Mon–Fri, winter 09.00–17.00 Mon–Fri, closed university & public holidays; admission free; free audio guide; wheelchair access to the museum's main entrance & 2nd floor*) This museum, one of the oldest in the Middle East, was founded in 1868, and is organised over two galleries charting man's journey from the Early Stone Age to the Islamic period. The first ground-floor gallery exhibits large archaeological finds from the Early Stone Age and Bronze Age periods in Lebanon and the wider region. The second first-floor gallery, and more archaeologically extensive, displays a range of smaller artefacts such as coins from the 7th century onwards, metal tools, weapons and jewellery from the Iron Age, Hellenistic, Roman and Byzantine periods to the Islamic (Umayyad to Ottoman) era.

In addition to housing a fine collection of antiquities, the AUB Museum is also engaged in ongoing archaeological digs in Downtown Beirut, the Bekaa Valley and in Syria. The museum also runs regular exhibitions, organises a wide programme of events for children related to archaeology and history, and holds regular lectures by both local and visiting foreign professors and archaeologists between October and June each year. Although not as extensive as the National Museum, the exhibits are all well presented and are labelled in Arabic and English. And is well worth visiting for its hive of information on, for example, the methods employed by the ancient Phoenicians in their manufacture of purple dye for garments sold to the rich and the royal (page 10) and the Phoenicians' glass making, navigational and trading skills amongst others.

CORNICHE A good place to start what is almost a Beirut ritual, and the obligatory stroll for any visitor, is opposite the Palm Beach Hotel [163 H1] in Ain Mreisse, and then walk west along this 8km strip of promenade dotted with palm trees to the public beach at Ramlet Al Baida. It's an attractive walking tour at any time of day but early morning is usually dominated by joggers and strollers, with women sporting designer tracksuits and men fishing from the Corniche. Itinerant tea and coffee vendors clunk their cups, whilst others cycle or push their carts along to tempt you with *ka'ik*, a circular type of bread with sesame seeds. But the people mosaic really comes to the fore in the evenings and at weekends when cyclists, rollerbladers, couples and families all take to the Corniche for what becomes one big social occasion with people bringing their own chairs to sit and smoke the *nargileh*.

Shortly after passing the famous Riviera Hotel, which basically epitomises the area you are now walking along, you come to the Manara Lighthouse, which, I was told by a hotelier, the Israelis spared during the 2006 July War, with their helicopter gunship only interested in taking out the light. **Luna Park** ✴ [126 A3] (☉ *10.00–midnight daily*) is unmissable, dominated by its large, colourful Ferris wheel (*admission: adults LBP4,000, children LBP2,000*), which illuminates the night sky. This compact funfair is a haven for families and couples, with a smattering of rides including dodgem cars and a café. A little further along this western stretch of the Corniche is the appropriately named Raouche, which is the Arabic version of the French word *rocher* meaning 'rock'. These two 60m-high **Pigeon Rocks** [126 A4], the city's sole geological attraction, are relics from one of the numerous earthquakes that have afflicted the city and are an enchanting and romantic sight come sunset where courting couples can often be seen leaning over the Corniche's railings admiring these natural wonders. There are a couple of small cafés overlooking the rocks, which offer a great vantage point and fantastic location at sunset. It is also possible to walk down the steep 100m path from the cliff edge for a closer look at these natural rock formations from sea level, and boat owners will take you around and through the rocks' inlets for a fee of around US$20 day or night.

DOWNTOWN Once the anarchic arena for rival militias during the 1975–90 civil war, the Downtown area of the city, also known as Beirut Central District (BCD) or Solidere, became the focal point of the war, devastating the former prosperous commercial district. This area was also the location for the most notorious symbol of the conflict, the Green Line, which divided the city into Muslim west and Christian east Beirut, making the area effectively a no-go zone for locals and visitors alike. Since the mid 1990s, however, the sound of machine gun and sniper fire has been replaced by the clattering machinery of reconstruction, filling the void of a once-desolate wartime landscape. The totally transformed area you see today has been undertaken by **Solidere** [139 F4] (*The Lebanese Company for the Development & Reconstruction of Beirut Central District; Bldg 149, Saad Zaghoul St;* \ *01 980 660;* e *solidere@solidere.com.lb; www.solidere.com*), which was founded in 1992 and initiated by former prime minister Rafiq Hariri. Hariri poured billions of his own personal fortune into this ambitious and futuristic project, which envisaged a completely new city of commercial and residential developments to drive Lebanon's economic rejuvenation and percolate through to other spheres of the economy following 15 years of negative economic fortunes.

Ironically, the 15 years of conflict also helped unearth the city's more illustrious past, with archaeologists working with Solidere in tandem with the bulldozers to uncover important ramparts, from antiquity to the Crusader eras. Some of these are still visible in Downtown, such as the Roman baths, while others are on display in **Beirut's National Museum** (pages 174–5). The heavily restored and pristine expanse of real estate that you see today has undoubtedly transformed this once-barren landscape and contributed to the oft-quoted cliché of Beirut's Phoenix-like revival from the ashes of war. However, the reconstructed French and Ottoman façades, plush designer stores, cafés and restaurants have not met with universal approval. Locals often bemoan the lack of character to the place and the almost clinical feel of reconstruction, not to mention the ongoing allegations of corruption pertaining to how Solidere acquired many of the war-damaged buildings from their owners in the first place. Nowhere is the glitzy and modernist construction more apparent than in the **Beirut Souks** [139 E4] (*Saad Zaghloul St, Downtown;* \ *01 989 040/1;* e *info@beirutsouks.com.lb; www.beirutsouks.com. lb;* ⊕ *10.00–22.00 daily*) in the northern section of Downtown. Here, spread over 128,000m², are a plethora of expensive boutiques, clothing and jewellery stores, an entertainment complex with 14 cinemas and more designer labels than Avery! Don't let the word 'souk' fool you into visions of traditional Arab markets full of intrigue and the aroma of spices – this area is a glitzy, modernist shopping mall through a concrete jungle of walkways, with not a hint or whisper of *1,001 Arabian Nights*, but is nonetheless a fascinating place to visit for taking in the great strides forward this city has made since the end of the 1975–90 civil war.

If you are travelling with young children and looking for a diversion from the shops and perhaps a more edifying and rewarding experience, there are a couple of excellent options close by. **Planet Discovery** ✳ [139 E4] (*Souk Ayyas, Beirut Souks, Downtown;* \ *01 980 650/660 ext 3440/1;* e *planetdiscovery@solidere.com.lb; www. solidere.com.lb;* ⊕ *08.30–18.00 Mon–Fri, 10.30–19.00 Sat–Sun & public holidays, closed New Year's Day; admission: museum LBP10,000, puppet shows LBP10,000, Kids Town LBP15,000, painting workshops from LBP5,000, chocolate factory LBP20,000, La Petite Académie LBP30,000; wheelchair access*) is Lebanon's sole permanent children's science museum, catering for families and kids from the age of three years. Another Solidere initiative, in conjunction with France's La Villette and Palais de la Découverte, the museum first opened in 1999 and moved to its current venue in June 2011. With its child-friendly bright and colourful décor, the museum provides a fun, hands-on scientific and social learning experience for youngsters (and adults) across a wide range of areas such as the life-cycle of the ant, the five senses, how genes make us who we are, the laws of physics, and how our bodies metabolise sugar; while the Unfinished House display lets children gain valuable social and physical coordination skills within a team environment, as workers wearing hard hats and high-vis vests on a pretend construction site, with a shared goal of completing a home. Among the other attractions and activities on offer at the museum are regular exhibitions and Polyspace, an interactive theatre with regular weekly puppet shows, arts and crafts, and educational workshops. The museum also runs Kids Town, where parents can drop off their children for up to a whole day in a professional and safe crèche-type environment. A short walk north of the souks to the waterfront there is also **KidzMondo** ✳ [139 E1](*Waterfront, Downtown;* ☏ *01 998 866;* e *info@kidzmondo. com; www.kidzmondo.com;* ⊕ *09.00–15.00 Tue–Thu, 10.00–21.00 Fri–Sun; admission: adults LBP20,000, children aged 1–3 LBP20,000, children aged 4–14 LBP40,000*), a fun, educational and interactive indoor theme park consisting of a child-size city, where kids take on roles essential to the city's day-to-day running such as airline pilot, banker, pharmacist and recycling operative, amongst many others. A short stroll west from the waterfront is the pristinely developed **Zaitunay Bay** (*www.solidere.com*), home to more luxury yachts than you can shake a stick at. Another Solidere project, the bay extends over some 20,000m² and makes for a pleasant stroll at any time of the day, but is especially attractive at night when the eclectic offerings at the marina's 17 restaurants makes this a pleasant and scenic dining experience. The area also hosts periodic arts, cultural and other events and is also the location for **Water Nation** (page 151), who offer boat rental, scuba diving and sailing activities.

To the south of the Beirut Souks is **Nejmeh Place** [139 E5], also referred to as Place de Étoile,where a series of roads containing cafés, restaurants and shops radiate out from the central Art Deco clock tower. The clock tower, with its Rolex face, dates back to the French Mandate era and is a stone's throw away from the Lebanese **Parliament Building** [139 E5], where soldiers may not always appreciate you taking photographs. The **Grand Serail** [138 C6], just west of Nejmeh Place, is nowadays the office of the prime minister. It has been nicely restored since its Ottoman roots as a military barracks in the 1850s and functioned as the office of the French governor during the French Mandate period (1920–43), but again, as was true at the time of writing, photographing this building could result in a telling-off from soldiers. The nearby **Ottoman clock tower** [138 C5] was built in 1897 in honour of the tenth anniversary of the coronation of Sultan Abdel Hamid. Just below and in front of the Serail are the quite extensive remains of some **Roman baths** [138 D5], which were discovered in the late 1960s but only restored since the late 1990s, with archaeologists carefully removing the rubble from the civil war to reveal them. They are in remarkably good condition, with the heating system devised by the Romans (hypocaust) clearly visible. Set in delightfully manicured gardens with seating, the baths are well worth a look for the fabulous restoration work done by the archaeological team. Though sectarian groups battled it out for supremacy here, Christian and Muslim architecture continues to stand in contented juxtaposition.

Lebanon's largest mosque, the distinctive blue-domed neo-Ottoman styled **Muhammad Al-Amine Mosque** [139 F6] (aka Khatem al-Anbiyaa Mosque), commonly referred to as the 'Hariri' mosque, resembles the Blue Mosque in

Istanbul and is unmissable southeast of Nejmeh Place, with its four 65m-high minarets. It is particularly impressive when lit up at night, a ray of light arrowing its beam towards Mecca and particularly atmospheric during Friday prayers with the overflow congregation filling the area outside the mosque, giving a moving display of the importance of faith. The ornate interior of the mosque is also worth a visit. Commissioned and financed by former premier Rafiq Hariri, it was four years in the making and, although Hariri himself didn't live to see its completion in 2006, the mosque, built with stone imported from Saudi Arabia, is the most striking visual legacy to the man credited with rebuilding the capital after the 1975–90 civil war. Adjacent to the mosque is the *darih* or **mausoleum** [139 F6] of the former Lebanese premier, who was slain by a car bomb on Valentine's Day 2005. The concrete shrine is free to visit and enveloped by the national flag and large-scale photographs of Hariri: a moving tribute to the man once the driving force behind Lebanon's post-war regeneration and the Downtown district you see today. More than a decade on from his death, the site continues to be one of pilgrimage for many Lebanese from across the sectarian divide of a man still regarded by many as a national, albeit still controversial, hero. Its Christian near neighbour is the neoclassical **St George Maronite Cathedral** [139 E6], dating from the 19th century, which has undergone extensive renovation since the war and is now the city's principal base for Maronite reverence.

Once the epicentre of the Downtown district, the former Beirut City Centre building [139 F7], variously known as 'the blob', 'Beirut Dome', 'egg' or 'bubble' by locals on account of its distinctive shape, is one of the only remaining examples of pre-war architecture in Downtown and sits just a short stroll across the road from the Muhammad Al-Amine mosque. This grey-looking structure dates back to the mid-1960s and was the brainchild of Lebanese architect Joseph Philippe Karam (1923–76), a leading exponent of modernism. The building was designed as a multi-purpose complex, complete with cinema, and could once boast the Middle East's largest shopping mall, but the intervention of the civil war halted construction and final completion of the project. Nowadays, the austere structure remains an icon of modernist architectural endeavour and a reminder of war amid the restored facades of Downtown, much like the similarly iconic and shell-shocked former Holiday Inn hotel in Ain Mreisse. The future of the building remains uncertain with continual talk of demolition and, latterly, preservation, by such organisations and pressure groups as Save Beirut Heritage.

To the north of the Al-Amine Mosque opposite the **Beirut Municipality** [139 F5], an imposing building dating from the 1920s, stands the **Al-Omari** or **Grand Mosque** [139 E5] (*Weygand St;* m *03 433 513* or *03 730 064*), which has had the builders in several times over the years. Originally the site of a Byzantine church, then a Roman bathhouse, it was converted by the Crusaders into a cathedral to St John in 1150, before finally being transformed into a mosque in 1291 by the Mamluks. In the author's view, this is the best of the mosques to visit in the area, with a fine interior and very friendly staff, but be sure to dress appropriately if visiting. Female visitors must cover their head.

A few minutes' walk east from the mosque and opposite the Le Gray Hotel is the attractive **Samir Kassir Garden** [139 F5], a compact and quiet little space spread over some 815m^2 with a cascading pool shaded by trees, and which contains a bronze statue, by French artist Louis Debré, in honour of the former *An-Nahar* newspaper journalist and vehement critic of Syria, who was assassinated by a car bomb on 2 June 2005, and whose former employers' towering building stands opposite. The garden has received numerous accolades including the Aga Khan Award for Architecture in 2007.

4

Although it has acted as an atmospheric backdrop to fashion shows and such-like, **Martyrs' Square** [139 F5], across the road from the Muhammad al-Amine Mosque, has been the setting for far less salubrious events over the years. A three-person statue, the creation of Italian Realist artist Marino Mazacurati (1907–69), stands in honour of the Lebanese nationalists murdered here by the Ottomans in 1915–16; the woman holding aloft a torch symbolising an array of light for the future. It was also the setting for the 14 March 2005 Cedar Revolution, when a quarter of the country's then population, around one million, descended on the square demanding the truth about the slaying of Rafiq Hariri and calling for an end to Syrian interference and military presence in Lebanon.

A short walk southeast of Martyrs' Square is **Saifi Village** [139 G7] (*01 980 650; www.saifivillage.com*), a leafy, commercial and residential enclave with just a hint of chocolate-box-type appeal with its pretty pastel hues, a welcome respite from the hustle and bustle of the main Downtown area. Another Solidere initiative, this pristine area of French colonial-style architecture, also referred to as the **Quartier des Arts**, is home to a variety of eateries, high-end boutiques and Lebanese designer fashion outlets, together with a number of art galleries. An unlikely presence, perhaps, but Beirut formerly had quite a thriving Jewish community with numerous schools and synagogues in the Downtown area and more than 10,000 Jews living in Lebanon during the 1950s. Today, estimates vary widely, but the Jewish population in Lebanon is now reckoned to be less than a few hundred. Tucked away between the less-than-kosher streets of France Street and Wadi Abou Jmil Street just north of the Grand Serial, is the **Maghen Abraham Synagogue** [138 C5]. Once the principal place of worship for Beirut's Jewish community, it dates back to 1926, built by Moses Abraham Sassoon of Calcutta. Heavily damaged during Lebanon's civil war, ironically by Israeli bombardment during its 1982 invasion, the synagogue has recently been restored following a five-year renovation programme costing some US$5 million, with financial support coming from, amongst other sources, Solidere, and with blessings across the sectarian divide, including from Hezbollah. At the time of writing a date had not yet been finalised for when the synagogue would reopen to visitors.

Robert Mouawad Private Museum [138 B6] (*Al Jeish (Army) St,* \01 980 970; e *rmpm@mouawad.com;* *www.rmpm.info;* ⊕ *09.00–17.00 Tue–Sun; admission: adults LBP9,000, children & students LBP1,500*) Not far from the Grand Serail, this cornucopia of opulence contains an eclectic mix of jewellery, metalwork, antiques, carpets, Chinese porcelain, Islamic pottery and books dating from the 12th to the 20th centuries. A former home of Lebanese art collector and connoisseur Henri Pharaon (1901–93), it was transformed by the prominent artist and jeweller Robert Mouawad, who has continued to expand the collection. The building itself is also of grand proportions and the extensive gardens, often the location for concerts and weddings, are adorned with Greek and Roman figurines.

EAST BEIRUT Situated to the east of Downtown, this is the traditional heartland of Beirut's Christian community and evinces a less frenetic daytime pace than many other areas of the capital. This district is home to innumerable cafés, restaurants and shops and is the main hub for the city's nightlife, where at weekends, especially in Achrafieh's Rue Monot, Gemmayze's Gouraud Street and Mar Mikhael, it buzzes with affluent young and style-conscious Beirutis. It also makes a pleasant place for a stroll to admire traditional neighbourhood houses, which have a very French ambience, and the well-respected Francophone St Joseph University (USJ), founded in 1875 by the Jesuits and housing a very engaging prehistory museum.

Gemmayze A few minutes walk east from Downtown's Martyrs' Square, Gemmayze is basically defined by its main Gouraud Street. This long, narrow road is festooned with bars, cafés and restaurants and its traditional old houses with balconies give the area a very rustic and faded sense of grandeur, a nice contrast if you have just emerged from Downtown. Although it is slowly losing its night-time dominance, due in part to pressure from local residents who have managed to get a curfew introduced to curb late-night noise in the area, the street makes for an interesting stroll and is a great place to eat or drink at any time. Just past the excellent Le Chef Restaurant and on the same side of the road are the **Mar Nicolas Steps** [172 C3], which will take you up towards Achrafieh. Usually held twice a year since the early 1990s, these 125 steps and walls are festooned with Lebanese and international artists displaying their creations at the **Gemmayze Stairs Art Festival (Festival Escalier des Arts)** every June and October.

Achrafieh Broadly, Achrafieh extends from Damascus Road in the west to the banks of the Beirut River in the east and reaches as far south as the National Museum with its northern limit roughly coinciding with Charles Malek Avenue. If visiting the area from the top of the Mar Nicolas Steps after walking along Gouraud Street, you will arrive on Sursock Street which, just a short walk to your left, has arguably the most beautiful building in the whole city, the **Sursock Museum** [172 C3] (*Archdiocese Orthodox St, Achrafieh;* ℡ *01 202 001;* e *info@sursock.museum; www.sursock.museum;* ⏱ *10.00–18.00 Mon, Wed, Fri–Sun, noon–21.00 Thu; admission free; wheelchair access; exhibits labelled in Arabic & English*). This ornate house with its impressive white façade, built in an Italianate-Lebanese style, has two graceful winding staircases, which lend the building an exquisite symmetry supplemented by stained-glass windows, which enhance the beauty of this building when illuminated at night. Former residence of wealthy aristocrat and fine-art collector Nicolas Ibrahim Sursock, the mansion dates back to 1912 and upon his death in 1952 was bequeathed in his will to the city of Beirut with the proviso that it be turned into a 'museum for arts, ancient and modern, originating from … Lebanon, other Arab countries or elsewhere'. Opening to the public for the first time in 1961, through its Salon d'Automne the museum began regularly to showcase the work of Lebanese artists of the period, alongside other exhibitions from the region and beyond, including Europe, in accordance with Mr Sursock's wishes. The museum closed in 2008 for a wholesale renovation and expansion programme, which has cost some US$12 million. The combined work of French architect Jean-Michel Wilmotte and Lebanese architect Jacques Aboukhaled, the building's interior has been sympathetically transformed above and below ground, creating a state-of-the-art museum whilst preserving the character of the original building of

BEIRUT East
For listings, see pages 140–7

🛏 **Where to stay**

1	Al-Naim	B2
2	The Grand Meshmosh	C3
3	Hayete Guesthouse	C4
4	Hostel Beirut	E3
5	Hotel Albergo	A4
6	O Monot	A3
7	Pension al-Nazih	A2
8	Port View	D2
9	Saifi Urban Gardens	C2
10	Talal Hostel	B2
11	Villa Clara	F2

Off map
Lancaster Tamar Hotel....D7

✖ **Where to eat and drink**

12	Abdel Wahab	A4
	Al Dente	(see 5)
13	Al Falamanki	A5
14	Bread Republic	B4
	Café Em Nazih	(see 9)
15	Godot	C3
16	Kahwet Leila	B2
17	Le Chef	B3
18	Makhlouf Café	A1
19	Paul	A2
20	Seza	F2
21	Tawlet	F2
22	Torino Express	C3
23	Varouj	H3

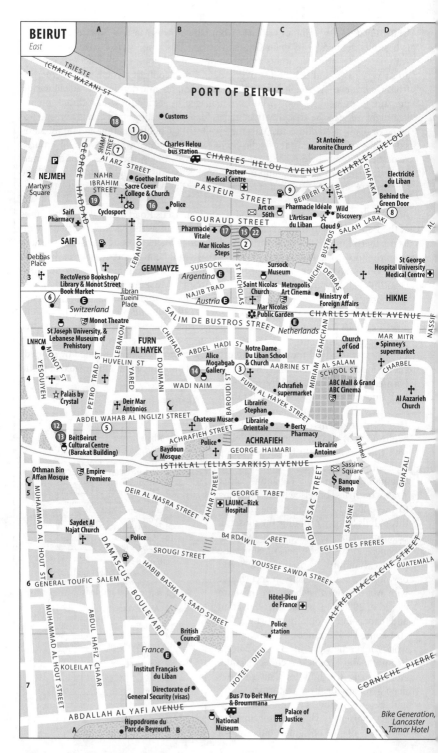

BEIRUT
East

PORT OF BEIRUT

● Customs

(18)

(1)(10)

● Charles Helou
bus station

A **B** **C** **D**

1

TRIESTE
(CHAFIC WAZANI) ST

St Antoine
Maronite Church

CHARLES HELOU AVENUE

CHARLES HELOU

(7)

AL ARZ STREET

SHAMY STREET

GEORGE HADDAD

P

NEJMEH
Martyrs' Square

2

NAHR
IBRAHIM
STREET

● Goethe Institute

(19)

Sacre Coeur
College & Church

Saifi
Pharmacy

(16)   ● Police

Cyclosport

SAIFI

Debbas
Place

PASTEUR STREET

Pasteur
Medical Centre

Art on
56th

(9)

BERBERI ST

RIZK

Pasteur
Medical Centre ✚

Pharmacie Idéale

L'Artisan
du Liban

Cloud 9

Electricité
du Liban

CHAFAKA

Behind the
Green Door

(8)

SALAH LABAKI

AL

GOURAUD STREET

Pharmacie ✚
Vitale

(17) (15)(22)

(2)

Mar Nicolas
Steps

Wild
Discovery

St George
Hospital University
Medical Centre ✚

3

GEMMAYEH

RectoVerso Bookshop/
Library & Monot Street
Book Market

(6)

E
Switzerland

SURSOCK

Argentina **E**

NAJIB TRAD

Austria **E**

Jibran
Tueini
Place

ST NICOLAS

Saint Nicolas
Church

Sursock
Museum

Mar Nicolas ❀
Public Garden

MICHEL BUSTROS

Metropolis
Art Cinema

Ministry of
Foreign Affairs

CHARLES MALEK AVENUE

HIKME

NASSIF

SALIM DE BUSTROS STREET

Netherlands **E**

St Joseph University, &
Lebanese Museum of
Prehistory

LNHCM

Monot Theatre

LEBANON

PETRO TRAD ST

TRAD ST

HUVELIN ST

YARED

CHEHADE

DOUMANI

**FURN
AL HAYEK**

ABDEL HADI ST

WADI NAIM

Alice
Mogabgab
Gallery

(14)

BAROUDI ST

Notre Dame
Du Liban School
& Church

(3)

FURN AL HAYEK STREET

AABRINE ST

Achrafieh
supermarket

MIRIAM AL SALAM

Church
of God

SCHOOL ST

ABC Mall & Grand
ABC Cinema

MAR MITR

● Spinney's
supermarket

CHARBEL

Al Aazarieh
Church

YESOUIYEH

MONOT ST

✩ Palais by
Crystal

Deir Mar
Antonios

ABDEL WAHAB AL INGLIZI STREET

Chateau Musar

Librairie
Stephan

Librairie
Orientale

Berty
Pharmacy

(12)

(13)

BeitBeirut
Cultural Centre
(Barakat Building)

(5)

ACHRAFIEH STREET

Police ●

Baydoun
Mosque

ACHRAFIEH
GEORGE HAIMARI

Librairie
Antoine

Empire
Premiere

Othman Bin
Affan Mosque

ISTIKLAL (ELIAS SARKIS) AVENUE

Sassine
Square

Banque
Bemo

$

GHAZALI

Tunnel

5

MUHAMMAD AL HOUT ST

DEIR AL NASRA STREET

ZAHAR STREET

GEORGE TABET

LAUMC–Rizk
Hospital ✚

ADIB ISSAC STREET

SASSINE

EGLISE DES FRERES

Saydet Al
Najat Church

● Police

BARDAWIL STREET

DAMASCUS BOULEVARD

SROUGI STREET

YOUSSEF SAWDA STREET

6

GENERAL TOUFIC SALEM

MUHAMMAD AL HOUT STREET

ABDUL HAFIZ CHAAR

KOLEILAT ST

HABIB BASHA AL SAAD STREET

British
Council

France **E**

Institut Français
du Liban

Directorate of
General Security (visas)

Hôtel-Dieu
de France ✚

Police
station

HOTEL DIEU

Bus 7 to Beit Mery
& Broummana

ALFRED NACCACHE STREET

GUATEMALA

CORNICHE PIERRE

7

ABDALLAH AL YAFI AVENUE

Hippodrome du
● Parc de Beyrouth

National
Museum

Palace of
Justice

Bike Generation,
Lancaster
Tamar Hotel

A **B** **C** **D**

172

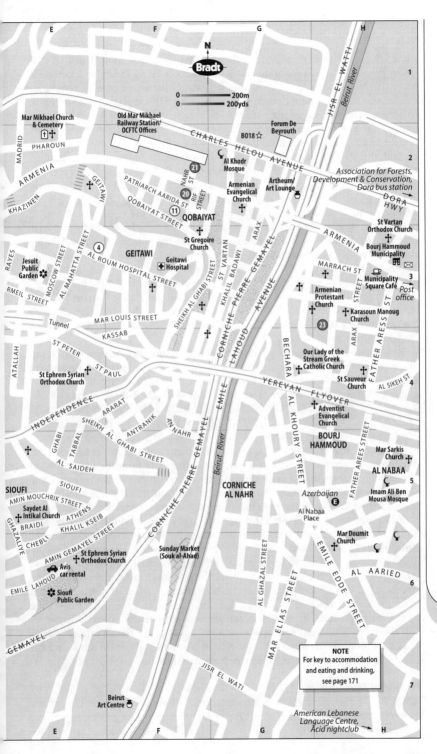

which the late Mr Sursock would surely have been proud. Re-opened on 8 October 2015, the museum's greatly enlarged exhibition area (from an original 1,500m^2 to some 8,500m^2), now extends over five floors, with two of these more than 20 metres below ground level and accommodating a new auditorium, library and exhibition space. Highlights include the ground-floor Twin Galleries, showcasing temporary exhibitions; the permanent Collection Galleries on the first and second floors, home to portraits and landscapes from artists such as Lebanon's late Impressionist painter Omar Onsi (1901–69); and the fascinating and insightful Fouad Debbas Gallery of over 30,000 photographs from the region, dating from 1830 to the 1960s. Below ground, the 168-seat auditorium is the venue for regular film screenings, lectures, talks and conferences, whilst the new **library** (⊕ *13.00–18.00 Mon, Wed, Fri & Sat, 13.00–21.00 Thu; free internet access for visitors using the library's 4 computers*) has an extensive collection of historical and modern art publications. Check the museum website for its schedule of events. The museum's **Resto Café** (✆ *01 200 512;* m *71 448 441;* e *resto@sursock.museum; www.sursock.museum;* ⊕ *11.00–16.00 Mon, Wed, Fri–Sun, 19.00–23.00 Thu*) outside the main entrance has indoor and al fresco dining and serves good *mezze* using ingredients sourced from local farmers. The obligatory adjoining gift shop (✆ *01 202 009;* ⊕ *11.00–19.00 Mon, Wed, Fri–Sun, noon–21.00 Thu*) sells a range of souvenirs, art books, glass and handicrafts. Behind the museum and facing St Nicholas Church, the 22,000m^2 **Mar Nicolas Public Garden** [172 C3] (*Charles Malek Av;* ⊕ *winter 06.00–17.00 daily, summer 06.00–20.00 daily; admission free*) makes for a pleasant pause if on a walking tour of the area and has a colourful tiled pool and plenty of seating.

Heading west along Charles Malek Avenue back towards west Beirut will bring you to the francophone St Joseph University, which operates the **Musée de Préhistoire Libanaise (Lebanese Museum of Prehistory)** [172 A3] (*University of St Joseph, St Joseph University St, nr intersection with Monot St;* ✆ *01 421 860/1/2;* e *mpl@usj.edu. lb; www.mpl.usj.edu.lb;* ⊕ *08.30–15.00 Tue–Fri, 08.30–13.00 Sat; admission: adults LBP5,000, students & under 18s LBP3,000*). Opened in 2000, this museum holds an extensive archaeological collection of more than 500 artefacts, gathered by Jesuits, of agricultural and hunting implements from Lebanon and the wider Middle East. The intriguing array of mainly small artefacts, which date from the Palaeolithic to Chalcolithic periods, offer a fascinating insight into a rich history dating back some one million years. The museum also screens a short documentary film. The nearby Rue Monot is the epicentre for the area's nightlife and boasts several cafés and restaurants.

If you continue heading south from the university or from Monot Street towards Sodeco Square, you will eventually come across the large war-damaged **Barakat Building** [172 A5] (*Sodeco Sq; www.beitbeirut.org*), which less than eloquently illustrates what it meant to be located right on the Green Line between east and west Beirut during the civil war. Known as the Yellow House, the bullet-ridden structure is currently undergoing restoration works and, when complete, will open as a museum and major cultural centre documenting the civil war and history of the city. A major project, undertaken in conjunction with the city of Paris, BeitBeirut will also stage exhibitions and lectures and will house a café, restaurant and a state-of-the-art multi-media library. A further 10–15-minute walk down the Damascus Road will bring you to Beirut's must-see National Museum.

National Museum ✴ [172 B7] (*Cnr Damascus Rd & Av Abdallah al Yafi;* ✆ *01 426 703;* e *info@beirutnationalmuseum.com; www.beirutnationalmuseum.com;* ⊕ *09.00–17.00 Tue–Sun, closed Mon, Christmas & New Year's Day, & Muslim holidays; admission: adults LBP5,000, students & under 18s LBP1,000; wheelchair access at the entrance & lifts to the 1st floor)* Without a doubt Lebanon's premier-league museum, this, arguably, should be first on your itinerary in order to gain an overview of the history and peoples that have helped shaped the development of this multi-faceted country. Construction of the museum, known as *matHaf* in Arabic, commenced in 1930 and was completed in 1937, finally opening to the public for the first time in 1943. Located right on the former Green Line, which divided the warring factions during the civil war, it was forced to close in 1975 with the onset of hostilities. To protect the larger items such as statues, sarcophagi and friezes, they were encased in concrete but still some were destroyed through a combination of neglect and saltwater corrosion. The imposing façade also suffered a heavy pounding from gun and shellfire, and the pillars were riddled with bullet holes. Restoration work on the building itself and the artefacts began in 1995, and, after lengthy and costly reconstruction work, the museum reopened to the public in 1999. A fascinating 15-minute documentary film, *Revival*, is screened every hour between 09.00 and 16.00, offering a poignant insight into how the museum was painstakingly restored by its staff and volunteers, and shouldn't be missed. Today, the museum's extensive archaeological collection spans the salient eras from prehistory and the Bronze Age to the Mamluk period.

The ground floor contains more than 70 of the largest items in the museum's collection, including a beautifully preserved mosaic from CE300, just inside the entrance, depicting the Seven Wise Men and which hails from Baalbek and once adorned a Roman villa. The other important exhibits include a marble statue of Hygeia, the goddess of health from the Roman period, 2nd-century CE Roman sarcophagi decorated with inebriated cupids and scenes of battles with the Greeks, and a bas-relief of Pharaoh Ramses II. From the Phoenician era, statues of children associated with Echmoun, the god of healing, are particularly impressive, but the most prestigious relic from this period is the sarcophagus of King Ahiram, the 10th-century King of Byblos, which contains the earliest inscriptions of the Phoenician alphabet. Continuing up to the first floor, around 1,000 smaller, delicate and more ornate items are no less impressive for their exquisite craftsmanship. Artefacts here date from prehistory, the Neolithic and Chalcolithic eras. There, Bronze Age figurines depict hippopotami, hedgehogs, cats, dogs, sphinxes and various grotesque faces, found in Byblos and Beirut. From the Iron Age and Greek Hellenistic periods, pottery, copper and flint tools, together with terracotta figurines, testify to the rich archaeological heritage left by Lebanon's early civilisations. One of the highlights of this floor is the display of lithe Phoenician figures with their gold-leaf pointed hats arranged in platoon-like fashion. The Ministry of Tourism office in Hamra has free brochures about the museum but for more extensive information the shop inside the museum (✆ *01 612 298;* ⊕ *10.00–17.00 Tue–Sun*) has more detailed publications plus numerous other memorabilia for sale. All exhibits within the museum are labelled in Arabic, English & French.

BOURJ HAMMOUD The location of Beirut's Armenian community, who fled here in great numbers following the 1915 genocide in eastern Turkey, this district is often overlooked by visitors, yet provides another perspective on the city. Though the area has few specific sites of note, except for a few traditionally built Armenian churches, the attraction of this part of town, easily reached by bus numbers 2 and 8 or by walking from Downtown and continuing along Gouraud Street, is its distinctive Armenian identity evidenced in its food, the Armenian script on shop and street signs, and the shopping. Wandering through the area's streets, especially around the main busy Armenia and Arax streets, you will encounter traditional Armenian embroidery such as scarves and tablecloths, spices, fruit and vegetable vendors, wandering tea sellers and a range of other bric-a-brac items.

What the capital lacks in historical sites it more than makes up for in its sheer range of annual cultural offerings with something to cater for most interests all year round. The following details and listings comprise the current principal events of most interest to the visitor and tickets can usually be purchased from the festival organisers themselves or at the **Virgin Megastore Ticketing Box Office** (page 153) in Downtown Beirut.

BEIRUT FASHION WEEK (*5th Fl, Osaka Bldg, Minet Al-Hosn, Downtown;* m *03 070 703;* e *info@beirutfashionweek.com; www.beirutfashionweek.com*) This annual extravaganza of fashion, usually held in March, has counted supermodels such as Claudia Schiffer, Eva Herzigova and Naomi Campbell among the icons who have strutted their stuff on the catwalk showing off regional and international designers' latest creations.

BEIRUT INTERNATIONAL FILM FESTIVAL (*4th Fl, Tekeyan Centre, 418 Nahr Ibrahim St, Saifi;* ℡ *01 448 141/2;* e *info@beirutfilmfestival.org; www.beirutfilmfestival.org*) Held annually in October, this well-established and also the largest film festival in the Middle East screens both short and feature films from Lebanon and the wider MENA region.

BEIRUT INTERNATIONAL MARATHON (*4th Fl, Makateb Bldg, Mar Takla, Hazmieh;* ℡ *05 959 262;* m *70 898 151;* e *info@beirutmarathon.org; www.beirutmarathon.org*. Since its inaugural run in 2003 which attracted 6,000 runners from 49 countries, this annual event, usually held in November, has grown year on year, with more than 37,000 runners from 94 countries taking part in 2014. As well as the full marathon (42.195km) for over 17s only, there is a 10km run for those with disabilities, a 5km youth run for those aged 7–17 years, and a 1km fun run for all age groups and families. Wheelchair users can also participate in the 10km race and full marathon.

BEIRUT INTERNATIONAL PLATFORM OF DANCE (*1st Fl, Habis Bldg, Independence St, Achrafieh;* ℡ *01 218 040;* m *71 616 624;* e *info@maqamat.org; www.maqamat.org*) Tickets can be purchased in advance either at the theatre, from branches of Librairie Antoine (page 155) or online (*www.antoineticketing.com*). This annual festival, which celebrated its 11th anniversary in 2015, takes place during April at various Beirut theatres, showcasing a range of performers from Lebanon and the Middle East and beyond. The organisers, Maqamat Dance Theatre, also run dance classes across a range of styles including contemporary, oriental, *dabke* and hip-hop.

BEIRUT INTERNATIONAL TANGO FESTIVAL (℡ *01 511 894;* m *03 872 013, 03 011 782;* e *info@tangolebanon.com; www.tangolebanon.com*) Held annually towards the

The narrow streets off the main drag are also worth exploring for the aroma of spices and cheap goods. What is striking about this enclave is the understated prosperity of the area and the friendly and welcoming people. The small **Municipality Square Café** [173 H3] (⊕ *11.00–01.00 daily*) is a very pleasant space to sit for a drink amid some nice greenery and to watch the world go by, although there are numerous other decent cafés and cheap eateries all within easy walking distance. The area has a good supply of banks and pharmacies. If you are visiting on a Sunday, the nearby market **Souk al-Ahad** [173 F6] (*Corniche al-Nahr, parallel to Emile Lahoud Av;*

end of April (check website for the schedule), this event runs dance classes, as well as concerts and shows, and is one of Lebanon's more recently established festivals, which was first held in 2009.

DOCUDAYS (*PO Box 113-7222, Hamra;* m *03 167 824, 03 075 870;* e *info@docudays.com; www.docudays.com*) Founded in 1999, the Beirut International Documentary Festival usually takes place in November/December and is a celebration totally devoted to the non-fiction film genre, attracting filmmakers from the Arab and international film world.

THE GARDEN SHOW & SPRING FESTIVAL (*Beirut Hippodrome;* \ *01 480 081;* e *garden@the-gardenshow.com; www.the-gardenshow.com*) Lebanon's answer to London's Chelsea Flower Show, this floral delight is held annually over five days towards the end of May with 200+ exhibitors from Lebanon, the Arab world and beyond showing off their finest floral wares, plus master classes in gardening, art exhibitions, food tasting and workshops, and plenty of activities for kids too. Tickets can be purchased online (*www.ticketingboxoffice.com*) and from branches of Virgin Megastore in the capital (page 153).

INTERNATIONAL FESTIVAL FOR EXPERIMENTAL MUSIC IN LEBANON (IRTIJAL) (m *03 323 339;* e *sound@irtijal.org; www.irtijal.org*) Usually held over four days in April, this is currently Lebanon's only showcase of innovative music across a variety of music genres. Check their website for dates and prices of upcoming events.

SUNFLOWER THEATRE SUMMER FESTIVAL (*Sami Solh Av, Tayouneh;* \ *01 381 290;* m *03 035 298, 70 126 764*) Held in July/August each year, this month-long festival showcases music, song, contemporary dance, theatre, puppetry and drama workshops from throughout the Arab world and Europe. Tickets can be purchased from the venue (prices in 2013 ranged from LBP15,000 to LBP20,000).

VINIFEST (*3rd Fl, Bou Eid & Hakin Bldg, Damascus St, Furn Al Chebbak;* \f *01 280 085;* m *03 260 986;* e *info@eventionslb.com; www.vinifestlebanon.com*) This annual four-day celebration of Lebanese wine is usually held at the Hippodrome du Parc de Beyrouth around the first week in October. In addition to the obligatory tasting sessions and Lebanese food, the festival hosts a wide range of cultural and musical events, games, quizzes, exhibitions and film screenings. The organisers also arrange various wine-tasting tours to the vineyards in Batroun and the Bekaa Valley through their summer Vinitour scheme. Take a look at the festival website for further information, full itineraries and prices.

⊕ *07.00–17.00 Sun*), or Sunday Market, could be worth a visit either *en route* to or on the way back from Bourj Hammoud, as this sprawling and extremely popular market sells everything from antique items, bric-a-brac and books to wedding dresses.

CILICIA MUSEUM (*Armenian Catholicosate of Cilicia, Antelias;* \ *04 410 001, 04 410 003;* e *museum@armenianorthodoxchurch.org; www.armenianorthodoxchurch.org;* ⊕ *10.00–17.00 Tue–Sat, 10.00–13.00 Sun; admission free*) Although located outside Bourj Hammoud, this museum is interesting for the light it sheds on a fascinating

Unveiled in August 1995, and coinciding with the 50th anniversary of the founding of the Lebanese army, outside the Lebanese Ministry of Defence at Yarze is one of the world's largest modern sculptures, the *Hope for Peace*. A monument to the debacle of the 1975–90 civil war, it was the brainchild of the French New Realist artist Arman Fernandez (17 November 1928–22 October 2005; *www.armanstudio.com*), who believed that art is a vital requirement for peace and prosperity in any society. In his trademark style of using found objects for his assembled creations – which have previously included household waste, car and bicycle parts, buttons, musical instruments and typewriters to aid social commentary and challenge received ideas about art and society – Fernandez's creation is a 100ft-high structure weighing in at over 5,000 tonnes and designed to transform objects of death and destruction into symbols of peace and a hope for the future. The ten-storey memorial contains real Soviet T-55 tanks, guns and armoured vehicles encased in masses of concrete: relics of endless militia battles. Each piece of military hardware was sandwiched between the concrete sandbags. Then, once the concrete had set, the tanks, guns and artillery pieces were given a fresh coat of camouflage paint. The artist believes that: 'embedding objects in something else changes the time of the object. Instead of a present object, you have a fossil of the object, as you might find an organic fossil in a rock formation … objects are by their nature rather impermanent, and I like that. I also like fossils.'

To visit the monument, a taxi from Beirut should cost somewhere between LBP10,000 and LBP20,000; or take bus number 14 or 15 from Cola to Yarze and ask to be dropped off outside the Ministry of Defence. There is no charge to visit the monument. Although photography of the sculpture is not officially prohibited, it has been relayed to the author that some visitors have been refused permission to take pictures, but this seems to depend on who is on guard duty on the day.

and traumatic aspect of Armenian history. The museum takes its name from the See in Sis church in Cilicia, former Armenian Turkey, following the genocide of Armenians by the Ottoman Turks in 1915. Hastily removing their artefacts from their monastery, the monks transported what they could of their treasures and travelled to Syria before finally arriving in Antelias and making it their home in 1930. The beautiful artefacts on display in the museum, which is continually receiving new exhibits, includes the first ever Armenian printed Bible, tapestries and sculptures, along with exquisitely decorated gold and silver metal items.

Getting there The museum is located about 30 minutes north of Beirut just off the main Antelias Highway and is easily reached by bus number 2, which commences its route in Hamra and terminates at Antelias. Alternatively you can take bus number 6, which starts its journey from Cola station [127 E7] for Byblos (Jbail), alighting at Antelias for the short walk to the museum. Expect to pay around LBP20,000+ for a taxi from Beirut.

SOUTHERN SUBURBS Known as *Dahiyeh* in Arabic ('the suburbs') but often referred to locally as the 'Belt of Misery', this sprawling mass of poverty and urban degradation couldn't be more different from the glitz and glamour of the

Downtown area of the city. Reached by following the road further south from the public beach at Ramlet Al Baida and then turning inland, this area is 'home' to thousands of Palestinian refugees at the Bourj Brajneh and the infamous Sabra and Shatila refugee camps, which witnessed appalling massacres during Israel's 1982 occupation of the city (page 24). These shanty-type dwellings accommodate the unfortunate thousands forced to flee their homeland in Palestine following the creation of the State of Israel in 1948. Supplementing these camps are those areas housing Shi'ite refugees from south Lebanon who have migrated north to escape the intermittent conflict between Israel and Hezbollah.

This area was also where many foreigners were kidnapped during the civil war and lost their liberty for years, including the UK's John McCarthy. As a Hezbollah stronghold the area was heavily bombed during the 2006 July War with Israel, and continues to show the effects to this day. The suburbs are by no means on the traditional tourist trail and the 'sites' in this area are predominantly ones of poverty with posters and placards of martyrs killed fighting Israel. It is more of an edifying, albeit sombre, experience of the effects of war and conflict on displacing people and destroying their livelihoods. It is perfectly safe to wander around the streets and area, but bear in mind that with a large Shi'ite population, this is a more conservative part of Beirut and you should dress appropriately. Although it is normally possible to visit the Palestinian camps as a lone traveller or on a group visit, at the time of writing many government travel advisory departments, including the UK's Foreign and Commonwealth Office (FCO; *www.gov.uk/foreign-travel-advice/lebanon*), are urging travellers against visiting the camps. If you are intent on visiting any Palestinian refugee camps in the capital or elsewhere around the country during your visit, it would be a good idea to keep abreast of the FCO travel advice and to make contact with UNRWA (*Lebanon Field Office;* \ *01 840 490; www.unrwa.org*), the United Nations humanitarian agency responsible for the provision of education, health and social services to registered Palestinian refugees.

GREEN SPACES AND PUBLIC PARKS Some of the main parks are detailed here, but for a more comprehensive listing and further details about each park and the ongoing campaigns for the preservation and extension of the city's public spaces, take a look at the **Beirut Green Guide** (*www.beirutgreenguide.com*), which has a useful directory of the capital's parks, and the related **Beirut Green Project** (*www.beirutgreenproject.wordpress.com*) for a series of blogs where Beirutis 'dream of a greener Beirut'.

Khalil Gibran Public Garden [138 D7] (*Nr General Fouad Chehab Av, south of the Roman Baths, Downtown;* ☉ *24hrs daily*) Named after the revered Lebanese poet and philosopher, this 6,000m^2 garden contains a bust of the famed writer plus a fountain, lawns, trees and plants.

Horsh Beirut (Pine Forest) [127 G7] (*Opposite the Hippodrome, entrance on Hamid Franjieh Bd, Tayouneh;* ☉ *07.00–17.00 daily*) A lovely green diversion from the hustle and bustle of the city, this c40,000m^2 space, Beirut's largest public park, is adorned with pine trees and also has a children's playground, seating areas, tennis and basketball courts and football pitches.

Sanayeh Public Garden [163 G5] See page 164.

Sioufi Public Garden [173 E6] (*Jean Jalkh St, Sioufi;* ☉ *07.00–17.00 daily*) Perfect for kids with its swings and climbing activities, alongside a range of

sculptures, plants and great views. In June 2011 the garden became Lebanon's first Wi-Fi internet park, offering free, high-speed internet access with further zones planned for the capital and beyond in the future.

Jesuit Public Garden [173 E3] (*Moscow St, off Charles Malek Av, Achrafieh;* ⊕ *07.00–17.00 daily*) One of the city's smaller parks and mainly patronised by the mature generation of Beirutis, but worth a look/stroll for the slice of life that takes place here, such as men playing backgammon. There is also a nice library located within the gardens which is worth a look in (page 155).

ART GALLERIES Beirut has a flourishing arts scene showcasing a range of Lebanese and non-Lebanese art across a variety of genres and themes. The venues listed represent a small selection of those currently available, which range from small-scale spaces to the large expanse of the cutting-edge Beirut Art Centre, and all are free to visit. The *Daily Star* newspaper often publicises details of current and forthcoming exhibitions together with profiles of and interviews with artists, whilst the French-language *Agenda Culturel* is also a good source of timely information on the capital's art and culture scene.

Agial Art Gallery [163 E3] (*63 Abdul Aziz St, nr the American University of Beirut, Hamra;* \ *01 345 213;* m *03 634 244;* e agial@cyberia.net.lb; www. agialart.com; ⊕ *10.00–18.00 Mon–Fri, 10.00–13.00 Sat*) Puts on seven to eight exhibitions a year which showcase the work of young and emerging 'Lebanese and Arab Contemporary Art' and artists across a range of genres. The gallery also houses a permanent collection of works from across the Arab world.

Alice Mogabgab Gallery [172 B4] (*1st Fl, Karam Bldg, Achrafieh St, Achrafieh;* \ *01 204 984;* m *03 210 424;* e info@alicemogabgab.com; www.alicemogabgab.com; ⊕ *10.00–19.00 Tue–Sat, closed Sun & Mon & month of Aug*) A well-respected multi-media gallery showcasing regularly rotating works from both local and international artists working in the fields of painting, photography and sculpture.

Art Circle [162 C4] (*Assaf Bldg, Antoine Gemayel St, Hamra;* m *03 027 776, 03 774 510;* e info@art-circle.net; www.art-circle.net; ⊕ *11.00–19.00 Tue–Fri, 11.00–15.00 Sat*) Hosts a whole range of artworks and multi-media installations by Lebanese artists with around 12 different exhibitions annually, and houses a permanent collection of artworks across a range of genres from both upcoming and established artists.

Art on 56th [172 C2] (*56th Youssef Hayeck St, across the road from Saifi Urban Gardens Hotel, Gemmayze;* \ *01 570 331;* m *70 570 333;* e info@arton56th.com; www.arton56th.com; ⊕ *10.00–19.00 Tue–Fri, 10.00–18.00 Sat*) One of the many new galleries on the Beirut art scene with regularly rotating shows, this delightful space is housed within a heritage building of some character. Whilst Lebanese talent is well represented, the gallery also showcases the work of international artists working in the fields of painting, photography, sculpture and video ranging from the abstract and conceptual to art that engages with society. The gallery is also active at art fairs and organises periodical art workshops.

Artheum [173 G2] (*Quarantina;* m *71 781 783, 78 901 313;* e info@artheum.com; www.artheum.com; ⊕ *16.00–20.00 daily; hours can vary according to current events & exhibitions – phone the gallery in advance of your visit*) A large, bright multi-media exhibition space specialising in showcasing a wide range of contemporary art forms and also a venue for fashion, book and art fairs. Adjoining the gallery is **Art Lounge** (m *03 997 676;* e *nino@artlounge.net, hala@artlounge.net; www. artlounge.net;* page 149), which also showcases modern art with the addition of a performing art and cultural space and a well-stocked bookshop.

Ayyam Gallery [138 B3] (*Ground Fl, Beirut Tower, Zaitunay St, Downtown;* \ *01 374 450/1;* e *beirut@ayyamgallery.com; www.ayyamgallery.com;* ⊕ *10.00–20.00 Mon–Fri, noon–18.00 Sat*) This large international gallery chain with additional venues in Damascus, London, Dubai and Jeddah is a bright and contemporary space specialising in showcasing the work of both emerging and established artists from all over the Middle East. Regular exhibitions display works across a range of themes and media including paintings, photography and sculpture. Well worth a look in.

Beirut Art Centre (BAC) [173 F7] (*Bldg 13, St 97, Zone 66, nr Jisr Al Wati, off Corniche Al Nahr & Emile Lahoud Av;* \ *01 397 018;* m *70 262 112;* e *info@ beirutartcenter.org; www.beirutartcenter.org;* ⊕ *noon–20.00 Mon–Sat*) Opened in January 2009, this not-for-profit gallery is one of the major venues on the city's art scene. The bright and airy 1,500m² space puts on around five solo and themed exhibitions a year specialising in contemporary Lebanese art across a variety of media. Past exhibitions have included work by famed Lebanese architect Bernard Khoury. In addition to its gallery space, the centre houses a bookshop and a multi-media digital database of contemporary art, and holds regular workshops ranging from art history and theory to photography and video. The website contains full details of both past and present exhibitions and forthcoming shows.

Beirut Exhibition Centre (BEC) [139 E2] (*Waterfront District, Allenby St, Downtown;* \ *01 962 000 ext 2883;* e *bec@solidere.com.lb; www.beirutexhibitioncenter. com;* ⊕ *11.00–20.00 daily*) A Solidere initiative, this large, bright and airy 1,200m² exhibition space is dedicated to showcasing local and international artists across a range of media to help boost public awareness of contemporary art. The strikingly sleek and reflective aluminium façade is intended to convey the dynamism of the city and its ever-changing landscape.

Zamaan Art Gallery [162 C4] (*Ground Fl, Abou El Hasan Bldg, Sadat St, Hamra;* \ *01 745 571/2;* e *info@zamaangallery.com; www.zamaangallery.com;* ⊕ *10.00– 19.00 Mon–Sat*) This gallery specialises in young and emerging Lebanese and Arab artists and holds two to three exhibitions a month. It is also home to a private collection of some 1,700 paintings.

4

5

Mount Lebanon

Telephone code 09, unless otherwise stated

Probably Lebanon's most varied region, the country's western range of mountains, which often climb steeply from the coastal districts, extends geographically practically the entire length of the country, but for the purposes of this guide stretches from Beirut to just south of the coastal town of Batroun in the north. The area as a whole encompasses a diverse range of terrain including forests, rivers, valleys and waterfalls and also contains Lebanon's highest point at Qornet es Saouda (3,083m) in the northeast portion of the territory (page 249). This is also the region from which the country derives its name, Lubnan, which is Arabic for 'white', a reference to the snowy peaks of Mount Lebanon. Given its undulating landscape and relative remoteness, the area has long been a safe haven for both the Christian and Druze populations seeking refuge from persecution, and during the Ottoman period managed to retain a semi-autonomous status.

Today, the region is predominantly Christian, with the effects of altitude lending the area a more cordial and temperate feel in many parts. In summer there are a range of offerings for the visitor including the summer resort towns of Beit Mery and Broummana, the ancient sites and charming fishing port at Byblos, which has resisted modernisation over the years, and the geological wonders at Jeita Grotto. The ski season runs from December through to April and sometimes even later, with the Mount Lebanon region home to five of the country's main resorts, catering for the beginner and intermediate skier, with superb après-ski facilities for individuals and families alike. Although the Chouf Mountains fall geographically within the southeast section of Mount Lebanon, owing to the area's distinctive history, landscape and culture, they merit separate treatment with their own chapter (pages 277–96).

BEIT MERY AND BROUMMANA *Telephone code 04*

These two towns, lying to the east of Beirut in the group of mountains known as the Metn, are Mount Lebanon's quintessential summer playgrounds and resort towns, just as they were for the Romans, who also appreciated the cool mountain air and breezes for their pleasant respite from sultry summer conditions on the coast. Beit Mery, Arabic for 'House of the Master', is just 16km east of the capital and sits 800m above sea level in the Metn, offering commanding views over Beirut and the Mediterranean coastline which are even more spectacular at night.

The town boasts a good range of eateries, an internationally renowned hotel, which hosts a similarly famous annual winter festival, and a couple of historical sites which make Beit Mery an extremely easy and pleasant day trip at least. Nearby Broummana, about 6km northeast, has a far less tranquil feel, and in summer sees its population balloon fourfold to some 60,000 as pleasure-seeking Lebanese and well-heeled Gulf Arabs flock here for the food, drink and often

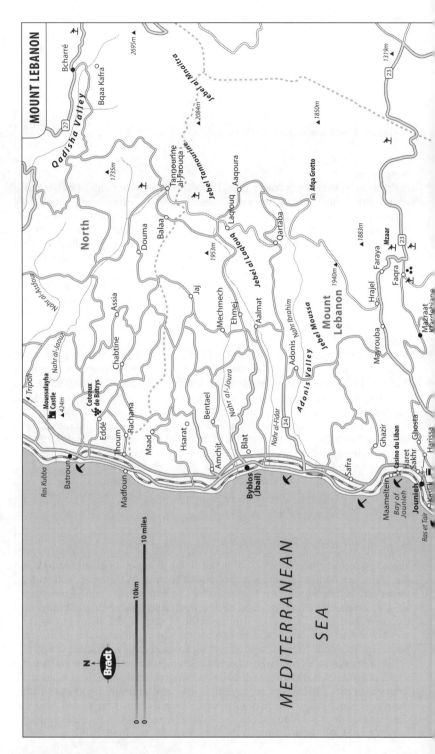

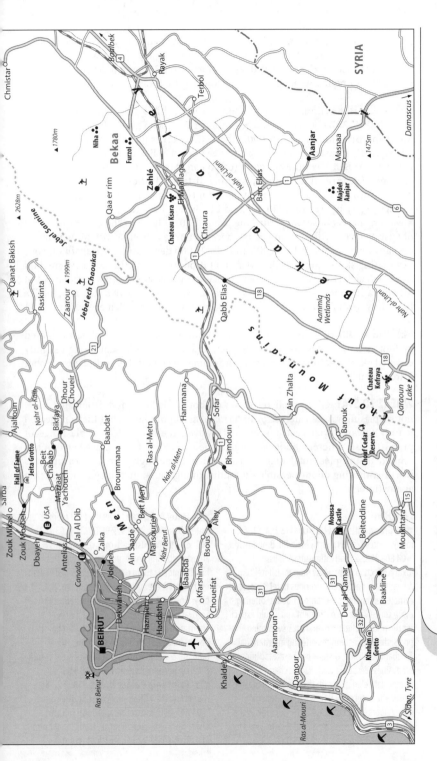

pulsating music scene. Although Broummana has equally good, if not better, panoramic views over the capital and coast, it has a dearth of historical sites to engage the visitor. However, it does hold a couple of annual summer festivals worth attending if you happen to be in town at the time.

GETTING THERE From Barbir, a short walk behind the National Museum (*MatHaf*) [172 B7], you can take bus number 7, which travels through both Beit Mery and Broummana (*LBP2,000*). The journey takes just under an hour and is an extremely pleasant one with terrific views down to Beirut as you ascend Mount Lebanon. At Beit Mery the bus will drop you off at the roundabout, where the sites and amenities are all within easy walking distance. It should also be possible to catch a minivan or service taxi leaving from Beirut's Dora intersection [173 H2]. Expect to pay between LBP20,000 and LBP30,000 for a taxi. It is worth noting, however, that as buses stop running around 20.00 (as was the case at the time of writing), you will need to get a service taxi or taxi back to Beirut, which can cost anywhere between LBP5,000 and LBP25,000 depending once again on your negotiating skills. To reach Beit Mery and Broummana by the self-drive method from Beirut, drive eastwards from the capital towards the large roundabout at Mkalles and continue travelling east towards Mansourieh, Ain Saade and, finally, Beit Mery, with Broummana a further 6km northeast from Beit Mery.

GETTING AROUND Both Beit Mery and Broummana are easily and best explored by foot as both towns are quite compact, and it's also a pleasant though slightly elevated 6km walk from Beit Mery to Broummana; taxis and of course bus number 7 are available.

WHERE TO STAY Given their resort status, both Beit Mery and Broummana are, not surprisingly, well catered for in terms of accommodation but they are geared mainly towards well-heeled visitors. However, there is a reasonable range of prices to suit different budgets, though the choice for the backpacker is really limited to the pleasant Hotel Kanaan. Outside the high summer season, it is worth enquiring about possible discounts, though it is, of course, worth asking at any time.

Luxury

Grand Hills Hotel & Spa [189 C4] (164 rooms, suites & apartments) Main Rd, Broummana; 04 868 888; e reservations.grandhills@ luxurycollection.com; www.grandhillshotel.com. A beautifully decorated, luxurious hotel & resort complex extending over some 35,000m² offering every conceivable accoutrement you would expect for the price, including gym, spa, 3 swimming pools, theatre, restaurants offering international & Lebanese cuisine, & state-of-the-art facilities for business & social events. Oozes charm & immaculate elegance with the bonus of fantastic views. The hotel's Royal Residence, extending over 7 floors & 4,131m², holds the Guinness World Record for the world's largest hotel suite: yours for only US$80,000 per night. $$$$$

Hotel Al Bustan [189 B4] (117 rooms & suites) Beit Mery; 04 972 980/1/2; m 03 752 000; e hotel@albustan-lb.com, reservations@ albustan-lb.com; www.albustan-lb.com. This hotel's unique selling point is its unrivalled views over Beirut & the surrounding mountains, & it plays host to the prestigious annual Al Bustan Festival (page 190) each Feb/Mar. A pricey alternative to the area's other hotels, but boasts decent business & conference facilities, the intimate & scenic Scottish Bar & its popular French & Italian restaurants. Free Wi-Fi. $$$$$

Printania Palace Hotel [189 F2] (86 rooms & suites) Chahine Achkar St, Broummana; 04 862 000; e printania@printania.com; www.printania.com. A large, traditional hotel in a nice sedate location with pleasant &

spacious rooms, swimming pool, good views from the rooms & a pleasant outdoor garden & seating area. Decent business & conference facilities & an onsite ATM. Free Wi-Fi. **$$$$$**

Mid range

🏠 **Garden Hotel** [189 F2] (50 rooms & suites) Chahine Achkar St, Broummana; 04 860 444, 04 860 777, 04 960 579; e info@gardenhotellb.com, garden@inco.com.lb; www.gardenhotellb.com. A decent enough hotel with clean & spacious, if unexciting, rooms, a swimming pool & pleasant outdoor bar area. All rooms have AC, TV & balcony. Discounts available in low season. B/fast inc. **$$$**

🏠 **Hotel Belvedere** [189 B4] (27 rooms) Main Rd, Broummana; 04 861 192; m 03 050 610. Although the rooms are a bit pricey for basic & bland, but clean accommodation, it is in a good central location & all rooms have AC & TV. **$$$**

🏠 **Le Crillon Hotel** [189 D3] (75 rooms) Main Rd, Broummana; 04 865 555/6/7/8/9; e c@lecrillon.com; www.lecrillon.com. Situated in a nice secluded setting just off the main road, this place caters mainly for families & older, expat Lebanese. Pleasant & clean rooms with swimming pool & lovely views over Mount Sannine. For those wanting a cosy, peaceful & quiet stay, this is a good choice. Wi-Fi & b/fast inc. **$$$**

Budget

🏠 **Hotel Kanaan** [189 C3] (17 rooms) Main Rd, Broummana, facing Broummana High School; 04 960 084, 04 960 025; m 03 826 725. This hotel, family-run since 1955, represents the best value in town. Though the en-suite rooms are a little simple with rather bland décor, this place has lovely old-world charm with a guest lounge area akin to a Victorian drawing room. Between Jul & Sep guests are permitted to use the Broummana High School swimming pool opposite for LBP10,000/day. **$$**

✖ **WHERE TO EAT AND DRINK** Broummana has by far the widest choice of drinking and eating options and all are very close together, on or just off the town's main road; the following establishments represent a good selection.

Expensive

✖ **Deir al-Kalaa Country Club** [189 B4] Beit Mery; 04 972 989; m 03 655 958; e info@dakcc.com; www.dakcc.com; ⏰ winter 08.00–23.00 daily, summer 08.00–midnight daily. An extremely pleasant club with terrific views & open to non-members which every Sun provides a buffet meal for US$24pp. Very family-friendly, the swimming pool & other facilities are open to non-members for a charge. **$$$$$**

Above average

✖ **Calvados** [189 D2] Fabraka St, behind Le Gargotier, Broummana; m 03 487 150, 03 979 597; ⏰ 20.30–late daily. Lively & atmospheric with a Spanish feel, located in a converted 300-year-old house. Good pub atmosphere with live music, serving decent steaks & other pub food. **$$$$**

✖ **Le Gargotier** [189 D2] Main Rd, Broummana; 04 960 562; ⏰ noon–15.00 & 19.00–midnight Tue–Sun. A favourite with locals serving good French food with an equally pleasant French & cosy ambience. Can get very busy at weekends, so best to book ahead. **$$$$**

✖ **Manhattan Centre** [189 G2] Main Rd, Broummana; 04 961 967, 04 963 370; ⏰ 09.00–00.30 daily. Serves Lebanese & international dishes. A good place to sit outside & watch the world go by. **$$$$**

✖ **Mounir** [189 E2] Just off Main Rd, Broummana; 04 873 900; e ffadel@mounirs.com; www.mounirs.com. Delightful Lebanese food including meat & seafood dishes in equally delightful & picturesque surroundings. *Nargileh* LBP13,750–16,000, glass of *arak* LBP6,750, Almaza beer LBP5,500. **$$$$**

Mid range

✖ **Crepaway** [189 F2] Main Rd, Broummana; 04 964 965; e info@crepaway.com; www.crepaway.com; ⏰ 10.30–00.30 Mon–Thu & Sun, 10.30–midnight Sun. Part of the nationwide chain serving decent standard fare of burgers, salads, pizza & pasta in the heart of the town. **$$$**

✖ **Tiger** [189 B4] Nr Deir al-Qalaa, Beit Mery; 04 870 564, 04 870 264; ⏰ noon–midnight daily. Serves decent Lebanese cuisine in a great rooftop setting with superlative views of Beirut below. **$$$**

Rock bottom

✗ **Chez Nassim** [189 G1] Main Rd, Broummana; ☎ 04 964 137; ⏰ summer 06.30–23.00 daily, winter 06.30–20.00 daily. Great patisserie serving Arabic sweets. $

ENTERTAINMENT AND NIGHTLIFE You are spoilt for choice in Broummana but the following are two of the best places in the author's view; there are plenty of others on or just off the main street.

♟ **Cheers** [189 B4] Main Rd, Broummana; m 03 211 420; ⏰ 18.00–late daily. Next door to Moods, this hostelry caters to a young crowd bopping away to pop & dance music.

♟ **Moods** [189 B4] Main Rd, Broummana; m 03 361 426, 70 184 382; ⏰ 20.00–03.00 daily. This small, intimate & lively watering hole has karaoke on Mon & a DJ spinning techno, house & Arabic discs on Fri/Sat nights. Doesn't serve food.

SHOPPING Whilst both towns have a range of general shops and stores, there is nothing here that you would travel especially to buy, but the well-stocked **Bechara Supermarket** [189 D2] (*Main Rd, Broummana;* ☎ *04 960 617 or 04 862 330;* m *70 175 050;* ⏰ *07.00–21.00 Mon–Sat, 07.00–13.00 Sun*), selling a wide range of groceries, fresh meat, frozen foods, dairy products and pastries should meet most travellers' daily needs.

OTHER PRACTICALITIES All the banks below have at least one ATM machine for cash withdrawals.

$ **Bank Med** [189 C3] Rizk Plaza, Bechara El Khoury St, Broummana; ☎ 04 860 995/6/79; m 03 760 023; www.bankmed.com.lb; ⏰ 08.30–13.00 Mon–Fri, 08.30–noon Sat.

$ **Credit Libanais Bank** [189 E2] ☎ 04 960 664, 04 960 349, dial 1518 within Lebanon; e info@ creditlibanais.com.lb; www.creditlibanais.com.lb; ⏰ 08.00–13.30 Mon–Fri, 08.00–11.30 Sat.

$ **SGBL Bank** [189 E2] Main Rd, Broummana; ☎ 04 961 538, 04 963 652, dial 1274 within Lebanon; www.sgbl.com.lb; ⏰ 08.30–13.30 Mon–Fri, 08.30–noon Sat.

✉ **Post office** [189 D3] Ogero Bldg, Bareed St, Broummana; ☎ 04 960 005; www.libanpost.com; ⏰ 08.00–17.00 Mon–Fri, 08.00–13.30 Sat

WHAT TO SEE AND DO

Beit Mery The town's small but engaging historical sites, which you can visit any time free of charge, revolve around the 18th-century Maronite monastery to St John of **Deir al-Qalaa (Monastery of the Fortress)**. Built c1748, it is thought to occupy the site of a much earlier Phoenician sanctuary and temple where they honoured their god of music and dance, Marqod, which the Romans later adapted to their own temple in the 1st century CE after their god Baal Marqod or Lord of the Dance, a reference to his power to control earthquakes and thunder and the ritual-like dances in which worshippers engaged in his honour. Until 2005, the site was used as an army barracks by the Syrian army, who looted and vandalised many of the artefacts before their departure; graffiti by the former occupiers can still be seen.

Restoration of the monastery and interior, which is well worth seeing, is ongoing and there are a series of photographs inside the monastery showing the extent of the destruction by the Syrian soldiers. In the reception area there is also a stone statue of Baal Marqod. A short walk downhill from here reveals a small, unattended site where there are some fine and well-preserved **mosaics**, which form the floor of a former 5th-century Byzantine church. In the vicinity are also

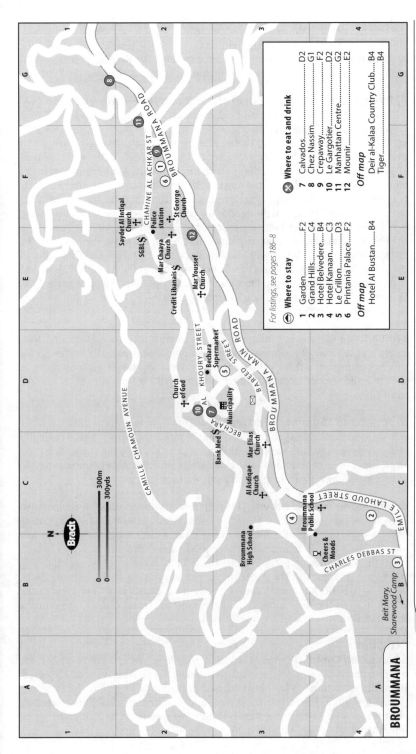

BROUMMANA

N

Bradt

0 ___ 300m
0 ___ 300yds

CAMILLE CHAMOUN AVENUE

Saydet Al Intiqal Church
Police station
SGBL$
Mar Chaaya Church
Credit Libanais $
Mar Youssef Church
St George Church

CHAHINE AL ACHKAR ST

BROUMMANA ROAD

Church of God

AL KHOURY STREET

Bechara Supermarket

BAB EL REED STREET

Municipality
Bank Med $
Mar Elias Church

BECHARA STREET

BROUMMANA MAIN ROAD

Al Asdiqae Church

Broummana Public School

Broummana High School

Cheers & Moods

CHARLES DEBBAS ST

EMILE LAHOUD STREET

Beit Mary, Sharewood Camp

For listings, see pages 186–8

Where to stay
1 Garden.............................F2
2 Grand Hills....................C4
3 Hotel Belvedere..........B4
4 Hotel Kanaan...............C3
5 Le Crillon......................D3
6 Printania Palace..........F2

Off map
    Hotel Al Bustan.........B4

Where to eat and drink
7   Calvados........................D2
8   Chez Nassim..................G1
9   Crepaway.......................F2
10 Le Gargotier.................D2
11 Manhattan Centre.......G2
12 Mounif............................E2

Off map
     Deir al-Kalaa Country Club....B4
     Tiger...............................B4

the remains of some **Roman baths** with the tiles that formed the heating system clearly visible, together with the remnants of a small temple dating from the reign of the emperor Trajan and dedicated to Juno, the Roman goddess who is reputed to have had a variety of roles, including guardian of women and fertility.

Al Bustan International Festival of Music and the Performing Arts (✆ 04 972 980/1/2; m 03 752 000; e *festival@albustan-lb.com; www.albustanfestival.com; London office: Al Bustan Festival, Mail Box 343, 56 Gloucester Rd, London SW7 4UB; e festival@albustan.co.uk*) This annual, themed, winter festival, which is held over a five-week period during February and March, celebrated its 23rd year in 2016 and takes place mainly at the 483-seat Emile Bustani Auditorium next to the Hotel Al Bustan, as well as in the hotel itself. This showcase of highbrow culture is a platform for a wide range of performing arts, from chamber and choral music to dance, jazz and theatrical productions, with many international artists having performed here over the years including Spanish flamenco guitarist Paco Peña, the English Shakespeare Company, and cellist Julian Lloyd Webber. In 2017, the festival dates are 15 February–19 March with 'Women, Queens and Empresses of the Orient' as its theme. Tickets can be purchased from the Al Bustan Hotel and from various branches of the Librairie Antoine bookshop in Beirut (page 155). For more information on the year's theme and performers, and for full booking details, visit the festival website.

Broummana Although Broummana is a pleasant town to walk around with lovely scenic views, it lacks any real sites of note, but it partially makes up for this by hosting a couple of well-established events, which take place annually in the town and are well worth attending if you are visiting Broummana around the same time.

Broummana Summer Festival (*www.brummana.org.lb*) This summer festival, held throughout July each year, sees Broummana's streets free of vehicular traffic and replaced with outdoor exhibitions of artists showing and selling their work, sales of Lebanese food, and a variety of entertainers perambulating the streets including clowns, jugglers and stilt walkers.

Broummana Tennis Festival [189 C3] (*Broummana Sports Club, Broummana High School Campus;* ✆ 04 960 430/1/2; e *info@bhs.edu.lb; www.bhs.edu.lb*) Dating back to 1927, this annual tennis tournament takes place towards the end of July and the beginning of August using the tennis courts at Broummana High School. Over the years the competition has attracted players of international standing from Asia, Europe and the Americas. If you are staying at the Kanaan Hotel, which is opposite the tennis courts, you'll get a decent bird's-eye view of the action from its top-floor terrace; if not, entry to the tennis club for spectators is free of charge.

Activities
Sharewood Camp (*PO Box 1474, Beit Mery, Metn;* ✆ 04 870 592; m 03 294 298; e *info@sharewoodcamp.com; www.sharewoodcamp.com*) This is a well-respected, fully equipped camping and activity-based organisation located in the Metn and geared towards families, providing tents and a full range of facilities including electrical power, 24-hour hot showers and toilet facilities. Outdoor activities on offer include abseiling, archery, donkey rides, hiking, rafting and trampolining.

This quaint Maronite mountain village is just 15km southeast of Beirut in the *qada* (district) of Aley in the Mount Lebanon Governorate. Although lower in height than Beit Mery and Broummana at between 200m and 700m, it is still a popular summer resort for Lebanese and Gulf Arabs, with a cooler summer climate than the capital. The village's main appeal for the visitor is its **Silk Museum (Musée de la Soie)**, which is less than an hour from Beirut (traffic permitting) by bus or taxi.

GETTING THERE If coming from Beirut, you can board bus number 14 or 15 from Cola intersection [127 E7] or the National Museum [172 B7] which terminates at Aley. Depending on traffic, the journey time can take up to an hour, with the fare costing LBP2,000. Alight at Jamhour and catch a taxi for the remaining 4km journey to the Silk Museum. Expect to pay around LBP20,000–35,000 for a taxi from Beirut; it would be a good idea to ask the driver to wait (which will obviously inflate the cost of the basic taxi fare) whilst you visit the museum which takes up to 2 hours to view at a leisurely pace. If you are on a self-drive visit, the museum's website has a clear map and directions to the entrance from Beirut.

WHAT TO SEE
The Silk Museum (Musée de la Soie) (*Bsous, Aley;* \ *05 940 757/767;* e *info@thesilkmuseum.com; www.thesilkmuseum.com;* ⊕ *May–Oct 10.00–18.00 Tue–Sun; admission: adults LBP8,000, students LBP5,000, children under 4 free, gardening workshop LBP10,000*) Opened in 2001, this fascinating eco-museum takes you through the many threads of the history and processes of sericulture, which in Lebanon traces its origins back to the Byzantine period and was once a flourishing, domestic and export industry during the Ottoman era and by the 19th-century employed over 10,000 women in Mount Lebanon's silk mills. One of the most enduring legacies of the rule of the emir Fakhreddine Maan II was to cultivate a silk industry, and under his reign *khans* were built from Sidon and Deir al-Qamar to Tripoli. Run by husband-and-wife team George and Alexandra Asseily, the museum is housed in what was once for around 50 years, until 1945, a working silk factory amidst delightful scented terraced gardens, mulberry trees and olive groves, and makes for a fascinating and edifying tour of what is a dying artisanal activity. There is a small gift shop selling silk garments, olive oil and soap, and the museum houses a couple of engaging permanent exhibitions (*Wild Silk from Madagascar* & *Living Silk: From the Worm to the Finished Product*) in addition to showing periodic silk-related exhibitions from around the globe.

Animal Encounter ✳ (*Al-Zouhour St, Ras al-Jabal, Aley;* \ *05 558 724;* m *03 667 354/5;* e *mabisaid@cyberia.net.lb; www.animalencounter.org;* ⊕ *11.00–18.30 Sat & Sun; voluntary contribution of around US$10 for family of 3–4 appreciated*) This non-profit organisation is dedicated to the welfare of abused and abandoned animals, and runs educational and lecture programmes together with hiking and camping during the summer months. This is a great venue for families which houses a wide range of animals such as bears, deer, foxes, jackals, ostrich, pelicans, imperial eagles and wild boar amongst others.

Aley EquiClub (*Ras al-Jabal, Aley;* \ *05 558 112;* m *03 818 112, 78 818 112;* e *info@aleyequiclub.com; www.aleyequiclub.com;* ⊕ *summer 24hrs daily, winter by prior appointment only; admission free, charged per activity only*) Another excellent place for families and not too far from the Silk Museum (page 191). This large outdoor space of nearly 4,000m² offers a range of adventurous activities in delightful rural surroundings for adults and children alike, including hiking and trekking, camping (*LBP25,000 pp per night*), horseriding (*LBP35,000 for 50min*), paintballing (*LBP35,000 for 200 balls*), etc. Every Saturday night is karaoke night. For a complete list of activities and services, visit the website.

SKIING AND SKI RESORTS

Lebanon has six ski resorts (a seventh, at Sannine Zenith, is in the planning stage with state-of-the-art facilities, including a helipad), with the season generally running from around mid-December to mid-April. Bear in mind that climate change has, and will continue to have, an impact on the ski season, with recent years having seen a marked decrease in its duration. Transport to the slopes other than in winter is, like the snow, sparse, and many of these resorts have little to offer the visitor outside the ski season. Even during the ski season, at the time of writing, there are no direct bus routes serving the resorts, and your transport options are confined to self-drive, or taxis, which will mostly have to be negotiated. **Ski Lebanon** (m *70 103 222, 70 211 503;* e *info@skileb.com; www. skileb.com*) offers excursions and a range of ski-related packages and tours, and is highly recommended for the quality and range of snow-related activities and information they offer, and if you want someone else to take care of the travel and ski arrangements. **Lebanese Ski Federation** (\ *09 914 550;* e *info@lebskifed. com; www.lebskifed.com*) and the **Skiing Society** (m *03 861 868, 70 444 450; www. skiingsociety.org*) should also be able to provide a wealth of information about skiing and associated activities and events in Lebanon such as snowboarding, snowshoeing, tobogganing, etc for the keen skier.

QANAT BAKISH AND ZAAROUR These two resorts, on the foothills of Mount Sannine, are not only the closest to the capital, at 47km and 54km respectively, but also two of Lebanon's smallest and most laid-back resorts; ideal for beginners, families and cross-country skiers. For climbing enthusiasts, the town of Baskinta also makes a good starting point for a 6km journey east to Nebaa Sannine, where in the summer months you can climb the 2,628m-high Jebel Sannine. This requires an ascent of around 3 hours if you are in reasonable health, and no special equipment is required except a plentiful supply of water. Be aware that the mountain has two peaks, with the higher summit, about 1km away, less interesting than its lower neighbour. From the top of the lower peak the views are stunning, affording panoramas all over Lebanon, including the Bekaa Valley, Anti-Lebanon Mountains, and the country's highest mountain peak, at Qornet es Saouda (3,083m).

Qanat Bakish (*North of Baskinta Village;* \ *04 340 300;* ⏱ *08.00–15.30 Mon–Fri, 08.00–16.00 Sat, Sun & public holidays; adult ski-lift pass prices: US$10 Mon–Fri, US$18 Sat/Sun; half-day & seasonal passes also available*) First opened in 1967, this resort ranges from 1,910m to 2,050m above sea level with three ski lifts and five ski slopes.

Zaarour (*South of Baskinta Village;* \ *04 310 010;* ⏱ *08.00–15.30 Mon–Fri, 08.00– 16.00 Sat, Sun & public holidays; ski-lift pass prices: adult LBP35,000 Mon–Fri, LBP65,000 Sat/Sun; children under 12 & senior citizens 64+ LBP25,000 Mon–Fri, LBP45,000 Sat & Sun; half-day & seasonal passes also available*) Destroyed on two occasions during the 1975–90 civil war, this tiny, privately run resort has been completely rebuilt, but, owing to its lower altitude of between 1,700m and 2,000m, has a shorter season than the others. Its main advantage is the excellent quality of its snow and a good 4km trail for lovers of cross-country skiing along Mount Sannine. There are six ski lifts catering for the beginner and advanced skier.

Getting there Both Qanat Bakish and Zaarour are best reached by car or taxi. Expect to pay somewhere around LBP90,000 for a taxi from Beirut. If on a self-drive visit from the capital, take the road to Sin al-Fil passing through Mansourieh, Beit Mery, Broummana, Baabda and Bikfaya, before turning east towards Dhour Choueir and Mrouj, and keep an eye out for the signs to the Snow Land Hotel. Alternatively, take the coast road north from Beirut and turn inland at Antelias towards Bikfaya, then follow the route above.

Where to stay The options are fairly limited at present to the sole venue below for the best access to the slopes at Qanat Bakish and Zaarour.

Snow Land Hotel (35 rooms & suites) Qanat Bakish; 04 252 222; m 03 345 300; e info@snowland.com.lb; www.snowland.com. lb. A clean, no-frills hotel with dated décor but with good access to the ski slopes. The hotel can provide ski tuition for beginners, equipment hire & purchase. Use of the nice outdoor pool is free to guests. B/fast inc. Dorm US$27pp. **$$**

LAQLOUQ (*Ihmij Village, between Mzaar & Cedars ski resorts;* m *03 441 112;* ☺ *08.00–15.30 Mon–Fri, 08.00–16.00 Sat, Sun & public holidays; adult ski-lift pass prices: US$17 Mon–Fri, US$23 Sat, Sun & public holidays; half-day & seasonal passes also available*) Located at between 1,650m and 1,920m above sea level, Laqlouq first opened as a ski resort in 1958 and offers nine slopes catering mainly for the beginner and intermediate skier. This is probably the best resort for cross-country skiing and an ideal choice for families and those content with more laid-back and sparser après-ski facilities amid stunning alpine scenery. Ski equipment and lessons for the novice to intermediate skier are also available.

Getting there Laqlouq is 62km from Beirut and 28km east from Byblos. For a taxi from Byblos, expect to pay somewhere around US$50 for a one-way trip. The journey time by car is alittle under 1½ hours from the capital. A taxi from Beirut should cost somewhere in the region of LBP100,000. If on a self-drive visit, take the coast road from Beirut to Byblos (Jbail) and then turn inland eastwards towards Annaya past St Charbel Monastery. Laqlouq ski resort is around 2km north of the main town of Laqlouq.

Where to stay

Hotel Shangri-La (20 rooms) Ihmij Village; m 03 441 112; e info@lakloukresort. com; www.lakloukresort.com. Conveniently located less than 5mins' walk from the slopes, this is a decent & popular choice with a nice homely feel. It is also open outside the ski season & offers a range of summer outdoor activities including archery, horseriding, mountain biking & tennis, as well as swimming in the hotel's own pool. **$$$$$**

What to see Apart from the skiing, Laqlouq is reasonably close to some interesting **natural rock formations** at Balaa, about 3km northwest of Laqlouq, which comprise a series of ancient dwellings cut into the rock face. A further 3km along from here is the **Balaa Sinkhole**, discovered only in 1952, a series of Jurassic limestone caverns separated by a natural rock bridge carved by water and more than 250m deep. Although an extraordinary sight, the utmost care is needed if exploring close up as there are no barriers or fences and the drops are sheer.

MZAAR (*Kfardebiane;* ☎ *09 341 501;* e *info@skifarayamzaar.com; www.skimzaar.com;* ⊕ *08.00–15.30 Mon–Fri, 08.00–16.00 Sat, Sun & public holidays; ski-lift day pass prices: adults US$27–33 Mon–Fri, US$47–63 Sat & Sun; children under 12 & senior citizens 64+ US$20–27 Mon–Fri, US$37–50 Sat & Sun; half-day & seasonal passes also available*) Previously known as Faraya Mzaar, this is Lebanon's premier, most modern, glitzy and best-equipped ski resort situated just above the village of Faraya. A relative ghost town in summer, it gets very busy in winter and has by far the country's best facilities, including a well-developed après-ski scene to international standards. With its 80km of ski trails and 42 slopes, Mzaar is also Lebanon's largest ski resort, varying in height from 1,830m to 2,465m above sea level and affording outstanding views over the Bekaa Valley, the Cedars and Beirut from its zenith. The resort's slopes are split into three categories based upon their access and are known as Refuge, Jonction and Wardeh.

Getting there Mzaar is 46km from Beirut and the journey time by taxi from the capital is around 1½ hours. Expect to pay around LBP90,000 for a taxi from the capital. If driving yourself from Beirut, take the coast road north until you get to Dog River (Nahr al-Kalb), then turn right to follow the road to Jeita Grotto. Keep following the roads ahead through the villages of Ajaltoun, Raifoun, Faitroun, Mayrouba and Faraya village, and on to Aoyoun al-Simane.

🏠 Where to stay

🏠 **InterContinental Mzaar (Mountain Resort & Spa)** (140 rooms & suites) Ouyoun El Simane, Kfardebiane, Mzaar; ☎ 09 340 100; e reservations.icmzaar@ihg.com; www.icmzaar.com. The classiest & most expensive place in town has everything you would expect from this luxurious chain for both the business & leisure visitor including pool, spa, cinema & a range of restaurants serving Lebanese & international dishes. The hotel also has direct access to the slopes from the Refuge category slope. **$$$$$**

🏠 **Coin Vert** (23 rooms) Main Rd, Faraya; ☎ 09 321 556; m 03 724 611. Simple, clean rooms with dated décor & dark wood panels, this friendly hotel is a good budget option with bar & restaurant, ski & snowboard equipment rental. **$$**

What to see and do

Mzaar Winter Festival (*Mzaar Ski Resort, Faraya;* m *70 444 450; www.skimzaar.com, www.skiingsociety.org*) Usually taking place each February, this annual event features an Air & Style competition with the Atomic Riders, an exhibition of skiing by the Lebanese army on the Refuge slope, a complimentary evening of free skiing and, of course, the obligatory after-ski party with a band and music.

FAQRA CLUB (*Kfardebiane;* ☎ *09 300 601;* ⊕ *08.00–15.30 Mon–Fri, 08.00–16.00 Sat, Sun & public holidays; ski-lift pass prices: US$12 Mon–Fri, US$20 Sat & Sun, night ski pass US$12 Sat & Sun only*) Some 45km from Beirut and with only four slopes, Faqra, at between 1,735m and 1,980m above sea level, is one of the smaller resorts. As the club is for private members only, you will only be permitted to ski here if you take out membership of the club or are a guest of a member. Staying at the club's hotel does not permit you to use the slopes, though on quiet days the club may make an exception. It would be sensible to call the club before visiting and certainly before booking a room. The club can provide ski tuition for beginners and also organises non-ski events such as hiking and horseriding.

Getting there A taxi from Beirut to Faqra should set you back between LBP90,000 and LBP100,000. If on a self-drive trip, take the coast road from Beirut north until just after the Nahr al-Kalb (Dog River), and turn right towards Jeita Grotto to follow the road ahead, passing through Ajaltoun, Raifoun, Faitroun, Mayrouba, through Faraya, and follow the signs to Faqra.

Where to stay

L'Auberge de Faqra (28 rooms) Faqra; 09 300 600; e info@faqraclub.com; www. faqraclub.com. This hotel underwent extensive renovation in recent years, & offers rooms of a decent size & comfort with all the modern accoutrements you would expect for the price; guests can use the hotel's outdoor swimming pool & there are a range of activities such as hiking & horseriding available to guests. **$$$$$**

Terre Brune Hotel (40 rooms & suites) Faqra, Kfardebiane Main Rd; 09 300 060, 09 300 065; m 03 030 301; e info@terrebrunehotel. com, reservation@terrebrunehotel.com; www. terrebrunehotel.com. Tasteful décor with lovely warm & cosy rooms are supplemented by the hotel's stunning mountain vistas, gym, pool & spa. B/fast inc, free Wi-Fi. **$$$$$**

What to see One of the most interesting of Faqra's sites is its 35m-long limestone **Natural Bridge** or Jisr al-Hajar, on the road between Faqra and Faraya, which looks so beautifully sculpted as if to be the work of skilled craftsmen but is in fact the work of nature. Apart from its Natural Bridge and of course its skiing, Faqra possesses the most extensive **archaeological remains** (*09 710 160;* ⏰ *08.00–19.00 daily; admission LBP3,000*) in all of the Mount Lebanon region; during the Roman epoch it functioned as an important centre of ecclesiastical worship. On his forays around Lebanon in the 19th century, the French archaeologist Ernest Renan (box, page 213) observed that Faqra's temple remains were 'the most spectacular ruins on the mountain', with the site comprising a broad array of lithe-like columns, altars, tombs and temples. The most intriguing, though its origins remain the subject of some scholarly debate, is the cube-like 15m-long **Claudius Tower**. The structure contains a weathered Greek inscription over its portal stating that it was renovated by the Roman emperor Claudius in CE43–44 in homage to the 'very great god', who is widely believed to be Adonis. At one time this cube-shaped building contained a pyramid-shaped top, resembling the one at Hermel in the Bekaa Valley (pages 274–5), but today it is the views from the top of the tower accessed by a staircase which will most interest the visitor.

ADONIS VALLEY AND AFQA GROTTO

Legendary associations and scenic beauty aside for one moment, if you want to live the cliché 'ski in the morning, swim in the afternoon', this is as good a spot as any to do it. The pure waters of the Nahr Ibrahim, or Adonis River, rush over a 200m-high cliff and are ideal for bathing, as well as being close to the ski resort at Laqlouq (pages 193–4). To supplement the swimming and skiing, you can also hike along the banks of the river. This area of stunning natural beauty is ideal for exploring on foot and has numerous caves and inlets, and a Roman temple near the 3,600m-long cave at Afqa Grotto, which feeds the river. In the spring and summer months, when the water level and flow are at their lowest, it's possible to explore inside the cave, which has a long mythological history, and like many a Hollywood movie has spawned a number of sequels. According to the Phoenician version, this is where Adonis met Astarte – Afqa means 'source' in Arabic – and stole his first passionate kiss with her (Aphrodite to the Greeks, Venus to the Romans). Unfortunately for Adonis, by the next date things turned rather Oedipal and Astarte's jealous husband despatched a wild boar to kill Adonis, who died in her arms, but not before they had managed to exchange one last kiss. Astarte succeeded in her quest for Adonis's reincarnation, well for part of each year anyway, and each spring the river takes on a reddish tint believed to be the blood of Adonis, which allegedly is responsible for the carpet of crimson anemones that adorns the landscape during this season. A more likely explanation for the hue of the river and seasonal blooms, however, is the speed of the water as it flows downstream picking up mineral deposits from the soil. This also just happens to be the best time to visit this spot.

GETTING THERE As the valley and grotto are somewhat isolated and remote from any bus or service taxi route, the best option for getting there is to negotiate a taxi from Byblos. Expect to pay somewhere in the region of LBP50,000–60,000 for the return fare.

MOUNT LEBANON COAST

NAHR AL-KALB (DOG RIVER) This 7km-long river, the Lycus or Wolf River to the ancient Greeks, originates at the nearby Jeita Grotto and forms the natural boundary between the Metn and Kesrouan administrative districts. It has witnessed, literally, the march of history for more than 3,000 years since the Egyptian pharaoh Ramses II felt the need to record, and perhaps give thanks for, his successful crossings. The route through the narrow, steep gorge for invading armies was potentially a precarious one, owing to the barriers created by mountain and water which necessitated a single-file march by the invaders, leaving them vulnerable to attack. One journeyman in 1232 remarked that 'a few men could prevent the entire world from passing through this place'.

Continuing the tradition set by Ramses II, subsequent foreign conquerors left their own calling cards. The result is that Dog River is a kind of a cross between an art gallery and open-air museum, with some 22 stelae (stone slabs with a commemorative inscription) in their native scripts serving as commemorative documents to the presence of icons from history. With the exception of one stela on the north or left bank of the river by the 6th-century neo-Babylonian king Nebuchadnezzar II, all of the stelae are on the right or south bank of the river. Some stelae are located higher up on the mountainside, a short walk up a specially constructed footpath with railings. Many of the stelae are labelled in Arabic, English and French, which is especially useful for those that have been weathered over time. Among the fascinating inscriptions to see are those depicting Assyrian kings, the pharaoh Ramses II with a prisoner about to be sacrificed to the god Harmarkhs, and Emperor Napoleon III, which overlays a former stela by Ramses II, commemorating his 1860 presence during the Christian–Druze conflict. There is also a selection of stelae from the more modern era, including the 25 July 1920 entry of French troops under General Gouraud into Damascus, whilst another documents French troops going the other way with their final withdrawal from Lebanon in 1946. Not all of the stelae deal directly with conflict. For instance, one commemorates construction work on the road during the Roman period under Emperor Caracalla.

Getting there At around 12km north from Beirut, Nahr al-Kalb is easily reached from the capital in less than 40 minutes, traffic permitting, with plenty of buses and taxis plying the route northbound. From Zone B of Beirut's Charles Helou bus station [172 B2], both Connexion Transport (*LBP4,000*) and Tripoli Express (*LBP3,500*) can drop you off on the highway right next to the stelae. From Dora [173 H2], buses and minivans also regularly ply the route north (*LBP1,500–2,000*); if coming from Cola intersection [127 E7], bus number 6 (*LBP1,500*) departs regularly, as do other minivans. If you are on a self-drive visit, just follow the signposted coast road route north and look out for the sign on the bridge saying *Vallé Historique de Nahr El Kalb*, which is impossible to miss and on your right just after the bridge.

Activities

Rio Lento ✳ (*c1,500m from Nahr al-Kalb;* ☏ *04 915 656;* e *riolentowaterpark@ gmail.com; www.riolento.com;* ☉ *summer 10.00–18.00 daily; admission: adults LBP35,000 Mon–Sat, LBP40,000 Sun & public holidays, children under 10 LBP25,000 Mon–Sat, LBP30,000 Sun & public holidays*) Lebanon's first water park makes for a great family day out and an easy add-on activity if visiting the inscriptions at the nearby Nahr al-Kalb. A host of water activities are on offer here ranging from the 30m-drop Kamikaze ride, Bumper Boats, and the banana-shaped Sidewinder ride to the more laid-back Lazy River. There are also a number of children's pools and a decent range of food including *mezze*, burgers and pizzas is available, plus a wide selection of hot and cold alcoholic and non-alcoholic beverages including *arak*.

JEITA GROTTO ✳ (*Main Rd, Jeita;* ☏ *09 220 840/1/2/3;* e *mapas@jeitagrotto. com; www.jeitagrotto.com;* ☉ *Jul–Sep 09.00–17.30/18.00 Tue–Sun, Oct–May 09.00–17.00 Tue–Sun, closed Mon except during Jul/Aug & closed for 3 weeks during Feb; admission: adults LBP18,150, children aged 4–14 LBP10,175, children under 4 free*) Outside the capital itself, Jeita Grotto is one of the country's biggest tourist attractions. Situated about 22km north of Beirut and the source of the Nahr al-Kalb, or Dog River, this karstic limestone landscape, fashioned by geology, time and water, has resulted in a stunning array of stalactite and stalagmite rock formations. Human habitation of the caves dates back to the Palaeolithic period, but it wasn't until a chance encounter by American missionary Reverend William Thomson, in 1836, whilst out on a hunting expedition, that its lower cavern was discovered. Upon hearing the rush of water, Thomson fired his gun and the resultant echo from inside the cave seemed proof enough that this was a substantial and important structure, which he reported back to the Ottoman authorities in Beirut. However, it wasn't until 1873 that a team of engineers from the Beirut Water Company began exploration of the caverns, lasting over a two-year period, and which concluded that there was sufficient water present to supply much of the capital's needs, which it continues to do to this day.

Additional explorations of the caverns took place in 1902, by a team from the American University of Beirut (AUB), in 1927 by a French team and, most intensely, in the 1940s and 1950s, by the Speleo-Club of Lebanon, who were responsible for discovering the upper cavern in 1958, with the lower cavern opening as a tourist attraction in the same year. When the upper cavern opened in January 1969, it did so to great fanfare. Exploiting the acoustic potential of the caves, a concert was held featuring the music of French composer François Bayle, and later the same year the cavern hosted a concert at which the German composer Carl-Heinrich Stockhausen performed. With the onset of civil war in 1975, the caverns changed from tourist site to munitions dump for the

5

Lebanese Forces militia, and the grotto was forced to close, not reopening until July 1995, following completion of extensive renovation and modernisation.

Previously on the shortlist to become one of the 'New 7 Wonders of Nature' (*www.new7wonders.com*), Jeita is a visual feast for both adults and kids alike, and a visit to the 9km-long grotto is divided into two parts: an upper and a lower cavern, which are separated by some 108m. The upper cavern, reached by a short cable car ride and then a 120m-long walkway, can be toured on foot for some 750m of its 2,200m length, where the temperature is kept constant at 22°C, and reveals a series of eerily peaceful and beautifully lit chambers containing bizarre rock formations, including the world's longest stalactite, measuring 8.2m. The 7,000m lower grotto, as the origin of the Nahr al-Kalb, can only be visited via a short boat ride through 500m of its accessible length and is equally beautiful, though cooler at 16°C, but is sometimes closed in winter when the water level is too high. What definitely won't win any awards, however, is the manmade and superfluous Disney-esque toy train ride outside the grotto. Apart from the obligatory gift shop there are also cafés and restaurants serving decent enough food. Allow 2 hours for your visit. Photography and video-recording is strictly forbidden inside the grotto, and cameras and mobile phones have to be deposited in secure lockers at the entrance.

Getting there The best way to get to Jeita if using public transport is to take bus number 6 from Beirut's Cola station [127 E7] (*LBP1,500*) and ask to be dropped off just past the Nahr al-Kalb Bridge, which is about a 40-minute journey, traffic permitting, from the capital. Over the road to your right will be a legion of taxis all waiting to convey you on the last leg of your journey to the grotto. The taxi fare shouldn't cost more than around LBP15,000–20,000 one-way, though be prepared to be quoted more! If you are visiting the grotto by hire car from the capital, take the coast road heading north and turn right shortly after passing Nahr al-Kalb; stay on this (scenic) road, which will also take you past the Hall of Fame (see below) *en route* to Jeita, which is c5km from the turn-off. A taxi to the Grotto from Beirut shouldn't cost more than around US$50–60 including the time the driver will have to wait while you explore the grotto.

Tourist information In addition to keeping brochures on the grotto itself, the **Ministry of Tourism Office** (*nr ticket office, Jeita Grotto;* \ *09 218 451;* e *tourisme_bureau_jeitaa@hotmail.com; www.mot.gov.lb;* ⊕ *09.00–17.00 Tue–Sat, 09.00–14.00 Sun*) should have a range of leaflets for other regions of the country.

HALL OF FAME (*Main Rd, Jeita;* \ *09 225 202/3; www.halloffamelb.com;* ⊕ *Aug–May 09.00–19.00 daily, Jun/Jul 09.00–20.00 daily; admission: adults LBP15,000, children under 10 LBP10,000*) Proclaiming itself to be the world's 'first animated silicone museum', this manmade attraction makes for an amusing and entertaining side trip when visiting Jeita Grotto as it is located on a side turning, clearly signposted, just off the same road to the grotto. Home to some 50 very lifelike moving and talking silicone figures from the worlds of celebrity, politics and culture, together with other more bizarre and famous people, the collection includes former Lebanese premier Rafiq Hariri, Fidel Castro, Tony Blair, Yasser Arafat, Lebanese singer Sabah, Bill Clinton, the towering frame of the world's former tallest man, Robert Wadlow, and a shifty-eyed, former US president George W Bush among its immortalised incumbents. There is also a small gift shop inside the museum selling souvenirs.

JOUNIEH

Just 15km or so north up the coastal highway from Beirut in the Kesrouan *qada* (district) to the north of the Metn region, this Maronite Christian town, with its picturesque 5km bay with mountains tumbling down into the sea, is a hedonist's paradise, its twin towns of Las Vegas, Monaco and Rio de Janeiro more than hinting at Jounieh's main preoccupation. Unfortunately, Jounieh has also become a developers' paradise with an urban sprawl of tower blocks of concrete-jungle proportions, and these monstrosities cascade down the mountainside as you approach from Beirut, with the town itself now dominated by hotels, restaurants, nightclubs and resorts. How times change. Prior to the civil war, Jounieh was a green and quiet, almost anonymous, little town with banana plantations and citrus groves.

With the onset of hostilities in 1975 and the divisive Green Line, Christians flocked here *en masse* and the area became a haven for uninhibited development,

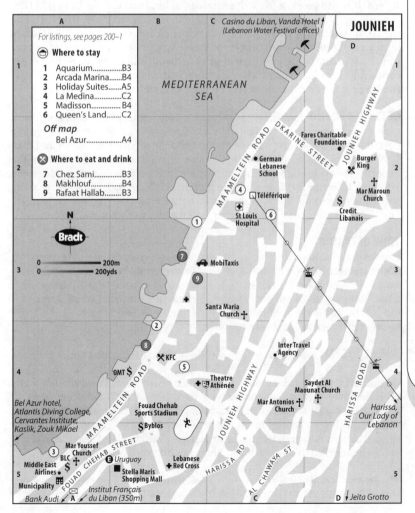

For listings, see pages 200–1

Where to stay

1 Aquarium...............B3
2 Arcada Marina.......B4
3 Holiday Suites........A5
4 La Medina.............C2
5 Madisson...............B4
6 Queen's Land........C2

Off map

Bel Azur...................A4

Where to eat and drink

7 Chez Sami.............B3
8 Makhlouf...............B4
9 Rafaat Hallab........B3

JOUNIEH

as well as a party capital both during the war and after. Although usurped somewhat by the ongoing reconstruction and ever-expanding nightlife options in the capital, Jounieh remains a popular summer resort retreat for Lebanese and wealthy Gulf Arabs alike, keen to indulge in luxurious retail therapy at nearby Kaslik, and visit expensive restaurants, nightclubs and that icon of glamour and wealth, the Casino du Liban (box, page 204). Given its primarily decadent culture, Jounieh is a little light on sites to visit but a cable car ride on the Téléférique (page 203) and a visit to the Christian shrine at Harissa (page 203) make a visit worthwhile, made more appealing by the fact that the town is in close proximity to other places of interest such as the stelae at Nahr al-Kalb (Dog River; page 196) and the essential Jeita Grotto (pages 197–8).

GETTING THERE From Beirut's Cola intersection [127 E7], bus number 6 (*LBP1,500*) departs regularly from the eastern side of the station and takes just under an hour, depending on traffic, to the centre of Jounieh *en route* to Byblos. It is also possible to catch a minivan or bus from Cola or Dora [173 H2], heading north, for between LBP1,500–2,000. If on a self-drive trip, just take the coast road north from Beirut: Jounieh is clearly signposted. The journey up the coastal highway will not be the most scenic travail you can undertake in Lebanon, consisting mostly of huge advertising billboards marketing every conceivable product and service, together with large shopping malls. A taxi from Beirut to Jounieh should set you back around US$30.

GETTING AROUND Jounieh is easily managed on foot from the main town, with everything from eateries to nightclubs all close together. You shouldn't have any need to take a bus or taxi unless you are planning to visit the Casino du Liban [199 D1], which is a longish walk along the main Rue Maameltein, where the majority of hotels, clubs and restaurants are located, as well as the Téléférique [199 C2]. If you do decide to continue walking this long road, you will eventually reach the Casino du Liban, with its superlative view over the Bay of Jounieh. Further north, this coast road continues all the way to Byblos and beyond.

TOUR OPERATOR
Lebanon Roots Tourism and Pilgrimage Opposite Holy Spirit University of Kaslik, Kaslik; ⟍09 600 444; m 03 199 338; e info@lebanonroots.com; www.lebanonroots. com. This Christian Maronite-based tour operator specialises in religious tours of the area & pilgrimages throughout the region & country. Their website also has a useful downloadable brochure of 'alternative lodgings' in Lebanon, such as those in convents & schools, providing a different option from the hotels.

WHERE TO STAY Jounieh is by no means short of accommodation options, though there is little to bring a smile to the face of the budget traveller. The hotels here do not really offer anything out of the ordinary, with the following being pretty representative. In any case, unless you find the sea and mountain views so irresistible or want to partake in Jounieh's nightlife, and the dubious attractions of the many 'super-nightclubs' invariably patronised by males enticed by seductively dressed eastern European females into paying for vastly inflated priced drinks that you feel compelled to stay overnight, Jounieh is best visited as a day trip.

⌂ **Bel Azur** [199 A4] (60 rooms) Port entrance; ⟍f 09 937 752, 09 932 162 or 09 930 621; m 03 288 894; e info@belazur.com; www. belazur.com. The quite average rooms, all with

TV & AC, are a little overpriced, but this hotel has a full complement of resort-type facilities, including swimming pool, jet- & waterskiing, & paragliding. One of the better-value options in Jounieh. **$$$$**

🏠 **Aquarium Hotel** [199 B3] (43 rooms & suites) Rue Maameltein; 📞09 936 858, 09 936 860 or 09 936 863; e info@hotelaquarium.info; www.hotelaquarium.info. Although there is no denying the fine sea views, the rooms look a little tired & dated, but all have TV & AC & there is a swimming pool in this resort complex. Otherwise it is a clean & adequate hotel for 1 or 2 nights. **$$$**

🏠 **Arcada Marina Hotel** [199 B4] (64 rooms & suites) Rue Maameltein; 📞09 640 613; m 03 117 667; e reservations@arcadamarina.com; www.arcadamarina.com. Wonderfully spacious rooms (though they don't quite match the grandness of the lobby), all with sea or mountain views, & popular with business travellers. **$$$**

🏠 **Holiday Suites Hotel** [199 A5] (45 rooms & suites) Mina St; 📞09 933 907; e info@holidaysuites.com; www.holidaysuites.com. A decent & comfortable option & pretty representative of Jounieh's lodging options with sea views & easy access to the beach with its own swimming pool & watersport activities. They can also arrange tours throughout Lebanon. Free Wi-Fi. **$$$**

🏠 **La Medina Hotel & Resort** [199 C2] (40 rooms) Rue Maameltein, next to Téléférique; 📞09 935 652/653, 09 918 044; e info@ lamedinahotel.com, reservation@lamedinahotel. com; www.lamedinagroup.com; ⏲ May–Oct only. A slightly cheaper option than the others, this hotel is pleasant & clean enough with large rooms, but not all have sea views. There is a nice communal lounge for relaxing & a swimming pool, & the hotel rents out jet skis. **$$$**

🏠 **Madisson Hotel** [199 B4] (65 rooms & suites) Haret Sakhr, opposite Fouad Chehab Stadium; 📞09 931 722/3/4 or 09 832 066; e info@madissonhotel.com; www. madissonhotel.com. Though the rooms are slightly less salubrious compared with some of the other mid range lodging options, this is still a decent hotel offering a good level of comfort for the price, with a nice indoor swimming pool, health suite, spa & sauna. All rooms have AC & TV. B/fast inc. **$$$**

🏠 **Queen's Land Hotel** [199 C2] (52 rooms & suites) Haret Sakhr, nr Téléférique; 📞09 917 333 or 09 918 333; m 71 888 820; e info@ queenslandhotel-lb.com; www.queenslandhotel-lb.com. A very modern, clean & comfortable hotel with the spacious rooms all having sea &/ or mountain views. The hotel restaurant (**$$$**) serves decent mainly international cuisine. Free Wi-Fi. **$$$**

✕ **WHERE TO EAT AND DRINK** What Jounieh lacks in sights and historical interest, it more than makes up for in its eating and drinking options. Cheap and convenience food including Burger King, KFC and Dunkin' Donuts et al is supplemented by a whole host of cafés, restaurants and watering holes serving up Lebanese and international dishes within easy walking distance of each other. The selection below is just a slice of the gastronomic choices on offer.

✳ ✕ **Chez Sami** [199 B3] Rue Maameltein; 📞09 646 064/164, 09 910 520; www.chezsami. org; ⏲ noon–midnight daily. Specialising in fresh seafood & established for over 40 years, this is one of those rare places where fine dining is complemented by the equally fine surroundings, whether it is the sea views from its terrace tables or the traditional stone interior of this converted house. Highly recommended, great service. **$$$$$**

✕ **Makhlouf** [199 B4] Rue Maameltein; 📞09 645 192; ⏲ 24hrs daily. One of the cheaper eateries, the Lebanese food served here is tasty &

filling with burgers & pizzas also available. The *plat du jour* is LBP12,000. Pleasant sea views; just a pity the KFC opposite partially obscures the mountains, but there's always the sea on the other side. **$$**

✕ **Rafaat Hallab** [199 B3] Rue Maameltein, opposite Chez Sami; 📞09 635 351; e info@hallab. com; www.hallab.com; ⏲ 07.00–midnight daily. One to avoid for weight-watchers, but this branch of renowned sweet makers from Tripoli who have been established since 1881 have a delicious range of speciality sweets such as *baklava*, cakes, pistachios, jams, coffee & ice cream. Ironically, they also stock diet products! **$$**

ENTERTAINMENT AND NIGHTLIFE You didn't decide to spend an evening in Jounieh for the peace and quiet – which is just as well, as there isn't much! It may have been usurped by Beirut's ever-evolving and pulsating club and pub scene, but Jounieh certainly knows how to have a good time, and the options are numerous. Of course, for those with large wallets there is always the Casino du Liban a little further up the road [199 C1] (box, page 204) for a decadent night out, as well as a plethora of 'super-nightclubs'. The theatre below should appeal to families with children.

❋ 🎭 **Theatre Athénée (children's theatre)** [199 B4] Haret Sakhr, opposite Fouad Chehab Sports Stadium; ☎09 912 321; e info@theatreatheneejounieh.com, roula@georgesnfrem.org; www.georgesnfrem.org, www.theatreatheneejounieh.com; ⊕ 08.00–17.00 Mon–Fri, 14.00–late Sat–Sun. A specialist children's theatre, run by the charitable NGO Georges N. Frem Foundation (*www.georgesnfrem.org*) to foster a sense of community, family values & interest in the arts, it organises drama & singing workshops for kids aged 4 & over & stages regular musical & other productions. Plays are performed in Arabic, French & English & sometimes a mixture of all 3! Ticket prices range from LBP10,000 to LBP50,000 & reservations can be made in person at the theatre or by phone. Check the website for details of current & forthcoming workshops & productions.

SHOPPING Jounieh has a bog-standard range of retail outlets including men's and women's clothing boutiques, pharmacies and supermarkets which between them stock enough items to cater for most daily needs, but there are few, if any, things you would come here specifically to buy.

OTHER PRACTICALITIES ATMs, banks and pharmacies abound, but the following useful and centrally located services are mostly clustered near to or a short walk from the **Municipality Building** [199 A5].

$ **Bank Audi** [199 A5] Fouad Chehab St; ☎09 641 660/1/2/3/4; www.banqueaudi.com; ⊕ 08.30–14.00 Mon–Sat

$ **BLC Bank** [199 A5] Stephan Bldg, opposite Municipality Bldg; ☎09 910 800 or 09 934 558, dial 1510 within Lebanon for 24hr call centre; e jouniehbranch@blcbank.com; www.blcbank.com; ⊕ 08.30–17.00 Mon–Fri, 08.30–noon Sat. 24hr ATM.

$ **Byblos Bank** [199 B5] Fouad Chehab St, Haret Sakhr, opposite Fouad Chehab Stadium; ☎01 205 050; www.byblosbank.com; ⊕ 08.30–15.30 Mon–Fri, 08.30–13.00 Sat. 24hr ATM.

$ **Credit Libanais** [199 D2] Just off main Jounieh Hwy; ☎09 832 063/065 or 09 832 069/070; www.creditlibanais.com.lb; ⊕ 08.15–14.30 Mon–Fri, 08.15–noon Sat. Has a couple of ATMs.

Institut Français du Liban [199 A5] Pere Boutros Abi Akl St; ☎09 644 427/8; www.institutfrancais-liban.com

Inter Travel Agency [199 C4] Richa Bldg, Jounieh Hwy; ☎09 934 465; m 03 656 580; e info@intertravel-lb.com; www.intertravel-agency.com. Can provide tours throughout the country, hotel reservations & car rental.

✈ **Middle East Airlines (MEA)** [199 A5] Khoury Bldg, Main Rd, facing Municipality Bldg; ☎09 932 120; e jounieh@mea.aero, spu-jouso@mea.aero; www.mea.com.lb; ⊕ 07.50–17.15 Mon–Fri, 08.50–13.15 Sat

🚗 **MobiTaxis** [199 B3] ☎09 936 107; e info@mobigates.com; www.mobitaxis.com. Free downloadable app for smartphone users for booking/paying for taxi services.

✉ **Post office** [199 A5] Fouad Chehab St, behind Municipality Bldg; ☎09 832 563 or 09 914 984; www.libanpost.com; ⊕ 08.00–17.00 Mon–Fri, 08.00–13.30 Sat

✚ **Lebanese Red Cross** [199 B5] ☎09 832 260 or 09 830 799, dial 140 within Lebanon in emergency; www.redcross.org.lb

✚ **St Louis Hospital** [199 C2] ☎09 912 970

ⓔ **Uruguay Embassy** [199 A5] opposite Stella Maris Shopping Mall; ☎09 636 529/30; e uruliban@dm.net.lb; www.embauruguaybeirut.org; ⊕ 08.30–13.30 Mon–Fri

WHAT TO SEE AND DO

Téléférique ✳ [199 C2] (*Téléférique Station, Rue Maameltein;* ✆ *09 936 075, 09 914 324;* e *comments@teleferiquelb.com; www.teleferiquelb.com;* ☉ *summer 10.00–22.00 Tue–Sun, winter 10.00–18.00 Tue–Sun; admission: adults: LBP7,000 one-way, LBP11,000 return trip Fri–Sun & public holidays, LBP5,500 one-way, LBP9,000 return trip Tue–Thu; children: LBP4,000 one-way, LBP6,000 return trip Fri–Sun & public holidays, LBP3,000 one way, LBP5,000 return trip Tue–Thu; children under 4 free if accompanied by adult*) Without doubt the highlight – with the emphasis on high – of a visit to Jounieh is this nine-minute ride by cable car from the town centre to Harissa. A white-knuckle experience for those who suffer from vertigo, but voyeuristic heaven for others who will enjoy the 'peeping Tom' experience of glimpses into people's kitchens, bedrooms and living rooms as the cable car climbs between the mountainside apartments. The final part of the journey is completed by funicular railway to Harissa and culminates in a fantastic symmetrical vista of the Bay of Jounieh, where you can sit down at the café and enjoy the view over a meal/snack and a drink.

Harissa, and Our Lady of Lebanon (Notre Dame du Liban) [199 D4] (*Harissa;* ✆ *09 263 660, 09 263 893* or *09 263 895;* m *70 203 040;* e *info@ololb.com; www.ololb. com;* ☉ *24hrs daily; admission free*) The reward for vertigo sufferers who have survived the 530m ascent on the Téléférique is this important 19th-century 15-tonne bronze statue (painted in white) of the Virgin Mary with her arms outstretched, an icon of Christianity and of Jounieh's Maronite religious persuasion and a site of pilgrimage for Christians and other sects from all over the world. Built in France and erected here in 1908, the base of the structure houses a tiny chapel, and when you reach the top of the 8.5m shrine via its 104-step spiral staircase, there are fine panoramic views over the Bay of Jounieh. There is a small souvenir shop close by selling miniature scale models of Harissa and other religious icons; and the unmissable and imposing modernist glass-fronted St Paul's Basilica, which can seat a congregation of some 3,500 worshippers, is situated just behind the statue and is also well worth a look in.

Jounieh International Festival (*Athene Bldg, Jounieh;* ✆ *09 832 263;* e *jouniehfestival@hotmail.com, phellipolis@hotmail.com; www.jouniehinternationalfestival. com*) This annual summer music festival, usually held during July at the Fouad Chehab Stadium [199 B4] and various other venues around the town, sees a range of entertainment for adults and children alike including spectacular firework displays, parades, street entertainers and competitions. Well-known artists who have performed here in recent years include Charles Aznavour, Chris De Burgh, Mika and French actor and singer Johnny Hallyday. Check the website for details of the coming year's festival. Tickets can be purchased from Virgin Megastore [139 F5] in Downtown Beirut or by logging onto www.ticketingboxoffice.com.

Adventure activities For adrenalin seekers and sporty types, paragliding (*US$120 for a 20-min flight with an instructor, US$155 inc souvenir video footage*) from Harissa to Jounieh is offered daily in summer from 14.00 to 18.00, and waterskiing (*US$110*) can also be undertaken daily around the Bay of Jounieh, offered by **Skileb** (✆ *09 231 611 Mon–Fri only;* m *70 103 222;* e *info@skileb.com; www.skileb. com*). **Paragliding Lebanon** (m *03 260 245;* e *contact@paraglidinglebanon.com;* ⨍*Paragliding.Lebanon*) is a well-respected company offering tandem flights over the Bay of Jounieh. Another excellent company is **Atlantis Diving College** [199 A5] (*located inside Bel Azur Hotel;* m *70 195 231;* e *info@atlantisscubadiving.com;*

f *Atlantis.Diving.College*), a National Geographic Dive Centre offering dive courses at all levels for both adults and children including certification for the PADI (Professional Association of Divers International) licence.

Lebanon Water Festival [199 C1] (*Organisers main office: Vanda Hotel, Naaman St, Maameltein;* ✆ *09 636 114;* m *03 940 990* or *03 275 882;* e *organization@ lebanonwaterfestival.com; www.lebanonwaterfestival.com;* **f** *lebanonwaterfestival*)

Between July and September each year, Lebanon's extensive coastline from Tripoli to Tyre is a haven for water lovers with an array of courses, competitions and activities such as jet-skiing, surfing, waterskiing, scuba diving, kite-boarding and underwater photography for both beginners and experienced pros alike. Check the festival website for details of the coming year's programme of events and information about how to register for the many courses and lessons on offer.

ZOUK MIKAEL [map, pages 184–5] If whilst in Jounieh you can tear yourself away from the nearby designer shopping outlets at Kaslik, a detour a little further inland to the attractive town of Zouk Mikael is well worth considering. This little 17th-century town has a nicely restored souk area and was once of some importance in the silk trade. Today, it retains many of its traditional old houses

---

CASINO DU LIBAN

[199 D1] *Maameltein Hwy, Jounieh;* ✆ *09 855 888* or *09 853 222;* e *customerservice@cdl.com.lb; www.cdl.com.lb;* ⏲ *slot machines 10.00–06.00 daily, except Good Friday, gaming tables 16.00–04.00 daily except Cercle D'or Room & Salles Privees 22.00–04.00 daily, except Good Friday*

This iconic showcase of 1960s and 1970s glamour and prosperity is nestled high up on the mountains commanding stunning views over the Bay of Jounieh a little over 20km north from Beirut. Lebanon's sole gambling venue, the 34,000m^2 casino complex, first opened in 1959, continues to evoke the era of extravagance and hedonism which saw the likes of Johnny Halliday, Julio Iglesias, Omar Sharif, Sasha Distel and, of course, Lebanon's very own diva Fayrouz (box, page 57), visit and entertain the famous and the wealthy. Forced to close for much of the civil war, the casino reopened on 4 December 1996, following a US$50 million restoration project. Amid the chandeliers, grand entrance and plush décor, the casino boasts around 500 slot machines, four restaurants, four gaming rooms offering American Roulette, Black Jack, Punto Banco and stud poker, and including the ultra-exclusive and private six-table Salles Privees for the gambling elite where the minimum bet is LBP250,000. If you think Las Vegas, which, coincidentally, just happens to be Jounieh's twin town, you will have a good idea of the general ambience.

Assuming you haven't just lost all your money on the gaming tables or slot machines, the casino offers equally lavish entertainment in its 1,000+ seat theatre, where performances have ranged from ballet, jazz and opera to plays, and the 600-seat Salle des Ambassadeurs, the venue for many an extravagant and elegant cabaret and piece of performance art. Whilst Lebanese nationals aged 21+ years have to prove they have an annual income in excess of US$20,000 in order to gain entry, all foreigners over the age of 21 are welcome to the casino and gaming tables in smart dress.

and village ambience, and you can still see artisans at work and selling the fruits of their hand crafted labours. Although the town has a reasonable smattering of restaurants and decent accommodation, an overnight stay is not really warranted unless you are attending the annual summer festival (below) and prefer to stay overnight rather than make the journey back to Beirut or elsewhere.

Getting there Zouk Mikael is situated around 20km from Beirut. If you are on a self-drive visit, take the coast road north from the capital and when you reach Kaslik head inland and follow the signs for Zouk. The total journey time, as always depending on traffic conditions, should be around half an hour. Expect to pay about LBP30,000 for a taxi from Beirut and considerably less for a taxi from nearby Jounieh or Kaslik, which should cost no more than LBP10,000.

Other practicalities In addition to a branch of **Libanpost** (*Ogero Bldg, Main Rd;* \ *09 214 516; www.libanpost.com;* ☉ *08.00–17.00 Mon–Fri, 08.00–13.30 Sat*), there is a good supply of banks, pharmacies, petrol stations and shops around the town catering for most visitors' needs.

What to do
Zouk Mikael International Festival (m *71 491 939;* e *info@zoukmikaelfestival. org; www.zoukmikaelfestival.org*) Held annually since 2003 for a week in July, this summer festival brings together Lebanese and international musicians and singers in a range of styles, from classical and opera to blues and jazz, and takes place in a beautiful location within the environs of the town's 2,500-seat Roman ampitheatre overlooking the Mediterranean. In recent years, the festival has featured Plácido Domingo, the Argentinian soprano Virginia Tola, the Lebanese Philharmonic Orchestra, the aptly named US blues band Roomful of Blues, Blues icon Otis Grand, well-known opera singers Monica Yunus and Jose Carreras, and musician Ziad Rahbani, the eldest son of Lebanese icon Fayrouz. See the website for details of the year's upcoming performances. Tickets can be purchased from Virgin Megastore in Downtown Beirut [139 F5], or online at www.ticketingboxoffice.com.

BYBLOS (JBAIL)

As the saying often goes, the more things change, the more they stay the same. This certainly applies to Byblos (*Jbail* in Arabic), where, despite its 7,000 years of existence, making it a contender for the oldest continuously inhabited town in the world, it continues to evoke the past as much as the present. Whilst the legends and myths of Adonis and Astarte were revered here for some 3,000 years, from the Phoenician to the Roman eras, physical reminders of the town's past can be found in the wealth of archaeological layers of civilisations which span the Phoenician, Greek, Roman and Crusader periods. This historical importance was recognised by UNESCO in 1984, when it bestowed World Heritage site status on the town for its 'outstanding universal value'. With continuous habitation since the Neolithic period Byblos was the town, under the Phoenicians, that gave birth to the alphabet upon which our modern version is based and was suitably named by the ancient Greeks as 'Byblos' after their word for papyrus, which was traded here and shipped to Egypt.

As a nation founded by its port cities and settlements, Byblos must rank as Lebanon's finest. Charming and picturesque by day and night, the port is the quintessential picture-postcard scene. It would be a great shame to visit the country without stopping by here to see the still-functioning workaday harbour

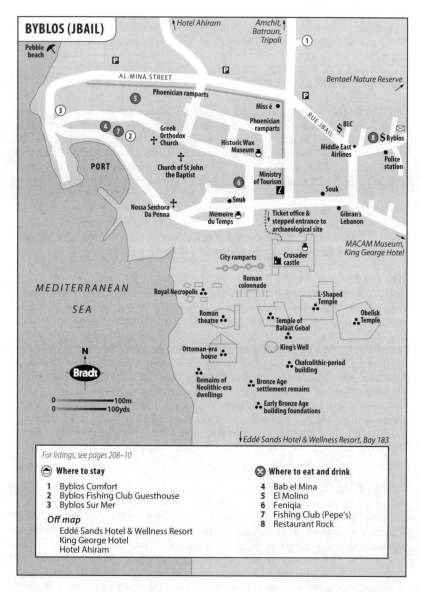

BYBLOS (JBAIL)

Pebble beach

Hotel Ahiram

Amchit, Batroun, Tripoli

AL-MINA STREET

Phoenician ramparts

Miss é

Phoenician ramparts

Bentaol Nature Reserve

RUE JBAIL

$ BLC

Greek Orthodox Church

Historic Wax Museum

Middle East Airlines

$ Byblos

Police station

PORT

Church of St John the Baptist

Ministry of Tourism

Souk

Souk

Nossa Senhora Da Penna

Mémoire du Temps

Ticket office & stepped entrance to archaeological site

Gibran's Lebanon

MACAM Museum, King George Hotel

City ramparts

Crusader castle

MEDITERRANEAN

Roman colonnade

Royal Necropolis

L-Shaped Temple

Obelisk Temple

SEA

Roman theatre

Temple of Balaat Gebal

N

Ottoman-era house

King's Well

Bradt

Chalcolithic-period building

Remains of Neolithic-era dwellings

Bronze Age settlement remains

0 — 100m
0 — 100yds

Early Bronze Age building foundations

Eddé Sands Hotel & Wellness Resort, Bay 183

For listings, see pages 208–10

⌂ Where to stay

1 Byblos Comfort
2 Byblos Fishing Club Guesthouse
3 Byblos Sur Mer

Off map
Eddé Sands Hotel & Wellness Resort
King George Hotel
Hotel Ahiram

✗ Where to eat and drink

4 Bab el Mina
5 El Molino
6 Feniqia
7 Fishing Club (Pepe's)
8 Restaurant Rock

and the tastefully restored souk (easily better than Beirut's), offering some of the most unusual and best souvenir items in the country. Byblos is dotted with fine seafood restaurants, including the Fishing Club (Pepe's), which has a splendid location by the port and offers a museum of photographs dedicated to the rich and famous who indulged their heady passions by day and night during the 1960s and 70s. In 2013, the United Nations World Tourism Organisation (UNWTO) voted Byblos the Arab world's best tourist city, whilst the Arab League's Council of Tourism also recognised the town's appeal and nominated Byblos the capital of Arab Tourism for 2016. At some 37km north of Beirut, Byblos is an easy day trip from the capital, though equally it is a delightful place to spend a few nights.

HISTORY From its humble beginnings as a modest Neolithic fishing port with small agricultural holdings some 7,000 years ago, Byblos's stature, like its coastal tides, has ebbed and flowed during its hosting of successive civilisations. During the Phoenician period the town was called Gubla, and the Greeks renamed the town 'Byblos' in recognition of the town's importance in the paper trade, papyrus being the Greek word for paper. It wasn't until around 3000BCE, however, with the arrival of the Canaanites, that Byblos expanded its sea trade and began to specialise in the export of Lebanese cedarwood to Egypt, receiving papyrus, gold and linen from the Egyptian pharaohs as part of the barter deal, which ushered in a period of economic prosperity for the town. Around 2300BCE, the Amorite tribe descended on the town, disrupting trade relations for the next two centuries which were further exacerbated by the arrival of another Asiatic clan from the desert lands of Syria and west Asia, the Hyksos, who introduced new equipment and tools of warfare hitherto unseen in the area, such as horse-drawn chariots and the composite bow. Following 500 years of Hyksos domination, the Egyptians finally managed to overcome them and restored economic and maritime prosperity, which was accompanied by a new period of cultural and religious osmosis between Byblos and Egypt.

From around 1200BCE, the Sea Peoples, probably from north Africa, arrived on the coast and, after a period of struggle, became assimilated into the fabric of the Phoenician city-states. Although this was the start of a golden era of overall Phoenician prosperity, Byblos very much played second fiddle to other ports such as Sidon and Tyre in the south. But this was also the period that witnessed perhaps the Phoenicians' greatest and enduring cultural legacy, the birthplace and development of the first 22-letter phonetic alphabet which was adopted by the Greeks in 800BCE and is the foundation of our modern alphabet. Inscriptions discovered on the sarcophagus of King Ahiram, including a curse on grave robbers, ranks as one of the most important archaeological discoveries in Byblos (now in the National Museum). By 1000BCE, Byblos was once again a victim of outside powers, this time by the Assyrians under King Ashurnasirpal II, who, along with the other Phoenician states, forced Byblos into paying annual tributes of precious metals and cedarwood in return for a semblance of economic and political independence.

Despite ongoing invasions by more powerful states, Phoenician prosperity continued apace, and under Persian rule in 539BCE, following Cyrus the Great's defeat of the Babylonians, the two entered into a pragmatic alliance, with Phoenician maritime skills and vessels used by the Persians in the Persian Wars against the Greeks. This mutually acceptable arrangement ended following Alexander the Great's defeat of Darius III in 333BCE at the Battle of Issus, paving the way for the Hellenisation of Byblos in which Greek became the lingua franca along with other Greek customs and mores. This endured during the Roman occupation from 64BCE under Pompey, when the town witnessed extensive Roman town planning and construction, including colonnaded streets, temples and a theatre. With the partitioning of the Roman Empire in CE395 into an eastern and a western branch, following the emperor Constantine's conversion to Christianity, the paganism of antiquity which had hitherto held sway now came under the banner of Christianity during eastern or Byzantine rule, and Byblos became, under the emperor Diocletian, a significant Christian bishopric, though there are few architectural remnants in the town from this period. The transition from Byzantium to Islamic rule, which occurred circa CE635, sustained this relatively uneventful and less illustrious period in Byblos's history. This was to change once more, with the arrival on Lebanon's shores of the Crusader knights from Europe in 1104, who exchanged the Arabic name Jbail to the more culinary Giblet. As in the other coastal towns, the Franks proved great early recyclers and utilised found Roman columns and stones to help construct the landmark Crusader fortress you see today.

Byblos remained under the Crusader yoke for the next two centuries until the Mamluks finally ousted them in 1289. Byblos again reverted to its rather anodyne existence, and after the onset of Ottoman rule in 1516, Fakhreddine Maan II incorporated Byblos into his emirate, which eventually became part of the Ottomans' northern administrative district. With the demise of the Turks following World War I, Byblos has become better known since for the efforts made by a number of archaeologists to unearth and document the town's rich historical legacy, which, though halted by the civil war, is still ongoing.

GETTING THERE Byblos is well served by both public transport and taxis heading north from Beirut. From Zone B of the capital's Charles Helou station [172 B2] both **Connexion Transport** (✆ *01 585 500;* m *03 206 308/384;* e *info@connexion-transport.com; www.connexion-transport.com; LBP4,000*) and **Tripoli Express** (m *03 327 625; LBP3,500*) can drop you off on the highway near the entrance to Byblos in a little under an hour, traffic permitting. From Beirut's Dora junction [173 H2], buses and minivans also ply the route to Byblos in around 50–60minutes where you can alight on Rue Jbail. From the eastern side of Cola intersection [127 E7], buses, including bus number 6, travel to Byblos in around an hour (*LBP1,500–3,000*). A taxi from Dora will set you back around US$20, whilst from Cola expect to pay in the region of US$50–60. If you are on a self-drive visit, Byblos, at less than 40km from Beirut, is a relatively easy drive north along the coastal highway past Jounieh with the clearly signposted route (Jbail) taking around 45–60minutes, traffic permitting.

GETTING AROUND Byblos is small and easy to navigate, centred on its small port, its archaeological ruins and souk area, which are all close together; you should have no need to use buses or taxis. The main street, Rue Jbail, contains most of the banks, shops, cafés and restaurants, and the post office is just off this main street. Slightly more outlying areas of interest such as Amchit, Camping Les Colombes and Rachana (pages 215–17) may require a service taxi or taxi.

TOURIST INFORMATION The friendly **Ministry of Tourism Office** (*Old Souk, facing Feniqia Restaurant & opposite castle;* ✆ *09 540 325;* e *mot_byblos@hotmail.com, sandykhoury.mot@gmail.com, pascalekhoueiry.mot@gmail.com; www.mot.gov.lb;* ⊕ *08.30–17.00 Mon–Sat*) has an excellent range of brochures & pamphlets on Byblos & other areas of the country in Arabic, English, French, German, Italian & Spanish.

WHERE TO STAY Map, page 206

Byblos Sur Mer Hotel (30 rooms & suites) Harbour; ✆09 548 000; e info@byblossurmer. com; www.byblossurmer.com. Byblos's most salubrious option, this boutique hotel has beautifully decorated & tasteful rooms in a terrific location overlooking the port & sea, & guests have free access to the beach in summer. All the luxury refinements you would expect for the price & restaurants serving great food including their glass-floored Dar L'Azrak-Masa restaurant (**$$$$$**), where diners sit above in situ ruins from antiquity

unearthed during the hotel's renovations. All rooms have sea views whilst the suites overlook the port. B/fast inc, free Wi-Fi. **$$$$$**

Eddé Sands Hotel & Wellness Resort: eBoutique Hotel (23 bungalows, rooms & suites) Port of Byblos; ✆09 546 666; e info@ eddesands.com, reservations@eddesands. com; www.eddesands.com. This resort complex boasts a couple of accommodation options catering to the mid range & luxury wallet. This is the 5-star option located within the resort itself

& has bright, colourful & tastefully decorated rooms in a nicely manicured & leafy hedonist's paradise. B/fast inc, free Wi-Fi. **$$$$$**

🏠 **Eddé Sands Hotel & Wellness Resort: é L'Hôtel** (28 rooms & suites) Port of Byblos; 📞 09 545 888; m 03 997 688; e hotelreception@ eddesands.com, info@eddesands.com, reservations@ eddesands.com; www.eddesands.com. The second of two accommodation options belonging to Eddé Sands, the 3-star é L'Hôtel has smart, comfortable rooms with good sea views & guests can use the facilities at the main resort (5mins away) free of charge, including spa, massage, bars, restaurants, adult & children's swimming pools, etc. **$$$$**

🏠 **Byblos Comfort Hotel** (46 rooms & suites) Main St; 📞 09 942 200; e info@ byblyoscomforthotel.com, byblyoscomforthotel@ hotmail.com; www.byblyoscomforthotel.com. A decent & spacious hotel with clean, comfortable rooms all with AC, TV & fridge, but with a slightly clinical resort-type feel to the place & located a short distance away from the ruins. B/fast inc. Free Wi-Fi in the hotel lobby but US$5/2hrs in guest rooms. **$$$**

🏠 **Hotel Ahiram** (25 rooms) 📞 09 540 440 or 09 944 726; e info@ahiramhotel.com; www. ahiramhotel.com. All rooms have sea views, AC & TV at this decent enough mid range offering & there are discounts for extended stays. The hotel can also help organise boat trips around the harbour. B/fast inc, free Wi-Fi. **$$$**

🏠 **King George Hotel** (25 rooms & suites) Mar Elias St, Blat; 📞 09 547 048; m 70 332 465; e info@king-george-hotel.com; www.king-george-hotel.com. Located about 1km southeast of Byblos itself in the village of Blat, a decent mid range hotel with bright, comfortable rooms, & a restaurant serving good Lebanese & international cuisine(**$$$**). Complimentary transport provided to the old town. B/fast inc. **$$$**

🏠 **Byblos Fishing Club Guesthouse** (8 bungalows) Harbour, behind the Fishing Club (Pepe's) (see below); 📞 09 540 213; e pepesfishingclub@gmail.com; rogerppabed@ hotmail.com. Run by Roger Abed of Pepe's, these comfortable bungalows are all en suite with AC, TV & private terrace. There is also a nice little garden for summer dining & drinking. **$**

✖ WHERE TO EAT AND DRINK *Map, page 206*

✳ ✖ **Fishing Club (Pepe's)** Rue Pepe Abed, Harbour; 📞 09 540 213; m 03 635 850; e pepesfishingclub@gmail.com, pepeabed@ pepeabed.net, rogerppabed@hotmail.com; ⏰ summer 10.00–midnight daily. Although it doesn't quite match the glitzy décor of the Casino du Liban, this place is a tourist attraction in its own right & was the other main hangout in the 1960s & 1970s for a variety of international celebrities & the jet set who came here as much for the *joie de vivre* as for the food. The owner, Pepe, died in 2007, & the club is now run by his son, Roger, a jeweller & Honorary Consul of Mexico who studied English in Hendon & lived in Golders Green. Although more sedate nowadays, the club is worth a visit to look at the gallery of black-&-white & colour photos of past patrons which included Marlon Brando, Anita Ekberg, Shirley Bassey, David Niven, Ray Milland, former French premier Jacques Chirac & Charles Aznavour, to name but a few. Do make time also to take a peak at the Club's museum, which has a variety of archaeological finds dating from the Phoenician era, collected by Pepe over the years. The seafood served here remains excellent, though a tad overpriced, but the set meal for 2 of seafood

mezze is good value for LBP45,000pp. For the summer months there is also the Hacienda de Pepe a short walk away, located amidst delightful verdant scenery & gardens serving Italian cuisine such as pizzas & homemade salad. **$$$$**

✖ **Bab el Mina** Harbour; 📞 09 540 475; m 03 540 475; e info@babelmina.com; www.babelmina.com; ⏰ noon–midnight daily. Located next door to Pepe's with a similarly nice port-side dining experience & the fresh seafood *mezze* every bit as good, but without the latter's ambience & history. **$$$$**

✖ **El Molino** Harbour; 📞 09 541 555; m 70 236 366; e elmolino@cyberia.net.lb; 🄵 elmolinobyblos; ⏰ 10.00–01.00 daily. Great Mexican restaurant with authentic atmosphere, excellent service & superb margaritas. **$$$$**

✳ ✖ **Feniqia Restaurant** Old souk, facing castle & Ministry of Tourism office; 📞 09 540 444; ⏰ noon–01.00 daily. A terrific restaurant with an excellent & varied menu of fish & meat dishes in the heart of Byblos & hugely popular with locals & visitors alike. The fish tampoura is highly recommended as is the restaurant's ice cream. Efficient & friendly service with a good range of beverages including *arak,* Almaza beer & wine from the Ksara vineyards. Highly recommended. **$$$$**

✕ Restaurant Rock Main St; ☎ 09 944 314 or 09 546 667; e info@restaurantrock.com; www. restaurantrock.com; ⏰ 08.00–02.00 daily. This mainstream fast-food eatery serves a decent range of burgers, seafood dishes, *shwarma* & hot & cold beverages. **$$$**

ENTERTAINMENT AND NIGHTLIFE Back in the 1960s and 1970s, Byblos had a pulsating and vibrant nightlife centred on the famed Fishing Club (Pepe's) Restaurant patronised by the rich and famous. Nowadays, Byblos has a much more restrained entertainment and nightlife scene, far less frenetic than the capital and revolving essentially around dining at one of the harbourside restaurants whilst admiring the picturesque views of the port, followed by an evening stroll around the harbour and nearby lanes. The town's annual festival (page 215) ups the *joie de vivre* ante during the summer months with its diverse music offerings. As a coastal town Byblos has some clean and excellent beaches, and the well-known Eddé Sands Beach Resort south of the ruins and the nearby Bay 183 are recommended for their range of relaxation and activity options.

Eddé Sands Beach Resort ☎ 09 546 666; m 03 997 688; e info@eddesands.com, reservations@eddesands.com; www.eddesands. com; ⏰ 09.00–19.00 daily; resort admission: adults LBP30,000 Mon–Fri, LBP42,000 Sat/ Sun, children under 12 LBP15,000 Mon–Fri, LBP15,000 Sat/Sun. Well suited to families, though not particularly cheap, a range of activities are on offer at this large 110,000m^2 complex, from jet-skiing to waterskiing. For those seeking more laid-back entertainment, there are bars, spas & a range of pampering & therapy treatments such as massage, yoga & homeopathy available in luxurious & picturesque surroundings. There is also regular weekday & w/end live music & DJs. All in all, the quintessential hedonist experience.

Bay 183 Just south of Eddé Sands Beach Resort; m 03 000 183 or 70 421 999; **f** Bay183; ⏰ 09.00–18.00 daily; admission: US$13 Mon–Fri, US$17 Sat & Sun. A lively, family-friendly & well-equipped resort offering activities such as beach volleyball, jet-skiing & water-skiing. For children there is a dedicated kiddies pool, trampoline, slides & play areas. The onsite eatery serves basic fare of meat & salad dishes.

SHOPPING Although the main Rue Jbail in Byblos contains the vast majority of banks, pharmacies and shops, including those selling the usual tourist tack, by far the best place to browse and buy is in the souk area, which offers a much more original and rewarding retail experience, with the following three outlets among the best options.

Gibran's Lebanon Old Souk; ☎ 09 542 226; e gibranslebanon@idm.net.lb; www.eddeyard. com/gibran_lebanon.html; ⏰ 09.00–19.00 Mon–Sat, noon–19.00 Sun. A superb bookshop in a lovely sandstone building & definitely worth a browse even if you are not buying. It sells a wide range of tomes on virtually every aspect of Lebanon – history, culture, cuisine & politics – in Arabic, English & French, including many rare titles. Also stocks a good selection of postcards & hard to find Lebanese stamps.

Mémoire du Temps (Memory of Time) Old Souk; ☎ 09 540 555; m 03 742 099; e memory@ memoryoftime.com, pierre@memoryoftime. com; www.memoryoftime.com; ⏰ summer 09.00–20.00 daily, winter 09.00–18.00 daily. This fascinating, part-museum part-shop, sells ancient fossilised fish remains dating back about 100 million years. Though some of the smaller items sell for US$5, many of the fossilised slabs are large enough to start paving a patio. Owned & run by Paleontologist Pierre Abi Saad, who carries on a tradition begun by his grandfather, excavating a number of mountain sites up to 800m above sea level east of Byblos, chipping away at the geological timescale and sediment which encased these creatures, including sharks, turtles, stingrays & many other varieties, which are then embedded in limestone rock & sold in his shop. Each purchase comes with a numbered certificate of authenticity with detailed background information on the fossil. They also have another shop across the road selling jewellery, books, mosaics & glass objects made by traditional glass blowers from Sarafand.

Miss é Old Souk; ✆ 09 943 023; **m** 03 370 007; **e** customerservice@miss-eboutique.com; ⏱ 10.00–20.00 daily. Sells some delightful & innovative clothing & accessories such as jewellery & handbags by Lebanese designers for the elegant & fashion-conscious woman.

OTHER PRACTICALITIES

$ BLC Bank BLC Bank Bldg, Rue Jbail; ✆ 09 540 150 or 09 546 956; **e** jbeilbranch@blcbank.com; www.blcbank.com; ⏱ 08.15–17.00 Mon–Fri, 08.15–13.00 Sat. 24hr ATM.
$ Byblos Bank Zaarour Bldg, Rue Jbail; ✆ 09 945 252; www.byblosbank.com; ⏱ 08.30–17.30 Mon–Fri, 08.30–13.00 Sat. Has a couple of 24hr ATMs.
$ Federal Bank Federal Bank Bldg, Rue Jbail; ✆ 09 949 295 or 09 547 172; **m** 03 184 494; www. fbl.com.lb. 24hr ATM

✉ **Post office** 2nd Fl, Rouhban Bldg, Rouhban St, off Rue Jbail; ✆ 09 540 003; www.libanpost. com; ⏱ 08.00–17.00 Mon–Fri, 08.00–13.30 Sat. As well as offering the usual range of postal services, they will also change US dollars to LBP.
✈ **Middle East Airlines (MEA)** Mansour Bldg, Rue Jbail; ✆ 09 949 467; **e** spv-jbeso@mea.aero; www.mea.com.lb; ⏱ 07.50–17.15 Mon–Fri, 08.50–13.15 Sat
🚕 **Byblos Taxi** ✆ 09 949 394/494; **m** 70 549 494/5; **e** info@byblostaxi.net; www.byblostaxi.net

WHAT TO SEE

Byblos Archaeological Site (✆ *09 540 001;* ⏱ *08.00–sunset daily; admission: adults LBP8,000, students & children over 6 LBP2,000, children under 6 free*) It wasn't until the latter period of the 19th century that Byblos's multiple layers of history began to be unearthed, when the French scholar Ernest Renan (box, page 213) started his excavations of the ancient *tell*, or mound, of the town, which paved the way for the discovery of seven different layers of civilisations across 7,000 years of history. Renan's work was followed by his compatriot, the Egyptologist Pierre Montet (1885–1966), who was responsible for bringing to light the sarcophagus of King Ahiram as well as providing evidence of trading links between Egypt and Byblos during antiquity. The archaeologist Maurice Dunand (1898–1987) was the driving force behind more than 40 excavations between 1926 and the mid 1970s, before work was halted owing to the onset of civil war. Today, ongoing archaeological work has resumed under the auspices of Lebanon's General Directorate of Antiquities.

From the ticket office, reached by walking through the old souk, the site's first and most conspicuous landmark is the omnipotent 12th-century **Crusader castle**, Château de la Mer to the Franks, which measures some 50m x 45m and was the final building in the Byblos historical jigsaw. Once inside the castle, it is worth stopping by the small museum, which has a few nice pottery items on display (labelled in Arabic, English and French) along with some interesting details and information about the architecture, trade and sea-going activities in Byblos down the years, as well as the history of the King Ahiram Sarcophagus, the jewel-in-the-crown exhibit in Beirut's National Museum (pages 174–5). The castle itself consists of five towers, one on each corner of the castle and a fifth centrally positioned in the north wall tower to protect the entrance, surrounding the courtyard and dungeon below. Constructed using pre-existing Roman columns and stones, the castle has been modified over the years with the Arabs, for instance, overlaying the moat with a bridge and adding vaulted ceilings and arches. Although the castle's monolithic appearance testifies to its once-strategic importance in guarding both port and town, for the visitor it is the commanding views over the entire archaeological site where its appeal lies.

In order to get the most from your visit set aside a minimum of 2 hours to view the site at a leisurely pace; guides from the main entrance can be hired for US$20 for one to six people and for US$27 for groups of seven or more.

Phoenician ramparts Once you exit the castle you are amidst the hub of the ancient Phoenician town dating from the 3rd and 2nd centuries BCE. The defensive 25m-thick walls, which curve from the castle to the coast, would have been a difficult obstacle for an invader to overcome. The ramparts have been modified and strengthened by succeeding civilisations.

Roman theatre Originally located between the city gate and the Obelisk Temple, this amphitheatre, a third of its original size and with only five of its original seating tiers remaining, is now arguably in a much better position, situated right on the coast. It affords glorious views over the Mediterranean and looks very enchanting at sunset. The theatre dates back to CE218, and was once adorned with a fine mosaic depicting Bacchus, which is now on display in Beirut's National Museum (pages 174–5).

Roman colonnade and the Temple of Baalat Gebal These six standing columns, dating from CE300, are all that remain of what was once a much more extensive collection of columns, built to form the route to the Baalat Gebal Temple or 'Lady of Byblos'. Built in 2700BCE, and located to the left of the colonnade, this is Byblos's most ancient temple and paid homage to Adonis's lover, the goddess Astarte, on a site considered so sacred it was built over many times and dedicated to Aphrodite under the Romans.

Obelisk Temple and the L-Shaped Temple These two temples, once revered as the dwelling of gods and used as sites where they were worshipped, date from the late Bronze Age. The Obelisk Temple, dating from 2150BCE at the height of the Egyptian presence in Byblos, occupies its current position just a short distance away from where it was originally built on the site of the L-Shaped Temple in order to facilitate ongoing archaeological work. The temple comprises a sacred courtyard with a number of standing obelisks including one built in the 19th century BCE at the behest of Abichemou, king of Byblos. The base of another obelisk is thought to honour Resheph, the Phoenician god of war. Aside from the obelisks, hundreds of other discoveries have been unearthed here, including iconic Phoenician figurines attired with gold leaf and wearing conical hats, providing further evidence of votive offerings to the gods; many of these are now on display in the National Museum in Beirut (pages 174–5). The L-Shaped Temple, so named for obvious reasons, though not as ancient or as well preserved as that of Baalat Gebal, ranks as one of the oldest in Byblos. The temple was partially destroyed by fire during offensives by the nomadic Amorite tribe around 2150–2000BCE and subsequently rebuilt with some design modifications. It is thought that this temple, too, may have been in honour of the Phoenician god Resheph.

King's Well (Ain al-Malik) This is a large crater sited on a promontory near the sea which was the town's principal water supply until the Romans began using water from the surrounding mountains via specially constructed aqueducts. The water here was reserved only for use in sacred rituals such as those at the Temple of Baalat Gebal. According to ancient mythology, Isis was discovered weeping for Osiris here by maidservants by the pool.

Royal necropolis Dating from the 2nd century BCE and located adjacent to the colonnaded street, these series of vertical burial shafts up to 10m deep represent probably the most significant archaeological find in Byblos. Of the nine tombs that have been unearthed, the most famous is that of the sarcophagus of the 1200BCE King Ahiram, which contains the earliest-known Phoenician script, now one of the most cherished exhibits in Beirut's National Museum (pages 174–5). Another tomb contains the resting place of the 19th-century BCE King Yp-Shemou-Abi. If you can ignore the Phoenician curse, which reads 'Warning, here! Thy death is below', you can walk down some of the shafts and between them.

Prehistoric Byblos settlement Further south towards the coast, dotted around the attractive 19th-century red-tiled **Ottoman-era house**, is evidence of Byblos's claim to be the oldest town in the world in the form of dwellings, barely visible limestone floors and low walls from the **Neolithic** and **Chalcolithic** periods (5000–4000BCE). Funerary or burial jars discovered here number around 1,500, with the skeletal remains arranged in the foetal position as if awaiting rebirth, and are now on display in the National Museum (pages 174–5).

Medieval Byblos The arrival of the Crusader knights from Europe did much to revitalise Christianity in the town, and in 1115, construction commenced on the attractive Church of St John the Baptist (Eglise St Jean Marc in French, or Mar Yuhanna as he is called in Arabic) built in a Romanesque style with an unconventional open-air baptistery. The church has seen later additions to its structure such as the 18th-century north door, which is of Arab origin, whilst the remnants of a mosaic in the garden west of the church date to the much earlier Byzantine period. The church suffered serious damage from an earthquake in 1170, and again in 1840 from British bombardments, but extensive restoration since 1947 has transformed the structure and the bell tower you see today was added during this period.

ERNEST RENAN

Born at Tréguier in Brittany in 1823 into a family of fishermen, the archaeologist, historian, philosopher and theologian Ernest Renan was responsible for undertaking some of the most important archaeological discoveries in Lebanon. Probably best known in his native France for his 1863 work *Vie de Jésus*, this book was both critically acclaimed and controversial for its less than sacred arguments and views. In 1860, the learned Renan travelled to Lebanon at the request of Emperor Napoleon III to undertake archaeological research into the country's Phoenician past, and lived in the coastal town of Amchit. The meticulous work and discoveries he made in nearby Byblos and elsewhere in the country paved the way for future work, and added significantly to our understanding of ancient cultures and their visible remains which we can enjoy today. His year-long stay in Lebanon formed the basis for his 1864 work *Mission de Phénicie*, in which he outlines the 'powerful impression' the country made on him. His treasured sister, Henriette, who accompanied him to Lebanon, died whilst they were staying in Amchit and she is buried in the town where her resting place can be seen. Renan himself died after a short illness in France in 1892 and is buried in the Montmartre Quarter of Paris.

Nossa Senhora Da Penna If you turn left out of the Crusader castle ticket entrance and walk down Rue Pépé Abed *en route* down to the port, you will come across this pocket-sized Christian stone chapel on your left with vaulted ceiling. This quaint, atmospheric shrine, with pictures of Mary and St Charbel, and burning candles inside, has nicely manicured gardens dotted with religious icons; well worth a quick look.

Byblos Historic Wax Museum (Musée de Cire Historique) (A *short walk up the road left out of Feniqia Restaurant;* ✆ *09 540 463;* m *03 395 537;* e *info@bybloswaxmuseum. com; www.bybloswaxmuseum.com; open: 09.00–18.00 daily; admission: adults LBP8,000, children under 10 & students LBP5,000)* This small museum, opposite the Church of St John the Baptist (Eglise St Jean Marc) displays a range of waxwork tableaux showcasing a variety of scenes from Lebanese history. Phoenician glass blowing, Alexander the Great at the burning of Tyre, a traditional village wedding, the imprisoned cabinet during the French Mandate era, and quite a scary-looking mermaid are some of the 25 different slices of Lebanese life on display here immortalised in 130 waxwork models. Worth a look in, but this is really one only for kitsch lovers.

Modern and Contemporary Art Museum (MACAM) (*Alita, c7km southeast of Byblos;* m *03 197 900 or 03 271 500;* e *info@macamlebanon.org; www. macamlebanon.com;* ⊕ *noon–18.00/sunset Fri–Sun, by prior appointment only outside these times, closed Mon; admission: adults LBP15,000, children under 18 LBP8,000, LBP15,000 inc creative workshop)* One of Lebanon's newest large-scale venues for the arts, founded by the owners of the RectoVerso bookshop in Beirut (page 156) opened in summer 2013 and has been converted from a former factory into an extensive indoor space showcasing a wide range of work by Lebanese artists. It houses a permanent exhibition of sculptures, is a venue for installation

---

BENTAEL NATURE RESERVE

Bentael; ✆ *09 738 330;* m *03 838 982 or 03 372 704;* e *info@bentaelreserve.org; www.bentaelreserve.org;* ⊕ *summer 08.00–18.00 daily, winter 08.00–17.00 daily; admission: no obligatory entrance fee but donations of LBP5,000 to aid ongoing environmental work in the reserve appreciated.*

Established in 1981, this is the first and smallest of Lebanon's protected natural environments and officially recognised as such in 1999. Established by Bentael's local residents in order to help safeguard the area from 'the misdeeds of development', this heavily wooded area covers just 2km^2 and sits between 250m and 850m above sea level and some 8km northeast of Byblos. An area of rich biodiversity, its 335+ species of flora include oak and pine trees, heather, orchids and cyclamen, whilst squirrels, voles, porcupines, shrews, wild boar, jackals, porcupines and foxes roam the verdant landscape. Recognised by the Ministry of Environment in 1999 as a nature reserve, it was also given the status of Important Bird Area (IBA) in 2008, and the white stork is a common visitor to the area during its annual migratory pattern. Also within the reserve is the small St John's Hermitage, which, during the 18th or 19th centuries, was home to a solitary monk of the Maronite order for some 40 years. The reserve is open all year and is ideal for hikers. For more information on the reserve and to arrange a visit, take a look at the official website (*www.bentaelreserve.org*), which also has directions on how to get there.

art and holds regular events such as conferences and workshops and engages with both the local and international communities. Plans are also underway to create a new 200-seat theatre in the MACAM complex. The museum also houses a café, children's activity area and museum bookshop.

Getting there As the museum is not on a main bus route, you will need to take a taxi from Beirut, which will cost around LBP50,000–55,000 whilst a taxi from Byblos will cost approximately LBP28,000. On the first Sunday of each month, however, MACAM operates a bus service to the museum (*for advance seat reservations* ℡ *01 330 994;* m *71 347 716*) departing from Martyrs' Square in Downtown Beirut [139 F5] (facing Virgin Megastore) at 11.00 with the return journey back to Beirut departing from the museum at 15.00. The total cost of the round trip at the time of writing was LBP10,000. which includes entry to the museum.

Byblos International Festival (*UNESCO Sq;* ℡ *09 542 020;* m *03 538 536;* e *info@ byblosfestival.org; www.byblosfestival.org*) An annual four-week event held during the months of July and August since 2003, the Byblos International Festival is held in a beautiful setting with the stage overlooking the ancient Phoenician harbour and Crusader ruins. The performances include a range of musical sounds and styles from flamenco, jazz and rock to opera, by both Lebanese and internationally acclaimed artists. Well-known names who have performed here over the years include Bryan Ferry, Placebo, Kool and the Gang, Blues icon B B King, UK band Gorillaz, Lebanese folk-music icon Wadih el-Safi, Irish rock band the Script and US R&B multiple Grammy winner John Legend. Log onto the festival website to see full details of the coming year's performers and festival programme. Tickets can be booked via the festival website, at Virgin Megastore in Downtown Beirut or online at www.ticketingboxoffice.com

AMCHIT

The hometown of former Lebanese president Michel Suleiman (b1948), the predominantly Christian Maronite town of Amchit is a little under 40km from Beirut and around 3.5km north from Byblos and home, literally, to dozens of attractive Ottoman-period houses, which are now all listed buildings and worth a wander around, as are the numerous churches dotted around the town. The town's other main claim to fame is that the 19th-century French archaeologist and writer Ernest Renan (box, page 213) once resided here, and described the town as 'paradise'. His sister, Henriette, is also buried here, and both the house in which they lived and her burial site can be visited. More recently, Amchit also has the distinction of being the location for Lebanon's first ever campsite, Camping Les Colombes (see below).

GETTING THERE From Beirut's Dora station [173 H2] buses & minivans travelling north can drop you off in Amchit (*LBP1,500–2,000*). A taxi from Dora will set you back around US$25 whilst a taxi from Byblos shouldn't cost more than US$10.

🏠 **WHERE TO STAY**

✴ ⚔ **Camping Les Colombes** (14 chalets & 25 'tengalows') Amchit; ℡ 09 622 401/2; e contact@campinglescolombes.com; www. campinglescolombes.com. For something a little different in an ultra-rural setting overlooking the sea, try this excellent budget campsite, which opened back in 1965, the first in Lebanon, and offers a variety of sleeping options, including camping (*LBP15,000pp/night, supply your own tent*), chalets (*from LBP60,000/night*), or a 'tengalow', a tent-shaped bungalow (*LBP40,000 per 2 people per night*), with AC, TV & fridge. At weekends, chalets

Association for the Protection of Jabal Moussa (APJM), Suites 205 & 207, 2nd Fl, Le Portail Bldg, Jounieh; \ *f 09 643 464;* m *71 944 405;* e *info@jabalmoussa.org; www.jabalmoussa.org;* f *jabalmoussareserve;* ⊕ *08.00–15.00 daily for walking tours, but the reserve is open for visits 24hrs daily; admission: adults & children over 16 LBP8,000, children under 16 LBP4,000; group hiking guide LBP50,000.*

Located in the Kesrouan district northeast of Jounieh, Lebanon's third and newest biosphere reserve at the time of writing was referred to by UNESCO in 2009 as 'a true mosaic of ecological systems', and achieved Important Bird Area (IBA) recognition in the same year. Jabal Moussa encompasses an area of some 6,500ha, extending 500m north beyond the Nahr Ibrahim river and a similar distance beyond the Nahr al-Dahab river in the south. The undulating and wild terrain in this reserve on the western slopes of the Mount Lebanon range varies in height from between 350m in the west to 1,700m in the east. This region has paid homage to the legend of Adonis and Astarte, and stairways were constructed to aid passing legions during the Roman occupation. During the 18th century, Jabal Moussa's cultural importance was supplemented by its economic significance in the silk industry, where the area's mulberry trees provided sustenance for the silkworms which were transported to the market villages at the bottom of the mountain. In the 2nd century CE, the emperor Hadrian practised an early type of environmental management when he prohibited the felling of specific trees such as the cedar, fir, juniper and oak. Today, the Association for the Protection of Jabal Moussa (APJM) has taken a few extra steps than the Romans in order to preserve the long-term sustainability of this region through its awareness and educational campaigns, research and field study programmes. The area's landscape of valleys, rivers and mountains are home to a variety of fauna including the hyena, the rock hyrax (*Procavia capensis*; the elephant's nearest living relative and known locally as *Tabsoun* and also the reserve's mascot), porcupines, squirrels, wild boar, wolves and more than 80 species of native and migratory bird. Of the genus of flora, cyclamen, Calabrian pine, kermes oak, manna ash, storax, maple, orchid, peony and the Lebanon marjoram dot the countryside.

As part of their environmental awareness programme, APJM operates a number of hiking trails of varying length and duration throughout the reserve with experienced and bilingual guides. They have a dedicated Ecotourism Manager (m *71 944 405*), who can advise and arrange tours and visits. Alternatively, visit the APJM website (see above) for further details on how to reach the reserve and hiking trail maps.

must be booked a week in advance, & 2 days ahead for tengalows. See the website for details of public transport and self-drive options for getting here from Beirut and the north. **$$**

OTHER PRACTICALITIES

$ Bank of Beirut Tony Michel Issa Bldg, President Suleiman St; \ 01 906 324 or 09 622 734/5/6/7/8/9, dial 1262 within Lebanon (24hr customer service line); www.bankofbeirut. com; ⊕ 08.00–17.00 Mon–Sat. 24hr ATM.

$ Byblos Bank Michel Rouhana Bldg, Main Rd; \ 09 620 815/6 or 09 620 996/7; e customerservice@byblosbank.com.lb; www. byblosbank.com; ⊕ 08.30–17.30 Mon–Fri, 08.00–13.00 Sat. 2 x 24hr ATMs.

RACHANA

A further 17km north of Amchit, this compact and hilly village just off the main coastal highway is the location for some extraordinary street art. This was created by the trio of the now-deceased Basbous Brothers, who since the 1950s had created an eclectic outdoor museum of conceptual, religious and sensual art forms, working with stone and wood. Since 1994, they have held the annual 'International Sculptor Atelier' during August and September, where sculptors from around the world can exhibit their work in a public setting and, in 1997, this prompted UNESCO to label Rachana the 'International Capital of Sculpture in Open Air'. The sculptures are still ubiquitous around the town.

GETTING THERE It is best to take a taxi from Byblos or Amchit as there were no buses operating to Rachana at the time of research; expect to pay around LBP30,000–35,000 for the journey from Byblos.

6

North Lebanon

Telephone code 06

North Lebanon comprises the area roughly north from the coastal town of Batroun to the tip of the Syrian border and inland to the western slopes of the Mount Lebanon range. The region is centred on the bustling and traditional coastal Sunni Arab city of Tripoli (Trablous), where, unlike the capital, time has virtually stood still as witnessed by its beautiful old buildings, anachronistic souks and a much more conservative lifestyle. The food is good too, with Tripoli renowned for its pastries and sweets. A visit to this city should be on every traveller's itinerary, but equally it would be a shame to overlook the region's other main attractions, with some of the best opportunities in the country to 'get back to nature'. The Christian town of Bcharré, some 50km southeast of Tripoli, is the birthplace and location of a museum dedicated to the country's greatest literary figure, Khalil Gibran (box, pages 250–1), ideally situated at the head of the UNESCO World Heritage site-listed Qadisha Valley. This rugged and wild region of both great natural and manmade beauty is home to numerous rock-carved chapels, grottos, monasteries and waterfalls, and is where the Maronites established their roots and shelter in the 7th century, fleeing their Arab persecutors; there are also innumerable opportunities for hiking and trekking in the area.

Above Bcharré is one of the last and oldest remaining stands of Lebanon's iconic cedar tree (*Cedrus libani*). Ownce carpeting the Lebanese countryside, the cedars provided the raw material for many a Phoenician trading vessel and were used in the building of King Solomon's Temple in Jerusalem. Today a fiercely protected species, some of the trees are estimated to be 2,000 years old, but age has not withered them, especially when snow-covered in winter. Adventurous travellers will find that the raw and rustic appeal of Lebanon's northernmost region offers a quite different experience from the chic and gloss of the capital. Modernisation *en masse* has been largely resisted, providing an opportunity to obtain an alternative view of Lebanon which goes beyond media and touristic clichés.

BATROUN

This attractive Christian Maronite coastal town, some 50km north of Beirut and 20km north of Byblos, is the first principal town you reach in the north. Batroun traces its ancient roots back to Phoenician times and its founder was King Ithobaal of Tyre, father of the infamous Jezabel. It is also referred to in the ancient 14th-century BCE Egyptian *Armana Letters*. Under the Greeks, the town was called Botrys, and in CE551 it succumbed to a massive earthquake, which destroyed the town's prosperity and which is believed by some historians to have created its natural harbour. Today, Batroun has the look and feel of a charming traditional fishing port and provincial town with attractive streets and sandstone buildings, plus houses and a workaday souk.

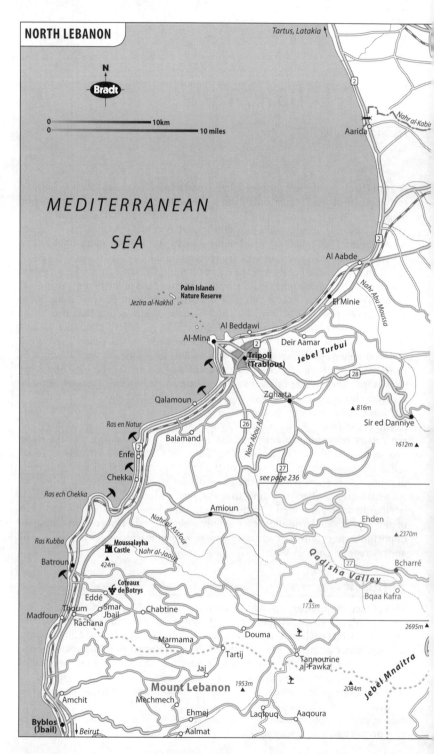

N

Bradt

0   10km
0   10 miles

Tartus, Latakia

Nahr al-Kabir

Aarida

2

2

MEDITERRANEAN

SEA

Al Aabde

Palm Islands
Nature Reserve

Jezira al-Nakhil

El Minie

Nahr Abou Moussa

Al Beddawi

Al-Mina

Deir Aamar

2

Jebel Turbui

**Tripoli
(Trablous)**

28

Qalamoun

Zgharta

▲816m

Sir ed Danniye

Ras en Natur

26

1612m ▲

Balamand

2

Enfe

27

Chekka

see page 236

Ras ech Chekka

Amioun

Ehden

Nahr al-Assfour

▲2370m

Ras Kubba

Moussalayha
Castle

Nahr al-Jaoua

Qadisha Valley

27

Bcharré

Batroun

424m

Coteaux
de Botrys

1735m

Bqaa Kafra

Eddé

2695m ▲

Madfoun

Smar
Jbail

Chabtine

Thoum

Rachana

Douma

Marmama

Tannourine
al-Fawka

Tartij

2084m ▲

Jebel Mnaitra

Jaj

Mount Lebanon *1953m*
▲

Amchit

Mechmech

**Byblos
(Jbail)**

Ehmej

Laqlouq

Aaqoura

Beirut

Aalmat

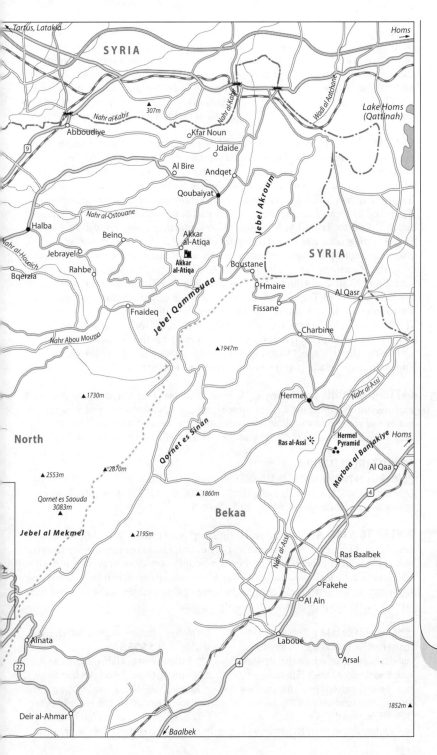

Renowned for its lemonade from the citrus groves that surround the town, and more recently for its burgeoning number of wineries (see pages 224–5 for a selection of the main ones), which you can visit, Batroun is now also a hub of nightlife for the north, with a good range of bars and clubs and a number of beach club bars and cafés just a few kilometres south of town, which keep the Batroun party rolling until late. Despite its small-town feel, Batroun is certainly the most cosmopolitan and lively place in the region and, especially at night, is a lively contrast to Tripoli.

GETTING THERE Batroun is well served by public transport as it is on the coast road north from Beirut. Buses and taxis pass by here *en route* to Tripoli and can drop you off on the highway exit, with a journey time from the capital of around an hour. From Zone B of Charles Helou station [172 B2] in Beirut **Tripoli Express** (m 03 327 625) have regular daily departures to Tripoli between 07.30 and 17.15 and can drop you off in Batroun, but you will still be charged the full fare to Tripoli (*LBP3,500*). Also departing from Zone B of Charles Helou station is **Connexion Transport** (☏ 01 585 500; m 03 206 308/384; www. connexion-transport.com), whose modern air-conditioned coaches depart at roughly 30-minute intervals between 07.30 and 19.30 Monday to Saturday and from 08.10 to 19.00 on Sunday, and you can alight at the Batroun exit for the full fare to Tripoli (*LBP5,000*). There are also a number buses serving Batroun *en route* to Tripoli departing from the capital's Dora station [173 H2] (*LBP2,000–3,000*). If you are on a self-drive visit, Batroun is around an hour's drive from the capital, just follow the coast road north if coming from Beirut or Byblos (Jbail). Expect to pay about US$40–50 for a taxi from the capital and approximately US$70 if you want the driver to wait around 2 hours.

GETTING AROUND Like many of Lebanon's towns, Batroun is easily and best explored on foot covering a fairly compact area, and walking will give you a much better feel for the town. Slightly more outlying areas and sites such as Batroun's beach clubs, Moussalayha Castle and the wineries will require a short taxi ride.

TOURIST INFORMATION
🛈 **Ministry of Tourism Office** Nr St Stephen's Cathedral, Old Souk; ☏ 06 741 522; e rafkanasr. mot@gmail.com, pascaledaaboul.mot@gmail. com; www.mot.gov.lb; ⏱ 08.30–17.00 Mon–Sat, 08.30–13.00 Sun, closed public holidays

🏠 **WHERE TO STAY** As a principally summer resort town popular with local couples and families, Batroun's resort-type complexes are geared more towards this more affluent local market. For the budget-conscious traveller, however, Batroun is an easy and affordable day trip from either Beirut or Tripoli, and these two cities, with their cheaper lodging options, could make an ideal base from which to explore the town and its regions.

🏠 **L'Auberge de la Mer** (9 rooms & suites) Port; ☏ 06 740 824/5; e reservation@ laubergedelamer.com; www.laubergedelamer. com. Housed within a lovely 19th-century stone building with port views, this charming boutique hotel combines a great location, a stone's throw from the souks, with character, its vaulted stone ceilings nicely complemented by the modern furnishings & airy ambience. B/fast inc, free Wi-Fi. **$$$$$**

🏠 **Batroun Village Club** (23 rooms, suites & bungalows) Off hwy, about 2km from centre of Batroun; ☏ 06 744 333; e info@batrounvclub. com; www.batrounvclub.com. Perched on a hill with lovely sea views, this is a fine & charming resort complex with some character, managing to avoid the often glitzy & plastic look of many resort complexes. Very family-friendly with a nice tropical pool, spa, horseriding, basketball & tennis courts among the summer activities, & a children's crèche. **$$$$**

🏠 **San Stephano Resort** (64 rooms & suites) Sea Rd, around 1km north of the town; 📞06 740 366, 06 642 366 or 06 643 202; e info@ sanstephano.com; www.sanstephano.com. Comfortable, though with less charm than the

Batroun Village Club, with all the usual resort accoutrements such as swimming pool, beach bar & scuba-diving school. **$$$$**

🏠 **Sawary Resort & Hotel** (18 rooms & 150 chalets) Sea Rd; 📞06 642 100/1/2/3; e info@ sawaryresort.com; www.sawaryresort.com. A rather typical & uninspiring resort complex but nicely situated for Batroun's amenities; decent rooms with sea views, live music at the beach bar, & swimming pool. All rooms have TV, AC & Wi-Fi. **$$$$**

✖ WHERE TO EAT AND DRINK

✖ **Chez Maguy** Makaad al-Mir; m 03 439 147; ⏱ noon–midnight daily. Small, homely restaurant overlooking the ocean, serving excellent fish *mezze* & a menu that changes daily. This place can get busy, so book ahead. **$$$$$**

✳ ✖ **Batrouniyat** Hay El Dawra St; 📞06 744 510; e info@batrouniyat.org; www.batrouniyat. org; ⏱ 10.00–late Tue–Sun. Located in a lovely old renovated stone building, which functioned as a hospital & a centre for textile manufacture during the Ottoman period, the restaurant serves healthy cuisine prepared with ingredients sourced locally along with a good selection of Batroun's wines. There is an open buffet most Sundays (*US$35pp, booking essential*) & *nargileh* costs from US$7. Recommended. **$$$$**

✖ **Le Marin** Bahsa St; 📞06 744 016; m 03 328 678; ⏱ noon–23.00 daily. Popular no-frills, casual local haunt, serving excellent seafood & *mezze* with a pleasant outdoor terrace dining area with panoramic sea views. **$$$$**

✳ ✖ **Colonel** Bayadir St; 📞06 743 543; m 03 743 543; e info@colonelbeer.com; www.

colonelbeer.com; ⏱ 16.00–midnight Mon–Fri, 10.00–01.00 Sat & Sun. This novel place is a one-stop shop for beer lovers as it combines a small brewery, pub & restaurant in a lovely green & pleasant setting with beer garden. The list of craft lagers produced here is pegged to its restaurant menu offering a tasty range of salads, sandwiches & platters. Tours of the brewery & the brewing process are also available by prior appointment. It's also worth checking the website for a whole host of beer, food & music events held here. Recommended. **$$$**

✖ **Le Garage** Facing St Stephen's Maronite Cathedral; m 03 323 897; ⏱ 06.30–midnight daily. A good place to try Batroun's speciality, lemonade, & a range of delicious Lebanese snacks such as *manoushe, shish tawouk* & other quick eats. **$$**

✳ ✖ **Chez Hilmi** Main Rd, nr the souk; 📞06 640 068; m 03 043 117; ⏱ 08.00–22.00 daily. Good patisserie selling Batroun's ubiquitous lemonade, pastries & sweets. **$**

ENTERTAINMENT AND NIGHTLIFE Bars and nightclubs abound in Batroun along its main street and this, with its annual summer festival annual (page 225) creates a vibrant nightlife scene in the town. An alternative to the clubs and drinking dens are the following selection of beach clubs, around 5km south of Batroun and easily reached by taxi, which offer a more chilled-out atmosphere than the bars and clubs in the main town and all serving good seafood and *mezze* dishes. A range of water-based activities are also available such as kayaking, sailing, scuba diving and windsurfing.

Loco Beach Resort Thoum; m 76 744 844; e fawaz@karamelevents.com; 📘 Locobeachresort; ⏱ 09.30–late daily; admission: adults & children LBP10,000 Mon–Fri, LBP15,000 Sat–Sun (no children at w/ends).

Pierre & Friends Thoum; m 03 352 930; e pierre-and-friends@outlook.com ⏱ 10.00–02.00 daily; admission free

White Beach Thoum; 📞06 742 404 or 06 742 505; m 03 732 404; e info@whitebeachlebanon. com; www.whitebeachlebanon.com; ⏱ 08.00–23.00 daily; admission: LBP5,000 Mon–Fri, LBP7,000 Sat & Sun

SHOPPING Despite having an old and still-working souk, Batroun's retail offerings are pretty much geared to local needs, with few things that you would come here specifically to buy. If you are planning to venture further north to Tripoli, your money would be better spent in the souks there.

OTHER PRACTICALITIES Batroun's Main Street is home to all the banks, cafés, eateries, shops, banks and ATMs for cash withdrawals.

$ BLC Bank BLC Bank Bldg, Main Rd; \06 642 166, 06 741 599; e batrounbranch@blcbank.com; www.blcbank.com; ⏰ 08.30–13.30 Mon–Fri, 08.30–noon Sat. ATM.

$ Byblos Bank Ground Fl, Royal Centre, Main Rd; \06 642 360/370; www.byblosbank.com;

⏰ 08.00–15.30 Mon–Fri, 08.00–noon Sat. 2 ATMs.

✉ **Post office** Ogero Bldg; \06 740 302; www.libanpost.com; ⏰ 08.00–17.00 Mon–Fri, 08.30–13.30 Sat

➕ **Lebanese Red Cross** \140 (emergency), 06 642 588, 06 742 916; www.redcross.org.lb

WHAT TO SEE AND DO As a charming and scenic town, Batroun is best explored on foot to admire its residential buildings and houses. Despite the renovations of recent years, however, it remains an essentially traditional town. Start off by the pleasant old harbour, where you can see a slice of life, with fishermen in their boats mending their nets, and take a look at Batroun's 225m long **Phoenician wall**, which was hewn from natural rock during the Phoenician era and is overlooked by the charming yet compact **Our Lady of the Sea** (Sadiyat al-Bahr) Greek Orthodox church. Behind the harbour is the triple-arched and imposing **St Stephen's Maronite Cathedral**, which dates from 1860. The nearby **St George's Greek Orthodox Church**, built in a Byzantine style, dates from the latter period of the 18th century. There are many other religious buildings and icons dotted around this predominantly Christian Maronite town, but Batroun's principal attraction is its sandstone **souks**, where local shopkeepers ply their trade as fishmongers, grocers and woodworkers behind large wooden doors. Just under 4km north of Batroun is **Moussalayha Castle**. This solitary and strategically located structure was once thought to be of Crusader origin but many authorities now attribute it to the work of Fakhreddine Maan II during the 17th century, intended to function as a lookout post to protect the coast road from Tripoli to Beirut. There are some rock-cut steps leading up to the top and the relatively steep climb is worth it for the views alone. The Nahr al Jaouz or Walnut River runs beneath an ancient bridge below the castle, which is easily reached by service taxi or taxi from Batroun and easily accessible from the main highway.

Wines of Batroun Whilst the Bekaa Valley remains Lebanon's historical and principal wine-producing region, the hills above Batroun have witnessed a burgeoning number of vineyards sprouting up over the last few years, and the following is a selection of wineries which all welcome visitors for guided tours and tasting sessions. Although opening times are given where applicable, it would still be a good idea to call or email in advance of your visit.

Atibaia Smar Jbail, Batroun; m 03 363 941; e info@atibaiawine.com; www.atibaiawine.com; ⏰ by prior appointment only. Set in a traditional 17th-century house amid extremely picturesque & verdant scenery, this boutique winery limits itself to producing 12,000 bottles annually of just

a single red wine, though there were plans to add a white wine in future years. You could combine a trip here with a visit to the nearby ruins of a Crusader castle and the Mar Nohra Church, whose name derives from a Persian missionary who was blinded by the Romans and continues to this day to draw pilgrims from far and wide seeking treatment for eye ailments.

Château Sanctus Marmama, Batroun; 04 417 974; m 03 661 699; e info@ chateausanctuslebanon.com, ramaouad@yahoo. com; www.chateausanctuslebanon.com; w/ends in spring & summer by prior appointment only. Covering just 4ha & with an annual output of just 12,000 bottles, this organic boutique winery has been widely lauded for the quality of its wines owned by former orthopaedic surgeon & wine connoisseur Ramez Aouad.

Clos du Phoenix Eddé, Batroun; 06 720 366; m 03 271 672; e info@closduphoenix.com; www. closduphoenix.com; summer & winter by prior appointment only. This family-owned winery extending over some 6ha employs traditional wine-making methods & techniques to produce 3 reds, a white & a rosé.

Coteaux de Botrys Main Rd, Eddé; 06 721 300; m 03 238 937 or 03 517 508; e info@ coteauxdebotrys.com; www.coteauxdebotrys. com. This château has been producing wine since 1998 & is now among the best known of the area's 8 wineries. The brainchild of the late army general Joseph Bitar, the château produces 3 varieties of red, together with a white & a rosé, & its Arak Kfifane has been hailed the best in Lebanon. Spread over more than 16ha, production continues

today by the late general's 2 daughters, who, in 2009, corked some 40,000 bottles with output anticipated to increase to 65,000 within 5 years. Each year, from June to September, on the first and last Sunday of each month, the château plays host to a lunch and wine-tasting event held in the picturesque & pleasant surroundings of the vines & overlooking the Mediterranean below. It is best to phone in advance for any tour of the winery or tasting session outside these days.

Domaine S Najm Chabtine, Batroun; m 70 623 023; e info@domaine-snajm.com; www.domaine-snajm.com; by prior appointment only. A long-established, family-run winery well known for its olive oil and *arak* for over 6 decades, & since the early 1990s it has added a red wine to its portfolio.

IXSIR Basbina, c7km above Batroun; m 71 631 613 (winery tours); m 71 773 770 (restaurant); e info@ ixsir.com.lb; www.ixsir.com.lb; winter 10.00–16.00 Tue–Sun, summer 10.00–18.00 Tue–Sun, closed Mon. Located in a 300-year-old stone house, IXSIR was founded in 2008 and corks some 300,000 bottles of wine annually from grapes grown in its 3 vineyards at Jezzine, the Bekaa Valley and Basbina, where visitors can take a tour of this eco-friendly winery to learn about the process of wine-making together with free tasting sessions, and have lunch at the winery's Nicolas Audi à La Maison d'IXSIR restaurant, including a weekend buffet.

Getting there As the above wineries are not on a bus route you will need to take a taxi from Batroun. Expect to pay around LBP15,000+ for the one-way trip from the centre of Batroun. Try the local company **Botrys Taxi** (06 744 111; m 70 744 111; e botrys_taxi@hotmail.com) who operate 24 hours, seven days a week.

Batroun International Festival (06 642 262; m 03 105 700 or 71 440 071; e info@batrounfestival.org; www.batrounfestival.org) Held annually during July, this festival has a more local feel than many of Lebanon's other festivals and showcases dance, song and comedy acts, and hosts open-air party nights in the town's main street and Phoenician wall area, as well as a variety of exhibitions by visual artists. Well-known artists who have performed here include Ali Campbell, former lead singer with UK band UB40, and the French/Armenian singer-songwriter and veteran of more than 1,000 songs and 50 albums, Charles Aznavour. Check the festival website for full details of the current years' programme of events. Tickets can be purchased from any branch of Virgin Megastore, online at www. ticketingboxoffice.com or from the Batroun Festival Office (*Main Rd, Batroun*).

TRIPOLI (TRABLOUS)

With a population of around 250,000, Tripoli – a heartland of the Sunni Muslim community – is Lebanon's second-largest city and port, and capital of the North

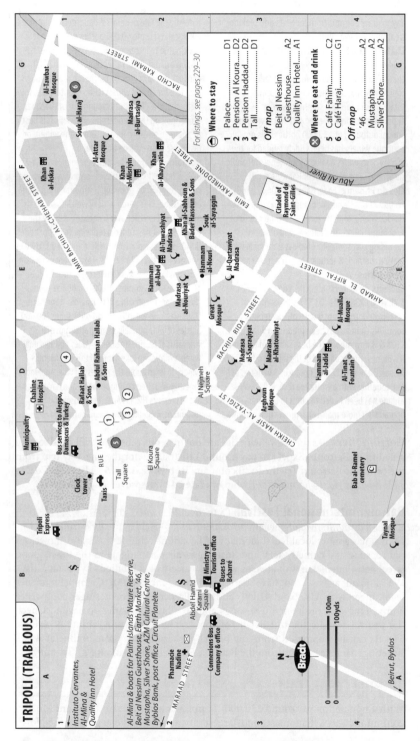

TRIPOLI (TRABLOUS)

Instituto Cervantes,
Al-Mina &
Quality Inn Hotel

Al-Mina & boats for Palm Islands Nature Reserve,
Beit al Nessim Guesthouse, Earth Market, '46,
Mustapha, Silver Shore, AZM Cultural Centre,
Byblos Bank, post office, Circuit Planète

Beirut, Byblos

Municipality

Chahine Hospital

Bus services to Aleppo,
Damascus & Turkey

Rafaat Hallab & Sons

Abdul Rahman Hallab & Sons

Tripoli Express

Clock tower

Taxis

RUE TALL

Tall Square

El Koura Square

Pharmacie Nadine

Abdel Hamid Karami Square

Ministry of Tourism office

Buses to Bcharré

Connexions Bus Company & office

MARAAD STREET

N

Brandt

0   100m
0   100yds

AMIR BACHIR AL-CHEHABI STREET

Al-Tawbat Mosque

Souk al-Haraj

Khan al-Askar

Al-Attar Mosque

Madrasa al-Burtasiya

Khan al-Misriyin

Khan al-Khayyatin

RACHID KARAMI STREET

Al-Tuwashiyat Madrasa

Hammam al-Abed

Madrasa al-Nouriyat

Khan al-Sabhoun & Bader Hassoun & Sons

Souk al-Sayaggin

Hammam al-Nouri

Al-Qartawiyat Madrasa

Great Mosque

EMIR FAKHREDDINE STREET

Citadel of Raymond de Saint-Gilles

Abu Ali River

RACHID RIDA STREET

Madrasa al-Saqraqiyat

Madrasa al-Khatoumiyat

Arghoun Mosque

Al-Nejmeh Square

CHEIKH NASIR AL-YAZIGI ST

Hammam al-Jadid

Al-Tinat Fountain

Al-Muallaq Mosque

AHMAD EL RIFFAL STREET

Bab al-Ramel cemetery

Taynal Mosque

Where to stay
For listings, see pages 229–30

1 Palace	D1
2 Pension Al Koura	D2
3 Pension Haddad	D2
4 Tall	D1

Off map

Beit al Nessim
Guesthouse........ A2
Quality Inn Hotel.... A1

Where to eat and drink

5 Café Fahim	C2
6 Café Haraj	G1

Off map

'46........................ A2
Mustapha................ A2
Silver Shore............ A2

Lebanon Governorate (*Muhafazat*). Despite its size, it has been estimated that only some 2% of visitors to the country actually visit Tripoli and those who do mostly arrive on organised coach tours as day-trippers rather than on an extended tour of the city and its environs. Yet Tripoli, 85km north of Beirut, contains after Cairo the largest and most significant set of Mamluk-period architecture in the world, with other vestiges of its past highlighted by the old-fashioned souks, as redolent of *1,001 Arabian Nights* as you will experience anywhere north of Sidon.

Here you can still see artisans, from jewellers to tailors, toiling over their labours in factories and workshops used by their forebears over the past five centuries. Keeping watch over this authentic Arab city is the Crusader castle of Raymond de Saint-Gilles, which has seen many alterations over the years and is Tripoli's most recognisable monument. One 'monument' that hasn't seen much in the way of modification since construction started in the early 1960s and halted with the onset of civil war in 1975, is the large domed expanse of the Rashid Karami International Fair, which was intended to become a major international commercial and exhibition space. Located west of the Old City, it was commissioned to enhance the profile of Tripoli as a business hub. The unfinished structure is the work of the late renowned Brazilian modernist architect Oscar Niemeyer (1907–2012) of *Brasilia* fame. Though there has been talk of restarting the project, it remains at the present time just a rather sorry blot on the landscape, overlooked by the Quality Inn Hotel, but will be of interest to architectural enthusiasts for Niemeyer's trademark use of curves in his work.

HISTORY Settlement in Tripoli dates back to the 14th century BCE, and perhaps even earlier, but the foundations of a prosperous city-state were not established until the 9th century BCE with the arrival of the Phoenicians. The city became part of a loose coalition of trading centres which included Sidon, Tyre and Arvad (along the coast of modern-day Syria) and grew into three separate districts, which the Greeks named Tripolis (Three Cities) and later amended to its current name Trablous with the inception of Arab rule. Tripoli has always been a centre for business and commerce, though it never surpassed the importance of the southern cities of Byblos, Sidon or Tyre, and its Phoenician roots survive in name only. The roll call of conquerors and occupiers is a familiar one – Assyrians, Persians, Greeks, Romans, Byzantines, Arabs, Crusaders and Ottomans – and all contributed to the city's general affluence over the centuries, interrupted only by the devastating earthquake that afflicted the city and other coastal cities in CE551. Tripoli was later rebuilt by the Byzantine emperor Justinian I. But it wasn't until the Middle Ages that Tripoli was to experience its greatest period of building, creating the fine architectural legacies we see today. The arrival of the Crusaders from Europe in 1109 wreaked havoc on the city, including the burning of Tripoli's famous Dar il-ilm library, which was once held in as high esteem as the famed Bibliotheca Alexandrina in the Egyptian city of Alexandria. But nearly two centuries of Frankish rule left a magnificent castle, which still oversees the city. Tripoli was the capital of the 'County of Tripoli' until 1289, when, under Sultan al-Mansur Qalawun, the Mamluks sacked the knights and destroyed the city, building *hammams, madrasas* and the innumerable mosques we see today.

The city's more recent history, however, has been marked more by destruction than construction. Tripoli suffered heavy Syrian bombardment in 1983 during the civil war and endured equally heavy fighting between Palestinian factions during the conflict. Tripoli's environs are also the location for two of Lebanon's 12 Palestinian refugee camps, at Beddawi, 5km north of Tripoli, and at Nahr al-Bared some 16km north of the city centre. Between 24 May and 5 September 2007, fighting erupted for control of the latter camp between the Sunni militant group Fatah al-Islam (allegedly assisted by Syrian military intelligence) and the Lebanese army, which in more than three months of struggle destroyed some 95% of the camp's infrastructure and displaced nearly 30,000 Palestinians to surrounding areas and the nearby Beddawi camp. With the cessation of hostilities, which left more than 400 dead including 170 Lebanese soldiers, UNRWA has embarked on a wholesale reconstruction of the Nahr al-Bared camp, the largest project it has ever undertaken at a cost of some US$345 million, which remains ongoing at the time of writing, with former residents returning on a piecemeal basis as elements of the reconstruction process are completed.

GETTING THERE As Lebanon's second city and capital of the north, Tripoli is well connected by public transport. Tripoli is also a hub for transport to Bcharré (pages 237–42) and the Cedars (pages 247–51) and so is a good place to base yourself for a few days if planning a day trip(s) to these areas.

By bus The following two companies have regular departures from Beirut's **Charles Helou** [172 B2] bus station, and are recommended. They can also drop you off at various points *en route* such as Jounieh, Byblos (Jbail), Batroun and Chekka. There are also departures from the capital's **Dora** station [173 H2] with buses & minivans leaving from near the tall building housing a branch of Byblos Bank in Dora which also ply the route north to Tripoli and cost LBP2,000–3,000 depending on which company you choose

🚆 **Connexion Transportation & Tourism** Zone B, Charles Helou Station, Rmeil, east of Downtown, Beirut; 📞 01 585 500; 📱 03 206 308/384 (Beirut); 📞 06 626 969; 📱 03 206 718 (Tripoli); e info@ connexion-transport.com; www.connexion-transport.com. This excellent company operates a fleet of large, modern, deluxe air-conditioned coaches. Buses depart daily for Tripoli from 07.30 to 19.30 Mon–Fri with some 25 departures at roughly 25–30min intervals; whilst on Sat & Sun there are

19 departures between 08.10 and 19.00 about every 30–40mins. A one-way fare costs LBP5,000, with a journey time of up to 2hrs. They have a useful departure timings board outside their office.

🚆 **Tripoli Express** Zone B, Charles Helou Station, Rmeil, east of Downtown, Beirut; 📱 03 327 625 (Beirut); 📱 03 575 844 (Tripoli). Their buses depart daily at roughly 30min intervals between 07.30 and 17.15. A one-way fare costs LBP3,500 with a journey time of around 1½hrs.

By taxi There are numerous taxi companies in Beirut. As a rough guide, expect to part with around LBP80,000–100,000 for a taxi to Tripoli from the capital and in the order of US$100 for a return journey including a 2-hour wait by the driver if your visit is just a brief one. A few reliable & trusted companies to try are:

🚕 **Charlie Taxi** ☏01 285 710; e operations@ charlietaxi.com; www.charlie-group.com
🚕 **Lebanon Taxi** ☏01 353 153; www. lebanontaxi.com

🚕 **Trust Taxi** ☏01 427 777, 01 613 573 or 01 613 398; m 03 601 806; e info@trust-taxi.com; www.trust-taxi.com

By car If you have a rental car, Tripoli is easily reached in less than 2 hours (traffic permitting) along the coastal highway north from Beirut, an extremely scenic and pleasant journey and clearly signposted.

GETTING AROUND Although Tripoli is quite a large city, it is perfectly manageable by foot, and this is actually the best option to appreciate this busy Arabian metropolis and its sites. The city is divided into the contrasting medieval Old City, situated around 3km inland, and the port, or Al-Mina district, which extends from the peninsula towards the Old City. As in Beirut, though, service taxis are readily available and prices are generally a little lower than what you would pay in the capital.

TOURIST INFORMATION The **Ministry of Tourism Office** [226 B2] at Abdel Hamid Karami Square (☏ *06 433 590*; e *manalayoubi.mot@gmail.com, rimtizani. mot@gmail.com; www.mot.gov.lb;* ⊕ *08.00–18.00 Mon–Thu, 08.00–16.00 Fri–Sat*) is a small, friendly branch offering a range of brochures and pamphlets in Arabic, English, French and Spanish. Also, and highly recommended by visitors for their edifying content & for dispelling the cliché of Tripoli as a 'taboo city', **Mira's Guided Tours** (m *70 126 764*; e *mirasguidedtours@gmail.com;* f *mirasguidedtours;* weekend group tours from US$20, see Mira's Facebook page for other group & private tour rates), led by local Mira Minkara, a tourism graduate from the Lebanese University, take an entertaining look at Tripoli's past & present from the Rashid Karami International Fair, the port district (Al-Mina) to the old city & its souks.

🏠 **WHERE TO STAY** Tripoli is a budget traveller's paradise compared with Beirut, with only one hotel in the city at present catering to those seeking more salubrious or international-type accommodation.

🏠 **Beit al Nessim Guesthouse** [226 A2] (5 rooms) Labban St, Al Mina; ☏06 200 983; m 03 308 156; e info@beitelnessim.com; www.beitelnessim. com. A small boutique lodging in a nicely restored, old, stone house with clean rooms, full of character yet with all the comforts of home in a relaxed & quiet setting. The hotel also runs weekly yoga classes (*LBP20,000pp*). B/fast inc, free Wi-Fi. Closed Feb. Highly recommended. **$$$**

🏠 **Quality Inn Hotel** [226 A1] (112 rooms & suites) Rashid Karami International Fair; ☏06 211 255/6/7/8; e info@qualityinnlebanon.com, sales@ qualityinnlebanon.com; www.qualityinnlebanon. com. Although clean & boasting the usual range of tourist & business facilities you would expect of a 4-star hotel, including 2 swimming pools & conference facilities, the rooms are quite bland & the stark, monochromatic bathrooms feel more on a par with budget offerings. The hotel's location is also about 2km from Tripoli's main city & attractions. **$$$**

🏠 **Pension Al Koura** [226 D2] (8 rooms) Tall St; ☏06 425 451; m 70 211 503; e contact@ alkourahotel.com; www.pensionalkoura.com. Tripoli's best-value hotel. Excellent, clean rooms, with character stone walls, flatscreen TV, AC & fridge, plus use of communal kitchen facilities. Laundry is an extra US$7–10 for a 5–6kg load. B/fast inc. **$$**

🏠 **Palace Hotel** [226 D1] (14 rooms) 📞 06 429 993. The grandeur of its exterior belies a darker & bleaker interior & the rooms could be cleaner, but it is adequate for a night or 2 for those on a tight budget. **$$**

🏠 **Tall Hotel** [226 D1] (13 rooms) Rue Tall; 📞 06 628 407. Although this hotel can't spell its name correctly (look for the red-lettered 'Tell Hotel' on a yellow sign), this is still a reasonable, though very basic place, for a night or two. 7 of the rooms have their own bathroom, are clean enough & the location is nice & central. No b/fast served. **$$**

🏠 **Pension Haddad** [226 D2] (8 rooms) Tall St, close to Fahim Café; m 03 507 709, 03 361 349; e haddadpension53@hotmail.com; www. pensionhaddad.8m.com. A good, decent, family-run budget hotel hosted by a friendly grandma, mother, sister, aunt & daughter. A house of some character with simple but clean rooms: Tripoli's best backpacker option. Dorm room US$10pp, b/fast US$5 extra, laundry US$1/US$2 for small/ large items respectively. Free Wi-Fi. **$**

✕ **WHERE TO EAT AND DRINK** Eating and drinking options are many in the city, but they tend to be more of the informal street snacking variety with few formal restaurants, which actually adds to the traditional charm of the city anyway. Just don't expect the options that you find in Beirut. Tripoli is famed for its sweets and in addition to the outlets below there are many others dotted around the city. The Al-Mina (port) area has an excellent seafood restaurant.

✕ **'46** [226 A2] Ibn Sina Rd, Al-Mina, Corniche; 📞 06 212 223; e contact@restaurantfourtysix.com; www.restaurantsilvershore.com; ⏰ 11.00–23.00 Tue–Sun. If you don't like fish, then this place, next door to Silver Shore, serves decent international & Italian cuisine with equally nice views. **$$$$**

✕ **Silver Shore** [226 A2] Ibn Sina Rd, Al-Mina, Corniche; 📞 06 601 384; m 03 691 385; 📘 Silver-Shore/226747037466646; ⏰ 11.15–20.00 daily. Something of an institution, which means advance booking is recommended, this specialist seafood eatery is easily the best in town for ultra fresh-fish *mezze* accompanied by lovely sea views. This is a good place to try the local & popular spicy fish known as *samkeh harrah*. **$$$$**

✕ **Mustapha** [226 A2] Rear of Omar bin-Khattab Mosque, Al-Mina; 📞 06 205 821; ⏰ 10.00–22.00

daily. An unpretentious café & restaurant serving freshly caught fish & *mezze*. A good-value choice for filling & tasty food. **$$**

☕ **Café Fahim** [226 C2] Rue Tall, close to the Ottoman clock tower; ⏰ 06.30–22.00 daily. Anachronistic with old-world charm, this large indoor & outdoor café is the place to head to for a *nargileh* (*LBP1,500–6,000*), coffee, tea, soft drinks & to play (or watch) backgammon & cards amidst some traditional Arab atmosphere. This place doesn't serve food. **$**

☕ **Café Haraj** [226 G1] Souk al-Haraj; 📞 06 440 154; m 03 956 458; ⏰ 09.00–sunset daily. Good homely feel about this place for watching the world go by in the souk, puffing on a *nargileh* pipe or snacking on a decent falafel or *shish tawouk* sandwich. **$**

ENTERTAINMENT AND NIGHTLIFE As a predominantly conservative city, Tripoli certainly doesn't exude nightlife options like the capital, with most places shutting up shop (and restaurant) by around midnight. The port area of Al-Mina has a handful of bars that stay open until midnight or thereabouts, or for a night at the movies there is **Circuit Planète** [226 A2] (*Planete City Complex, Riad al-Solh St;* 📞 06 442 471; e *cineklik@cineklik.com; www.cineklik.com*), a typical multiplex cinema complex showing films in English, including the latest Western blockbusters.

Tripoli Film Festival (*Office 204, Gibran National Committee Bldg, Bechara Al-Khoury Bd;* m *71 400 101;* e *info@tripoli-filmfestival.org; www.tripoli-filmfestival. org*) Launched in 2014, this annual festival, usually held towards the end of April each year, at the Safadi Cultural Centre & Azm Cultural Centre (Beit El Fann; page 234) showcases a wide range of Lebanese & international films including animated shorts, features, documentaries & short films. Check the festival website for detailed information on the coming year's screenings and online catalogue.

SHOPPING The contrast with the glitz and glamour of Beirut couldn't be more pronounced in Lebanon's second city as the ubiquitous boutiques and shopping malls of the capital are largely absent in Tripoli, giving way to a much more antiquated and authentic Arab shopping aesthetic. It probably goes without saying that the best and most satisfying shopping, unless modern designer labels are your thing, is in the city's old-style souks and *khans*. Each has its own special character and goods, which are well worth a look even if you are not intending to buy, just to watch the craftsmen at work. Tripoli has long been famous for the manufacture of soap and sweets, and the two shops below are well worth searching out, both for the products themselves and the still-traditional processes involved in making them.

✳ **Abdul Rahman Hallab & Sons** [226 D1] Kasr El Helou (Castle of Sweets), Riad al-Solh St; 📞06 444 445; e contact@hallab.com.lb; www. hallab.com.lb; ⏱ 05.00–23.00 daily. Established in 1881, this is Tripoli's best-known & favourite sweet shop selling a huge variety of everything your dentist advised you against, including *baklava*, jams, nougats, the Lebanese favourite *knefeh* & the delicious *nammoura* slice, containing a concoction of semolina, sugar, coconut, butter, syrup, milk & almonds. They also serve coffee.

Bader Hassoun & Sons [226 E2] Khan al-Saboun; 📞06 438 369; m 03 438 369; e info@khanalsaboun. net; www.khanalsaboun.net; ⏱ 09.00–19.00 daily. The Hassoun family has been making soap for generations & a cornucopia

of varieties are on sale at this 16th-century khan, ranging from a variety of aromatic soaps (amber, cinnamon, jasmine, etc) to those purporting to be for medicinal purposes. They come in all shapes & sizes, including a double-page spread of the Koran, former prime minister Rafiq Hariri, & soap in the shape of a cedar tree. Highly recommended.

Earth Market [226 A2] Outside Bou-Khalil Supermarket, Al-Mina; 📞06 411 300; m 03 347 957; e shuruk71@hotmail.com; www. earthmarkets.com, www.fondazioneslowfood. com; ⏱ 08.00–15.00 Thu. This weekly market sees numerous Lebanese vendors selling their local produce, which ranges from fruit juice, honey & olive oil to seasonal fruit & veg.

OTHER PRACTICALITIES In addition to the branch of Blom Bank listed below, there are numerous other unmissable banks with ATMs dotted around the roundabout at Abdel Hamid Karami Square near the tourist office. Similarly, the branch of Libanpost below is supplemented by others in the Al Mina area.

$ **Blom Bank** [226 B2] Abdel Hamid Karami Sq; 📞06 430 153 or 06 628 200/2; e tripolitell@blom. com.lb; www.blombank.com; ⏱ 08.15–17.00 Mon–Fri, 08.15–12.30 Sat. ATM.

$ **Byblos Bank** [226 A2] Jabadou Bldg, Chiraa Sq, Al Bawabe St, Al Mina; 📞06 205 943/4; www. byblosbank.com; ⏱ 08.30–15.30 Mon–Fri, 08.30–noon Sat. ATM.

✉ **Post offices** [226 A2] Bilsan Bldg, Maarad St; 📞06 425 690; www.libanpost.com; ⏱ 08.00–17.00 Mon–Fri, 08.00–13.30 Sat. Libanpost has additional branches in Al-Mina (*Batsh Bldg, Jamarek St;* 📞06 601 181), at El Kobeh Sq (*Safsouf Bldg;* 📞06 388 107) & at Abi

Samra (*Al Siyadi Bldg, Saadoun Sq, behind the old mosque, Al-Bareed St;* 📞06 430 096).

✚ **Chahine Hospital** [226 D1] Rue Muhammad Karame, nr Municipality Bldg; 📞06 430 250, 06 625 796; e hop-chahine@hotmail. com. A small, 28-bed hospital with a range of departments including paediatrics, radiology, surgery & general medicine.

✚ **Pharmacie Nadine** [226 A2] Maarad St; 📞06 440 470; m 03 809 480; e pharm_ abboudeh@hotmail.com; ⏱ 08.00–22.00 Mon–Sat, 10.00–22.00 Sun. Next door to the post office this is a friendly & well-stocked pharmacy selling a wide range of cosmetics, & prescription & non-prescription drugs.

WHAT TO SEE AND DO

Old Tripoli Although Tripoli has a history dating back to antiquity, the surviving architecture and principal historical sites are mainly those spanning the 14th and 15th centuries from the period of Mamluk rule, such as *hammams, khans, madrasas*, mosques and souks (pages 232–4). Revered as fine warriors, this caste of former Ayyubid servants were equally fine designers and builders, and the city possesses some of the finest examples of their handiwork outside their former capital in Cairo, with their trademark style of alternating layers of black and white stone, geometric shapes and highly decorated niches apparent in many of the city's buildings. There are some 45 buildings in the city designated as listed monuments and, although many are numbered, it may take some detective work to locate the often well-hidden plaques. The following sites are just a selection of the main places of interest in the city; just wandering through the alleyways and roads of the town will reveal many more. It is worth bearing in mind that as a traditional Arab city, a more modest mode of attire is very much the order of the day for both males and females so as not to offend local sensibilities, and females should bring a headscarf if intending to enter any of Tripoli's mosques.

Citadel of Raymond de Saint-Gilles

Citadel of Raymond de Saint-Gilles [226 F3] (✆ *06 430 495; Old City;* ⊕ *08.00–sunset daily; admission: adults LBP5,000, students LBP2,000*) Tripoli's largest and most recognisable landmark covers some 10,000m^2 with its rectangular structure measuring some 140m x 70m. Known as Qalaa Sinjil in Arabic, this 12th-century Crusader fortress dates back to the time of the First Crusade and the Count of Toulouse, Raymond de St Gilles, who built the castle after entering the city in 1102. For the next 180 years of Crusader presence in Tripoli, the castle, with its strategic location, on a hill that the Crusaders named Mount Pilgrim, kept watch over the city until the arrival of the Mamluk dynasty, who laid siege to it and demolished the castle in 1289, only for it to be rebuilt two decades later by the Mamluk sultan Essendir al-Kurji. It was then destroyed once again by the Mamluks with the onset of Ottoman rule, and reconstructed under Suleiman the Magnificent, whose stone-carved inscription testifying to his hope for the eternal existence of this 'fortified stronghold' can still be read today over the large Ottoman gate by which you enter the castle. Once through the gate, proceed across the bridge, which is built over a moat constructed by the Crusaders. Inside the vast castle complex you are confronted by an array of arches, courtyards and staircases that represent something of a mish-mash of architectural influences and styles, and are testimony to the castle's history. It is interesting just to wander around and look at the various ramparts. It is the views from the fortress's battlements, however, that make a visit most worthwhile, with stunning panoramas over the Old City and the Abou Ali River.

Hammams

Hammam al-Abed [226 E2] (⊕ *08.00–21.00 daily; bath with 'full works' of steam bath, body scrub & massage around US$20*) Tripoli's sole working *hammam*, for men only, dates from the end of the 17th century and bears all the hallmarks of traditional bathing, with vaulted ceilings and sunlight shafting through the pierced Mamluk and Ottoman domes, accompanied by the sound of running water, contributing to an almost hypnotic Arabian ambience and mood.

Hammam al-Nouri [226 E2] This now-obsolete public baths traces its origins back to 1333, when it was constructed by a former governor of the city, Nu red Din, and is notable for its cluster of perforated domes which allow light to percolate through to the baths below.

Hammam al-Jadid [226 D4] Although 300 years old, this public bath, also known as the 'New Bath' as, comparatively speaking, it is the newest of the city's baths, was a fully functioning *hammam* up until the 1970s. Located northeast of the Taynal Mosque, it was built during the Ottoman era in 1740 by the Damascus governor Asad Pasha al-Azem. It is also Tripoli's largest baths and still manages to evoke its former splendour. The huge stone interior with numerous recessed arches and central fountain is nicely complemented by the beautiful multi-coloured and geometrically decorated marble floor. The lofty-domed ceiling allows shafts of light to pierce through to the fountain below. Another fine feature of this *hammam* can be seen over the entrance, which is adorned with a 14-link chain, from a single slab of hewn stone.

Madrasa
Al-Qartawiyat Madrasa [226 E3] Adjoining the Great Mosque, this Islamic school is an excellent and typical example of Mamluk architecture and a contender for Tripoli's most opulently decorated monument, with its prayer hall the city's sole building with an oval dome. The *madrasa* has an attractively adorned honeycombed pattern ceiling and the hallmark black and white, layered stonework on the building's façade is nicely complemented by its distinctive geometric patterning. Built by the Governor of Tripoli in the early period of the 14th century, after whom the building is named, it is thought that it may occupy the site of a former Frankish church, with some of the stonework at the entrance typical of that period and style.

Al-Tuwashiyat Madrasa [226 E2] Built in 1471, this sandstone-constructed school is part *madrasa*, part mausoleum, with a good example of layered, black-and-white striped stonework (*ablaq*), and the nicely decorated portal with zig-zag motifs is unique in that it is located above the main entrance.

Mosques
Al-Muallaq Mosque [226 D4] This simple and compact mosque, with an attractive garden in the courtyard, dates from the middle part of the 16th century but is more famed for its location, on the second floor of a building. Hence its name, the 'Hanging Mosque'.

Madrasa al-Burtasiya [226 G2] Situated on the bank of the Abu Ali River opposite the Khan al-Khayyatin, this impressive domed mosque dating from the beginning of the 14th century is well worth a visit to appreciate its large square minaret and the exquisite interior with its fine stonework and colourful mosaic-adorned *mihrab*.

Great Mosque [226 E3] Also referred to as Jami al-Kabir, the Great Mosque shows a fusion of Western and Mamluk styles of architecture, and was completed in 1315 after some 20 years under construction. It is built over the burnt remains of the St Mary of the Tower Cathedral, and numerous porticos surround its sizeable courtyard. The interior of the mosque is typically Islamic with its large domed and vaulted prayer hall, but vestiges of the former Frankish shrine can still be discerned at the mosque's northern entrance, together with the mosque's minaret, which was the former cathedral's Lombard bell tower.

Taynal Mosque [226 B4] If you visit only one mosque during your stay in Tripoli, make it this one: a superb and representative example of Mamluk architectural magnificence. Approximately a 5–10-minute walk southwest of the Great Mosque, this multiple green-domed shrine dates back to 1336, and was built by Saif ed-Din Taynal. It occupies the site of a former Carmelite church seen by the nave in the first prayer hall, and whose two granite columns, which support the large, vaulted ceiling, may themselves have been borrowed from an earlier Roman structure. It is the grand portico leading to the second prayer hall which is this mosque's greatest feature, with its use of layered, black-and-white striped stonework (*ablaq*), a decorative honeycomb-like niche, stone-carved geometric patterns and intricate Arabic calligraphy.

Khans and souks
Khan al-Askar [226 F1] This early 14th-century *khan* was originally built as a garrison to house Mamluk soldiers, and thus is known as the 'Soldiers' Khan'. At its northern entrance it consists of two buildings, which are connected to the southern building by a very narrow, vaulted alleyway. Although heavily restored during the 18th century, the original Mamluk architecture can still be discerned such as arches and columns, together with decorative palm leaf motifs.

Khan al-Khayyatin [226 F2] This elongated 'Tailors' Khan' is one of the oldest in the city, dating back to the 14th century, and probably occupies a much earlier Byzantine and Crusader site. It is a great place to watch tailors fashioning all manner of clothing for locals and tourists alike.

Souk al-Haraj [226 G1] With a totally traditional and rustic atmosphere, this is Tripoli's only covered souk, dating back to the 14th century. A series of 14 granite columns support its high, vaulted roof and these are believed to be the remnants of much earlier Roman or Crusader structures. This workaday market specialises in a range of household utilities such as mats, mattresses and pillowcases.

Port (Al-Mina) [226 A2] Whilst the Old City has an abundance of medieval sites, the port area has just one site of any historical note, the **Burj es-Sabaa** or **Lion's Tower**, so-called owing to the carvings of lions which formerly adorned the building's façade. This large, rectangular, mid 15th-century Mamluk defensive tower is the last remaining of a whole series of seven coastal fortifications which were once built to protect Tripoli. With its high, vaulted ceilings and monochromatic *ablaq*, it is typical of Mamluk architectural design. The monument is located about a 1km walk northeast of the coast just past the disused railway tracks.

AZM Cultural Centre (Beit El Fann) [226 A2] (*Mar Elias St, Al-Mina, Corniche;* m *03 387 714;* e *beitelfann@hotmail.com; www.azmculturalcenter.com;* ⊕ *08.00–18.00 daily; admission free*) Beit El Fann means 'House of Art', and this centre for the promotion of culture is housed within a lovely old building, full of character, where they hold workshops, theatrical shows, concerts and exhibitions, as well as working closely with local and overseas arts groups and organisations. One of the screening venues for Tripoli's annual film festival (pages 230–1), its patron is former prime minister Najib Mikati (b1955).

Palm Islands Nature Reserve [map, pages 220–1] (*www.moe.gov.lb/protectedareas/palmislands.htm, www.tripoli-city.org/palm.html*; ⊕ *Jul–Sep; admission free, voluntary donations to the reserve appreciated*) Lebanon's only protected area not on the mainland, this group of three flat islands located about 5.5km off the northwest coast of Tripoli was designated protected area status by UNESCO in 1992 and is recognised

---

LEBANON MOUNTAIN TRAIL (LMT)

Lebanon Mountain Trail Association, 1st Fl, Ghaleb Centre, Sacré Coeur Hospital St, Baabda; ☎ *05 955 302/3;* e *info@lebanontrail.org; www.lebanontrail.org*

This is one of Lebanon's most exciting major developments, pioneering long-distance hiking and walking trails in the country, intended to foster ecotourism and bring economic development and improved prosperity to its rural towns and villages. The idea was conceived back in 2002 by Joseph Karam and Karim El-Jisr, who were also inspired by the success of the Appalachian Trail in the USA which stretches some 2,190 miles (c3,530km) from the state of Georgia in the south to Maine in the north. Although slightly less extensive in Lebanon at 470km, the LMT was finally given the green light to be put into practice in 2005, with the awarding of a two-year development grant of US$3.3 million by USAID (United States Agency for International Development; *www.usaid.gov*) to ECODIT (*www.ecodit.com*), Karam's US company specialising in environmental and social welfare projects and responsible for consultancy and developmental work on the LMT project. The LMT finally opened in 2008, following delays caused by the 2006 July War between Israel and Hezbollah (box, page 32), and this hiking and walking trail now stretches down the spine of the country from Andqet in the far northern Akkar region to the southern town of Marjayoun at the foothills of Mount Hermon (see the essential travel advice on page 301 for hiking the southern sections of the LMT). The signposted 27-section trail, with accommodation options available on each section if required, includes bike-friendly sections, with individual trails varying in length between 10 and 24km, which can be walked in entirety in around a month or individually as day hikes, taking in the great variety of Lebanon's terrain and passing through some 75 towns and villages varying in altitude from over 600m to 2,000m above sea level, two biosphere reserves and a UNESCO World Heritage site (Qadisha Valley; pages 237–44). For aficionados of Lebanese culture and literature, the LMT also incorporates the 24km-long Baskinta Literary Trail (BLT), whose route takes you through 22 landmarks and sites associated with the country's most celebrated writers including Amin Maalouf, Abdallah Ghanem, Georges Ghanem and Mikhail Naimy, whilst other sections of the LMT provide the opportunity to take part in numerous activities such as snowshoeing, mountain biking and camping. Working closely with a variety of government departments, NGOs, schools and local tour guides, the LMT is not a tour operator but it does organise two events annually which are open to all: the Thru Walk in April, a month-long hike of all 27 sections of the trail (the theme in 2016 was food heritage); and a Fall Trek each October in aid of good causes. For further information, the LMT website (*www.lebanontrail.org*) contains a wealth of practical information for hikers and walkers, including detailed descriptions of each trail, advice and contact details on accommodation, child- and family-friendly routes, cultural considerations, local guides and tour operators, bike riding the trail, and what to bring, etc.

as an Important Bird Area by BirdLife International. In 1993, the Lebanese Ministry of the Environment established the area as a National Nature Reserve. The largest of the three islands, covering some 180,796m^2 is **Palm Island** (*Jezira al-Nakhil*), also known as Rabbits Island (*Jezira al-Araneb*), owing to its formerly large population of the floppy-eared creatures, which were introduced to the island during the French Mandate era for breeding and hunting, but which have since been removed for the threat they posed to the local flora. The island also contains the remains of human habitation in the form of a Crusader church and a freshwater well. Southeast of Palm Island is **Sanani Island**, covering an area of 45,503m^2 whilst the smallest of the three is **Ramkine (Fanar or lighthouse) Island**, at just 34,903m^2. Together, they comprise a unique and delicate ecosystem of flora and fauna and are a stop-off point for some 156 species of migratory bird including the Audouin's gull (*Larus audouini*), grey heron (*Ardea cinerea*), white wagtail (*Motacilla alba*) and the ruff (*Philomachus pugnax*). The area is also a preferred site for the green sea turtle (*Chelonia mydas*) and the loggerhead turtle (*Caretta caretta*) – both of which are globally endangered species – and the Mediterranean monk seal (*Monachus monachus*).

Prevalent species of flora on the islands are rock samphire (*Crithmum maritimum*), sea poppy (*Glaucium flavum*), and sea daffodil (*Pancratium maritimum*). The islands have designated hiking trails, and swimming and snorkelling can be undertaken. Normally, the islands are open for visitors only from July until September when no special permit is required. Outside these times, a permit must be obtained for which 72 hours' notice is required; contact the **Palm Islands Nature Reserve Committee Office** (*Al-Mina;* ✆ *06 615 938;* e *r-jaradi@cyberia.net.lb*) with the date of your proposed visit. There is no obligatory entrance fee to visit the islands but voluntary donations are welcome to aid with ongoing environmental work.

Getting there There are a number of boat owners at the Al-Mina port who can convey you to the islands in around half an hour. Fares will need to be negotiated with the port's fishermen, but expect to part with up to US$20 for a group return

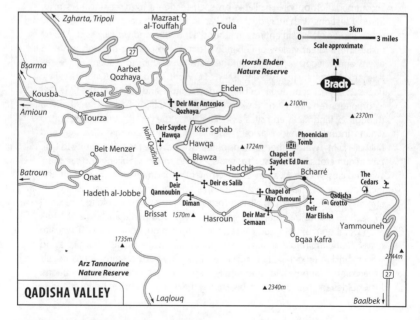

trip, and be prepared to pay US$130+ as an individual to charter a boat. If you prefer to visit as part of an organised day cruise, **Sharewood Camp** (m *04 870 592;* m *03 294 298;* e *info@sharewoodcamp.com; www.sharewoodcamp.com*) offer day trips to the islands, with opportunities for fishing, swimming, snorkelling, hiking and photography. Lunch and a tour of Tripoli's Old City are usually included. Another excellent option to consider for visiting the islands is tourism operator **Adventures in Lebanon** (m *71 443 323;* e *info@adventuresinlebanon. com; www.adventuresinlebanon.com*), who in July 2016 ran a return shuttle bus from Beirut to Tripoli's Al Mina (port) followed by a boat tour and guided visit around the islands, with lunch and soft drinks included for US$65 per person.

QADISHA VALLEY

This elongated steep-sided gorge extending for approximately 50km from Koura east of Batroun in the west to the town of Bcharré and the Cedars in the east possesses arguably the most spectacular scenery in the country. Unlike at many of Lebanon's natural and manmade attractions, the Qadisha Valley offers little in the way of concessions to tourists. Raw, rugged and wild, with often treacherous and steep mountain passes dotted with waterfalls, the valley is a scenic place to visit at any time. In spring, Lebanon's varied and colourful flora like buttercups and poppies carpet the landscape with the melting snow drizzling down the mountain forming an extremely picturesque backdrop. Spring, along with summer, is ideal for hiking and trekking in this largely unspoilt and undulating terrain of outstanding natural beauty.

Translated from the Syriac language, Qadisha means 'Holy', and until a little over a century ago, this was the lingua franca of the valley and remains the language of the Maronite liturgy to this day. When UNESCO incorporated the valley into its World Heritage site listing in 1998, it did so with the comment that Qadisha is 'one of the most important early Christian monastic settlements in the world'. Although not the first inhabitants in the valley, the Maronites sought refuge and spiritual solitude here from the dawning of Christianity as ecclesiastical debates and conflicts raged concerning the very essence of Christ and whether he had a divine or human will, or both. The arrival of the Arabs in the 7th century accentuated the exodus to the safety of the valley, where the natural and inaccessible landscape was fashioned into a plethora of caves and rock-cut monasteries, which provided shelter from persecutors. The head of the valley is dominated by the picturesque town of Bcharré, which, with the Cedars close by, makes a logical and ideal choice for a base from which to explore the valley below.

BCHARRÉ

This small Maronite Christian town of red-roofed buildings around 130km from Beirut commands one of the most spectacular natural locations in the country. Situated 1,500m above sea level, the town sits above the Qadisha Valley and is framed by the snow-capped mountains and Cedars. Apart from its scenic location, Bcharré is also well known as being the birthplace of Lebanon's most revered literary figure, Khalil Gibran (1883–1931; box, pages 250–1), who is also buried here, and there is a museum dedicated to his life and work. This is also the hometown of Lebanese Forces leader Samir Geagea (b1952), who in 1995 stood trial for a series of political assassinations, including that of the rival Christian leader Dany Chamoun (1934–90) and former prime minister Rashid Karami (1921–87). Sentenced to life imprisonment in 1995, Geagea was released in 2005 following the Cedar Revolution and is now a prominent member of the 14 March political coalition. This laid-back and welcoming

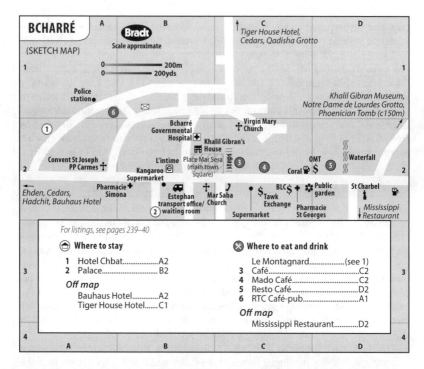

BCHARRÉ

(SKETCH MAP)

Bradt

Scale approximate

0 ——— 200m
0 ——— 200yds

Tiger House Hotel,
Cedars, Qadisha Grotto

Police station ●

⊠

Khalil Gibran Museum,
Notre Dame de Lourdes Grotto,
Phoenician Tomb (c150m)

①

Bcharré
Governmental
Hospital ✚
Khalil Gibran's
House

✝ Virgin Mary
Church

Convent St Joseph
PP Carmes ✝

L'intime
Kangaroo
Supermarket

Place Mar Sera
(main town
square)

③ ④

steps

OMT
Coral ⬛ $

⑤ ≋ Waterfall

Pharmacie ✚
Simona

Ehden, Cedars,
Hadchit, Bauhaus Hotel

②

Estephan
transport office/
waiting room

✝
Mar Saba
Church

$
Tawk
Exchange

BLC $ ✚
Supermarket

Public
garden

Pharmacie
St Georges

St Charbel

Mississippi
Restaurant

For listings, see pages 239–40

🛏 **Where to stay**

1 Hotel Chbat..................A2
2 Palace.............................B2

Off map
 Bauhaus Hotel..............A2
 Tiger House Hotel.......C1

✖ **Where to eat and drink**

 Le Montagnard..................(see 1)
3 Café..................................C2
4 Mado Café.......................C2
5 Resto Café........................D2
6 RTC Café-pub...........................A1

Off map
 Mississippi Restaurant.............D2

little town is located some 50km southeast of Tripoli, and as the principal town of any size in the region with a decent range of amenities and accommodation options catering to most budgets, it is the obvious place to base yourself for a few days if planning an extended tour of the Qadisha Valley and the Cedars, and is a good transit stop if on a day trip to see the Khalil Gibran Museum (pages 240–1).

GETTING THERE
From Beirut

Bcharré is well connected by bus from Beirut's Dora station [173 H2] and served by the two companies listed below, with buses departing from outside their respective offices. Both charge LBP7,000 for the one-way journey, which takes about 2½ hours and brings you to the centre of town, outside the main Mar Saba Church [238 B2]. If you intend travelling to Bcharré by taxi from Beirut, be prepared to be quoted a fare somewhere around US$100–120 and a similar price for the return fare.

🚌 **Cedar Taxi** 🖀 01 265 205 Dora office, 🖀 06 672 166 Bcharré office; m 03 660 965. This company operates daily bus services to Bcharré departing every 2 hours between 08.15 & 18.15. From Bcharré to Beirut, buses also leave every 2 hours from 05.00 daily, with the last bus departing at 17.30. Their office in Beirut is the first turning left after the green-lettered 'Felafel Arax' eatery & clearly signposted.

🚌 **Estephan Transport** [238 B2] m 03 534 701; 🖀 06 671 108 Bcharré office. At the time of writing operating 16 daily departures to Bcharré from 06.30 to 19.30 Mon–Sat & 10 departures from 07.00 to 20.00 on Sun. It's worth noting if you are on a day trip to the town from the capital, that their last bus back to Beirut (as at the time of research) leaves from outside their office in Bcharré at 16.30 Mon–Sat & at 18.00 on Sun. To reach their office in Dora, walk along the road on which the statue of the Virgin Mary is located & the office is in a café just behind the Total petrol station, opposite the signposted street named Rue Maguy El Hajj.

From Tripoli Buses depart from near the Ministry of Tourism office [226 B2] and are operated by the **Bcharré Transport Company** (↘ *06 672 166;* m *70 353 135; LBP5,000–6,000 one-way*), with the journey taking around 1¼ hours. A taxi from Tripoli will set you back around US$50.

Self-drive If you are using a rental vehicle from Beirut, take the coast road north towards Tripoli past Jounieh, Byblos and Batroun and then head inland at Chekka passing through the town of Amioun on the road towards Ehden, the Cedars and Bcharré.

GETTING AROUND Bcharré is tiny and you certainly won't require a taxi to get around as it is easily explored on foot with all the 'what to see and do' options, with the possible exception of Qadisha Grotto, all eminently walkable. The nucleus of the town is the main square or Place Mar Sera [238 B2], overlooked by the red-roofed Mar Saba Church, which is the main transport hub for taxis and vans. The main east–west road is where most of the amenities such as the bank, internet café, pharmacies, cafés and restaurants are situated, with the post office just to the north of this road.

WHERE TO STAY

Hotel Chbat [238 A2] (41 rooms) Khalil Gibran St; ↘ 06 672 672; m 03 292 494; e info@ hotelchbat.net; www.hotelchbat.net. Although the rooms tend to look a little tired & possibly too retro for some people's taste, this is nonetheless a decent & cosy enough option with its on-site restaurant, Le Montagnard (below), serving filling & tasty food. A good-value stay with stunning views over the Qadisha Valley. B/fast inc, free Wi-Fi. **$$$**

Palace Hotel [238 B2] (30 rooms) Main Rd, opposite L'Intime internet cafe; ↘/f 06 671 460 or 06 671 005; m 76 581 560; e jaydeeb6@hotmail. com; www.palacehotelbsharry.com. Very central & unmissable with its brightly painted, geometric patterned blue façade. It seems a bit out of sync with the town's more traditional ambience but offers decent accommodation catering to most budgets in clean, spacious & well-equipped rooms. The older-style section consists of 12 cheaply priced rooms all of which are a decent size with en-suite facilities. The newer & more expensive 18-room section has more sophisticated & modern facilities including AC. The management can also

organise group eco-tourism packages in the area. B/fast inc for all rooms & free Wi-Fi. **$$$**

Bauhaus [238 A2] (12 rooms, suites & chalets) Gibran Khalil Gibran St; ↘ 06 672 220; m 03 329 294; e info@bauhauslb.com; www. bauhauslb.com. Run by the friendly owner Tony, this place is nicely located for the Cedars, Qadisha & the Khalil Gibran Museum. The rooms are spacious & exceptionally clean with shared bathrooms. 2-person chalet US$70, inc Wi-Fi. Dorm room US$10pp per night. **$**

Tiger House Hotel [238 C1] (5 rooms) Rue Cedre, c1km north of Bcharré main square; ↘ 06 672 480; m 03 087 126, 03 378 138; e fereztawk@ gmail.com. An excellent hotel for the backpacker in clean but basic accommodation with a nice communal area complete with central fountain. B/fast is an extra LBP6,000, Wi-Fi LBP4,500/hr & laundry is cLBP10,000/8kg load. A dorm room costs US$10pp per night. This friendly hotel can also arrange walking tours of the Qadisha Valley & has good free maps of the area. Highly recommended for a few days if touring the valley & environs. **$**

WHERE TO EAT AND DRINK

Mississippi Restaurant [238 D2] Southern end of Bcharré; m 71 309 065; ⊕ 10.00–02.00 daily. This long-standing Lebanese restaurant providing excellent service serves equally excellent fish, meat & *mezze*, in a fabulous location affording superlative views over the Qadisha Valley. One of those

rare venues where the atmosphere, cuisine & location are in perfect harmony. **$$$$**

Le Montagnard [238 A2] Inside Hotel Chbat, Main Rd; ↘ 06 672 222; m 03 571 154; ⊕ 11.00– late daily. Friendly eatery serving a wide range of standard fare from burgers to pizzas, salads, pasta & steak with a pleasant terrace area affording

North Lebanon BCHARRÉ

6

terrific views over the valley & town. Serves alcohol, & *nargileh* is LBP7,000. $$$

✗ **Café** [238 C2] Midway up the steps opposite Mar Saba church; ☎06 671 549; m 03 213 070; ☼ 06.00–14.00 daily. Small café in the heart of the town with outside seating only. A decent stop-off for coffee, *manoushe*, *shawarma* or *nargileh*. $$

✗ **Mado Café** [238 C2] Main Rd, opposite Tawk Exchange; ☎06 671 246 m 03 256 734; ☼ 08.00–22.00 daily. Decent restaurant & café serving *shish tawaouk*, *labneh*, salads, chicken & sausages. An Almaza beer will set you back LBP3,500, & *nargileh* LBP5,000. $$

✗ **Resto Café** [238 D2] Main Rd, next to the waterfall; ☎06 671 131; m 03 158 641; ☼ summer 10.00–02.00 daily, winter 11.00–

19.00 daily. Friendly, pleasant & spacious eatery serving up a good, tasty selection of *mezze* & platters together with wines from the Kefraya & Musar vineyards. An Almaza beer costs LBP4,000 & *nargileh* LBP8,000. $$

✗ **RTC Café-pub** [238 A1] Main Rd; m 03 432 226; ☼ noon–midnight daily. A cool, relaxing & stylish venue for a beer, spirits & *nargileh* (*LBP8,000–12,000*), serving a varied menu of salads, pizzas, burgers, sandwiches & desserts at good prices. There is a terrace for the summer months with lovely views over the Qadisha Valley which is very popular with the locals, & regular disco nights are held during the high-season months of Jun–Aug. They also run a shop across the road which sells cakes & sweets. $$

OTHER PRACTICALITIES

$ **BLC Bank** [238 C2] Elie Geagea Bldg, Main Rd; ☎06 671 101, 06 672 767; e becharrebranch@ blcbank.com; www.blcbank.com; ☼ 08.00–13.30 Mon–Fri, 08.15–13.00 Sat. 24hr ATM.

$ **OMT (Online Money Transfer)** [238 D2] Main Rd, next to the Coral Petrol Station; ☎06 671 032; ☼ 10.00–18.00 Mon–Sat

$ **Tawk Exchange** [238 C2] Main Rd; ☎06 671 305; ☼ summer 09.00–15.00, winter 09.00–13.30 Mon–Sat

✉ **Post office** [238 B1] Just north of the Main Rd; ☎06 671 025; www.libanpost.com; ☼ 08.00–17.00 Mon–Fri, 08.00–13.30 Sat

✚ **Bcharré Governmental Hospital** [238 B2] Just north of the Main Rd; ☎06 671 357/8, 06 678 488; m 03 540 585; e bghosp@gmail.com; ☼ 24hrs daily. This small, modern & well-equipped hospital has a range of departments

including gynaecology, paediatrics, obstetrics, urology & 24hr emergency admissions.

✚ **Pharmacie St Georges** [238 C2] Main Rd; ☎06 671 800; m 03 631 080; ☼ 08.30–22.00 daily. Stocks a good range of medicines, cosmetics & baby provisions.

✚ **Pharmacie Simona** [238 B2] Main Rd; ☎06 672 727; m 03 291 492; ☼ 08.00–20.00 Mon–Sat, 08.00–18.00 Sun. Small but well-stocked pharmacy.

Kangaroo Supermarket [238 B2] Main Rd; ☎06 672 160; m 76 394 477; ☼ 08.00–midnight daily. A number of mini-markets dot the main street, but this one is the most extensive, stocking most grocery, toiletry & other utility items to meet most day-to-day needs.

L'Intime Internet Café [238 B2] Main Rd; ☎06 671 327; m 70 167 974; e g_rahme67@ hotmail.com; ☼ 10.00–01.00 daily. This internet café has 15 computers with access charged at LBP2,000/hr.

WHAT TO SEE AND DO

Khalil Gibran's House [238 B2] (☼ *winter 09.00–17.00 daily, summer 10.00–18.00 daily; admission free*) Located just across the road from the main square (signposted 'Maison Gibran') the renovated exterior of Khalil Gibran's birthplace and home is worth a quick look and there is a bust of Lebanon's famed literary icon in the gardens.

Khalil Gibran Museum [238 D1] (*Main Rd;* ☎ *06 671 137;* m *03 314 695;* e *gibranmuseum1975@hotmail.com; www.gibrankhalilgibran.org;* ☼ *May–Oct 10.00–18.00 Tue–Sun, Nov–Apr 10.00–17.00 Tue–Sun; admission: adults LBP8,000, students LBP5,000, children under 10 free; audio guide LBP3,000*) Built into the rock-face, the site housing the Khalil Gibran Museum dates back to the 7th century, when it began life as a hermitage for the monks of the Mar Sarkis (Saint Sergio) order seeking a safe haven from persecution. In the 17th century, it was bequeathed to the local Carmelite monks, who finished construction of a new monastery and the building you see today, in 1862. Whilst living in New York, it was on Gibran's wish list to purchase the monastery so he could live out his final days there, and finally be buried there. Though he died before he could fulfil the first part of his dream, his one surviving sister, Mariana, and benefactor Mary Elizabeth Haskell eventually purchased the site in 1932, and Gibran is laid to rest in a casket in the basement along with a number of his personal possessions, which were shipped over from New York such as his bed, his paintings and easel, cases, notebooks, table and a crucifix. Finally opening as a museum in 1975, the site comprises some 16 rooms plus Gibran's below-stairs resting place spread over three floors, and in many respects resembles more an art gallery and house. The museum is home to 440 of Gibran's artworks, of which 130 are on public display. His drawings and paintings exhibit an extraordinary corpus of work affording an insightful look at Gibran's aesthetic and tormented psychology, including the relationship between man and nature, nudes and death. His portraiture in particular makes for compelling viewing and includes paintings of some of the most iconic individuals of his age, including Swiss psychiatrist and psychoanalyst Carl Jung (1875–1961), Irish poet and playwright W B Yeats (1865–1939), French composer Claude Debussy (1862–1918) and French sculptor Auguste Rodin (1840–1917).

Notre Dame de Lourdes Grotto [238 D1] (⊕ *24hrs daily; admission free*) A stairway signposted to 'Grotte Notre Dame Lourdes' leads the way up to this quaint little cave and spring, located behind the Khalil Gibran Museum. According to local folklore, the Virgin Mary took pity on a Carmelite monk who trekked each day with heavy loads of water up the mountainside to irrigate his vegetable patch; thus she created the spring to relieve him of this daily toil. The cave, with its serene sound of running water and altar dotted with religious icons, including the Virgin herself, and lit by candles, is definitely worth the short walk up the steps from the museum.

Phoenician Tomb [238 D1] (⊕ *24hrs daily; admission free*) Although it's a bit of a scramble to reach the Phoenician Tomb, further on up the same path from the Notre Dame de Lourdes Grotto, it's worth the little extra effort for the wonderful views over Bcharré and the surrounding Qadisha Valley. Thought to date back to around 750BCE, the tomb itself is the principal evidential remains that Bcharré was once a Phoenician settlement of some importance. This large conical obelisk has an opening at its base where you can wander inside and see the recesses and partitions, which were cut into the rock to hold four coffins.

Qadisha Grotto [map, page 236] (*Off the top of the Old Rd between Bcharré & Cedars;* ✆ *06 671 088;* m *03 568 251;* ⊕ *May–Sep 10.00–19.00 daily, Oct–Nov 10.00–17.00 daily; admission LBP5,000*) A sign points the way to the grotto from near the Tiger House Hotel [238 C1]. Follow the road to the Cedars as far as the L'Aiglon Hotel, where there is a small parking area, and from here it is an extremely picturesque level 10–15-minute walk (c1.5km) along a designated footpath to the cave. Arguably, the stroll along the mountain path with its superlative views over the Qadisha Valley is more engaging than the grotto itself. Nowhere near as spectacular as Jeita Grotto or as nicely lit as Kfarhim Grotto in the Chouf, this small cave of stalactites and stalagmites is nonetheless still worth a visit if you are travelling around the region. Like the aforementioned grottos, Qadisha has been fashioned over millions of years, but was only a relatively recent discovery, in 1903. It was to be another two decades before serious excavation of the cave started, and work is still ongoing. Although some 778m of the grotto have been explored, only a portion is accessible to visitors at present. A positive for visitors, however, is that, unlike at Jeita, photography was permitted inside the cave during the author's last visit. A further plus point is that the views from outside the grotto over the valley are superb. A cafeteria near the grotto entrance serves coffee and standard fare and is a nice place to sit down and admire the vista of the valley below.

QADISHA VALLEY FLOOR: CHAPELS, CAVES AND MONASTERIES

To explore the most interesting and scenic 20km section of the Qadisha Valley from Tourza in the west to the source of the Qadisha River in the east at the Qadisha Grotto, you can walk down into the valley from roads that lead out of Bcharré. You should allocate a whole day to exploring the sites mentioned below independently, but if you would like a more guided and organised tour of the valley and its history, the following ecotourism organisations should be able to help.

Footprints Nature Club m 03 876 112; e info@ footprintsclub.com, hiking@footprintsclub.com; www.footprintsclub.com
Lebanese Adventure m 03 081 620, 03 214 989; infos@lebanese-adventure.com; www. lebanese-adventure.com
Lebanon Mountain Trail (LMT) \05 955 302/3; e info@lebanontrail.org; www.lebanontrail.org. Part of the LMT goes through the valley & there is

an extensive list of local guides & eco tour operators on their website if you prefer an escorted visit. For more details on the LMT, see box, page 235.
Liban Trek \01 329 975; m 03 291 616; e info@libantrek.com; www.libantrek.com
Sharewood Camp \04 870 592; m 03 294 298; e info@sharewoodcamp.com; www. sharewoodcamp.com

WHAT TO SEE
Deir Mar Elisha This important monastery is where the Maronite Order of Lebanese Monks was founded in 1695, but is first mentioned back in the 14th century as the home of a Maronite bishop. As is apparent from its façade, the Deir Mar Elisha underwent renovation in recent years and since 1991 is now part museum, with a number of exhibits explaining the history of the building. In one of its four chapels is the tomb of a French hermit, Father François de Chasteuil, who died in 1644. One of the most picturesque and spectacularly situated of the valley's many religious shrines, the monastery is cut into the rock face and appears almost part of the surrounding geology. Located south of Bcharré, the monastery is accessed via a steep road.

Deir Mar Semaan Located in the southern section of the valley, this rock-cut hermitage, supposedly the former residence of Saint Simon (Mar Semaan), is reached by a 15-minute walk down a steep path just past the turning for the village of Bqaa Kafra. This hermitage dates from 1112 and was reputedly founded by Takla, the daughter of Basil, a priest from Bcharré. Although the hermitage contains a number of rooms built into the cliffs, the main points of interest are the remnants of some frescoes, cisterns for collecting and storing water, and terrific views over the valley.

Chapel of Mar Chmouni Occupying a position beneath a rocky ledge, this three-nave chapel – two manmade and one part of the local geology – dates from the Middle Ages. Until the late 1990s, the entire chapel walls were finely decorated with 13th-century Byzantine-style paintings. Regrettably, 20th-century artisanal endeavours have not been as creative, and the paintings are now obscured behind a layer of plaster.

Deir es Salib Though now abandoned and in a very poor state of repair, Deir es Salib, or Monastery of the Cross, still has traces of frescoes dating to the Byzantine era and a number of ecclesiastical scenes. In addition there is a chapel and a few caves formerly used as hermits' cells. The monastery can be reached by taking a 30-minute walk down a steep path to the valley from the village of Hadchit.

Deir Qannoubin Partially cut into the rock face with lovely views over the valley in a serene and spectacular setting, Deir Qannoubin takes its name from the Greek word *kenobion* meaning 'monastery', and is reputedly the oldest Maronite monastery in the valley, dating back to the Byzantine period. Although a working convent nowadays, this was formerly the seat of the Maronite patriarchs between the 15th and 19th centuries, and there are frescoes dating from this time together with the remains of 17 Maronites buried in a nearby chapel to the west of the monastery. Also close by is the chapel-cum-cave dedicated to St Marina. According to local legend, St Marina entered the monastery disguised as a monk and, following unfounded allegations of being the father of a child, decided to rear the baby herself using her own milk. Close to the monastery's entrance are the mummified remains reputedly of the 18th-century patriarch Yousef Tynan. Deir Qannoubin is about another hour's walk further along the valley floor from Deir es Salib.

Deir Saydet Hawqa This compact cliff-side monastery, known as Our Lady of Hawqa, has a delightful little chapel and a number of monks' cells which date from around the end of the 13th century. It is mainly known for an attack by Mamluk forces and the betrayal by one of the local populace who suggested pouring water from a cistern, a cave and natural fortress called Aassi Hawqa above the monastery, to drown out the inhabitants. The fortress above the monastery is not easy to get to, and this is one place where you really need to be an experienced rock climber. Mainly secluded and unoccupied, the monastery comes to life each year on 14 August, when it hosts the Feast of the Assumption of the Virgin, which culminates in a high mass during the evening. To reach here, continue along the valley past Deir Qannoubin. If you have a car, you can drive from Blawza to Hawqa, which is then a 30-minute walk down a steep path.

Deir Mar Antonios Qozhaya (✆ 06 995 504/5; e *qozhaya@qozhaya.com; www.qozhaya.com*) A fully functioning monastery since the mid 12th century, this is one of the largest in the valley, and its setting, partially cut into the rock face, with lovely views, has one of the most attractive façades of all the monasteries in the area. Since 1995, it has also housed a museum exhibiting ecclesiastical and ethnographic artefacts. Perhaps the most important object on display is the Arab world's first printing press, which dates from the 16th century, and which was used to print the Book of Psalms in the Syriac language which remains in use by the Maronites today during their religious rituals. Close to the monastery's entrance is the 'Cave of the Mad', as locals refer to St Anthony's Grotto, where you can still see the chains that were used to restrain those deemed to be mentally ill or possessed by demons. If the chains eventually opened by themselves, it was believed that those they had been restraining had been visited and cured by St Anthony. If you are travelling on foot, continue along the valley floor. If driving, the monastery can be reached from Aarbet Qozhaiya, though you may need to ask locals for directions, as it is not clearly marked.

Chapel of Saydet Ed Darr A path down into this compact rock-cut sanctuary reaches the Our Lady of Abundant Milk, between Bcharré and Hadchit. Breastfeeding

6

women, who would come here to give thanks, revered it. The walls of the chapel contain some 14th-century paintings, including a portrayal of the Baptism of Christ.

Diman Since the 19th century, this modern church at Diman has been the Maronite patriarch's summer residence. Located in the southern part of the gorge with lovely views over the valley from the rear of the church, it houses a nice collection of religious paintings from the 1930s and 1940s by the late Lebanese artist Saliba Doueihy (1915–94).

Arz Tannourine Nature Reserve (*Main entrance: Tannourine al-Fawka;* ✆ *06 500 550;* m *03 815 029, 03 277 618;* e *info@arztannourine.org; www.arztannourine. org;* ⊕ *Apr–Nov 08.00–18.00 daily; admission LBP5,000, LBP3,000pp for groups, optional guide LBP10,000*) A few kilometres south of Qadisha, and around 85km from Beirut, Tannourine is one of Lebanon's less-visited nature reserves owing to its more rocky and undulating terrain, making it more demanding for hikers and walkers than many of the other protected areas. Yet it is well worth a visit: with some 80% of the trees in the forest being cedars, it also contains the densest and largest cedar forest in Lebanon spread over some 600ha. Though one of Lebanon's smaller reserves, protected by law since 25 February 1999 and varying in height between 1,350m and 1,850m, this 12km^2 reserve also has a rich biodiversity, containing more than 20 varieties of mushroom (of the edible and non-edible variety), the prickly juniper tree (*Juniperus oxycedrus*), the Lebanon prickly thrift (*Acantholiman libanoticum*), and the mountain tulip (*Tulipa montana*). In addition, the reserve is home to more than 16 species of mammal including hedgehogs, hyenas, cape hare, badgers, foxes, porcupine, wildcat, wild boar and wolves. Both spring and summer are good times to visit, with the forest's flora in full bloom; whilst autumn sees a variety of bird species stopping off here on their annual migratory routes and the reserve has been designated an Important Bird Area (IBA). The reserve has a number of designated hiking trails of 2–4.5km in length, ranging from easy to difficult, and trail maps and further information can be obtained from the reserve's information office at the entrance.

Tour operators There are a number of ecotourism-based organisations who operate daily and periodic guided tours to the reserve (and other areas of Lebanon) if you prefer a more organised visit, with the following just a few of the possibilities worth contacting for further details.

Cyclamen ✆ 04 419 848; m 03 486 551; e contact@tlb-destinations.com; www.tlb-destinations.com
Footprints Nature Club m 03 876 112; e info@footprintsclub.com, hiking@footprintsclub.com; www.footprintsclub.com
Lebanon Mountain Trail (LMT) ✆ 05 955 302/3; e info@lebanontrail.org; www.lebanontrail.org.

Although the LMT do not provide tours, they can help organise trips & the LMT website contains a list of recommended local guides with their contact details, together with advice on the approximate fees you should pay (box, page 235).
Vamos Todos ✆ 09 635 145; m 79 115 001; e info@vamos-todos.com, mark.aoun@gmail.com; www.vamos-todos.com

EHDEN

Like many of Lebanon's mountainous regions, Ehden is principally a resort town, often referred to as Lebanon's 'Summer Bride'. This attractive, friendly and pleasant little Christian Maronite town is popular with residents from nearby

Zgharta, many of whom have holiday homes in Ehden to take advantage of the town's more temperate summer climate. Between June and October the town is buzzing with couples and families enjoying the pleasant atmosphere of its main square and its gastronomy. Famed especially for its meat, and in particular its variety of *kibbeh*, the popular and traditional Lebanese dish of raw or minced meat with cracked wheat, Ehden made it into the *Guinness World Records* book in 2009 for making the biggest-ever *kibbeh*, which weighed in at a very filling 233kg (514lb). Outside the summer season, however, the town is extremely quiet, with many cafés and restaurants closed for the winter, and there is little reason to visit unless you are exploring the nearby Horsh Ehden Nature Reserve (page 247).

GETTING THERE At an altitude of 2,000m above sea level, Ehden sits on the northern edge of the Qadisha Valley and is around 110km from Beirut and 40km southeast of Tripoli.

By car If on a self-drive arrangement **from Beirut**, take the coast road north and turn inland at Chekka. Then follow the road that goes through Amioun, Kousba and Tourza towards Ehden. If driving **from Tripoli**, take the road southeast towards Zgharta and continue on this road for around 26km, until you reach the town. The Horsh Ehden Nature Reserve is then a further 4km (10 minutes' drive) or so north from here. This is a particularly scenic route.

By taxi Service taxis from Tripoli pass through Ehden *en route* to Bcharré and should cost between LBP10,000 and LBP15,000. Expect to pay around LBP25,000–30,000 for a taxi from Bcharré to Ehden.

GETTING AROUND Ehden's chief area of interest is its central square, or Al-Midan, and is easily walkable, with all the main eateries, watering holes and the town's handful of sites all close by.

WHERE TO STAY

Ehden Country Club (85 rooms & suites) 06 560 651/2/3; m 03 252 700/701; e info@ehdencountryclubhotel.com; www. ehdencountryclubhotel.com. In many ways a typical resort complex with modern, spacious but minimalist rooms. The restaurant ($$$$$) serves international & Lebanese food. A well-equipped gym, large outdoor pool & lively piano bar make this ideal for couples & families, but there is little in the way of character. $$$$$

Hotel Ehden (36 rooms & suites) 06 560 100; m 03 560 100; e info@hotelehden. com; www.hotelehden.com. A nice, comfortable hotel with modern décor & spacious rooms with mountain views, TV, AC & free Wi-Fi. The restaurant serves a good range of international dishes & there is a small pool & gym. B/fast inc. $$$$$

Master's Hotel (40 rooms) Nabaa Jouit Rd; 06 561 052/3/4; m 70 727 711; e info@ mastershotel-ehden.com; www.mastershotel-

ehden.com. Very scenically located surrounded by wonderful mountain views, the rooms are warm & cosy & the good hotel restaurant ($$$$) dishes up a wide-ranging menu. With childcare services, a spa, tennis court & outdoor pool for the summer months, this hotel is a good choice for families. They can also help organise sightseeing trips around Ehden. B/fast inc, free Wi-Fi. Usually closed during the winter months of Jan–Mar. $$$$$

Hotel Abchi (43 rooms & suites, 21 apartments) 06 560 001, 06 561 101/2; e info@abchi-hotel.com; www.abchi-hotel.com; ⊕ Jun–Oct. Within walking distance of Ehden's main square, this hotel has well-decorated & comfortable rooms with all the usual modern accoutrements. There is a large outdoor pool, & a decent restaurant ($$$) serving Lebanese & international cuisine, with nightly entertainment including belly dancing. $$$$

✘ WHERE TO EAT AND DRINK The beating heart of Ehden is the pleasant Al-Midan, or central square, shaded by trees and thronged with cafés and restaurants. In summer the town gets very busy, with couples and families enjoying the indoor and outdoor ambience of the town's setting. Attractive, Ottoman-period café **Platanus** (*Al-Midan;* ✆ *06 560 678;* m *70 117 058;* ⊕ *08.00–03.00 daily;* $$$$) has a great local atmosphere and good service and serves up standard pub fare of pasta, pizza and sandwiches,.

ACTIVITIES Ehden Adventures (✆ *76 556 887;* e *info@ehdenadventures.com; www.ehdenadventures.com*) is a specialist outdoor activity organisation striving to make Ehden a year-round destination for families & individuals interested in the great outdoors & the natural world. An excellent range of activities is on offer including camping, caving, hiking, paragliding & rock climbing in and around Ehden. This company also organises day visits to many other areas such as Baalbek, the Chouf & Harissa.

OTHER PRACTICALITIES As primarily a summer bolthole for residents from nearby Zgharta, gastronomy and nightlife easily take precedence over such practical matters as banking, post offices and pharmaceuticals in Ehden. The following are the best options located just over 20km away in Zgharta.

$ **Credit Libanais** Kareh & Mouawad Bldg, Main Rd, Zgharta; ✆06 668 600/1/2/3; www. creditlibanais.com.lb; ⊕ 08.00–14.00 Mon–Fri, 08.00–13.00 Sat. ATM.

✉ **Post office** Zgharta; ✆06 660 001; www. libanpost.com; ⊕ 08.00–17.00 Mon–Fri, 08.00–13.30 Sat

✚ **Ehden Governmental Hospital** ✆06 561 701/2

✚ **Care Centre Pharmacy** Zgharta; ✆06 550 655; m 03 101 063; ⊕ 08.30–22.00 Mon–Fri, 08.30–21.00 Sat, closed Sun

WHAT TO SEE AND DO Although Ehden functions predominantly as a summer resort town, it has a few engaging centrally located sites, in addition to the slightly further afield ecotourism attraction of Horsh Ehden Nature Reserve, all of which are worth a look. To the west of the main square stands the CE749 Mar Mama, or Saint Mamas Chapel, which is reputedly the oldest Christian Maronite church in Lebanon. The town's main St George's Church is also nearby, which houses the glass-topped sarcophagus of the local nationalist hero Youssef Bey Karam (1823–89), who led several military campaigns against the Ottomans but was finally killed by the Turks. His mummified body is dressed resplendently in his ceremonial finery of gold-embroidered costume, and there is also a statue of 'Lebanon's hero', as the locals refer to Karam, on horseback next to the church. For a marvellous view of the surrounding valley and countryside, you can take a trip up to the 9th-century Our Lady of the Fort, or Saydet al-Hosn as she is known locally, which is perched atop a hill sitting atop a geometric structure in the shape of a star.

Ehdeniyat International Festival (*1st Fl, Kabalan Ghaleb Centre, Al Abeh, Zgharta;* ✆ *06 664 466;* m *76 908 020;* e *info@ehdeniyat.org; www.ehdeniyat.com; tickets can be purchased online from www.ticketingboxoffice.com*) Held annually throughout the month of August since 2004 this summer festival has a wide range of activities for children and an impressive programme of live music concerts and performances which has seen artists such as Demis Roussos, Julio Iglesias, Gloria Gaynor and the Royal Moscow Ballet perform here.

Horsh Ehden Nature Reserve (*Ehden;* ✆ *06 660 120, 06 663 120;* 📱 *70 601 601;* ℮ *info@horshehden.org; www.horshehden.org; information centre* ⏲ *08.00–18.00 daily; admission free, but voluntary donations are appreciated*) This comparatively tiny nature reserve, varying in altitude between 1,200m and 2,000m, covers just 17km^2, but contains one of the most concentrated varieties of flora and fauna of any of Lebanon's natural reserves. Representing less than 1% of the country's total landmass, the reserve is home to 1,058 types of flora which account for 40% of the country's total species and contains some 20% of Lebanon's stands of cedar trees, the largest in the country. Of the varieties of fauna, 156 varieties of bird have been recorded in the reserve, including the globally endangered corncrake (*Crex crex*), greater spotted eagle (*Aquila clanga*), imperial eagle (*Aquila heliaca*), and lesser kestrel (*Falco naumanni*). In addition, there are 26 mammal species including badgers, deer, hyena, squirrels, wildcats and wolves, and 23 species of reptile such as the Lebanon viper (*Montivipera bornmuellen*), Palestinian viper (*Vipera palaestinae*), and the delightfully tongue-twistingly named Schreiber's fringe-fingered lizard (*Acanthodactylus schreiberi*). The reserve is best visited in spring and autumn when the variety of flowers are in full bloom and the trees are at their most vibrant. A stunning location for walking, the reserve has a number of short designated hiking trails that vary in length from just under 1km to just over 2km, with varying degrees of difficulty.

THE CEDARS (ARZ AL-RAB)

(✆ *06 672 562;* ⏲ *1 May–30 Nov 09.00–18.00 daily; admission free, but voluntary contributions between LBP5,000 & LBP10,000 appreciated to aid ongoing preservation work*) Located around 5km above Bcharré on the slopes of Jebel Makmel between 1,900m and 2,050m above sea level, the Cedars is home to Lebanon's oldest stands of cedar tree, with only some 375 trees remaining of a copse that once carpeted the Lebanese mountains. But they are held in the most esteem for their grandiose proportions, attaining heights up to 40m and with a few dating back 1,500–2,000 years. With their huge girth of up to 14m, the trees are a scenic sight at any time of year, but particularly beautiful in winter when draped with snow against a mountain backdrop – arguably the best time to see them. Known locally as Arz al-Rab or 'Cedars of the Lord', numerous civilisations over the millennia have left their mark on the Cedars, from the ancient Phoenicians, who felled the trees to build their trading vessels, to, more latterly, the British army in World War II who cut down the trees to build a railway line from Tripoli to Haifa.

Others decided to leave their mark in different ways including the 19th-century English poet Lord Byron (1788–1824), who saw fit to carve his initials onto one specimen, an example followed by the French aristocrat and poet Lamartine, whose tree has since been resculptured by the Bcharré-born artist Rudy Rahme (b1967; *www.rudyrahme.com*). Britain's Queen Victoria (1819–1901), however, was certainly not amused when she learnt that the cedar grove was under threat from goats with a taste for the young saplings, and, perhaps following the conservationist example of the emperor Hadrian in the 2nd century, personally financed the construction of a wall around the copse to protect the trees. Today it is the Maronite patriarchs who are the guardians and protectors of the cedar forest, and in 1843 they built a small chapel in the centre of the grove which is the location for a blessing and service to honour the trees in the first week of August each year.

GETTING THERE The Cedars are located about 5km from Bcharré. A taxi from outside the town's main St Saba church and square to the Cedars should not cost more than LBP20,000, with a service taxi costing somewhere around LBP8,000 and with a journey time of 20 minutes or so. If driving from Beirut, take the coastal road north towards Tripoli and at Chekka, a few kilometres south of Tripoli, turn inland and follow the road towards Amioun, continuing towards Kousba, Tourza, Hadath el Joubbe, Hasroun, Bazoun and Bcharré, with the Cedars just a few kilometres beyond Bcharré and clearly signposted.

GETTING AROUND The Cedars are easily manageable by foot but, if you prefer to visit by taxi, it would be best to arrange this and negotiate a price in Bcharré as there is a distinct lack of public transport options in the Cedars.

WHERE TO STAY The accommodation options in the Cedars are very much geared towards the visiting skier and all offer a decent level of comfort and facilities. If coming here in the much quieter months outside the ski season, however, it could be worth enquiring about discounted room rates, as significant savings could be available. The hotels below all serve food.

Le Cedrus Boutique Hotel (40 rooms & suites) Cedars; 06 678 777; m 70 413 777; e info@cedrushotel.com; www.cedrushotel.com. A salubrious & cosy option, located very close to the ski slopes, with warm décor & an excellent French Le Pichet Restaurant & piano bar ($$$$). Free Wi-Fi. $$$$$

L'Auberge des Cèdres (18 chalets, suites & luxury tents) Cedars; 06 678 888; m 03 566 953; e res@smresorts.net; www.smresorts.net. The Cedars' most luxurious option, with a great range of accommodation options & with all the bells & whistles you would expect for the price, including roaring fire & good restaurant menu. The hotel can also organise a range of winter & summer outdoor activities, including paragliding. $$$$

La Cabane Hotel (12 rooms) Cedars, above Bcharré; 06 678 067; m 70 103 222; www.lacabanecedars.com. In a superb location a minute's walk from the ski resort, with some of the best views over the Qadisha Valley. Rooms in this lodge are simple but spotlessly clean. Very friendly & helpful owner. B/fast LBP8,000 extra. $$$

Hotel St Bernard (23 rooms & suites) Above the Cedars; 06 678 100/101; m 03 289 600, 79 189 600; www.hstbernard.com. Very homely rooms & atmosphere combined with outstanding views over the Cedars from its terrace. The hotel's Cedria Restaurant ($$) serves a Lebanese & international menu. $$

Mon Refuge Hotel (16 rooms) Main Rd, Cedars; 06 671 397, 06 678 050. A clean & comfortable hotel with simpler rooms than the other options, & with a nice friendly atmosphere. Free Wi-Fi. $$

WHERE TO EAT AND DRINK In addition to the venues below, the hotels reviewed above all have good restaurants where non-guests are welcome to dine.

La Casa Night Club Main Rd; m 03 555 829, 70 555 829; ⊕ Oct–Jun 21.00–late Sat, Jul–Sep 21.00–late Fri & Sat. A great fun & friendly venue serving a wide range of alcoholic & non-alcoholic drinks in a party atmosphere, which includes karaoke & a DJ spinning discs from electro to R&B. $$

Tombe La Neige Main Rd; 06 678 800; m 70 953 577; ⊕ 07.00–midnight daily. Very much a home-from-home eatery & pub, with fireplace & welcoming atmosphere, serving a varied menu including fondue, steak & salad. $$

OTHER PRACTICALITIES For day-to-day practicalities such as banking, post office and pharmacies, etc, nearby Bcharré is your best option given the dearth of these facilities in the area (page 240).

ACTIVITIES

Skiing *(Cedars; above Bcharré;* m *03 399 133;* ☉ *08.00–15.30 Mon–Fri, 08.00–16.00 Sat & Sun; adult ski-lift pass prices: US$30/day Mon–Fri, US$40 Sat & Sun, half-day pass after noon US$30 Mon–Fri, US$30 Sat & Sun)* About 3km further up the road from the trees, the Cedars ski resort, around 130km from Beirut, is also the location for Lebanon's oldest ski resort, where skiers have been negotiating its slopes since the 1920s, well before its first ski lift was installed back in 1953. At well over 2,000m altitude, the Cedars is also Lebanon's highest ski resort with the resulting higher altitude giving a longer ski season than the others in the country – it can run from as early as November or early December right through towards the end of April. The resort is probably the most picturesque of Lebanon's ski locations, with superlative views over the cedar forest and Qadisha Valley. Of the resort's eight ski lifts, five are for beginners, making this an ideal choice for the novice. Although its *après-ski* facilities can't compete with those at Mzaar, there has recently been ongoing investment in the resort to the tune of US$15 million, including new chair lifts, a six-person gondola to take skiers from base level to the highest accessible point of 2,870m, and a new road to reduce journey times from Bcharré to the slopes.

Hiking and climbing (Qornet es Saouda) Around 6km northeast of the Cedars, the northern portion of the Mount Lebanon range is dominated by Qornet es Saouda (the Black Horn or Nook), Lebanon's highest mountain peak at 3,083m on Mount Mekmel, towering over the surrounding landscape. From its summit it affords unrivalled views over the coast, eastwards to the Bekaa Valley, the Anti-Lebanon Mountain range and neighbouring Syria. A good time to climb this mountain is generally between April and late October, and it can take up to around 5 or 6 hours to reach the summit, depending upon your level of fitness. It would be a good idea to allocate a whole day to making the ascent, wear warm clothing to help offset the effect of the year-round strong winds and to take plenty of water. You can start the climb from a location within the Cedars ski resort or arrange a guided hike with one of the many organisations such as **Skileb** (m *70 103 222 or 70 211 503;* e *info@ skileb.com; www.skileb.com)*, whose guided hike includes accommodation in the Cedars and lunch *(US$143pp at the time of writing)*, and **Lebanese Adventure** (✎ *03 081 620 or 03 214 989;* e *infos@lebanese-adventure.com; www.lebanese-adventure. com)*, who also run day hikes from Beirut and come highly recommended.

Paragliding Paragliding has been gaining in popularity over the last few years, and it is now possible to chase the thermals high up over the Cedars. If gaining an aerial view of the surrounding landscape appeals, paragliding flights over the Cedars are offered by a couple of excellent and reputable organisations. During the summer months, **Skileb** (m *70 103 222, 70 211 503;* e *info@skileb. com; www.skileb.com)* offers flights daily, taking off between 13.00 and 18.00. At the time of writing an approximately 20-minute flight cost US$125 per person with an instructor. The **Cedars Paragliding School** (m *03 544 449;* e *george@ cedarsparagliding.com; www.cedarsparagliding.com)* has been established since 1992 and offers year-round tandem flights with an instructor, as well as 5-day *ab initio* training for those interested in becoming a qualified gliding pilot. See their website for details of current pricing and schedules.

WHAT TO SEE AND DO
Cedars International Festival *(Al Malak St, Zouk Mosbeh;* ✎ *09 218 267;* e *info@ cedarsinternationalfestival.org; www.cedarsinternationalfestival.org)* Established in

When love beckons to you, follow him, though his ways are hard and steep. And when his wings enfold you yield to him, though the sword hidden among his pinions may wound you. And when he speaks to you believe in him, though his voice may shatter your dreams as the north wind lays waste the garden. For even as love crowns you so shall he crucify you. Even as he is for your growth so is he for your pruning. (The Prophet, 1923)

Born on 6 January 1883 in the mountain town of Bcharré in northern Lebanon, Khalil Gibran is Lebanon's best-known and loved literary figure and philosopher. After William Shakespeare (1564–1616) and China's Lao-tzu (died c531BCE), he is the best-selling poet of all time and his prose has been a source of inspiration for the political rhetoric of world leaders such as India's former prime minister Indira Ghandi (1917–84) and former US president John F. Kennedy (1917–63), with his words even influencing the music of The Beatles. Gibran was born into a poor Christian Maronite family and was the second eldest of four children. His father, Khalil, was never a good family provider, opting instead to drink and gamble away what little income the family possessed. In 1891, whilst working as a tax collector, he was imprisoned by the Ottoman authorities for embezzling funds, leaving the family destitute and homeless. In order to carve out a better life, in 1895 his stronger-willed wife, Kamila, took her four children – Khalil, his half-brother, Boutros, and sisters, Mariana and Sultana – to the USA, settling in the poor immigrant quarter of South End in Boston, Massachusetts. Although the family's financial hardships continued, despite Kamila working as a seamstress and peddler, Gibran began to attend school for the first time where his interest and talent for art, nurtured back in his native Bcharré, was recognised by his teacher. He was introduced to Fred Holland Day (1864–1933), an intellectual, publisher and photographer who was one of the early exponents for recognising photography as a fine art form. Holland took Gibran under his wing as assistant and student, and the young man's cultural world began to blossom. Returning from a three-year stay back in Lebanon, where he pursued studies in Arabic and French in Beirut, Gibran returned to South End in 1902. A little over a year later he had suffered the triple loss of his mother to cancer and his half-brother, Boutros, and sister Sultana to tuberculosis, the latter condition then endemic to the poverty-stricken area of South End. But in 1904 Gibran held the first exhibition of his drawings in Boston, where he met and formed a life-long professional and

1963, this festival has had a chequered history being postponed during the civil war years of 1975–90 and for many years since then but was revived in 2015 to once again become an annual event held during August. In 2016 the festival was headlined by a number of Lebanese icons including the renowned Caracalla dance company and singers Nancy Ajram and Magida Al Roumi. See the festival website for details of the coming year's programme of performances, how to book tickets and getting there via public transport or by self-drive.

BQAA KAFRA At an elevation of 1,750m above sea level, Bqaa Kafra, 4km south of Bcharré on the road to Hasroun, is the highest village in Lebanon. Located up a steep side road between Deir Mar Elisha and Deir Mar Semaan, this little village of traditional and well-preserved rural houses and slender streets is also famed as the birthplace of Lebanon's revered Maronite saint, St Charbel, whose personal association with a woman nearly ten years his senior, the headmistress Mary Elizabeth Haskell (1873–1964) who would become Gibran's benefactor. Following two years in Paris from 1908 where he studied art under the Symbolist August Rodin (1840–1917), paid for by Haskell, who likened Gibran's work to that of William Blake (1757–1827), he moved to New York to concentrate on painting (he would eventually create more than 700 artworks) and writing. Until 1918 most of Gibran's works were written in Arabic but after this time he began to write more in English, and of his 17 published books, nine are in Arabic and eight in English, including his best-known 1923 book, *The Prophet*. Gibran's seminal work is a series of 26 prose poems containing his heartfelt and poignant musings on such things as beauty, children, love, marriage, pleasure, religion, time, etc. It is a book that has never gone out of print, has been translated into around 50 different languages, and to date has sold some 100 million copies worldwide and is, reputedly, the best-selling book in the USA after the Bible, famed for its depth of feeling and almost mystical qualities. Gibran's wide popular appeal was not always universally shared in his Arab homeland, where he was regarded in some quarters as something of a maverick both in style and content. He vehemently opposed the oppression of women, eschewed sectarianism emphasising the oneness of religion, he was excommunicated by the Maronite church for what he saw as its autocratic role, and his opposition to Ottoman rule resulted in his 1908 work *Spirits Rebellious* being burnt in a Beirut *souk* following publication. A tortured soul, Gibran embarked on a number of romantic relationships, including with his patron Haskell, to whom he proposed and was refused on two occasions; and although the theme of love resonates throughout his work, it is often tinged with loss and pain and he never married. Plagued by ill health throughout his life, Gibran was a heavy smoker which was supplemented by a poor diet and a penchant for *arak* as a substitute for more traditional pain relief. After a lengthy battle with his health Gibran passed away in a New York hospital on 10 April 1931 from a deadly cocktail of cancer, cirrhosis of the liver and tuberculosis. Despite residing in exile for much of his life outside Lebanon, in the USA, he never forgot the beauty of his hometown landscape which had inspired him in his work. His wish to be buried back in Lebanon was fulfilled and his body now lies in a tomb in the former rock-cut Mar Sarkis Monastery (now converted into the Khalil Gibran Museum; pages 240–1), along with a number of his personal effects.

house is now converted into a museum-art gallery, with his life-story told in a series of paintings. On the third Sunday of July each year, a feast in the saint's honour is held in the village. A convent in honour of St Charbel has been built in the village, and there is also the Notre Dame Church near the museum.

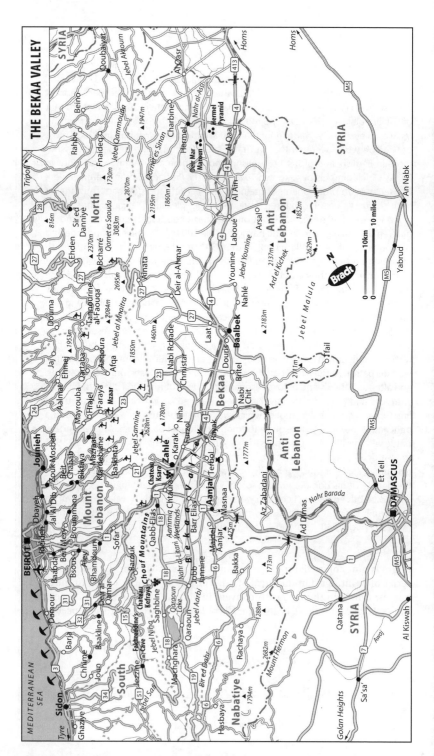

THE BEKAA VALLEY

7

The Bekaa Valley

Telephone code 08

Geographically, the Bekaa Valley is the result of earthly forces residing outside Lebanon, a vast geological fault that extends from east Africa northwards to neighbouring Syria, known as the Great Rift Valley. Separated by the Mount Lebanon and Anti-Lebanon mountain ranges, the Bekaa is an elongated plateau but still reaches up to 1,000m above sea level in places. It stretches for some 120km and averages only 16km in width. With its favourable climate of warm, dry summers and cold, wet winters, the valley has been an important agricultural region since antiquity. Referred to as Coele-Syria (Hollow Syria) by Alexander the Great, it was also the 'bread basket' of Rome during that empire's era. The Bekaa retains its agricultural importance to this day, comprising some 40% of Lebanon's arable farmland, thanks to its fertile soil, drained by the Orontes and Litani river systems. A variety of crops are grown including wheat, vegetables and fruits such as grapes and olives. Both wild and beautiful, the landscape is characterised by a patchwork of cultivated fields, grazing sheep and goats, and a variety of Bedouin encampments. Nonetheless, despite the area's rural importance, the Bekaa remains a largely traditional, poor and underdeveloped part of Lebanon with none of the frenzied rebuilding and construction seen in the capital.

The region has perhaps become more familiar to many Western eyes as a Hezbollah area, and it suffered greatly during its 2006 war with Israel with an estimated one-fifth of its buildings destroyed. It also has long been, though a now much-diminished, centre for cannabis production, the famous (or infamous, depending on your point of view) 'Red Leb', which has no doubt seen many a visitor depart these lowlands on a high. It was also the main base for Syrian occupation troops until their withdrawal from Lebanon in 2005. The region as a whole nowadays has a much more sedate and less troubled feel. The archaeological evidence of the great Arab and Roman civilisations that have passed through here in history are reason enough to visit, with the impressive UNESCO World Heritage sites at Aanjar and Baalbek demanding any visitor's time. Adding in a visit to a winery or two to appreciate Lebanon's long tradition of viniculture can only serve to enhance a rich cultural visit to this region. While the Bekaa is easily reached by bus, taxi or organised tour on a day trip from Beirut, to get the most from a visit to the region, a few days' touring by car or van would be a more rewarding experience.

ZAHLÉ

The town of Zahlé, around 54km east from Beirut, is Lebanon's only major town not located on the coast. As the capital of the Bekaa Governorate, it is quite different from other parts of the more conservative Bekaa Valley. The hometown of former president Elias Hrawi (1925–2006), parental home of the late Egyptian film star Omar Sharif (1932–2015) and birthplace of the grandparents of pop icon Shakira (b1977), Zahlé is the country's largest Christian Greek Catholic town and is often referred to as Arousat al-Beqaa or the 'Bride of the Bekaa' by locals. This friendly, pleasant and picturesque town numbering around 150,000 souls spread over numerous neighbourhoods lends the place more of a small-town feel, with its Ottoman-era red-tiled dwellings sitting on the eastern slopes of Mount Sannine and the Bardouni River flowing through its centre. The town has, however, known darker days. Sectarian conflict between Christian and Druze militias in 1860 all but razed the town to the ground, with the latter's victory helping to initiate the migration *en masse* of the town's inhabitants to Brazil, hence the name of Zahlé's principal street. During the civil war, the 'Arab Deterrent Force' of the Syrian army in the Bekaa, with the aim of staving off Palestinian influence in the area, came into conflict with the Lebanese Forces of Bashir Gemayel (1947–82). The Phalangist leader decided to construct a road link connecting Zahlé to Mount Sannine for the benefit of the Christian population. The Syrians, perceiving this as a threat by giving Israel a strategic advantage in allowing their forces access to the Bekaa and even Syria itself, decided to take military action against the Phalange. During the spring and summer of 1981, relentless Syrian bombardments not only left 300 dead and 3,000 wounded, according to Phalange estimates, but also set in motion the first stage of Syrian–Israeli conflict during the civil war.

No traces of note remain of Zahlé's bloody past and a good clue to the preoccupation and prosperity of the town today is seen on the roundabout at the entrance to Zahlé in the statue of the goddess Erato, the Greek muse of love and poetry, holding aloft a bunch of grapes. For the town is also known as the City of Wine and Poetry, and over the past century or so numerous literary figures such as Riad Maalouf (b1912) and the late Said Akl (1912–2014) were born here. Not surprisingly, Zahlé has been incorporated into the gastronomic category of UNESCO's Creative Cities Network and is one of the best places in the country to sample some of the best *mezze*, wine and *arak* (box, page 274) in Lebanon, especially around the cluster of eateries known as the Cafés du Bardouni. With a varied selection of hotels to suit all budgets and good minivan and taxi links to the nearby ancient sites at Aanjar and Baalbek, Zahlé also makes an excellent base for an extended tour of the Bekaa region. Be aware, however, that the main summer season is between June and mid-September, and outside this period, during the colder winter months, Zahlé can resemble a ghost town, and many of the town's eateries may well be shut.

Celebrated annually since 1825, Zahlé hosts the **Corpus Christi Festival** on the first Thursday in June, with torchlight displays and processions through the streets as locals pay thanks for the town being saved from the devastating effects of the bubonic plague. For about half a week in September – coinciding with the grape harvest – the town also celebrates its annual **Festival of the Vine** (e *zahle@zahlefestival.org; www.zahlefestival.org*), with a packed programme of concerts, exhibitions, theatrical performances and poetry readings, capped by the crowning of the local beauty queen, Maid of the Vine, and a procession of floats.

GETTING THERE
By bus Buses to Zahlé leave regularly from the southwest section of the Cola bus station [127 E7] in Beirut. The one-way bus fare costs LBP6,000 for the 1¼-hour journey, though this can sometimes take slightly longer depending on traffic. The

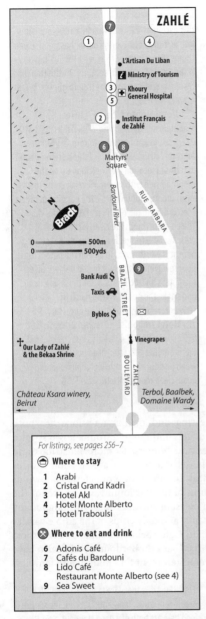

ZAHLÉ

- L'Artisan Du Liban
- Ministry of Tourism
- Khoury General Hospital
- Institut Français de Zahlé

Martyrs' Square

Bardouni River

RUE BARBARA

0 ——— 500m
0 ——— 500yds

BRAZIL STREET

Bank Audi $
Taxis
Byblos $

Vinegrapes

Our Lady of Zahlé & the Bekaa Shrine

ZAHLÉ BOULEVARD

Château Ksara winery, Beirut ◄

► *Terbol, Baalbek, Domaine Wardy*

For listings, see pages 256–7

Where to stay

1 Arabi
2 Cristal Grand Kadri
3 Hotel Akl
4 Hotel Monte Alberto
5 Hotel Traboulsi

Where to eat and drink

6 Adonis Café
7 Cafés du Bardouni
8 Lido Café
Restaurant Monte Alberto (see 4)
9 Sea Sweet

bus will drop you off at the highway turn-off around 1km from the centre of Zahlé. A service taxi from here to the centre should cost no more than LBP2,000 for the 5-minute journey.

By taxi A taxi should cost somewhere around US$60 to the centre of Zahlé from Beirut.

Self-drive If you have rented a car to visit the Bekaa, a popular route option is to take the Damascus Road in Beirut which travels through Hazmieh, Aley and Bhamdoun. Keep on this road as you descend Mount Lebanon into the Bekaa Valley, travelling east towards Chtaura and finally Zahlé, a further 3km or so from Chtaura. Traffic permitting, the journey time to Zahlé should be around an hour from Beirut.

GETTING AROUND For the most part, the town of Zahlé is easily navigated on foot. All of the hotels (with the exception of the Monte Alberto), banks, eateries and post office are all easily reached on or nearby the main Brazil Street. Taxis are plentiful, as are buses and minivans serving other areas of the Bekaa Valley and, of course, Beirut, with regular departures every day. Slightly more outlying areas such as the Our Lady of Zahlé shrine and vineyards such as Ksara, 2km outside Zahlé, may require a short service taxi ride (*LBP2,000*). As in many areas of the country, driving outside the main town at night, whether in a hire car or taxi, is not something that is recommended owing to the often poorly or even unlit roads, which can make travelling a somewhat hazardous undertaking, especially when combined with an often total lack of awareness of other drivers from locals. Caution and alertness is advised if you do decide to travel at night.

TOURIST INFORMATION The seasonally open **Ministry of Tourism Office** (*nr Cafés du Bardouni & L'Artisan du Liban;* \ *08 801 804;* e *dalia.mouhasseb@hotmail. com; www.mot.gov.lb;* ⏱ *Jun–Sep 09.00–13.00 Mon–Thu, 09.00–11.00 Fri, 09.00–noon Sat*) has leaflets and pamphlets on Zahlé and other regions of Lebanon.

🏠 WHERE TO STAY *Map, page 255*

🏠 **Cristal Grand Kadri Hotel** (84 rooms & suites) Brazil St; ☎ 08 800 038; e info@cristalgrandkadri.com; www.cristalgrandkadri.com. Zahlé's 5-star option, which has undergone extensive renovation in recent years, was formerly home to an army hospital during the Ottoman period, & the building retains its period charm to this day. It has all the business & leisure facilities you would expect for the price, including outdoor swimming pool, tennis court, health club & spa, children's play area, restaurants (**$$$$**) serving Lebanese & international dishes & a comprehensive business & conference centre with secretarial services & Wi-Fi. The hotel can also organise winery tours & cultural tourism packages. **$$$$$**

🏠 **Arabi Hotel** (10 rooms) Wadi Zahlé; ☎ 08 821 214, 08 800 144; m 03 276 545; e racharabi@hotmail.com. A very average hotel, though all rooms have AC & TV, but in a great location in the thick of the town's eateries next to the popular Cafés du Bardouni. There is a large outdoor seating area, which is popular in summer for eating & drinking. **$$**

🏠 **Hotel Akl** (10 rooms) Brazil St, virtually opposite Khoury Hospital; ☎ 08 820 701; m 03 820 701; e contact@akl-hotel.com; www.akl-hotel.com. A delightful & friendly hotel, this excellent-value option in a 100-year-old house, full of old-world charm, has good, clean rooms (6 en suite) with stove heating in winter & fan-cooled rooms in summer. At the time of research Wi-Fi access was free to guests. B/fast is an extra US$5pp. **$$**

🏠 **Hotel Monte Alberto** (20 rooms) Mountainside overlooking Wadi Zahlé; ☎ 08 810 912/3; e info@montealberto.com; f Monte-Alberto-240150056076641. Zahlé's premier hotel in terms of location, perched high up on the mountainside with superb views over the town & surrounding countryside – 'the hanging paradise' – according to the hotel's marketing literature. The en-suite rooms are clean & comfortable with AC, TV & fridge. Even if you are not staying here, it is worth a visit to dine in the hotel's top-floor revolving restaurant (listed below). Given the hotel's hillside location, for those unable to undertake the uphill walk to reach the hotel a *servees* taxi (*LBP2,000*) may be necessary. **$$**

🏠 **Hotel Traboulsi** (3 rooms) Brazil St; ☎ 08 812 661; m 03 727 400. Very close to Hotel Akl, this is another character-filled house with dark-wood furniture & chandeliers complemented by good, clean rooms, all with AC & TV. **$**

✖ WHERE TO EAT AND DRINK *Map, page 255*

As principally a resort town, Zahlé's eating and drinking options are both numerous and varied, catering to most budgets and ranging from a few fast-food places serving up the usual fare of chips and burgers, to more illustrious and formal feasts of *mezze*, wine and *arak*. The selections below are all good choices for either a quick snack or full-blown meal, but the group of eateries known as **Cafés du Bardouni**, nestled along the banks of the Bardouni River, make for the quintessential Zahlé dining experience in pleasant surroundings. Although many are called 'casinos', they are in fact restaurants, and only chips of the edible variety are served. A few eateries, such as the Lido Café (below), double as nightspots with discos and live music, as do those at the Cafés du Bardouni, which also have dodgems and other fairground rides and entertainment for children and families.

✖ **Restaurant Monte Alberto** Mountainside overlooking Wadi Zahlé; ☎ 08 810 912/3/4; e info@montealberto.com; f Monte-Alberto-240150056076641; ⏱ 08.00–late daily. The most eclectic restaurant in Zahlé with the best views in town has a small rotating restaurant, winter & summer terrace dining areas, the Al Ourzal Restaurant, with thatched ceiling & wooden beams, & the Alberto Café, serving Lebanese & international dishes. The Oriental Room, although a little kitsch, is the place to enjoy a *nargileh* & Arabic coffee in an 'authentic' setting. The service & food here are both of a good standard. **$$$$**

✖ **Lido Café** Brazil St; ☎ 08 818 656; ⏱ 10.00–midnight daily. Specialising in mainly international cuisine such as pasta, steaks & pizzas, this centrally located eatery offers great service & excellent food. They also serve a range of wines from the Domaine Wardy, Kefraya & Ksara vineyards. There is live music 22.00–

midnight every Sat. The statue outside the café has replaced the former clock tower & has been renamed Martyrs' Square, in honour of those who died fighting the Syrians in 1981. $$$

⎕ **Adonis Café** Brazil St (opposite Lido Café); ☏ 08 820 329; m 03 877 379; ⊕ summer 07.00–02.00 daily, winter 08.00–23.00 daily. A good place for fresh fruit juices, cocktails &

snacks such as sandwiches. Also serves a decent b/fast menu including *mannouche* & *labneh*. $

⎕ **Sea Sweet** Zahlé Bd; ☏ 08 822 379; e seasweet@lebanon.com; www.lebanon.com/seasweet; ⊕ 06.30–22.00 daily. This Lebanese chain of patisseries specialises in delicious varieties of take-away *baklava*, cakes, chocolates, ice cream & *knefeh*. $

SHOPPING There is no shortage of shopping options in Zahlé, including a couple of decent pharmacies, and you will be able to buy almost anything you could want for your day-to-day needs. But perhaps the best and most interesting retail experience is at the **L'Artisan du Liban** (☏ 08 809 229; ⊕ May–Nov 11.00–19.00 daily, Dec–Apr 11.00–16.00 Mon–Sat), a couple of doors along from the Ministry of Tourism office near the Cafés du Bardouni, which has a wide selection of locally made products manufactured by Lebanese craftsmen and women. Items you can buy here, in the knowledge that you are supporting Lebanese artisans and the local economy, are glass, purses, tablecloths, ornaments, jewellery, kaftans, *nargileh* (sheesha) pipes and postcards, all at reasonable prices.

OTHER PRACTICALITIES

$ **Bank Audi** Beshwati Bldg, Zahlé Bd; ☏ 08 813 592; www.banqueaudi.com. 2 ATMs.

$ **Byblos Bank** Zahlé Bd, opposite Libanpost; ☏ 08 818 330; e customerservice@byblosbank.com; www.byblosbank.com; ⊕ 08.30–17.30 Mon–Fri, 08.30–13.00 Sat. 24hr ATM.

✉ **Post office** Ogero Bldg, Zahlé Bd; ☏ 08 820 126 or 08 822 127; www.libanpost.com; ⊕ 08.00–17.00 Mon–Fri, 08.00–13.30 Sat

✚ **Khoury General Hospital** Brazil St, opposite Hotel Akl & Hotel Traboulsi; ☏ 08 807 000/1/2/3 or 08 811 181/2/3; e info@khouryhospital.com; www.khouryhospital.com. This 120-bed hospital has a comprehensive

range of medical services & facilities, including a 24hr Accident & Emergency Department.

✚ **Lebanese Red Cross** ☏ 140 (emergency), 08 800 735, 08 808 145; www.redcross.org.lb

Fire brigade ☏ 175 (emergency), 08 822 222

Institut Français de Zahlé Brazil St, opposite Cristal Grand Kadri Hotel; ☏ 08 821 293; e zahle@if-liban.com; www.institutfrancais-liban.com; ⊕ winter 08.30–13.00 & 14.30–18.00 Mon–Fri, 09.00–13.00 Sat, summer (Jul–Aug) 08.00–15.00 Mon–Fri. This very active French Cultural Centre organises exhibitions, conferences, music concerts & an annual international theatre festival in May. It also houses a library with a small children's section.

WHAT TO SEE AND DO Apart from the surrounding **vineyards** (pages 258–61), and the nearby **Terbol Museum** (page 258), the main town of Zahlé is not over-endowed with sights to visit and there is not much to distract you from the principal pursuits of eating and drinking. However, a short service taxi ride east of the main town is the **Our Lady of Zahlé and the Bekaa shrine** which yield, from atop the 54m-high structure, unparalleled and stunning views of the town, its trademark red-roof-tiled buildings, looking resplendent amid the surrounding valley and mountains. A lift (*LBP1,000*) takes you to the summit of the viewing platform, which is topped by the 9m-tall bronze statue of the Virgin Mary, a work by Italian artist Pierotti. The small chapel at the base of the shrine can accommodate up to 100 worshippers. It's well worth the visit.

A few kilometres northeast of Zahlé, just off the main road to Baalbek, are some interesting remains of caves, rock-cut tombs and Roman temples at **Furzol** and **Niha**, which could make for an interesting detour if *en route* to the temples at Baalbek from Zahlé.

Terbol Museum (*Terbol, nr Municipality Bldg, c8km southeast of Zahlé;* ✎ *05 455 104;* e *terbol@fnp.org.lb; www.fnp.org.lb;* ⊕ *May–Nov 10.00–18.00 Tue–Sun; admission: adults LBP3,000, children LBP1,000*) One of a number of projects undertaken by Lebanon's National Heritage Foundation (*www. lebanonheritage.com*), who are responsible for the cUS$50,000 refurbishment of this 150m² old farmhouse, is an interesting eco-museum 'dedicated to bringing the heritage of the Lebanese countryside back to life'. The L-shaped house, built from sun-dried bricks coated with clay and marl, complete with wooden beams supporting the roof, which is made of reeds and tamped clay, houses a number of primitive agricultural and household tools affording a fascinating glimpse into the past; whilst the picturesque and verdant gardens are shaded by poplar and juniper trees, which were used in the construction of the house. Documentary videos on the history of the museum are shown in the audio visual room and the museum shop sells locally produced handicrafts, produce and books. Allow up to 2 hours for a comprehensive tour.

LEBANON'S WINE INDUSTRY AND VINEYARDS

It may not be the first thing that springs to mind when one thinks of Lebanon, but the country produces some excellent wines, which have won many international awards over the years. In fact, Lebanon has a viniculture tradition as old as the Lebanese themselves, making the country one of the most ancient wine producers in the world, estimated by many authorities to date back to 7000BCE. The Bekaa Valley has always been the epicentre for viniculture – the predominantly chalky soil, wet winters and long, dry, hot summers with some 240 days of continuous sunshine, provide ideal growing and ripening conditions for the grape. The ancient Phoenicians were prolific producers and oceanographic and archaeological evidence from shipwrecks suggest that this entrepreneurial race produced and exported the drink throughout the Mediterranean region, ushering in a golden era for wine production from 3000BCE to 350BCE. The era of Roman rule continued the tradition, with the Temple of Bacchus at Baalbek paying homage to their god of wine. Production declined with the onset of Islamic rule, but picked up again during the Ottoman period. The French Mandate era, following the end of World War I, was influential in popularising wine, and this impact survives to this day.

Production was severely hampered during the 1975–90 civil war, though many producers continued to flourish. With Lebanon once again experiencing a period of stability, the industry is once more a prosperous one and the country is now starting to market itself as a boutique wine destination. The number of producers has risen from a mere five in 1995 to around 40 in 2014, and this figure is expected to rise further. Lebanon now produces some seven million bottles annually with the industry currently worth over US$40 million per annum. This figure is small by the standards of other major international producers, with Lebanon producing less than 1% of the wine made by France, for example. Nonetheless, Lebanese wine is exported to more than 30 countries, with the UK, followed by France and the USA the largest importers amongst Lebanon's main western markets. Amongst other Arab countries, Lebanese wines are bought by the UAE, Syria, Iraq, Jordan and Bahrain. For more information on the country's wine industry take a look at the website of Lebanon's association of wine producers, **Union Vinicole du Liban** (e *info@lebanonwines.com; www. lebanonwines.com*).

CHÂTEAU KSARA [Map, page 252] (*Caves of Ksara, entrance to Ksara village, nr Zahlé;* ✆ *08 813 495 or 08 801 662;* e *info@ksara.com.lb; www.chateauksara.com;* ⊕ *Jan & Feb 09.00–16.00 Mon–Sat except 1 Jan (New Year's Day), Mar, Nov & Dec 09.00–17.00 daily except 25 Dec (Christmas Day), 1 Apr–31 Oct 09.00–18.00 daily, except Easter Day*) If there is one winery that symbolises the tradition and importance of wine-making in Lebanon, it is the multi-award-winning Ksara. The château celebrated its 150th anniversary in 2007, and is the oldest winery in Lebanon and the Middle East, and the largest producer, exporting some 40% of its current output of around 3 million bottles to more than 35 countries including the USA, UK, Canada, Australia and France. Ksara began life in 1857, when the religious order of the Jesuits inherited a 25ha parcel of land and began to produce wine for religious purposes, importing the vines from Algeria. In 1898, they discovered over 2km of labyrinthine Roman-era caves beneath the château which to this day, with their humidity and stable temperature of c13–15°C, provide optimum conditions for storage of the wine. By 1972, Ksara was producing 1.5 million bottles, accounting for 85% of Lebanon's total wine production. The Jesuits sold the winery to a consortium of local businessmen in August 1973 under pressure from the Vatican, who deemed their increasing commercial affairs incompatible with their religious calling. Today, the Ksara estate extends over some 440ha and harvests some 3,000 tons of grapes from its ten vineyards around the central and western areas of the Bekaa Valley. Without doubt, Ksara is the best of Lebanon's many vineyards to visit and welcomes some 70,000 visitors annually. Daily tours lasting c45 minutes commence with a short 15-minute film telling the history of the château and the process of wine-making followed by a free tasting session in the purpose-built tasting rooms; and conclude with a fascinating guided visit to the cobwebbed and dusty cellars (caves), which hold some 900,000 bottles of the tipple including their 1918 vintage. In the on-site shop you can purchase Ksara wine, including its famed *arak*, together with a range of Ksara memorabilia such as books and DVDs.

OTHER NOTABLE BEKAA VALLEY VINEYARDS Although opening hours are given where available, it is still advisable to call in advance to arrange an appointment before setting off for a tour of the following wineries. Alternatively, **Club Grappe** (✆ *04 871 421;* m *70 432 640 or 03 611 603;* e *ck@clubgrappe.com; www. clubgrappe.com*), Lebanon's first wine-tasting club, runs one- to two-day group trips to the wineries in the Bekaa, as well as to other vineyards in the country if you would prefer a more guided visit.

Château Kefraya (*Kefraya;* ✆ *08 645 333/444;* m *03 322 005/6;* e *reservations@ chateaukefraya.com; www.chateaukefraya.com;* ⊕ *10.00–18.00 (cellar tours), noon– 22.00 (restaurant) daily; 50min train tour of vineyards LBP6,000, 30min train tour of* hypogea *(rock-cut tombs) LBP6,000; 90min train ride to vineyards & hypogea LBP10,000*) One of Lebanon's newer wineries, and after Ksara the country's largest producer, Kefraya corks some two million bottles annually and exports to in excess of 35 countries. With vineyards spread over more than 300ha, Kefraya began producing its own wine in 1979, and its mantra '*semper ultra*' (Latin for 'always better') has resulted in its label winning an array of national and international accolades, including numerous awards for its Chateâu Kefraya Celebration red wine. Located just over 20km south of Chtaura, the majority shareholder is Druze leader Walid Jumblatt. Set amid picturesque and verdant gardens named after famous composers from the world of opera, the delightful 350-seat Le Relais Dionysos restaurant serves fine *mezze* as well as international cuisine (*Sunday buffet lunch US$50*). The daily tours of the winery, including free tastings, consist of a train ride through the attractive vineyards of the château, as well as visits to the cellars and museum.

Château Khoury (*Overlooking Zahlé;* ✆ *08 801 160;* m *03 075 422;* e *info@chateaukhoury.com; www.chateaukhoury.com;* ☉ *by prior appointment*) Run by the Khoury family since 2004, this small, boutique winery produces only around 50,000 bottles annually from its 13ha vineyard, with quality over quantity the prime concern. The chateâu is credited with introducing new grape varieties to Lebanon such as Pinot Noir, Pinot Gris and Riesling. Call a couple of days in advance to arrange your visit.

Château Massaya (*Relais de Tanail Property, nr Chtaura;* ✆ *08 510 135;* m *70 103 656;* e *massaya@massaya.com, www.massaya.com;* ☉ *summer 08.30–16.00 Mon-Fri, closed 1 Jan, 25 Dec, Easter Good Fri, Eid al-Adha & during Ramadan*) The château is predominantly owned and run by brothers Sami and Ramzi Ghosn, who returned to Lebanon in 1992 after the civil war to kick-start the family's vineyard estate. Having respectively pursued careers as an LA architect and French-based restaurateur, they re-established the production of *arak* and, in 1998, added red and white wine production to their viniculture portfolio. They now produce on average 200,000 bottles a year.

Château Musar (*Sopenco Bldg, Baroudy St, Achrafieh, Beirut;* ✆ *01 201 828, 01 328 111* or *01 328 211;* e *info@chateaumusar.com.lb; www.chateaumusar.com.lb;* ☉ *by prior appointment*) Probably Lebanon's most recognisable label internationally, Château Musar began life back in the vault of a 17th-century castle in 1930 as a pastime of Gaston Hochar. Upon meeting the famous British viticulturalist Ronald Barton during his posting to Lebanon during World War II, Hochar's hobby quickly blossomed into a 'passion', and since 1962 the 180ha vineyards have been run by Hochar's youngest son, Ronald, producing 500,000 bottles annually, almost exclusively for the overseas market, together with its own variety of *arak*, the liquorice aromatic L'Arack de Musar, which is aged for 12 months before bottling. Unlike the other Bekaa wineries, the chateâu is located away from the vineyards in the Bekaa Valley in the village of Ghazir, above Jounieh, north of Beirut.

Clos St Thomas (*Qabb Elias, c6km from Chtaura;* \ *08 500 812/3;* e *info@ clossthomas.com; www.clossthomas.com;* ⊕ *09.00–16.00 Mon–Sat, group guided tours by prior appointment only*) Run by the Touma family since its founding in 1990, this 50ha vineyard has been a long-time major *arak* producer, with wine production added later in the 1990s. Daily tours, except on Sundays, take place in lovely surroundings which encompass attractive gardens, a picnic site and a chapel devoted to St Thomas.

Domaine des Tourelles (*Main Rd, Chtaura;* \ *08 540 114;* m *03 775 943;* e *info@domainedestourelles.com; www.domainedestourelles.com;* ⊕ *by prior appointment*) Founded in 1868, this is one of Lebanon's oldest wineries, producing c100,000 bottles a year. Originally renowned for its *arak*, whose Arak Brun Special Reserve is aged for five years in clay jars, wine production has increased and its red Marquis de Beys has won a slew of awards. Guided tours of the delightful cellars, 7,000m^2 gardens and winery are by appointment only.

Domaine Wardy (*Industrial Park, Zahlé;* \ *08 930 141/2/3 or 08 930 777;* e *info@domainewardy.com; www.domainewardy.com;* ⊕ *08.00–17.00 Mon–Fri, 08.00–noon Sat*) Another relatively new winery, Wardy was established in 1997, and in 2004 became the first winery in the country to donate a portion of sales to its Cedars Campaign, the winery's own initiative to help preserve Lebanon's natural heritage. The winery produces a variety of reds, a rosé, two varieties of *arak* and a selection of whites including a fruity, aromatic Sauvignon Blanc.

AANJAR

With an area of only some 20km^2, Aanjar is more a village than a town. Around 58km from Beirut and close to the Syrian border, the area takes its name from a large spring, Ain Gerrha, a few kilometres northeast of Aanjar's main archaeological site. It is also often referred to locally as Haouch Moussa or Moses' Farm. It has a small, almost exclusively Armenian, population numbering around 2,500 and was settled by those fleeing the 1915 genocide in Turkey – which is estimated to have cost the lives of 1.5 million Armenians under the Ottoman Turks – and their descendants. (Three centuries earlier the maverick Fakhreddine Maan II had managed to subdue Ottoman forces at the Battle of Aanjar in 1623.) During the more recent Lebanese civil war, Aanjar was the main base for Syrian occupation troops and *mukhabbarat* (security service) until their departure from the country in 2005 following the Cedar Revolution. Today the town evokes a splendid aura of peace and tranquillity, set in very picturesque surroundings against the snowy backdrop of the Anti-Lebanon Mountains, and offers some fine waterside dining of *mezze*, Armenian food and the local speciality, farmed trout, at many of its restaurants. But the main draw of Aanjar is its much earlier historical settlement built during the Umayyad period, which has left a beautiful and unique architectural legacy from the earliest years of Islamic rule.

GETTING THERE Public transport to Aanjar is best taken from either Zahlé or Chtaura with a journey time of less than half an hour and costing around LBP5,000. If you are on a self-drive visit, Aanjar can be reached from Chtaura, which is around 15km to the northwest of Aanjar, by taking the road to Damascus.

If based in Zahlé, drive to Chtaura and follow the above road. Aanjar is also quite close to the border crossing point to Syria at Masnaa, a few kilometeres south of Aanjar. A taxi from Beirut will cost in the region of US$60–70.

⌂ WHERE TO STAY

⌂ **Hotel Anjar** (23 rooms & suites) Al Nabeh St; ☎ 08 620 753; m 03 212 300, 03 620 753; e contact@hotelanjar.com; www.hotelanjar.com. A 10min walk from the Aanjar ruins, this unremarkable yet modern & clean hotel has good en-suite rooms with AC, TV & fridge. There is a pleasant communal lounge area with TV & the large terrace hosts live music during the summer months. B/fast inc. **$$**

✕ WHERE TO EAT AND DRINK Although there is a cluster of signposted eateries near the Aanjar ruins, the establishment below is definitely the pick of the bunch and a favourite of locals and visitors alike.

✕ **Shams Restaurant** Nr the main entrance to Aanjar; ☎ 08 620 567/8; m 81 620 567; e info@shamsrestaurant.com, contact@ shamsrestaurant.com, shamsrestaurant@ hotmail.com; www.shamsrestaurant.com; ⊕ year-round 11.00–midnight daily. This large, sprawling restaurant complex can accommodate around 2,000 diners. A favourite with locals & visitors alike for more than 30 years, this family-friendly eatery has a wonderfully friendly & fun atmosphere backed up by a varied & tasty menu of Armenian & Lebanese dishes including *mezze* & fresh, locally farmed trout. A range of non-alcoholic & alcoholic drinks including *arak* & the Lebanese beer Almaza are served. It gets very busy during the summer months so it's advisable to book ahead if visiting during this period. There is also a pleasant children's play area, & kids can watch 5D films. A takeaway service is also available. **$$$$**

OTHER PRACTICALITIES Being a small rural town, Aanjar is not the best place for exchanging currency, making cash withdrawals or using the post office, and you would be best advised to seek out the plentiful supply of banks and the post office in either Chtaura, or better still Zahlé.

WHAT TO SEE

Aanjar Archaeological Site ✳ [Site plan, page 264] (☎ 08 623 008; ⊕ winter 08.00– 30min before sunset daily, summer 08.00–19.00 daily; admission: adults & children over 10 LBP6,000, students LBP1,500) Unlike at Lebanon's other archaeological sites, there are no onion layers to peel away in order to reveal the seams of existence of successive civilisations. Aanjar is, uniquely, the product of only one historical period: the 8th-century Umayyad caliphate, the first and most short-lived of the Arab dynasties, which founded an Islamic empire extending from the Indus Valley to southern Spain. Strategically located at the intersection of important trade routes linking Damascus and Homs in Syria, and Baalbek and Sidon in the south, Aanjar is also Lebanon's sole example of an inland trading centre. It is believed that the city was built by Caliph al-Walid I around CE710 and prospered for only around half a century until the Umayyads were overthrown by the Abbasids.

Incorporated into UNESCO's list of World Heritage sites in 1984, the site was discovered by chance in 1949, when archaeologists from the General Directorate of Antiquities were searching for the old city of Chalcis but unearthed Aanjar instead. Today this historic city has been comprehensively excavated to reveal an important and hitherto missing part of the Lebanese architectural jigsaw puzzle, making this a must-see, but often overlooked, site on any visit to the Bekaa Valley. Being compact and well organised, Aanjar makes for a pleasant couple of hours perambulating its delicate structures.

(The ticket office usually has free Ministry of Tourism brochures available in Arabic, English, French, Italian, Portuguese and Spanish.)

Comprising an area of some 114,000m^2, the site is rectangular in form, 385m long by 310m wide, enclosed by 2m-thick walls on all sides to help secure the town against the threat of invaders. Possessing a wonderful symmetry of design, two main 20m-wide streets, north–south (Cardo Maximus) and east–west (Decumanus Maximus), divide the town into more or less four equal quarters, a design feature indicating the influence of Roman town planning. To the left as you enter from the main northern entrance are some very eroded but still discernible **mosaics** next to the **public baths**, and in front of these lies the **Little Palace** adorned with lovely little carvings of acanthus leaves, eagles and birds. But the main highlight is to walk from the main entrance up the principal north–south street, lined with shops and residential houses on either side to get an insight into the former life of the town. Some 600 shops have been uncovered, testifying to the importance of Aanjar's role as a hub of trade and retail activity. At the midway point is the restored **Tetrapylon**, a structure consisting of four columns, which stands at the crossroads of the two main streets. With its alternating stonework, it once again shows how the Umayyads drew upon earlier architectural styles, in this case that of the Byzantines. Although there are scant remains of a mosque just across the east–west road from the Little Palace, Aanjar's undoubted jewel in the crown is the nearby **Great Palace**, the first part of the town to be excavated by archaeologists. With one of its walls and two tiers of fragile and slender arches beautifully restored, it doesn't take much imagination when standing in the 40m^2 courtyard to envisage the palace enveloped by the lithe-like structures in its heyday.

Majdel Aanjar (✆ 08 621 300; ☼ 08.00–17.00 daily; admission free) Located a little over 1km south from the main Aanjar site, this seldom-visited, small, 1st-century Roman temple with a scattering of fallen entablature and subterranean passages, later fortified during the 7th and 8th centuries by the Abbasid dynasty, sits atop a hill affording superb views over the Bekaa Valley. In the past the area has suffered from sporadic conflict between the Lebanese army and groups and individuals sympathetic to al-Qaeda, so to find out if the area is safe to visit, ask at the ticket office at the main Aanjar site or at the small café just outside its main entrance, or telephone the site number given.

Aammiq Wetlands An ecotourist's delight, these marshes in the western Bekaa Valley are Lebanon's largest freshwater reserve and one of the few remaining in the Middle East. This elongated area of land consisting of over 250ha of marshes, lakes and swamps lies at the foothills of Jebel Barouk and the Litani River. This entire area is a delicate ecosystem and lies on one of the most important migratory bird routes in the eastern Mediterranean. More than 250 species of bird have been identified here including the endangered great spotted eagle (*Aquila clanga*), imperial eagle (*Aquila heliaca*), lesser kestrel (*Falco naumanni*), great snipe (*Gallinago media*) and ferruginous duck (*Aythya nyroca*). In addition to our feathered friends, Aammiq is an important habitat for 20-plus species of animal such as the swamp cat, otters, hedgehogs, foxes and a variety of lizards and snakes. In recognition of the area's importance, Aammiq was made an Important Bird Area by Birdlife International in 1994, and was designated a UNESCO Biosphere Reserve in 2005.

Until a few years ago, the area was under threat from the impact of a range of man's activities such as hunting, the dumping of waste and less than environmentally friendly agricultural practices. In 1996, however, a Christian environmental organisation, **A Rocha Lebanon** (*Main St, Aana;* \ *08 566 578;* m *71 451 410;* e *lebanon@arocha. org; www.arocha.org, www.wildlebanon.org*) was founded, dedicated to conserving the marshes' flora and fauna. A Rocha have taken great strides in curtailing the threats to the marsh through a variety of practical measures such as restricting hunting, limiting vehicular access to the area and working with local farmers to protect the most vulnerable parts of the marsh by reducing the number of goats and putting in place a more environmentally friendly grazing management scheme. A Rocha's ongoing tasks include research, conservation and working with the local population. An important part of their remit is collaborating with schools and universities and organising group visits to the area to give schoolchildren and students hands-on experience of the importance of the wetland environment.

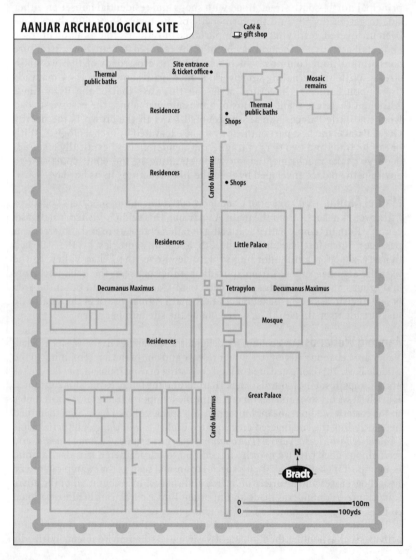

AANJAR ARCHAEOLOGICAL SITE

Café & gift shop

Thermal public baths

Site entrance & ticket office •

Mosaic remains

Residences

Thermal public baths

• Shops

Cardo Maximus

Residences

• Shops

Residences

Little Palace

Decumanus Maximus

Tetrapylon

Decumanus Maximus

Residences

Mosque

Cardo Maximus

Great Palace

N

Bradt

0 ━━━━━━ 100m
0 ━━━━━━ 100yds

Getting there Aammiq is situated around 7km south of the town of Qabb Elias between Zahlé and Lake Qaraoun. The area is not on a service taxi or main bus route and so, unless you have your own car, you will need to negotiate the fare with a taxi driver. If you are on a self-drive visit from Chtaura or Zahlé, take the road south which goes through the town of Qabb Elias; Aammiq Wetlands is around 1km before the main village of Aammiq. It may be best to combine a visit to the marshes with a trip further south along this road to Lake Qaraoun and the Litani Dam.

Lake Qaraoun and the Litani River Dam Project (*www.litani.gov.lb*) What

its neighbours lack – water – Lebanon has been able to successfully capitalise on to great economic and social benefit. Located about 10km south of Aammiq, the 12km^2 Lake Qaraoun, Lebanon's biggest artificial lake, was created by the Litani River Dam Project in 1959. This is Lebanon's most ambitious hydroelectricity project to date, providing electricity and irrigation throughout the Bekaa Valley and the south of the country. The harnessing of the waters of the Litani – the country's largest river, flowing south some 170km from its source near Baalbek before emptying into the Mediterranean Sea north of Tyre – has also created an extremely scenic area to visit. Although the 6km-long lake is not suitable for swimming due to the water's bacterial contamination, in spring, when the water level reaches its zenith, boats are available to take visitors around the lake. There are also a few fish restaurants nearby serving locally farmed trout.

Where to stay, eat and drink

West Bekaa Country Club (54 rooms) Nr Khirbet Qanafar; 08 645 601/2/3; m 03 485 695; e info@wbccbekaa.com; www.wbccbekaa. com. Located north of Lake Qaraoun, nestled amidst delightful verdant scenery, this country club has a nice, homely feel. The rooms are comfortable, & with an outdoor swimming pool, large bar & restaurant & a range of activities catering to adults & children alike, this is an especially good choice for a few nights for those exploring the region with children. B/fast inc, free Wi-Fi. **$$$$**

Blue Lake Hotel (30 rooms) Saghbine, above the Blue Lake Restaurant; 08 670 146/254/611; m 71 999 592; e info@bluelake-hotel.com; www.bluelake-hotel.com. Whilst the rooms are clean & comfortable though rather anodyne, the lake & mountain views are anything but, thus making this a great choice for 1 or 2 nights if you are touring the area. Free Wi-Fi. **$$$**

Macharef Saghbine Hotel (40 rooms & suites) Saghbine, overlooking Lake Qaraoun;

08 671 200; m 03 423 307. An average hotel with quite ordinary, but clean & spacious rooms, with superb views over Lake Qaraoun. Dining in the 1st-floor restaurant is also a good opportunity for absorbing the picturesque vistas. The hotel also has a swimming pool which is open from Jun to Oct. B/fast US$7 extra. **$$**

Blue Lake Restaurant Saghbine, approx 500m from Macharef Saghbine Hotel; 08 670 146/254/611; m 71 999 592; e info@bluelake-hotel.com; www.bluelake-hotel. com; ⊕ summer 10.00–midnight daily, winter 10.00–20.00 daily. Serves a variety of Lebanese food including *mezze*, grills, wine & *arak* from the Kefraya & Ksara vineyards, & Lebanese Almaza beer. Dining on the restaurant's terrace is almost obligatory given the astounding views overlooking the Litani Dam & mountains. A variety of flavours of *nargileh* are also available for those wanting to puff on the water pipe or *sheesha*. **$$$$**

BAALBEK

Located around 35km northeast of Zahlé and 85km northeast of Beirut, the town of Baalbek should be on every visitor's schedule. Despite some recent regeneration, the area has a raw, rugged feel and retains its long-standing poor and traditional appearance. It has a mildly engaging souk, selling mainly standard tourist fare, but is nowhere near as atmospheric as those in Sidon and Tripoli. A predominantly Shi'ite town, Baalbek has become all too familiar to Westerners as a base for Palestinian and Syrian forces during the civil war and, more recently, as the 'home' of many high-profile Western hostages. It has also become synonymous with Hezbollah, whose presence today remains in the form of placards adorned with images of the Party of God's Secretary General, Sayyed Hassan Nasrallah, and of martyrs killed fighting Israel. Whilst these associations endure, the town today is a friendly and safe place to visit, with its main attraction on the outskirts of the town: a world-class archaeological and historical site, Heliopolis or 'Sun City', a short walk from the centre (pages 268–72; site plan, page 269).

There are also innumerable local tour operators (pages 136–40) offering day trips to Baalbek, and if you are planning on seeing only this main site or perhaps combining it with Aanjar or the wineries, then an organised tour, which often includes lunch and a guide, could be worthwhile if time is short or you would prefer not to organise a schedule yourself.

GETTING THERE Baalbek is quite well served by both taxis and minivans from the southwest area of Beirut's Cola station [127 E7]. A bus or van costs LBP7,000 for the journey of around 2 hours. Expect to pay somewhere between US$80 and US$100 for a taxi to Baalbek from Beirut. If you are coming from Zahlé, a minivan will cost around LBP5,000 for the 45-minute journey.

If you have a rental car, Baalbek is approximately a 2-hour drive from Beirut travelling east along the Damascus Road towards the Bekaa. When you reach Chtaura, take the road in the direction of Zahlé and continue north, following signs in the direction of Baalbek.

GETTING AROUND As a compact town, Baalbek is easily explored on foot. Its two main intersecting roads – Rue Abdel Halim Hajjar and Ras al-ain Boulevard – are home to most of its banks, eateries, hotels and post office, along with most other amenities useful to tourists and visitors.

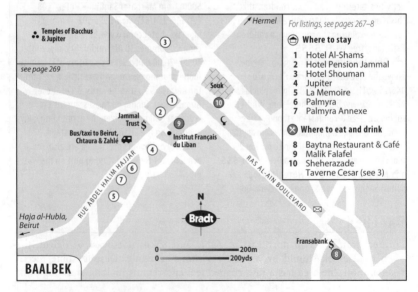

TOURIST INFORMATION There's a **Ministry of Tourism Office** at the Baalbek archaeological site (m *71 000 519*; e *baalbek.mot@gmail.com*; *www.mot.gov.lb*; ☾ *winter 08.30–16.00 daily, summer 08.30–18.00 daily*) which should have free pamphlets available on the Baalbek site.

WHERE TO STAY *Map, page 266*

🏠 **La Memoire Hotel** (9 rooms) approx 400m behind Jupiter & Palmyra hotels, next to Mar Jeorgous Church; ☎ 08 373 730/1; m 03 556 944. The modern façade & facilities are well complemented by nice dark wood furniture, stone walls, chandeliers & decorative doors, making this hotel a characterful, though not particularly cheap, boutique-style option. There is a nice terrace area for summer dining. B/fast is an extra US$5. Free Wi-Fi. **$$$**

🏠 **Hotel Pension Jammal** (30 rooms) Rue Abdel Halim Hajjar; ☎ 08 370 649; m 03 716 072. Housed within a 100-year-old building – with a selection of rooms also available across the street – this is a decent, clean hotel with all rooms en suite. Rooms are charged per person & there are discounts of 50% for children under 10. According to their promotional literature, this hotel is 'favoured by the German archaeologists working at the archaeological site'. **$$**

🏠 **Jupiter Hotel** (21 rooms) Rue Abdel Halim Hajjar; ☎ 08 376 715, 08 370 151; m 70 269 079. As its name suggests, this hotel has terrific views of the ruins opposite (rooms 13, 14, 15, 16 & 17) & is clean & friendly. All rooms are en suite with TV. Only 2 rooms have AC but all are equipped with fan & are oil heated in winter. The courtyard below the rooms is a pleasant area for relaxing & refreshments. A good & popular choice. Free Wi-Fi. **$$**

🏠 **Palmyra Hotel** (32 rooms) Rue Abdel Halim Hajjar; ☎ 08 370 011/230. Directly opposite the Baalbek ruins, this hotel is a tourist attraction in its own right & worth a look in even if you are not staying here. Those who have stayed here include General de Gaulle (room 30), Kaiser Wilhelm II, French Surrealist painter Jean Cocteau, whose works

& a handwritten letter still adorn the walls near the hotel's restaurant, Brigitte Bardot, Rudolf Nureyev & the King of Belgium, among many others. One of Lebanon's oldest hotels, dating back to 1874, it has a slightly melancholic look & feel nowadays, which has been accentuated by its lack of guests due to Baalbek's proximity to the Syrian border & the spillover effect of the conflict in that country, but still manages to evoke its old-world charm; creaky floors, a warren of long, narrow corridors with a ghostly feel, dark wood furniture & chandeliers. The rooms, all with bathroom, have changed little over time & have a wonderful faded grandeur, but are clean & cosy. The small, intimate bar on the ground floor is open from 18.00 to 23.00 & serves a range of spirits & beers. The Palmyra also has an **annexe** a few doors along from the main hotel whose 5 rooms all have character but with the addition of more modern bathroom facilities & AC. There is also a pleasant outdoor garden area for the summer months. B/fast US$7 extra. Annexe flat-rate US$100/room. **$$**

🏠 **Hotel Al-Shams** (5 rooms) Rue Abdel Halim Hajjar; ☎ 08 373 284; m 70 069 757 or 03 770 990. Extremely basic & run down with shared bathrooms, this place is best seen as a last resort. Dorm room US$10/pp. **$**

🏠 **Hotel Shouman** (7 rooms) Ras al-Ain Bd; ☎ 08 372 685; m 03 796 077; e shouman-hotel@ hotmail.com. Although this is a typical budget hotel with clean rooms which are stove-heated in winter & fan-cooled in summer, its main advantage is its great location opposite the Baalbek site. Not all rooms have bathrooms. Free Wi-Fi. A decent b/fast US$5 extra. Dorm room US$10pp. **$**

✗ WHERE TO EAT AND DRINK *Map, page 266*

Compared with Zahlé, Baalbek's eating and drinking options are nowhere near as varied or formal and veer more towards the informal and snacking variety; but the places reviewed below are excellent and representative of the town's eateries and watering holes.

✗ **Sheherazade Restaurant** 6th Fl, Yaghi & Sunbola Shopping Centre; ☎ 08 371 851; m 70 642 797; ☾ 09.00–22.00 daily. A window onto

the ruins, literally, this place is reached by lift (when working) or by stairs in a rather bizarre-looking shopping centre adjacent to the souk. It serves filling though unremarkable fish & meat dishes & desserts at very reasonable prices. $$$

✘ Baytna Restaurant & Café Ras al-Ain Bd, opposite Riviera Restaurant & Fransabank; 📞08 374 846; **m** 70 524 878; **f** baytnacafe; ⏱ 07.00–03.00 daily. Nice little café/restaurant serving tasty local & home-cooked food & a good Lebanese b/fast. No alcohol. $$

✘ Taverne Cesar Ras al-Ain Bd; 📞08 372 685; **m** 03 796 077 or 70 854 352; ⏱ 08.00–

01.00 daily. Located directly beneath Hotel Shouman & run by the hotel's friendly owner, Muhammad Shouman, this is an excellent choice for tasty & filling Lebanese snacks & fresh fruit juice. $$

✘ Malik Falafel Rue Abdel Halim Hajjar; **m** 70 735 526; ⏱ 08.00–22.00 daily except Fri. Malik means 'King' in Arabic & this small eatery certainly lives up to its name, with probably the best falafel in town at great prices. $

OTHER PRACTICALITIES

$ Fransabank Ras Al-Ain Bd, next to Baytna Café; 📞08 378 800/1/2, 08 371 800/1, dial 1552 within Lebanon; www.fransabank.com. 24hr ATM.

$ Jammal Trust Bank Rue Abdel Halim Hajjar, opposite taxi stand nr Palmyra Hotel; 📞08 371 198 or 08 377 575; www.jtbbank.com; ⏱ 08.30–13.30 Mon–Fri, 08.30–13.00 Sat. 24hr ATM.

✉ Post office Ogero Bldg, Ras al-Ain Bd; 📞08 371 169; www.libanpost.com; ⏱ 08.00–17.00 Mon–Fri, 08.00–13.30 Sat

Institut Français du Liban Pl de L'Evêche, just off Rue Abdel Halim Hajjar nr Jupiter Hotel; 📞08 377 436; www.institutfrancais-liban.com; ⏱ 10.00–13.00 & 15.00–18.00 Mon–Fri, 13.00–18.00 Sat. Has a well-stocked library & organises exhibitions & concerts.

WHAT TO SEE AND DO

Baalbek Archaeological Site ✳ [Site plan, opposite] (📞 *08 376 912;* ⏱ *08.00– 17.30 daily; admission: adults LBP15,000, students LBP5,000, children under 10 free*) The Baalbek complex, a homage to the gods of the Heliopolitan Triad – Jupiter, Venus and Mercury – contains some of the largest and most impressive Roman remains in the world. Lebanon's most feted archaeological attraction, Baalbek was made a UNESCO World Heritage site in 1984 with the comment that 'Baalbek, with its colossal structures, is one of the finest examples of imperial Roman architecture at its apogee'. On his journey through Asia in the 1930s, British writer Robert Byron (1905–41), in his acclaimed *The Road to Oxiana*, referred to Baalbek as a 'triumph of stone; of lapidary magnificence on a scale whose language, being still the language of the eye, dwarfs New York into a home of ants'. Despite a series of devastating earthquakes and a succession of conquering civilisations over the millennia, the Baalbek site is one of the most remarkably preserved complexes in the Middle East and should be on every traveller's itinerary while in Lebanon. Visiting the site early on in the day will ensure there are fewer crowds and coach parties and yield better, warmer photographs of the ruins. Available free of charge at the site entrance is a useful map from the German Archaeological Institute titled *Heliopolis Baalbek 1898–1998: Rediscovering the Ruins*, and is highly recommended to accompany you on a tour of the site. Knowledgeable and trilingual (Arabic, English, French) tour guides are also available at the entrance; you can expect to pay around US$20 (*LBP30,000*) for a guided tour lasting approximately 1 hour.

The history of settlement at Baalbek can be traced back to the ancient Phoenicians, when it was an important waypoint on their trade route from Tyre to Damascus, and they worshipped their god Baal, the sun god, here. By 333BCE the Greeks, under Ptolemy, who had been given Syria by Alexander the Great before he died, renamed the city Heliopolis, or City of the Sun. This name was retained following the onset of Roman rule in 64BCE, but, under Julius Caesar in 47BCE, the city was incorporated into the Roman Empire as a colony and renamed after his daughter, Julia, as Julia Augusta

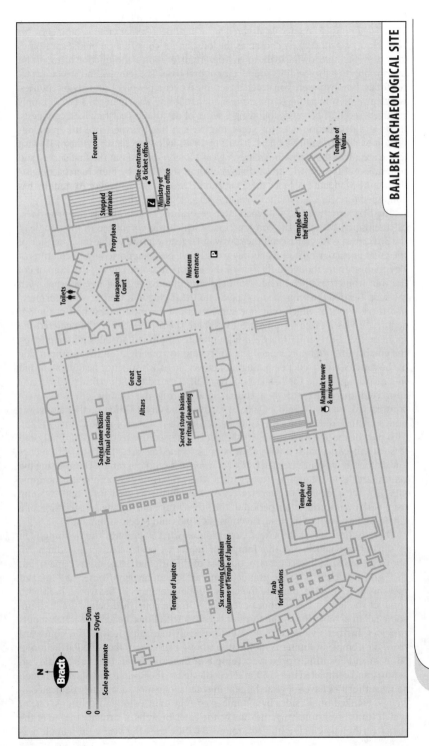

BAALBEK ARCHAEOLOGICAL SITE

N

Bradt

0 ⸻ 50m
0 ⸻ 50yds
Scale approximate

Temple of Jupiter

Six surviving Corinthian columns of Temple of Jupiter

Arab fortifications

Temple of Bacchus

Mamluk tower & museum

Sacred stone basins for ritual cleansing

Great Court

Altars

Sacred stone basins for ritual cleansing

Hexagonal Court

Toilets

Museum entrance

P

Propylaea

Stepped entrance

Forecourt

Site entrance & ticket office

Ministry of Tourism office

Temple of the Muses

Temple of Venus

Felix Heliopolis. Roman rule ushered in a period of remarkable prominence for Baalbek. It was most likely chosen as the location for construction of ancient Rome's largest-ever temples owing to the town's important location at the junction of important trade routes together with its sound agricultural base. The temples and structures we see today, however, were constructed piecemeal over a period of some two centuries, which gives new meaning to the expression that 'Rome wasn't built in a day'. It is only relatively recently, however, following a series of devastating earthquakes, conquests, thefts and destruction over the years, that we can finally experience the splendour of Rome's architectural wonders. It was in 1898, following Kaiser Wilhelm II's visit to the area, that the German Archaeological Mission carried out the first survey and restoration of the site which was followed some years later by French archaeologists during the Mandate era. Since then, Lebanon's Directorate General of Antiquities has continued this work, as has the German Archaeological Institute.

The first structure you will encounter beyond the ticket office is the **propylaea**, or ceremonial entrance, the construction of which was completed in the middle of the 3rd century. As you ascend the stairway, large towers are visible on either side of the great portico, which in its heyday would have been supported by 12 columns of Egyptian granite, though only four of these remain today. During the Roman era the roof would have been made from cedarwood and the floor area adorned with mosaics. Beyond the *propylaea* you pass into the **Hexagonal Court**, which formerly had three doors of which only one survives. Built during the first half of the 3rd century, it was a place for pilgrims to prepare themselves before they entered the more sacred courtyard. Thirty 8m-high granite-columned porticos for supporting the entablature originally ringed the court, and to your right on the northern side of the court is a bas-relief depicting Jupiter wearing a wheat-sheaf headdress, found in a nearby spring on the outskirts of Baalbek. Around the 5th century, Christians converted the courtyard to a church, and during the Islamic era walls were constructed, turning it into a Qalaa or fortress. The **Great Court** further along was built sometime during the 2nd century and covers a vast area of some 134m by 112m. This part of the site was where worshippers witnessed the sacrifice of animals and it is extremely decorative, with a variety of *exedrae* (recesses) adorned with niches and statues. It was once fronted by 84 columns of Egyptian granite. Dominating the central area is the altar and a tower from where pilgrims were afforded panoramic views of the spectacle of sacrifice. Two pools formerly used for ritual washing were destroyed in the latter period of the 4th century during the construction of a Christian basilica, but intricate carvings of Cupids and Medusas remain.

Directly in front of the Great Court looms what is perhaps the defining icon of the entire Baalbek site: the **Temple of Jupiter**. Constructed on a podium 7m above the surrounding courtyard, only six of the original 54 columns remain, but they give no doubt as to the grandeur and artistry of ancient Rome. At 22m, and measuring 2.2m wide, they are the tallest Roman columns in the world, built with some of the largest hewn stones ever made. In the courtyard below the podium, some fallen entablature in the form of cornices with lions' heads and water spouts provides further evidence of Rome's fine craftsmanship. Across the courtyard from the Temple of Jupiter is the smaller (though still larger than the Parthenon in Athens) and beautifully preserved **Temple of Bacchus**. It was built during the 2nd century and completed in CE150, and is dedicated to the Roman god of wine, though some authorities have suggested that it may in fact be more accurately dedicated to Venus. Flanked on all sides by a number of 19m-tall Corinthian columns, one of which leans precariously against one of the exterior walls, a casualty of one of the many earthquakes that rumbled around Baalbek over the years, the temple was built over a much earlier Phoenician structure. It is entered after walking up the stairway's 33 steps where a magnificent and extremely ornamental entrance door awaits, with its fallen keystone and stunning friezes of poppies, vine leaves and wheat, the subject matter for many an artist's work over the years. Inside, the inner temple, once a theatre for drinking, drug-taking and other scenes of debauchery, is richly and stunningly decorated with columns, niches and friezes. The nearby small museum is housed underground beneath the Mamluk tower, and within its dark confines it houses some quite engaging Roman artefacts: sarcophagi from the 2nd and 3rd centuries, an eagle symbolising life, and the basalt door of a tomb.

The main **Baalbek museum** (✆ *08 370 520*; ⏰ *10.30–17.00 daily; admission free, included with site entrance ticket*), however, is located in tunnels beneath the Temple of Jupiter. This elongated underground museum first opened in 1998 to commemorate the 100th anniversary of the visit to Baalbek of German emperor Wilhelm II, and is worth a look in to appreciate the history of the complex from the Bronze, Hellenistic and Roman eras, as well as learn details of the techniques used in construction of the temples. There is also a range of statues and other artefacts related to the site on display. A pictorial representation of life in Baalbek is provided in the form of excellent images in a permanent exhibition by the renowned German photographer Herman Burckhardt.

The **Temple of Venus**, a short distance south of the main ticket office, is definitely worth a look for its fine stonework. Despite being dwarfed in size by Baalbek's other temples, its cupola roof with a series of columns and niches depicting doves and seashells make it a charming little feature. In the Byzantine era, the temple was turned into a church and dedicated to the Christian martyr Saint Barbara. Folklore has it that Barbara's father, angered at her Christian beliefs, murdered her but was struck by lightning, as if by divine intervention, and engulfed in flames for his

STONE ME!

About 1km from the main Baalbek site, in a quarry that once supplied the stones for construction of the Baalbek complex on Sheikh Abdullah Hill, lies the biggest cut stone in the world. It is known as the Hajar al-Hubla or 'Stone of the Pregnant Woman', so called because, according to local legend, any woman who touches it will experience an increase in fertility. This huge monolithic limestone block weighs more than 1,000 tonnes and measures some 21.5m x 4.8m x 4.2m, and would have required more than 40,000 labourers to move it. Originally destined as the base rock for the Temple of Jupiter, it is an enigma why the stone was never used and it has remained *in situ* for over 2,000 years. If it wasn't for the efforts of 52-year-old local resident Abdul Nabi al-Afi, the stone would probably have disappeared into oblivion or, more accurately, under a pile of rubbish. In the early 1990s, Mr al-Afi, dismayed at the amount of household waste and other garbage that was filling the quarry, decided to undertake a one-man mission, to preserve the site for posterity. Since that time, he has managed to tidy up and prettify the quarry, construct a short footpath down to the structure, and open a small gift shop selling books and other memorabilia in order to support his charitable endeavours. Although the stone won't win any awards for its aesthetic qualities, it is free to visit and there is a certain caché for visitors in having someone take your picture whilst standing on top of the stone next to the Lebanese national flag.

treacherous act. In the English village of Stourhead in Wiltshire, a replica of the temple stands in the grounds of a country manor, built by its 19th-century owner.

Baalbeck International Festival (*Doursoumian Bldg, Osman Ben Affan St, Beirut;* \ *01 373 150/1/2;* m *03 041 006/7;* e *baalbeck@baalbeck.org.lb; www. baalbeck.org.lb*) Founded in 1955 and held annually during the months of July and August, the Baalbeck International Festival is the oldest and most impressive festival in the entire Middle East. Held within the historic courtyards of Baalbek's Roman temples amidst atmospheric and dramatic lighting displays, the festival serves up a full gamut of performing arts – ballet, classical music, jazz, opera, pop and rock music, together with a variety of theatrical productions. Since its inaugural season in 1956, the festival has played host to an eclectic range of national and international artists, including Lebanese icon Fayrouz, Duke Ellington, Ella Fitzgerald, Joan Baez, Rudolf Nureyev and the Bolshoi Ballet, the Royal Ballet and Dame Margot Fonteyn, the Berlin Philharmonic Orchestra, pop sensation Mika, jazz musician Eliane Elias and famed *Oud* artist Marcel Khalifé to name but a few. Visit the festival website for details of the current annual programme of events, transportation to and from the festival and accommodation options, plus details of prices and how to book tickets to the performances.

HERMEL

At around 140km from Beirut and 50km north of Baalbek, the predominantly Shi'ite town of Hermel is the Bekaa Valley's most far-flung rural outpost, sitting at some 700m above sea level and only a few kilometres from the Syrian border. For the area's inhabitants, agriculture is the mainstay of the local economy, with the region having remained relatively insulated from the conflicts and modernisation programmes that have engulfed many areas of the country. It therefore retains a rugged and wild appearance evinced in the landscape as well as in the traditional ways of life of its rural population, and remains perhaps Lebanon's poorest region in almost all of the indices used to measure development. This, coupled with its relative geographical isolation and lack of a well-developed transport infrastructure, means that the area is one of the least-visited places in the country.

Although not on the mainstream tourist trail, Hermel is still well worth a visit for a number of interesting monuments, including perhaps Lebanon's most puzzling, the Hermel Pyramid, whose origin remains the subject of scholarly debate to this day. Meandering past Hermel is the north-flowing Orontes River (Nahr al-Assi), making this area the country's premier location for water-based activities such as canoeing and kayaking. If you are intending to engage in any of these or the range of other outdoor adventure activities that are popular in the area, Hermel is a great place to stay for a night or two to sample an alternative slice of Lebanese life in authentic and traditional surroundings, far removed from the urbane existence of the capital. Otherwise, Hermel makes for an interesting trip extension if visiting the archaeological sites at Aanjar and Baalbek. Combining a visit to this area with one of the activity- and ecotourism-based organisations listed on pages 273–4 can also enhance the experience. Despite the area's attractions, however, given the ongoing hostilities in Syria and Hermel's proximity to the Syrian border, it would perhaps be prudent to check on the current security situation in the town and environs to ascertain whether the area is safe to visit as Hermel has in the past been targeted with bomb attacks as a result of the spillover from the ongoing war in Lebanon's larger neighbour.

GETTING THERE The sights and activities below are somewhat remote from the main town of Baalbek, being in the far north of the region; but, if you have your own vehicle, they make an excellent addition to an extended tour of the Bekaa Valley region. If driving from Baalbek, take the main road north towards Hermel and, when you reach Ras Baalbek, turn left and the Hermel Pyramid is about 10km further on. If you don't have your own car, minivans ply the route north for around LBP7,000, but expect to pay at least US$50–60 for a return trip by taxi from Baalbek to Hermel, which takes around 1½–2 hours.

WHERE TO STAY The accommodation options below all offer a completely different lodging and travel experience from anywhere else in the country in an area well off the beaten tourist track. This area is remote and wild, inhabited by Bedouin mountain dwellers and grazing sheep and goats, giving an insightful look at an alternative, relatively raw Lebanon, far removed from the ongoing urban development and sprawl of the city. These places can also organise a range of outdoor pursuits in the local and surrounding areas. In all cases it is best to phone ahead to book your accommodation in advance.

Al Kwakh Eco-lodge Hermel; m 03 454 996 or 70 359 659; www.tarhal.org/kwakh. Al Kwakh – which means 'huts' in English – is an eco-initiative by a collective of local women. Accommodation comprises 3 old traditional houses with mud chimneys & ceilings made of juniper wood, & the Bedouin-style bedding is made by the women themselves of goat hair. The lodge has capacity for 20–30 people & all meals are prepared by the women's co-operative. A variety of local outdoor pursuits are also arranged such as hiking, rafting, rock climbing, & even herb picking with the local women themselves. Hiking trips with a guide cost around US$7. **$**

Lazzab Club Hermel; m 03 797 569 or 71 146 915; e info@lazzab.net; www.lazzab.net. This eco-lodge is situated 20km from Hermel with mud-hut accommodation equipped with toilets & hot water. Meals are provided using ingredients from the local area. If you have your own tent, camping is charged at US$5 for a pitch per night. Lazzab also arranges 1–3-day hiking trips in & around Hermel with knowledgeable guides. If you do not have your own transport, Lazzab also runs a club bus, which, for US$5pp, will collect you from Hermel town & bring you back again after your stay. **$**

OTHER PRACTICALITIES

$ BLC Bank Shahine Centre, facing Seray Bldg, Main Rd; ✆08 201 771/2; e hermelbranch@ blcbank.com; www.blcbank.com; ⏲ 08.15–13.30 Mon–Fri, 08.30–noon Sat. 24hr ATM.
$ SGBL Bank Main Rd; ✆08 200 600, dial 1274 within Lebanon; www.sgbl.com.lb; ⏲ 08.30–13.30 Mon–Fri, 08.30–noon Sat. ATM.

Post office Main Rd, c200m from BLC Bank; ✆08 200 403; www.libanpost.com; ⏲ 08.00–17.00 Mon–Fri, 08.00–13.30 Sat
Al Assi Hospital Main Rd; ✆08 200 795 or 08 200 238
Lebanese Red Cross ✆140, 08 200 023, 08 200 098; www.redcross.org.lb

ACTIVITIES

Assi Club Hermel Chouaghir, Hermel; administrative office: 2nd Fl, Mkari Bldg, Makdissi St, Hamra, Beirut; m 70 755 131; e info@assirafting.com; www.assirafting. com. For the adventurous, this club runs rafting trips for both the beginner & advanced rafter along a 7km stretch of the Assi (Orontes) River, Lebanon's premier rafting area. Canoeing &

kayaking, together with activities such as basketball, fishing & volleyball, are also offered along with camping. For the less active, the club also runs historical tours of the Hermel region which take in Hermel Pyramid & the other ancient monuments that dot the area.
Aquassi Assi Village, Hermel; m 03 791 866 or 70 777 632; e info@aquassi.com; www.

aquassi.com. Excellent-value canoeing, rafting & camping trip provider. See website for their current activities & prices.

Tarhal 4th Fl, Youssef Centre, Fata St, Badaro, Beirut; \01 382 305; m 03 454 996; e ecotourism@mada. org.lb; www.tarhal.org. They run an expanding network of eco-lodges & guesthouses throughout the Hermel & Akkar districts at extremely competitive prices with lots of outdoor activities such as cycling, fishing, hiking & rafting on offer.

Vamos Todos m 03 917 190 or 79 115 001; e info@vamos-todos.com, mark.aoun@gmail.com; www.vamos-todos.com. This excellent ecotourism club (*Vamos todos* is Spanish for 'Let's all go!') organises hiking events, as well as a range of other eco-friendly activities all around the country.

WHAT TO SEE

Hermel Pyramid (Qamou el-Hermel) This isolated, but by no means forlorn-looking structure, also known as 'God's Pyramid' remains something of a mystery, though many legends and stories abound about just why it is here. The most likely explanation, given its similarity to tombs discovered in Palmyra (Tadmor) in Syria, is that it is the tomb of a Syrian prince dating from the 1st or 2nd century BCE. This 27m-tall column has a black marble base with two distinct, cube-shaped stone blocks, topped by a pyramid. It is decorated with a range of friezes, which show hunting scenes of deer, a wounded boar and wolves attacking a bull. Some fervent restoration carried out by the Department of Antiquities is clearly visible

---

ARAK

Lebanon's national drink, *arak*, tends to evoke that Marmite moment – you'll either love it or hate it. This potent aniseed-flavoured alcoholic grape tipple – typically made from Lebanon's indigenous Obaideh or Marweh grape varieties and green aniseed imported from the village of Hina in Syria on the slopes of Mount Hermon – has relatives all over the Mediterranean and beyond. It is known as *pastis* in France, *ouzo* in Greece, *sambuca* in Italy, *ojen* in Spain and *raki* in Turkey. *Arak* is most often drunk to accompany a *mezze* meal because it refreshes the taste buds when drunk after each dish, leaving the palate refreshed for the next course. Although dilution of the final concoction is a matter of personal preference, *arak* is usually drunk '*tilt bi tiltain*', as they say in Lebanon, meaning one-third *arak* to two-thirds water, with ice added last and perhaps a few fresh leaves of mint for additional flavouring. The addition of water, to help dilute the high alcohol content, causes the *arak* to cloud over, giving a milky-white colour: because aniseed oil is soluble in alcohol but not in water, this results in an emulsion, which is why *arak* is also sometimes referred to as 'lion's milk', a reference also to the masculinity and strength of the drink, which can also be used to embellish the flavouring of many a fish and meat dish. Literally translated from the Arabic, *arak* means a rather unpalatable 'sweat' from the still, basically what is left over after the three-stage distillation process involving heating, cooling, the removal of toxins and the production of a near pure form of alcohol, which is then aged in often traditional clay amphorae or containers. The ageing process of the final mixture is typically around 12 months but it can take up to five years to produce the best varieties. Available all over the country by the glass, or in quarter-, half- and full-litre bottles, the best brands are invariably produced in the vineyards of the Bekaa Valley, most notably Kefraya, Ksara, Domaine des Tourelles and Massaya, with the latters' El Massaya *arak* available in their unique slim, stylish blue bottles, which can make excellent gifts to take home.

on the sides of the monument. Visible for miles around, this ancient remnant is located some 50km north of Baalbek and 6km south of the town of Hermel.

Deir Mar Maroun About 6km southwest of the Hermel Pyramid 200m above the source of the Orontes River, are a series of caves interlinked by stone stairways and dominated by the Monastery of Mar Maroun or 'Caves of the Monks'. It was founded by St Maroun, founder of the Maronite sect and used as a place of sanctuary for Maronites fleeing from Emperor Justinian's war on heresy in the 7th century.

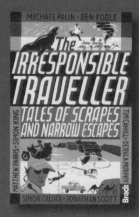

8

The Chouf Mountains

Telephone code 05

The Chouf Mountains, some 40km southeast of Beirut, lie within the southern governorate or *muhafazat* of Mount Lebanon. Although only an hour or so away from the capital, this region maintains a distinct geographical, cultural and ethnic identity quite unlike any other in the country. Its lush green vegetation, undulating terrain and cultivated fields of apples, grapes and olives is dotted with numerous picturesque towns and villages, making the Chouf one of the most scenic places in Lebanon. This is also the heartland of both the Maronite Christian and Druze communities; breakaway religious groups who have long made the area their home, fleeing persecution and sectarian rivalry. They have held steadfast to their traditions and it is here, especially in the towns of Baakline and Moukhtara, that you will see the eccentric moustaches, white skullcaps and baggy *sherwal* trousers worn by Druze men, and the white veil worn by women.

During the Ottoman era, the Chouf was the seat of power, given quasi-autonomous status by the Sublime Porte in Istanbul, first to the Druze Maan family, who first came to Lebanon c1120 from Mesopotamia (modern-day Iraq) fleeing persecution and settling in the Chouf Mountains and later the Sunni Shihab dynasty who administered the feudal kingdom from their capitals at Deir al-Qamar and Beiteddine respectively on behalf of Istanbul. Rule by the two emirs – the cosmopolitan and Machiavellian Fakhreddine Maan II (1572–1635; box, pages 284–5) and the more autocratic Bashir Shihab II (1767–1850) – brought a veneer of unification to the Christian and Druze orders, for a time at least; and they are today widely regarded as nationalist icons in Lebanese history. Nowadays, the nearby town of Moukhtara serves as the base for Druze power under the leadership of the charismatic Walid Jumblatt (b1949; box, page 291). Despite its present-day tranquility, the Chouf has seen its fair share of conflict over the years, most notably the 1860 clashes between Christians and Druze and more recently during the so-called War of the Mountain during Lebanon's civil war (1975–90). Today, however, visitors to the area will be most struck by the well-preserved Ottoman-era architecture in the peaceful town of Deir al-Qamar (pages 280–6) with many examples from the reign of Fakhreddine Maan II, whilst the opulent Beiteddine Palace (pages 287–90), the legacy of the emir Bashir Shihab II, also houses a remarkable collection of Byzantine-era mosaics. For outdoor and nature lovers, too, the Chouf makes a welcome respite from the hustle and bustle of Beirut and in addition to its many hiking and trekking possibilities is home to the Chouf Cedar Reserve, Lebanon's largest nature reserve containing a quarter of the country's cedar trees, as well as a wide range of other flora and fauna. A number of local tour operators offer day trips to the Chouf if you prefer a more organised visit (pages 136–40).

Despite a sign indicating otherwise in Deir al-Qamar, there was no tourist office in the Chouf at the time of writing, but useful and informative brochures

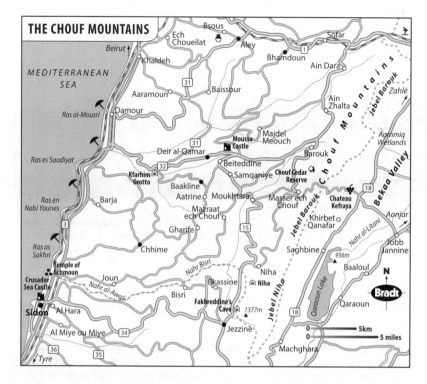

THE CHOUF MOUNTAINS

Bsous
Ech Choueilat
Beirut
Khaldeh
Aley
Sofar
Bhamdoun
Ain Dara

MEDITERRANEAN SEA

31
Baissour
Aaramoun
Ain Zhalta
Zahlé
Ras al-Mousri
Damour

Ras es Saadiyat
Deir al-Qamar
31
Moussa Castle
Majdel Meouch
Barouk

32
Beiteddine
Chouf Cedar Reserve

Kfarhim Grotto
Samqaniye

Baakline
Ras en Nabi Younes
Barja
Aatrine
Moukhtara
Masser ech Chouf
Chateau Kefraya
18

Mazraat ech Chouf
Khirbet Qanafar
Aanjar

Gharife
15

Chhime
Saghbine
956m
Jobb Jannine
Baaloul
N

Ras as Sakhri
Temple of Echmoun
Joun
Nahr Bisri
Niha
Bradt

Crusader Sea Castle
Nahr al-Awali
Bkassine
Niha

Sidon
Bisri
Fakhreddine's Cave
1377m
Qaraoun Lake
Qaraoun

Al Hara
Jezzine
0   5km
0   5 miles

Al Miye ou Miye
34
Machghara

36
35
Tyre

and pamphlets on the sites and towns covered in this chapter can be obtained from the Ministry of Tourism's Hamra office in Beirut (page 135).

DAMOUR

This coastal Christian town, birthplace of internationally renowned Lebanese costume designer Elie Saab (b1964), is the first settlement of interest *en route* to the Chouf, and about 20km south from Beirut just before where the highway turns east towards the village of Kfarhim and its small grotto, and the towns of Deir al-Qamar and Beiteddine. Once known for its silk factories, olive groves, orange trees and sandy beach, Damour was the scene of fierce fighting in World War II during an Australian operation as part of its Syrian–Lebanese offensive in 1941. The town hit the headlines for even more notorious reasons in 1976, during the tit-for-tat killings between Christians and Muslims which ensued in the early stages of the civil war. Following a Christian Phalangist massacre of 1,500 Palestinians in the Beirut district of Quarantina, Palestinians responded by executing around 150 Christians in Damour, largely destroying the town itself and proceeding to install their own people – victims of another atrocity at the Tel al Za'atar refugee camp in Beirut – into the abandoned Christian homes.

GETTING THERE Although the main towns and sites of interest to the visitor in the Chouf are clustered fairly close together, the region is not particularly well linked or served by public transport and becomes even less so come nightfall, when buses become almost non-existent and taxis equally scarce. This means that, if you are intending to explore this area in depth, you would be advised to hire a car or use a taxi to get to and around the region. Buses that do travel to the Chouf depart from the northern end of Beirut's Cola intersection [127 E7] and pass through or close by Damour, Kfarhim, Baakline, Beiteddine, Barouk and Moukhtara. At the time of writing there were no buses serving the town of Deir al-Qamar. From Cola a bus to Damour (*c30 minutes*) and Kfarhim Grotto (*c50 minutes*) will cost LBP2,500 and drop you off in the town and outside the grotto *en route* to Baakline. A taxi from Beirut to Damour or Kfarhim will set you back around US$40–50.

WHERE TO STAY, EAT AND DRINK As principally a region for beach and watersport enthusiasts, Damour is best visited as a day trip for the beach and clubs such as the Oceana resort (see below). However, the town does have a handful of resort-type hotels and eateries offering standard fare, with food also available at the beach clubs that dot the area. But with Damour's proximity to Beirut and the main Chouf towns of Deir al-Qamar and Beiteddine your LBP would be better spent in those places that offer a much more authentic dining and sleeping experience compared with what is on offer in Damour.

OTHER PRACTICALITIES Damour is extremely limited as regards banks and many other practical utilities for the visitor, so you would be advised to do any essential banking either from Beirut or from one of the following Chouf towns prior to journeying here. There's a **post office** at the Coral petrol station (\ *05 601 678; www.libanpost.com;* ◷ *08.00–22.00 daily*).

WHAT TO SEE AND DO Although Damour is an unremarkable town from a sightseeing perspective, this area is dotted with beach clubs and you will see their advertising hoardings as you travel south along the coast road towards the Chouf. One of the most popular of these for indulging in endless partying amid its banana orchard setting is the huge 25,000m² **La Suite Oceana Beach Resort** (*off the main Damour road;* m *03 998 080, 03 191 515;* e *lasuiteoceana@live.com;* f *la.suite.oceana.beach.resort/info;* ◷ *09.00–19.00 Mon–Thu, 09.00–01.00 Fri–Sun; admission: adults LBP30,000 Mon– Fri, LBP35,000 Sat & Sun, children aged 8–12 LBP12,000 Mon–Fri, LBP15,000 Sat & Sun, children under 7 free*), which proclaims itself to be 'Lebanon's ultimate destination for beach lovers'. It can accommodate around 700 hedonist sun worshippers, boasts four swimming pools, a number of fast-food outlets, coffee shops, walking trails and a children's nursery, and come nightfall transforms itself into a clubbers' paradise belting out house and techno sounds. For a comprehensive listing of other nearby and countrywide beach resorts, have a look at the **LebBeach** website (*www.lebbeach.com*).

Kfarhim Grotto (*c2km from Deir al-Qamar, Kfarhim Village;* \ *05 720 500;* m *03 380 588, 03 388 048;* e *info@kfarhimgrotto.com, kfarhimgrotto@hotmail. com, waelgbk@yahoo.com; www.kfarhimgrotto.com;* ◷ *winter 08.30–16.00 daily, summer 08.00–19.00 daily; admission: adults LBP15,000, children under 10 LBP10,000, students LBP5,000*) Around 11km from Damour, this grotto was discovered only in 1974 and opened for the first time a year later. Small and intimate, the grotto has neither the scale nor jaw-dropping appeal of its far more impressive relative at Jeita, and although the town itself possesses no other sites of note to detain the visitor, Kfarhim's limestone stalactites and stalagmites are still worth a visit and are quite nicely lit in colourful hues. The grotto houses a souvenir shop upstairs selling a wide range of postcards, jewellery items, woodcarvings, glassware and other handicrafts. There is also a small café outside the grotto serving drinks and snacks together with another small shop selling

8

ornamental souvenirs. Their website has self-drive directions if you are arriving by car from Beirut or Beiteddine.

DEIR AL-QAMAR

This overwhelmingly Christian Maronite town, with a small number of Greek Catholics, was where the ancient Phoenicians worshipped the moon, but it is Deir al-Qamar's more recent history that tells the story of modern Lebanon. With its red-roofed buildings, stone houses, cobbled walkways and serene atmosphere, the town became the capital of Mount Lebanon in 1590, following the emir Fakhreddine Maan II's decision to move it from Baakline owing to a chronic water shortage in his hometown. The well-watered Deir al-Qamar, fed by innumerable springs, remained the capital until the 18th century, when the Shihab dynasty moved the capital to Beiteddine. Despite the decline in the town's political stature from the 19th century, Deir al-Qamar retains the rich legacy of its medieval architecture in one of the most charming and best-preserved areas in the whole country.

GETTING THERE As no buses travel to Deir al-Qamar itself, one option is to take a bus from the northern section of Cola intersection in Beirut going to Kfarhim (*LBP2,500*) and from Kfarhim take a taxi (*LBP10,000–20,000*) the remainder of the way, though they are not plentiful. A more expensive alternative would be to take a taxi to Deir al-Qamar from Beirut and ask the driver to wait for a couple of hours or so while you visit the town and perhaps have a bite to eat, and then drive you back to Beirut. This should cost cUS$100–120 for the return trip.

GETTING AROUND Deir al-Qamar is small, making the town easily (and best) explored on foot with all of its main sites and amenities such as cafés, restaurants and stores pretty much adjacent to each other.

WHERE TO STAY *Map, opposite*
At the time of writing there was only one hotel in the town of Deir al-Qamar itself, with an additional accommodation option only 1km away on the outskirts of town, on the road leading to Moussa Castle and Beiteddine.

 Deir al Oumara (12 suites) c500m downhill by the signposted path opposite Germanos Pharmacy; 🌙05 511 557/8; m 71 119 935; e mycontact@deiraloumara.com; www.deiraloumara.com. Opened in 2012, this hotel is located within a lovely old heritage building dating back to 1827 & the brainchild of emir Bashir Shihab II. It was converted into a school in 1908 &, at the time of writing, is now the town's sole hotel. Still a venue of some character, it has lovely, spacious, clean rooms & welcoming staff, & its superb Soufrat restaurant serves local cuisine whilst the terrace offers superlative mountain vistas over Deir al-Qamar and the nearby villages of Beiteddine & Baakline. All rooms have TV & are fan-cooled in summer. B/fast inc, free Wi-Fi. **$$$$**

La Bastide (21 rooms) Around 1km from Deir al-Qamar on the main road to Beiteddine; 🌙05 505 320, 05 505 848; m 03 643 010; e bastideir@hotmail.com. In a good location with picturesque surroundings. The rooms are all en suite, spacious & clean with TV & internet, but feel a little sparse & don't quite match the character of the very homely & cosy reception area. B/fast inc. **$$**

WHERE TO EAT AND DRINK *Map, opposite*
In addition to the eateries below, there are a few shops selling take-away snacks, fruit and vegetables, and such like, just across the road from the Funky Monkey Café.

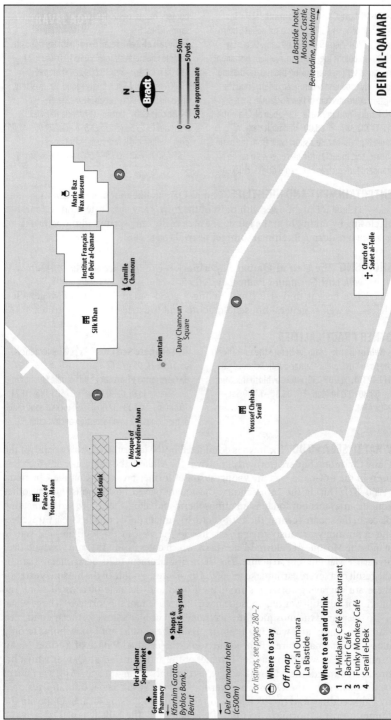

DEIR AL-QAMAR

La Bastide hotel,
Moussa Castle,
Beiteddine, Moukhtara →

**Palace of
Younes Maan**

Old souk

**Mosque of
Fakhreddine Maan**

Silk Khan

**Institut Français
de Deir al-Qamar**

**Marie Baz
Wax Museum**

Camille
Chamoun

Fountain

Dany Chamoun
Square

**Youssef Chehab
Serail**

Church of
Sadet al-Telle

Deir al-Qamar
Supermarket

Germanos
Pharmacy

Shops &
fruit & veg stalls

Kfarhim Grotto,
Byblos Bank,
Beirut ↓

Deir al Oumara hotel
(c500m) ↓

N

Bradt

0 ─── 50m
0 ─── 50yds
Scale approximate

For listings, see pages 280–2

Where to stay

Off map
Deir al Oumara
La Bastide

Where to eat and drink
1 Al-Midane Café & Restaurant
2 Bachir Café
3 Funky Monkey Café
4 Serail el-Bek

The Chouf Mountains   DEIR AL-QAMAR

8

281

✕ Al-Midane Café & Restaurant Main Sq; ☏ 05 511 651; m 03 763 768; e rafatabet@hotmail.com; ⊕ Jun–Sep 10.00–03.00 daily, Oct–May 10.00–midnight Tue–Sun. An excellent restaurant in a great setting overlooking the square, making for lovely Lebanese & European dining amid the history & architecture of Deir al-Qamar. $$$$

✕ Funky Monkey Café Pl Nabeh al-Chalout; m 03 782 382; ⊕ 08.00–midnight daily. A small & pleasant café a short walk from the main square, this friendly little place serves a range of standard fare such as hot & cold drinks, chicken burgers, pizzas, pasta dishes, salads doughnuts & sandwiches. $$

✕ Serail el-Bek Serail Bldg, Main Sq, opposite Camille Chamoun statue; ☏ 05 510 006; m 71 181 023; ⊕ Apr–Sep 10.00–22.00 Mon–Fri, 10.00–midnight Sat & Sun. A good-value eatery, specialising in tasty Lebanese *mezze*. $$

✕ Bachir Café Outside the Marie Baz Wax Museum (☏ *05 505 353;* ⊕ *Mar–Oct 09.00–23.00 daily*) selling basic fare such as hot dogs (*LBP4,500*), waffles (*LBP4,000*) and ice cream. $

ENTERTAINMENT AND NIGHTLIFE Deir al-Qamar, like much of the Chouf, is not really a place for night owls with most of the town's few bars, cafés and restaurants all closing by midnight at the latest. The area really only springs into nocturnal *joie de vivre* during its annual summer festival (page 286).

SHOPPING The **Deir al-Qamar Supermarket** (*nr entrance to Deir al-Qamar, a short walk past Germanos Pharmacy;* ☏ *05 505 166;* m *03 293 928* ⊕ *07.30–22.00 daily*) is a decent mid-size store, selling a good range of fruit and vegetables, cheese, as well as general household goods and toiletries.

OTHER PRACTICALITIES

$ Byblos Bank Main Rd before the entrance to the town, nr Deir al-Qamar public school; ☏ 05 511 173/4, 01 205 050; www.byblosbank.com; ⊕ 08.30–17.30 Mon–Fri, 08.30–13.00 Sat. 24hr ATM.

✚ Lebanese Red Cross ☏ 140 (emergency), 05 505 803, 05 473 637

✚ Germanos Pharmacy Bd Camille Chamoun, nr entrance to Deir al-Qamar; ☏ 05 505 196; m 71 297 000; ⊕ 07.30–22.00 daily. Stocks a good range of medicines & a small selection of cosmetics.

WHAT TO SEE AND DO The town is dominated by the large and central expanse of the **Dany Chamoun Square** (formerly known as the Midan), the namesake of which was born in the town and was the youngest son of former president Camille Chamoun (1900–87). During the 16th century, the square played host to jousting and other equestrian events but today is an atmospheric and altogether more sedate meeting place. In the square's centre, the 19th-century fountain once provided weary travellers the opportunity to satisfy their thirst. Just to the west of the fountain and square stands the **Mosque of Fakhreddine Maan**, which dates from 1493, and was built over an earlier Mamluk-era structure. The slight displacement of its octagonal minaret is the result of a severe earthquake in 1630. On the western side of the mosque's exterior there are engravings of verses from the Koran and the date of construction. The interior of this still-working mosque has a high stone roof supported by a large pillar.

To the rear of the mosque, the once-bustling **cobbler's souk** formerly contained numerous shops and working artisans plying their trade, but is now home to only a handful of small stores. Behind the souk, the original **Palace of Younes Maan** (Younes Maan was commander-in-chief of the army in Deir al-Qamar whilst his brother Fakhreddine Maan II was exiled in Italy from 1613 to 1618) was burnt to the ground by the Ottoman governor (*pasha*) Yusuf Sayfa, but later restored by Fakhreddine, and merits a look to see its fine, imposing façade. Opposite the fountain on the northern section of the square is the **Silk Khan** (Qaisariyah), constructed by Fakhreddine Maan II in 1595, and built in the traditional khan style with a central fountain, open-air courtyard and surrounding arches, formerly used by merchants to sell their silk wares which was once a thriving industry. Today, part of the *khan* is home to the active **Institut Français de Deir al-Qamar** (**French Cultural Centre**) (✆ *05 510 016;* e *deirelqamar@if-liban.com; www.institutfrancais-liban.com;* ⊕ *08.30–13.00 & 15.00–18.00 Mon–Fri, 10.00– 13.00 & 15.00–18.00 Sat*), which hosts a variety of mainly free cultural activities including theatre, a library, exhibitions and concerts, plus French language tuition for both adults and children (*LBP215,000 for 40hrs*). Just behind the khan are the remains of a 16th-century synagogue testifying to Fakhreddine Maan II's cosmopolitan reign.

The **Palace of Fakhreddine** lies just to the east of the Silk Khan. Constructed in 1620, once again in typical khan style, it is on the site of his former palace, which in 1614 was burnt to the ground by Yusuf Sayfa in an attempt to rein in Fakhreddine's authority and power. Vowing revenge on Yusuf upon hearing of its destruction whilst in self-imposed exile in Italy, Fakhreddine proceeded to dismantle the yellow stones from Yusuf's own palace in Akkar, northeast of Tripoli, and used some 20,000 defeated soldiers to transport them to Deir al-Qamar to rebuild the palace, which today is home to the **Marie Baz Wax Museum** (*Main Sq;* ✆ *05 511 666;* m *03 756 000;* e *museemariebaz@gmail.com;* ⊕ *Apr–Oct 09.00–19.00 daily, Nov–Mar 09.00–17.00 daily; admission: adults LBP15,000, children under 12 LBP10,000*). Spread over five rooms, this museum contains some 150 waxwork figures, giving a who's who of Lebanese history, with most of the main players – both Lebanese and non-Lebanese – involved in the country's history lined up as if in readiness for a press photocall. From, appropriately, an elderly Fakhreddine Maan II at the entrance, the collection ranges across religious, political and cultural figures such as singer Majida al Roumi, Egyptian presidents Mubarak and Sadat, current Parliamentary Speaker Nabih Berri, Hezbollah Secretary General Sayed Hassan Nasrallah, former prime minister Rafiq Hariri and former president Camille Chamoun, looking like a rock star in his dark sunglasses. There is even a nonchalant-looking Lady Hester Stanhope gazing down in her medieval garb as if ruminating on her impending downfall. In the main square between the museum and the Silk Khan is a **statue** of former president Camille Chamoun, who is probably best known for evoking the 1957 Eisenhower Doctrine in 1958, requesting US military assistance, code named Operation Blue Bat, to quell internal rebellion and pressure from Syria; he was also instrumental in granting women the right to vote for the first time in 1952.

On the southern side of the main square is the site of the **Youssef Chehab Serail**, which dates from the 18th century and whose courtyard, in 1860, was the scene of a massacre, which cost the lives of 1,200 Christians. It now serves as the offices of the local municipality (town hall) and from 08.00 to 14.00 Monday–Friday it is open to visitors to view its splendid rooms and courtyard, entered via its very decorative façade. Just behind and below the Serail and accessed by a flight of steps down is the **Church of Sadet al-Telle (Our Lady of the Hill)** dating from CE451 and built on the site of a much earlier Phoenician temple to the goddess Astarte. The church's contemporary structure, however, dates mainly from the 16th century after the earthquake of CE859 which destroyed most of the church. A much-revered site for pilgrims from both Lebanon and abroad, this church is also the venue for an annual feast devoted to the Virgin Mary which takes place on the first Sunday in August. It is thought that the stone carving of a rosette with a cross above an inverted crescent moon on the original doorway on the southern side of the church may explain why the town's name, Deir

Born in the Chouf town of Baakline in 1572, Fakhreddine Maan II endures as one of the most colourful and important figures who eclipsed the affairs of Mount Lebanon for more than three decades during the Ottoman era. Fakhreddine ascended to his hereditary title of emir, or prince, in c1590, when he was also appointed by the Ottomans to govern the Chouf region, and began carrying out his leadership duties three years later. He is often lauded, albeit controversially, as 'Father of the Nation' and national hero for his attempts to carve out an independent Lebanon free from the Ottoman yoke and, for a time at least, bringing together the Christian, Shi'ite, Sunni and Druze sects in an era when sectarian rivalries were commonplace. The Ottomans, keen to stave off nearly seven decades of internecine rebellions against their rule following their conquest of Arab lands in 1516, mostly led by the Maans, chose Fakhreddine to keep the peace, with due deference to the Porte in Istanbul and by the timely and full payment of taxes. His initial conciliatory stance towards his Turkish overlords, including bribes, saw him rewarded and he was appointed *bey* (governor) of the *sanjaks* (provinces) of Beirut and Sidon in 1593 followed by Safad (in northern Palestine) in 1602. Despite the emir's small stature – his rivals in the Sunni Sayfa clan in Tripoli would mock that he was so short 'an egg could fall from his pocket without breaking' – this would belie his lofty ambitions and in c1608 Fakhreddine formed an alliance with Ferdinando I, the Grand Duke of Tuscany, of the Medici family for military assistance in exchange for economic trading privileges in the Levant. Increasingly alarmed at their vassal's European Christian connections and attempts to usurp their power, the Turks dispatched an overwhelming land and sea force to rein in Fakhreddine. The resourceful prince proved as elusive as the Scarlet Pimpernel and, using a combination of bribery and cunning, managed to acquire two French galleons and one Flemish ship as the Ottomans were closing in. Fakhreddine and his entourage set sail from the port of Sidon on 16 September 1613, arriving at the port of Livorno following a near two-month voyage for what would be a five-year Italian exile where he would be hosted initially by Ferdinando's son, Cosimo II de' Medici, in Florence and latterly by the Duke of Osuna, the Spanish Viceroy of Sicily and then Naples.

The emir's Italian sojourn would prove to be a very edifying one. He observed and was captivated by the economic and cultural mores of Renaissance Florence, in particular the banking and monetary system, the architecture of the Duomo, the free medical system, the judiciary and militia, agricultural practices, Renaissance technology and the orderly nature of Florentine society. The emir's homecoming in September 1618, timed to coincide with Ottoman preoccupation with fighting the Shi'ite Safavids, saw him embark on

al-Qamar, may mean 'monastery of the moon' and that this symbolises the transition from the cult of Astarte's paganism to that of Christianity. This so-called Churches Quarter is also the setting for the nearby 17th-century **Our Lady of the Rosary** church and the small Greek-Catholic church of **Saint Elie** dating from c1741 and housing the tomb of Nicolas Turk, the emir Bashir Shihab II's favourite poet.

Apart from those sites mentioned above, the town is a pretty and charming place to go for a wander around the streets and alleyways to admire the traditional houses, gardens and architecture. There are also superb views over the town and surrounding mountains and valleys if you venture up the hillsides.

a concerted attempt to reclaim power and territories lost to rival clans and the Ottomans during his absence. Fakhreddine strengthened his force of *Soqmans* (mercenary troops) and claimed back Bcharré and Akkar and, in November 1623, defeated the numerically superior forces led by Mustafa Pasha, governor of Damascus, at the Battle of Aanjar in the Bekaa Valley, where, in exchange for the release of the captured Mustafa Fakhreddine and his sons, he regained the *sanjaks* of Safad, Ajlun (in Jordan) and Nablus, and was additionally granted Gaza, the *nahiye* (district) of the Bekaa and the *sanjak* of Lajjun (northern Palestine). Eventually asserting control over what now comprises modern-day Lebanon and beyond, the emir's power peaked c1630 and he extended his influence eastwards into Palmyra (Tadmor) in Syria, where he built the Qalaa ibn Maan (Castle of Fakhreddine) perched on a hilltop overlooking the ruins of this famous Roman city. In addition to his territorial expansion, the prince applied to his homeland much of what he had seen in the Italian city-states. He used Italian artisans and engineers to modernise agricultural practices, and built bridges and waterworks in Beirut and Sidon. He expanded the silk industry for export to Europe and encouraged Maronite Christians to relocate to Druze regions to engage in mulberry tree cultivation for silk production, as well as other agricultural tasks. In Sidon, Fakhreddine built the Khan al-Franj to attract foreign merchants to the Levant, and this, along with other remnants of his reign, can still be seen in his ancestral home of Deir al-Qamar and elsewhere.

A low point for Fakhreddine came in late 1632 when a battle-weary Ottoman force was denied access to spend the winter in the Bekaa Valley. The following year he extended his reach northwards to build forts in Antakya and Aleppo; this was unbearable to Istanbul and Sultan Murad IV (ruled 1623–40) sent his Syrian pashas to defeat Fakhreddine. The prince took flight to a cave near Jezzine, eventually surrendering to the Ottoman admiral Jaffar Pasha and, along with two of his sons, Hussein and Mas'ud, was taken to Istanbul where in all probability Fakhreddine spent the next two years in Yedi Kule (Seven Towers) prison. Fakhreddine was strangled and then beheaded on 13 April 1635 and his head publicly paraded on a pike at the *At meydam* (Hippodrome) as a warning to others of the consequences of rebellion. Mas'ud was also executed, whilst the young Hussein was spared and reared in Istanbul, becoming Ottoman ambassador to India.

Following the emir's death, the Maan dynasty was led by his nephew and then his grandson Ahmad Maan (1658–97); but in the absence of a male heir, the family died out and were succeeded by the Sunni Shihabs. The threat to Ottoman dominance from Lebanon was now over.

Moussa Castle ✳ (*Main Rd between Deir al-Qamar & Beiteddine;* ☎ *05 500 106;* m *03 273 750 or 03 411 144;* e *moussa@moussacastle.com, mcastle@cyberia.net.lb;* www.moussacastle.com; ⊕ *May–Oct 09.00–18.00 daily, Nov–Apr 09.00–17.00 daily; admission: adults LBP15,000, children LBP7,500*) A pleasant and picturesque 2km walk or service taxi ride from Deir al-Qamar on the road east to Beiteddine, this is one of Lebanon's (and possibly the world's) most offbeat and odd attractions. Its history and existence tell the story, not of omnipotent foreign conquest and rule, but of one man's childhood dream and ambition which endured for some 60 years, and reads as a variation on the theme of all those children's fairytales from Cinderella to a Disney animation. The story goes, as every Lebanese knows, that Moussa Abdel Karim al-Maamari as a 14-year-old schoolboy had a dream that he would one day 'turn sand into gold' and live in a castle. His teacher at school, Anwar, caught him in class drawing his embryonic architect's plans for his future creation and proceeded to berate and beat him, telling him he would never live in a castle; whilst the rest of the class, including his first love, Saideh, mocked him. Undeterred by the humiliation, Moussa left school and set to work with his uncle on helping to restore the sea castle in Sidon which, he says, provided the 'yeast' from which his future edifice would rise. Further forays at Beirut's National Museum and the Beiteddine Museum followed. Eventually saving enough money to buy some land, work started on the present castle with the foundation stone laid by his supportive mother, who had always told him that 'everyone holds billions in their brains'. Work was finally completed in 2005, with each brick in the wall, not just one of many as Pink Floyd would have us believe, telling its own story, having been cut and positioned by Moussa's own hands. Inside the castle a tableau of plaster figures give snapshots of scenes from traditional Lebanese life such as silk making, grape picking, corn workers and sheep shearing. On the ground floor is a classroom scene depicting Moussa's teacher about to strike Moussa with a cane, together with scenes of bread making, the Last Supper and *dabke* dancing.

Deir al-Qamar Festival (*Block B, Ivoire Centre, Moussa Nammour St, Sin El Fil, Beirut;* m *70 225 007;* e *info@deqfestival.org; www.deirelqamarfestival.org*) This festival in the town is held annually during the months of July and August, and hosts a wide range of music, concerts, exhibitions and other cultural events and acts as a stage for promotion of the town itself and for emerging and young Lebanese artists and performers. The festival website has a comprehensive downloadable diary of events for each season, and tickets can be purchased from any Virgin Megastore or online from www.ticketingboxoffice.com.

BEITEDDINE

Located 5km from Deir al-Qamar on the opposite side of a deep gorge some 50km from Beirut, Beiteddine (meaning 'House of Faith') is best known as the home of one of Lebanon's must-see attractions – Beiteddine Palace (pages 287–90) – nestled 850m up on a hilltop with outstanding views over the surrounding countryside, and which blends Italian and Arabic architectural design and skills, testifying to the grandeur and power of an important period in Lebanon's modern history. A further reason to visit is that the palace is the location for an annual summer arts and cultural festival within the grounds of the palace, attracting both Lebanese and international talent (page 290).

GETTING THERE Buses and vans from the northern section of Beirut's Cola station [127 E7] travel regularly to Beiteddine and cost LBP3,000, with a journey time of just over 1 hour. The bus will drop you off at the roundabout where a large Christian–Druze war memorial stands, and from there it is a 5-minute service taxi (*LBP2,000*) ride to the entrance of Beiteddine Palace. A taxi from Beirut to Beiteddine should cost around US$50.

WHERE TO STAY

 Mir Amin Palace Hotel (22 rooms & suites) On a hill overlooking Beiteddine Palace; \05 501 315/8; m 03 900 924/5; www. miraminpalace.com; closed 25 Oct–1 Apr annually. Built by emir Bashir Shihab II for his youngest son, Amin, this hotel is like a smaller sibling of the main palace itself, with its rooms of some character every bit as luxurious & boasting all the 5-star facilities you would expect for the price, including a delightful outdoor swimming pool. The hotel also has a couple of good conference rooms with state-of-the-art facilities for the business traveller, & a terrace restaurant with outstanding views of the palace & surrounding countryside. **$$$$$**

⌂ L'Hote Libanais m 03 513 766; www. hotelibanais.com. L'Hote Libanais has a network of B&B accommodation around the country offering a more authentic lodging experience staying with local people & with the added advantage of helping to sustain local communities. Booking can only be done online via their website & a minimum of 48 hrs' notice is usually required. They have a nice B&B option for Beiteddine on their website. **$$$$**

✕ WHERE TO EAT AND DRINK

✕ Mir Amin Palace Hotel ✆ 05 501 315; m 03 900 924; ⏱ noon–23.00 daily, year-round. The hotel's 3 main restaurants, serving excellent Lebanese, international & Italian cuisine, are supplemented by lovely outdoor terrace & garden dining areas affording panoramas of the mountains & Beiteddine Palace below. The best, though not the cheapest, place to eat in town. **$$$$$**

ENTERTAINMENT AND NIGHTLIFE Beiteddine's principal offering is its world-class annual summer festival (page 290), which has attracted audiences in their thousands to the environs of the opulent Beiteddine Palace.

OTHER PRACTICALITIES

✉ **Post office** Ogero Bldg, opposite police station, above Palace; ✆ 05 500 006; www. libanpost.com; ⏱ 08.00–17.00 Mon–Fri, 08.00–13.30 Sat

WHAT TO SEE AND DO

Beiteddine Palace [site plan, page 289] (✆ 05 500 077; ⏱ Apr–Oct 09.00–17.15 Tue–Sun, Nov–Mar 09.00–15.00 Tue–Sun; admission: adults LBP10,000, students LBP3,000) A necessary safe haven away from Deir al-Qamar and from opposition to his despotic rule, which had involved executions and cutting the throats of his opponents, emir Bashir Shihab II's Beiteddine Palace, or House of Faith, was to become the charming and regal-like architectural legacy of Lebanon's final ruling prince. Built over a 30-year period on the site of a former Druze hermitage, using Italian architects and highly skilled artisans from Damascus and Aleppo, construction commenced in 1788, and upon completion remained the emir's place of residence until 1840, when he was forced into exile to Turkey by the British and the Ottomans for forging an alliance with the Egyptian *pasha*, Muhammad Ali, against the Ottomans. Following Bashir's banishment to Turkey, the Ottomans utilised the palace for their own governmental purposes, and during the French Mandate period it served a similar function. When Lebanon achieved independence in 1943, the country's first post-independence president, Bechara al-Khoury (1890–1964), used it as his summer residence, a tradition that continues to this day. In 1947, Bashir's remains were returned to Lebanon from Istanbul, where he had died in 1850, and were buried in a tomb with his first wife, Sitt Shams, in the northwest section of the palace. Designated a historic monument by Lebanon's General Directorate of Antiquities in 1934, the palace has undergone impressive restorations over the years, culminating in 1984 when Walid Jumblatt, the current Druze leader, helped finance renovations and renamed it the Palace of the People. Today it remains a fine example both of 19th-century Lebanese architecture and of one man's quest to create a grandiose and stunning architectural legacy to his rule and supremacy. The emir Bashir II built a further three palaces for his sons in Beiteddine, but only one of these has survived and has been transformed into one of Lebanon's most luxurious hotels, the Mir Amin Palace Hotel (page 286). Depending on your interests, it would be wise to allow at least a couple of hours to view the palace at a leisurely pace in order to appreciate its finely crafted design and luxurious contents. There is ample parking space for vehicles outside the main entrance and there are a couple of male/female public toilets to your right in the first courtyard.

The palace is organised in a number of sections. The first you come to from the main entrance is the **Dar al-Baraniyyeh**, a large, open courtyard some 100m in length and which was once used as a meeting place for guests and horsemen, as well as for other public events. The **Al Madafa** on the right-hand side of the courtyard was formerly a two-storey accommodation block for visitors and, as was the custom of the time, a visitor could stay here and remain anonymous for three days before they were obliged to disclose their identity. One notable guest who did this was the famous French poet and politician Alphonse de Lamartine (1790–1869), who visited in 1833. On the upper level of the Madafa is the **Rashid Karami Archaeological and Ethnographic Museum** – named after Rashid Karami (1921–87) who served eight terms as prime minister of Lebanon at various times between September 1955 and June 1987 – which contains a huge collection of Bronze, Iron-Age and Islamic pottery, together with glass objects from the Roman era, gold jewellery, weaponry and costumes from the period. There is also an overview of the palace design in the form of a scale model.

The tranquil and exquisite middle-court section, or **Dar al-Wousta**, richly decorated with mosaics, marquetry, oriental furnishings and some fine Arabic calligraphy, is accessed via a dual stairway and was home to **Apartments for the Hamadeh Sheikhs**, offices of the emir's ministers, secretaries (**Dar al-Kataba**) and other dignitaries. Ahead, as you enter the main courtyard with a delightful baby fountain at its centre, is **Lamartine's room**. As was traditional in Lebanese architecture, the arcades surrounding the courtyard were left open on one side to allow views of the surrounding countryside and nature's wonders.

The third of the palace's main sections is the inner courtyard known as the **Dar al-Harim**, which comprise the **Lower and Upper Harems** or private lodgings and apartments for Bashir and his family. This portion of the palace also contains some of the most decorative elements in the entire complex. A major highlight is the huge façade of the richly decorated internal gate. Beyond here is the waiting room known as the **room of the column**, on account of the single column that supports the ceiling. The adjacent reception rooms or *salamlik* comprise two levels, and one of these has a fine mosaic floor and walls with marble carvings. Probably one of the most important areas in the palace, this is where Bashir carried out the day-to-day affairs of his administration and handed out justice. On one of the walls is one of his proverbs, which says: 'The homage of a governor towards God is to observe justice, for an hour of justice is worth more than a thousand months of prayer.'

Although closed to visitors at the time of writing, the **kitchens** once fed more than 500 people assembled in the reception area. The maze-like domed **hammam complex (baths)**, with ornate niches, marble floors, basins and fountains, comprised a series of cold (*frigidarium*), warm (*tepidarium*) and hot (*caldarium*) rooms for undressing, relaxation, massage and bathing and whose impressive décor is enhanced when light shafts through the domed ceiling, giving an almost heavenly look and feel. A short walk north of the baths is the site of the final resting place of Bashir's first wife, the **tomb of Sitt Shams**, which also contains Bashir's ashes transported here from Turkey in 1947. Beneath the main and central sections of the palace are the stables, which once kept 600 horses and accommodated 500 of the emir's soldiers, but are now home to a very impressive and eclectic array of

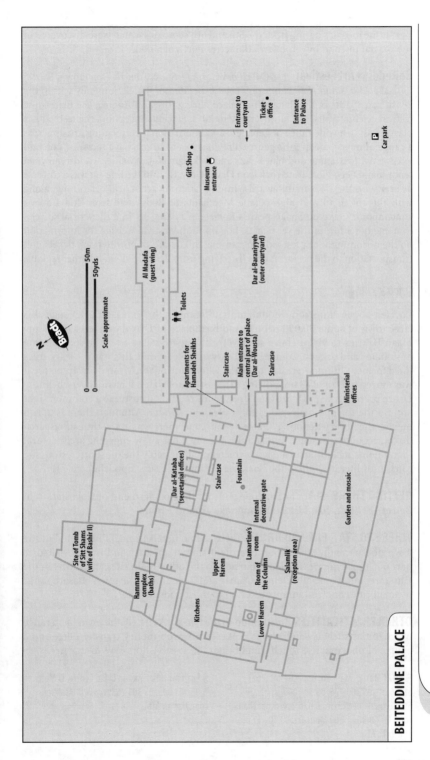

BEITEDDINE PALACE

Byzantine mosaics dating from the 5th and 6th centuries which were discovered in the coastal town of Jiyyeh, a few kilometres north of Sidon.

Beiteddine Art Festival [138 C4] (*Block C, 4th Fl, Starco Centre, Downtown, Beirut;* \ *01 373 430;* e *info@beiteddine.org; www.beiteddine.org*) Held annually within the lavish courtyards of the Beiteddine Palace during July and August, the Beiteddine festival celebrated its 30th anniversary in 2015. Since its inception, the festival has played host to a wide range of Lebanese and international performing artists across a range of music and artistic genres. Previous headline acts have included pop and R&B artist Joss Stone and blues, jazz and folk icon Katie Melua, world-renowned tenor Juan Diego Florez and rock icon David Gray. In 2016 the line-up was as diverse as ever with the UK's multi-award-winning Grammy artist Seal headlining, along with the colourful and high-octane Merchants of Bollywood from India and a contemporary take on Shakespeare's *Romeo and Juliet,* set in a dictatorial society, to name but a few of the year's acts. Log on to the festival website for information on the upcoming year's festival programme, full details of how to book tickets and transportation to the performances if arriving from Beirut, Sidon and other regions.

BAAKLINE

Located about 7km from Moukhtara and 4km south from Deir al-Qamar, this large town of some 30,000 people, and birthplace of Druze prince Fakhreddine Maan II, rises to 900m above sea level with superb views over the surrounding mountains and valleys. Compact and easy to walk around, this was the leafy, tree-lined former Ottoman-era capital of the Chouf during the Maan dynasty, before it was moved to Deir al-Qamar owing to a shortage of water. It has an overwhelming Druze presence, with Druze men dressed in traditional costume a common sight around the town, which makes for a pleasant wander. Although there is a sign outside the library denoting 'Office de tourisme' there was at the time of research no tourist office presence in Baakline. The town has a few engaging architectural monuments including an ancient cemetery, but possibly the most interesting site to visit for literary buffs is the Baakline National Library (opposite).

GETTING THERE Buses to Baakline go from the northern end of Cola station in Beirut [127 E7], cost LBP3,000, and take around 1 hour.

WHERE TO STAY, EAT AND DRINK There are no hotels in Baakline itself, but the town doesn't really warrant an overnight stay in any case and is best visited as part of a day trip or extended excursion to the other main sites and towns in the Chouf region, especially Deir al-Qamar and Beiteddine. The town boasts a range of small cafés and restaurants catering to most budgets.

OTHER PRACTICALITIES In addition to the two banks listed, the town has a range of amenities such as small **shops**, a **Western Union** money transfer office and a couple of **pharmacies**, which should cater for most visitors' day-to-day needs.

$ **BBAC Bank** Main Rd, opposite Total Gas Station; \ 05 300 776, 05 304 060; m 03 265 503; e baakline@bbac.com.lb; www.bbacbank. com; ◷ 08.30–14.00 Mon–Fri, 08.30–13.00 Sat. 24hr ATM.

$ **Fransabank** Akram El Eid Centre, El Marj; \ 05 303 005, 05 301 267; www.fransabank. com. Has an ATM.

WHAT TO SEE AND DO

Baakline National Library (✆ *05 304 050/1*; e *info@baakleenlibrary.com,*
baakleenlibrary@gmail.com; www.baakleenlibrary.com; ⏰ *08.00–18.00 Mon–Fri,*
08.00–16.00 Sat) This is one of the largest libraries in Lebanon, containing some
100,000 books in Arabic, English and French. Built in 1897, it functioned as the former
Grand Serail (Municipality Building) during the Ottoman era, later becoming a police

---

THE HOUSE OF JUMBLATT

The Jumblatt family is one of the most enduring and iconic names in Lebanese
history and politics. Originally descendants of the Kurdish Janbulad clan from
Aleppo in Syria, the Druze Jumblatt dynasty have survived persecution by the
Ottomans and a series of political killings and wars, yet remain at the forefront
of Lebanese affairs and politics. Making the Chouf their home since around
the 17th century, the Jumblatt line has been a powerful force since Ottoman
times. Following the murder of Fouad Jumblatt (1885–1921) in 1921, it was
left to his determined wife, Nazira (1890–1949), to assume the role of head of
the family and lead the Druze community for the next 25 years; a challenging
task for a woman during that period. Following her death, her son Kamal
(1917–77) assumed the helm and founded the Progressive Socialist Party
(PSP) in 1949, seeking to challenge the sectarian nature of Lebanese politics:
'Only a secular, progressive Lebanon freed of confessionalism could ever
hope to survive,' he argued. Educated in the social sciences and law at the
Sorbonne in Paris and at Beirut's Saint Joseph University (USJ), his socialist
leadership made him a revered and key player in the early years of the 1975–
90 Lebanese civil war. Along with Muslims, Pan-Arabic groups and other left-
wing organisations, he forged a coalition known as the National Movement
(NM), which was to become one of the strongest militias in the conflict. His
assassination in 1977 was widely attributed to Syrian involvement. Since
then, Kamal's only son, the litigious Walid Jumblatt (b1949), leads the Druze
cause and heads up the PSP. A graduate of the American University of Beirut
(AUB) and former secondary school history teacher, he has long campaigned
for a rewriting of Lebanon's history books to dispel the bias and myths, he
claims, propagated by Christians; historical accuracy being a precondition for
the country's long-term stability he argues. Known for his butterfly mentality
of constantly shifting allegiances according to the prevailing political tastes
and winds, he was a supporter of Syria after the civil war, but later began to
question their dominance in Lebanese political affairs, and today denounces
the 'terrorist regime' of Bashar al-Assad. He praised Hezbollah for ousting
Israel from south Lebanon, but became concerned that in the aftermath of
war they had an Iranian and Syrian agenda for Lebanon. Walid Jumblatt has
been called a 'rebel with a cause', survived an assassination attempt during
the civil war and says that it is 'down to fate' whether he too will fall prey to
assassins as many of his ancestors have done. His present (second) wife, Nora
(b1955), is daughter of a former Syrian defence minister and the president
of the Beiteddine Art Festival, and his son Taymour (b1982) is earmarked
eventually to succeed him. Responsible for the founding of the annual
Beiteddine Festival and a staunch advocate of preserving the Chouf's natural
environment, Walid Jumblatt returns to his hometown in Moukhtara weekly
to receive his fellow Druze followers and discuss their grievances.

CEDAR OF LEBANON *(CEDRUS LIBANI)*

The legendary cedar tree symbolically percolates through Lebanon: it is emblazoned on the national flag, it is inscribed on the Lebanese currency and postage stamps, it forms part of the logo of numerous banks, educational institutions and NGOs, and it decorates the livery of the national carrier, Middle East Airlines (MEA). It is also the emblem of choice among political parties such as the Phalangist Kataeb, the Lebanese Forces and the Future Movement and has inspired many artistic and other cultural mores. As a figure of longevity and strength, it has numerous references in the Bible, with Psalm 92 proclaiming that 'the righteous shall flourish like the palm tree: he shall grow like a cedar of Lebanon'. In the ancient Sumerian tale c2000BCE of the *Epic of Gilgamesh*, the King of Uruk raids the cedar forests to build his city, infuriating the gods. The 19th-century Romantic poet Alphonse de Lamartine (1790–1869) was so impressed that, in addition to carving his name onto one of the specimens, lauded the cedar tree as 'the most famous natural monuments in the world'. Politically, too, the widely venerated cedar tree has in more recent times come to represent freedom, justice and peace during the country's famous Cedar Revolution in 2005 calling for the withdrawal of Syrian forces from the country in the wake of the killing of former prime minister Rafiq Hariri with the one-million-strong crowd chanting 'Wahde Lubnaniyah, wahde wataniyeh' (one Lebanon, one nation). Outside the country, the cedar tree often serves to embellish the landscape including, famously, the Circle of Lebanon section in London's Highgate Cemetery, where a lone cedar tree is surrounded by numerous mausoleums.

The Lebanese cedar, which is also native to Syria and the Taurus Mountains in southern Turkey, is part of the pine family quartet of trees (Pinaceae), with the Atlas cedar (*Cedrus atlantica*) growing in the Tell Atlas Mountains of Algeria and Morocco, the Deodar cedar (*Cedrus deodara*) native to the western Himalayas and the Cyprus cedar (*Cedrus brevifolia*), which grows in the Troodos Mountains of central Cyprus. Characterised by a broad trunk, which can achieve a diameter of up to 10m, and dense, needle-like leaves, the evergreen Lebanese cedar can attain heights of up to 40m – though the trees are slow growing, and it can take up to 70 years for the tree to complete its greatest vertical growth, after which it gradually assumes its distinctive layered and flattened form. This robust

station and prison, before finally becoming a library in 1987. It's well worth a look inside to examine its collection of new and dusty tomes and the building itself, which has an impressive façade and interior. Internet access is available and there is a special children's section, which hosts a varied summer educational programme for kids.

MOUKHTARA

Around 10km southeast of Beiteddine, Moukhtara is an attractive town for a stroll amid picturesque buildings whilst on a day trip to the Chouf. The main reason for visiting is that this is overwhelmingly the Druze seat of power, dominated by the **Walid Jumblatt house and palace** (℘ 05 310 555; ⊕ 10.00–17.00 Mon–Wed; *admission free*; box, page 291), an imposing fusion of Italian and oriental architectural influences comprising a lovely curved staircase entrance, Roman sarcophagi, hammam and lush gardens complete with waterfall. Every Saturday, between 09.00

Lebanese conifer is highly resistant to extremes of temperature and achieves its optimal growth at high altitudes of between 900m and 1,800m, where the trees can attain a lifespan of thousands of years. As a monoecious tree, the cedar bears both male and female blossoms during summer and autumn respectively.

Since antiquity the Lebanese cedar has served many a utilitarian and ornamental use. This strong and aromatic tree was vital to the economic prosperity of the ancient Phoenicians, who used the wood to build their trading vessels, homes and palaces; the Egyptians used the resin, which they called the 'life of the dead', to embalm their pharaohs; the wood was used also in the construction of King Solomon's Temple in Jerusalem. The Romans, under Emperor Hadrian in CE119, practised an early form of conservation, restricting the felling of the tree for military purposes. In the 20th century, too, the cedar tree came under the axe of the Ottomans, who cut down the trees to use as fuel and as sleepers for the Hejaz Railway, with British forces undertaking similar deforestation during World War II.

Progressive deforestation by successive civilisations and empires over the years has severely depleted the number of cedars in existence, which once covered around 500,000ha of the Lebanese mountains; today they comprise an estimated 2,000ha spread across just six cedar forests, with those in the north of Lebanon at Akkar, Bcharré, Ehden and Tannourine supplemented by those at Jaj, east of Byblos, and the three cedar forests in the Chouf Cedar Reserve containing a quarter of the country's cedars and marking the southern limit of the tree's growth in the country. Fortunately, Lebanon's national emblem is now a fiercely protected species and enshrined in law, with numerous NGOs also working to ensure the cedar's survival through reforestation programmes – a slow process, though well under way. Although man's impact on the trees has now been much reduced compared with antiquity, there is a new threat: climate change. With warmer and shorter winters and the consequent reductions in rain and snowfall, global warming is having a detrimental effect on the tree's growth and ability to regenerate itself.

An excellent pictorial study packed full of fascinating facts, history and quotations about Lebanon's national floral icon, Gabriela Schaub's book *Cedrus Libani: The Cedar of Lebanon* (Beirut: Fine Arts Publishing, 2012) is well worth seeking out.

and noon, the Druze leader holds his weekly surgery here, and residents and visitors alike are welcome to attend. Even if your visit doesn't coincide with Mr Jumblatt's weekly surgeries, it is still possible to tour the public areas of this imposing house during the week, and guards at the entrance will happily show you around for free.

GETTING THERE There are buses and taxis from Cola station in Beirut [127 E7] to Moukhtara and buses from outside Baakline National Library which also serve the town, costing LBP1,500 for the 20-minute journey and stopping just across the road from the Walid Jumblatt house.

CHOUF CEDAR RESERVE

(Chouf Cedar Society Main Office: Park House, Masser Al-Chouf, Village Sq, opposite public gardens; \ *05 350 250/150;* m *03 964 495;* e *info@shoufcedar.*

org, arzshouf@cyberia.net.lb; www.shoufcedar.org; ⊕ *09.30–18.00 daily in summer, 10.00–16.00 daily in winter; admission: adults LBP7,000, students LBP5,000, children free)* To get up close and personal with Lebanon's iconic national symbol, a visit to this extremely scenic protectorate, which was made a protected Biosphere Reserve by UNESCO in July 2005, should be high on your list of things to see and do in the Chouf, and is a good example of Lebanon's burgeoning ecotourism potential. As Lebanon's largest nature reserve, covering some 5% (around 500km^2) of the country's landmass, it represents the most southerly point of Lebanese cedar growth and is home to a quarter of the last-remaining stands of cedar, with some thought to be c2,000 years old.

This delicate ecosystem contains more than 20 species of other tree, including juniper, oak and pine; numerous types of amphibian and reptile, including chameleons, frogs, lizards, snakes, toads and tortoises; more than 500 varieties of plant; and 250 species of bird, such as the Eagle Owl and the Syrian serin, and was designated an Important Bird Area by BirdLife International. Wild mammals such as the gazelle, hyena, Lebanese jungle cat, jackal, red fox, wild boar and wolf continue to roam the undulating landscape, which varies from 1,000m to 2,000m above sea level. The Chouf Cedar Society, who have administered and run the reserve since its opening in 1996 with Druze leader Walid Jumblatt as its president, operates a number of activities including animal spotting, guided walks and hikes, trekking, birdwatching and mountain biking, and snow-shoeing during the winter months. Ecotourism day and overnight packages are also offered by the society at very reasonable prices. The society aims to foster rural development and invigorate local rural economies, and they have an active engagement programme with local communities. You can purchase locally made foodstuffs such as jams and herbs, together with a range of handicrafts, from the huts at any of the reserve's entrances.

The reserve extends over three cedar forests. **Barouk**, covering 400ha, is the largest. **Masser Al-Chouf**, despite being the smallest forest and spread over some 16ha, is home to the most ancient cedars and the so-called Lamartine Cedar, named for the famous French poet who visited here. **Ain Zhalta** comprises around 240ha and is especially recommended for bird- and other animal watchers. Access to the three forests is via one of the four main entrances: Barouk, Masser Al-Chouf, Ain Zhalta and Niha. If you have a rental car, see the reserve's website for detailed self-drive directions to each of these entrances. There are 250km of designated walking trails which snake their way through the reserves inculding short-, medium- and long-distance trails catering for both adults and children of all fitness levels. A particular trail highlight is the c10km **Barouk River Valley Trail**, which commences from the Church of Our Lady in the village of Moukhtara. One of the benefits of this trail, which caters for most fitness levels, is the opportunity to get back to nature whilst seeing a number of relics such as bridges, forts and water mills from the Greek, Roman, Mamluk and Ottoman periods, which testify to the area's importance in the history of the country. As part of their inclusive philosophy, there is also a short, tailor-made **Handicap Trail** of 300m for those with physical disabilities, including wheelchair users, which commences from the Barouk entrance. Some of the trails also link up with sections 17–21 of the Lebanon Mountain Trail (LMT; box, page 235).

GETTING THERE
By bus and taxi Although not quite as frequent as buses to Beiteddine, buses from the northern section of Cola station in Beirut [127 E7] travel to the nearby

town of Barouk (*LBP3,000*). You can also catch a bus from outside the library in Baakline to Barouk for the Cedars, which takes around half an hour and costs LBP1,500. In both cases, the bus will drop you off in the town, from where you can take a taxi to the reserve, though they are not frequent. The reserve itself can also arrange transport if you call ahead; however, this is one place where having your own transport is definitely an advantage.

By car If you have your own car, the following routes, from Beirut, Aley and the Bekaa Valley will all take you to Masser Al-Chouf, the location for the Chouf Cedar Society main office. To reach the Barouk entrance from Masser Al-Chouf just continue heading north on the snaking main road.

From Beirut Take the coast road south and follow the signs to Damour, turning inland shortly after Damour. Then follow the roads to Deir al-Qamar, Beiteddine, Semkanieh, Moukhtara, Boutmeh and finally Masser Al-Chouf.

From Aley Head towards Dahr El Baidar, Ain Zhalta, Barouk and Masser Al-Chouf.

From the Bekaa Valley Start from Chtaura and drive south towards Aammiq. Shortly after this, turn east towards Kefraya and follow this road, which will bring you to Masser Al-Chouf.

TOURIST INFORMATION

i **Ministry of Tourism** Chouf Cedar Society Office, Park House, Masser Al-Chouf, Village sq, opposite public gardens; m 03 178 354; e nahedboudargham.mot@gmail.com; www. mot.gov.lb; ⏱ 08.30–14.00 Mon–Thu; Niha office, Jbaa Village Rd, Niha; m 03 178 354; ⏱ 08.30–11.00 Fri, 08.30–13.00 Sat

TOUR OPERATORS

Adventures in Lebanon m 71 443 323; e info@adventuresinlebanon.com; www. adventuresinlebanon.com. Runs hiking & snowshoeing trips to the reserve among its many other activities.
Footprints Nature Club m 03 876 112; e info@ footprintsclub.com, hiking@footprintsclub.com; www.footprintsclub.com. Runs day hikes to the Chouf plus a host of other activities.
Liban Trek ☏ 01 329 975; m 03 291 616; e info@ libantrek.com; www.libantrek.com. This well established & Lebanon's first ecotourism company operates scheduled hikes every Sun & they can also customise trips according to your needs. At the time of writing the cost of a day's hiking through all 3 cedar forests was around LBP40,000 for adults & LBP30,000 for children, inc return transport from Beirut & the services of a guide.

Safari Lebanon ☏ 01 360 227; m 03 954 052; e info@safarilebanon.com; www. safarilebanon.com. Operates a number of day excursions to the Chouf including tours by 4x4, & hiking & trekking in the reserve.
Vamos Todos m 03 917 190 or 79 115 001; e info@vamos-todos.com, mark.aoun@gmail.com; www.vamos-todos.com. Specialist ecotour operator offering regular day hikes through the reserve. Check the website for their upcoming schedule.
Wild Discovery [172 C2] Pasteur Bldg, Pasteur St, Gemmayze, Beirut; ☏ 01 565 646; e info@ wilddiscovery.com.lb; www.wilddiscovery.com.lb. In addition to their general tours to Deir al-Qamar & Beiteddine, this excellent company also offers full-day trips in winter for those interested in snowshoeing in the Chouf Cedar Reserve.

⌂ **WHERE TO STAY, EAT AND DRINK** The following places are all in or around the cedar reserve, and make an ideal stopover if you are planning an extended tour of the Chouf and want to combine the attractions at Deir al-Qamar and Beiteddine with an ecotourism experience. There is also an extensive list of recommended guesthouses on the Chouf Cedar Reserve's website (*www.shoufcedar.org*).

🏠 **Barouk Palace Hotel** (25 rooms & suites) Main Rd, Barouk, Chouf; ☎05 240 251/2; 📱03 630 056; e info@baroukpalace.com; www.baroukpalace.com. Although the rooms, all with AC & TV, are quite ordinary, the location is not, with stunning views over the mountains. This large hotel has 4 restaurants & a swimming pool, & can also organise excursions. Out of high season, room discounts of 15% are often available. **$$$**

🏠 **Association for Forests, Development & Conservation (AFDC)** (22 rooms) Ramlieh, Aley; ☎05 280 430; 📱03 711 386; e afdc@afdc.org.lb, hey@heyhostels.com; www.afdc.org.lb. A youth hostel 7km from the Chouf Cedar Reserve, offering clean, basic accommodation together with a range of educational & ecotourism activities. They also run another hostel in Dmit. See website for full details. **$$**

🏠 **Al Achkar Guesthouse** (5 rooms) El-Khreybeh, Chouf; ☎05 311 999; 📱03 354 558. A traditional, comfortable & clean old stone family house with wooden beams, situated on the outskirts of the cedar reserve & an ideal choice if you are planning an extended hiking tour of the area. There is a common room & use

of the kitchen for guests plus a delightful & picturesque outdoor area. They can also arrange tour guides (*cUS$40/day for groups*) & packed lunches for hikers (*cUS$7*). Lunch & dinner is an extra US$15. Discounts available for tour groups & those undertaking the Lebanon Mountain Trail (LMT; page 235). B/fast inc. **$**

🏠 **Auberge St Michel** (16 rooms & dorms) Masser Al-Chouf; ☎05 350 451; 📱03 107 182; e auberge@arcenciel.org; www.arcenciel.org; ⊕ May–Oct only. A former convent, this friendly & clean budget option also organises activities such as hiking & cycling, & there is a playground for children. Internet & laundry facilities are also available. Dorm room US$15 adults, US$10 children. B/fast an extra US$5. **$**

🏠 **Ecovillage** Dmit Valley, Chouf; ☎01 369 488; 📱03 211 463 or 03 381 733; e ecovillagelebanon@gmail.com; 🅕 Ecovillage-Lebanon-183793088335005 . Basic lodgings in huts & tents with a real back-to-nature feel. A range of activities is also on offer at this sustainable village, including donkey rides, hiking, painting, rock climbing, swimming & yoga, etc. Wi-Fi available. B/fast inc. **$**

UPDATES WEBSITE

You can post your comments and recommendations, and read the latest feedback and updates from other readers online at www.bradtupdates.com/lebanon.

9

South Lebanon

Telephone code 07

The region of south Lebanon is centred on the main towns of Sidon and Tyre, which have their origins in ancient port cities. Home to the ancient Phoenicians who sailed all over the Mediterranean exporting their luxurious and utilitarian goods, they were followed by other civilisations such as the Romans, Crusaders and Ottomans, who have all left important architectural footprints in the area. Castles, mosques, khans, temples, and caves where Jesus reputedly performed his first miracle serve to lend the area an open-air-museum feel, telling the story of Lebanon from ancient times. This is also a very fertile region, dotted with citrus, banana and olive groves and blessed with picturesque waterfalls, nature reserves and some of the best public beaches in the country. The presence of Islam is much more pronounced here and you will see women dressed in the *hijab* and full-length *chador*, whilst the anachronistic souks easily eclipse those in the capital. Yet, despite all these attractions, the south remains a poor relation of the north and over the years has often played second fiddle to the more affluent north in terms of economic development and regeneration. Partly, and understandably perhaps, this is because the region continues to suffer from an image problem.

Often at the heart of the country's – and the region's – tortured history, south Lebanon suffered greatly during the civil war years, especially during the 1982 Israeli invasion of the country. The 22-year Israeli occupation from 1978 to 2000 effectively severed any link with tourism and the region also became off limits for most Lebanese. The 2006 July War between Israel and Hezbollah, with its large loss of life and huge infrastructural damage, merely accentuated the image of the south as a virtual no-go area for locals and visitors alike. The continued presence of UN peacekeeping forces in the region, with their headquarters in Naqoura, which numbers some 10,000 United Nations Interim Force in Lebanon (UNIFIL) troops from 38 countries at the time of writing, testifies to the area's ongoing potential volatility; but a visit to the south is also an essential piece of the historical Lebanese jigsaw. The region possesses the same ingredients that characterise the north, such as friendly and hospitable people, engaging archaeological sites, and great food which combine to offer the traveller an authentic and much rawer experience.

SIDON (SAIDA)

Lebanon's third-largest city (after Beirut and Tripoli) and the largest town in the south, the old Phoenician port city of Sidon is only 45km south from Beirut along the coastal highway. As a conservative, predominantly Sunni Muslim town, surrounded by banana and citrus groves, it evokes a much more traditional and relaxed way of life compared with the capital, lacking the frenetic construction and nightlife of Beirut. Sidon is also the birthplace of former prime minister

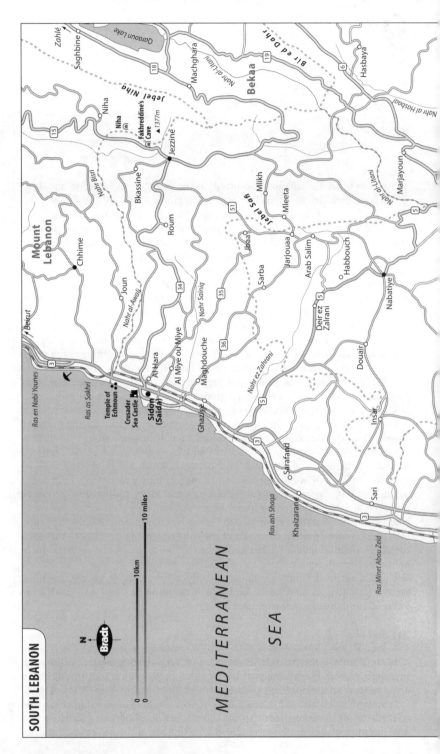

MEDITERRANEAN

SEA

Mount
Lebanon

Bekaa

Qaraoun Lake

Zahlé

Saghbine

Niha

Niha
Fakhreddine's
Cave
▲1377m

Jezzine

Bkassine

Roum

Chhime

Joun

Mlikh

Mleeta

Jebel Saib

Jebel Niha

Nahr Bisri

Nahr al-Awali

Nahr al-Hasbaal

Nahr al-Litani

Marjayoun

Hasbaya

Machghara

Bir ed Dahr

Ubaa

Jarjouaa

Sarba

Arab Salim

Habbouch

Nabatiye

Deir ez
Zahrani

Nahr Sainiq

Nahr ez Zahrani

Douair

Insar

Beirut

Ras en Nabi Younes

Ras as Sakhri

Temple of
Echmoun

Crusader
Sea Castle

Sidon
(Saida)

Al Hara

Al Miye ou Miye

Maghdouche

Ghaziye

Sarafand

Ras ash Shaqa

Khaizarane

Sari

Ras Minet Abou Zeid

N

Bradt

0   10km
0   10 miles

298

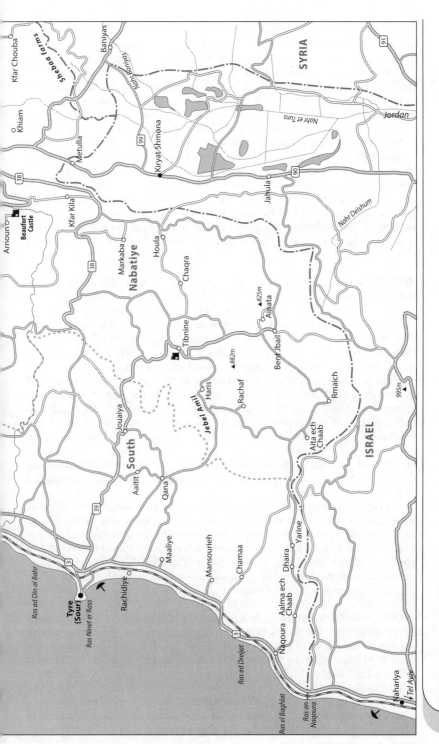

Rafiq Hariri (1944–2005) as well as the childhood home of Lebanon's first prime minister, Riad al–Solh (1894–1951), but its claim to fame over the last few decades has, unfortunately, come to be for wars and occupation. Heavily damaged during the Lebanese civil war, it was also hard-hit by the Israeli military machine during their occupation of the south. If visiting straight from the capital, the city's much more laid-back atmosphere will prove quite a contrast. But while Sidon may lack the eclectic entertainment and nightlife of the capital – alcohol is served in only one restaurant in the city at present – it more than makes up for this in being a largely authentic and traditional Arab city with old-style souks and artisans plying their trade like they have done for centuries. A famous sea castle, khans, a couple of excellent museums and a busy, picturesque fishing port make Sidon a very pleasant place for a few days; and with its excellent accommodation options and transport links, it is also a good base for an extended stay if you are intending to make a comprehensive tour of the south. At the time of writing, plans were afoot to build a new permanent museum in the town showcasing the ongoing archaeological artifacts unearthed in Sidon by the Directorate General of Antiquities and their colleagues from the British Museum.

HISTORY As one of Lebanon's main coastal cites, Sidon's illustrious past is intimately bound up with the earliest civilisations that took advantage of its favourable geography to carve out successive empires. In the Book of Genesis in the Old Testament, Sidon is referred to as the 'first born' of Canaan, making the city the earliest of the Phoenician city-states and, along with Tyre, one of its most important. During the Phoenician era the economy of Sidon prospered, with Phoenician artisans producing glass items and the famed purple dye which adorned many a royal and well-heeled citizen of the day, and who were praised in the writings of Homer for their artistry and skill. At the peak of their empire, around 550–330BCE, the Phoenicians equipped the Persians with vessels and sailors to stave off the Egyptians and Greeks. Sidon was also one of the Phoenician state's most important religious cities and around this time the Temple of Echmoun (pages 307–9) was constructed. Following the end of the Persian period, Sidon experienced wave after wave of invaders, its most famous being Alexander the Great in 333BCE, who ushered in the Hellenistic period, with Greek becoming the lingua franca of the area.

The city's comparative autonomy and freedom continued into the Roman epoch, which saw the Pax Romana with Sidon's citizens having a degree of parity of rights with their Roman occupiers. During the Byzantine era, the city continued to enjoy a relatively quiet period in its long history with many achievements in areas such as literature, the arts and science, etc; and it became the ideal choice for the relocation of Beirut's famous School of Law following a devastating earthquake in CE551. The Arabs conquered the city around CE636, and the city came under the banner of Islam for over 500 years until the advent of the Crusaders who, in 1111 under Baldwin, included Sidon alongside Jerusalem amongst its successes. The imposing sea castle remains the most salient reminder of this period of Sidonian history, along with the Castle of St Louis (Qalaa al-Muizz). The Crusader presence was quite short-lived, however, and they were defeated and forced out by the Mamluk forces in 1291, after which the city enjoyed a couple of centuries of relative calm.

It wasn't until the 17th century, during the reign of the Ottomans, that Sidon was once again to achieve a degree of illustrious existence not enjoyed since antiquity. Under the enlightened rule of Emir Fakhreddine Maan II, Sidon's port underwent major restoration and he built the famous Khan al-Franj or travellers' inn for foreign

Although south Lebanon is a rewarding region to visit, it needs to be borne in mind that the area has been the frontline in the on/off war between Israel and Hezbollah for many years, despite the former's withdrawal from the majority of the country in May 2000. The area also saw intense fighting during the civil war, which again embroiled Israel. More recently, the ongoing fighting in neighbouring Syria has served to sustain tensions between these two enemies, as witnessed in January 2015 when Israeli air strikes, which killed six Hezbollah fighters in the Golan Heights, saw the Party of God retaliate by killing two Israeli soldiers in the disputed Shebaa farms. In June 2013, the city of Sidon witnessed gun battles between the Lebanese army and followers of the radical Sunni sheikh Ahmad al-Assir, again linked to the Syria conflict, which claimed many lives on both sides. The current advice from the UK's Foreign and Commonwealth Office (FCO) along with other countries' security recommendations is to avoid all non-essential travel to Sidon and areas south of the Litani River. Keep abreast of developments by tuning into television and radio stations or perusing the English-language *Daily Star* newspaper. It would also be a good idea to check on the current security situation at the Ein el Helweh Palestinian refugee camp in Sidon if you intend visiting as a senior Fatah official, along with a passerby, were the victims of a car bomb attack in April 2016 near the Ein el Helweh camp.

Given the continued tensions between Israel and Hezbollah and the knock-on effect of the conflict in Syria, at the time of research any non-Lebanese citizen intending to visit areas south of Tyre must obtain a security pass number from the army security service in Sidon prior to travelling, and which must be presented at the army checkpoints. There is no charge for this and the relevant document is usually issued while you wait, but it can take longer. In practical terms, any visitors intending to travel to the Orange House in Naqoura (page 319) and those wishing to hike the southern sections, 22–26, of the Lebanon Mountain Trail (LMT; page 235) must have this numbered security pass. When in Sidon, take a service taxi (*LBP2,000*) and ask for the *'mukhabbarat al-jeish' (Army St;* \ *07 725 800 ext 221, 07 724 912;* ⏰ *08.00–14.00 Mon–Fri, 08.00–13.00 Sat)*, which is the headquarters of the army intelligence service in Sidon. It would be a good idea to bring a photocopy of your passport's main pages in addition to the passport itself, and you may be asked to deposit your mobile phone and/or camera prior to being admitted through the security gate. At the time of writing the English-speaking officer dealing with these security passes was Jalal Ghandour (m *03 264 274*) and he can be contacted for the most up-to-date information on the security permit procedure. It is also worth noting that, since the end of the summer 2006 Israel–Hezbollah conflict, a large number of cluster bombs and other unexploded devices remain in the region, which have subsequently killed dozens of civilians and wounded more than 200. Further fatalities and injuries have occurred to those responsible for de-mining the area. Operations are ongoing to rid the land of unexploded munitions but there is still much work to do, and until complete it is best to stick to well-trodden paths and highways. You can keep up to date with these issues by logging onto the official UNIFIL website (*www.unifil.unmissions.org*).

South Lebanon SIDON (SAIDA)

9

merchants trading in silk and cotton. During the 20th century, the town was heavily involved in the civil war and was also embroiled in the ongoing conflict between Israel and Hezbollah. Today, Sidon retains its traditional feel but trappings of modernity are evident in its newly opened shopping malls on the outskirts of town.

GETTING THERE From the southwest section of Beirut's Cola intersection [127 E7], buses and vans (*LBP1,500 and LBP2,000 respectively*) depart regularly for Sidon, arriving at Sahat al-Nejmeh in the town in around 50 minutes, from where it is only a 5-minute walk to Sidon's main attractions. The blue-and-white coaches of the Lebanese Transport Company (LTC; *Zantout Bldg, Sahat al-Nejmeh, Sidon;* ✆ *07 720 566* or *07 722 783;* e *lebanesetransportco@gmail.com*) are a slightly more roomy and salubrious option, and they operate air-conditioned coaches with daily departures from Cola to Sidon every 15 minutes or so between 07.00 and 21.00 with a journey time of around 45 minutes (*LBP2,500*). A taxi from Cola to Sidon will set you back around LBP25,000–30,000.

GETTING AROUND Like most of Lebanon's towns and cities, Sidon is easily explored on foot, with all the main sights (and sites) in the city reviewed quite close together. The slightly more outlying Temple of Echmoun (pages 307–9) can easily be reached by taxi (*approx. LBP10,000*) from Sidon's Sahat al-Nejmeh roundabout or by hailing a taxi on the street. Buses and minivans travelling north from here can also drop you off by the Stade De Saida (Sports Stadium), where you can flag down a taxi or walk the remaining 1km to the temple, which is signposted. This is a very picturesque route, as dotted along the riverbanks are a few outdoor cafés which make for a pleasant detour.

TOURIST INFORMATION A few doors along on the right as you enter the Khan al-Franj is the **Ministry of Tourism Office** (m *70 691 722;* e *sohaissa.mot@ gmail.com; www.mot.gov.lb;* ⊕ *08.30–14.00 Thu–Sat*). This small office has a range of free brochures and pamphlets in English, French, German, Italian and Spanish about south Lebanon, as well as other areas of the country. **Najwa Harb** (m *03 262 653;* e *najwa_harb@hotmail.com*) is an excellent and knowledgeable trilingual tourist guide offering guided visits around the city and the south in Arabic, French and Italian.

 WHERE TO STAY *Map, opposite*

🏠 **Al Qualaa Hotel** (12 rooms) Seaside Rd; ✆07 734 777; e info@alqualaa.com; www.lebhotels.com. In an excellent location right opposite the sea castle, this is Sidon's premier address, housed inside a lovely old medieval building. The characterful rooms are exceptionally clean & have ethnic décor, AC & TV. Recommended for those not on a tight budget. B/fast inc, free Wi-Fi. **$$$**

🏠 **Hotel Yacoub** (6 rooms) Moutran St, nr the old souk; m 70 103 222 e booking@lebhotels.com; www.yacoubhotel.com. The building dates from Ottoman times & the present hotel is converted from an old family house. Very clean with comfortable beds, AC, TV & en-suite rooms, this is a great place to base yourself for a few nights if exploring the south of the country. A very basic b/fast of *manoushe* & coffee is included. Free Wi-Fi. **$$**

🏠 **Convent De Terre Sainte** (8 rooms) Behind the Khan al-Franj (look for the sign 'Latin Church – Our Lady of the Annunciation') in the souk; m 03 442 141, 70 668 398. Basic, but clean, all rooms have fan, toilet & shower & there is a pleasant courtyard area for relaxing & dining. A characterful place & the delightful manager, Katia, will prepare evening meals on request (*US$10–15*). Sidon's best budget option right in the heart of the souk. Ask a local for 'Katia's' if you have problems locating the place, as many Sidonians in the souk seem to know the convent by her name. B/fast US$5 extra. **$**

SIDON (SAIDA)

MEDITERRANEAN SEA

Crusader Sea Castle

Temple of Echmoun, Beirut

Port

Khan al-Franj & Ministry of Tourism office

Bab al-Saray Mosque

Souk

Great (Omari) Mosque

Soap Museum (Musée Du Savon) & Hammam Saida

Debbané Palace & Museum

SHAKRIEH STREET

MOUTRAN STREET

COAST ROAD (CORNICHE)

Bus & service taxi station to Beirut, Nabatiye & Tyre

Sahât al-Nejmeh

Municipality

Arab Exchange bureaus

Blom

ATMs

LTC office & buses to Beirut, Jezzine & Tyre

Hisham Pharmacy

RUE HOUSSAM RAFIQ HARIRI

RIAD AL-SOLH ST

Le Mall (±800m), Mleeta

Bradt

N

0   200m
0   200yds

Castle of St Louis

Egyptian port

Murex Hill

Hammoud Hospital University Medical Centre, Tyre, Naqoura

For listings, see pages 302–4

Where to stay
1   Al Qualaa
2   Convent De Terre Sainte
3   Hotel Yacoub

Where to eat and drink
    Al Qualaa (see 1)
4   Falafel Abou Rami
5   Kanaan Sweets Co
6   Resthouse Sidon
7   Salloum Café
8   Zawat

✗ WHERE TO EAT AND DRINK *Map, above*

In addition to the places below, there are a number of other eateries thronging the road opposite and in the vicinity of the sea castle which offer good-value, filling meals and snacks in a nice location near the Corniche, though none of these places serves alcohol. There is also a range of cafés and snack bars in the nearby souks.

✗ **Resthouse Sidon** Seaside Rd, next to the sea castle; ☎ 07 722 469; m 03 103 603; ⊕ 09.00–midnight daily. At the time of writing this restaurant was the only place in the city serving alcohol including *arak*, wine, beers & spirits. It is housed within a converted Ottoman-era khan & has 2 restaurants: the smaller 'Italian Room' serves excellent Italian cuisine, whilst the much larger room specialises in delicious Lebanese food. It also has a nice outdoor area with in-your-face views of the sea castle. There is also a daily menu of fresh fish from the market. $$$$$

✗ **Al Qualaa Hotel** Seaside Rd; ☎ 07 734 777; m 03 759 395; e info@alqualaa.com; www. lebhotels.com; ⊕ 08.00–midnight daily. A good choice for *mezze* & international French & Italian cuisine. $$$$

✗ **Zawat** Seaside Rd, opposite the sea castle; ☎ 07 723 724; m 70 350 050; ⊕ 09.00–midnight daily. A lovely terrace restaurant overlooking the Corniche, serving delicious *mezze*, locally caught fish dishes & a variety of grilled meats. A very atmospheric place for puffing on a *nargileh*. $$$$

✗ **Falafel Abou Rami** Seaside Rd, directly opposite the sea castle; ☎ 07 721 907; ⊕ 07.30–

19.30 Sat–Thu. Specialising in tasty & extremely generous portions of falafel, this is a delightful little informal eatery with nice outdoor-only seating. A popular haunt & something of a long-standing institution for locals & visitors alike. **$**

☕ **Kanaan Sweets Co** Riad al-Solh St, nr Sahat al-Nejmeh; 📞07 720 271; e kanaan_sweets@ hotmail.com; www.kanaansweets.com; ⏰ 06.00–22.00 daily. The place to try Sidon's local speciality, the *sanioura*, an oval–shaped, deliciously sweet, crumbly biscuit, & a good place for a sit-down

coffee. They also serve a range of other sweets & cakes, including *baklava* & the delicious *knefeh*. **$**

☕ **Salloum Café** Next to Bab al-Saray Mosque; m 78 854 799; ⏰ 08.30–midnight daily. You can't miss this café right beside the mosque with its rather kitsch yellow plastic chairs scattered about a lovely old stone building with coloured glass windows & large arches. The lemonade on offer is something of a specialty & food such as *hummus*, *manoushe* & *labneh* is served in the mornings. A coffee costs a very reasonable LBP2,000. **$**

ENTERTAINMENT AND NIGHTLIFE Like other conservative towns in the country, Sidon's nightlife is not especially sophisticated or vibrant. Evenings tend to be dominated by a more restrained café culture, with couples and families eating and drinking whilst puffing on a *nargileh*. As a predominantly 'dry' city, your only possibility currently for drinking alcohol is at the Resthouse Sidon, beside the sea castle.

SHOPPING In addition to those places listed below, some of the best shopping in the city, whether for foodstuffs like fruit and vegetables or souvenirs, is to be had in Sidon's atmospheric **souks,** which offer a range of traditionally crafted products that can make great gifts. Away from the souks, the streets radiating off Sahat al-Nejmeh offer more modern retail outlets selling a whole range of items to meet day-to-day needs.

Hammam Saida Audi Bldg, Moutran St; 📞07 733 353; m 03 887 688; ⏰ 08.30–17.00 daily. Housed inside the Soap Museum, this small boutique shop sells an assortment of kaftans, jewellery & a range of different soaps, together with books about Lebanon, postcards, coasters & ornamental glass items, though prices are not particularly cheap. At the time of research there was talk of this shop possibly being transformed into a

museum/art gallery space to showcase the work of local & other artisans.

Le Mall Rue Houssam Rafiq Hariri, c800m from Sahat al-Nejmeh; 📞07 732 999; e info@lemall.com.lb; www.lemall.com.lb; ⏰ 10.00–22.00 daily. An ultramodern complex for everything from designer fashion-wear to Dunkin' Donuts. In fact, everything you can buy back home! A variety of cafés are housed on the top floor & there are a couple of ATMs.

OTHER PRACTICALITIES The area around Sahat al-Nejmeh, besides being the main hub for the city's transport network of buses and taxis, is where most of the banks, ATMs, larger stores and travel companies are located. The area also has numerous cafés and is home to the Municipality Building. Good, reliable internet cafés were not exactly widespread at the time of writing.

$ Arab Bank Riad al-Solh St; 📞07 751 070/2; e saida@arabbank.com.lb; www.arabbank.com.lb; ⏰ 08.30–16.00 Mon–Fri, 08.00–13.00 Sat. Has a 24hr ATM.

$ Blom Bank Riad al-Solh St; 📞07 723 266, 07 724 866; e saida@blom.com.lb; www.blombank. com; ⏰ 08.15–17.00 Mon–Fri (Jul–Aug 08.15–16.00), 08.15–12.30 Sat. Has 2 x 24hr ATMs.

✉ **Post office** Bizri Bldg, Riad al-Solh St; 📞07 721 604, 07 722 813; www.libanpost. com; ⏰ 08.00–17.00 Mon–Fri, 08.00–13.30 Sat. Provides the full range of postal services, including Western Union money transfer.

➕ **Hammoud Hospital University Medical Centre** Dr Ghassan Hammoud St; 📞07 723 111 or 07 720 152; e info@hammoudhospital.com; www.

hammoudhospital.com. A high-quality, 325-bed teaching hospital with A & E dept.

✚ Hisham Pharmacy Rue Houssam; ☏ 07 732 730; m 03 007 698; e hisham.dalibalta@ gmail.com; ⏰ 08.00–20.30 Mon–Thu & Sat, 08.00–15.00 Fri & Sun

WHAT TO SEE AND DO

Crusader Sea Castle (Qalaa al-Bahr) *(Seafront;* ☏ *07 722 491;* ⏰ *08.00–18.00 daily; admission: adults LBP4,000, students LBP1,000, children under 10 free)* This is Sidon's most recognisable landmark and popular visitor site. Known as Château de la Mer to the Franks, the castle is located offshore but connected to the mainland by an 80m causeway constructed by the Arabs. Built by the Crusaders in 1228, using the foundations of a much earlier Phoenician temple dedicated to their god Melqart, the rise to power of the Mamluks led to the destruction of the castle in order to deter future incursions by the medieval invaders. The castle comprises a west and an east tower either side of the main entrance; the former is in the better condition of the two. Following their defeat of the Mamluks, the Ottomans built a compact domed mosque on the castle's west side. The exterior walls of the castle show evidence of the use of Roman stonework used to strengthen the structure, indicating that the Crusaders were great early recyclers. Both towers are easily accessed on foot via staircases and from aloft yield great views over the town and the old fishing port.

Khan al-Franj (Inn of the Foreigners) ✳ (☏ *07 727 344;* ⏰ *summer 08.30– 17.00 daily, winter 08.00–17.00 daily; admission free)* A few minutes' walk south of the sea castle is this inland khan built by Fakhreddine Maan II in the early 17th century, as a one-stop shop for cotton and silk merchants trading locally and with overseas markets as part of his cosmopolitan philosophy to stimulate economic activity and assert his independence from the Ottomans. Architecturally, the building follows the design of other khans attributed to Fakhreddine. It consists of a large central courtyard dominated by arches and vaulted ceilings. The ground floor would have been used for storing goods, as stables for animals such as camels and horses, hostelries and a marketplace. The upper floor was reserved for traveller accommodation. This was Sidon's hub of economic prosperity during the 19th century, and which also housed the French consulate, to which Fakhreddine donated the khan. Nowadays it remains an icon of its time and until relatively recently offered accommodation to tourists and other visitors in superbly renovated and character rooms with high, vaulted ceilings in this delightful heritage building. It is once again at the time of writing undergoing further restoration work by the **Hariri Foundation** (☏ *07 728 746/9* or *07 730 929;* e *info@hariri-foundation.org; www.hariri-foundation.org)* but no longer, unfortunately, offers lodgings. When completed the khan will house on its top floor a French Cultural Centre. The khan should certainly be on your list of places to visit in Sidon. (The **Ministry of Tourism** office is a short distance along on your right as you enter the khan.)

Great (Omari) Mosque Dating from 1291, the mosque was originally a Church of St John of the Hospitallers Order (Knights of St John) during the latter period of the Crusader era, housing a chapel and stables. The onset of Mamluk rule saw the fortress converted into a mosque but retaining its original walls. The structure had suffered immense damage over the years from earthquakes, storms and war, especially the 1982 Israeli invasion that left the mosque in a perilous state. Between 1983 and 1986, the mosque underwent

extensive renovations, funded by Rafiq Hariri, and in 1989 received the coveted Aga Khan Award for Architecture (see *www.akdn.org/architecture*, which has interesting and extensive background notes on the architectural details and history of this building). The mosque today, entered via its main northern gate in the souk, is an impressive site, with its large courtyard surrounded by archways and impressive 10m-high, vaulted ceilings. The elongated prayer hall, with its customary niche pointing towards Mecca, stained-glass windows and imposing domes make this mosque a highly recommended site.

Bab al-Saray Mosque Built in 1201, the Bab al-Saray or Gate of the Palace is Sidon's oldest mosque. With its imposing dome supported by a series of large pillars, it has some newly renovated and beautiful medieval stonework with vaulted ceiling and large arches.

Port Just a couple of minutes' walk south from the sea castle, this traditional, still-working fishermen's port has an early-morning daily fish market from around 06.00 to 11.00 and is well worth getting up for to watch the fishermen bring back the product of their night-time scaly labours and to observe the frenetic trading activity.

Souk ✳ Whilst not as extensive as Tripoli's souks, Sidon's labyrinthine streets still make for a few hours of happy wandering to appreciate this atmospheric slice of traditional Arab and Sidonian life. This remains a living museum of tradition with artisans plying their trade as cobblers, furniture-makers and metalworkers tapping and hammering away at their tasks, as they have done for generations. It's probably best not to take a set route; just head straight across the road from the sea castle to begin your meanderings at the innumerable fruit and vegetable stalls and get lost amongst them and the crowded alleyways to soak up the medieval atmosphere, stopping *en route* at one of the many cafés to drink tea, smoke a *nargileh* and watch young and old play backgammon and cards. The souk is also a good place to try Sidon's very own *sanioura* crumbly biscuit in authentic surroundings.

Soap Museum (Musée Du Savon) ✳ (*Moutran St;* ☏ *07 753 599; admission: adults LBP5,000, children 12–16 years LBP2,500, children under 12 free;* ⏰ *08.30– 17.00 daily*) Sidon's tradition of soap manufacture dates back to the 17th century, when the city was a hub for exports to France. Although production has all but ceased today, Lebanon's first museum dedicated to the art and craft of this once-flourishing industry is absorbing and definitely worth a look. The museum's building dates from the Middle Ages, but it wasn't until the mid 19th century that it became a soap factory supplying local markets such as the bathhouses or hammams which once proliferated in the city. Towards the end of the 19th century, the building was purchased by the affluent Audi family, who continued soap making under their own brand label. Production finally came to a halt in 1975 with the onset of the civil war, and the ground floor of the building became a safe haven for refugees from the conflict. In 1996, the Audis began renovating the factory and it finally opened to the public as a museum in November 2000. The end result is a very well-designed and organised shrine over two floors with clear labelling of the exhibits in Arabic, English and French. The museum takes you on a journey through the history, raw materials and processes involved in soap manufacture in the countries of the Levant and includes the fascinating 'saponification' process, a two-stage, week-long procedure of fermentation and heating of the raw materials.

Debbané Palace and Museum (Musée Historique de Saida) (*Moutran St;* ✆ *07 720 110;* e *museedebbane@debbane.com; www.museumsaida.org;* ⊕ *09.00–18.00 Sat–Thu; admission free*) This little gem of a palace is hidden away inside the souk, though very close to the Hotel Yacoub, and is a must-see site in the city. Built by prominent local Ali Agha Hammoud as his private place of residence in 1721, it was later purchased by the affluent Debbané family in c1800 who proceeded to renovate and extend the property to the one you see today. It remained the family home until 1978, when the civil war forced them out to make way for hundreds of refugees who sought sanctuary there from the horrors of war. The building and house itself are an archetypal example of Ottoman-era architecture – a main courtyard as the centrepiece of the building and the very private layout of the entrance. Inside the house there are numerous exquisite decorative items, including a ceiling of cedarwood, paintings, a fountain and a variety of motifs. More recent renovations show the influence of the French presence with the addition of two extra storeys in the 1920s. The Debbané Foundation, inaugurated in 1999, was established to restore and showcase Ottoman-era architecture and, more widely, the history of the town of Sidon itself, and the building first opened to the public in 2001.

Castle of St Louis (Qalaa al-Muizz) Like many other archaeological remains in Lebanon this fortress occupies the site of an earlier 10th-century fortification built during the Fatimid era and with some evidence of much earlier settlement dating back to the Phoenician period. The castle we see today, a short walk south from the Soap Museum and sitting atop a large mound was the first crusader castle constructed in Sidon. It was built in 1254 by King Louis IX (1214–70) – the only French king to be later canonised, and popularly known as St Louis – who led the Seventh (1248–54) and Eighth (1270) crusades, but the castle also reflects later Mamluk- and Ottoman-era restoration efforts. The castle also served for a time as a safe haven for Palestinian refugees fleeing their homeland following the 1948 *nakba* or catastrophe of the first Arab–Israeli war and the creation of the state of Israel. Currently undergoing renovation once again, the site was at the time of research enclosed by metal fencing and the castle itself covered with scaffolding, with bulldozers working inside the grounds; but you can still view this once impressive structure from the roadside.

Murex Hill Located a few metres southeast and across the road from the Castle of St Louis is Sidon's 100m-long and 50m-high hill, the most 'invisible' evidence of its once-great importance during the Phoenician era. It was here that archaeologists discovered some 40m-high piles of discarded murex shells from the purple dye-manufacturing process, which hints at the once-massive scale of production. Alas, ongoing residential development and the advent of a Muslim cemetery now mark this spot, and you are likely to have more luck locating a murex shell on eBay.

Temple of Echmoun [site plan, overleaf] (⊕ *08.00–18.00 daily; admission free*) Located just over 1km north of Sidon, the Temple of Echmoun, or Bustan al-Sheikh as it is known locally in Arabic, is located in a picturesque location along the banks of the Awali River lined with lush green vegetation and citrus plantations. More importantly from an archaeological viewpoint is that this ancient site, which dates from the 7th century BCE, is the sole Phoenician site that preserves more than its stone foundations. Like many of Lebanon's archaeological ruins it has seen numerous additions over the centuries, illustrating how it has been revered by subsequent civilisations. The legend of Echmoun tells the tale of a handsome Beiruti hunter who attracted

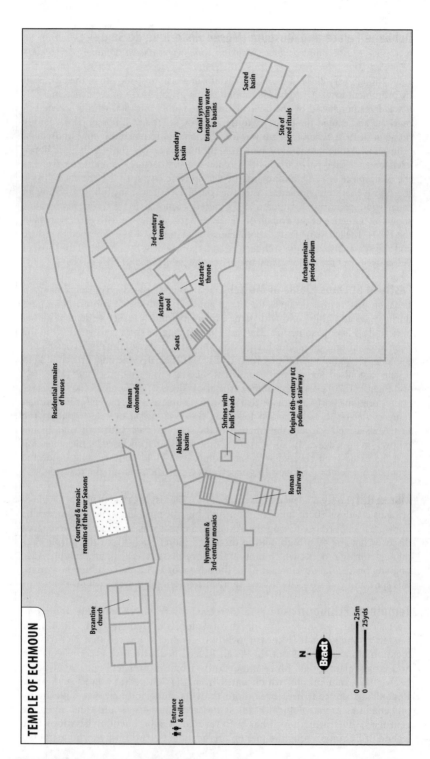

TEMPLE OF ECHMOUN

Entrance & toilets

Byzantine church

Courtyard & mosaic remains of the Four Seasons

Residential remains of houses

Roman colonnade

Nymphaeum & 3rd-century mosaics

Roman stairway

Ablution basins

Shrines with bulls' heads

Original 6th-century BCE podium & stairway

Seats

Astarte's pool

Astarte's throne

3rd-century temple

Secondary basin

Canal system transporting water to basins

Sacred basin

Site of sacred rituals

Archaemenian-period podium

N

Bradt

0   25m
0   25yds

the romantic attentions of the goddess Astarte, who subsequently fell in love with him. He rebuked her affections and in order to escape her persistent and amorous intentions proceeded to castrate himself, which resulted in his death. Astarte, venerating the young man even more, brought him back to life and transformed him into a god and as one who dies and is perennially reborn.

He became known as Echmoun, the god of fertility and healing, and the site's location, adjacent to an abundant water supply, was most likely chosen to facilitate in ritual ablutions. The custom of the times was to offer the god statues engraved with the names of the sick, and as many of these depict children it is possible that Echmoun was known as the local paediatrician during this period. Many of these marble statues of children are now housed in the National Museum in Beirut (pages 174–5). The Greeks later identified Echmoun with the medical arts and the Greek god Asklepios, and a gold plaque uncovered at the temple of a snake curled around a staff survives to this day as a symbol of the medical profession. Although work had commenced at the original temple some three centuries previously, beginning with the rule of King Eshmounazar II, successive civilisations (64BCE–CE330) further embellished the complex, with the Romans building a **colonnade, ritual basins** and a **nymphaeum** complete with mosaics and with the fountain containing in its niches three, now weathered, examples of nymphs. Just in front of the main entrance on the left-hand side are the foundations of a **Byzantine church,** and a little further along on the same side of the road are some very eroded but still discernible **Four Seasons mosaics,** which also date from the 3rd century CE. The **throne** of the heroine herself, Astarte, dates from the later Hellenistic period and is built in Egyptian style. A fine panoramic view of the temple complex can be gained by walking up the Roman stairway opposite the Four Seasons mosaics to the podium, the largest of the temples on the site built by King Echmounazzar II in the 5th century.

There is a small manned office on the site, which at the time of writing had no brochures, and toilet facilities are located just inside the entrance.

JEZZINE

The predominantly Christian Maronite town of Jezzine, 22km east of Sidon and 40km south from Beirut, takes its name from the Syriac word meaning 'store', suggesting that in antiquity, Jezzine's strategic location functioned as a depot for traders peddling their wares eastwards from the port of Sidon to the Chouf region, the Bekaa Valley, and beyond to Damascus in Syria. Today, Jezzine's 950m altitude and milder climate in an extremely picturesque location overlooking mountains, valleys and pine forests serves as the south's principal summer resort town, attracting scores of families to its cooler air, famous 40m-high waterfalls and the quality of its traditional handicrafts which go back generations. For the foreign visitor, too, Jezzine makes for a very laid-back and pleasant place to visit on either a day trip or as an overnight stay.

GETTING THERE Jezzine is easily reached by the LTC bus from Sidon which departs daily approximately every 20–25 minutes between 06.00 and 20.00 from the garage just behind the company's office on Sahat al-Nejmeh. The c50-minute journey costs LBP2,000, and the route is a very pleasant and scenic one. The bus can drop you off at the entrance to the town near the town hall (Serail Building). At the time of writing the last bus back to Sidon was at 20.00, so factor this into your visit if you don't want the extra expense of a taxi. The one-way taxi fare from Sidon to Jezzine will set you back around LBP30,000.

LADY HESTER LUCY STANHOPE: A LIFE LESS ORDINARY

The Arabs have never looked upon me in the light either of man or woman, but *un être à part.*

Lebanon has hosted a number of eccentric visitors to its shores over the millennia, but Lady Hester Stanhope as a woman of her time who defied the conventions of class and gender and from a young age possessing an adventurous, charismatic and formidable personality, must rank as one of the more unorthodox of travellers. Born in London into a wealthy aristocratic background on 12 March 1776, Lady Hester was the eldest daughter of the imperious Charles Stanhope (1753–1816), the third Earl of Stanhope, and his first wife, Lady Hester Pitt (1755–80), niece of England's long-serving and youngest ever prime minister William Pitt the Younger (1759–1806). Hester, a skilled horsewoman and adept with firearms, became close to her uncle and in 1803 Pitt invited his niece to reside at 10 Downing Street to perform the duties of political and social hostess to the unmarried Pitt. Hester soon gained a reputation for her social, and sometimes unconventional and blunt, social skills, which didn't always meet with approval in the upper echelons of politics and society. Following the death of Pitt in 1806, the state granted her a lifetime pension of £1,200 per annum, a tidy sum equivalent to c£100,000 in today's money; but this was never sufficient to match her lavish ambitions and spending. Lamenting the loss of Pitt and her associated influential status, Hester moved briefly across London to Montagu Square and then to Wales. In 1809, she suffered further loss when her first love, General Sir John Moore, and her brother were killed by French forces at the Battle of Corunna in Galicia, northern Spain during the Peninsular War. A year later, and with little now to detain Hester in England, she departed the country for the East, never to return again, embarking on a peripatetic sea voyage with her entourage of maids and her long-serving physician, Charles Meryon (1783–1877) – who after her death would publish numerous volumes of Hester's memoirs – joined later by her much younger lover Michael Bruce. Journeying to Malta, Greece, Constantinople and Cairo, Hester defied tradition and refused to wear the Muslim veil, choosing instead to dress in male Ottoman attire. In 1813, in what was probably her greatest moment, feeding her need for glory and status, Hester became the first European woman to enter Palmyra (Tadmor) in Syria, arriving on an Arabian horse, where the local Bedouin revered her as 'Queen of the East' akin to the legendary Queen Zenobia. By around 1821, Hester had moved from the Convent of Mar Elias and settled in Joun, a few kilometres northeast from Sidon, into a refurbished monastery with her retinue of servants. Here she dabbled in Ottoman politics, gave shelter to numerous refugees (Arabs, Albanians, Armenians and Jews) during

GETTING AROUND Jezzine is a straightforward town to navigate. Walking is by far the best and most pleasant method of getting around as the main town is really just one long street. Start a tour from the Municipality Building (near Infinity Blue nightclub and Al-Shallal Restaurant) and continue ahead, which will bring you to the town's other main eateries, shops, the souk and handicraft area.

 WHERE TO STAY

L'Étoile du Loup (15 chalets) c5min drive from the waterfalls; 07 781 425; m 03 425 525 or 03 505 016; e najmahaoun@yahoo.fr; www. etoileduloup.com. This resort-style complex

periods of civil strife and earned the enmity of Egyptian leader Mehmet Ali: 'The Englishwoman has caused me more trouble than all the insurgent people of Syria or Palestine.' She also gave money generously to needy elderly and pregnant women, was generally well liked by locals, who referred to her as 'Sitt' or 'Lady of Joun', and she forged influential relations with the Druze. Her reputation spread and, as in London, she played host to many well-known intellectuals including the French poet Alphonse de Lamartine (1790–1869), who observed that 'she has those features which years cannot alter' and writer Alexander William Kinglake (1809–91), author of *Eothen: Or Traces of Travel Brought Home from the East* (1844), who commented that Hester was 'a good, businesslike, practical prophetess'. Despite having affairs, Hester never married and as time went by her mental and physical health steadily declined, like her finances; she became a virtual recluse, rarely venturing outside her house and only receiving visitors come nightfall who were permitted to see only her face and hands. She consulted with the stars and her ever-dwindling number of guests were treated to endless monologues about her earlier life with Pitt. Hester's unstable condition deteriorated further and her grasp of reality seemed to become ever more tenuous. Travel writer Colin Thubron remarked how

she slapped her servants and beat them with a mace, and the rooms at Joun were fantastic with rubbish. Down the twilit corridors tiptoed black slaves, and in the halls stirred herbalists and astrologers and a lunatic soothsayer, an ex-general of Napoleon. Her stables were occupied by a white mare and its deformed foal, 'the horse born saddled', on which she and the Messiah would ride to Jerusalem at the second coming.

A couple of weeks before her lonely death on 23 June 1839, Hester wrote

I have done what I believe my duty, the duty of everyone of every religion; I have no reproaches to make myself, but that I went rather too far; but such is my nature, and a happy nature, too, who can make up its mind to everything but *insult*

By the time she died Hester's servants had already fled with what booty they could when it became apparent that they were not going to be paid, and her burial was left up to the British Consul, who hastily laid her to rest alongside her former lover, an officer in Napoleon's Imperial Guard, near her house. Today, Hester's former home can still be visited but is in a ruinous state, and her still discernible grave has long been plundered; but this undulating area is an attractive and peaceful one for a relaxing break and stroll amidst the olive groves.

of chalets beautifully located overlooking the picturesque vista of Jezzine is a comfortable, though not cheap option, with swimming pool, jacuzzi & sauna complementing the spacious & nicely furnished chalets equipped with all mod cons including kitchenette, living room, TV & AC. They can also recommend local guides for sightseeing & arrange visits to the caves at Niha, c2km from the resort. B/fast inc, free Wi-Fi. **$$$$$**

🏠 **La Maison de la Forêt** (25 bungalows) Bkassine; ☎ 07 800 222; m 78 828 252; e reservations@lamaisondelaforet.net; www. lamaisondelaforet.net. Delightfully located by the Middle East's biggest pine forest, at Bkassine, less than 5km north of Jezzine, this charming rural retreat, its accommodation in wooden bungalows with all the comforts of home, is an ideal choice for couples & families alike, with a range of activities on offer for both adults & children such as cycling, hiking & canyoning in a beautiful, scenic & tranquil setting. B/fast inc., free Wi-Fi. **$$$$**

🏠 **Iris Flower Hotel** (28 rooms & suites) General de Gaulle St; ☎07 781 999; m 70 449 305; e info@l-iris.com; www.l-iris.com. One of Jezzine's newer hotels, the Iris Flower is a friendly establishment in a good, central location but housed in a rather anodyne, modern tower block. But the spacious & comfortable rooms are fine for 1 or 2 nights. The hotel also has a well-equipped business centre for up to 30 delegates & guests have discounted access

to the nearby swimming pool (c5mins from the hotel) during the summer months. Free Wi-Fi. A decent buffet b/fast is an extra US$10. **$$$**

🏠 **Auberge Wehbé** (30 rooms) Off the main street, behind St Antoine Monastery; ☎07 780 217 or 07 781 009; ⏲ Mar–Oct only. A spotlessly clean, bright & airy hotel dating back to 1872 & full of character, with comfortable & homely reception area, & a pleasant terrace with good views over the town. The swimming pool is a nice addition for the summer months. B/fast US$5 extra. **$$**

✕ **WHERE TO EAT AND DRINK, AND NIGHTLIFE** There is no shortage of options in and around the town, from fast-food places to more formal dining, but the pick of the crop are undoubtedly those venues overlooking the waterfalls. The following represent a selection of the possibilities.

✕ **Beit El Ghâbeh** Bkassine; ☎07 800 222; m 78 828 252; e reservations@lamaisondelaforet.net; www.lamaisondelaforet.net. A short taxi ride away from the town itself, this restaurant is worth the trip even if you are not staying here (La Maison de la Forêt, page 311), for its lovely location amid the Middle East's largest pine forest & its wide-ranging & excellent Lebanese & international cuisine. On Sun & public holidays they provide an open buffet inc *arak* for LBP60,000. **$$$$**

✕ **Al-Shallal Restaurant** Opposite Infinity Blue, overlooking the waterfalls; ☎07 780 067; m 03 513 497, 70 442 444; ⏲ 11.00–02.00 daily. In a prime location for terrific views of the waterfalls & surrounding mountain, this venue

serves decent enough *mezze*, fried & grilled meats & *arak*. **$$$$**

☆ **Coin Rouge** Town centre; m 03 120 856 or 76 373 673; f Coinrouge; ⏲ 15.00–late daily; admission US$10 'disco charge', Sat inc free drink. Jezzine's liveliest venue combines a cosy downstairs pub with live music & DJ on Sat nights in a wonderfully intimate upstairs setting with compact dance floor. **$$**

☆ **Infinity Blue** Entrance to Jezzine, next to the Municipality Bldg; m 70 587 090, 71 208 092; ⏲ 22.00–late Thu–Sun; admission US$10, inc free drink. A lively nightclub venue offering karaoke on w/day nights with Arabic pop music, Latin tunes & a Sat-night DJ spinning the discs to English & Arabic sounds. **$$**

SHOPPING There are a number of everyday general stores and pharmacies catering to most visitors' needs, but by far the best shopping in Jezzine is in the town's small souk: only one street perhaps, but here skilled craftsmen continue to decorate distinctive, decorative and utilitarian household items. The two shops below are something of an institution, turning out quality products a cut above the rest, and are definitely worth a look in even if you have no intention of buying, to see the exquisitely crafted items. However, if ever there was a place to pick up authentic local souvenirs, then this is it – and so much more useful (but also more expensive!) than an 'I love Beirut' T-shirt or such like.

Eid Bou Rached Souk; ☎07 780 082; m 03 227 550; ⏲ 09.00–20.00 daily. A family-run business established since 1925, Rached fashions handmade daggers, swords & cutlery out of horn & ivory in a variety of colourful designs & will custom-make items on request. A hand-crafted cutlery

set will set you back LBP1,050,000, whilst smaller items such as bottle openers cost LBP9,000.

S & S Haddad Souk; ☎01 280 353; m 03 683 369, 70 293 231; e info@haddadcutlery.com; www.haddadcutlery.com; ⏲ 09.30–18.30 daily. Continuing a family tradition that stretches

above   Statue of Impressionist artist Omar Onsi (1901–69), Downtown Beirut, whose works captured the essence of Lebanon's people and the beauty of the country's natural landscape (PD) page 174

right   The Khalil Gibran Museum in Bcharré houses the artistic and written works of Lebanon's revered literary figure (EH/S) pages 240–1

below   The opulent Beiteddine Palace is the setting for an annual summer arts festival attracting Lebanese and international performing artists (MTL) page 290

YOUR ESCAPE IN BEIRUT
STARTS HERE!

Summer in Beirut has an ambiance of its own.
Pay a visit to the city of lights and enjoy an unforgettable experience of a unique kind.

www.fourseasons.com/beirut
1418 Professor Wafic Sinno Avenue, Minet El Hosn, Beirut 2020 - 4107, Lebanon
Tel: 961 1 761000

O MONOT
hotel

back to 1770, when the Haddad family began manufacturing hand-crafted knives, swords & later rifles for the Lebanese army, the business now specialises in making more widely used practical items from bottle openers & desk, dessert & manicure sets to their popular colourful & decorative cutlery sets of up to 114 items, often embellished with brass, copper or mother-of-pearl but always adorned with their trademark handles bearing the Phoenix, a symbol of the rising & falling fortunes of Lebanon itself. As Jezzine's most famed cutlery makers they have supplied politicians such as former French premier Jacques Chirac, popes & other world dignitaries. Well worth a look in even if you are not buying, & you may get an opportunity to see their craftsman at work in their nearby workshop.

OTHER PRACTICALITIES Banks and ATMs proliferate in Jezzine, so you will have no problem obtaining cash and changing currency. The town also boasts a couple of decent pharmacies.

$ Byblos Bank Ground Fl, St Antoine Centre; ☎ 01 205 050; www.byblosbank.com; ⏱ 08.30–15.30 Mon–Fri, 08.30–noon Sat. Has an ATM.

✉ **Post office** Ogero Bldg, towards the far end of town just after the Aoun Tex bedlinen store; ☎ 07 780 003; www.libanpost.com; ⏱ 08.00–17.00 Mon–Fri, 08.00–13.30 Sat

WHAT TO SEE AND DO Although Jezzine's biggest pull is its more palatable climate in summer and its attractive 40m-high waterfalls, which cascade down the mountainside, lending the area a very picturesque air following the winter rains, it does possess a handful of engaging sites for the visitor on a day or overnight visit. The grand Ottoman-style **Farid Serhal Palace** (☎ *03 353 293; ⏱ by prior appointment only; admission free*) is the result of a long-term dream and passion of the late Farid Serhal, a local politician, to erect a 'great palace' showcasing numerous *objets d'art* from antiques, books and carpets to sculpture housed within an ornate interior. The **Old Serail** or Municipality Building at the entrance to the town is also worth a look. The building dates from 1898 and has an interesting façade with arched doorways and wooden-shuttered windows. Also located in the town centre area is the attractive Maronite **St Antoine Monastery** (*nr Auberge Wehbé Hotel;* ☎ *07 780 131;* e *sec.oam@gmail.com; www.antonins. org;* ⏱ *07.00–19.00 daily; admission free*), which dates back to 1774 and the lovely arched stone interior makes the building worth a quick look in. Nestled deep in the valley beneath the town is **Fakhreddine's Cave (Grotte de Fakhreddine)**, a place of refuge for Fakhreddine II's father, Qurqmaz, who died there, and Fakhreddine II himself, who was eventually discovered by the Ottomans in 1633 and taken prisoner to Istanbul, where he was strangled and then beheaded two years later. This is not an easy site to visit, however, and really requires elementary climbing equipment and the services of a local guide. Try contacting the **Spéléo Club of Lebanon** (*Speleo Club Du Liban;* m *71 727 929;* e *info@speleoliban.org; www.speleoliban.org*), who should be able to help with putting you in touch with a local guide. If all that sounds too much like hard work, you could always seek out **Karam Wines** (*Jezzine;* ☎ *01 370 519, 01 367 518;* m *03 402 538;* e *contact@ karamwines.com; www.karamwines.com;* ⏱ *spring/summer 10.00–17.00 daily; call in advance for lunch & tasting sessions*), south Lebanon's first commercial vineyard producing some 55,000 bottles of red and white wine annually, 50% of which is destined for export. The tipple is also available all over Jezzine, with the Coin Rouge club (page 312) stocking a large range.

Beaufort Castle (Qalaa al-Shaqif Arnoun) ✳ (*Above Arnoun village, c7km southeast of Nabatiye;* ☎ *01 426 703;* m *03 655 905;* ⏱ *summer 08.00–19.00 daily,*

winter 08.30–17.00 daily; admission: adults LBP6,000, children LBP1,000) This fortress, known as Qalaa al-Shaqif Arnoun in Arabic and Château de Beaufort or 'beautiful fortress' in French, remains a symbol both of Lebanon's multi-faceted and tortured past and one of the very few examples of a medieval stronghold that has proven its military worth in contemporary warfare. Though there is some debate about its history, with some scholars contending that Beaufort's origins hark back to the Roman and Arab eras, according to the chronicles of William of Tyre (c1130–86) the castle dates from 1139 during the crusader period and built to defend the Kingdom of Jerusalem against Arab incursions. The castle remained under Frankish control until around 1190, when, following a protracted siege, it was captured by Saladin after the success of his cunning plan to entice Renaud, Prince of Sagette, out of the fortress who was then tortured in full view of his men and taken in chains as a prisoner to Damascus. In 1240, the castle once again reverted back to the Franks following a deal done with the Ayyubid sultan of Damascus, despite some stiff resistance from the sultan's own forces. Then in 1260 the castle was sold to the Knights Templars, whose ownership would prove to be short-lived as the revered Mamluk sultan Baybars reclaimed the castle for Islam in 1268. A period of relative calm now descended over Beaufort until the early part of the 17th century when the forces of Druze emir Fakhreddine Maan II occupied it until expelled by Ottoman forces. Beaufort's strategic significance came to the fore once again in the 20th century during Lebanon's 1975–90 civil war when *fedayeen* fighters of the Palestine Liberation Organisation (PLO) occupied the site from 1976, until driven out under heavy aerial bombardment by the Israelis in June 1982. The Israelis then proceeded to install their own forces in the castle, where they remained for the next 18 years until their military withdrawal from Lebanon in May 2000, leaving a wave of destruction in their wake despite appeals from the Lebanese government to respect this important piece of the country's heritage.

From 2011, Beaufort began to undergo extensive restoration works undertaken by Lebanon's Directorate General of Antiquities with support from the Kuwait Fund for Arabic Economic Development, and the renovated structure finally re-opened to visitors in 2015. Whether or not you are a history buff, the journey to Beaufort is worth it for the views alone. At an elevation of more than 700m above sea level it is easy to see why it is perfectly sited for strategic purposes; but for the tourist it will be the stunning panoramic vistas over northern Israel, the Golan Heights, the foothills of Mount Hermon and the Litani River that will most impress. Just below Beaufort is the family-friendly **Kalaa Resort** (*Arnoun;* \07 571 444/888; m *03 650 793 or 70 022 704;* e *info@kalaaresort.com; www.kalaaresort.com;* ⊕ *noon–midnight daily),* a very pleasant hotel (*25 rooms; double room US$70, b/fast inc, free Wi-Fi*) and restaurant complex with a very pleasant outdoor space for enjoying their Lebanese and international dishes. A main course meal for two will set you back around LBP45,000, with a *nargileh* costing LBP8,000. There's also a children's play area and cinema. Note that it gets very busy here in the summer, and no alcohol is served.

Getting there There are no direct public transport buses to the castle. If you are travelling here from Beirut take a bus from Cola station [127 E7] to Sidon (*LBP1,500–2,500, around 45–50mins*). From Sidon catch a bus to Nabatiye (*LBP2,000–3,000, about 30mins*). Then from Nabatiye you can take a taxi (*cLBP20,000–25,000*) the remainder of the way to Beaufort. Alternatively, catch a taxi from Sidon to Beaufort, which will cost around US$30, or a taxi from Beirut to Beaufort which will set you back US$100–120.

MLEETA

Located 82km from Beirut and around 27km southeast of Sidon, Mleeta was formerly just one of many remote and scenic, but strategically important, hilltop positions fought over by Israel and Hezbollah. Since 2010, however, this former stronghold of the resistance and theatre of conflict has hit the media headlines after being transformed into what some have called Hezbollah's Disneyland.

GETTING THERE At the time of writing, Mleeta was not the easiest of places to visit by public transport, as it was not on any direct bus route from Beirut. The Mleeta website (*www.mleeta.com*) suggests some self-drive and public transport route options together with an estimate of the cost from Beirut and Sidon. From Beirut, the journey time by car, traffic permitting, is less than 2 hours. From Sidon, the journey time shouldn't take much more than about 45 minutes by taxi; expect to be quoted somewhere between LBP50,000 and LBP60,000 by drivers for a return trip. If travelling from Beirut by taxi, the one-way fare should cost somewhere between US$80 and US$100. If you intend visiting Mleeta on a day trip from the capital, expect to pay around US$150 for the round trip which includes the time the driver will need to wait (usually up to 2 hours) whilst you view the site.

WHAT TO SEE AND DO
Where the Land Speaks to the Heavens: Mleeta Resistance Tourist Landmark ✳ (*Iklim al Tuffah, Jarjou-Ayn-Boswar Rd;* ✆ *07 210 211* or *07 211 210;* m *70 076 060;* e *info@mleeta.com; www.mleeta.com;* ⊕ *09.00–sunset daily; admission: adults LBP4,000, children under 10 LBP2,000*) As an in situ open-air and subterranean museum of war, the 60,000m^2 complex at Mleeta, which opened in May 2010 to coincide with the tenth anniversary of Israel's military withdrawal from Lebanon, must rank as one of the most unique and extraordinary shrines to military endeavour in the world. Some two years in the making, using the skills of 50 engineers and at an estimated cost of US$4 million, the site is a very graphic account of the conflicts between Israel and Hezbollah from 1982 to 2006. Although the site already has a large cafeteria, parking for more than 200 vehicles and a gift shop selling Hezbollah DVDs, T-shirts and books, further expansion is planned, including a Téléférique (cable car) linking Mleeta with the former Israeli outpost of Sujud, along with hotels and restaurants to put this site firmly on the theme park map. The site has proved very popular so far, and within the first six months of opening some 700,000 visitors have viewed the complex, both Lebanese and foreign. Except for the red-coloured Mleeta emblem of a sparrowhawk in flight, a bird that refuses to accept defeat, there are few insights into the defining ideology and philosophy of the Party of God (see box, pages 34–5 for more details on Hezbollah), with the site's principal aim devoted to showcasing the spoils of war.

The ideal starting point for the visitor is to view the two short films that document the site's construction, followed by a short history of the conflict between Israel and Hezbollah, before proceeding to the 350m^2 Exhibition Hall to view captured Israeli war relics from 1982–2006, which includes uniforms, aircraft drones, medical supplies and an interesting breakdown of the Israeli military command structure. Outside the hall is the crater-like 3,000m^2 Abyss, which showcases the 'Zionist enemy defeat' in the form of a captured Israeli Merkava tank with its gun turret in a twist, together with all manner of shells and rockets imbued with geometric and symbolic meanings. Following The Pathway from The Abyss takes you through a maze of former resistance positions: lifelike mannequins of Hezbollah fighters in battle readiness, together with the different fighting units and roles of the resistance including a field hospital and rocket launch sites. The 200m-long Cave, built over a three-year period with a careful disposal of debris to avoid the attentions of Israeli surveillance, finally became home to more than 7,000 resistance guerillas. Above ground, the final landmark, The Hill, at over 1,000m above sea level, gives commanding views over the mountains and valleys and former Israeli positions.

Informative free maps, containing a suggested walking route around the complex, with background information on the reverse side, are available at the entrance.

TYRE (SOUR)

Once dubbed the 'Queen of the Seas' for its mercantile and seafaring activities, Tyre was previously a flourishing commercial centre for international trade and appears in the classical writings of Herodotus and Homer. Some 80km from Beirut, and a little over 40km from Sidon, Tyre today evokes a battered and slightly melancholic feel with very few traces left of its once illustrious past. As the last major town before the Israeli border, Tyre's more recent and less salubrious past has tended to be dominated, like Sidon, by the intermittent Israel–Hezbollah conflict, but the city also suffered greatly during the civil war years. As an overwhelmingly Shi'ite town, Tyre wears its heart on its sleeve, with effigies of the resistance movement and shops selling Hezbollah souvenirs and photos of its leader, Hassan Nasrallah, ubiquitous. Although economically less developed and visited than other areas of the country, Tyre's wealth for the visitor today lies in its still traditional and functioning fishing port, its lively and engaging souk area and its 1984 UNESCO-designated World Heritage site of Roman-era architecture. During the summer months, an international arts and music festival is held within the environs of these Roman ruins (page 323).

HISTORY Although the Greek historian Herodotus dates settlement at Tyre back to 2750BCE, with further evidence of Neolithic-era occupation from 5000BCE, it wasn't until the 10th century BCE that the city began to experience the zenith of its power and wealth. Tyre was the largest and most successful city during the Phoenician era and under its most important leader, King Ahiram, the city expanded both geographically and economically. Formerly consisting of an island and mainland settlement, Ahiram connected the two areas and added a second port to take advantage of changing wind conditions. But it would take a chance discovery, according to legend, to usher in the golden age of Tyrian prosperity. According to mythology, Tyre's god Melqart was walking along the beach one day with Tyrus, a nymph, whose affections he coveted, when her dog chewed on a mollusc, turning the mutt's mouth purple. Desiring a dress of the same colour, Tyrus requested the garment be made for her or she would not see Melqart again. Thus the high-maintenance nymph's request was granted and so was born the manufacture of Tyre's greatest product, which became revered by the rich and royals alike. But economic prosperity had a flip side, and as the ancient Greek geographer Strabo pointed out: 'the great number of dye works renders the city unpleasant as a place of residence, but the superior skill of these people in the practice of this art is the source of its wealth'.

Tyrian trade of luxury and practical goods, in line with their skills in shipbuilding, expanded throughout the Mediterranean, and in 814BCE Phoenician princess Dido sailed west and founded Carthage in modern-day Tunisia. Towards the end of the 7th century BCE, the Babylonian king Nebuchadnezzar besieged the city for 13 years, but was unable to conquer it on account of its strong fortifications. With the fall of the Babylonians the Persians ushered in a period of stability and co-operation from around 539BCE, with the Tyrians assisting the Persian navy with ships and personnel during their wars with the Greeks. But the city suffered a major setback to its commercial strength in 332BCE when Alexander the Great, fresh from his success over Darius at the Battle of Issus, laid siege to the city for seven months (January–July), the most protracted battle in his short but illustrious military career, finally breaking the city's staunch resistance and massacring and enslaving Tyre's 30,000 inhabitants as the city came under Hellenistic rule, absorbing and adopting Greek culture and influences. The onset of Roman rule in 64BCE was a period of remarkable peace and prosperity for Tyre, the so-called Pax Romana, with Tyre's citizens granted parity with Rome's own subjects under the law, whilst the Byzantine era saw Tyre become one of the first cities to welcome Christianity to its shores. A change of master doesn't necessarily mean a change in fortune, and when the Arab dynasties arrived around CE634, they met with no resistance from Tyre's citizens and the port was transformed into a naval base for the Arab fleet. The Middle Ages, however, did bring a marked change of fortune to the city, as the Crusader knights from Europe forced Tyre's leaders to pay heavy tributes and besieged the city for months until ousted by the Mamluks in 1291, who proceeded to destroy the city to prevent the Franks' return. Tyre then sunk into relative obscurity and came under the banner of the Ottoman Empire from the 16th century, before finally becoming part of the newly formed Lebanese Republic after the end of World War I.

GETTING THERE From Beirut's Cola station [127 E7] catch a bus to Sidon (*LBP1,500–2,500, 45–50 minutes*) or take a taxi (*approx US$30*) to Sidon. From Sidon's Sahat al-Nejmeh there are regular buses and vans plying the route to Tyre costing LBP1,500–2,000 with a journey time of around 1 hour, arriving at the city's Al-Bass Roundabout & transport hub, which is a 5–10–minute walk from the Al-Bass archaeological site. The LTC buses depart Sidon (*LBP1,500*) every 20 minutes for Tyre between 06.00 and 18.00 daily. A taxi to Tyre from anywhere in Beirut should cost somewhere between US$50 and US$70 with a journey time of around 1½ hours.

GETTING AROUND Tyre is eminently walkable, with the main sites, souks, port and utilities all quite close together, though some may want to take a short *servees* (*LBP2,000*) or taxi to the inland Al-Bass archaeological site (page 322) if coming from the coast. Otherwise, it's about a 20–30-minute walk to the ruins.

⌂ WHERE TO STAY *Map, overleaf*

⌂ **Al-Yasmine Guest House** (16 rooms & 1 cottage) Maaliye, between Tyre & Naqoura; m 03 372 888; e info@alyasmineguesthouse.com; www.alyasmineguesthouse.com. Although around a half-hour's drive south from Tyre, the scenic & tranquil location of this guesthouse, set amid lovely greenery with deer, ducks & flamingos roaming the local landscape, makes this a perfect rural retreat for couples & families who don't mind paying a little more for that back-to-nature experience. The comfortable, en-suite rooms all with AC are spacious & tastefully decorated, & the homely feel is complemented by a range of facilities & activities such as outdoor swimming pool

(summer only), tennis courts, horseriding, cycling & hiking. B/fast inc. **$$$$$**

⌂ **Tyre Rest House Hotel & Resort** (62 rooms & suites) Sea Rd; ☎ 07 742 000 or 07 740 677/8; m 03 356 663; e info@resthouse-tyr.com.lb; www.resthouse-tyr.com.lb. Although character is largely absent from this establishment, it is nevertheless Tyre's most salubrious option with the majority of rooms having sea views together with all the refinements you would expect of a top-end hotel. The hotel also benefits from its own exclusive beach, swimming pool, health & massage facilities & has good conference & business amenities & services. Good discounts available

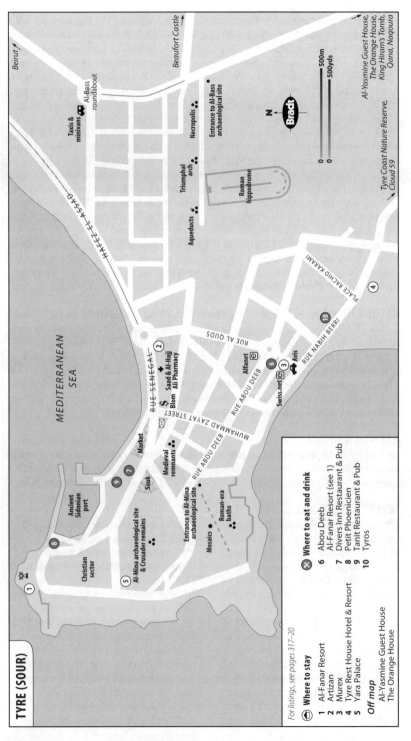

TYRE (SOUR)

MEDITERRANEAN SEA

Beirut

Beaufort Castle

Al-Bass roundabout

Taxis & minivans

HAFEZ EL-ASSAD

RUE SENEGAL

Blom

Saad & Al-Hajj Ali Pharmacy

Ancient Sidonian port

Christian sector

Market

Souk

Medieval remnants

Al-Mina archaeological site & Crusader remains

Entrance to Al-Mina archaeological site

Mosaics

Roman-era baths

MUHAMMAD ZAYAT STREET

RUE ABOU DEEB

RUE ABOU DEEB

Alfanet

Swiss.net

Avis

RUE AL QUDS

RUE NABIH BERRI

PLACE RACHID KARAMI

Aqueducts

Triumphal arch

Roman hippodrome

Necropolis

Entrance to Al-Bass archaeological site

N

Bradt

0   500m
0   500yds

Al-Yasmine Guest House,
The Orange House,
King Hiram's Tomb,
Qana, Naqoura

Tyre Coast Nature Reserve,
Cloud 59

For listings, see pages 317–20

Where to stay
1 Al-Fanar Resort
2 Artizan
3 Murex
4 Tyre Rest House Hotel & Resort
5 Yara Palace

Off map
  Al-Yasmine Guest House
  The Orange House

Where to eat and drink
6 Abou Deeb
   Al-Fanar Resort (see 1)
7 Divers Inn Restaurant & Pub
8 Petit Phoenicien
9 Tanit Restaurant & Pub
10 Tyros

on room rates outside the high summer season (Oct–May). B/fast inc. **$$$$$**

⌂ **Murex Hotel** (29 rooms & 10 apartments) Nabih Berri Bd; ☏07 347 111; e info@murex-hotel.com; www.murex-hotel.com. Renovated in recent years to a high standard, this is an ultra-modern hotel situated right on the Corniche with great sea views & boasting all the comforts of home. All rooms have AC, TV & free Wi-Fi. The hotel also has good business & conference facilities. B/fast inc. **$$$$**

⌂ **Yara Palace** (4 suites) Al-Kharab St, Tyre, opposite beach; ☏07 346 622; e info@yarapalace.com; www.yarapalace.com. A decent, though unexciting mid range option with the rooms situated above their restaurant. The en-suite rooms all have sea views but the teak-style décor & furnishings make this place feel a little claustrophobic. All rooms have TV, AC & kitchenettes. B/fast extra on request, free Wi-Fi. **$$$**

THE ORANGE HOUSE PROJECT

'My little peace of heaven' is how Mona Khalil describes her restored family home and ecotourism venture. Having left Lebanon for the Netherlands in 1975 after the onset of the country's civil war, she returned in 1999, with the aim of resettling in the abandoned family beach home. In memory of the country where she had spent more than 20 years, the house was repainted orange and called, unsurprisingly, The Orange House. Located in the village of Mansourieh, c14km south of Tyre at Naqoura, close to the border with Israel, the renovated solar-powered residence, surrounded by banana groves, citrus plantations and a garden brimming with orange trees and pretty flowers in beds and pots, is shared with Mona's friend and fellow environmental enthusiast Habiba Fayed, five goats, a black cat, two dogs and an African grey parrot. Whilst out walking one evening on the beach, a chance sighting of a turtle *en route* to lay her eggs gave birth to Mona's passion and 'dream' to preserve and protect the turtles, their eggs and new hatchlings, which was put into action in 2000. There are two species of sea turtle that come to lay their eggs on Lebanon's coastline each summer: the green turtle (*Chelonia mydas*) and the loggerhead (*Caretta caretta*) turtle, both of which are endangered species but can have a lifespan of up to 100 years and typically take up to 30 years to reach maturity and lay eggs. Fortunately, the female leaves traces of her tracks in the sand, so it is relatively easy to locate where the eggs have been laid and camouflaged, with each nest usually producing around 100 golf ball-like, soft-shelled eggs. Together, Mona and Habiba cordon off the area with 1m² wire mesh to protect them from marauding predators such as crabs, dogs and foxes. Following some 45–60 days of incubation, depending on the warmth of the sand, the eggs hatch and the young make their way down the beach at nightfall to the sea to begin their orphan life. The overall survival rate is not high, however, with roughly one hatchling per thousand reaching maturity. Mona and Habiba's tasks also include ensuring the beaches are kept clean and educating the local people about the turtles and the importance of correct waste disposal, so vital to the environment and the turtles themselves. In order to continue funding the project, the women decided to provide bed-and-breakfast accommodation (page 320), including a homemade breakfast made from their own garden produce, where guests can not only enjoy the beauty and tranquillity of the house, and beach area, but can also help out with keeping the beach clean and assisting with new hatchlings. If you wish to stay during the popular period of May–October, the turtles' nesting season, it is advisable to book well in advance.

🏠 **Al-Fanar Resort Hotel** (12 rooms) Rachid Nakhlé St, next to the lighthouse (Fanar); ☎07 741 111; m 03 665 016; e info@alfanarresort.com; www.alfanarresort.com. Great seafront location in a lovely, character-filled & centuries-old building. Rooms are fairly basic, but clean, & the feeling is one of a cosy, cottage-like atmosphere. There is a large open-plan lounge area, & outdoor space overlooking the sea for relaxing & dining. All 12 rooms have AC & en-suite bathrooms, & 10 have sea views. The hotel's Cave Club downstairs is regularly open for drinking & dance nights, enlivening an otherwise quiet, but excellent hotel. B/fast inc. **$$**

🏠 **Artizan Hotel** (17 rooms) Senegal St; ☎07 346 739; m 03 964 927; e info@artizanhotel.com; www. artizanhotel.com. A clean, but unremarkable hotel, with AC & TV in all rooms. It's decently located for shops & amenities but really only a place if there is no room at the inn elsewhere. B/fast is an extra US$5. **$**

✳ 🏠 **The Orange House** (3 rooms) Mansourieh Village, c15km south of Tyre on the Tyre–Naqoura Main Rd; ☎07 320 063; m 03 383 080; e monahabiba@yahoo.co.uk, orangehouseproject@gmail.com; 🅵 TheOrangeHouseProject. They may only have 3 rooms, but this is a delightful little place for those interested in ecotourism & conservation or just looking for something a little different from more mainstream lodging options (box, page 319). B/fast inc & guests have use of the kitchen. **$**

🍴 **WHERE TO EAT AND DRINK** *Map, page 318*

🍴 **Al-Fanar Resort Restaurant** Rachid Nakhlé St, next to the lighthouse; ☎07 740 111; ⏰ noon–late daily. This venue has a decent enough fresh fish & *mezze* menu but the prices are a little steep. The beach location is its greatest asset. **$$$$$**

🍴 **Tyros Restaurant** Nabbi Berri Bd; ☎07 741 027; m 03 048 954; ⏰ noon–midnight daily. A nice, friendly eatery with a hard-to-miss wood-panelled exterior, & very popular with local families. The restaurant is very roomy with a varied fish & *mezze* menu, & there's live Arabic music every Sat night. **$$$$$**

🍴 **Petit Phoenicien** Port; ☎07 740 564; m 03 655 177; ⏰ noon–midnight daily. The best location in the city for fish meals, this well-established & intimate, no-frills restaurant is located right on the port, where you can watch fishermen bringing in their catch & mending their nets. Delicious fish *kibbeh*, crab, shrimps & a host of the day's catches are served along with wine from the Bekaa Valley, Almaza beer & spirits. **$$$$**

🍴 **Tanit Restaurant & Pub** Port; ☎07 347 539; m 03 308 928; ⏰ 10.00–midnight daily. Small, intimate eatery with only 4 tables & a well-stocked bar area, with vaulted ceiling & the walls adorned with old black-&-white photos of Tyre, & guns & swords. This atmospheric restaurant serves an eclectic range of seafood, mixed grills & stir-fry dishes, & gets quite lively in the evenings & at w/ends. Many off-duty UNIFIL staff patronise this restaurant & are a useful source of information on travel south of Tyre & the overall security situation in this region. **$$$$**

🍴 **Divers Inn Restaurant & Pub** Port; m 03 359 687 or 03 740 987; ⏰ 10.00–late daily. Run by active diver Nazih, this is a great place for delicious, locally caught fish dishes, *mezze* & paella. Its cellar-like appearance with vaulted stone roof & walls has a great atmosphere & screens live football matches. Beer, whisky & wine are served, & a *nargileh* costs from LBP7,000. **$$$**

🍴 **Abou Deeb** Abou Deeb St; ☎07 349 372/808 or 07 740 808; m 03 234 630; ⏰ 08.00–midnight daily. Family-run & friendly Lebanese restaurant & take-away, serving tasty food in cheerful & pleasant surroundings. **$$**

ENTERTAINMENT AND NIGHTLIFE Despite its predominantly Shi'ite population, alcohol is readily available in the city, and during the summer months Tyre's beaches come alive with late-night beach parties, with many also serving delicious food. The pick of the current crop is **Cloud 59** (m *03 517 996* or *03 238 837*; 🅵 *Cloud59*; ⏰ *May–early Oct 10.00–02.00 Mon–Thu, 09.00–02.00 Fri–Sun*), serving seafood and *mezze* alongside cocktails and accompanied by music and dancing. The bar of the **Al-Fanar Resort Hotel** (☎ *07 740 111*; ⏰ *noon–late daily*) is also a popular nightspot, with its cellar-like vaulted pub serving alcohol until the early hours.

SHOPPING Despite its once illustrious trade in purple-dyed garments worn by the rich and royal, Tyre's shopping options are today much more anodyne and this is not really the place for serious souvenir hunting. The city's numerous shops and stores, however, do cater for most visitors' day-to-day needs, and you will have no problem buying food, cosmetics and other toiletries or any additional or replacement items of clothing you may require. The busy **souk** area is well worth a browse for handicrafts but can't compete with the offerings, or atmosphere, of the souks at Sidon and Tripoli. Tyre is, however, one of the best towns in Lebanon to purchase Hezbollah souvenirs (the other is Mleeta; pages 315–16). Whether you want a yellow T-shirt emblazoned with the Party of God's logo, a DVD, framed portraits of Secretary General Sayyed Hassan Nasrallah or other ornamental items, you're in the right place.

OTHER PRACTICALITIES

$ Blom Bank Senegal St; 07 740 900, 07 741 649; e blom.tyr@blom.com.lb; www.blombank. com; ⏰ 08.15–17.00 Mon–Fri (Jul–Aug 08.15–16.00), 08.15–12.30 Sat. Has 2 x 24hr ATMs.

✉ Post office Ogero Bldg, Senegal St; 07 740 565; www.libanpost.com; ⏰ 08.00–17.00 Mon–Fri, 08.00–13.30 Sat

✚ Saad & Al-Hajj Ali Pharmacy Senegal St; 07 344 227; m 03 165 653; ⏰ 08.00–23.00 daily. A friendly & well-stocked pharmacy.

e Swiss.net Al Quds St, behind Abou Deeb Restaurant; m 03 256 978 or 70 122 720; ⏰ 09.00–midnight daily. A good place to log on & check your email. LBP1,000/30mins, LBP1,500/hr.

e Alfanet Al-Quds St, 2min walk from Abou Deeb Restaurant; 07 347 047; e awad54@ hotmail.com; ⏰ 10.00–22.00 daily. LBP1,500/hr.

🚗 Avis Nabbi Berri Bd; 07 347 777; e reservation@avis-lebanon.com; www.avis. com.lb

WHAT TO SEE AND DO Tyre's port, like Sidon's, remains a hive of activity and is even more atmospheric, with colourful boats, mounds of nets dotting the harbourside and plenty of seafood dining right on the edge of the harbour. Here you can watch fishermen mending their nets, fashioning a new craft and repairing an old one, drinking tea, playing cards and smoking a *nargileh*, lending the whole area a lovely old-world charm. The city's souks, however, while busy and bustling and engaging enough, don't quite evoke the same anachronistic feel of those in Sidon, though the maze of alleyways of the Christian sector with their old traditional houses and churches are certainly worth a look. Lebanon's southernmost city's main draw is in its excellent collection of Roman-era artefacts and ruins at the Al-Mina and Al-Bass sites.

Roman archaeological sites Tyre's UNESCO-listed Roman archaeological legacy is spread over a couple of different sites, which have been extensively excavated over the course of half a century by Lebanon's Directorate of Antiquities. They are generally remarkably well preserved and give an excellent insight into the Roman and Byzantine period of Tyre's history. The Al-Bass ruins are the most extensive and imposing of the two main sites. At the time of writing the sites didn't have any detailed Ministry of Tourism pamphlets and, like at many other of Lebanon's sites, it is often best to pick up everything you will need for your visit from their main Hamra office in Beirut (page 135).

Al-Mina archaeological site (07 740 115; ⏰ *summer 08.00–19.00 daily, winter 08.00–17.00 daily; admission: adults LBP6,000, children over 10 LBP3,000, children under 10 free, students LBP1,000*) Also known as the Al-Medina or city ruins to locals, this site occupies a picturesque location leading onto the coastline on what was once the Phoenician island settlement. A pleasant 10-minute walk along the Corniche if coming from the Al-Fanar Resort Hotel, the main entrance is dominated by the 170m-long Mosaic Road flanked by columns and once covered in Byzantine **mosaic paving**, some of which can still be seen. The smaller road to the right, containing some 26 columns tapering away to the coastline, sits adjacent to the 1st-century sporting arena, a large rectangular space with rows of stepped seating able to accommodate 2,000 spectators, who would once have enjoyed the spectacles of boxing and wrestling. Across the main Mosaic Road towards the coast is a series of nine columns denoting the palestra, a 30m^2 area dating back to the 2nd century CE, which appears to have had a number of functions over the years, ranging from a sporting venue, a marketplace and, following the 6th-century CE earthquake, may have been used as a purple-dye factory. As was customary, adjacent to the palestra were the bathing areas: there are extensive remains of these 2nd- and 3rd-century CE **Roman baths** and their hypocaust clay discs, which supported the marble floor allowing hot air to circulate and provide underfloor heating. A couple of minutes' walk to the north of Al-Mina is the **Crusader cathedral**. More than a little imagination is required to imagine this site in its heyday. This 12th-century cathedral offers up little of its history, save for a wall and a few fallen granite columns strewn around the site, which in parts is often eclipsed by the amount of domestic rubbish dumped around the area. Built on a much earlier site dedicated to Tyre's Phoenician god Melqart, during the Crusader period, the cathedral was the setting for the coronation of the Kings of Jerusalem and archaeological digging here has revealed a system of earlier Roman and Byzantine roads beneath the shrine.

Al-Bass archaeological site (✆ 07 740 530; ☉ summer 08.00–19.00 daily, winter 08-00–18.00 daily; admission: adults LBP6,000, children over 10 LBP3,500, children under 10 free, students LBP1,000) The most grandiose of Tyre's Roman past, this second site covers a much larger area than the Al-Mina ruins with a cornucopia of archaeological finds spanning the 2nd to 4th centuries CE. Entering the site from the east–west Byzantine Road is a vast **necropolis** revealing an array of ornately decorated sarcophagi in marble and stone, followed further ahead by a 6th-century funerary chapel with patterned marble flooring within its compact courtyard. Undoubtedly one of the two main highlights of the Al-Bass site is the 2nd-century **triumphal arch**, probably built during the reign of the emperor Hadrian and marking the point at which the Byzantine Road becomes the older, Roman Road. At 20m tall, the arch has been beautifully restored by the Directorate of Antiquities, which had suffered almost total destruction during the devastating earthquake of CE551. Just along the Roman Road beyond the arch are the remains of an **aqueduct**, which once supplied water from the Ras al-Ain Springs 6km away to the south.

To the left of the aqueduct is Al-Bass's other key highlight, the unmissable U-shaped **Roman hippodrome**. Built during the 2nd century CE and measuring 480m by 160m, it is the largest and best preserved in the world, having once staged spectacular chariot races and other sporting events, with the grandstand able to seat more than 30,000 spectators. Beneath the grandstand, still walkable, was a marketplace and shops. Today, the Hippodrome plays host to less death-defying activities in the form of a summer festival (opposite).

Tyre Coast Nature Reserve (TCNR) Southeast of Tyre (✆ 07 351 341; m 03 483 331; e tcnr98@hotmail.com; www.moe.gov.lb, www.ramsar.org; ☉ 08.00–17.00 Mon–Sat, closed Sun unless visitors call ahead; admission free, but suggested voluntary donation of around LBP10,000 per group of 3) Covering an area of some 380ha and containing the largest sandy beach in the country, the reserve was established in November 1998 and designated a Ramsar Site in 1999, named after the Iranian city

where the convention for the protection and use of wetland areas was signed. The TCNR contains a whole gamut of flora and fauna including birdlife and is a nesting site for the green sea turtle (*Chelonia mydas*) and the loggerhead turtle (*Caretta caretta*). The activities on offer here include birdwatching, cycling, swimming and snorkelling, turtle watching and kayaking. The area also comprises the **Ras al-Ain Springs**, about 6km south of the city, which have provided irrigation and drinking water for the city since Phoenician times.

Festivals in the south

Ashura This annual Shi'ite 'festival' of remembrance in Nabatiye is of overriding religious importance to this sect, which commemorates the martyrdom of the Prophet Muhammad's grandson Hussein, who was slain at the Battle of Karbala, southern Iraq, in CE680. Spread over nine days, it is quite unlike any festival you will experience anywhere in Lebanon, with processions of sadness building to a crescendo on the tenth day of Muharram, the actual date Hussein died, accompanied by women screaming and men and children chanting while lacerating themselves with razors, knives and swords, drawing blood, re-enacting the pain and suffering of the third *imam* Hussein. The best place to see this is in Nabatiye, an unremarkable, sprawling and nondescript town, which is overwhelmingly Shi'ite. As the date is calculated according to the Muslim lunar calendar based on an actual sighting of the New Moon, it is a 'moveable feast', but at the time of writing is due on or around 30 September in 2017 and around 10–11 days earlier in subsequent years. Given the passion and grief attached to the occasion, it may be sensible to seek out the services of a trusted guide if you wish to attend, and to be sensitive by wearing conservative attire. From Sidon's transport hub at Sahat al-Nejmeh, buses travel regularly to Nabatiye and cost LBP2,000, taking between 30–45 minutes, while the taxi fare is around LBP10,000.

Tyre and South Festival (✆ *01 791 140* or *01 791 252; www.tyrefestival.com*) First held in 1996, this annual festival of performing arts takes place during July and August within the environs of the spectacular Hippodrome at the Al-Bass site and showcases a range of local and international artists, dancers, musicians, singers, poets, puppetry and theatrical performances. The festival's 2010 line-up included a colourful collection of 46 dancers, poetry readings and singers from the Gulf. Tickets can be obtained locally from the Tyre Rest House Hotel and Resort (page 317), or from any branch of Virgin Megastore (page 153). See the festival website for details of the year's upcoming performances.

AROUND TYRE

KING AHIRAM'S TOMB (☺ *24hrs daily; admission free*) Although not one of Lebanon's most illustrious sites, King Ahiram's Tomb, or Qabr Hiram in Arabic, is still worth a quick look. Located around 6km southeast of Tyre on the road to Qana, the limestone sarcophagus, unfortunately a little daubed with some 20th-century graffiti additions, is subject to some academic debate but often attributed to Ahiram, Tyre's most prominent king, famous for his assistance in building King Solomon's Temple in Jerusalem during his 34-year reign. The tomb itself is not much more than a series of stone blocks, reaching a height of 6m, and is part of a larger excavated area that has unearthed Roman and Byzantine tombs. During his excavations in the 19th century, the French philosopher and writer Ernest Renan (1823–92) discovered the remains of an earlier stairway and chamber beneath the tomb (inaccessible), but its presence continues to remain a mystery. The tomb is about 20 minutes by car on the right-hand side of the road *en route* to Qana from Tyre, and there is a Ministry of Tourism sign for 'Tombe de Hiram' just before the structure.

QANA This small, mainly Shi'ite town of around 10,000 people, is a further 6km or so along the road from King Ahiram's Tomb and some 11km southeast of Tyre, and is where, according to the Gospel of St John, Jesus reputedly performed his first miracle, turning water into wine at a local wedding ceremony. Although the authenticity of the claim has been the subject of ongoing debate (some scholars have advocated that in fact it was in the town of Kafar Qana near Nazareth in Israel), Lebanon's claim appears to be reinforced by the ecclesiastical 4th-century historian Eusebius, which in turn is backed up by the 3rd-century writings of St Jerome. **Qana Grotto** (*1km from Qana town;* m *03 963 932;* ⊕ *08.00–16.00 daily; admission: adults LBP4,000, children LBP2,000*), the site of the alleged miracle, restored by the Ministry of Tourism, is well worth a visit, and contains a bas-relief of Jesus and the Apostles, and other carvings, ancient stone water basins and a cave with a wooden cross leaning beside the entrance which is still visited by Christian pilgrims each Christmas. A small gift shop sells postcards and souvenirs, and there is ample free parking outside the entrance and onsite toilet facilities.

More recently, Qana has come to be associated with a couple of less palatable religious associations, specifically the conflicts between Israel and Hezbollah. During the former's Operation Grapes of Wrath in 1996 against the Shi'ite resistance, Israel launched relentless shelling on the Fujian UNIFIL compound, where refugees were sheltering from the conflict. The continuous 17-minute bombardment killed 106 civilians and wounded many others. Subsequent investigations revealed that the attack was most likely a deliberate one. The date of the genocide, 18 April, is now an annual day of mourning and remembrance in Lebanon. There is a monument and a series of photographs near the UN base that can be viewed. A decade later, during the 2006 July War between Israel and Hezbollah, 28 civilians were killed, mostly children, in night-time air attacks by the Jewish state, and a small and very poignant graveyard is a shrine to those who died.

Appendix 1

LANGUAGE

Arabic is the official language in Lebanon but the amount you will need to speak whilst in the country will very much depend on the type of trip you are taking. If you are spending just a few days in Beirut or on a week-long organised tour, then you will most likely be able to get by with just a few words such as those in *Essentials* (below) as many people speak English and French in the capital. If you are planning on more extensive or independent travel around less cosmopolitan regions of Lebanon which will bring you into closer contact with the locals, then a more extensive vocabulary will be both practically beneficial and will win you many friends along the way, as it is a well-known and true cliché that Arabs really do appreciate foreigners' attempts to communicate in their language. If arriving on business, English is widely spoken in commercial circles, but once again a pidgin command of Arabic will do you no harm in establishing a rapport. French is also widely utilised, especially in east Beirut and in many parts of the Mount Lebanon region, a hangover from colonial rule, and in the sections below French is included alongside the Arabic words and phrases for a more comprehensive vocabulary and to help you negotiate your way in most linguistic situations. In some cases there is more than one way to stay the same thing, and this is indicated by the forward slash in the relevant entry.

In written form spoken Arabic can show great variation in spelling and it is far from being an exact science as to the 'right' or 'wrong' way to spell words and phrases, which can sometimes be confusing for the visitor trying to decipher street and place names. Thus the words and phrases used here are as phonetically friendly as possible and employ spellings as 'conventional' as can be realistically accomplished. For those with a desire or need to go beyond the rudiments of the language, the basic 28-character Arabic alphabet, written from right to left, is given below together with a rough guide to pronunciation. Appendix 3 (page 351) details some further reading and listening on the Arabic language, and the author would particularly recommend either the BBC Active *Talk Arabic* or *Colloquial Arabic (Levantine)* books and CD package for those readers wanting to delve more deeply into the details of the spoken Arabic in Lebanon and the Levant.

ESSENTIALS

English	Arabic	French
Welcome!	*ahlan wa sahlan!*	*Bienvenue!*
Good morning	*sabaaH al-khayr*	*Bonjour*
Good evening	*masaa al-khayr*	*Bonsoir*
Hello	*marHaba*	*Salut*
Goodbye (one leaving)	*bikhaa Trak*	*Au revoir*
Goodbye (one staying)	*ma' as-salaameh*	*Au revoir*
My name is...	*ismi...*	*Je m'appelle...*
What is your name?	*shoo ismak? (m),*	*Comment vous*
	shoo ismik? (f)	*appelez-vous?*

I am from England	ana min Ingilterra	Je viens d'Angleterre
I am from America	ana min Amerika	Je viens des Etats-Unis
I am from Australia	ana min Uustralia	Je viens d'Australie
How are you?	keefak? (m), keefik? (f)	Comment allez-vous?
Pleased to meet you	tasharrafna	Enchanté
Thank you	shukran	Merci
Thank you very much	shukran jazeelan	Merci beaucoup
Don't mention it	ahlan/afwan	De rien/Je vous en prie
Please	min faDlak (m), minfaDlik (f)	S'il vous plaît
Yes	aywa/na'am	Oui
No	laa	Non
I don't understand	ana maa faahim (m)	Je n'ai pas compris
	ana maa faahma (f)	Je n'ai pas compris
Please would you speak more slowly?	mumkin tiHki 'ala mahlak (m), mahlik(f)?	Pouirriez-vous parler plus lentement?
Sorry	assif (m), asfa (f)	Pardon
Enjoy your meal!	sahtein!	Bon appétit!
Congratulations!	mabrook!	Félicitations!

THE ARABIC ALPHABET

Final	Medial	Initial	Alone	Transliteration	Pronunciation
ـا			ا	aa	as in 'after'
ـب	ـبـ	بـ	ب	b	as in 'but'
ـت	ـتـ	تـ	ت	t	as in 'tin'
ـث	ـثـ	ثـ	ث	th	as in 'think'
ـج	ـجـ	جـ	ج	j	as in 'jam'
ـح	ـحـ	حـ	ح	H	emphatic, breathy 'h'
ـخ	ـخـ	خـ	خ	kh	as in the Scottish 'loch'
ـد			د	d	as in 'den'
ـذ			ذ	dh	as in 'that'
ـر			ر	r	as in 'red'
ـز			ز	z	as in 'zero'
ـس	ـسـ	سـ	س	s	as in 'sit', hard 's'
ـش	ـشـ	شـ	ش	sh	as in 'shut'
ـص	ـصـ	صـ	ص	S	emphatic, strong 's'
ـض	ـضـ	ضـ	ض	D	emphatic, strong 'd'
ـط	ـطـ	طـ	ط	T	emphatic, strong 't'
ـظ	ـظـ	ظـ	ظ	Z	emphatic, strong 'z'
ـع	ـعـ	عـ	ع	'	gutteral stop, hardest sound for non-Arabs to make, called 'ayn'.
ـغ	ـغـ	غـ	غ	gh	like a gargling sound
ـف	ـفـ	فـ	ف	f	as in 'fire'
ـق	ـقـ	قـ	ق	q	like a guttural 'k'
ـك	ـكـ	كـ	ك	k	as in 'king'
ـل	ـلـ	لـ	ل	l	as in 'lady'
ـم	ـمـ	مـ	م	m	as in 'mat'
ـن	ـنـ	نـ	ن	n	as in 'not'
ـه	ـهـ	هـ	ه	h	as in 'hat'
ـو			و	w	as in 'will', or 'oo' as in 'food'
ـي	ـيـ	يـ	ي	y	as in 'yet', or 'ee' as in 'clean'

QUESTIONS

Do you understand?	'aam tefham? (m), tefhami? (f)	Comprenez-vous?
How?	keef? kiif?	Comment?
What?	shoo?	Quoi?
Where?	wayn?	Où?
What is it?	shoo hayda?	Qu'est-ce que c'est?
Which?	'ayy...?/ayahoo?/ayeh?	Quel...?
When?	aymta? emta?	Quand?
Why?	laysh? lay?	Pourquoi?
Who?	meen?	Qui?
How much?	addayish?	Combien?

NUMBERS

1	wahad	un
2	itnayin	deux
3	talaata	trois
4	arba'a	quatre
5	khamseh	cinq
6	sitteh	six
7	sab'aa	sept
8	tamanyah	huit
9	tisaa	neuf
10	shara	dix
11	hidaash	onze
12	ithnaash	douze
13	talataash	treize
14	arba'ataash	quatorze
15	khamsta'ash	quinze
16	sitta'ash	seize
17	saba'ata'ash	dix-sept
18	tamenta'ash	dix-huit
19	tisi'ta'ash	dix-neuf
20	ishreen	vingt
30	talateen	trente
40	arba'een	quarante
50	khamseen	cinquante
60	sitteen	soixante
70	sab'een	soixante-dix
80	tamaaneen	quatre-vingts
90	tes'een	quatre-vingt-dix
100	miyya	cent
1,000	alf	mille

TIME

What time is it?	ayy as-sa'a?	Quelle heure est-il?
It's am	es-saa'a... SabaaH	Il est...du matin
It's pm (afternoon)	es-saa'a...ba'ed aD-Dohr	Il est...de l'après-midi
It's pm (evening and night)	es-saa'a...al-massa	Il est...du soir
today	al-yawm	aujourd'hui
tonight	al-layla	cette nuit/ce soir

tomorrow	*bookra/bukra*	*demain*
yesterday	*imbaariH*	*hier*
morning	*SabaaH*	*le matin*
evening	*al-massa*	*le soir*

DAYS

Monday	*al-itnayn*	*lundi*
Tuesday	*al-talaata*	*mardi*
Wednesday	*al-arba'a*	*mercredi*
Thursday	*al-khamees*	*jeudi*
Friday	*al-juma'a*	*vendredi*
Saturday	*al-sabt*	*samedi*
Sunday	*al-ahad*	*dimanche*

MONTHS

January	*kanun thani*	*janvier*
February	*shbaaT*	*février*
March	*adhar*	*mars*
April	*neesan*	*avril*
May	*ayyar*	*mai*
June	*Hzayran*	*juin*
July	*tammooz*	*juillet*
August	*'aab*	*août*
September	*aylool*	*septembre*
October	*techreen al-awal*	*octobre*
November	*techreen at-thaani*	*novembre*
December	*kanun al-awal*	*décembre*

GETTING AROUND
Public transport

I'd like...	*biddee/baddee...*	*Je voudrais*
... a one-way ticket	*...tadhkara rowHa/ tadhkarat zahab*	*...un billet aller simple*
... a return ticket	*...tadhkara rowha raj'aa/ tadhkarat zahab wa owda*	*un billet retour/un aller retour*
I want to go to	*baddee rooH 'aala*	*Je veux aller à...*
How much is it?	*addaysh?*	*Combien ça coûte?*
What time does it leave?	*aya sa'a biemshi/birooH?*	*A quelle heure part-il?*
What time is it?	*ayy as-sa'a?*	*Quelle heure est-il?*
The bus has been delayed	*ta'akhar maw 'aad el-baaS*	*Le bus a été retardé*
The bus has been cancelled	*eltagha maw 'aad el-baaS*	*Le bus a été annulé*
first class	*darajeh oola*	*...de première classe*
second class	*darajeh taniyeh*	*...de seconde classe*
ticket office	*maktab bay' et-tadhaker*	*guichet/bureau de vente des billets*
timetable	*jadwal el-mawa'eed*	*horaire*
map	*khaariTa*	*carte*
from	*min*	*de*
to	*ila*	*à*
bus station	*maHaTTat il-baaSaat*	*gare d'autobus/gare routière*

airport	maTar	aéroport
port	marfa' mina	port
bus	(s), baaSaat (pl)	autobus/autocar
plane	Tayaara	avion
boat	markab/safeena	bateau
ferry	ferry	ferry/traversier
car	sayaara seeyara	voiture
4x4	4 by 4	quatre quatre
taxi	taxi taksi	taxi
shared taxi	servees	servees
minibus	minibaaS	minibus
motorbike	motoceecle/darrajeh nariyeeh	moto
moped	mobilette	cyclomoteur/vélomoteur
arrival	wussool wuSuul	arrivée
departure	el-inTilaa lyimshi	départ
here	hawn	ici
there	honik	là-bas
Safe journey!	safra muwaffaqa/bis-salaameh!	Bon voyage!

Private transport

Is this the road to...?	min hawn Tareeq...?	C'est par là la route de...?
Where is the service station?	wayn maHaTet el-benzine?	Où se trouve la station-service?
Please fill it up	faowilha please/'aabiha law samaHt	Faites-le plein, s'il vous plaît
I'd like...litres	baddee...litre	Je voudrais ...litres
diesel	deesel	diesel
leaded petrol	benzine bi-raSaSS	essence au plomb
unleaded petrol	benzine bala raSaSS	essence sans plomb
I have broken down	ta'a Talet sayartee	Je suis en panne

Road signs

give way	afseH eT-Tareeq	céder le passge
danger	kha Tar	danger
entry	madkhal	entrée
detour	taHwila	déviation
one way	Tareeq fee ettejah waHed	voie à sens unique
toll	rasem muroor	péage
no entry	mamnoo' ed-dukhool/ 'itijah mamnoo	entrée interdite/ sens interdit
exit	makhraj	sortie
keep clear	ibqa ba' eed	défense d'entrer/ dégager la voie

Directions

Where is...?	Wayn...?	Où se trouve...?
Go straight ahead	rooH deghree (m), rooHee deghree (f)	Allez tout droit
Turn left	brom (m), bremee (f) 'alash-shmel/'alal-yassar	Tournez à gauche

Turn right	brom (m), bremee (f) 'alal-yameen	Tournez à droite
...at the traffic lights	...'àla isharet el-muroor	...aux feux de signalisation
...at the roundabout	...'àlal-mustadira	...au rond-point
north	shmel	nord
south	jnoob	sud
east	sharq	est
west	gharb	ouest
behind	wara	derrière
in front of	edam	devant
near	janb	près
opposite	muqaabil	en face de/opposé

Street signs

entrance	madkhal	entrée
exit	makhraj	sortie
open	maftooH	ouvert
closed	ma'fuul	fermé
toilets-men	Hammam rijal	toilettes des hommes
toilets-women	Hammam sayidat	toilettes des dames
information (desk)	iste'alamat	accueil
information	ma'loomat	renseignements/ informations

ACCOMMODATION

hotel	funduq	hôtel
soap	saboun	savon
Where is a cheap hotel?	wayn fee funduq rkhiSS?	Où trouver un hôtel bon marché?
Where is a good hotel?	wayn fee funduq mneeH?	Où trouver un bon hôtel?
Could you please write the address?	mumkin tekteblee el-'iinwan?	Pourriez-vous m' écrire l'adresse s'il vous plaît?
Do you have any rooms available?	'iindak ghoraf fa Dyee?	Aves-vous des chambres libres?
I'd like...	baddee...	Je voudrais...
...a single room	...ghorfee la-shakheSS waHed	...une chambre simple
...a double room	...ghorfee la-shakheSeiyn/double	...une chambre double
...a room with two beds	...ghorfee fiha sarirayn	...une chambre à deux lits
...a room with a bathroom	...ghorfee ma'à Hammam	...une chambre avec salle de bains
...to share a dorm	...manameh mushtarakeh fi marqad	...partager un dortoir
How much is it per night?	adeish el-layleh?	C'est combien la nuit?
How much is it per person?	adeish la-shakheeSS waHed?	C'est combien par personne?
Where is the toilet?	wayn el-Hamman?/ et-twaleet?/el-mirHaaD?	Où sont les toilettes?
Where is the bathroom?	wayn el-Hamman?	Où est la salle de bains?
Is there hot water?	fee mai sokhneh?	Y a-t-il de l'eau chaude?

Is there electricity?	*fee kahraba?*	*Y a-t-il de l'électricité?*
Is breakfast included?	*fee terwiqa/fee fuToor ma' el-ghorfee?*	*Petit déjeuner compris?*
I am leaving today	*raH etrok el-funduq el-yom*	*Je quitte l'hôtel/je pars aujourd'hui*

FOOD

Do you have a table for ... people?	*'iindak Towlee la...ashkhaSS?*	*Avez-vous une table pour...personnes?*
...a children's menu	*...menu lel-owlad?*	*...un menu pour enfants?*
I am a vegetarian	*ana nabati nabatee*	*Je suis végétarien*
Do you have any vegetarian dishes?	*'iindak aSnaaf lel-nabateyeen?*	*Auriez-vous des plats pour végétariens?*
Please bring me...	*jiblee min faDlak...(m), jiblee min faDlik...(f)*	*Apportez-moi, s'il vous plaît...*
a fork	*showkeh*	*une fourchette*
a knife	*sekkeen*	*un couteau*
a spoon	*mal 'aaqa*	*une cuillère*
Please may I have the bill?	*mumkin el-Hissab min faDlak?*	*Puis-je avoir l'addition, s'il vous plaît?*

Basics

food	*akl*	*nourriture*
bread	*khebez khubz*	*pain*
butter	*zebdeh*	*beurre*
cheese	*jebneh*	*fromage*
eggs	*bayd*	*oeuf*
oil	*zeyt*	*huile*
pepper	*bahar filfil*	*poivre*
salt	*meleH*	*sel*
sugar	*sukkar*	*sucre*
yoghurt	*laban*	*yaourt*

Fruits

fruit	*fawaakih/fweké*	*fruit*
apples	*tuffaah*	*pommes*
bananas	*mawz mooz*	*bananes*
grapes	*'iinab*	*raisins*
mango	*manga*	*mangues*
olives	*zaytoon*	*olives*
oranges	*burtuqal burtu'aan*	*oranges*
pears	*njass*	*poires*
watermelon	*batik*	*pastèque*

Vegetables

vegetables	*khodra*	*légume*
broccoli	*broccoli*	*brocoli*
carrots	*jazar*	*carottes*
garlic	*toom*	*ail*
onion	*baSSal*	*oignon*
peppers	*flayflee*	*poivrons*

potato	*batata*	*pomme de terre*
salad	*salata*	*salade*

Fish

fish	*samak*	*poisson*
mackerel	*makreel*	*maquereau*
mussels	*balaH el-baHer*	*moules*
salmon	*salamoon*	*saumon*
tuna	*balamida*	*thon*

Meat

meat	*lahem*	*viande*
beef	*baqar*	*boeuf*
chicken	*dajaj*	*poulet*
goat	*ma'ez*	*chèvre*
pork	*khanzeer*	*porc*
lamb	*kharouf*	*agneau*
sausage	*maqaaneq*	*saucisse*

Drinks

beer	*beera/biira*	*bière*
coffee	*ahwa*	*café*
fruit juice	*'aSSeer*	*jus de fruit*
milk	*Haleeb/Haliib*	*lait*
tea	*shai shaay*	*thé*
water	*mai/mayya*	*eau*
wine	*nabeed*	*vin*

SHOPPING

I'd like to buy...	*baddee ishtiree...*	*Je voudrais acheter...*
How much is it?	*adeish Haqo?*	*Combien coûte?*
I don't like it	*ma Habbayto (m),* *ma Habbayta (f)*	*Je ne l'ai pas aimé (m),* *aimée (f)*
I'm just looking	*aam betfarraj bass*	*Je voudrais juste regarder/* *je regarde seulement*
It's too expensive	*ghalee kteer*	*C'est trop cher*
I'll take it	*raH bekhdo (m),* *raH bekhdo (f)*	*Je le prends (m),* *Je la prends (f)*
Please may I have...?	*mumkin akhod...?*	*Puis-je avoir...?*
Do you accept...	*btiqbal (m)..., btiqbali (f)*	*Acceptez-vous...*
...credit cards?	*...biTaqat i'itimad?*	*...des cartes de crédits?*
...traveller's cheques?	*...chiccat el-musafer?*	*...des chèques de voyage*
more	*aktar*	*plus*
less	*aqal*	*moins*
smaller	*aSghar*	*plus petit*
bigger	*akbar*	*plus grand*
market	*souk*	*marché*

COMMUNICATIONS

I am looking for	*wayn...*	*Je cherche...*
bank	*masraf*	*banque*

castle	qalaa	château
chemist	Saydaliyeh/Saydaliyya	pharmacie
church	kaneesa	église
embassy	safaara	ambassade
exchange office	maktab Sayrafa/Sarraf	bureau de change
hospital	mustashfa	hôpital
telephone centre	markaz hawatef	centre téléphonique
market	souk	marché
mosque	masjid	mosquée
museum	matHaf	musée
post office	maktab bareed	bureau de poste
tourist office	maktab siyaHa	office de tourisme

HEALTH

diarrhoea	ishal	diarrhée
nausea	ghathayan/là ayan nafess/mareeD	nausée
doctor	Hakeem	médecin
prescription	waSfeh Tibbeyeh	ordonnance
pharmacy	Saydaliyeh	pharmacie
paracetamol	paracetamol	paracétamol
antibiotics	muDadat Hayaweeyeh	antibiotiques
antiseptic	mu Tahher	antiseptique
tampons	fatila tampon	tampon hygiénique
condoms	waqee dhakaree	préservatif
contraceptive (pills)	huboob mana'a el-haml	pilules contraceptives
sun block	waqi min esh-shams	écran solaire
I am...	ma'ii...	Je suis...
...asthmatic	...raboo	...asthmatique
...epileptic	...daa' eS-Saraa'/epilepsiya	...épileptique
...diabetic	...sukkaree	...diabétique
I'm allergic to...	ma'ii Hassassiya 'ala...	Je suis allergique...
...penicillin	...el-penicillin	...à la pénicilline

EMERGENCY

Help!	sa'idoonee!/an-najdeh!	Au secours!
Call a doctor!	talfen lal-Hakeem!/laT-Tabeeb!	Appelez le médecin!
There's been an accident	Sar Haadeth	Il y a eu un accident
I'm lost	ana Diy'eh (m), Diy'aa(f)	Je suis perdu (m), perdue (f)
Go away!	rooH min hawn! (m), rooHi min hawn! (f)/imshi!	Allez-vous-en!
police	shurta/shorTa	police
fire	Hareeq	incendie
ambulance	is'aaf	ambulance
thief	Haramee	voleur
hospital	mustashfa	hôpital
I am ill	ana mareeD	Je suis malade
Stop!	wa'af/wa'eif	arrêt

| ...nuts | ...el-mukassart | ...aux fruits secs à coque |
| ...bees | ...el-naHel | ...aux abeilles |

TRAVEL WITH CHILDREN

Is there a...	fee...	Y a-t-il...
...baby changing room?	...ghorfee lataghyier el-HifaDat?	...une salle à langer?/ pour changer les couches?
...children's menu	...menu lel-owlad?	...un menu pour enfants?
Do you have...	'iindak... (m), ' iindak... (f)	Avez-vous...
...infant milk formula?	...Haleeb lel-aTfal?	...du lait maternisé?/ pour enfants?
nappies	HifaDat	couches
potty	asriyeh/nooneyeh lel-aTfal/ pot lel-aTfal	pot
babysitter	babysitter/jaleesat aTfal	baby-sitter
highchair	kirsi akl lel-aTfal	chaise haute
Are children allowed?	masmooH lel-owlad?	Acceptez-vous les enfants?

OTHER

my/mine	zaherti	mon/le mien (m), ma/la mienne (f)
your/yours (s)	zahertak (m), zahertik (f)	ton/le tien (m), ta/la tienne (f)
your/yours (p)	zahretkom	votre/le vôtre (m), la vôtre (f)
our/ours	zahretna	notre/le nôtre (m), la nôtre (f)
and	wawi	et
some	shwayee/kam	un peu de/quelques
but	walaaken/bass	mais
this	hayda (m), haydee (f)	ceci/celui-ci (m), celle-ci (f)
that	haydaak (m), haydeek (f)	cela/celui-là (m), cella-là (f)
expensive	ghalee/ghali (m), ghaliyeh/ ghatilya (f)	cher (m), chère (f)
cheap	rakheeSS (m), rakheeSa (f)	bon marché/pas cher
beautiful	Helu (m), Helueh (f) /jamiil (m), jamiila (f)	beau (m), belle (f)
ugly	bashe'a/mush Helu	laid (m), laide (f)
old	adeem (m), adeemeh(f)	vieux (m), vieille (f)
new	jdeed (m), jadeed (f)	nouveau (m), nouvelle (f)
good	kuwayyis	bon (m), bonne (f)
good (food)	Tayeb (m), Taybeh (f)	bon (m), bonne (f)
bad	mush mneeH/'aaTel (m), 'aaTleh (f)	mauvaise (m), mauvaise (f)
bad (food)	mush Tayeb	mauvais/gate avené
early	bakkeer	tôt/de bonne heurel en avance
late	mit'akhar	en retard
hot	sokhn (m), sokhenh (f)	chaud (m), chaude (f)

cold	*baarid*	*froid (m), froide (f)*
difficult	*Sa'eb (m), Sa'abeh(f)*	*difficile*
easy	*sahel (m), sahleh(f)*	*facile*
boring	*mumel (m), mumelleh (f)*	*ennuyant (m), ennuyante (f)*
interesting	*mufeed/muhimm/lazeez/ mutheer lil-ihtimaam*	*intéressant (m), intéressante (f)*
mobile phone	*mubayl/maHmool*	*mobile*

LEBANON ONLINE

For additional online content, articles, photos and more on Lebanon, why not visit www.bradtguides.com/lebanon.

SEND US YOUR SNAPS!

We'd love to follow your adventures using our *Lebanon* guide – why not send us your photos and stories via Twitter (@BradtGuides) and Instagram (@bradtguides) using the hashtag #lebanon. Alternatively, you can upload your photos directly to the gallery on the Lebanon destination page via our website (*www.bradtguides.com*).

Appendix 2

GLOSSARY

Abbasid Caliphate
(CE750–1258)   Dynasty of Sunni Muslims who overthrew the Umayyad caliphate and ruled from their capital, Baghdad, until finally defeated by the Mongol Empire.

ablaq   The technique of using patterns of alternating shades of stonework in a mosque or other building; a characteristic feature of Islamic architecture during the Mamluk and Ottoman eras.

acropolis   The fortified upper section of a (usually) Greek city, containing sacred, political or economic buildings of some importance.

ahd   The term of office for Lebanon's president.

Ahl al-Kitab   Arabic phrase for *People of the Book* comprising non-Muslims such as Christians and Jews who followed earlier, pre-Koranic teachings and texts.

ain   Spring or well

agora   Literally 'assembly'. Open-plan meeting area such as a marketplace.

Allah   God

Al-Nakba   Arabic name for the defeat and expulsion of the Palestinian people from their homeland in 1948 following the first Arab–Israeli war and the creation of the State of Israel. Literally, the 'catastrophe' or 'disaster'.

Amal Movement
(Harakat Amal)   Arabic acronym for 'Hope'. Founded in 1975 by Imam Musa al-Sadr. Amal is a Lebanese anti-Israeli, Shi'ite military and political organisation led by current parliamentary speaker Nabih Berri.

Arab League   Association of 22 Arab countries established in Cairo on 22 March 1945 by Egypt, Iraq, Jordan, Lebanon, Saudi Arabia and Syria to foster ties and unity across economic, social, military and political fronts.

Arab Spring   Generic term for a series of popular pro-democracy uprisings which began in Tunisia in 2010 challenging dictatorship, corruption and human rights abuses, which rapidly spread across the MENA region.

architrave   Lowest horizontal segment of the *entablature* resting on columns; can also refer to any moulded elements framing a door or window.

Arz al-Rab   'Cedars of the Lord'; the local name for the stands of cedar trees near Bcharré.

Ashura   Annual sacred Shi'ite 'festival' commemorating the Battle of Karbala in CE680 and the martyrdom of Imam Hussein, grandson of the Prophet Muhammad on the tenth day of Muharram (Islamic New Year).

AUB   American University of Beirut

Ayyubids
(1183–1250)   Founded by Saladin, the Ayyubids succeeded the Fatimid *caliph* and ruled from Cairo until superseded by the Mamluk dynasty.

bab	Door or gate
baksheesh	Tip or tipping
BCD	Beirut Central District
beit	House, also spelt *bait*
Belt of Misery	Generic name for the southern suburbs of Beirut inhabited by Shi'ite refugees from south Lebanon and the Palestinian *diaspora* in the Sabra and Shatila refugee camps.
Black September (1970)	Palestinian name for the defeat and expulsion of the Palestine Liberation Organisation from Jordan by the forces of King Hussein (1935–99) and the relocating of the organisation's headquarters to Beirut.
burj	Tower
Caliph	Generic title for all Islamic civil and religious leaders who ruled after the Prophet Muhammad.
Cardo Maximus	The principal north–south-oriented street in a typical Roman city.
Cedar Revolution (2005)	A series of demonstrations that followed the assassination of former prime minister Rafiq Hariri on 14 February 2005, calling for an end to nearly 30 years of Syrian military presence, its involvement in Lebanese politics and the establishment of an international investigation into Hariri's murder. Under international pressure Syria withdrew the last of its forces on 26 April 2005. Also known as Independence Intifada (Intifadat al-Istiqlal).
CIA	Central Intelligence Agency
chador	A full-body-length, usually black, garment worn by some Muslim women.
Chalcolithic Age (c4000–3500BCE)	Transitory era between the Neolithic (New Stone Age) and the Bronze Age characterised by the simultaneous use of both stone and copper and an increase in trade and urban living.
confessionalism	Government system that proportions political power amongst the various religious groups. Also called consociationalism.
cornice	Uppermost section of the *entablature* in classical architecture.
corniche	Coast road or promenade
cuneiform	A Sumerian invention c3200BCE composed of wedge-like inscriptions etched onto clay tablets and regarded as the earliest known form of writing.
cupola	Dome-like structure atop a building, eg: a mosque.
dabke	Lebanon and the Levant's lively national folk dance.
Dar al-Islam	House of Islam. Land or territories under Muslim rule.
Decumanus Maximus	The principal east–west street in a typical Roman city which crosses the Cardo Maximus.
deir	Convent or monastery
dhimmis	Protected non-Islamic peoples such as Christians and Jews.
diaspora	General term for the 'dispersion' of the Arab, Jewish and Palestinian peoples from their homelands.
Doha Agreement (2008)	The accord reached by opposing Lebanese factions in Dohar (Qatar) on 21 May which ended an 18-month political impasse and averted possible civil war.
Druze	Religious sect derived from Shi'ite Islam which arose in Cairo around the 11th century during the Fatimid era and the tenure of the *caliph* Al-Hakim. The Druze account for over 5% of Lebanon's

	population with additional communities in Israel and the Palestinian Territories, Syria and Jordan.
eid	Muslim feast or festival
Eid al-Adha	A four-day Muslim festival and feast following the annual pilgrimage to Mecca.
Eid al-Fitr	A Muslim festival and feast lasting up to three days at the end of the fast of Ramadan.
Eisenhower Doctrine (1957)	Formulated by former US President Dwight D Eisenhower (1890–1969), it stated that any country could request military assistance from the USA if threatened by aggression. First used at request of pro-Western Maronite president Camille Chamoun in July 1958, when c14,000 US marines landed in Beirut to quell Arab nationalism.
emir	Generic term for a 'prince', Islamic leader or other high-ranking official, eg: Fakhreddine Maan II; also spelt *amir*.
entablature	Upper section of a building characteristic of classical architecture (Greek/Roman) and usually comprising *architrave*, *frieze* and *cornice*, supported by columns.
exedra (*pl.* exedrae)	A normally semi-circular or rectangular recess in a structure such as a wall, room or columns often containing decorative niches. Popular in Roman architecture, eg: the Great Court at Baalbek.
Fakhreddine Maan II (1572–1635)	Druze prince often revered to as Lebanon's first national hero for unifying the Mount Lebanon region during the Ottoman era. His expansionist ideology was perceived as a threat to Ottoman dominance and he was executed in Istanbul.
Fatimid Caliphate (CE909–1171)	Cairo-based Shi'ite dynasty whose founder, Abdullah al-Mahdi Billah, claimed descent from the Prophet Muhammad's daughter, Fatima, and her husband Ali ibn-Abi Talib, until abolished by Saladin.
Fertile Crescent	Arc of fertile agricultural land extending from Egypt to Iraq.
forum	Open marketplace or other meeting area typical of a Roman city.
French Mandate (1920–43)	The lands comprising modern-day Lebanon and Syria which were mandated to France during the 19–26 April 1920 San Remo Conference in Italy, in accordance with the earlier secret Sykes-Picot Agreement (1916) and ratified by the League of Nations in 1921.
frieze	Central portion of *entablature* between the *architrave* and *cornice*.
funduq	Hotel
Grand Liban	Greater Lebanon
Green Line	The border in Beirut which divided the Muslim western and Christian eastern sections of the city during the 1975–90 civil war.
hajj	Muslim pilgrimage to Mecca.
hammam	Traditional Turkish steam bathhouse usually offering a sauna followed by a massage.
Hezbollah	Party of God. Lebanese Shi'ite Muslim resistance movement, political party and social care provider formed in 1982; also spelt *Hezbullah* or *Hizbullah*.
hijab	Headscarf covering the head and neck leaving the face visible worn by some Muslim women.
Hegira	Arabic word for 'migration' referring to the Prophet Muhammad's journey from Mecca to Medina in CE622, which heralded the start of the Islamic calendar; spelt *hijra* in Arabic.

Hyksos	Nomadic Semitic tribe from central Asia who conquered Egypt, interrupting Phoenician–Egyptian trade relations for about three decades from c1600BCE to 1570BCE. They introduced new weapons and tools of warfare such as bronze armour, the composite bow and the horse-drawn chariot.
hypocaust	A system of under-floor heating devised by the Romans to heat their public baths and houses by means of a raised floor held up by ceramic tiles through which hot air would freely circulate.
IDF	Israel Defence Forces
ifranj	Franks. Arabic term for the European Crusaders in the Levant, especially those from France.
iftar	Evening meal that breaks the day's fast of Ramadan.
imam	Islamic religious leader or cleric.
IS	Islamic State; also referred to as Daesh.
Islam	The religion practised by Muslims; literally, 'submission' or 'surrender' to God
jebel	Mountain, also spelt *jabal*.
jihad	Ambiguous word that is Arabic for 'struggle' or 'striving in the way of Allah'. It commonly refers to a Muslim Holy War against non-Muslims, but also has a more personal or spiritual dimension that can be expressed by words and/or literature in the sense of attaining perfect faith and living a moral and virtuous life.
jumhuriyah	Republic
Kaaba	Islam's most revered and sacred shrine, a black cube-shaped building within the Masjid al-Haram (Great Mosque) in Mecca, Saudi Arabia, which is circumnavigated anti-clockwise many times by *hajj* pilgrims.
Khalwat	Druze place of retreat and worship.
khan	Generic name for a travellers' inn in the Middle East, consisting of a central courtyard usually surrounded by the upper-level living quarters, a ground floor for stables and a storage area and marketplace (eg: Khan al-Franj in Sidon). Sometimes referred to as a *caravanserai*.
Koran	Islam's holy book, which, according to Muslim tradition, contains the actual words of God as recited to the Prophet Muhammad by the angel Gabriel; also spelt *Quran* or *Qur'an*.
Levant	Eastern Mediterranean landmasses including Egypt, Israel and the Palestinian Territories, Jordan, Lebanon, Syria and the island of Cyprus. Literally, the land of the 'rising sun'.
madrasa	Arabic for 'school' and usually associated with educational institutions offering instruction in the Koran and theology; also spelt *madrasah*.
Mamluks (1250–1516)	Islamic dynasty comprising former Turkish slaves who ruled over large parts of Lebanon and Syria from their capital in Cairo until overthrown by the Ottoman Empire.
mar	Saint
Maronite Christians	Breakaway Monothelite Lebanese Christians whose origins date back to Saint Maroun in CE400 and whose doctrinal faith holds that Christ had two natures but operated with a divine will.
Mashriq	The eastern region of the Arab world. This usually includes the states of Egypt, Sudan, the Palestinian Territories, Lebanon, Jordan, Syria, Iraq, Saudi Arabia, Yemen, Oman, United Arab Emirates, Qatar, Kuwait and Bahrain.

masjid	Mosque. Literally, a place of prostration for Muslims.
MEA	Middle East Airlines–Air Liban, Lebanon's national carrier.
Medina	Old walled city; the word also refers to Islam's second holiest city, after Mecca.
MENA	Middle East and North Africa
mihrab	Semi-circular niche in a mosque indicating the direction of prayer towards Mecca.
Millet system	Hierarchical system of governing during the Ottoman Empire in Mount Lebanon according to religion and sect.
minaret	The slender and tallest architectural feature of a mosque comprising the base, shaft and gallery from which the *muezzin* traditionally announces the call to prayer.
minbar	Pulpit in a mosque from where the imam preaches to the faithful, situated to the right of the *mihrab*.
moqawama	Resistance, eg: Hezbollah.
muezzin	Muslim cleric or other official who calls the faithful to prayer.
mufti	Islamic religious official or legal expert approved to issue an Islamic legal edict or *fatwa*.
Mukhabbarat	Intelligence/security services.
Murex	Shellfish or mollusc from which the ancient Phoenicians extracted the coveted purple dye of Sidon and Tyre.
Muslims	Adherents of Islam who thus submit to God's will.
Mutasarrifiyah	Administrative unit during the Ottoman Empire, eg: Mount Lebanon.
nahr	River
nargileh	Water-pipe, *argileh, sheesha* or hubbly bubbly for smoking fragrant tobacco.
National Pact (1943)	An unwritten or gentlemen's agreement negotiated by Sunni, Shi'ite and Maronite leaders which paved the way for the country's independence and established Lebanon's present-day confessional system of politics in which the main political posts are distributed amongst the various religious sects.
necropolis	Ancient burial site.
Neolithic	New Stone Age. Characterised by the increased use of stone tools and weapons, domesticated use of livestock and settled urban communities.
odeon	Compact building used for theatrical and musical performances during Greek and Roman times.
outremer	French-derived word meaning 'lands beyond the sea' referring to the Crusader states that were established following the First Crusade, eg: County of Tripoli etc.
Pan-Arabism	A concept that seeks the political unification of the Arab world and a united front against its enemies. Popularised in the 1950s and 1960s by Egypt's president Gamal Abdel Nasser (1918–70).
pasha	Governor, general or other high-ranking official of the Ottoman Empire.
Phalange (Kataeb Party)	Right-wing Lebanese Christian political party and militia founded in 1936 by Pierre Gemayel (1905–84) which played a major role during the Lebanese civil war (1975–90) and is now part of the March 14 political coalition of parties.

PLO	Palestine Liberation Organisation, formed in 1964, which advocated armed struggle to restore the Palestinian homeland.
propylaea	Grand or ceremonial entrance to a temple complex, eg: Baalbek.
qalaa	Castle or fort.
qibla	Direction to which Muslims turn during prayer, ie: towards Mecca, as indicated by the *mihrab* in a mosque.
Ramadan	Ninth month of the Islamic calendar, during which practising Muslims fast, abstaining from eating, drinking, smoking and sexual activity from sunrise until sunset.
ras	Headland
Rashidun	Literally, the four 'rightly guided caliphs' who were the supporters and direct successors of the Prophet Muhammad: Abu Bakr (CE632–4), Omar ibn al-Khattab (CE634–44), Uthman ibn Affan (CE644–56) and Ali ibn Abi Talib (CE656–61).
sahat	Square
Saladin (c1137/8–93)	Kurdish military leader, founder of the Ayyubid dynasty who recaptured Jerusalem, Aleppo, Beirut, Byblos and Sidon from the Crusaders.
sanjak	Administrative subdivision within an Ottoman *vilayet*.
saray	Generic word for 'Palace', also spelt *serai*.
Seleucids (312–64BCE)	Monarchical dynasty founded by Seleucus Nicator following the death of Alexander the Great and the partition of his Macedonian Empire among his generals. At its height, the empire ruled over Lebanon and a vast swathe of Asia.
Seljuk Turks (1058–1157)	Turkish sultanate of Sunni Muslims who ruled from their capital in Isfahan conquering large areas of the eastern Islamic world including Jerusalem, Syria and defeated the Byzantine army at the Battle of Manzikert in1071.
serail	Ottoman-era palace, also spelt *seraglio*.
servees	Service (shared) taxi
Sharia	Islamic law that informs the everyday life and conduct of Muslims.
Shi'ite	Islamic sect who believe that only the Prophet Muhammad's son-in-law and cousin Ali and his successors – the 'partisans' of Ali – can be rightful *caliphs*. Although Shi'ites represent around 15% of the world's Muslims they are probably Lebanon's largest single religious group. Also spelt *Shia*.
Solidere	The Lebanese Company for the Development and Reconstruction of Beirut Central District
souk	Arabic market; also spelt *souq*.
Special Tribunal for Lebanon (STL)	International tribunal which started work in 2009, at the request of the Lebanese government and under the auspices of the UN, to bring to justice those responsible for the killing of former prime minister Rafiq Hariri and 21 others on Valentine's Day 2005. Trials *in absentia* for five accused commenced in January 2014.
stela (*pl.* stelae)	Stone slab(s) usually containing carvings or inscriptions such as those at Nahr al-Kalb (Dog River).
sultan	Muslim leader or ruler, eg: Saladin, Süleyman the Magnificent.
Sunni	The larger or orthodox of the two main Islamic sects. Sunnis follow the tradition of *sunna* or life of the Prophet Muhammad and the Koran. They believe that successive *caliphs* unrelated to the prophet can succeed him. Sunnis represent about 85% of the world's Muslims.

Sykes–Picot Agreement (1916)	A secret agreement between the governments of Britain and France which established their respective regions of interests and control over Ottoman lands following the anticipated Allied victory over the Central Powers in World War I.
Taif Agreement (1989)	The accord reached at Taif, in Saudi Arabia, which modified Lebanon's confessional power sharing system between Christians and Muslims and ended the 1975–90 civil war.
Tanzimat	Ottoman-era economic, social, religious and constitutional modernising reforms between 1839 and 1876, initiated by Sultan Abdul Mejid; literally, 'reorderings'.
tell	Artificial archaeological hill or mound resulting from successive generations of earlier human settlement.
tetrapylon	A typically Roman-style structure consisting of four pillars, often built at a crossroads or junction in a town. The term derives from the Greek word tetra meaning four, eg: Aanjar in the Bekaa Valley.
Umayyad Caliphate (CE661–750)	A family of leading Meccan traders during the time of the Prophet Muhammad which became the first Arab dynasty of Sunni Muslims who ruled from Damascus.
UN	United Nations
UNESCO	United Nations Educational, Scientific and Cultural Organisation
UNHCR	United Nations High Commissioner for Refugees
UNIFIL	United Nations Interim Force in Lebanon
UNRWA	United Nations Relief and Works Agency
USAID	United States Agency for International Development
vilayet	Principle administrative province during the Ottoman Empire, also spelt wilaya, eg: Beirut.
wadi	Seasonal valley or river.
waqf	Islamic religious (charitable) endowment.

FOOD AND DRINK

ahweh	Strong, dark and thick Arabic coffee usually drunk from small cups; similar to Turkish coffee.
akhtabout	Octopus
Almaza	Lebanon's local bottled and draught lager beer.
arak	National drink of Lebanon; this highly alcoholic aniseed-flavoured beverage distilled from grapes is often drunk to accompany mezze.
baklava	Very sweet dessert made from filo pastry stuffed with nuts, syrup or honey and pistachios.
balamida	Tuna
djaj	Chicken
falafel	Round balls of fried chickpeas or fava beans often served in a pitta bread wrap or as part of a mezze dish.
farride	Sea bream
fattoush	Bread-based mixed salad comprising cucumber, garlic, lemon, lettuce juice, olive oil, mint, onions, parsley, sumac, tomatoes and toasted bread.
haleeb	Milk
hummus	Creamy dip dish made from mashed chickpeas, lemon juice, olive oil and garlic and eaten with pitta bread.
ka'ik (ka'ak)	Large, ring-shaped bread, served either plain or filled with za'atar (dry thyme) or cheese and garnished with sesame seeds.

khodra	Vegetables
kibbeh	National dish comprising *burghol* (crushed wheat), chopped beef or lamb and fried in olive oil. They resemble a cross between Scotch eggs and a torpedo. Sometimes eaten raw.
knefeh	Warm, often square-shaped pastry dessert filled with cheese and topped with cream or syrup and nuts. Often eaten for breakfast and the preferred sweet after the *iftar* meal.
labneh	A delicate creamy cheese made from strained yoghurt (similar to fromage frais) and garnished with olive oil and garlic.
karakand	Lobster
laban	Yoghurt
lukos	Sea bass
maamoul	Small, rounded, shortbread pastries containing dates, pistachio and walnuts and a popular snack for Muslims following Ramadan and eaten by Christians during Easter festivities.
manoushe	Type of pizza topped with cheese or thyme; a popular breakfast dish.
mezze	Hors d'oeuvres. An assortment of small, hot and/or cold dishes which comprise a Lebanese meal, eg: *tabbouleh*, *hummus*, *fattoush*, *labneh*, etc.
mouneh	Stored provisions of seasonal foods for the pantry such as beans, dried vegetables, olives, oils, spices, pickles, fruits, *awarma* (preserved lamb), etc for consumption throughout the year.
moutabel	Slices of grilled aubergine with lemon juice and olive oil.
mujaddara	Dish consisting of lentils, rice and onions.
qamareddine	Thirst-quenching apricot beverage, often drunk during *iftar*.
sabideg	Squid
salata	Salad
samak	Fish
sanioura	Sweet, sugary crumbly biscuit from the southern city of Sidon.
sayadieh	Sliced fish – usually sea bass – with onions and rice and flavoured with cinnamon and lemon juice
shai	Tea, often served with mint and sweetened with sugar, without milk.
shawarma	Chicken or lamb döner kebab.
shish tawouk	Grilled boneless chicken flavoured with olive oil, garlic and lemon juice, often served in flat or pitta bread.
sujuk	Dry, spicy Armenian sausage of ground beef, containing mixed spices such as cumin, garlic, red pepper and salt.
sultan ibrahim	Red mullet (aka red snapper) variously served baked, fried or grilled.
sumac	Lemony-tasting wild berry from the mountains which is dried and used for seasoning on salads. An essential ingredient in *za'atar*.
tabbouleh	Parsley-based mixed salad consisting of parsley, mint, chopped onions and tomatoes, cracked wheat with lemon juice and olive oil.
tahini	Versatile sesame paste used as a dip, sauce or side accompaniment with fish and meat dishes such as *sayadieh*.
za'atar	A spice blend of dried and crushed thyme, dried sumac, toasted sesame seeds and salt which is then blended with olive oil and spread over bread, often eaten with *manoushe*.

Appendix 3

FURTHER INFORMATION

BOOKSHOPS In London, **Foyles** (*Main branch: 107 Charing Cross Rd, London WC2H 0DT;* ✆ *020 7440 3240;* e *travel@foyles.co.uk; www.foyles.co.uk*) is the UK's largest bookshop and stocks an extensive selection of works on Lebanon and the wider Middle East region and will deliver books worldwide. The specialist travel bookshop **Stanfords** (*12–14 Long Acre, Covent Garden, London WC2E 9LP;* ✆ *020 7836 1321;* e *sales@stanfords.co.uk; www.stanfords.co.uk*) is considered the world's largest travel bookshop, with an additional branch in Bristol (*29 Corn St, Bristol BS1 1HT;* ✆ *0117 929 9966;* e *bristol@stanfords.co.uk*) and is a good place to pick up a copy of the latest ITMB Lebanon travel map as well as the *Zawarib Beirut and Beyond* street atlas; they also offer worldwide delivery when ordering from their website. With a large nationwide chain of stores in the UK, **Waterstones** (*Main branch: 203–206 Piccadilly, London W1J 9HD;* ✆ *020 7851 2400;* e *piccadilly@waterstones.com; www.waterstones.com*) is also a decent literary source for travel as well as more general books on Lebanon and the region. The following additional bookshops below, however, will be of particular interest to those readers in search of more specialised and/or academic works on Lebanon and the wider Middle East region.

UK

Al Saqi Books 26 Westbourne Grove, London W2 5RH; ✆ 020 7229 8543; e orders@alsaqibookshop. com; www.alsaqibookshop.com. This is the largest Middle Eastern bookseller in the UK.

Arthur Probsthain 41 Great Russell St, London WC1B 3PE, opposite the British Museum; ✆ 020 7636 1096; e arthurprobsthain@hotmail. com; www.apandtea.co.uk. Established in 1903 and specialising in antiquarian & hard-to-find works covering the arts, culture, languages & religions of the world, with a good selection covering the Middle East. The on-site gallery holds periodic art exhibitions from around the world & previous shows have included works on Islamic Calligraphy.

Darf Publishers 277 West End Lane, West Hampstead, London NW6 1QS; ✆ 020 7431 7009; e enquiry@darfpublishers.co.uk, info@ darfpublishers.co.uk, orders@darfpublishers.co.uk; www.darfpublishers.co.uk. A source of hard-to-find, historical & out-of-print literature covering the Middle East & north Africa on the culture, geography, history & religion of the region.

Daunt Books 83 Marylebone High St, London W1U 4QW; ✆ 020 7224 2295; e orders@ dauntbooks.co.uk; www.dauntbooks.co.uk. Also has 5 other London branches at Belsize Park, Cheapside, Chelsea, Hampstead & Holland Park.

The Maghreb Bookshop 45 Burton St, London WC1H 9AL; ✆ 020 7388 1840; e Maghreb@maghrebreview.com; www. maghrebbookshop.com. Stocks new, rare & out-of-print works on the Middle East & Islam.

SOAS Bookshop Brunei Gallery Bldg, School of Oriental & African Studies, Thornhaugh St, Russell Sq, London WC1H 0XG; ✆ 020 7898 4470; e bookshop@soas.ac.uk; www.soas.ac.uk/visitors/ bookshop. A branch of Arthur Probsthain books housed within this highly regarded university stocks an excellent range of academic, historical & cultural books from across the Middle East region.

Republic of Ireland

Easons 40 Lower O'Connell St, Dublin 1; ✆ (0)1 858 3800; e support@easons.com; www. easons.com. One of Ireland's biggest book retailers with more than 60 stores in the North & Republic of Ireland stocking an eclectic selection of works on Lebanon & the region.

USA

Brookline Booksmith 279 Harvard St, Coolidge Corner, Brookline MA 02446–2908; ☎ +1 617 566 6660; e thestore@brooklinebooksmith.com; www. brooklinebooksmith.com. A leading independent bookseller stocking an excellent range of well-

known & more obscure titles on Lebanon & the Middle East.

Longitude Books 2838 Vicksburg Lane, Plymouth, MN 55447; ☎ +1 800 342 2164 or +1 952 252 1203; e info@longitudebooks.com; www.longitudebooks.com. An Aladdin's Cave of old, rare & new travel reading & maps from around the world with an excellent selection of material on Lebanon & the Middle East.

PUBLISHERS These specialist independent book publishers are also worth keeping an eye on, as they produce an extensive range of new titles annually on a variety of Middle Eastern countries and topics. In addition to the range of bookshops mentioned in the relevant regional chapters, Lebanese publisher Turning Point is also worth looking at as they issue a variety of titles specifically about Lebanon, from novels, lifestyle and children's books to a variety of guides about Beirut and the country.

UK

Hurst Publishers 41 Great Russell St, London WC1B 3PL; ☎ 020 7255 2201; www.hurstpublishers. com. Established in 1969, this excellent, leading independent non-fiction company publishes 60+ titles annually, including in their specialist fields of Islam, Lebanon & the Middle East generally.

I B Tauris & Co Ltd 6 Salem Rd, London W2 4BU; ☎ 020 7243 1225; e accountspayable@ibtauris. com, reception@ibtauris.com; www.ibtauris.com. Currently publishes around 300 new titles annually.

Ithaca Press 8 Southern Court, South St, Reading, Berkshire RG1 4QS; ☎ 0118 959 7847; www.ithacapress.co.uk. Predominantly publishing academic works on the Middle East & Islam across a wide range of subjects.

Lebanon

Turning Point Books 14th Fl, Concorde Bldg, Dunant St, Verdun, Beirut; ☎ 01 752 100; e info@ tpbooksonline.com; www.tpbooksonline.com

BOOKS The literature on Lebanon is extensive and ever growing, and dates back to the time of antiquity with Strabo, Homer and Herodotus among the classical scholars who have written about the country, not to mention the numerous references to Lebanon in the Bible. The selections below should give the reader further illuminating insights into the country and the wider Middle East region; and all the books listed should be available at the outlets mentioned above, second-hand bookshops or at the very least online at www. amazon.com. Failing that, try www.usedbooksearch.co.uk, which at the last count had a worldwide database of more than 100 million used books, giving details of suppliers and prices. For children's books on Lebanon, see page 85.

Civil War (1975–90)

Fisk, Robert *Pity the Nation: Lebanon at War* Oxford: Oxford University Press, 1992. First published 1990. Thorough and poignant analysis of Lebanon's civil strife by the *The Independent* newspaper's veteran Middle East correspondent.

Folman, Ari *Waltz with Bashir: A Lebanon War Story* New York: Metropolitan Books, 2009. One man's recurring and disturbing dream and consequent psychoanalytic journey to uncover his role in the 1982 massacres at the Palestinian camps of Sabra and Shatila. This graphic book was also made into an award-winning animated film.

Gilmour, David *Lebanon: The Fractured Country* Basingstoke: Palgrave Macmillan, 1983. A good account of the history of the country's civil unrest from 1975.

Hage, Rawi *De Niro's Game* New York: Harper Perennial, 2008. First published 2006. Photographer turned writer, Hage's multi-award-winning debut novel focuses on a life's journey for two childhood friends set against the backdrop of war-ravaged Beirut.

Haugbolle, Sune *War and Memory in Lebanon* Cambridge: Cambridge University Press, 2010. An intriguing and insightful analysis of the ways in which intellectuals and activists used cultural mores such as media, art, literature, film, and architecture in an attempt to make sense of Lebanon's protracted 1975–90 civil war, in opposition to a state that was more interested in engendering a collective amnesia of the events.

Hiro, Dilip *Lebanon: Fire and Embers – A History of the Lebanese Civil War* London: Weidenfeld & Nicolson, 1993. An account of the minutiae of internal and external events leading to the 1975–90 civil war.

Keenan, Brian *An Evil Cradling* London: Vintage Books, 1993. First published 1992. A now classic and poignant account of this former hostage's time in captivity in Lebanon during the civil war, focusing on both his own and his peers' experiences.

McCarthy, John and Morrell, Jill *Their Own Story: Some Other Rainbow* London: Transworld Publishers Ltd, 1994. John McCarthy's experiences as a hostage for five years in Lebanon, his friendship with Brian Keenan and the tireless endeavours of partner Jill Morrell to secure his release, together with her own psychological deprivation.

Makdisi, Jean Said *Beirut Fragments: A War Memoir* New York: W W Norton, 2004. First published 1990. Personal musings on living amid the carnage that was Beirut during the civil war years.

Reed, Eli and Ajami, Fouad *Beirut: City of Regrets* New York: W W Norton, 1988. Penetrating and insightful photojournalism of the 1975–90 civil war from Magnum photographer Reed.

Cookery

Accad, Joumana *Taste of Beirut: Delicious Lebanese Recipes from Classics to Contemporary to Mezzes and More* Florida: HCI Books, 2014.

Al-Faqih, Kamal *Classic Lebanese Cuisine: 170 Fresh and Healthy Mediterranean Favorites* Connecticut: Three Forks, 2009.

Dekmak, Hussein *The Lebanese Cookbook* London: Kyle Cathie Ltd, 2006.

Hage, Salma *The Lebanese Kitchen* London: Phaidon, 2012.

Hage, Salma *The Middle Eastern Vegetarian Cookbook* London: Phaidon, 2016.

Hamadeh, Mona *Everyday Lebanese Cooking* Oxford: How to Books, 2013.

Hamady, Mary Laird *Lebanese Mountain Cookery* Boston : David R Godine, 1995.

Helou, Anissa *Lebanese Cuisine: More than 250 Authentic Recipes from the Most Elegant Middle Eastern Cuisine* New York: Grub Street, 1994.

Karam, Michael *Arak and Mezze: The Taste of Lebanon* London: Saqi Books, 2008.

Karam, Michael *Lebanese Wines: An Independent Guide* Beirut: Turning Point Books, 2013.

Karam, Michael *Wines of Lebanon* London: Saqi Books, 2005.

Kehdy, Bethany *The Jewelled Kitchen: A Stunning Collection of Lebanese, Moroccan & Persian Recipes* London: Duncan Baird Publishers, 2013.

Khalife, Maria *The Mezze Cookbook: Over 90 Delicious Appetizers from Greece, Lebanon and Turkey* London: New Holland Publishers Ltd, 2008.

Kitous, Tony and Lepard, Dan *Comptoir Libanais: A Feast of Lebanese-Style Home Cooking* London: Preface Publishing, 2013.

Malouf, Greg and Malouf, Lucy *Saha: A Chef's Journey Through Lebanon and Syria* London: Quadrille, 2006.

Massaad, Barbara Abdeni *Mouneh: Preserving Foods for the Lebanese Pantry* Barbara Massaad, 2010.

Saleh, Nada *Fragrance of the Earth: Lebanese Home Cooking* London: Saqi Books, 1996.

Whatever your culinary preferences, one of the practical advantages of having a large Lebanese diaspora are the ample opportunities that this provides to try Lebanese – meat and/or vegetarian – food and drink before and after you travel. There are plenty of Lebanese restaurants in Australia, the USA and the UK together with those in countries such as Brazil, where the Lebanese expatriate community is well represented. In the UK, London has a substantial number of Lebanese eateries, especially in and around the Edgware Road district, including the long-established **Maroush** (*21 Edgware Rd, London W2 2JE;* ✆ *020 7723 0773; www.maroush.com;* ⊕ *noon–02.00 daily*) chain of restaurants, where you can enjoy its good food to the accompaniment of nightly live music and belly dancing from 21.30 onwards. Named after Lebanon's most famous singer **Fairuz** (*3 Blandford St, London W1U 3DA;* ✆ *020 7486 8108/82;* e *info@fairuz.uk.com; www.fairuz.uk.com;* ⊕ *noon–23.00 Mon–Sat, noon–22.30 Sun*) is a cosy little restaurant with an excellent and wide-ranging *mezze* menu (including a take-away service) and serves *arak* and wines from the Kefraya, Ksara and Musar labels accompanied by the haunting lyrics of Lebanon's diva. The UK's first Lebanese restaurant to be located outside of London and still going strong is the **Al-Shami Lebanese Restaurant** (*25 Walton Crescent, Oxford OX1 2JG;* ✆ *01865 310066;* e *food@al-shami.co.uk; www.al-shami.co.uk;* ⊕ *noon–midnight daily*) has been established for more than 25 years and serves first-rate Lebanese meat and vegetarian dishes, and of course *mezze* with a take-away service also available. This restaurant has also had regular mentions in *The Good Food Guide* and in addition to its excellent food serves *arak* and Lebanese wine from the Kefraya, Ksara and Musar labels.

Salloum, Mary *A Taste of Lebanon: Cooking Today the Lebanese Way* New York: Interlink Books, 2001. First published 1988.

Taouk, Nouha *Whispers from a Lebanese Kitchen: A Family's Treasured Recipes* London: Murdoch Books, 2011.

Flora and fauna

Aspinall, Simon and Porter, Richard *Birds of the Middle East* London: Christopher Helm, 2010. Second edition. First published 1996. An excellent field guide for the ornithological enthusiast.

Benson, Vere S *Birds of Lebanon and the Jordan Area* London: International Council for Bird Preservation, 1970. Currently out of print but should be available in some Beirut bookshops or via Amazon etc.

El-Hibri, Hana *A Million Steps: Discovering the Lebanon Mountain Trail* Beirut: Turning Point Books, 2010. A glossy, coffee-table book documenting the author's month-long trek along the entirety of the Lebanon Mountain Trail (LMT) vividly evoking the diversity and beauty of Lebanon's animal and plant life, the stunning natural landscapes together with the people and cuisine encountered in some of Lebanon's least explored areas. Highly recommended for those interested in the environment and ecotourism.

Haber, Ricardus M and Haber, Semaan Myrna *Floral Enchantment to Lebanon* Beirut: Edition Terre du Liban, 2009. Large format book with lovely colour photos of Lebanon's wide-ranging flora.

Haber, Ricardus M and Haber, Semaan Myrna *Orchids of Lebanon* Beirut: 2009. Another coffee-table book with attractive colour photos.

Houri, Ahmad and Houri, Machaka Nisrine *Photographic Guide to Wild Flowers of Lebanon (Vol 2)* Beirut: AFDC, 2008. Pocket-size guide, with colour photos, giving detailed Latin and English names of Lebanon's flora.

Larsen T B *Butterflies of Lebanon* Beirut: Librairie du Liban, 1974. Nicely illustrated book on the subject.

Schaub, Gabriela S. *Cedrus Libani: The Cedar of Lebanon* Beirut: Fine Arts Publishing, 2012. Excellent pictorial and written study of Lebanon's iconic national emblem and the enduring importance of this ancient tree culturally, economically and politically.

Tohmé, Georges and Tohmé, Henriette *Illustrated Flora of Lebanon* Beirut: National Council for Scientific Research, 2014. The outcome of a 50-year ecological career, the husband-and-wife team have documented Lebanon's varied flower and plant species across the country's numerous ecosystems stretching from the sea to the mountains.

Health

Ellis, Matthew Dr and Wilson-Howarth, Jane Dr *Your Child Abroad: A Travel Health Guide* Bucks: Bradt Travel Guides, 2014. Second edition. An invaluable guide for those travelling or resident overseas with babies and children of all ages.

History, economics and politics

Abulafia, David *The Great Sea: A Human History of the Mediterranean* London: Allen Lane, 2011. Although not dealing with Lebanon specifically, this is an excellent and vivid approach to the subject, which brings to life the eclectic characters and civilisations, including the Greeks, Phoenicians and the Sea Peoples, who have sailed the Mediterranean and Levant from antiquity to the present day. An excellent read for an overview of this 'sea between the lands'.

Achcar, Gilbert and Warschawski, Michel *The 33-Day War: Israel's War on Hezbollah in Lebanon and its Aftermath* London: Saqi Books, 2007. Examination of the local and regional basis for Israel's 2006 July War in Lebanon against Hezbollah together with the roles played by the USA and European political machines. Penned jointly by an Israeli and Lebanese author.

Anderson, Scott *Lawrence in Arabia: War, Deceit, Imperial Folly and the Making of the Modern Middle East* London: Atlantic Books, 2014. An absorbing book on the personality and career of T E Lawrence which goes beyond the mere biographical, placing him in the context of the other main foreign players – German, Jewish, American – in the Levant during the First World War.

Arsan, Andrew *Interlopers of Empire: The Lebanese Diaspora in Colonial French West Africa* London: Hurst, 2014. An original and engaging historical analysis of the Lebanese diaspora in colonial French west Africa since late Ottoman times and the complexity of their existence, vis-à-vis their migrant status, homeland and the reaction of the French colonial rulers.

Asbridge, Thomas *The Crusades: The War for the Holy Land* London: Simon and Schuster, 2012. First published 2010. Meticulously researched, highly readable and colourful account of this period by a renowned authority in the field which brings to life this salient era in the Middle Ages with excellent detail on iconic protagonists such as Richard the Lionheart and Saladin.

Barr, James *A Line in the Sand: Britain, France and the Struggle that Shaped the Middle East* London: Simon & Schuster, 2011. A thorough account that focuses on the 1916 Sykes–Picot Agreement and the internal conflicts that ensued between Anglo-French interests together with the consequences for the modern Middle East.

Blanford, Nicholas *Killing Mr Lebanon: The Assassination of Rafiq Hariri and Its Impact on the Middle East* London: I B Tauris, 2006. An absorbing and highly detailed account drawing on interviews with many of Lebanon's key political figures and main players in the country's affairs, together with background information on Hariri himself to elucidate the dynamics at work in his killing and why it continues to resonate throughout the region and beyond.

Bowen, Jeremy *The Arab Uprisings: The People Want the Fall of the Regime* London: Simon & Schuster, 2012. A good journalistic overview of the early stages of the regional upheavals, the so-called Arab Spring, affecting Lebanon and the wider Arab world by the BBC's Middle East Editor.

Bregman, Ahron and El-Tahri, Jihan *The Fifty Years War: Israel and the Arabs* London: Penguin, and BBC Books, 1998. A good general overview of the origins of the Arab–Israeli conflict for the lay reader.

Cammett, Melani, Diwan, Ishac, Richards, Alan and Waterbury, John *A Political Economy of the Middle East* Boulder, CO: Westview Press, 2015. Fourth edition. This detailed, wide-ranging and easily digestible tome will appeal especially to academic and business readers for its economic, political and social coverage of regional dynamics both before and since the advent of the Arab Spring with plenty of insightful detail about Lebanon.

Catherwood, Christopher *A Brief History of the Middle East* London: Constable & Robinson, 2006. An excellent introduction and basis for further reading.

El Cheikh, Nadia Maria, Choueiri, Lina & Orfali, Bilal (eds) *One Hundred and Fifty* Beirut: American University of Beirut Press, 2016. A coffee-table tome published to coincide with the AUB's 150th birthday in December 2016, this is an absorbing historical analysis that places this iconic, and at times controversial, institution of learning in its wider regional and global context, which at certain historical junctures has tended to mirror developments in Lebanon's wider history. A fascinating read.

Fawaz, Tarazi Leila *An Occasion for War: Civil Conflict in Lebanon and Damascus in 1860* California: University of California Press, 1994. An account of the Druze/Christian Mountain War of 1860.

Felsch, Maximilian and Wählisch, Martin (eds) *Lebanon and the Arab Uprisings: In the eye of the hurricane* Oxon: Routledge, 2016. An excellent and insightful series of essays exploring the multi-faceted events of the Arab Spring, war in Syria, the country's recent citizen protests over garbage collection and the repercussions of these conflicts for the internal and external dynamics of Lebanon's present and future delicate sectarian balance.

Fisk, Robert *The Great War for Civilisation: The Conquest of the Middle East* London: Harper Perennial, 2006. A mighty paperback tome but worth the effort for its insightful analysis and regional sweep of events.

Friedman, Thomas *From Beirut to Jerusalem* London: HarperCollins, 1995. Journalistic account of two cities at the epicentre of the Middle East conflict.

Gorton, T J *Renaissance Emir: A Druze Warlord at the Court of the Medici* London: Quartet Books, 2013. An excellent, vivid and rare biographical study of former Druze prince, Fakhreddine Maan II, which brings to life the man himself, his edifying exile in Renaissance Florence and the interplay between East and West during this important period in Ottoman and Lebanese history.

Harris, W W *Lebanon: A History, 600–2011 (Studies in Middle Eastern History)* New York: Oxford University Press, 2012. A scholarly and readable account covering an unusually large swathe of the country's timeline which does an excellent job of unravelling the complexities of the country's various communities and sects, together with a compelling account as to why Lebanon has yet to achieve an internally cohesive society. One of the best books available for an insightful history of Lebanon.

Hirst, David *Beware of Small States: Lebanon, Battleground of the Middle East* London: Faber & Faber, 2010. A book that places Lebanon's past woes in the context of the wider international scene.

Hourani, Albert *A History of the Arab Peoples* London: Faber & Faber, 2005. First published 1991. A seminal work on the subject from the late renowned Lebanese historian. Highly recommended.

Jaber, Hala *Hezbollah: Born with a Vengeance* New York: Columbia University Press, 1997. Excellent account of the foundation and philosophy of this organisation with illuminating insights, which go beyond the media stereotypes.

Kassir, Samir *Beirut* California: University of California Press, 2010. Translated into English by M B DeBevoise. First published 2003, in French, as *Histoire de Beyrouth*. Evocative and comprehensive history of the capital from ancient times to the modern era by the late and prominent journalist who was assassinated in 2005.

Khatib, Lina, Matar, Dina and Alshaer, Atef *The Hizbullah Phenomenon: Politics and Communication* London: Hurst, 2014. An original work which transcends discussions of the Party of God's military operations focusing instead on the group's ideology and its adaptable dissemination through the various media, including poetry, the rise and prominence of its charismatic leader Hassan Nasrallah and the challenges facing the group's communications strategy in the wake of the Arab Spring and ongoing Syrian crisis.

Knudsen, Are and Kerr, Michael (eds) *Lebanon: After the Cedar Revolution* London: Hurst, 2012. The assassination of former premier Rafiq Hariri heralded the start of wide-ranging political and social upheavals in Lebanon. This eclectic collection of essays addresses the sectarian conflicts, the polarisation of Lebanese politics and the influence of foreign powers amongst other topics to help understand the state of Lebanese society in the post-2005 era. Highly recommended.

Levi, Tomer *The Jews of Beirut: The Rise of a Levantine Community, 1860s–1930s* New York: Peter Lang Publishing, 2012. A detailed account of Jewish settlement in Beirut during the late Ottoman and French Mandate eras.

Levitt, Matthew *Hezbollah: The Global Footprint of Lebanon's Party of God* Washington: Georgetown University Press, 2013. As the title suggests, this book focuses on the group's activities and impact beyond Lebanon's borders.

Llewellyn, Tim *Spirit of the Phoenix: Beirut and the Story of Lebanon* London: I B Tauris, 2010. Interesting attempt by a former BBC correspondent to 'explain how the Lebanese survive the punitive rigours of their geography and history and the never-ending attempts of myriad outsiders to give them every assistance in aggravating their own internal contradictions'.

Maalouf, Amin *The Crusades through Arab Eyes* London: Al Saqi Books, 1984. A now classic account by the Lebanese author chronicling this period of history from the standpoint of Arab consciousness.

Mackey, Sandra *Mirror of the Arab World: Lebanon in Conflict* New York: W W Norton, 2009. Another book that places Lebanon's crises and problems in a wider Middle East context.

Man, John *Saladin: The Life, the Legend and the Islamic Empire* London: Bantam Press, 2015. A decent, insightful and readable biography of the oft-called 'hero of Islam' but does have a tendency to be a little too honorific at times.

Mansel, Philip *Levant: Splendour and Catastrophe in the Mediterranean* London: John Murray, 2010. An excellent social history tale of three port cities – Smyrna (Turkey), Alexandria (Egypt) and Beirut (Lebanon) from the last decades of the Ottoman Empire.

Mansfield, Peter *A History of the Middle East* London: Penguin, 2010. Third edition. First published 2003. Historical and political overview of the region over the past 200 years.

Miles, Richard *Carthage Must Be Destroyed: The Rise and Fall of an Ancient Civilisation* London: Allen Lane, 2010. Although dealing with Carthage, this book is interesting reading for its historical sweep of the Levant in general and the ancient Phoenicians' presence in Lebanon.

Rawlinson, George *Phoenicia: History of a Civilisation* London: I B Tauris, 2005. Good account of this enterprising and innovative civilisation.

Rogan, Eugene *The Arabs: A History* London: Allen Lane, 2009. Highly readable, colourful and scholarly account of Arab history ranging widely across the Arab world from the Ottoman Empire to the present with insightful analysis of Arab antipathy towards the West today.

Rogan, Eugene *The Fall of the Ottomans: The Great War in the Middle East, 1914–1920* London: Allen Lane, 2015. An account of the final years of the Ottoman Empire, which sowed the seeds of the modern Middle East, and its conflicts, focusing on the Arabs, Turks and the Armenian genocide.

Salamey, Imad *The Government and Politics of Lebanon* Oxon: Routledge, 2014. A first rate account of the origins and institutions of Lebanon's modern political apparatus with analysis of the pros and cons of the country's sectarian system of government, its place in the region and on the wider international political stage. A rare book devoted to this important subject. Highly recommended for those wishing to understand better Lebanon's past and present.

Salibi, Kamal *A House of Many Mansions: The History of Lebanon Reconsidered* London: I B Tauris, 2009. First published 1988. The late Lebanese author eschews a linear interpretation of Lebanese history in favour of a more analytical and critical approach to his country's conflicts and divisions.

Schulze, Kirsten E, *The Jews of Lebanon: Between Coexistence and Conflict* Sussex: Sussex Academic Press, 2001 (2nd edition, 2009). Political analysis of the Jewish presence in Lebanon in the 20th century which challenges widely held preconceptions that Jews were a persecuted minority.

Traboulsi, Fawwaz *A History of Modern Lebanon* London: Pluto Press, 2007. A classic and scholarly history of Lebanon since Ottoman times.

Young, Michael *The Ghosts of Martyrs Square: An Eyewitness Account of Lebanon's Life Struggle* New York: Simon & Schuster, 2010. A book that details the minutiae of Lebanon's political and religious landscape in the post-Cedar Revolution era as seen through the main characters and tensions in the country, with interesting personal musings from the *Daily Star* columnist.

Language

Al-Masri, Mohammad *Colloquial Arabic* (*Levantine*): *The Complete Course for Beginners* Oxford: Routledge, 2015. Third edition. First published 1982. Available as a book-and-CD package or separately, this is recommended if you want a good grasp of Arabic including the linguistic nuances that make up everyday life in Lebanon and the Levant.

Arnander, Primrose and Skipwith, Ashkhain *Upload Your Own Donkey* London: Stacey International, 2002. Although not a conventional language guide, this book is full of Arabic proverbs and sayings with their English translations and makes for an edifying and humorous read.

Featherstone, Jonathan *Talk Arabic: The Ideal Course for Absolute Beginners* London: BBC Active/Pearson Education, 2015. Second edition. A book and two 60-minute CD package concentrating on the Arabic spoken in Lebanon and elsewhere in the Levant (Jordan, Palestine, Syria). An easy-to-follow and well-structured course providing a good foundation for business and leisure travellers alike. Highly recommended.

McGrew, Suzanne E (ed) *In-Flight Arabic: Learn Before You Land* New York: Living Language, 2005. A crash course (so to speak).

Religion

Armstrong, Karen *Fields of Blood: Religion and the History of Violence* London: Bodley Head, 2014. Interesting book that seeks to challenge the widely held belief that religious ideology is responsible for wars.

Armstrong, Karen *Islam: A Short History* London: Phoenix Press, 2001. Clear and concise introduction to the subject by a former nun which cuts through the clichés, prejudices and stereotypes that often surround Islam.

Goldsmith, Leon T *Cycle of Fear: Syria's Alawites in War and Peace* London: Hurst, 2015. Informative account of the foundation and development of this hitherto little-known sect and its role in the current Syrian crisis, facilitating understanding of the impact of the war's fallout on Lebanon's own Alawite community. Highly recommended.

Holland, Tom *In the Shadow of the Sword: The Battle for Global Empire and the End of the Ancient World* London: Little Brown, 2012. A controversial book that focuses on the birth of Islam and the Koran, challenging received knowledge on the faith's very foundation. The subject of a BBC television documentary.

Kadri, Sadakat *Heaven on Earth: A Journey through Sharia Law* London: Bodley Head, 2012. A book that attempts to demystify the clichés and stereotypes surrounding *Sharia* or Islamic Law.

Russell, Gerard *Heirs to Forgotten Kingdoms: Journeys into the Disappearing Religions of the Middle East* London: Simon & Schuster, 2014. An account of the Middle East's more esoteric religions analysing their history and the threats to their survival, with good coverage of the Alawite, Copt and Druze sects.

Travel writing, novels and biographies

Al-Shaykh, Hanan *The Locust and the Bird: My Mother's Story* London: Bloomsbury, 2009. The themes of forced marriage, infidelity, resilience and survival are explored in this account of Lebanese author Al-Shaykh's mother and her home life.

Bell, Gertrude *The Desert and the Sown: Travels in Palestine and Syria* New York: Dover Publications, 2008. First published 1907. Highly regarded personal account of Bell's insightful forays around the Middle East in 1905.

Bruce, Ian *The Nun of Lebanon: The Love Affair of Lady Hester Stanhope and Michael Bruce* London: Collins, 1951. An excellent read about the impact of the author's great-grandfather Michael Bruce on Lady Hester, told mainly via their personal correspondence, as well as being an insightful glimpse into the period.

Dalrymple, William *From the Holy Mountain: A Journey in the Shadow of Byzantium* London: Harper Perennial, 2005. First published 1997. Much-acclaimed book in which the author retraces the steps of two Byzantine monks, taking him from Greece through Turkey, Syria, Lebanon, Israel, Jordan and Egypt, and analysing the legacy of Christianity.

Ellis, Kirsten *Star of the Morning: The Extraordinary Life of Lady Hester Stanhope* London: Harper Collins, 2008. A meticulously researched, comprehensive and evocative account of this adventurous and independent woman traveller who refused to follow the rules. A feature film of Stanhope's life titled *The Lady Who Went Too Far*, with a screenplay adapted from Ellis's book, was in the development stage at the time of writing (*www.bedlamproductions.co.uk*).

Gibb, Lorna *Lady Hester: Queen of the East* London: Faber & Faber, 2006. A very vivid account exploring the eccentricities of the life of the nonconformist Lady Hester.

Gibran, Khalil *The Prophet* New York: Alfred A Knopf, 1992. First published 1923. Gibran's seminal work ranges deeply across the whole gamut of human life from clothes to love, pain and pleasure.

Gorton, Andree Féghali and Gorton, Ted *Lebanon: Through Writers' Eyes* London: Eland, 2009. An eclectic collection of writings by numerous authors spanning antiquity to the modern era, vividly illustrating the contradictions, diversity and complexity of the country.

Herodotus *The Histories* London: Penguin, 2003. Known as the 'Father of History' the peripatetic 5th century BCE Greek historian's magnum opus devotes plenty of highly readable references to Lebanon.

Khalaf, Roseanne Saad (ed) *Hikayat: Short Stories by Lebanese Women* London: Telegram Books, 2006. An anthology of writings from Lebanese authors exploring such issues as identity, love, marriage and sex.

Khoury, Elias *Yalo* London: Quercus, 2009. Psycho-social novel in which the crimes, confusions and contradictions of a young man, Yalo, are set against the similarly chaotic background of Lebanon's civil war.

Najjar, Alexandre *Kahlil Gibran: A Biography* London: Saqi Books, 2008. Good book on Lebanon's well-loved writer and philosopher.

Shadid, Anthony *House of Stone: A Memoir of Home, Family and a Lost Middle East* London: Granta, 2012. The late Pulitzer Prize winning journalist's story of the restoration of his family's ancestral home in the south Lebanese village of Marjayoun is set against the backdrop of personal, local and regional musings of a bygone world as he yearns for an 'older, more tolerant, more indulgent Middle East' that in reality is no longer attainable.

Shimon, Samuel (ed) *Beirut39: New Writing from the Arab World* London: Bloomsbury, 2010. Poems and short stories across a range of subject areas from 39 emerging writers, all aged under 40, from across the Arab world.

Thubron, Colin *The Hills of Adonis: A Quest in Lebanon* London: Vintage Books, 2008. First published 1968. A now classic account of the author's four-month journey through Lebanon in 1967 vividly illustrating what is now a bygone age in the country. His descriptions of his encounters with the Druze, Maronites and Shi'ites *en route* are both absorbing and insightful.

FILMS There are a number of cinematic offerings that deal, unsurprisingly, with various aspects of Lebanon's bloody past and include *Beirut Oh Beirut* (1975), directed by Cannes award winner Maroun Baghdadi, and *Beirut: The Last Home Movie* (1987), directed by US filmmaker Jennifer Fox and examining the attempts of a wealthy Beirut family to maintain their privileged lifestyle amid the carnage of war. Palestinian director Mai Masri's *Children of Shatila* (1998) looks at this infamous camp through the video narratives of the children who live there. Ziad Doueiri's *West Beirut* (1998) tells the often funny and touching rites-of-passage tale of two young boys growing up during the initial phase of the Lebanese civil war. Nadine Labaki's award-winning and often funny *Where Do We Go Now* (2011) deals with women's solidarity and their attempts to pacify their men-folk from fighting in a remote Christian–Muslim village during Lebanon's civil strife. For a slick and stylish Hollywood take on the civil war, director Tony Scott's *Spy Game* (2001), starring Robert Redford, Brad Pitt and Catherine McCormack, vividly evokes the carnage and chaos during the War of the Camps in Beirut in 1985 accompanied by Harry Gregson-Williams's wonderfully atmospheric and inventive music score.

A unique perspective on the 1982 First Lebanon War – shot almost entirely from inside an Israeli tank – is the autobiographical and cathartic *Lebanon* (2009), which charts the catastrophic journey, geographically and psychologically, of the film's writer and director, Samuel Maoz, and his cohorts, as the young recruits negotiate the raw realities of war. The film won the Golden Lion Award for Best Film at the 2009 Venice Film Festival, and also the Satyajit Ray Award. Another film that looks at the events of 1982 is *Waltz with Bashir* (2008) by Israeli author and filmmaker Ari Folman, who also produced and directed this animated film about the Lebanon War and the massacres of Palestinians at refugee camps in Beirut and which subsequently became a best-selling graphically illustrated novel. The film has won numerous awards including a Golden Globe for Best Foreign Language Film (*www.waltzwithbashir.com*). The final months of the IDF occupation of south Lebanon in 2000 is explored by Israeli director Joseph

Cedar in *Beaufort* (2007), which chronicles the day-to-day lives of Israeli soldiers encamped aloft the crusader-era Beaufort Castle. This is another film that has received widespread praise, winning the Best Director award for Cedar at the 2007 Berlin International Film Festival.

A few other films worth tracking down, and notable for their move away from the war genre, are: *Lady of the Palace* (2003) directed by Samir Habchi, which chronicles the history of the Jumblatt family from the 17th century to the present day concentrating on Nazira Jumblatt and her 25-year reign as head of the household and her foray into the political sphere; *Caramel* (2007), which saw the directorial debut of Lebanese actress Nadine Labaki and premiered at the 2007 Cannes Film Festival, telling the stories of five women in a beauty salon and exploring issues such as ageing, lesbianism, religious tradition and other universal human issues; and *What's Going On?* (2010) from Jocelyne Saab, veteran of some 20 documentary films, which ventures into the realm of the surreal, exploring issues of women, identity and equality against the background of the complexities of life in modern-day Beirut.

There are many more films about Lebanon (and the wider Middle East region) and these are available via mail or online order from **Arab Film Distribution** (*3619 Greenwood Av, N. Seattle, WA 98103-8518, USA;* \ *+1 206 322 0882;* e *info@arabfilm.com; www.arabfilm.com*).

WEBSITES
Blogs
www.beirutspring.com All manner of society and political topics are discussed here, from Hezbollah to *hummus*, by former Tripoli resident Mustapha.

www.ginosblog.com 'Everything you love & hate about Beirut' discussed in a forthright manner by former AUB student Gino Raidy.

www.lebaneseblogs.com An index of Lebanon's best and latest blogs covering a wide gamut of issues and subjects.

www.mashallahnews.com Emphasis is on the little-known stories from Lebanon and the Middle East focusing on 'urban issues, culture and society'.

www.mayazankoul.com Maya, a young Lebanese designer, uses a series of cathartic cartoons as release for the 'daily hassles' she experiences living in Lebanon.

www.moulahazat.com Political debates and musings with 'a pinch of sarcasm', from Ramez Dagher.

www.nogarlicnoonions.com A good food and travel blog.

www.onoffbeirut.com All manner of topics are discussed here, from the cost of living, social media, music and nightlife to what's happening generally on the streets of the capital.

www.plus961.com Interesting and humorous musings about Lebanon from citizen journalist, Rami.

www.shankaboot.com This Emmy Award-winning docu-drama, first broadcast in March 2010 and in its fifth series at the time of writing, is enlivened with humour and is the first Arabic-based web series in the world, offering a slice of Beiruti life through the eyes and experiences of its young protagonists.

Government
www.cas.gov.lb Central Administration of Statistics government website providing data on the economy, population, housing and a range of other society indicators.

www.dawlati.gov.lb Government portal with links to a whole host of information including Lebanese private and public sector organisations and numerous international bodies.

www.isf.gov.lb Website of the Internal Security Forces (ISF).

www.justice.gov.lb Official website of the Ministry of Justice with a good overview of the Lebanese legal system.

www.lp.gov.lb Website of the Lebanese parliament. In Arabic only at the time of writing.

www.nna-leb.gov.lb Lebanon's official National News Agency (NNA) from the Ministry of Information with timely national and international current affairs coverage.

www.pcm.gov.lb Website of the Council of Ministers (cabinet). Only in Arabic at the time of writing.

www.presidency.gov.lb Lots of interesting information about the President and the Constitution.

Newspapers and magazines

www.agendaculturel.com Bi-weekly magazine and website, in French, giving details of the capital's arts scene and cultural events.

www.annahar.com *An-Nahar* is one of Lebanon's leading daily Arabic newspapers (website in Arabic, English and French).

www.dailystar.com.lb Lebanon's sole English-language daily newspaper, with excellent coverage of local, national and international current affairs, culture and sport.

www.femmemag.com.lb Women's lifestyle magazine serving the usual journalistic diet of lifestyle, hair and beauty, together with profiles of local and international personalities and celebrities.

www.lorientlejour.com The French daily newspaper equivalent of the English-language *Daily Star*.

www.naharnet.com An excellent, up-to-date and non-sectarian online news source for Lebanon and the region in Arabic and English.

www.prestigemag.com Monthly lifestyle magazine, in French, for well-heeled socialite women concentrating on celebrity, parties, weddings, health and beauty. Website in English and French.

www.yalibnan.com An online-only news resource in English from Lebanese journalists following the 2005 Cedar Revolution, offering a less partisan view than many of Lebanon's other newspapers.

Tourist and travel information

www.adventuresinlebanon.com Excellent website devoted to less mainstream and off-the-beaten track touristic pursuits, with outdoor activities such as boating, rafting, snowshoeing, medical and rural tourism, etc, offering an alternative and edifying view of Lebanon. Runs an excellent range of tours at competitive prices with an ethos of care and concern for the environment.

www.facebook.com/BeyondBeirut Another excellent website from a Lebanese NGO with a cornucopia of information aiming to take visitors on a 'journey to discover Lebanon differently', emphasising environmental, cultural and rural tourism.

www.cia.gov *The World Fact Book* providing a range of factual country data across economic, political, social indicators, etc.

www.culture.gov.lb Informative website from the Ministry of Culture.

www.destinationlebanon.gov.lb Lebanon's official Ministry of Tourism website. A useful resource for both the business and leisure visitor.

www.eturbonews.com eTurboNews is a global online travel news site with useful country articles on tourism developments and trends.

www.freedomhouse.org A US organisation and watchdog that has been championing the causes of freedom (civil, media, political, women's rights, etc) around the world since 1941. Publishes an annual *Freedom in the World* report covering nearly 200 nations and other world entities.

www.general-security.gov.lb Website of Lebanon's General Directorate of General Security with lots of useful information on visas and obtaining residency permits.

www.gov.uk/foreign-travel-advice/lebanon Website of the British Foreign and Commonwealth Office (FCO) offering timely advice on travel safety and security in Lebanon, with some useful links for the business traveller.

www.lebanesestudies.com Website of the Centre for Lebanese Studies (CLS), an independent scholarly research organisation covering the whole gamut of issues affecting Lebanese society. An insightful resource for the leisure and business traveller alike.

www.lebanonroad.blogspot.com A good and well-organised site with useful background and practical information on the country, together with a decent overview of where to eat and stay, what to do and useful suggestions for tours around Lebanon

www.lebrecord.com An online news site devoted to the visual arts in Lebanon featuring interviews with artists and a diary of upcoming events.

www.lebtivity.com An excellent site which gives a month-by-month guide to the major and lesser well-known events happening all over the country. A good site to help you plan your visit.

www.now.nmedia.me/lb/en Acronym for New Opinion Workshop. Now is a non-sectarian online news forum established in the wake of the 2005 Cedar Revolution (Independence Intifada) to champion the cause for an independent Lebanon through debate of the key economic, political and social issues affecting the country and the region.

www.skileb.com Contains a wealth of detail on winter (and summer) sports and outdoor adventure activities around the country together with prices and detailed itineraries. Highly recommended for the active and sporty traveller and another site good for advance trip planning.

www.xe.com World currency converter.

www.yellowpages.com.lb An excellent online (and print) resource with listings for everything from banks, car rental companies, guesthouses and hotels, hospitals to entertainment and leisure facilities nationwide.

Index

Page numbers in **bold** refer to main entries; those in *italics* refer to map entries

INDEX OF ADVERTISERS